THE RIGHT TO LIFE AND THE VALUE OF LIFE

The Right to Life and the Value of Life: Orientations in Law, Politics and Ethics is a cohesive and engaging set of essays that addresses many of the difficult issues that arise in conversations about human life and human death. Bringing together legal questions about the right to life, ethical or economic questions about the value of life, and aesthetic or philosophical questions about the good life or prosperous life, the contributors make clear that a reliable discussion of human life in the contemporary world demands a nuanced, multidisciplinary approach. This collection represents precisely such an approach – weaving together analyses of such seemingly disparate topics as war, detention, capital punishment, suicide, euthanasia, reproductive technologies, and the biosciences, while drawing on methodologies from political theory, literature, history, public policy, law, and sociology. In the process, *The Right to Life and the Value of Life* moves beyond existing frameworks of analysis to open up exciting and sometimes unexpected new spaces for inquiry and dialogue.

Ruth A. Miller, University of Massachusetts Boston, USA

The Right to Life and the Value of Life: Orientations in Law, Politics and Ethics is a valiant effort bringing the questions of life and death under academic scrutiny. Traditionally, studies referring to the right to life and the value of life have been analyzed from isolated standpoints. This work weaves together science, political awareness and life, and its meritorious and ample endeavor may well entice and enlighten those questions mankind has asked itself repeatedly since the dawn of times.

Antonio Muñoz Aunion, Universidad de Castilla-La Mancha, Spain

For my mother, Elizabeth, who fought for her right to life, and my grandmother, Laura, who has shown her whole family the value of life.

The Right to Life and the Value of Life

Orientations in Law, Politics and Ethics

Edited by
JON YORKE
Birmingham City University, UK

ASHGATE

Published by
Ashgate Publishing Limited
Wey Court East
Union Road
Farnham
Surrey, GU9 7PT
England

Ashgate Publishing Company
Suite 420
101 Cherry Street
Burlington
VT 05401-4405
USA

www.ashgate.com

British Library Cataloguing in Publication Data
The right to life and the value of life : orientations in law, politics and ethics. -- (Law, justice and power series)
1. Right to life. 2. Life. 3. Life and death, Power over.
I. Series II. Yorke, Jon.
342'.085-dc22

Library of Congress Cataloging-in-Publication Data
Yorke, Jon.
The right to life and the value of life : orientations in law, politics, and ethics / by Jon Yorke.
p. cm.
Includes index.
ISBN 978-0-7546-7761-1 (hardback) -- ISBN 978-0-7546-9506-6 (ebook)
1. Right to life. I. Title.

K3252.Y67 2010
179.7--dc22

2010006003

ISBN 9780754677611 (hbk)
ISBN 9780754695066 (ebk)

Mixed Sources
Product group from well-managed forests and other controlled sources
www.fsc.org Cert no. SA-COC-1565
© 1996 Forest Stewardship Council
FSC

Printed and bound in Great Britain by
MPG Books Group, UK

Contents

List of Contributors

Professor David Benatar is Professor and Head of the Department of Philosophy at the University of Cape Town in South Africa. He is the author of numerous articles, the editor of a number of books and the author of *Better Never to Have Been: The Harm of Coming into Existence* (Oxford University Press, 2006).

Professor Bill Bowring is an acknowledged expert on human rights legislation and Russian law. He was appointed Professor of Law at Birkbeck College, University of London in September 2006 and is a practising barrister. He is International Secretary of the Haldane Society of Socialist Lawyers, and President of the European Lawyers for Democracy and Human Rights (in eight European countries). He serves as an Executive Committee Member of the Bar Human Rights Committee of England and Wales, a Member of the Council of Liberty, and a Trustee of the Redress Trust, working for torture survivors. Prof. Bowring founded and is Chair of the International Steering Committee of the European Human Rights Advocacy Centre (EHRAC), which, in partnership with the Russian NGO *Memorial* and the Bar Human Rights Committee, is assisting with over 150 cases against Russia, Georgia and Latvia to the European Court of Human Rights. In his role as a barrister, he has represented applicants before the ECHR in cases against Azerbaijan, Georgia, Latvia, Russia, and Turkey. He regularly acts as expert for the Council of Europe (DGI, DGII and DGIV) on human and minority rights issues, and works as a trainer and expert for the Council, the European Union, Amnesty International and others. He has written many publications on topics of international law, human rights, minority rights and Russian law.

Dr Susan Breau is currently Reader in International Law at the University of Surrey and Assistant Associate Dean for Research in the Faculty of Management and Law. She was formerly the Dorset Fellow in Public International Law at the British Institute of International and Comparative Law conducting an active research agenda in International Law and the International Protection of Human Rights. She was awarded her doctorate from the London School of Economics and Political Science for her research into Humanitarian Intervention. Her book on this topic entitled *Humanitarian Intervention: The United Nations and Collective Responsibility* was published by Cameron May in 2005. She has also co-written a book on State Immunity and co-edited three books; two on international humanitarian law and one on religion and human rights. She has authored several chapters and articles on various aspects of international law and the international protection of human rights. Dr Breau is a barrister and a solicitor in the province of Ontario, Canada (called to the Bar in 1981) and she practised law in Kingston, Ontario for 18 years. In her academic career, she has also taught international law at Queen's University Belfast, the London School of Economics, Pepperdine University and King's College London.

Dr Caroline Fournet (LLM Lund, DEA Strasbourg, PhD Leicester) is a senior lecturer in law at the University of Exeter (United Kingdom). Her research interests are Public International Law, Human Rights Law, International Humanitarian Law and International Criminal Law, with a particular emphasis on the law of genocide and the prohibition of torture. Her publications notably include two monographs: *International Crimes – Theories, Practice and Evolution*, with a foreword by Professor Malcolm N. Shaw QC (Cameron May, 2006) and *The Crime of Destruction and The Law of Genocide: Their Impact on Collective Memory* (Ashgate Publishing, 2007).

Professor Steven Freeland is Professor in International Law at the University of Western Sydney, Australia, where he teaches both postgraduate and undergraduate students in Public International Law, Human Rights Law, International Criminal Law and Commercial Aspects of Space Law. He is also Associate Head of School (Research) and coordinator of the School's International Law Mooting Program. He is a Visiting Professor in International Law at the University of Copenhagen, Denmark and has taught courses and presented guest lectures at Universities in The Netherlands, Denmark, United States, Australia, Austria, Bulgaria, Thailand and Singapore. He is also a Visiting Professional within the Appeals Chamber at the International Criminal Court, The Hague and has been a Special Advisor to the Danish Foreign Ministry in matters related to the International Criminal Court. After completing his LLB and BCom (with merit) in 1980, he worked in Australia, the United States, England and Belgium as an attorney with an international law firm, and is admitted to practice in Australia, the United Kingdom and Hong Kong. Subsequently, he worked as an investment banker for twelve years based primarily in Hong Kong with Asian regional responsibilities. After a professional career of almost twenty years, he returned to university studies and research in 1999 and completed his LLM in International Law at the University of Utrecht/University of New South Wales in 2000. Among other appointments, he is Chair of the International Law Action Group of the Lawyers Reform Association, a member of the Management Committee of the Australian Human Rights Centre, a member of the Transnational Enforcement of International Environmental Law Committee of the International Law Association, a member of the Space Law Committee of the International Law Association, a member of the Executive Committee of the International Law Association (Australian Branch), a member of the Australian and New Zealand Society of International Law, a member of the Directorate of Studies of the International Institute of Space Law, a member of the SUR/United Nations Human Rights University Network and a Fellow of the Tim Fischer Centre for Global Trade and Finance. He sits on the Editorial Board of both the

Australian Journal of Human Rights and the *Australian International Law Journal*, as well as a series of books entitled *Studies in Space Law*. He is also actively involved in the publication of a series of casebooks annotating the jurisprudence of the International Criminal Court, the International Criminal Tribunals for the former Yugoslavia and for Rwanda, the Special Court for Sierra Leone and the Special Panels for Serious Crimes in East Timor. He has published extensively on various aspects of International Law and is a frequent speaker at national and international conferences, having been invited to present conference papers and keynote speeches in Australia, Austria, Belgium, Canada, China, Denmark, France, Germany, India, Japan, The Netherlands, New Zealand, Singapore, Spain, Sweden, United Kingdom and United States.

Professor Johanna Gibson is Herchel Smith Professor of Intellectual Property Law and Director of the Queen Mary Intellectual Property Research Institute, Queen Mary University of London, where she researches and teaches in intellectual property law and policy, public health and traditional knowledge. Johanna maintains research interests in intellectual property policy and development, including medicine, public health and human rights. She has reported to the Scottish Executive on the ethical and legal aspects of public sector databases and has also been supported by the AHRC in her work on life patents and socio-cultural development. Johanna is the author of numerous articles as well as three books, all published by Ashgate: *Creating Selves: Intellectual Property and the Narration of Culture* (2006); *Community Resources: Intellectual Property, International Trade and Protection of Traditional Knowledge* (2005); and *Intellectual Property, Medicine and Health* (2009). She is the editor of the collection, *Patenting Lives: Life Patents, Culture and Development* (Ashgate, 2008).

Ms Agnieszka Jachec-Neale has over five years experience working with international organisations in South-Eastern Europe, where she specialised in monitoring domestic war crimes trials and human rights observation. Recently Agnieszka has served as a research fellow for the British Institute of International and Comparative Law (BIICL) and taught for three years at the Centre for International Studies and Diplomacy (SOAS). She is currently teaching the Laws of Armed Conflict course at the University of Essex. Her studies at the University of Gdansk (Poland) specialise in international criminal law, and she is currently pursuing doctoral studies in the law of armed conflicts at the University of Essex.

Ms Kerstin Klein, is currently a PhD student at the Bios Centre, London School of Economics and Political Science (LSE). She completed her Masters in Sociology and STS in the Department of Sociology and Institute of Science and Technology Studies (IWT) at Bielefeld University, Germany. She also worked as a researcher at the Social Science Research Centre Berlin (WZB), Free University Berlin; at the School of Archaeology and Anthropology, Faculty of Arts, Australian National University (ANU) and at St Petersburg State University, Faculty of Sociology.

Her research interests including conference presentations and up-coming publications, comprises of life science and society, biopolitics, political culture, and authoritarianism.

Professor Andrew Norris received his PhD from the Department of Rhetoric at UC Berkeley. Currently, he is Associate Professor in the Department of Political Science at the University of California, Santa Barbara. He is the editor of *The Claim to Community: Essays on Stanley Cavell and Political Philosophy* (Stanford University Press, 2006) and *Politics, Metaphysics, and Death: Essays on Giorgio Agamben's Homo Sacer* (Duke University Press, 2005), the co-editor of *Truth and Democratic Politics* (University of Pennsylvania Press, forthcoming), and the author of *Publicity and Partiality: Political Reflection in the Work of Stanley Cavell* (Stanford University Press, forthcoming).

Professor Mark Olssen is Professor of Political Theory and Education Policy in the Department of Political, International and Policy Studies, University of Surrey. He is author of *Toward A Global Thin Community: Nietzsche, Foucault and the Cosmopolitan Commitment* (Paradigm Press, 2008); *Michel Foucault: Materialism and Education* (Paradigm Press, 2006). He has also published a book with John Codd and Anne-Marie O'Neill titled *Education Policy: Globalisation, Citizenship, Democracy* (Sage, 2004); and an edited volume *Culture and Learning: Access and Opportunity in the Classroom* (IAP Press, 2004). He has published extensively in leading academic journals in Britain, America and in Australasia.

Professor Nikolas Rose is Martin White Professor of Sociology and Director of the BIOS Centre for the Study of Bioscience, Biomedicine, Biotechnology and Society at the London School of Economics and Political Science. The main focus of his current research is on the social implications of developments in the new brain sciences. His most recent books are *The Politics of Life Itself* (Princeton, 2006) and *Governing the Present* (with Peter Miller, Polity, 2008.)

Dr Stephen Smith is a Lecturer in Law at the Birmingham Law School and the Deputy Director of the Institute of Medical Law at Birmingham. Dr Smith has both a PhD from the University of Manchester, which he received in 2003, and a JD from Washington University School of Law, St. Louis, Missouri, USA, which he received in 1998. His research is primarily in the fields of medical law and bioethics especially issues of end of life care. He has published articles in the *Medical Law Review*, *The American Journal of Law and Medicine*, *Clinical Ethics* and *Medicine and Law*. He is currently working on a monograph about end of life decision-making.

Dr Ayo Wahlberg is Postdoctoral Research Fellow in the Department of Anthropology, University of Copenhagen, Denmark. He holds a PhD in Sociology from the London School of Economics and an MSc in International Development

Studies and Social Science from Roskilde University, Denmark. Academic publications include: 'Measuring progress – calculating the life of nations' in *Distinktion: Scandinavian Journal of Social Theory*, 2007, 'Bio-politics and the promotion of traditional herbal medicine in Vietnam', *Health: An Interdisciplinary Journal for the Social Study of Health, Illness and Medicine*, 2006, 'Above and beyond superstition – western herbal medicine and the decriminalising of placebo' in *History of the Human Sciences*, 2008, and 'Reproductive medicine and the concept of "quality"', in *Clinical Ethics*, 2008.

Dr Helen Watt is Director of the Linacre Centre for Healthcare Ethics, London. Before taking up this post in 2001, she held the position of Research Fellow at the Centre. From 1993 to 1996, she was also Senior Research Associate at Peterhouse, Cambridge. She holds a PhD in Philosophy from the University of Edinburgh, and an honors degree in Italian from the University of Western Australia. She is the author of *Life and Death in Healthcare Ethics: A Short Introduction* (Routledge, 2000) and the editor of *Cooperation, Complicity and Conscience* (Linacre Centre, 2005).

Dr Elizabeth Wicks is a Senior Lecturer in the Birmingham Law School at the University of Birmingham. Her research and teaching interests are in constitutional law, medical law and human rights. She is the author of two books: *The Evolution of a Constitution: Eight Key Moments in British Constitutional History* (2006) and *Human Rights and Healthcare* (2007), both published by Hart Publishing. She is currently writing a book on the Right to Life and Conflicting Interests, to be published by Oxford University Press.

Dr Jon Yorke is a Reader in Law, BCU Law School, Birmingham City University. His teaching and research interests are in medical law, public law, human rights and the death penalty. He has acted as a consultant for the British Institute of International and Comparative Law project on the death penalty in Commonwealth Africa, and has worked on state and federal capital cases in Oklahoma. He is on the editorial board of the death penalty journal *Amicus Journal* and is the editor of *Against the Death Penalty: International Initiatives and Implications* (Ashgate, 2008), and has published journal articles including in the *European Law Review*, *European Public Law* and the *International and Comparative Law Quarterly*. He is currently writing a book entitled *Europe and Abolition of the Death Penalty*, to be published by Cambridge University Press.

Acknowledgements

I am extremely grateful to the marvellous scholars who contributed to this book, and who engage and promote the right to life and the value of life around the world. I am also grateful to my new academic home in Birmingham City University Law School, and especially to Professor John Fairhurst, Head of the School, and Valerie Humphreys, Deputy Head, for their academic leadership, and to Dr Haydn Davies, Director of Research, for his constant generative ideas on law and rights. This collection has also benefited from discussions with other BCU colleagues, Professor Julian Killingley, Dave Keefe, Sarah Cooper, Chipo Mwale, Lisa Rodgers, Timothy James and Chris King.

The idea for this book manifested from a tributary of my doctoral research at Warwick Law School, and I am very thankful to Dr Andrew Williams for his extreme generosity and wonderful academic guidance as my doctoral supervisor, and also at Warwick, to Professor Upendra Baxi for his incredible grasp of all things 'human rights.' This book has also benefited from informative discussions with Professor Roger Hood and Dr Carolyn Hoyle, at the Centre for Criminology, University of Oxford, Dr. Susan Breau and Professor Mark Olssen, at Surrey University, Professor Panos Koutrakos at the University of Bristol, and Dr Stephen Smith and Dr Elizabeth Wicks at the University of Birmingham Law School, and the discussions at a seminar led by Stephen in the Institute of Medical Law. Finally, this work has been collated with the benefit of conversations with some of the remarkable people at the Council of Europe. I am indebted to the generosity of Günter Schirmer of the Committee on Legal Affairs and Human Rights, at the Parliamentary Assembly of the Council of Europe, and also to Michelle Lafferty and Paul Harvey, of the Registry of the European Court of Human Rights. Also for making an intellectual home for me, and guiding me to the resources I needed, I wholeheartedly thank the wonderful librarians in the Library of the European Court of Human Rights, Nora Binder, Head Librarian, and Genevieve Woods, Deputy Librarian.

This collection includes two chapters which are reproduced with permission from other publications. These are: Nikolas Rose, 'The Value of Life: Somatic Ethics and the Spirit of Biocapital,' from *Daedalus*, Winter, 2008, 36-48, and Andrew Norris, 'The Exemplary Exception: Philosophical and Political Decisions in Giorgio Agamben's *Homo Sacer*,' from *Radical Philosophy* 119 (May/June 2003). Also included are chapters which are substantially edited, updated, and expanded versions of previous publications. These are: Mark Olssen, 'Politics and the Philosophy of Life: Towards a Normative Framework,' from *Toward a Global Thin Community* (Paradigm Publishers, 2009), Chapter 6; Jon Yorke, 'The Right to Life and Abolition of the Death Penalty in the Council of Europe,' from (same title) *European Law Review* 2009 32(2): 205-229; and Helen Watt, 'Conjoined Twins: Separation as Lethal Mutilation,' from 'Conjoined Twins: Separation as Mutilation,' *Medical Law Review* 2001 9(3):237-245.

List of Abbreviations

AbCHR	Arab Charter on Human Rights
ACHPR	African Charter on Human and People's Rights
ACHR	American Convention on Human Rights
ADRDM	American Declaration on the Rights and Duties of Man
AID	Artificial insemination by donor
AIH	Artificial insemination by husband
ANH	Artificial nutrition and hydration
ART	Assisted reproductive technologies
BBC	British Broadcasting Corporation
BIICL	British Institute of International and Comparative Law
CAS	Chinese Academy of Science
CCW	Convention on Certain Conventional Weapons
CESCR	Committee on Economic, Social and Cultural Rights
CIHL	Customary International Humanitarian Law
CISCHRFF	Commonwealth of Independent States Convention on Human Rights and Fundamental Freedoms
CPC	Communist Party of China
CRO	Contract research organisation
CSDH	Commission on Social Determinants of Health
DGD	Day of General Discussion
DNA	Deoxyribonucleic acid
DPH	Direct participants in hostilities
ECHR	European Convention on Human Rights (Convention for the Protection of Human Rights and Fundamental Freedoms)
ECOSOC	Economic and Social Council
ECtHR	European Court of Human Rights
EHRAC	European Human Rights Advocacy Centre
FTA	Free trade agreement
GMC	General Medical Council
hESCR	Human embryonic stem cell research
HFEA	Human Fertilisation and Embryology Authority
HMO	Health Maintenance Organization
IAC	International armed conflict
ICC	International Criminal Court
ICCPR	International Covenant on Civil and Political Rights
ICESCR	International Covenant on Economic, Social and Cultural Rights
ICJ	International Court of Justice

ICSI	Intracytoplasmic sperm injection
ICTR	International Criminal Tribunal for Rwanda
ICTY	International Criminal Tribunal for the Former Yugoslavia
IGWG	Intergovernmental Working Group on Public Health, Innovation and Intellectual Property
IHCT	Iraqi High Criminal Tribunal
IHL	International humanitarian law
IHRL	International human rights law
ILC	International Law Commission
IUI	Intrauterine insemination
IVF	*in vitro* fertilisation
MBE	Member of the British Empire
MDG	Millennium Development Goal
MOD	Ministry of Defence
MOH	Ministry of Health
NATO	North Atlantic Treaty Organization
NGO	Non-governmental organisation
NIAC	Non-international armed conflict
NICE	National Institute for Clinical Excellence
NSA	Non-state actors
OSCE	Organization for Security and Cooperation in Europe
PACE	Parliamentary Assembly of the Council of Europe
PFII	Permanent Forum on Indigenous Issues
PVS	Permanent vegetative state
PRC	People's Republic of China
QALY	Quality adjusted life year
R&D	Research and development
RSFSR	Russian Socialist Federation of Soviet Republics
RPE	Rules of evidence and procedure
S&T	Science and technology
SCNT	Somatic cell nuclear transfer
SOL	Sanctity of life
STS	Science and technology studies
TRIPS	Trade-Related Aspects of Intellectual Property Rights (Agreement on)
USSR	Union of Soviet Socialist Republics
UDHR	Universal Declaration of Human Rights
VOL	Value of life
WHA	World Health Assembly
WHO	World Health Organization
WIPO	World Intellectual Property Organization

Chapter 1
Introduction: The Right to Life and the Value of Life: Orientations in Law, Politics and Ethics

Jon Yorke

The biological and political processes which create, maintain, and end life, are assessed within the evolving parameters of the 'right to life' and the 'value of life.' These processes are the product of a multi-dimensional relationship between individuals, companies, and governments, and it is necessary to place these relationships under scrutiny to ensure that mortal choices are made legitimately (see Ramcharan 1985; Hood and Hoyle 2008; Schabas 2002 and Rose 2007). The assessment of the evolving spectrum of life scenarios from an isolation of life in its biological existence (Mathieu 2006, 9) through to life as a political expression requires a multi-disciplinary analysis. It is not enough for the right to life to remain within the ambit of law and legal critique, political science and philosophical exposition and other systems of thought (for example, those considering autopoietic sociology, feminism and religion) are also required.[1] Furthermore, the value of life cannot remain within the realm of economics and actuarial calculation, it must include a consideration of the ethical and sentimental circumstances (Rorty 1993) which infiltrate financial exchange. Hence there is a need for '*orienting* ourselves in thought' (Kant 1970, 241),[2] to continue the assessment of the questions which are currently in the public domain, for example the debates concerning the legitimacy of war, the death penalty and retribution in punishment, abortion and

1 Bertrand Ramcharan argued that human rights lawyers should not remain static in their understanding of the juridical boundaries of the right to life and he stated, '[t]he branch of international law concerned with the promotion and protection of human rights must, therefore, of necessity, be in the forefront of the discipline, charting new courses, breaking new grounds, and establishing new models and methods' (Ramcharan, 1985, 1).

2 Immanuel Kant explained in a footnote in 'What is Orientation in Thinking?' that '[t]hus to *orient* oneself in thought means to be guided, in one's conviction of truth, by a subjective principle of reason where objective principles of reason are inadequate' (Kant 1970, 240). Current examples of Kant's 'subjective principle of reason' dismantling inadequate 'objective principles,' can be found, *inter alia*, in the history of the worldwide campaign against the death penalty, the growing momentum for the legalisation of assisted suicide and certain forms of euthanasia, and the debates over the various cut-off dates for legalised abortion.

the propositions of the pro-life and pro-choice movements.[3] There are also new and developing questions which require scrutiny, for example, those concerning human embryonic stem cell research, and therapeutic and non-therapeutic cloning, which seek to contribute to the health and macro-eugenic governmental strategies, and the micro-eugenic considerations by parents (see Rose, Wahlberg and Klein, this collection).[4]

What will become clear throughout this book is that there is uncertainty over the application of the right to life and the value of life to many of the different questions of life and death. Indeed, as life and death concepts become more nuanced a greater degree of sensitivity is required to engage the right to life and the value of life in legitimate ways. In the presence of the (different) decisions made by governments, companies and individuals, it becomes fundamental to determine how people and organisations act. What follows in this introduction is an overview of these issues and then it is proposed that the legitimate application of the boundaries of the right to life and the value of life are contingent upon the transparency of the various decision making processes (including those made by governments, the commercial sector and different religious organisations and theocracies) and the dissemination of information for the specific issues concerning life and death. It is argued that perceived legitimate life and death decisions can only be made, by all parties, after an adequate consideration of the most up-to-date information: following Gibson, this collection, this information must be sensitive to cultural variations and plural sentiments within society.

The Right to Life and the Value of Life

The right to life has been both 'defined' and 'enumerated' in the international human rights instruments following World War Two, but there is still uncertainty over its scope. There are many instances where the drafters of various treaties were unsure, and in some cases in conflict, over the textual formulation of the

3 For the 'pro-life' position see, the International Right to Life Federation, www.internationalrighttolife.com, the Society for the Protection of Unborn Children, www.spuc.org.uk, and Prolife America, www.prolifeamerica.com. For the 'pro-choice' position see, Pro-Choice Majority, www.prochoicemajority.org.uk, and Prochoice, http://prochoice.com. Indeed, the issue of abortion not only involves antagonistic debates surrounding the right to life of the foetus, but also, the right to life of physicians, as is witnessed when pro-life activists kill pro-choice physicians administering abortions. An example in the United States was the shooting of Dr George Tiller in Kansas on 31 May 2009.

4 This collection is not concerned with identifying any *per se* 'meaning of life.' However, the chapters in this book do provide a certain level of 'meaning' within the specific juridical, political and philosophical boundaries with which the contributors are concerned. For the appropriateness of the question of an inherent meaning of life see the excellent introductions by Cottingham 2003 and Eagleton 2007, and see also Grayling 2001 and Belshaw 2005. For an overview of the converse issues surrounding 'death,' see, Enright 1983.

right (Colon-Collazo 1985; Ramcharan 1985), and specific examples can be seen from the recorded drafting debates of both the International Covenant on Civil and Political Rights (see Schabas 2002, 45-92) and the European Convention on Human Rights (see Council of Europe 1975; Wicks 2000; Yorke, this collection, and 2010). The right to life is included in the Universal Declaration of Human Rights, article 3, as an 'enumeration' that '[e]veryone has the right to life, liberty and security of person.'[5] The text is recorded through a basic articulation which gives room for a reflexive interpretive mechanism to encompass the different life and death concepts as they evolve. While other instruments provide 'definitions' of the scope of the right to life, for example, the International Covenant on Civil and Political Rights, article 6, which begins with an enumeration that '[e]very human being has the inherent right to life,' and then details that no one shall be arbitrarily deprived of life, and then specific issues concerning the death penalty are recorded, including the prohibition on the reintroduction of the punishment once abolished, the right of pardon, and the non-application of the punishment for people below the age of eighteen, and pregnant women.[6] There are both advantages and disadvantages in using definitions. An advantage is that the text may produce certainty in the law with regard to the specific listed circumstances, but a disadvantage may be that it renders the text inflexible to the evolving, and new, life and death questions.[7]

The textual variation supplied by the enumeration or definition of the right to life has not created a clear legal position. Hugo Bedau stated that the 'salient fact about this right is the considerable disagreement over its scope' (Bedau 1968, 550). In the 1980s and 1990s the Association of International Consultants on Human Rights investigated the parameters of the right to life and identified the expanding and varying boundaries of the right (Association of International Consultants on Human Rights 1992, 3). William Schabas has observed that the right is 'intangible in scope, and vexingly difficult to define' (Schabas 2002, 8), and James Griffin notes that the 'scope of the right seems irresistibly to expand,' and that there is a 'ballooning of the content' (Griffin 2008, 212-213). As a consequence this right does not have a 'clear boundary' because what 'starts off as the least problematic of rights becomes, on reflection, distinctly problematic' (ibid., 213). Torkel Opsahl affirmed that the right to life, and the 'context in which it operates will show that what at first seemed simple may have problematic points' (Opsahl 1993, 207), and Jacques Derrida goes

5 Other international instruments providing enumerations are the: American Declaration on the Rights and Duties of Man, article 1; African Charter of Human and People's Rights article 4; Arab Charter on Human Rights, article 5.

6 Other international instruments providing definitions are the: European Convention on Human Rights, article 2(1); American Convention on Human Rights article 4; Commonwealth of Independent States Convention on Human Rights and Fundamental Freedoms, article 2.

7 One way around this problem is the adoption of additional instruments and most of the contributors to this collection engage with this possibility.

as far to argue that the right to life is 'highly precarious,' as its 'concept and axiom are more than problematic' (Derrida and Roudinesco 2004, 153).

Even with the uncertainty concerning the scope of the right to life, it has not thwarted an attempted definition of the right in absolute terms. It has been described as a 'natural' and 'inalienable' attribute of every human being, an 'absolute' right (Bedau 1968, 553), and as 'undoubtedly the most fundamental of all rights' (van Boven 1988; Delafield Smith 1955), 'the supreme right,'[8] 'the foundation and cornerstone of all other rights,'[9] and as 'ranking the highest,' 'primordial,' 'imprescriptible,' a 'cardinal human right' (Ramcharan 1985, 18, 19), the 'irreducible core of human rights,' (Jachec-Neale, this collection) and as an 'imperative norm of international law' (Ramcharan 1985, 12). With such apparent incontrovertible mandate, the right to life has been identified as a 'norm of *ius cogens*' (Redelbach 1985, 182) which may not be derogated from in any circumstances. No government may deny its existence.

The duty on the state to protect the right to life has negative as well as positive applications. In the negative, governments must take all reasonable measures to *prevent* unlawful deprivations, including arbitrary deprivation.[10] In the positive, governments must take all reasonable measures to *promote* the right to life, by for instance, reducing infant mortality and increasing life expectancy, which will involve having an adequate healthcare service to tend to the population's health needs. However, the right to life does not mean that life must exist under all circumstances as Ramcharan observed, '[i]t is not life, but the right to life which is protected by law' (Ramcharan 1985, 2). For example, William Schabas notes there are some 'rather obvious exceptions to the right to life,' for instance the 'right to self-defence, including the right to take another person's life where his or her own life is threatened by that person' (Schabas 2002, 7), and Fiona Leverick argues that within the right to life itself, 'the most convincing explanation of the permissibility of killing in self-defence can be found' (2006, 54). The permissibility of self-defence is derived from the inalienability of the right to life that is possessed by innocent people(s) and states. The basic position may be explained in that if an attacker applies violence (towards an individual in a domestic criminal law circumstance, or a country or a terrorist, in an act

8 General Comment 6(16), UN Doc. CCPR/C/21/Add.1.

9 Annual Report of the Inter-American Commission on Human Rights, 1986-1987, OAS Doc. OEA/Ser.L/V/II.71, doc. 9 rev. 1, p. 271.

10 Daniel Nsereko states that the framers of the international instruments, 'recognized the existence of situations in which it may be legitimate to sacrifice an individual's right to life for the sake of averting harm to or of protecting other compelling state interests,' (Nsereko 1985, 247), but he observes that:

'[d]eprivation of life would be arbitrary if: (a) it is made without due regard to the rules of natural justice or the due process of law; or (b) it is made in a manner contrary to the law; or (c) it is made in pursuance of a law which is despotic, tyrannical and in conflict with international human rights standards or international humanitarian law' (ibid., 248).

of war), the innocent party may initiate a proportionate response. If an attacker aims to kill (individual(s) or a state's political infrastructure) he/she may forfeit the right to life and be killed. As Ramcharan argued above, it is not 'life' that must be protected in every circumstance, but only the 'right' to life. The innocent party maintains the 'right,' but the attacking party advancing violence may lose the protection of the 'right.' This example is best placed within the state's negative duty to refrain from putting to death (because of the inalienability of the right to life) unless there is a legal basis for such killing (as the forfeiture of the right to life has been demonstrated), and we can also interpret this as a principle applying in a negative way to individuals (although the assessment of an individual's actions will be within domestic criminal law and not human rights). There can also be exceptions to the right to life in its positive application, for instance, allowing the death of an individual on a life support machine when it is not in his best interest to be (artificially) kept alive, or the separation of a conjoined twin where the continued biological existence of Childs A and B was killing Child B and B would eventually die of natural causes (and die following surgery), but A might survive following a surgical separation (see Wicks and Watt, this collection). The extent of the application, and the manifestation of an exception, of the right to life to the beginning, continuance, and ending of life, will depend upon societal and political sentiments (Rorty 1993),[11] and the economic resources of the country. Sylvanus Okechukwu observes that:

> the right to life...shows that the nature and scope of the rights protected, guaranteed and promoted, depend fundamentally on the different levels of development attained by various societies and on the different ideologies they propound (Okechukwu 1990, 323).

At the beginning of life, scientific research on the ova and sperm, infertility treatment, studies in embryology and stem cells,[12] neonatal care, and advances in obstetrics and gynaecology, will affect the opinions on when (the right to) life begins, which, for instance, will have implications for the debates surrounding abortion. For the continuance of life the extent of the government's promotion of the right to life will depend upon the level of a country's development and available resources to meet basic needs; including the provisions for adequate water and food, the delivery of a certain level of protection against internal

11 Richard Rorty argued for the use of a discourse on 'sentimentality' in creating the boundaries of human rights, and he stated that the past 'two centuries are most easily understood not as a period of deepening understanding of the nature of rationality or of morality, but rather as one in which there occurred an astonishingly rapid progression of sentiments, in which it has become much easier for us to be moved to action by sad and sentimental stories' (Rorty 1993, 134).

12 For the possibility that stem cells could be extracted from skin, as opposed to being derived from embryos, see 'Skin transformed into stem cells' (BBC, 2007).

individual(s) threatening other individuals or a population, and also externally from outside threats to the survival of the population.[13] The government should also implement reasonable measures to provide paediatric care to reduce infant mortality, improve care of the population to increase life expectancy, and take steps to provide an adequate environment where the population may thrive. If an individual experiences an accident, illness or disease an adequate medical service should be readily available.[14] To provide this service to a population, it requires adequate funding, infrastructure, management, and delivery of care.

Death occurs either by perceived natural causes, for example, disease, illness or old age, or by perceived unnatural causes, including, accidents, trauma, neglect, poisoning, suicide, euthanasia, and homicide. When death occurs the analysis of the right to life requires that the relationship of the government with the deceased individual is placed under scrutiny. For example, whether during the targeting of a person in a combat zone he or she can be recognised to be an enemy combatant or a civilian. If a civilian, then it is not legitimate to kill the individual as he/she is not threatening the security of the attacking government. However, if the person is identified as an enemy, the killing will be a legitimate, and legal, cause of action (see Jachec-Neale and Breau, this collection). Furthermore, the boundaries of the state control over the life and death of its population (Foucault 2004) is placed under question when it seeks to implement a death penalty (see Freeland, Yorke, and Bowring, this collection). The question will be whether the right to life can be used to protect an individual, who has committed a murder, from being executed. The sovereign right of the death penalty has been applied at some point in the history of most countries of the world. However, the right to life has evolved as a defensive mechanism to argue that the state no longer has the right to administer an execution. In another example, if an individual seeks to obtain the right to end their own life through assisted suicide or voluntary euthanasia (see Benatar and Smith, this collection), the question will be whether the right to life can include a right to end one's own life. For now the majority of the world does not allow the right to life to include a right to cause one's own death, but there is a growing sentiment to promote change. The ethical positions on autonomous decisions for determining that one's life has lost value, are gaining momentum.[15]

13 On the use of 'emergency powers' by governments see, Gross and Ní Aoláin 2006, and for the emerging scholarship on 'law and catastrophe' see, Posner 2004; Sarat, Douglas and Umphrey 2007.

14 The World Health Organization notes that '[g]lobally in 2006, expenditure on health was about 8.7% of gross domestic product, with the highest level in the Americas at 12.8% and the lowest in the South-East Asia Region at 3.4%. This translates to about US$ 716 per capita on the average but there is tremendous variation ranging from a very low US$31 per capita in the South-East Region to a high of US$ 2636 per capita in the Americas' (WHO 2009, 107).

15 For example, in the United Kingdom, the intricate debates on assisted suicide have led to the House of Lords instructing the Director of Public Prosecutions to formulate specific guidelines to determine when people assisting a person to travel abroad end their

What is also noticeable is that the issue of the right to life is becoming more and more infused with the calculations on the 'value of life' (see Rose and Smith, this collection).[16] As a general proposition, the value of life is assessed by the individual, the commercial sector, and governments. An individual may view his own value of life through the two traditional positions of either that life has an inherent or basic value (via the doctrine of the 'Sanctity of Life' (SOL)), or by a quality of life assessment (via the doctrine of 'Quality of Life' (QOL)). The traditional SOL position maintains that in its religious articulation that a transcendent religious entity bestowed life and it is only for that entity to allow the beginning, continuance or ending of life. In its secular articulation, the SOL position maintains that life is a basic, foundational, good and consequently it is not permissable to intentionally end life. Hence, those advocating the SOL position, generally, are against abortion, assisted suicide and euthanasia. The traditional QOL position lies in the utility of life, in that life should exist if it has a certain quality and/or function. Hence, if an individual decides that his/her quality of life has now diminished to such an extent that it is cognitively and physically unbearable that a right to end one's own life should be granted. As such, those advocating the QOL position may allow for the possibility of abortion, assisted suicide and euthanasia (this is the general bifurcation of the positions but see the cogent argument for a fusion within one principle in Smith, this collection). The government, and the commercial sector (increasingly occupied by the biotechnology industry), assess life on utility and cost, which encompasses the general running of a country, including, for example, healthcare, population fluctuations, and compensations in wrongful death claims.

However, the value of life does not have a clear boundary and the observations on the multifaceted approaches above problematise the 'value' assessment (see Rose and Gibson, this collection). Part of the difficulty lies in the fact that value in life encompasses what may be termed 'measurable aspects' and 'immeasurable aspects.' The measurable aspect of the value of life can be calculated by governments, companies, and international organisations, such as the World Health Organization and the United Nations. Individuals can measure the value of themselves financially, by how much they earn and invest, and if appropriate, how much the family earns and invests collectively. Assessments can be made on these figures to make financial plans for security and the increase in profit. However, the

life through assisted suicide in clinics such as Dignitas in Switzerland, will and will not be subject to prosecution, see *R (Purdy) v. Director of Public Prosecutions (Society for the Protection of Unborn Children intervening)* [2009] UKHL 45; [2009] 3 W.L.R. 403. Life ending procedures are legally available in Europe in the Netherlands, Belgium, Switzerland and Luxembourg, and in the United States in Oregon and Washington, and in 2009, there has been litigation in Montana questioning whether the state's constitution protects assisted suicide (see Srinivas 2009).

16 'Value' is as problematical as 'right.' Slavoj Žižek identifies that when we discuss 'values' then we have, 'a priori postulated values as something relative, contingent, whose preserve is not unquestionable' (Žižek 2002, 132).

immeasurable aspect of the value of life is not based upon any financial calculation, as it is determined by personal (or collective) sentiment (Rorty 1993); for example, a parent's love for their newborn baby, or one's own claim that *my life still has value to me*, or a group or a people's claim that *our life has value to us*. The determination of the value of life for both individuals, and within groups and people's identity, is symbiotic with political identity. Martha Nussbaum observed that individuals and groups (for example, Nussbaum emphasises the need to recognise the rights and political choices of the disabled and ethnic minorities in the theory of the social contract) should possess 'minimum core social entitlements,' and included within this entitlement is '[*c*]*ontrol over one's environment*...[b]eing able to participate effectively in political choices that govern one's life' (Naussbaum 2006, 75-76). The immeasurable aspect of the value of life should not be curtailed by the more objective criteria established through the measurable aspect of the value of life, but should be placed on an equal footing. Calculating the value of life can be a product of autonomous assessment, and where appropriate, the outcome of dialogue with companies and governments. However, there is scope for governments and companies to prevent or curtail the autonomous voice.[17] Hence a fair application of the value of life, and indeed, the right to life, is required, which involves not only a transparent assessment of current circumstances, but also necessitates a recalling of past decisions and the weighing of future projections. To achieve this requires an adequate access to information by all parties.

Access to Information for the Determination of the Boundaries of the Right to Life and the Value of Life

Jacques Derrida provides a deconstruction which is useful here. In the dialogue with Elisabeth Roudinesco, he stated, '[b]eginning with the word "life." It would be necessary to think [of] life on the basis of heritage,' and through such heritage Derrida argues that life involves a process which must be allowed 'to select, to filter, to interpret, and therefore to transform' in order for there not to be a complete 'refraining from all killing or putting to death' (Derrida and Roudinesco 2004, 4). We must review our past and current practices and question whether we want to continue with what we have done before, or view our previous actions as somehow de-legitimised, and in need of political and legal modification. Here Derrida is approaching a deconstruction of the processes which determine the beginning, continuing and ending of life, and he does not see that in every circumstance life should be protected. For Derrida, this 'heritage,' is determined by not only

17 Ronald Dworkin argued the importance of validating the deontological expression of life and death choices, when he stated, 'decisions about life are the most important, the most crucial for forming and expressing personality, that anyone makes: we think it crucial to get these decisions right, but also to make them in character, and for ourselves' (Dworkin 1994, 239).

viewing our pasts, but also carefully considering what we have in the present and how this bears on 'life.' He argued that this process:

> demands two gestures at once both to leave life in life and to make it live again, to save life and to 'let live' in the most poetic sense of this phrase…To know how to 'leave' and to 'let,' and to know the meaning of 'leaving' and 'letting' – that is one of the most beautiful, most hazardous, most necessary things I know of. It is in close proximity with giving up and giving over, the gift, and forgiveness. The experience of 'deconstruction' is never without this, without this love, if you prefer that word (ibid.).

The questions concerning life and death involve a sensitive inter-play between governments and individuals, and it is necessary for governments to know when to affirm control over the parameters of life (in both the negative and positive application of the right to life), and when to relinquish control (through facilitating individual autonomy), and such decisions may be a 'hazardous' exercise for the governmental decision making process. Derrida explained 'the idea of heritage implies…a filtering, a choice, a strategy. An heir is not only someone who receives, he or she is someone who chooses, and takes the risk of deciding' (ibid., 8). Certainly questions of life and death involve elements of filtering, choice and strategy, and so this 'heritage' informs the identification of when sovereign governments can legitimately establish themselves as the 'heir' to create circumstances where life may or may not begin, be continued, be protected, and when it shall be ended. Furthermore, individuals must be able to make their own claims, and if they so wish, attempt to establish themselves with the authority of the 'heir,' through an autonomous, unfettered, testimony (Lyotard 1989) to sovereign governments, that; '*I do not want you to take my life*,' '*I want you to provide me with the means for my life to exist*,' '*I want you to allow me to obtain the means for the existence and continuation of my life*,' '*I want you to allow me to determine when my life has value to me and when it does not*,' and '*If I so desire, I want you to allow me to take my own life or provide me with the means to take my own life*.' The issue then becomes: how are these life and death questions to be determined?

An important factor is the control of information and whether there is transparency in the decision making process. As scientific knowledge and techniques for the beginning and ending of life advance, it opens up the possibility for individuals to have greater information for informed decisions, and it also allows governments to use that knowledge for the biological and penological calculations which it makes concerning its population, and for some governments, to impinge upon the wider international community. Here Michel Foucault is illuminating when in, 'The Subject and Power,' he outlined the importance of knowledge transfer for 'anti-authority struggles.' These struggles manifest:

> an opposition to the effects of power linked with knowledge, competence, and qualification – struggles against the privileges of knowledge. But they are also an

> opposition against secrecy, deformation, and mystifying representations imposed by people…What is questioned is the way in which knowledge circulates and functions, its relations to power. In short, the regime of knowledge (Foucault 2001, 330-331).

We strive for transparency in government decision making over the full spectrum of life and death, because the knowledge-base for the determination of the questions cannot be privileged information. Governments should not keep 'secret' or 'mystify' the information that is constantly being developed by scientists, philosophers, political scientists, lawyers, anthropologists, sociologists, feminists, and economists, but must ensure that this information circulates and functions within what are considered to be legitimate boundaries of life and death. Governments must act transparently and disseminate information in a way which is coherent and lucid, and the political (including legislative) and scientific language used should not hide illegitimate governmental actions, or blur them behind euphemistic phrases. Politicians, and indeed, certain parts of the commercial sector, may hide behind selective wording and cloud the true consequences of their policies and applications for the populace. Albert Camus referred to the journalistic articles and death penalty scholarship during mid-twentieth century Europe and stated that '[p]eople write of capital punishment as if they are whispering...since everyone strives to refer to it only through euphemisms' (Camus 1988, 176), and Sigmund Freud helped us to understand a psychoanalytical view of death when he stated, '[w]e have shown the unmistakable tendency to "shelve" death, to eliminate it from life. We tried to hush it up' (Freud 1968, 15).[18]

There may be good reasons for governments (and companies, see Gibson, this collection) to control the dissemination, or filtering of knowledge. However, the evolving standards of legitimacy determine that transparency in decision making is a fundamental principle. The difficulty is that in such circumstances, we must *trust* governments to know when the reservation of information is on the one hand a *means* to an *end* for the protection and enhancement of society, and on the other hand, when it is a *means* to an *end* for protecting and concealing illegitimate political and commercial decisions (see Wagner-Pacifici 2009, 25-50).[19] It must

18 Although Ludwig Wittgenstein sought to distil the structure of language to display how 'grammar deceives' (Eagleton 2007, 9), at the end of *Tractatus Logico-Philosophicus* he resigned that the question of life and death could not be adequately dealt with as, '[w]e feel that even when all *possible* scientific questions have been answered, the problems of life remain completely untouched. Of course there are then no questions left, and this itself is the answer. The solution of the problem of life is seen in the vanishing of the problem. (Is not this the reason why those who have found after a long period of doubt that the sense of life became clear to them have been unable to say what constituted that sense?) There are, indeed, things that cannot be put into words. They *make themselves manifest*. They are what is mystical' (Wittgenstein 1974, 88-89).

19 Herbert Spencer observed that, '[s]tate-authority as thus derived, is a means to an end, and has no validity save as subserving that end: if the end is not subserved, the authority,

be realised and acknowledged that sovereignty, in its application by governments, may determine that such actions are for the 'good of the people,' but in many ways sovereignty itself creates the very problems concerning life and death which it seeks to solve; a recent example being the invasion of Iraq (Arnold 2009, 51-82). When adequate information is obtained we can correctly utilise Derrida's deconstruction of 'heritage,' and be able to keep what was legitimate from the past, such as self-defence in war, and reject past practices which are now considered to be illegitimate, at least by the majority of the world's governments, and this may be viewed as an on-going political and legal project. We have inherited *inter alia* the past of the death penalty, mass death in war, deaths in prisons, few medical discoveries for both therapeutic and non-therapeutic treatment,[20] but the majority of the world's governments reject the death penalty (Hood and Hoyle 2008; Johnson and Zimring, 2009; Sarat 1999, 2001a, 2001b; Schabas 2002; Yorke 2008), and attempt to restrain war via political means and as a practical political task (Freud 2005, 221), there are strong arguments for denouncing the 'no-one to blame' excuse for deaths in prisons (Bizos 1998; and see Fournet, this collection) and science and medicine are pushing the boundaries of biotechnological and medical research, for the improved healthcare of the world's populations.

Walter Benjamin had argued that when the death penalty is applied it manifests what is 'rotten in law' (Benjamin 1997, 242) and Derrida engaged with Benjamin's phenomenology, and extended the analysis to identify that the punishment is a 'contamination at the very heart of law' (Derrida 1992, 56). The various questions of life and death which are demonstrated to be in violation of evolved legitimate standards, should be considered a *rotten element of law* and as *contaminating law and society*. If we can continue this phenomenology, we need to produce what Paul Craig proposed as a 'healthy public law' (Craig 2008, 111). This can be formulated through John Rawls's identification in *Political Liberalism* that '[a]t some point, the injustice of the outcomes of a legitimate democratic procedure corrupts its legitimacy' (Rawls 2005, 428) and Austin Sarat confirms this corrupting element as 'law cannot work its lethal will and ally itself with the killing state while remaining aloof and unstained by the deeds themselves' (Sarat 2001a, 21). When there is an acceptance that a past or present law is rotten, corrupting, contaminating, stained, and unhealthy, then it needs to be removed or amended. Indeed the various innovations which penetrate the parameters of life and death may problematise the current legitimate standards, and place stress upon

by the hypothesis, does not exist…the end for which the authority exists, as thus specified, is the enforcement of justice-the maintenance of equitable relations' (Offer 1994, 143).

20 Medical science has come a long way since Jean-Jacques Rousseau's question in, *A Discourse on the Origin of Inequality*, that, '[w]ith respect to sickness…I shall ask if any solid observations have been made from which it may be justly concluded that, in countries where the art of medicine is most neglected, the mean duration of man's life is less than in those where it is most cultivated' (Rousseau 1993, 56).

legal interpretation (Cover 1986),[21] and although Robert Cover noted the pressure applied by the irrevocability of the death penalty, it is just as significant when judges decide the full spectrum of cases which are concerned with the beginning, the continuing, and the ending of life, including, questions of assisted suicide, euthanasia, abortion, advances in biotechnology and patent law, deaths in prison, and the legality of acts in wartime.

Overview of the Book

The Right to Life and the Value of Life: Orientations in Law, Politics and Ethics contributes to the study of the application of choices over life and death by focusing on selected examples within both the 'right to life' and the 'value of life.' Hugo Bedau observed that the right to life itself is an 'enormous topic' (Bedau 1968, 562), and an engagement with every argument of the legal, political and philosophical disciplines which contribute to the debates would necessitate many volumes. This collection provides a selected collage to introduce the reader to the possibilities of interweaving the right to life and the value of life, through the cords of law, politics and ethics, and to do this, it is divided into four themes: firstly, theoretical discourse on life and death; and then specific questions concerning armed combat and detention; the death penalty; and finally, medical scenarios for the causing of death and the easing of passing, and which both promote and enhance the continuation of life.

Part I of the book, entitled *Approaching the Horizons of Life and Death*, has four chapters. It opens with 'Politics and the Philosophy of Life: Towards a Normative Framework,' in which Mark Olssen presents a *tour de force* of life philosophy beginning with Herbert Schnädelbach's three forms of life philosophy, and then an engaging analysis of *inter alia*, Spinoza, Nietzsche and Foucault, to delineate a political philosophy of life as 'continuance.' Olssen provides the Nietzschian observation that 'the only basis for sound evaluations is related to that which supports or does not support life,' and that such evaluation is a necessary component of the 'quest for life's continuance.' For Olssen this is not mere self-preservation, but involves a more nuanced pursuit of '*well-being.*' And this well-being has an inherent political context, which Olssen positions within a cogent

21 Robert Cover began his seminal article, 'Violence and the Word,' in the *Yale Law Review*, with the statement, '[l]egal interpretation plays on a field of pain and death,' and he argued that, '[b]ecause in capital punishment the action or deed is extreme and irrevocable, there is pressure placed on the word – the interpretation that establishes the legal justification for the act. At the same time, the fact that capital punishment constitutes the most plain, the most deliberate, and the most thoughtful manifestation of legal interpretation as violence makes the imposition of the sentence an especially powerful test of the faith and commitment of the interpreters…Capital cases, thus, disclose far more of the structure of judicial interpretation than do other cases (Cover 1986, 1622-1623). See also, Sarat 2001b.

critique of Aristotle's *zoē* and *bios* bifurcation,[22] as he argues that, 'Aristotle was wrong to discern ontic states of *zoē* and *bios*: *zoē* exists within *bios*, but is distinct from it. Life is always political, for politics expresses nothing but the relations between life that mediate the one and the many.'

For Olssen, continuance in life is importantly contingent upon the determination of space boundaries. He maintains that if 'life operates through energy, or power, the limits of its excesses are ultimately determined by life in a particular relationship to space,' and that pressures on space 'determine the limits of growth and the prospect of death.' Within this space, life is not isolated, but dependent upon relationships, as '*life* is always a *form of life*, for humans at least, it always takes place in a community.' Central to life in this community is the concept of the 'good,' as Olssen argues:

> continuance, then, in my conception, is postulated as the strategic dimension of *life*. Life seeks to *continue*. It continues in terms of practices. Such practices constitute a good toward which societies and humanity aim.

It appears that for Olssen, once the good is no more, then the choice of continuance can be discontinued, as 'it raises the issue of suicide, and one must concede, I believe, a right in this regard.' Indeed, for Olssen, the 'good' is identified by positing what allows life to 'survive, to prosper, to flourish, *to continue to live.*' And Olssen identifies three categories of what is 'good,' 'bad' and 'indifferent' for a politics and philosophy of life, and as such these three categories provide a guiding mechanism for governments and what they 'ought to encourage; what ought to be outlawed, or discouraged; and what ought to be left to the discretion of individuals and communities free from the constraints of the state.' Such distinguishing features have important ramifications for identifying the legitimacy of governmental actions with regard to the ever expanding spectrum of the beginning and end of life circumstances, and that, 'decisions for economics, politics, or education require constantly adjusted settlements constitutive of temporary closures around norms, which must be always open to doubt and questioning if they are to sustain a democratic polity.'

---

22 Aristotle in *The Politics* termed life in its biological existence as, *zoē,* and life in the political realm, *bios*, and he stated, '[t]he *good* life is indeed their chief end, both communally and individually; but they form and continue to maintain a political association for the sake of life itself [*zoē*]. Perhaps we may say that there is an element of good even in mere living, provided that life is not excessively beset with troubles. Certainly most men, in their desire to be kept alive, are prepared to face a great deal of suffering, as if finding in life itself a certain well-being and a natural sweetness' (Aristotle, 1992, 187). Giorgio Agamben explained that '[t]he Greeks had no single term to express what we mean by the word "life." They used two terms that, although traceable to a common etymological root, are semantically and morphologically distinct: *zoē*, which expressed the simple fact of living common to all living beings (animals, men or gods), and *bios*, which indicated the form or way of living proper to an individual or a group' (Agamben 1998, 1).

This continual quest for challenging 'temporary closures around norms' must be placed within a political model which constantly renews itself within a transparent formulation. Indeed, Olssen observes Foucault providing that 'life is able to contain and democratise sovereignty,' and as such, '[l]ife is an immanent force that permits infinite ways to continue.' This is contrary to Giorgio Agamben's *Homo Sacer* project, which essentially maintains that sovereignty is recognised in the opposite, as it contains life, and disposes of it outside juridical control in an archaic state of exception (Agamben 1998, 2004). In this way Olssen supports the arguments presented by Andrew Norris in his chapter, 'The Exemplary Exception: Philosophical and Political Decisions in Giorgio Agamben's *Homo Sacer*.' Norris provides a deconstruction of Agamben's theory on 'bare life,' which is derived from the original political decision of the 'ban' where 'a mode of life is actively and continuously excluded or shut out (*ex-claudere*) from the *polis*,' and that the life which is 'taken outside of the *polis* is a sovereign decision.'

Norris provides a very technical critique of the *Homo Sacer*, and particularly, Agamben's use of Carl Schmitt's constitutional theory based on the Weimar Constitution, Article 48, and its possibility for the sovereign to act outside of legal norms which protect the rights of individuals (see also, Agamben 2005). In his critique of Agamben, Norris engages with Martin Heidegger and Hannah Arendt, to demonstrate the political construct in which 'life is placed into question.' And it is this questioning that Norris uses to critique Schmitt, as he observes:

> [f]or Schmitt, any legal system rests upon a decision that cannot itself take the form of law. Both the origin and the border of the law require a political power that exceeds legal justification, and in a state of emergency this power must re-emerge from the system of positive norms appropriate to the normal situation.

For Schmitt, the 'sovereign is he who decides on the exception,' and this '[s]overeignty operates at the outermost sphere; it is here, at the borderline, that it establishes and violates limits.' However, there is an intrinsic flaw in that the exception itself can only be identified through the dichotomy of what is inside and outside, of this borderline concept. Norris notes that this borderline concept is also problematical as 'exceptional cases are clearly defined as such by the rule – itself a paradoxical position.' So the exception requires law for its own identification.[23] The problems do not end there. Agamben uses the camp, and specifically the Nazi camp (the Cambodian killing fields or the Russian Gulags are not intrinsic for Agamben's analysis), and he maintains that 'today it is not the city but rather the camp that is the fundamental biopolitical paradigm of the West.' Through the camp, and specifically the Jewish Holocaust, Norris identifies that for Agamben, 'all of politics, including the liberal regimes devoted to human rights, is implicated and *can be understood in terms of* the Shoah.' Norris has grasped the mantel here,

---

23 On this point, and also in rejection of Agamben's mechanisms for placing the sovereign in an extra-juridical position, see the arguments by Peter Fitzpatrick 2005.

as the recorded debates in the *travaux préparatoires* of the European Convention on Human Rights displayed a denunciation of the Nazi camps, and in London and Strasbourg they were described as the repugnant 'doctrines of death' (Council of Europe 1975 1, 40). Indeed, Norris observes, 'what is needed is the *reinstatement* of legal protection rather than a critique of law – that is the fascist imitation of law that results in the inclusive exclusion of life, and not law itself.' We need a stalwart mechanism for the enforcement of the human rights of individuals over sovereign acts which seek to destroy life, against the life-bearer's will. On this theme, Norris engages with John Locke's thesis of resistance against despotical government, and advancing Locke's argument that in the state of nature freedom involves the right of self-defence, observes that:

> [t]his robust, normative identification of life with individual freedom is part and parcel of Locke's defense of our ability to recognise when a political ruler has put himself into a state of rebellion, and to depose him.[24]

Such rebellion is central to the social and political processes which formulate the evolving discourse on the right to life and how we assign value to life. These processes determine the autonomous, deontological, expression that the sovereign does not have the right to take life in certain circumstances. Life must be protected and not arbitrarily destroyed, and the norms of human rights and the discourse of cosmoplitanism (see Fine 2007) are providing more accurate paradigms of law and political structures for the protection of life, against any rogue sovereign continuously advancing exceptional circumstances to capture and destroy life. Perhaps Agamben's paradigm of the 'camp' is best reserved within phenomenology rather than concrete empirical scrutiny, as Norris maintains:

> [i]t is one thing to suggest, as philosophers like Heidegger working in the phenomenological tradition are bound to do, that one is giving descriptions rather than arguments. It is quite another to say that the aptness or accuracy of a description is something that is appropriately determined only by a sovereign decision.

Norris concludes that 'Agamben's acceptance of Schmitt's decisionism makes it impossible for his analysis to claim any general validity.' On a point of positive law, this is because within post-World War Two constitutional construction, there has been a European, and specifically the Council of Europe's,[25] rejection of the

---

24 See also Bedau 1968.

25 The work of the European Commission for Democracy through Law (the 'Venice Commission'), has been instructive in the formulation of human rights standards within Council of Europe's member state constitutions, see www.venice.coe.int, and for the Venice Commission's contribution to the abolition of the death penalty in the Council of Europe, see Yorke 2010.

principle of the Weimar Constitution, Article 48, and in the deconstruction of the borderline concept, the denunciation of the *inside* and *outside*, human rights seeks to keep the sovereign within law, and severely restrict the circumstances where the sovereign may legitimately take life. The sovereign can no longer decide to create an exception, it must be curtailed by legally identified states of emergency, which include a legally defined protection of life.

Nikolas Rose, in the next chapter, 'The Value of Life: Somatic Ethics and the Spirit of Biocapital,' positions an ethical argument for the value of life within the advances of biocapital. At the beginning of his chapter, Rose engages with the calculations made by England and Wales' National Institute for Clinical Excellence (NICE), for the distribution of the drugs, Avastin and Erbitux, for treatment of late-stage bowel cancer. NICE uses the 'quality adjusted life year' (QALY) calculation to place a financial value on life. Rose takes us to the juncture between the state's fiscal assessment, in a biopolitical calculation, and the individual's desire to live through an 'instructive intertwining of the ethical and the economic.' He identifies that the ethical boundaries of life and death should be 'framed in terms of dignity,' and states:

> [t]he value of life here seems to exist in a kind of transactional space between the claim that existence itself has some intrinsic value, and the claim that value should attach, not to life as vitality, but to life as a subjective state – to the 'dignity' of those who live it.

Rose notes that some economists place a value on life calculated by the state's 'willingness to pay,' and that this will be determined by the wealth of a country and the proportion of net wealth to national health provisions, and also for compensation in cases of state negligence. Rose reveals that the extent of the compensation will not only depend upon the government, but also, on the nationality of the victims. For instance, in 1998 the United States gave almost $2million to the Italian victims' families when a US marine jet hit aerial tramway cables, and then in 2003, a US gunship shot at villages in Afghanistan and the innocent victims' families received only $200, and consequently, 'we know that in practice, some forms of life are judged more valuable than others.'

Rose then shifts from biopolitical practices initiated by governments, to emphasise the role of individuals, and the family network, in maximising the value of life, when he observes, '[t]he notion of human capital links to ways in which, in advanced liberal ethics, each individual is urged to live his or her life as a kind of enterprise to maximise lifestyle or potential, to become a kind of entrepreneur of oneself and one's family.' Rose is absolutely right when he identifies the importance of human capital for the value of life, and it can also be seen that those successful entrepreneurs of 'oneself and one's family,' are more equipped to protect the parameters of their own life. Consequently, when considering the industrialisation of life through the, 'laboratory, the factory, and the stock market,' Rose notes an evolution through a 'bioeconomics,' which has a more global emphasis on 'biovalue,' because, 'the language of bioeconomics brings into existence a new space for thought and action. The bioeconomy has appeared as a space to be mapped, managed and understood.'

Such calculations, which map and manage, are manifested within the growth of investment and consultancy organisations worldwide, as Rose notes the '[p]rojects to govern the bioeconomy sometimes involve surprising alliances between political authorities and promissory capitalism.' Indeed, biotechnology has become one of the essential economic drivers within the global economy, and essential to this is biomedicine. Rose observes that '[p]oliticians across the globe continue to foster the growth of a biotech sector,' and this is because, in many ways, both the governments and individuals, agree that the vitality of the population is a worthwhile goal of politics and ethics. Rose states:

> [h]uman beings identify and interpret much of their unease in terms of the health, vitality, and morbidity of their bodies; they judge and act upon their soma in their attempts to make themselves not just physically better, but also to make themselves better persons. This is what I call a 'somatic ethic.'

Rose identifies that 'the somatic, the bodily, the "bio," have become so central to our form of life,' it is essential that we supervise 'all those practices in which life is the object, target, and stake.' This ethic is 'in key respects, somatic, this is because it is our soma – our genome, our neurotransmitters, our "biology" – that is given salience.' Essentially Rose is uncovering a global dissymmetry facilitated by the transcendent 'corrupt pursuit of profit and personal gain.' It is reflected within the 'capitalisation of life itself,' as located within the juxtaposition of rich and poor countries, or between the rich and poor individuals within countries. As such, there is a crucial need to understand that the 'differential value of life is very much at stake.' The very realisation of a right to life, in many respects, is determined, or contingent upon, the distillation of this differential value in life.

Stephen Smith, in his chapter, 'How We Value Life: George Bailey and the Life Not Worthy of Being Lived,' focuses upon healthcare situations at the end of life, through the lenses of the 'Sanctity of Life' (SOL) and the 'Quality of Life' (QOL) positions. Smith provides a novel enquiry into the two traditional schools on the value of life, through the use of the character George Bailey from the film, *It's a Wonderful Life*. In utilising this fictional character, or as he terms an 'example life,' Smith is able to deconstruct the two positions and provide a hybrid calculation on the value of life which no longer follows the demarcated approach. He argues that:

> [d]espite the importance of concerns about the value of life, no overriding conception about how best to value life has evolved. Indeed, in many ways, the debate is more polarised now than it was previously. The two sides which have emerged in the debate over the value of life have become entrenched positions and very little headway has been made in repeated discussions about the issue.

Smith provides a new analysis based upon a hitherto unrecognised fusion of the two positions, which produces a 'more inclusive viewpoint about how we value life.' Smith identifies that for the SOL position 'life has an inherent or basic value,' and for the QOL position, 'there is no inherent value in life. Instead, life is valuable because it allows you to do things which are valuable.' Smith effectively deconstructs these positions through Bailey's claim that the world would have been better off without him,[26] and Clarence the angel's rebuttal by showing Bailey the degrading depiction of what the world would have been like without him. Smith identifies that '[i]n the end, then, his simple existence matters as much as the choices he has made throughout his life.' Smith observes:

> [t]he conclusion of the film seems to be that George's life matters both because of some inherent value in existence and because of the things he accomplishes during that existence. In other words, both the essential valuations of the SOL position and the QOL position appear to be correct. This, however, is the one result which is supposed to be impossible under the current formulation.

Smith provides a rupture of the current bifurcated position and when the issues of the beginning and ending of life are encountered, Smith's thesis proves cogent and illuminating, and not just for medical law, but for the wider consideration of the boundaries of life and death. Reflective of the struggle outlined in the introduction above, Smith confirms that:

> [d]etermining our lives have value may not be easy. It is a struggle because what we value is a multi-faceted and complex notion about not only ourselves but how we interact with the people, events and things around us. It causes us to examine those things we take for granted and our failures as well as our successes. Despite this, the examination is worth doing. At the very least, it shows us that even so-called 'ordinary lives' have great meaning.

Part II, *The Vicissitudes of Armed Conflict and Detention*, begins with a chapter by Agnieszka Jachec-Neale, 'The Right to Take Life: Killing and Death in Armed Conflict.' Jachec-Neale provides a probing assessment of the extent of the right to life of combatants in armed conflict, the difficulties of correctly classifying when individuals may be recognised by law as a combatant, and when they are citizens in a non-military function, and the circumstances determining oscillation between the two. For the determination of these issues, Jachec-Neale manoeuvres through both international humanitarian law and international human rights law and identifies that there is an 'ongoing debate about how these two regimes are to be applied to armed conflict situations,' and that '[a]t the heart of the problem

26 On the issue of whether the world would be *better off* without humans, see Benatar, 2006.

are questions of how these two regimes relate to each other in armed conflict situations.'

Jachec-Neale argues that the killing of enemy combatants within the international legal framework is a complicated exercise and it is of fundamental importance that those in command have a detailed understanding of the legal parameters of the right to life and its exceptions. She notes the complex calculation for using weapons which, by their nature, do not discriminate between persons on the ground. Such weapons do not enable a specific targeting of enemy combatants and as a consequence the indiscriminate nature of the weapon renders the possibility that civilians may be injured or killed. Fundamental for Jachec-Neale's arguments is the need to distinguish between legitimate and arbitrary killings. She notes, '[a]s a rule, civilians, who are not directly participating in hostilities, must not be the subjects of direct attack, and any deaths resulting from a direct intentional attack on them could be construed as arbitrary killings.' As a result, '[a]n attacker should take all feasible precautions with the view to avoid or to minimise incidental loss of life.' To illustrate this point Jachec-Neale argues:

> [t]he problem is acute in cases when people are rotating in and out of direct participation in hostilities and this makes it very difficult for the armed forces to correctly assess not only the substance and degree of the individual conduct, but also to identify whether it is legal to apprehend or kill the individual.

Jachec-Neale has effectively identified that the high pressure circumstances on the ground in armed conflict situations will mean that it is extremely difficult for armed forces to always correctly identify when an individual is an enemy combatant, and when he/she is not, and therefore whether it is legitimate to apprehend or, if necessary, kill, this person(s). Jachec-Neale argues that the difficulty presented by the situation, must not neutralise the responsibility of the forces for arbitrary deaths or unjust detentions.

The apprehension and detention of individuals in armed conflict is then considered by Susan Breau, in 'The Right to Life of Detainees in Armed Conflict.' Breau intricately explores the extent to which the right to life is protected when individuals are detained in combat situations, and she uses as a case study the death of Baha Mousa whilst in the custody of United Kingdom armed forces during the conflict in Iraq.[27] Breau utilises the two regimes of legal protection provided by international humanitarian law and international human rights law, and she also investigates the possibility of adopting the International Law Commission's Draft Articles on State Responsibility. After considering the international law provisions, Breau argues that within:

---

27 Argued in the case, *Mazin Jumaa Gatteh Al-Skeini v. the Secretary of State for Defence*, 2007 UKHL 26.

> treaty and customary law, there are extensive provisions establishing protection for the right to life in detention, but the next step within the purview of international humanitarian law is to ensure criminal accountability if these protections are not respected.

The Mousa litigation demonstrates that during and following armed conflict it is necessary to scrutinise the knowledge and actions of the military personnel up to the highest position in the chain of command. Breau maintains that the:

> criminal responsibility extends not only to those who directly perpetrate the crime but also to those in command, who bear the burden of training and supervising troops under their command. This has been a long standing rule within international criminal law that those who bear the greatest responsibility should be tried.

Breau reveals that in the case of Baha Mousa, the 'thorny question of command responsibility' was the major issue, and she notes that there was a disparity between those charged with grave breaches of international law, being the junior ranked officers, and those who were charged with tortous offences, being the more senior officers. Breau also identifies the importance of human rights law in this case as she states:

> [h]uman rights law provided the mechanism of enforcing violations of human rights but at the same time was dealing indirectly with violations of international humanitarian law. This is particularly important as although the senior officers were relieved of criminal responsibility, the United Kingdom could be held liable under its human rights obligations for failing to absolutely prohibit robust methods of interrogation, known in this case as 'conditioning techniques' and for failing to live up to their positive obligations to preserve and protect life.

The Mousa decision demonstrates that during detention in armed combat situations, the right to life cannot be infringed, even within emergency situations that threaten the life of a nation. Breau argues 'in the case of deaths in detention, the onus shifts to the detaining power to explain how the death occurred lawfully, something that would be impossible in the circumstances of the death of Baha Mousa.' As such, Breau positions the doctrine of state responsibility 'as a core concept of customary international law,' and along with international humanitarian law, and international human rights, the International Law Commission's Draft Articles of State Responsibility can preserve a claim involving a three pronged analysis of, 'a call for preventative measures, a claim for the punishment of those responsible and a demand for payment of compensation.' Breau argues for there to be greater clarity in the law on two central issues; the jurisdictional grounds of international humanitarian law and international human rights law, and the designation of 'command responsibility.' She warns that the Nuremberg and subsequent military tribunals which 'attached responsibility for massive violations of human rights to the highest level of military and government command seems to be fading into obscurity.' The Mousa decision is a partial inroad into these determinations, and Breau is clear that there is still more to do as this 'part of international law is just beginning to be developed and it remains to be seen how the global community will respond to systematic and pervasive violations of the rights of detainees in armed conflict.'

From detention in armed conflict, Caroline Fournet considers the deaths of inmates in domestic detention circumstances in, 'At the Hands of the State: When Arrest and Imprisonment Prove Fatal.' Fournet surveys the international standards, with a focus upon the Council of Europe's Convention system of human rights, and as case studies, she analyses the situations in the United Kingdom and France. Fournet argues that deaths following arrest and imprisonment are 'too often met with social indifference and state tacit approval,' that 'state authorities appear to be less than willing to fully investigate such deaths,' and further, that in many instances such deaths 'generate little interest within public opinion.' This is a startling observation concerning the systemic failure of the protection of the life of inmates, but Fournet argues that there is a life-line as 'respect for human rights – including human dignity, the right to physical integrity and the right to life – transcend penitentiary walls.' She notes the importance of the European Convention on Human Rights, article 3, which prohibits torture and inhuman treatment and punishment, and article 5, which prohibits arbitrary deprivation of liberty, and she engages with how these articles scrutinise the protection of inmate's lives and then places them within the context of the right to life provision under article 2. Fournet affirms that article 2 should be utilised to protect the right to life of detainees, and positions the European Court of Human Rights case *Osman v. United Kingdom* as a key decision identifying the vulnerability of detainees.

She argues that state authorities must 'take preventive operational measures to protect an individual whose life is at risk' and that this principle must apply, 'to individuals placed in detention.' Fournet also questions the 'almost total disregard by legal doctrine of self-inflicted deaths,' and that 'cases of suicides in custody fail to attract the interest of legal scholars,' and remains predominantly within sociological analysis. Following her survey of the above issues, Fournet argues that this scholarly lacuna is primarily because of the difficulty of meeting the legal standards of proof for determining responsibility for homicides in detention, and that secrecy and coercion play a major role in the ineffectiveness of prosecutions for such deaths. This flaw, argues Fournet, maintains the lacuna in current understanding of deaths in prisons and the failure, 'to explore the occurrences of suicides in detention prevents [lawyers] from adequately assessing the way in which prisons operate.' Fournet's important work reveals that there is a dearth of information on deaths in prisons within the United Kingdom and France, and strategic polices should be implemented to generate data from not only sociological perspectives, but from a legal basis as well.

Part III, *The Denunciation of the Death Penalty*, opens with a critical review of the abandonment of the death penalty within international criminal justice. Steven Freeland in 'International Criminal Justice and the Death Penalty,' provides a probing genealogy of the cases from the post-World War Two Nuremberg and Tokyo Military Tribunals, which imposed the death penalty, to the recent International Court of Justice cases and the various United Nations international criminal tribunals, which impose a maximum punishment of a term of imprisonment. Freeland places the non-application of the death penalty by these international institutions, within a wider consideration of the 'evolution of the nature of international criminal justice,' over the past 60 years, and identifies this process as an 'internationalisation of justice.' Freeland surveys the discussions at the United Nations which involved the International Law Commission on the appropriate punishment for future defendants charged with international crimes. Following the 'era of impunity' where the death penalty was imposed, Freeland observes how the Cold War made it 'impossible for the international community to find the common will to build upon the foundations laid by the Nuremberg and Tokyo Military Tribunal processes.' One of the issues which caused controversy was whether the death penalty was an appropriate punishment for any future formulated international tribunal.

Freeland outlines the tide of change in the 1990s. It was after the 'shackles of the Cold War were loosened,' that the United Nations was able to focus upon addressing international crimes and create a system of international criminal tribunals. Freeland notes that under Chapter VII of the United Nations Charter, the United Nations Security Council established two *ad hoc* tribunals in Rwanda and the former Yugoslavia. The statutes for the International Criminal Tribunal for the Former Yugoslavia (ICTY), and the International Criminal Tribunal for Rwanda (ICTR), do not include the possibility of the death penalty. For Rwanda, this posed an intricate legal conundrum, as at the time of the drafting of the statutes, while those responsible for the atrocities during the genocide did not receive a capital trial under the ICTY, in the domestic criminal justice system the death penalty remained a possible sentence. Freeland notes that this penological conundrum led Rwanda to reassess their criminal justice policy and in 2007 it abolished the death penalty. He also notes that the death penalty was not included within the Statute for the International Criminal Court. However this positive process of abolitionism was not witnessed in The Iraqi High Criminal Tribunal, following the death sentence and execution of Saddam Hussein on 20 December 2006. Freeland provides a probing analyses of the Dujail and Genocide trials, and concludes:

> [a]s a result of the flawed processes involved in his trial, an important opportunity was missed. The Saddam trial simply failed to promote reconciliation in Iraq. The circumstances leading up to, and including, the death sentence significantly undermined the credibility and potential for positive consequences that might otherwise have possibly stemmed from the trial of the former dictator. Instead, what it demonstrated was that, unlike the process that was actually implemented,

> if international criminal justice is to make an important contribution to peace, then it must respect the rule of law and ensure the rights of the accused, so as to limit any suggestions that it simply represents 'victors' justice.'

Freeland also surveys the international standards to argue that the evolution of international criminal law is towards a denunciation of the death penalty. But he provides a note of caution, in that, in his opinion, there is not yet a *per se* international rule against the death penalty or that the abolition of the punishment is a 'norm' of customary international law as:

> there is an undeniable trend towards abolition, so that the illegality of the death penalty might more accurately be described as an 'emerging norm' of international law...However, we are simply not there yet as far as being definitive as to the illegality of the death penalty under customary international law.

Importantly Freeland concludes with a visionary proposition that 'the internationalisation of criminal justice might...be seen as a way of "persuading" countries to acknowledge the irreversible momentum towards universal abolition of the death penalty' (see also Bae 2007). The domino effect of complete abolition is in motion.

In the next chapter, the Council of Europe is considered by Jon Yorke in 'The Right to Life and Abolition of the Death Penalty in the Council of Europe.' Yorke outlines a history of the legislation on the right to life and investigates the compatibility of the European Convention on Human Rights, article 2(1), which *prima facie* allows for the application of the death penalty, with Protocol No. 6 to the Convention, which provides for abolition of the punishment in peacetime, and Protocol No. 13 to the Convention, which provides for abolition in all circumstances. Yorke provides new readings of the political discussions on the death penalty within the Parliamentary Assembly and the Committee of Ministers, and also engages with the jurisprudence of the European Commission of Human Rights and the European Court of Human Rights on article 2(1). In analysing the legislation restricting and abolishing the death penalty within the Council of Europe, Yorke reveals the early disagreements within the political organs, and then the pivotal date of 1980, when the Parliamentary Assembly unified itself and laid the groundwork for abolition through a report, resolution and recommendation, which provided the impetus for Protocol No. 6. Yorke notes that during the debates on the death penalty in the Parliamentary Assembly, the issue of the right to life was of crucial importance, and it was used for the breaking down of the member state's monopoly on the right of the death penalty. He refers to the work of various Parliamentarians, including Carl Lidbom and Renate Wohlwend, and argues that a political position was being created which demonstrated that 'the death penalty was no longer to be seen as an exclusive issue for the state,' and that the 'renunciation of this sovereign state right was then affirmed through recourse to the individual's right to life.'

Following the expansion of the Council to Central and Eastern Europe in 1993, the journey to the adoption of Protocol No. 13 is explored. Although Protocol No. 6 had provided for the removal of the death penalty in peacetime, the text of Convention article 2(1) remained. The Parliamentary Assembly, and particularly Renate Wohlwend, the *rapporteur* to the Committee on Legal Affairs and Human Rights, saw Protocol No. 13 as the ideal opportunity to provide for the change in the text by a removal of the second sentence of article 2(1). However, to the astonishment of the *rapporteur*, the final draft provided by the Committee of Ministers did not include a provision for amendment, and so the European Court of Human Rights was left to adjudicate on the compatibility of the two protocols with the text of article 2(1). Yorke provides a history of the jurisprudence on the right to life, and engages with the key decisions of *Soering v. United Kingdom* and *Öcalan v. Turkey*, and discusses the extent to which the Court considers the death penalty to be (in)compatible with article 2(1). Even with the text of article 2(1) remaining, the jurisprudence of the Court on this article has positively developed in its holding that the death penalty is a violation of the right to life in peacetime, and that following *Bader v. Sweden* there may now be scope for determining that an execution does not need to take place to initiate a violation of article 2(1). Yorke concludes that the maintenance of the Council of Europe 'death penalty-free zone' may not only be contingent upon the event of amendment of article 2(1), but that 'the abolition of the death penalty in the Council of Europe should be viewed as an on-going legal and political project' and that central to this is the role of the Committee on Legal Affairs and Human Rights of the Parliamentary Assembly.

In the next chapter, 'The Death Penalty and Russia,' Bill Bowring provides a multi-disciplinary investigation into the reasons why the death penalty is still preserved within Russian criminal law, and presents a prognosis for the future removal of the punishment. Bowring analyses the recent coverage of the death penalty in the Russian media, and engages with how this is reflective of the religious, political and philosophical issues. Notably Bowring uncovers how the work of the Enlightenment humanist, Cesare Beccaria, manifests within Russian political thought and he also presents a corrective exegesis of Karl Marx's opinions on the death penalty. This scholarly exposition is then positioned within the gradual demise of the punishment and the role in the 1990s of the Constitutional reformists in Russia.

Bowring highlights the important role of Anatoly Pristavkin, the former Chairman of the Presidential Pardons Commission of Russia (Pristavkin 1999) for the promotion of abolitionism in the 1990s, and he situates this within the current reluctance of Russia to adopt the Council of Europe's abolitionist instruments. Russia currently has a moratorium, but it has not yet removed the punishment from its statutes and has signed but not ratified Protocol No. 6, and has not signed Protocol No. 13. Bowring notes that although in 1996, President Yeltsin issued a decree on the 'gradual curtailing of the application of the death penalty,' there is still a discrepancy between what Russia initially agreed with the Council of Europe, and what has subsequently been achieved. Bowring effectively brings to light the differences in the approaches to the status of the death penalty within the State Duma, the President, and the Federal Constitutional Court. While both Presidents Putin and Medvedev have stressed the importance of the continuation of the moratorium in Russia, the State Duma has repeatedly refused to ratify Protocol No. 6, and in 1999 the Federal Constitutional Court held that in the absence of trial by jury in every part of Russia, the death penalty is unconstitutional.

Furthermore on 19 November 2009 the Court held that even if trial by jury is completely reinstated in Russia, this will not provide the mechanism to reintroduce the death penalty. The Court affirmed that because Russia had signed Protocol No. 6, the death penalty is now abolished in this vast country. Bowring argues that this is a significant legal reasoning which may act as a bulwark against any political moves to bring back the punishment.

The next two sections engage with medical scenarios and how they relate to questions of life and death. Part IV, *Medical Countenance at the End of Life*, focuses on medical circumstances at the passing of life, both in the form of a killing and circumstances of letting die. In the first chapter, 'Assisted Suicide, Voluntary Euthanasia, and the Right to Life,' David Benatar provides an ethical argument for autonomous decisions at the end of life, and he positions his thesis outside of the traditional human rights framework. Benatar identifies that although liberal societies provide competent adults 'extensive freedom to *lead* their lives in the ways they choose, all but a handful of such societies deny people freedom to obtain assistance to *end* their lives.' From this observation, Benatar makes an illuminating analysis which leads him to conclude that a right to assisted suicide and voluntary euthanasia (this chapter does not consider non-voluntary or involuntary euthanasia) can be adequately constructed without recourse to a specific human rights mandate.

Benatar observes the possibility (and perhaps the necessity) of separating the ethical and legal questions when he maintains, '[m]any people fail to recognise that there are two distinct moral questions one can ask about suicide and euthanasia. The one is whether these practices are morally acceptable, while the other is whether they ought (morally) to be legal.' Benatar engages with the moral/immoral and legal/illegal distinction, and in isolating the right to life, he states that there is no need for a separate 'right to die,' because such a position can be made through observing the possibility of the relinquishing of the right to life as:

> [w]ith regard to assisted suicide and voluntary euthanasia the crucial question about the right not to be killed is whether it can be waived. The right not to be killed obligates others not to kill the right-bearer. However, if the right-bearer is entitled to waive this right, then he is entitled to release others from their duty not to kill him.

A further prong with regard to the 'power' over our own lives is provided when he states:

> [o]bviously, if a right not to be killed included the power to waive the right, then the right not to be killed would not preclude assisted suicide and voluntary euthanasia. Indeed such a power would positively permit these practices.

Benatar explains that the right to waive the right to life, and the vested power in allowing the ending of our own lives, has an intrinsic moral basis. The morality of this calculation lies in the assessment of continued life and this assessment maintains that 'continued life is *ordinarily* in our interests, it is not always so. The quality of one's life can be so bad that one reasonably judges death to be less bad than continuing to live in one's condition.' The assessment of such quality of life must be a subjective, deontological, position arrived at by the person wishing to die, and on this point Benatar provides a most useful analysis:

> [o]nce we recognise that life could become so bad that continued life is no longer in one's interests, we must recognise that a right not to be killed can outlive its moral purpose – to protect an individual's important interests. If a right to life does not include a power to waive the right then instead of the right serving the interests of the right-bearer it becomes the right-bearer's master. And the worse the quality of life is, the more cruel a master it is.

Healthcare professionals providing palliative care must take on board Benatar's claims, because if the SOL arguments are demonstrated to have failed, then the QOL argument becomes an assessment of the severity of pain an individual experiences before life loses its meaning for that person and whether palliative care can ensure that this pain threshold is not reached. Such a position would ignite public policy questions. However, Benatar deals with the claims that a slippery slope of mass death awaits if these forms of passing are legalised, and also the possible problems associated with voluntariness. Although Benatar grounds his analysis within a moral framework he does see the importance of law for regulating any system of assisted suicide and voluntary euthanasia. In dealing with the concerns, he states that governments would be required to 'build robust safeguards into the legislation that legalises these practices.' The slippery slope can be prevented.

In the next chapter, 'Positive and Negative Obligations under the Right to Life in English Medical Law: Letting Patients Die,' Elizabeth Wicks provides an excellent overview of the different medical scenarios within English law, which attract an analysis of the right to life. Wicks outlines the current prohibition of 'all forms of positive assistance in causing death,' and engages with the questions concerning the negative application of the right to life in the separation of conjoined twins, the killing of the unborn, and in the positive application of the withdrawal of life-sustaining treatment, the refusal of life-sustaining treatment, and the issues of funding treatment. Wicks provides a probing analysis of these issues, including a rejection of the 'designated for death' thesis within the conjoined twins case, *Re A*, as she explains:

> [t]he designated for death argument must be rejected as a means of reducing the protection afforded by the right to life. We are all designated for death and the imminence of an expected death is not a sufficient reason for abandoning legal and ethical protection for that life.

Wick's argument strengthens the mechanisms for protecting the right to life in English medical law and ethical reasoning. She displays a sensitive understanding of the political and legal thresholds, for example, in considering the right to life of the unborn, vis-à-vis the right to bodily integrity of the mother, Wicks argues:

> [w]hat is crucial is that a viable foetus, even though it has a right not to be killed, cannot depend upon a continued violation of another person's bodily integrity. The right to life never guarantees to anyone that their life will be preserved.

Wicks explains the need for the importance of clarity concerning the nuances of the discourse on the protection of the right to life which in some circumstances call for life to be allowed to die or caused to die, and in others for life to be protected. In placing these variables in context, Wicks critiques the application of the right to life in the case of Anthony Bland, and she argues:

> [t]he patient in PVS [permanent vegetative state] is not bereft of rights and interests, as the case-law regrettably implies, but rather it is the very continuance of these rights and interests that may justify the state withdrawing life-sustaining treatment and ceasing to take positive steps to preserve that patient's life.

Wicks also provides a cogent observation with regard to placing a human right to life within the QALY test, and she observes that '[u]nder the right to life, equality of protection is vital. Everyone's life should be protected by law, regardless of life expectancy, quality of life, or the conflicting needs of healthier or younger individuals.' Wicks has achieved an intricate weaving together of the multifaceted challenges to medical law in dealing with the right to life, and in unraveling her heterogeneous consideration she concludes, '[w]hile the right to life offers fundamental protection for human life, it has to operate within the real world in which we will all die and some invariably sooner rather than later.' But even so '[t]he right to life is far less forgiving of positive acts that cause death,' and is 'less about preserving life in all circumstances and more about the need for a sufficiently compelling justification before the legal protection for life can be overridden.'

Then in the next chapter, 'Conjoined Twins: Separation As Lethal Mutilation,' Helen Watt provides a detailed critique of the *Re A* case. *Re A* concerned the legality of surgery for the separation of the conjoined twins named by the court as 'Jodie' and 'Mary.' Mary was so physically disabled that she depended upon Jodie for her survival. However, Mary's reliance on Jodie's organs was killing her sister. If separated Jodie had the highest chance of survival and the medical opinion was that Mary would die following surgery. Watt places this case within an analysis of how persons with disabilities are perceived. She argues:

> [i]n identifying human beings or human bodily subjects, we need to bear in mind that human bodies do not all look the same. Even healthy bodies go through major changes as they grow and develop. Disabled bodies also look different from the kind of bodies to which we are accustomed. We need to go back to the concept of an organism – a living, self-organised whole – to count how many human subjects were present in the case of *Re A*.

The complexities of identifying the changing human body (see also Herring and Chau 2007) which is assigned a right to life, and indeed the ways in which the right to life should be used for people with disabilities are identified. In analysing the *Re A* decision, Watt maintains that the 'suggestion that a conjoined twin should be given a more normal-looking body at the cost of her life represents a new low point in the way we see disabled people.' As such, Watt argues that Mary's biological existence should have reflected an essential good in and of itself as:

> [i]t is surely part of what it means to be an organism that one has certain biological interests, including the interest in survival. If this is true of lower organisms, it is true in a much richer sense of human beings, whose presence in the world carries with it the meaning and value of the kind of being they are. Mary was a member of the rational human species, whose interests in the range of 'human goods' were those of her species. Even if most of these interests were doomed to be thwarted in Mary's lifetime, this did not mean that her existence itself was a bad or worthless thing.

However, a limit calculation is acknowledged as '[j]ust because life retains a certain value, even in a highly damaged state, this does not mean we should go to all possible lengths to promote or safeguard that value. The good of life must compete with other goods, and with life in other people, when it comes (for example) to allocating resources.' So Watt does not make a 'vitalist pursuit of life for one person, at any cost to other people's lives and well being,' and following a probing engagement with the issues of unjust aggression, the principle of double effect, the mutilation of Mary, and the cognitive issues associated with this case, Watt formulates a useful means/ends distinction when she states:

> [i]n this as in any other field, it is not enough to have a good end; we also need to have a good means…In *Re A*, there were two patients, each of whom had the right to immunity from harmful bodily invasions. Cutting into Mary, in a way which did her only serious permanent harm, was a bad means to the good end of saving her twin sister's life.

Part V, *Access to Medical Treatment and the Preservation of (New) Life*, concludes this collection, with chapters concerning the promotion of life as continuing in a healthcare context, through the concept of access to healthcare provisions, and the availability of assisted reproduction and research on human embryos in China. Johanna Gibson, in 'Access to Medicines and the Right to (Cultural) Life,' identifies the importance of scientific research and access to medical provisions and she argues that the information about such provisions must be 'delivered in a culturally relevant and meaningful context.'[28] She argues for the recognition of the importance of knowledge transfer, and the need for identification that the heterogeneous considerations require that governments provide a more nuanced approach to healthcare delivery. Gibson demonstrates the connectedness of culture and healthcare as:

> [t]he cultural and physical health and well-being of the individual underpins the full realisation of the right to cultural life, comprising the individual's access to the public sphere and to the institutions within that sphere, including the institution of medicine and healthcare.

And in affirmation, 'the full realisation of the right to health includes fulfillment of the cultural, social and political determinants relevant to health.' In our multi-cultural world, nothing less will do than to facilitate an autonomous decision making process concerning the full spectrum of medical and healthcare decisions to be made by both doctor and patient. Gibson's observation is powerful, and it is necessary for a research agenda which promotes healthcare as being sensitive to cultural variations.

The political economics of such policies are crucial to Gibson, and she demonstrates the need for effective development and the contribution of the World Health Organization for the special considerations in developing countries. Gibson outlines the importance of the WHO's Intergovernmental Working Group on Public Health, Innovation and Intellectual Property (IGWG). The IGWG has a mandate to 'develop and prepare a global strategy and work programme, with particular regard to the special issues for developing countries.' Fundamental to the promotion of development is the 'moral' use of patents for the benefit of the community, as Gibson explains:

> [t]his central value of use is critical to questions of morality in the application and exercise of patent law. When examining the concept of use in patent rights, not only the scope of the patent (the legal rights in the invention) but also the accessibility for users (the beneficial interests in the invention) will be manifest. This characterisation of use is furthermore critical to an appreciation of the

28 On the issue of healthcare delivery being sensitive to cultural issues, see also Prado 2008 and Dundes Renteln 2004.

> cultural life of patents and provides for a foundation for maintaining access to the beneficial interests of the invention, on behalf of the whole society.

This moral application has much to commend it. Gibson's framework here would help ensure that medical care and treatment is more effectively distributed globally than it currently is. The ethical aspects of access to healthcare are crucial, as Gibson calls for an 'ethical oversight for medicines,' and such ethics will facilitate 'life chances' which are maintained through medical care, as '[m]eaningful access to medicines is fundamentally a question of the right to life.'

The next two chapters concern questions of fertility in China. Ayo Wahlberg, in 'Assessing Vitality: Infertility and Good Life in Urban China,' analyses the reproductive technologies used in China to improve life, and he investigates what kind of life it is that requires such improvement. To do this he focuses on four IVF clinics in Beijing and Changsha, and investigates how different viewpoints on the vitality of life contribute to the ways in which infertility and assisted reproductive technologies are considered and used. Wahlberg argues that:

> assisted reproductive technologies in urban China are best understood as assemblages of practices aimed at improving human *life* (shēng). Yet, it is not a singular kind of life, it is life that is at once biological and social, cellular and psychological, individual and collective.

In his assessment of life in China, Wahlberg analyses the 'interlinkages between certain concepts of "quality" and the very practical and normative assessments of "good life" that they make possible.' Wahlberg outlines what constitutes good life in assisted reproduction in China, and he reveals that there are certain sentiments which transcend political ideologies; essentially, for China, even in this vast population with a one child policy, the inherent longing to conceive a child. Wahlberg describes the harrowing circumstances in and around the fertility clinics, with couples searching for 'answers as to why they are unable to conceive a child,' and the 'landlords hawking rooms to rent for those who have traveled afar.' Inherent within the need to procreate is a deep psychological phenomenon closely intertwined with Chinese culture, as Wahlberg observes that 'the resulting involuntary childlessness is seen to disrupt and indeed devastate the cultural, social and/or psychological *well-being* of those who are infertile.' Wahlberg informs us that the problems of infertility do not rest with the biological, but infuse a burdened life in existential terms. Infertility is contra to 'filial piety' which is an 'obligation to honour and respect one's parents and ancestors as well as to extend the life of one's ancestors indefinitely through patrilineal birth.' Ancestral worship places a burden on the lives of those infertile in China, and renders of such believers *inter alia* an 'incomplete life,' and 'matrimonial failure.'

Wahlberg makes the illuminating observation that due to these multifaceted vicissitudes placed on the Chinese family, '[w]e can see then how it is burdened life rather than pathological life *per se* that assisted reproductive technologies are called upon to redress in urban China today,' and because of this, '[b]iological treatments…are a means to the end of improving a couple's and family's quality of life by eliminating their agony and suffering.' Wahlberg informs us that, unlike in the liberal context, the concept of 'quality of life' is relatively new in China. Even so, we can see that the Chinese concept is nuanced as he argues:

> [i]t is important to note that in Mandarin, there are three common ways of conveying a concept of 'quality of life': *shēngcún zhìliàng* (生存质量), *shēngmìng zhìliàng* (生命質量) and *shēnghuó zhìliàng* (生活质量), where *shēngcún* denotes the minimum requirements for life (to exist, to survive), *shēngmìng* refers to life as a vital force and *shēnghuó* conveys a sense of life as an activity (being alive, living, working). And so, in Chinese terminology, one might distinguish between physiological and health-related forms of quality of life on the one hand and a more social form of quality of life on the other.

Wahlberg observes that China's promotion of the good life is found in the improvement of facilities for fertility treatment so that families can have their own children and he argues that '[e]very successful assisted birth is, in a sense, a victory over the "bad life" (inferior quality sperm, bad quality embryos, tubular blockages, endometriosis, etc.) that would otherwise prevent it.' And this inferior quality is also transposed for the creation of a greater 'population quality' at the macro level, as a collective 'good life' 'animates a healthy, vibrant and strong collective free of persons suffering from genetic diseases of a serious nature, congenital defects of a serious nature, target infectious diseases as well as so-called "relevant mental diseases."'

Kerstin Klein, in 'Illiberal Biopolitics and "Embryonic Life": The Governance of Human Embryonic Stem Cell Research in China,' provides a scholarly enquiry into the work of Michel Foucault and his liberal biopolitical thesis, to uncover whether the French philosopher's arguments can be utilised to assess human embryonic stem cell research in the illiberal Chinese context. Klein explains the major advances in reproductive technologies in China and argues that under the premise of 'scientific development,' the Chinese population is called upon to become an 'innovation-oriented society.' One of the central issues for this orientation is the advances in human embryonic stem cell research and in this field although China is recognised to be an illiberal democracy, their policies on the regulation of stem cell research appear to be extremely liberal. Klein observes, 'cautious stem cell policies and the ongoing controversy in large parts of the developed world offer unprecedented research and commercialisation opportunities,' because in China:

> the government and bioethics experts pertain an official view according to which China has a cultural environment with fewer moral obstacles to the use of human embryos in stem cell research than many other nations.

Klein notes that 'under the premises of "scientific development" the "population" and human embryos are harnessed as "experimental" resources for national development through scientific progress.' This progress has now taken the identification of what life itself *is* beyond the biopolitical thesis which originally attached itself to modern liberal democracies. Klein explains:

> [w]hat the two forms, liberalism and authoritarianism, share is that they inhere elements of sovereignty and a biopolitical imperative of the optimisation of the population. The fundamental difference between liberal and illiberal biopolitics, however, lies in the extent to which both deploy this sovereign power. While new forms of self-governance, choice, liberties and more indirect forms of regulation may be a new trend in some areas of life in late-socialist China…the regulatory control of life in China, to a greater extent than liberal governmentality, is linked up with a power that is sovereign.

It is this recognition of the transcendent use of sovereign power that leads Klein to argue that the Chinese one-party state's control over life and the population is an example of Foucaultian 'excess of biopower.' Klein argues that this is firstly, exemplified in the disparity of harvested eggs, and the eggs required for reproduction, secondly, that the one-child policy creates the category of 'illegal' pregnancies, and also transforms human embryos into 'illegal embryonic life,' and thirdly, that embryos do not attract any *enforced* rights to protect them from harmful usage, and consequently, there are no political or juridical mechanisms for their protection. As such, Klein argues that in China the embryo does not have a '*per se* right to life. Its value does neither derive from public discourse about culture and morality nor from ethical guidelines, but the value that the created surplus of "life" derives is that of its usefulness as "experimental" resource.'

Bibliography

Agamben, G. (2005) *State of Exception* (Chicago: University of Chicago Press).

—— (1998) *Homo Sacer: Sovereign Power and Bare Life* (Stanford: Stanford University Press).

Aristotle (1992) *The Politics* (London: Penguin Books).

Arnold, J. (2009) 'Oedipal Sovereignty and the War in Iraq', in Sarat, A. and Culbert, J. (eds) *States of Violence: War, Capital Punishment, and Letting Die* (Cambridge: Cambridge University Press).

Association of International Consultants on Human Rights (1992) *Proceedings of the symposium on the right to life: 40 years after the adoption of the Universal Declaration of Human Rights: evolution of the concept, norms and case-law* (Geneva: ACIDH).

Bae, S. (2007) *When the State No Longer Kills: International Human Rights Norms and Abolition of Capital Punishment* (Albany: State University of New York Press).

BBC (2007) 'Skin transformed into stem cells', 20 November, http://news.bbc.co.uk/1/hi/health/7101834.stm.

Bedau, H. (1968) *The Right to Life*, Monist 52.

Belshaw, C. (2005) *10 Good Questions About Life and Death* (Oxford: Blackwell Publishing).

Benatar, D. (2006) *Better Never to Have Been: The Harm of Coming into Existence* (Oxford: Oxford University Press).

Benjamin, W. (1997) 'Critique of Violence', in Bullock, M. and Jennings, M.W. (eds) *Walter Benjamin: Selected Writings Vol. 1, 1913-1926* (Cambridge: Harvard University Press).

Bizos, G. (1998) *No One to Blame? In Pursuit of Justice in South Africa* (Cape Town: David Philip Publishers).

Camus, A. (1988) 'Reflections on the Guillotine', in *Resistance, Rebellion, and Death* (New York: Vintage Books).

Colon-Collazo, J. (1985) 'The Drafting History of Treaty Provisions on the Right to Life', in Ramcharan, B.G. (ed.) *The Right to Life in International Law* (Dordrecht: Martinus Nijhoff Publishers).

Cottingham, J. (2003) *On the Meaning of Life* (London: Routledge).

Council of Europe (1975) *Collected Edition of the 'Travaux Préparatoires' of the European Convention on Human Rights* (The Hague: Martinus Nijhoff Publishers).

Cover, R. (1986) 'Violence and the Word', 95 *Yale Law Review* 1601.

Craig, P. (2008) *Administrative Law*, 6th edn (London: Sweet and Maxwell).

Delafield Smith, A. (1955) *The Right to Life* (Chapel Hill: The University of North Carolina Press).

Derrida, J. (1992) 'Force of Law: The "Mystical Foundation of Authority"', in Cornell D., Rosenfeld, M. and Gray Carlson, D. (eds) *Deconstruction and the Possibility of Justice* (New York: Routledge).

Derrida, J. and Roudinesco, E. (2004) *For What Tomorrow…A Dialogue* (Stanford: Stanford University Press).

Dundes Renteln, A. (2004) *The Cultural Defense* (New York: Oxford University Press).

Dworkin, R. (1994) *Life's Dominion: An Argument about Abortion, Euthanasia, and Individual Freedom* (New York: Vintage Books).

—— (1977) *Taking Rights Seriously* (Cambridge: Harvard University Press).

Eagleton, T. (2007) *The Meaning of Life* (Oxford: Oxford University Press).

Enright, D.J. (1983) *The Oxford Book of Death* (Oxford: Oxford University Press).

Espiell, H.G. (1988) 'The Right to Life and the Right to Live', in Association of International Consultants on Human Rights, *Essays on the Concept of a*

Rights to Live (Bruxelles: Association of International Consultants on Human Rights).

Fine, R. (2007) *Cosmopolitanism* (London: Routledge).

Fitzpatrick, P. (2005) 'Bare Sovereignty: Homo Sacer and the Insistence of Law', in Norris, A. (ed.) *Politics, Metaphysics, and Death: Essays on Giorgio Agamben's Homo Sacer* (Durham: Duke University Press).

Foucault, M. (2008) *The Birth of Biopolitics: Lectures at the Collège de France 1978-1979* (Basingstoke: Palgrave Macmillan).

—— (2004) *Society Must be Defended: Lectures at the Collège de France, 1975-76* (London: Penguin Books).

—— (2001) 'The Subject and Power', in Faubion, J.D. (ed.) *Michel Foucault: Power: Essential Works of Foucault 1954-1984, Vol. 3* (London: Penguin Books).

—— (1981) *The Will to Knowledge: The History of Sexuality, Volume One* (London: Penguin Books).

Freud, S. (2005) *On Murder, Mourning and Melancholia* (London: Penguin).

—— (1968) *Civilization and its Discontents* (New York: W.W. Norton and Company).

Grayling, A.C. (2001) *The Meaning of Things: Applying Philosophy to Life* (London: Phoenix Paperback).

Griffin, J. (2008) *On Human Rights* (Oxford: Oxford University Press).

Gross, O. and Ní Aoláin, F. (2006) *Law in Times of Crisis: Emergency Powers in Theory and Practice* (New York: Cambridge University Press).

Herring, J. and Chau, P-L. (2007) *My Body, Your Body, Our Bodies*, 15 *Medical Law Review*, 34-61.

Hood, R. and Hoyle, C. (2008) *The Death Penalty: A Worldwide Perspective*, 4th edn (Oxford: Oxford University Press).

Johnson, D.T. and Zimring, F.E. (2009) *The Next Frontier: National Development, Political Change, and the Death Penalty in Asia* (New York: Oxford University Press).

Kant, I. (1970) 'What is Orientation in Thinking?', in Reiss, H.S. (ed.) *Kant: Political Writings* (Cambridge: Cambridge University Press).

Leverick, F. (2006) *Killing in Self-Defence* (Oxford: Oxford University Press).

Lyotard, J-F. (1989) *The Differend: Phrases in Dispute* (University of Minnesota Press).

Matthieu, B. (2006) *The Right to Life in European Constitutional and International Case-law* (Strasbourg: Council of Europe Publishing).

Nietzsche, F. (2004) *Human, All Too Human* (London: Penguin Books).

Nserenko, D.D. (1985) 'Arbitrary Deprivation of Life: Controls on Permissible Deprivation', in Ramcharan, B.G. (ed.) *The Right to Life in International Law* (Dordrecht: Martinus Nijhoff Publishers).

Nussbaum, M.C. (2006) *Frontiers of Justice: Disability, Nationality, Species Membership* (Cambridge: The Belknap Press of Harvard University Press).

Offer, J. (1994) *Spencer: Political Writings* (Cambridge: Cambridge University Press).

Okechukwu, S.N. (1990) *The Right to Life and the Right to Live: Ethics of International Solidarity* (European University Studies) (Frankfurt: Peter Lang Press).

Opsahl, T. (1993) 'The Right to Life', in Macdonald, R.St.J. et al. (eds) *The European System for the Protection of Human Rights* (Dordrecht: Martinus Nijhoff Publishers).

Posner, R.A. (2004) *Catastrophe: Risk and Response* (New York: Oxford University Press).

Prado, C.G. (2008) *Choosing to Die: Elective Death and Multiculturalism* (New York: Cambridge University Press).

Pristavkin, A. (1999) 'A Vast Place of Execution – The Death Penalty in Russia', in Council of Europe, *The Death Penalty: Abolition in Europe* (Strasbourg: Council of Europe Publishing).

Redelbach, A. (1985) 'Protection of the Right to Life by Law and by Other Means', in Ramcharan, B.G. (ed.) *The Right to Life in International Law* (Dordrecht: Martinus Nijhoff Publishers).

Ramcharan, B.G. (ed.) (1985) *The Right to Life in International Law* (Dordrecht: Martinus Nijhoff Publishers).

Rawls, J. (2005) *Political Liberalism* (New York: Columbia University Press).

Rorty, R. (1993) 'Human Rights, Rationality, and Sentimentality', in Shute, S. and Hurley, S. (eds) *On Human Rights: The Oxford Amnesty Lectures 1993* (New York: Basic Books).

Rose, N. (2007) *The Politics of Life Itself: Biomedicine, Power, and Subjectivity in the Twenty-First Century* (Princeton: Princeton University Press).

Rousseau, J-J. (1993) 'A Discourse on the Origin of Inequality', in *The Social Contract and Discourses* (London: Everyman).

Sarat, A., Douglas, L. and Umphrey, M.M. (2007) *Law and Catastrophe* (Stanford: Stanford University Press).

—— (2001a) *When the State Kills: Capital Punishment and the American Condition* (Princeton: Princeton University Press).

—— (2001b) *Pain, Death and the Law* (Ann Arbor: University of Michigan Press).

—— (1999) *The Killing State: Capital Punishment in Law, Politics and Culture* (New York: Oxford University Press).

Schabas, W.A. (2002) *The Abolition of the Death Penalty in International Law*, 3rd edn (Cambridge: Cambridge University Press).

Srinivas, R. (2009) 'Exploring the Potential for American Death Tourism', 13 *Michigan State University Journal for Medicine and Law*, Winter 91.

van Boven, T.C. (1988) 'The Need to Stop Deliberate Violations of the Right to Life', in Prémont, D. (ed.) *Essais sur le Concept de 'Droit de Vivre' en Mémoire de Yougindra Khushalani* (Brussels: Bruylant).

Wagner-Pacifici, R. (2009) 'The Innocuousness of State Lethality in an Age of National Security', in Sarat, A., and Culbert, J. *States of Violence: War, Capital Punishment, and Letting Die* (Cambridge: Cambridge University Press).

Wermiel, S.J. (1999) 'Law and Human Dignity: The Judicial Soul of Justice Brennan', 7 *William and Mary Bill of Rights Journal* 223.

World Health Organization (2009) *World Health Statistics 2009* (Geneva: WHO).

Wicks, E. (2000) 'The United Kingdom Government's Perceptions of the European Convention on Human Rights at the Time of Entry', *Public Law* 2000, Aut, 438-455.

Wittgenstein, L. (1974) *Tractatus Logico-Philosophicus* (London: Routledge).

Yorke, J. (2010) 'Inhuman Punishment and Abolition of the Death Penalty in the Council of Europe', *European Public Law*, Volume 16, Issue 1.

—— (2008) *Against the Death Penalty: International Initiatives and Implications* (Farnham: Ashgate Publishing).

Žižek, S. (2002) *For They Know Not What They Do: Enjoyment as a Political Factor* (London: Verso).

PART I
Approaching the Horizons of Life and Death

Chapter 2
Politics and the Philosophy of Life: Towards a Normative Framework

Mark Olssen

Introduction

This chapter argues that a philosophy of life can provide a new conception of the good which can provide a useful framework for the resolution of political and ethical disputes.[1] Building off Spinoza, Hume, Nietzsche, Bergson, Foucault and Deleuze, it outlines what is central to life philosophy and how these thinkers can be represented as providing a new basis for normative political philosophy which avoids the consequences associated with the mechanical and deterministic philosophies of Galileo and Newton as well as the teleological organicism of the Romantics and Hegel. It goes on to explain how such an approach was developed by philosophers such as Friedrich Nietzsche and how life philosophy can function to steer evaluations which are genuinely cross-cultural, thus avoiding both moral and epistemological relativism in relation to the assessment of other cultures.

The History of *Lebensphilosophie*

Herbert Schnädelbach (1984) has identified three forms of life philosophy. The first form is what he refers to as metaphysical life philosophy which posits a conception of life as an objective noumenal substance beyond (or underneath) the domains of human perception and consciousness. Schnädelbach gives the example of Henri Bergson's *élan vital* to illustrate. For Bergson élan vital refers to an inanimate ahistorical principle or substance beyond the realm of the human experience which could ultimately only be verified through 'intuition' or direct apprehension. In this conception life represents a permanent universal substrate which lies behind and explains human and non-human experience. It relies upon a fundamental dualism between the conceptual experience and the supposition of something beyond the realm of experience which is ahistorical. Life philosophy in this sense is something which functions as a permanent animating principle or basic metaphysical force.

---

1 This chapter draws from chapter 6 of *Toward A Global Thin Community*, published by Paradigm Publishers in 2009.

Schnädelbach's second form refers to life philosophy as a philosophy of history. This form of life philosophy is represented by historians such as Oswald Spengler who theorizes the rise and fall of historical cultures as forms of growth and decay, where historical cultures are treated as parallel to organisms, and where history involves a process of struggle equivalent to the struggle depicted by Darwin between species and life forms within history. Societies in this model are depicted metaphorically as life forms like species, or vegetation, which unfold, decay, burst forth, and develop. As Alastair Morgan (2007, 9)[2] notes, such a perspective 'collapses any distinction between culture and nature in a fateful identification of the processes of life with those of a politics that emphasizes growth, vigour and the healthy. The move from such a philosophy to the concepts of race and Social Darwinism intrinsic to National Socialist ideology is obvious.'

Schnädelbach's third form of life philosophy is ethical life philosophy which he identifies with Friedrich Nietzsche. This form distinguishes between what is living and what does not live and identifies a normativity immanent in life itself. What enhances and sustains life in this sense grounds a conception of value and becomes the basis for establishing all value. As Morgan (2007, 9) puts it, it 'becomes the grounding for all values and norms.' It is primarily this conception that is the subject of focus in this chapter. Although my focus will be derived from a wide variety of thinkers, including Spinoza, Hume, Heidegger, Bataille, Deleuze, and Foucault, it is Nietzsche who is the central inspiration. For Nietzsche, as reason and ideology coalesce, the only basis for sound evaluations is related to that which supports or does not support life. This is why he recognizes authentic existence as that which seeks to sustain and enhance; concerned, as Ansell-Pearson (1994, 18) says, with 'abundant health and strength.' It is why Nietzsche writes in *Beyond Good and Evil* (1966, sect. 4), '[t]he falseness of a judgement is to us not necessarily an objection to the judgement… .The question is to what extent it is life-advancing, life-preserving, species preserving, perhaps even species breeding; and our fundamental tendency is to assert that the falsest judgements…are the most indispensable to us…'. If things are valued for the sake of life, Nietzsche defines life as 'a multiplicity of forces connected by a common mode of nutrition' (ibid., sect. 641) in which 'the different contenders grow unequally' (ibid., sect. 642). As Lester Hunt (1991, 126) puts it, '[l]ife is a hierachically integrated system the members of which have a common means of support. Perfection is the state in which this integration is fully achieved (*volkommen*). To "enhance life," then, is to increase the extent to which this state has been achieved.'

Bataille also identifies the theme of a concern with life as pervading Nietzsche's thought, most prominently expressed in his concept of the Overman and Nietzsche's concern with the future, as expressed forcefully in *Thus Spoke Zarathustra*, *Beyond Good and Evil*, and notes and commentaries that eventually constituted *The Will to Power*. For Bataille, Nietzsche's philosophy represents a concern with

2 I am indebted to Morgan (2007) for originally drawing my attention to Schnädelbach's work.

life that represents a specifically non-moral yearning once God is Dead, a goal that stretches out before one, as Bataille (2004, xviii) puts it 'independently of moral goals or of serving God,' and yet paradoxically itself becomes articulated as a moral obligation, imposing an object that 'surpasses all others in value' (ibid., xvii) and translating 'as a demand for definite acts' (ibid., xvii). This concern with life's continuance in Nietzsche is not substantive or developmental, as in Hegel, but expresses a relationship to the environment manifesting both a historicity and consequent contingency in terms of how that relationship is traversed. It is the concern with life's continuance that Zarathustra teaches. It is the *bridge* that Zarathustra seeks to cross, the new dawn, midday, noontide, and beyond.

The quest for life's continuance need not be seen as coming from an essential cause in human nature. Nietzsche rejects the idea of *conatus* as an instinct for self-preservation. It is not through an instinct or drive to self-preservation that survival primarily ensues. As we have seen above, there must be something 'more' than self-preservation. For Nietzsche, too, life and survival are responsive to the effect of will (as opposed to an instinct). This is also evident in his criticisms of Darwinian evolution theory, which he saw as deficient in this key respect. As Elizabeth Grosz (2004) says, Nietzsche dissented from Darwin's view of natural selection, asserting a thesis of survival plus excess as the aim of development. This was the idea of a higher order than that to which Darwin subscribed. Centrally where Nietzsche differed from Darwin, says Grosz, is that:

> Nietzsche wants to bring forth from Darwin's own heritage an activity that Darwin did not recognize adequately: the active force of seizing hold of a thing, of matter. Life is not a reaction to matter or nature, but a seizing of matter and a rendering it for one's own purposes to come. Life is not simply a subjective interpretation imposed on matter that leaves matter absolutely intact and untouched; interpretation is itself the activity of making matter over, overcoming its form by one's own forces, the wills to power that compete to make life more than itself. Nietzsche understands clearly that evolution is overcoming, and that evolution is thus a process that, if it occurs at all, occurs equally for ideas, customs, and social practices as much as it does for organs, morphologies, and instincts (ibid., 107).

Nietzsche thus differs from Darwin in that life is not simply about survival, but about excess or abundance. Darwin is too preoccupied, for Nietzsche, with the struggle for existence, and the mere avoidance of death.

Life: *zoē* and *bios*

If Nietzsche serves as a general inspiration in creating a normative philosophy of life, what other writers are important, and what elements should we include? We can start by saying that life constitutes itself as both *strategy* and *telos*. It is orientated to the future, or as I will say more often, life seeks to *continue*. To represent it in terms of *continuance* is to represent it in terms of *survival* and *well-being*. Continuance is thus intended only as a short-hand descriptor to represent these dimensions of *life*. It is *life* that is the important concept, but life must be understood as a force which seeks to continue on the basis of a will. For Agamben (1999, 239) '"life" is not a medical and scientific notion but a philosophical, political, and theological concept.' For Foucault (1998, 476), following Georges Canguilhem, 'life…is that which is capable of error' (Canguilhem 1978, 476).[3] It is this fact, he continues, that 'life has led to a living being that is never completely in the right place, that is destined to "err" and to be "wrong."' Indeed, 'if one grants that the concept [of error] is the reply that life itself has given to that chance process, one must agree that error is the root of what produces human thought and its history' (ibid., 476).

As Georges Bataille (1985, 171) notes, 'men act in order to be.' Such action is central to the idea of *life*. At the strategic level, it requires continuance and maintenance of being; but more, it involves a striving for *well*-being. Rather than view such a striving naturalistically, it should be represented as the effect of a will. I would maintain that the quest for being is always the quest for *well-being*. Life is regarded as inherently normative in this sense that it strives for continuance and the maintenance of well-being. It represents what the Greeks called *zoē*, which refers to simple living, what referred to for Aristotle 'mere living' (see Aristotle 1905, 1278b), as opposed to *bios*, which pertained to the historical or cultural form of living of a group or polis, and was represented as the good life. Yet, Aristotle thought that some normative principle possibly resided in *zoē*. As he says in the *Politics*:

> [a]nd therefore, men, even when they do not require one another's help, desire to live together all the same, and are in fact brought together by their common interests in proportion as they severally attain to any measure of well-being. This is certainly the chief end, both of individuals and of states. And also for the sake of mere life (in which there is possibly some noble element) mankind meet together and maintain the political community, so long as the evils of existence do not greatly overbalance the good (ibid.)

Despite his view that some noble element comprises bare life, Aristotle is usually interpreted as presupposing a distinction between natural (or animal existence) and social and political life. For Foucault, on the other hand, the political is seen as simply extending out of, or sitting on top of, bare life, as necessary to it. Thus, in the last chapter of the *History of Sexuality, Volume One*, Foucault states, '[f]or millennia, man remained what he was for Aristotle: a living animal with an

---

3 This is perhaps why, Canguilhem says, the issue of anomaly 'permeates the whole of biology' (Canguilhem 1978, 476).

additional capacity for political existence; modern man is an animal whose politics places his existence as a living being into question' (Foucault 1978, 143).

Foucault's central thesis is a temporal one. Shifts in form occur at particular times in history. At a certain level of complexity, both coordination and justice become indispensable. Aristotle was wrong to discern distinct ontic states of *zoē* and *bios*: *zoē* exists within *bios*, but is distinct from it. Life is always political, for politics expresses nothing but the relations between life that mediate the one and the many.

Although Foucault sees a continuity between bare life and political life, it is Agamben's (1998) so-called 'correction' or 'completion' in *Homo Sacer* to reinsert the non-identity between bare life and political life in terms of which political life fails continually to be able to reconcile the relationship with bare life itself. Although one nestles within the other, politics must repeatedly seek a synthesis of relations between men's bare existence and the good of all; to the extent it fails, the result is violence or death.

Although Foucault never utilized the concept of life in a normative sense, there is a possible way forward on this basis. Mere life does not just 'possibly' contain a 'noble element', but *always* contains at least some sort of normative element, in that life must, if it is to remain as life, seek its own continuance and well-being. This at least is a possible extension, and one that possibly makes sense of Nietzsche's *Zarathustra*. A similar claim could be extended to Georges Canguilhem, for whom the norm of medicine maintained its existence because of the normativity in life itself. In his book, *On The Normal and the Pathological*, Canguilhem (Canguilhem 1978, 73) argues that 'it is life itself and not medical judgment which makes the biological normal a concept of value and not a concept of statistical reality.' Such a program to achieve well-being requires *definite acts*. It can thus (I will argue) function as a support for a moral and political theory. The shift from *zoē* to *bios* is in this view simply a function of complexity. Such 'mere living' is thus not primarily natural, but is always a *form of living*, and hence, exists within *bios*. If mere life is always a historical form of life and contains its own normative principle for continuance and well-being, the distinction between *zoē* and *bios* is one of scale, or complexity. This incorporates that the distinction can usefully mediate between the individual and collective, or between the social and the political. Hence, the sense that Plato has Socrates say, in the *Crito* (Plato 2003, section 48b), that 'the really important thing is not to live but to live well' doesn't conflict with such a view and doesn't necessarily imply a dualism of nature/culture.[4] This will give rise to various theses. Politics entails a relation

4 Agamben seems to conflate a distinction between the one and the many (individual and collective) with a distinction between nature and culture. As such, he essentializes sovereignty and presumes a naturalization of bare life as being prior to the social, because sovereignty always dominates biopower. As he says in *Homo Sacer*, for instance, '[t]he entire character of homo sacer shows that it was not born on the soil of a constituted juridical order but goes all the way back to the period of pre-social life' (Agamben 1998,

between *zoē* and *bios* that must be managed. It need not require that we posit a theory of nature. In an overcrowded global world, the achievement of continuance and well-being *for any* – I will argue – will necessitate complex collective political and institutional structures *for all*. In Heidegger's sense (Heidegger 1993, 326), an 'enframing' [*Ge-stell*] will be required that 'entraps nature,' and reduces the world to a 'calculable coherence of forces.'

Within Foucault's writings on life, as Peter Fitzpatrick (Fitzpatrick 2005, 57) points out, there is a certain 'vitalist excess,' in that Foucault, as we will see further below, does not foreclose the possibilities of resolving the problems of war and catastrophe or arbitrary violence in the way Agamben does, in the way he privileges sovereignty, following Schmitt (1985), based on the ability to define the state of exception as an invariant historical form. Hardt and Negri (2000) reject the dominance of life by an all-powerful conception of sovereignty in Agamben in support of Foucault's more historically open and optimistic thesis. Foucault believes it possible to find 'a way of living in complete mobility and not of immobilizing life' (Foucault 1988, 60). Through his notions such as 'resistance', life is able to contain and democratize sovereignty. In such a view, Foucault asserts the theoretical openness of his historicism and his similarity to Deleuze on the issue of life. It supports an adherence to a critical vitalism of the sort associated with Nietzsche, Heidegger, and Bergson, in the shift in the nineteenth century from a 'matter-based physics to an energy-based model' (Marks 1998, 67).[5] Also, to a conception of immanence in the sense utilized by Deleuze and Guattari, for whom immanence means 'openness' in relation to complexity management or chaos and without transcendent values. As Deleuze and Guattari (1994, 35-8), and Deleuze by himself (1993, 4) have stated, immanence describes the 'movement of the infinite,' it is equivalent to 'chaos,' 'formless, unlimited, absolute,' it 'escapes every transcendence'. Life is an immanent force that permits infinite ways to continue. Although these may invoke universals (such as the requirement for sustenance, for example), such universals are always contingently realized and therefore always have a (potentially) variable contingent dimension or aspect. In this sense, as for Hegel, the universal is *in* the particular. Immanence, say Deleuze and Guattari (1994, 45), is 'never *to* Something', such as sovereignty, for if it is '*to* Something' it fixes it as a historical constant. Peter Fitzpatrick (2005, 64) has used

104). Or, again, he relates 'bare life' to 'a fragment of the primitive life of Indo-European people' (ibid.). He maintains further that the 'Hobbesian state of nature is…a condition in which everyone is bare life and homo sacer for everyone else' (ibid., 106). For him, thus, homo sacer has a 'pre-legal' quality (ibid.). The distinction can only be valid, for Foucault, as indicating a tension, or continuum, between the one and the many. Foucault does not essentialize sovereignty, and is thus more optimistic about the future than Agamben, as sovereignty does not necessarily stand outside the law, or on the borderline between law and exception, but is capable of being democratized, or controlled.

5 Deleuze documents the criticisms that Bergson encountered as being against his rejection of eternal or foundational values. See Marks (1998), 68.

such a view to underscore the differences between Agamben and his ahistorical prioritizing of sovereignty on the one hand, and Foucault and Deleuze's more historically open perspective on the other. According to Fitzpatrick, in Foucault, the theme of 'an excess of life over death [exists] in [his] combining sovereignty and biopower,' whereas in Agamben the 'death-driven reign of sovereignty is unavoidable' (ibid., 68).

If the term 'survival' is sometimes used to designate the strategic aspect of *life* as the striving for continuance and well-being, it does not equate to 'bare survival', or 'minimum bare subsistence', or 'bare humanness', but indicates a strategy that is common to all of life – to animals, humans, and gods, as was 'mere' or 'simple' life for Aristotle. More carefully stated, this strategy is one concerned with either 'conservation' or 'growth'. It is characterized, as Bataille (1991, 23) says, not just with struggle and conservation of energy, or struggle to avoid death, but with 'excess' and superabundance, for '[on] the surface of the globe, for living matter in general, energy is always in excess; the question is always posed in terms of extravagance.' If the organism always 'has at its disposal greater energy resources than are necessary for the operations that sustain life' it means that the term survival does not fully convey what is implied by life. For, as Elizabeth Grosz (2004, 103) says, the mere 'struggle for existence aims too low: it aims only for existence, for bare survival, for mere life itself….[T]his struggle for self-preservation, for survival, is by definition a losing fight. If survival is the goal of life, life fails in every case!' Thus the conception of life is always something more than mere survival or existence, for it must be conceived as an active force by which an organism achieves continuance and maintains (well)being. Hence, it cannot mean what it did for Darwin, as mere adaptation, accommodation, or passive reaction to external forces.

If life operates through energy, or power, the limits of its excess are ultimately determined by life in a particular relationship to space. As Bataille (1991, 29) says, 'the immediate limitation, for each individual or each group, is given by the other individuals or other groups. But the terrestrial sphere (to be exact, the *biosphere*), which corresponds to the space available to life, is the only real limit.' Space, and other life, for Bataille, constitutes the 'local conditions [which] determine the intensity of the *pressure* exerted in all directions by life.' Such pressures determine the limits of growth and the prospect of death. While it is difficult to define them, one can adduce their effects. One effect is sheer quantitative extension of occupation of space as life continues; another effect is poverty or luxury. Bataille continues, '[b]eside the external action of life (climatic or volcanic phenomena), the unevenness of pressure in living matter continually makes available to growth the place left vacant by death. It is not a new space, and if one considers life as a whole, there is not really growth but a maintenance of volume in general' (Bataille 1991, 33).

Bataille maintains that '[m]an's activity is basically conditioned by this general movement of life. In a sense, *in extension*, his activity opens up a new possibility to life, a new space' (ibid., 35-6). In that *life* is always a *form of life*, for humans, at least, it always takes place in a community, in the sense at least that it involves always an *outside* of norms, meanings, rules, and institutions, organized in a net or web, expressing the context of development and continuance and also the interconnectedness between things. Although, in this sense, modes of articulation within any determinate historical terrain are patterned, and maintain their regularity, they are also capable of infinite variety and expression.

Life, then, is reproduced and transformed by practices linked by norms of continuance. In addition to Nietzsche and Bataille, Hume is an important influence here. For Hume, continuance (or continuous existence, or continuity) is an external relation not given in experience of either the senses or understanding. It is the horizon that all of life presupposes. It is achieved through the association of ideas and through impressions 'torn from the senses' and made possible in terms of a 'schematizing immagination' (Deleuze 1991, 80-81). As Hume says in the *Treatise*, we 'advance rather than retard our existence' (1978, 432). Association operates 'secretly and calmly on the mind' (ibid., 334). Reason is the 'slave of the passions' (ibid., 415) and operates on the basis of fancy, ideology and good sense as we set about the tasks of living. In this sense, Hume saw the subject in terms of succession. This highlights for him the importance of habit and anticipation. The imagination coordinates how to live in a process of moving from present to future. As Deleuze (1991, 92-93) says of Hume, the subject is 'a synthesis of the present and the past in the light of the future.' This highlights also the importance of 'anticipation', which is 'a synthesis of the past and the present brought about by habit. Anticipation, or the future, is the synthesis of time constituted by the subject' (ibid., 93), and '[i]n short, the synthesis posits the present as the rule for the future' (ibid., 94). Hence, 'anticipation is habit, and habit is anticipation: these two determinations – the thrust of the past and the élan toward the future – are, at the centre of Hume's philosophy, the two aspects of the same fundamental dynamism' (ibid., 92). In Hume's terms, survival and continuance thus constitute *relations* (of association) between disparate ideas and impressions, which are subject to constant reflection and guided by the passions through to the imagination. What underpins such a conception, which Hume articulated in his writings on religion, is a concept of *purpose*.[6]

Continuance, then, in my conception, is postulated as the strategic dimension of *life*. Life seeks *to continue*. It continues in terms of practices. Such practices constitute a good toward which societies and humanity aim. A thick conception of life thus entails (1) *continuance* of all life forms, involving both conservation and expenditure of energy; maintenance and growth; (2) a conception of survival, or the maintenance of existence; and (3) a conception of well-being or flourishing, constitutive of (a) both structures or conditions, (b) capabilities which express a positive conception of freedom, and a role for the state, and (c) safety and security, indicative of negative rights and protections from interference. The notion of continuance does not preclude change, and involves, as it did for John Dewey, various types of process, including the intentional and unintentional reproduction

6 See Hume (1970) and Deleuze (1991, 109).

of structures and practices and various types of learning (from habitual or repetitive, to meaningful or deep).[7] The concern with survival involves a concern to ward off death and continue with 'bare life', in Agamben's sense. The conception of well-being includes many possible different factors, which involves individuals with complex practices of self, and an engagement with politics, in a quest for the good life. At the macro or institutional level, it involves factors such as a problem-solving approach as the basis of education and policy or a conception of security for all, incorporating a dimension of negative liberty. Within these conditions, necessary for the continuance of life of each and all, there exists the possibility of many different forms of life. The quest to sustain life is thus not primarily an instinct, or drive, and must not be interpreted naturalistically. Rather, in the sense I mean it, it constitutes a relationship to an environment, and a goal, based on a choice, and ultimately, a will.[8] It involves beliefs and deliberations, guesswork, foresight, knowledge, and anticipation. Because it is at one level a choice, it raises the issue of suicide, and one must concede, I believe, a right in this regard.[9] The continuance of humanity is, we can say, conditional upon the human will to continue. Unlike the Darwinian conception, life's continuance is not conceptualized as a purely individual orientation to survival, but must be seen as involving both individual and collective practices. Although the modern state is a historically recent entity, forms of collective action, governments of one sort or another, are as old as history itself. In that the individual cannot even survive today without the collective, both individual and collective increasingly presuppose each other. Sustaining and developing life thus expresses a relationship to our common humanity, as Bhikhu Parekh (1997) observes. It is because we acknowledge our common struggles to survive and prosper that we recognize our common humanity. Violations of such values, such as genocide, are typically seen as crimes.[10] As

7 Although Dewey's writings on continuity are insightful, his concept of growth betrays a Hegelian influence which is rejected in my conception. Growth for Dewey indicates continued progress and an inevitable direction to history as characterized by improvement. The notion also suggests a dialectical process of the reconciliation of contradictions through successive syntheses. Continuance in my conception is simply saying that the quest to continue is immanent within life.

8 Even if it is an instinct, it can be overridden by an act of choice, as in suicide. It is conceptualized here as both a relation to an environment and as a goal.

9 There is no need to deny that life might initially 'decide' on itself biogenetically, given sustainable ecological and environmental conditions, and that there may be 'instincts' that 'facilitate' transition to life. But, ultimately, life continues confirmed by a choice, if not actively, then by default. The active potential of life should not be denied or neglected.

10 This need not be justified according to something called nature, or natural law, but, rather on the basis that, within finitude and the limitations that that imposes, no overriding evidence can support why any group or individual who wills survival should be excluded. The reader may accuse me of playing with words. The point, however, is that to say that life has a quest for continuance immanent within it is not necessary to invoke nature. The pro-value on life is itself the vote of life. Who shall demur?

such, a common concern for survival and the achievement of (well)-being goes beyond states, classes, races, or gender. It provides a commonality cross-cutting a terrain in terms of which manifold differences express themselves.

Establishing *Life* as a Good

If life has immanent within it its own quest for continuance and well-being, expressing itself both as strategy and telos, can we say it constitutes both a strategic modus vivendi and a substantive conception of good? This I will try at least to argue on the basis that life dictates certain *shared functions and interests*; and also that – increasingly (and therefore contingently) – the preconditions for sustaining *any* life require, more perhaps today than at any time hitherto previously in history, the collective coordination of structures, practices, and arrangements *for all*.

Continuing life, then, constitutes both a strategic modus vivendi and a substantive conception of good. As a modus vivendi, it functions instrumentally as an accord or settlement. Its strategic focus on values like continuance or continuity gives it a pragmatic focus on securing settlements over norms between the deeply divergent and pluralistic interests that constitute the contemporary world. This was Hobbes' position in *Leviathan*. Yet, in the sense that it stipulates common aims and requirements, such as stability and security, that allow all to survive and flourish, it also posits a good. If it were purely instrumental, then support for the values and institutions required would hardly command sufficient common allegiance. Even acknowledging the deep pluralism of our contemporary world, the tasks of life's continuance represent shared goals, and for most are important in promoting the good life. But, in this sense, such a good is not convergent, meaning it does not seek integration or unity, except within broad limits. Although all want to survive, and achieve well-being, the reasons, values, motives, and interests may be very different in different groups and individuals. By positing such a good, it enables collective responsibilities to be taken seriously, and yet, as we shall see, pluralism to be maintained and for the claims of individuals to be arbitrated or balanced with the democratic majority. Difference is maintained in relation to the tasks of sustaining life in that although all share a will to prosper and flourish, all inhabit social networks and communal solidarities discursively differentiated in relation to space and time. Such embodied modalities constitute different styles of life, values, beliefs, aspirations, and anticipations of the future. Sustaining life establishes necessary and legitimate boundaries to such commitments as liberty and toleration, and yet it is non-metaphysical in that it does not posit 'a domain beyond discursive verification to which truth and falsity do not apply and about which no assertion may meaningfully be made' (Richardson 1990, 7). In other words, it grounds certain commonalities in a *chosen* or *willed* order of being, from which certain normative principles follow. No super-sensible entities are posited. No assumptions are made about the nature of the individual, or the nature of reason beyond that individuals are learning beings, and to the extent they have a will to survive and maintain (well)-being. The conditions it specifies are conditions within history. These conditions will reflect age-old concerns and needs, such as the need for sustenance, and yet manifest an inescapable contingency in the way that different groups and individuals, at different times and places, are orientated to the real conditions of their existence.

Not only is life not metaphysical in the way that offends liberals, but the commonalities specified do not preclude pluralism except within certain obvious necessary limits. This is to say, what such a good does is specify certain intelligible limits to pluralism. What it does not do is specify the detail, or claim to resolve arguments in any complete way as to how disputes over such value differences as abortion or affirmative action or euthanasia should be resolved. It constitutes a good that will in this sense *underdetermine* outcomes on specific issues. In this sense, it does not resolve the issue of the incommensurability of values in some domains (religion, abortion, appropriate punishments), but specifies a formula for arbitrating disputes and conflicts, and allows and makes possible for convergences in other areas. In this sense, a philosophy of life specifies a range of values and interpersonal standards that will be common to all participants, no matter how intractable the disputes they may otherwise be engaged in, and by which disputes can be arbitrated. In this sense, survival and life constitute values that have a high priority: higher than other values, such as impulsive desires. To resolve disputes in this way indicates a form of rationality in terms of what enhances life. Sometimes, where this is not obvious, value disputes will need to be resolved on pragmatic or instrumental grounds.[11]

To continue life forces concordance over the necessary, for if we are to continue, it leaves the determination of what is discretionary, and its separation from what is necessary, as something for each age to decide. Although a non-metaphysical conception of the good, in that it doesn't presuppose foundational precepts, it doesn't allow for just anything, but specifies particular preferences or prohibitions for specific normative orderings, or rankings. The values associated with 'life' carry greater importance than do values such as 'nationalism', or 'sporting achievement', yet it does not specify all outcomes or determine all possibilities. This is because – apart from putting a pro-value on life itself – the concept of life does not suggest an easy answer in relation to complex issues such as abortion, euthanasia, and the like. It does, however, place the same sort of pro-value on all of human life, and in this sense would appear to be broadly egalitarian, as regards moral and political status. In this sense, as a good, it is 'wide' rather than 'narrow', in Richard Arneson's sense:

> [t]he 'wider' a perfectionist doctrine, the more it values goods that virtually all humans can reach, and the smaller is the gap between the value assigned to

11 Continuance in this context asserts that it is preferable to achieve a settlement for the purposes of 'continuing', when conflict threatens life itself, rather than to fight endlessly over incommensurable value positions.

> these lower goods compared to the value assigned to the higher goods that few can attain. Wide perfectionism need not be elitist as narrow perfectionism is (Arneson 2000, 55).

In a way not dissimilar to Arneson, Richardson (1990) classifies theories of the good in relation to their scope.[12] Unlike Aristotle, for whom *eudeimonia* specifies a narrow perfectionist scope as the highest good for individuals, or John Rawls, who limits the good to the political, the concept of life constitutes a broad scope and a robust conception of the good, in the sense that it is not exclusively concerned with rights, but also gives importance to responsibilities and duties, as well as in the sense that it is multifaceted and balances values such as liberty with those like security. Such rights and duties emerge from the common good of continuance. Such a good is objective in the sense that it exists independently of individuals and collectivities, but will vary reflecting the specificities and imperatives of both time and place and mode of social economic and political organization. Such a good, although objective, is itself conditional on the human will to survive, and hence, arises – like the Phoenix – once the project of life is underway. Although objective, it is also infinitely variable. Just as the tasks of survival vary from culture to culture, so all the forms of continuance and flourishing have their cultural and historical specificity. Because it manifests a high degree of variability according to time and place, it requires its constitutional articulation in relation to the varied domains of human life – sexuality and gender relations, work and economy, politics and democracy, rights and liberties – to be (re)articulated, (re)expressed and (re)implemented in both national and transnational institutional sites on an ongoing basis. It is through these processes of (re)articulation, (perpetual) deliberation, and (re)implementation that such a good can be democratically mandated, and that, if not strict neutrality, then certainly a conception of 'justified reasonable fairness' or 'impartiality' can be accorded to all participants in the contract based upon their different relations to, and interests in, the project called life.

As a substantive conception of good, I mean to suggest that the quest to sustain life is specific enough to prohibit certain actions and specify limits to a conception to the reasonable, and in this sense to function normatively, and yet is broad enough to encompass many different lifestyles and value systems. What is good, as Richard Kraut (2007) states, 'is always *for something.*' It is what enables something to survive, to prosper, to flourish, *to continue to live*. Just as things

12 Richardson (1990) distinguishes theories of the good in relation to (1) metaphysical depth, detailing the types of foundational postulates it contains; (2) critical structure, pertaining to what enables it to prohibit or support a certain normative ordering; (3) scope, pertaining to the range of subject matter to which it applies, and whether it is narrow or broad; and (4) degree of detail of the conception, pertaining to whether it stipulates a few general principles, or sub-principles, and the degree of detail it requires to be specified in relation to them. This framework has guided me to some extent in the considerations in this section.

may be good for life, so things may be bad for life, or indifferent for life. A list of these three categories – of *goods, bads, and indifferents* – would specify what governments ought to encourage; what ought to be outlawed, or discouraged; and what ought to be left to the discretion of individuals and communities free from the constraints of the state.[13]

The good in this sense is not as the utilitarian philosophers conceived it, as related to preferences and desires. Preferences and desires can be distorted by oppressive social conditions, warped by tradition, or may be dysfunctional for life, and has tended historically to limit the focus of concern to humans rather than all forms of life.[14] This is also why the utilitarian good of pleasure, although certainly a good under many circumstances, is not *necessarily* a good for life's continuance in all times and places. We could say that there is more to life than individual pleasure or utility. Even the quest of bare life, or basic survival, although projected onto the world by life itself, and in this sense constructed, constitutes an objective framework of value for all species, and for life itself. The concept of 'objective' used here is not intended to deny social relativity, or historical variability, nor that different amounts of resources may need to be provided due to different initial conditions. Objective in this sense is also not referring to any metaphysical reality. This is to say that it is not there in the world independent or irrespective of humans; rather its objectivity is dependent and *conditional upon* a will to survive. This will to survive must be exercised both individually and collectively. The good is what is objectively necessary *if* we are to survive. This is to say that, *if* we are to survive, either as individuals or as a species, *then* certain objective things will follow. Collectively, this will include certain moral, political, and social structures, and so on; individually, it will include appropriate nurturance, education, skills, and training. Thus, *if we want to survive* then certain moral categories and certain institutions would best be established. This is the constructivism as regards value and practice that informs my approach.

Continuing life is objective, then, in the sense that values and standards and rules will be independent of an individual's own choices and judgments. This is the sense by which, to use Thomas Scanlon's (1975, 658) conception, it posits 'a criterion which provides a basis for appraisal of a person's well-being

13 I believe that this typology is more useful and adequate to a global age than Mill's 'harm principle', for instance. The harm principle depends upon a whole sub-structure of assumptions about 'self-regarding/other-regarding' behavior, or 'private/public' spheres, and is of limited use when considering complex issues, such as, '[w]ould allowing "Faith schools" to organize and recruit students solely on the grounds of religion cause harm to other groups or to a democratic polity as a whole?' to be answered. The issue is simply too complex to be considered in such simplistic terms. The 'harm principle' also permits too greater indeterminacy, and it is noteworthy that Mill himself thought that 'drug taking' was an exclusively private affair, which no one had any right to interfere over.

14 Utilitarians such as Peter Singer have of course sought to make up for this neglect in recent years by focusing on animals.

which is independent of that person's tastes and interests, thus allowing for the possibility that such an appraisal could be correct even though it conflicted with the preferences of the individual in question.' Scanlon's approach thus seeks to combat the subjectivist approach based on preferences and desires as well as the classical liberal approach based on rights. As he summarizes his position:

> [w]hat I take to be central to the objectivist position…is the idea that, insofar as we are concerned with moral claims that some interests should be favored at the expense of others in the design of distributive institutions or in the allocation of other rights and prerogatives, it is an objective evaluation of the importance of these interests, and not merely the strength of the subjective preferences they represent, that is relevant (ibid.).

As a consequence of globalization, and also events like 9/11, the importance of this sort of objectivism has increased. This is no more evident than in international law, where, as the former president of the International Court of Justice has maintained, 'the resolutely positivist, voluntarist approach of international law still current at the beginning of the [twentieth] century has been replaced by an objective conception of international law, a law more readily seeking to reflect a collective juridical conscience and respond to the social necessities of States organized as a community.'[15] While recognition of the importance of objective values has increased, there is a very real sense in which sociologists have always recognized their centrality as dimension to life, in relation to defining inhibitions and sanctions, both in public and in private. We all do act in publicly agreed upon ways, and both our social and our moral behaviors are measured in relation to socially negotiated norms, which we contradict at our peril.

In a way not dissimilar to Scanlon, Richard Arneson (2000) also defends an objective theory of good. For Arneson (ibid., 38), an objective, or perfectionist, doctrine of the good 'holds that what is good for its own sake for a person is fixed independently of her attitudes and opinions toward it,' whereas in the subjective good account, 'things that are intrinsically good for an agent…acquire this status only in virtue of how she happens to regard them' (ibid., 37). For Arneson, it should not be ruled out that perfectionism, in certain cases, might possibly be able to justify paternalism. Restriction of choice in certain senses may also be necessary to justify choice in others. Rather than perfectionism being thought of as forcing upon the agent 'a single option thought to be good,' it could more plausibly be seen as prohibiting 'some tempting bad options while leaving many other options open' (Arneson 2000, 44). For Arneson, then, arguments on conceptual grounds against a 'perfectionist-inspired paternalism' do not succeed. John Stuart Mill's view that 'strict no-paternalism does best to maximize the sum of human good…predictably tends to diminish the welfare of some agents who are poor choosers.' One might add

15 President Bedjaoui, *Legality of the Threat or Use of Nuclear Weapons* (Advisory Opinion, ICJ Reports, 1996), 226.

that it is not simply 'poor choosers', but 'the impressionable', 'the younger', 'the less experienced', 'the elderly' 'the unfortunate', or 'generally less capable', who conceivably would be most protected from such policies. Arneson concludes that 'in principle coercive state interference with individuals' personal lives for their own good might be warranted, if it boosts the coerced individual's achievement of perfection and is part of an overall best strategy for maximizing the appropriately weighted sum of perfection' (ibid., 46). Liberals traditionally, as he concedes, will be suspicious of increasing state intervention and will have reasons for 'doubting that such paternalistic interference will very often do more good than harm' (ibid.). This is because, as Arneson puts it, '[t]he perfectionist propounds her doctrine in the shadow cast by Plato and Nietzsche' (ibid., 52), not to mention, relatedly, many years of exposure to the liberal theory of totalitarianism. He recommends what he terms 'a partial solution' which resonates closely with those like me who advocate constitutional approaches to global politics, based on the qualities of *specification*, *articulation*, and *institutionalization*. A 'partial solution', for Arneson, involves a response that:

> begins by distinguishing a life that is good [objectively]...and a life that is good for the person who is living it. The theory of objective human good should deliver an account of what constitutes a life that is good for the person who lives it.... Once one distinguishes a good life and a life that is good for the one living it, it becomes immediately plausible to maintain that even if great accomplishment is one dimension of the human good or well-being, there are other important dimensions that are objectively important constituents of it. These other components include having relations of love and friendship, having experiences that are interesting and pleasant, fulfilling one's important reasonable life aims or at least a subset of them, having a rudimentary understanding of the world one inhabits including its people, having ordinary bodily vigor and good health, and the sustaining of all of the above through a life whose span contains more rather than fewer years. (ibid., 52-53)

Rawls's approach is inadequate precisely because he lacks a theory of the good. We clearly need a conception of the good that does not constitute a unified all-encompassing doctrine of the good in the way Rawls configured it. Although, for Rawls, 'the two main concepts of ethics are those of the right and the good' (1971, 21), for him the right is prior to the good. He believes that there is a category of reasons that is more important than those that attach to good, and that moral decisions can be justified according to self-legislation based purely upon a reformulation of Kant's categorical imperative. Central to Rawls's individualist conception is that such a good is unified, or homogeneous, and that it excludes, proportionately to its degree of extension, as a matter of logic and history, the ability of the individual to exercise choice or agency. Rawls has classified the problem in terms of the concept of 'perfectionism' (ibid., 286). Whereas utilitarianism is a 'want-regarding principle', perfectionism is an 'ideal-regarding principle' (ibid., 287). A perfectionist principle 'must provide some way of ranking different kinds of achievements and summing their values' (ibid., 287). Although such a conception need not, he says, provide a very accurate assessment, 'it should be accurate enough to guide the main decisions concerning the basic structure [of society]' (ibid.).

Rawls's understanding of good is not the way I understand the concept. For Rawls, the conception of perfection not only suggests that any promulgation of a good can only be concerned with an impossibly narrow ideal of achievement, but his very understanding of the concept of good resonates with a concern with 'maximization' in very much the same way as the utilitarians conceived it. As Richard Kraut (2007, 254) notes:

> [t]he utilitarian assumes that good is to be maximized, and that it consists in the satisfaction of rational desire; both ideas should be rejected. Rawls mistakenly agrees that the good consists in the satisfaction of rational desire; he holds, again mistakenly, that there is a general category of reasons that take precedence over those that avert to good. We should reject both the good-maximizing and right-prioritizing alternatives.... Practical reasoning must always proceed by way of premises that have to do with what is good…but good must be understood developmentally.

My only qualification to Kraut's wonderfully clear exposition is that the good should be understood, not developmentally, but *constructively*. Rather than see the good as the outcome, unfolding, or development of nature, as if caught in the evolving web of Aristotelian teleology, we must see it as *constructed* and as *conditional upon our will to survive*, in a way that is not naturalistic. *Will* must be seen as stronger than nature; or as surpassing nature in this important sense.

Although Rawls takes the concept of perfectionism to stand for any comprehensive conception of good, and sees it as synonymous, we could envisage a situation where the good in question promoted only a level of *sustainability*, rather than *perfection*, or where perfection is defined as referring simply to a structure comprising positive values, or a threshold, rather than as an ultimate point or value in a hierarchy. In this sense, the 'maximizing' thrust of utilitarianism is avoided. As Kraut (2007, 42) notes, '[t]he maximizing thrust of utilitarianism drives it ever outward, to exclude nothing from its concern that can contribute to the total amount of good. That is the result of its fundamental commitment to quantitative thinking: the larger the sum total of good that exists, the better the state of the universe.'

Certainly if we take a value like 'excellence', which Nietzsche is meant to have proffered, then the argument is well set up for Rawls to win it. This was certainly Rawls's characterization of Nietzsche. Such a conception promotes elitism, says Rawls, and certainly it would. But if Nietzsche is seen as advocating, not 'excellence for a few', but 'life for all', what then? If Zarathustra's crossing the bridge is not to advance the elite of superman, but to construct new norms for the survival of humanity, how should this be represented? While Anglo-American scholars have systematically characterized Nietzsche as being elitist, and fascist, it is interesting that a whole group of continental thinkers, including those who identified with the 'new' Nietzsche, dispute the evidence for such a view.[16]

What is distinctive about the notion of life, of the strategies by which life is continued, is that, as a form of the good, its derivation is solely within history, its content alters in many respects in different societies and at different times, and it leaves a large degree of latitude as to what that content is at any particular time. There are in this sense certain distinct and identifiable limits as to which values and practices should be allowed and which should not. Life not only manifests multiplicities as a consequence of time and place, it also permits of a multiplicity of specifications, trajectories, and styles in relation to its form. If norms of life as a strategy are articulated they are specific to a particular historical terrain. While, of course, there are certain constancies as to what it takes to sustain life, or maintain bare survival in all periods, neither the tasks of life, nor those of bare survival, can provide a court of transcendental truth that can dictate for the present what should hold for all time. Rather, what sustains and promotes life will be relative to a particular horizon. Such a contingency goes very deep.[17] For Leibniz, as Deleuze (1993) reads him, we can say that life and the tasks of surviving it, are always *folded* differently. The concept of the fold expresses the multiplicity of life's challenges as infinitely complex, and 'a conception of matter as multiple and continuous. In short it is the triumph of the wave over the particle' (Marks 1998, 76). Just as the tasks of survival vary from one era to another, and even within a particular horizon, the perspectivism entailed does not mean truth is relative

16 Nietzsche's position on this has already been touched upon. The difficulty here is Rawls viewing the good as always representing an ideal which is *perfect*, and then, after having set the situation up in this way, deciding that it is *elitist*. The counterargument to Rawls is that his detection of elitism, excellence, fascism, etc., in the good, is an artifact of the manner in which he constructs his argument.

17 Even the neoliberal theory of the self-interested subject, as developed by game theorists in America during the 1940s and 1950s, must be seen as contingent, rather than, as was supposed, foundational and universal. The game theorists postulated the idea that self-interested egoism was always the preferred rational choice, and that shared or cooperative behavior was not rational. (Such was the scenario of the classic Prisoner's Dilemma, for instance). But in a situation where life's limits to the biosphere are altered as a consequence of either population pressure, climate change, nuclear stalemate, or for any other reason, the boundaries between – and indeed *the very conceptions of* what *is* – 'self-interest' versus 'shared interest', or 'public interest', *radically alter*. In a situation of a nuclear nightmare, for example, my self-interest becomes *identical to yours*! (i.e., *shared*!). Similarly, in a period of climate environmental crisis, new shared concerns emerge. Even adopting game theory logic, once intense enough as a threat, the rational choice is to opt for the cooperative, or shared strategy.

to its social conditions, 'but rather constitutes a "truth of the relative"' (ibid.).[18] Where life establishes new limits in relation to the biosphere, it has new global consequences. Decisions for economics, politics, or education require constantly adjusted settlements constitutive of temporary closures around norms, which must be always open to doubt and questioning if they are to sustain a democratic polity.

Although, at one level, a focus on the strategic aspects of life, such as survival and continuance, generates a form of consequentialism, unlike utilitarianism it does not privilege aggregate or averages, nor does it exclude certain groups or individuals, nor does it privilege certain values, like happiness, at the expense of others, like well-being, security, or continuity. In this sense, by emphasizing both consequences and harm, it avoids the criticism frequently made against Utilitarianism. As Kraut (2007, 43) puts it:

> [u]tilitarianism is committed to a regime of constant sacrifice – sacrificing some for the sake of others – in order to increase the quantity of good. And the wider our circle of concern becomes – the more beings there are for whom some things are good and others bad – the greater must be our readiness to diminish the well-being of some.

In addition, it is not narrowly consequentialist in that morality need not be conceptualized purely in terms of outcomes in the manner of the utilitarian. For my own conception is committed to both *harm* as well as *consequences*. As a relation to the real, or qualitative mode of being, life's quest to continue is deeply interiorized as it is willed and can thus be represented as *intrinsically* worthwhile. As the quest to continue life and achieve (well)-being is immanent within life, to trade life against life goes against the principle of life itself.[19] It is on this basis that Bataille considered life as *sacred*.[20] Sacred does not pertain in his sense to an objective religious truth, but simply expresses a sense of 'utmost value.'[21]

18 Marks is citing Gilles Deleuze from *What is Philosophy?* (see Deleuze and Guattari 1994).

19 This is as near as one gets to natural rights. But, of course, life's immanent quest for continuance gives only a right to be included – life and liberty – but not property, except as is sufficient to continue.

20 Spiritual could also allude to values of commonality and connectedness between life forms, *sensed*, but poorly articulated and *therefore unable to be expressed*, within liberal discourses which were atomistic. Also, see Agamben (1998).

21 It is rational for the religious person to claim a defense of agnosticism, within the bounds of finitude, but not atheism, or absolute definite knowledge. Such a sacred attitude, premised on the basis of an insufficiency of knowledge as the ontological condition of existence, may conceivably justify arguments, like those of Habermas (2003), that the active manipulation of the human genome would confuse or change morally important distinctions between life and non-life, the grown and the fabricated. Such issues are beyond the scope of this chapter.

In addition, rights are not to be neglected in a life philosophy approach. As liberty and a certain amount of property are necessary to continuance, rights are one mechanism for safeguarding entitlements in the complex interactions between part and whole, and in reconciling the individual and collective. But rights, like responsibilities, must be articulated in each age and arise, not from nature, but as necessary as a consequence of a commitment to democratic proceduralism, which is justified in this account as crucial to continuance in the coming age.

Establishing Life as a Bad: The Organization of Life by Biopower

I have argued above that a philosophy of life can serve our purposes for establishing a conception of good. Life has immanent powers that are to survive and flourish. A philosophy of life can also enable us to criticize the practices of other communities. Hence, it can save political theory from localism, patriotism, and nationalism, and solve the problem of moral and epistemological relativism, for which writers like Michael Walzer have been criticized. This is to say that life continuance expresses real necessities and immanent qualities which characterize all communities, indeed which characterize humanity, and indeed, *life itself*. It is in this sense that life necessities, such as sustenance, are universal in all times and places. What communities do is organize life's immanent tendencies in distinctive ways at the discursive level of cultural and linguistic practice. It is this distinction between the discursive and the pre-discursive that enables us to avoid relativism and localism. While a community constitutes a configuration that is always unique, and where even problems of translation from one community to another will always exist, inter-cultural criticism is possible in relation to the immanent tendencies that are universally recognizable as part of the forces of life itself.[22]

Discursive

(Language, discourse, culture, practices, states of affairs)
Configurations depend on time and place (therefore, infinite possibilities of configurative form)

Pre-discursive

Life/non-life necessities Labour
(Non-Discursive materialities: facts, things, regularities – e.g., birth, death – finite regularities, technologies, etc.)

Figure 2.1 Dualistic ontology of discursive and pre-discursive

22 Hence, we can distinguish the cultural form of articulation from the practice of life continuance it represents.

This distinction between discursive and pre-discursive, as schematically represented in Figure 2.1, permits the elaboration of a dualistic ontology and is familiar in writers like Foucault and Adorno and others with the general orbit of neo-Kantianism, including Marx and Marxism. Central to both Foucault and Adorno was an impossibility of avoiding conceptual mediation and a refusal to accept that objectivity could be achieved through the application of universally valid laws of reason. Both also rejected other familiar attempts to posit objectivity, and thus solve Kant's paradox, including Bergson's appeal to 'intuitionism', Husserl's phenomenological reduction via 'intentionality', or via the 'protocol sentences' of positivism. There could be no knowledge except through reflexiveness and mediation. Although Foucault, at least in a formal sense, left the issue unresolved, for Adorno, all that grounded a limited conception of objectivity was life itself, or rather, the *experience* of life. In this sense, too, the positing of life necessities as historical represents a commitment for we can only know them indirectly via mediation. As Alastair Morgan (2007) notes, it was the impossibility of escaping conceptual mediation that characterizes Adorno's solution to Kant's paradox in reinstating life experience as the indirect route by which the real is apprehended and understood. As Morgan argues, such a concept of life enables Adorno to construct a normative theory which permits him to delineate the contours of a 'damaged life', as exemplified by Auschwitz, and to postulate more fundamentally enriched modes of living, without – hopefully – presuming an essential, ahistorical way of life that in some sense constitutes a 'natural way of living.'

A philosophy of life can also help us understand life as a bad, by which I mean it can provide us with materialist categories whereby we understand violence, deceit, fraud, war, genocide, murder, and exclusion. In this section I want to consider Foucault's account of *racism* and the collusion of sovereign and biopower, which culminated in Nazism. If power can organize life for good, it can also do so for bad. It is this latter prospect we now seek to understand.

For Foucault, it is around life that power organizes itself, the importance of life and death being a dissymmetrical in different systems of power. In the *History of Sexuality, Volume 1*, the transition of power from the Middle Ages to modernism alters the way life is focused upon. Prior to the seventeenth century, life was focused upon in terms of death, or the right to end it, which was the prerogative of the sovereign. The sovereign 'exercised his power over life only by exercising his right to kill,' or by refraining from killing, '[h]e evidenced his power over life only through the death he was capable of requiring' (1978, 136). 'The right which was formulated as the 'power of life and death' was in reality the right to *take* life or *let* live. Its symbol, after all, was the sword' (ibid.). Power in this sense was juridical in that 'power was exercised mainly as a means of destruction (*prélèvement*)' or as a 'subtraction mechanism' (ibid.).

Early modernism witnessed the rise of new forms of power over life – related to administrating it, and enabling it, in a more *productive* sense. This was crucially a form of *positive* power in that, rather than controlling it according to the simple axis of destroying it, or letting it be, it sought to constrain or alter forms of life as given in order to shape the ends and purposes desired; to *improve it*, to *make it better*, to *foster it*. The modern era witnessed two forms of such positive power – first, *disciplinary* power, centered on the body as a machine, aiming to integrate it into a specific system of control. Although such a system was exemplified by Foucault in relation to the prison, as a technology it could be applied to different settings. A second form of positive power that complimented sovereign power after modernism, Foucault called *biopower*. This form focused on man as a global mass, species, or population and concerned such phenomena as propagation, birth, mortality, health, and life expectation. Rather than being primarily juridical, centered on law as prohibition or destruction, its legal orientation was regulatory, its political vision teleological, and its epistemology constructivist. Biopower became especially important from the second half of the eighteenth century with the rise of demography, utilizing statistical knowledge, enabling new forms of control and new types of interventions, and enabling the individual to be compared on the same conceptual space to others and to the population. New types of knowledge, such as political arithmetic, statistics, and eugenics, led to new knowledge of aggregates and wholes, which gave rise to concepts such as 'population' and new developments in relation to 'insurance', 'planning', and 'interventions' in relation to health, childcare, and the administration of welfare and security. Biopower thus operates at a more general level than disciplinary mechanisms and results in a more general form of knowledge. Its mode of operation is regulatory and it enables security as a discipline which aims to optimize life and protect it from dangers – both internal and external – by regulating them and rendering them secure. Both biopower and discipline constitute new positive forms of power whose focus is regulatory and broadly pedagogical rather than juridical, and focus on optimization rather than mere policing through control over death. Regulatory law relies on a knowledge of contexts, populations, and needs, as opposed to the formal nature of the juridical subject whose relation to others and characteristics as part of a population were not known, indeed, could not be known, prior to the modern era. These new forms of knowledge, together with the rise of capitalism and consequent urbanization and industrialization, thus constitute the material basis of these new positive forms of power, in the sense that *they make them possible*. Although, to a large extent, disciplinary and biopower were harnessed as technologies by the state, they were also utilized, increasingly, through society in the eighteenth and nineteenth centuries, by all manner of groups and organizations: religious, social, political, and charitable. Such an emergent form of power, which Foucault sees as materially grounded in the changes of the early modern period, linked to the rise of capitalism, the emergence of new conceptions of science, and the developments in philosophy related to the rise of liberalism. Biopower introduces new mechanisms of power such as forecasts, statistical estimates, and overall measures. It ushered in the importance and rise of the norm at the expense of the juridical system of law (1978, 144). Although norms, for Foucault, constitute standards around an average, they are themselves based on the immanent capabilities of life. Hence, Foucault says, '[t]he "right to life," to one's body, to health, to happiness, to the satisfaction of needs, and beyond all the oppressions or "alienations," the "right" to rediscover what one is and all that one can be, this "right" – which the classical juridical system was utterly incapable of comprehending – was the political response to all these new procedures of power which did not derive, either, from the traditional right of sovereignty' (ibid., 145).

Foucault thus contrasts the negativity of sovereign power with a positive power over life that parallels the classical liberal mindset of the seventeenth century as constituting the condition for the rise of capitalism and new forms of political order. The forms of power that the liberal philosophers later identified as dangerous were materially inscribed in the social conditions of modernity emerging from the seventeenth century. The model for sovereign power, he says (2003, 265), 'is a subject of natural rights or primitive powers' and it encapsulates a negative power over death, while biopower parallels the emergence of positive forms of power of the era of social democratic state of the eighteenth and nineteenth centuries. The emergence of such power introduces dangers in relation to the abuse of power by the state. This is what Foucault meant when he said that biopower inscribes *racism* in the mechanisms of the state, in dividing the species into sub-species based on race and introducing a new logic into the operation of the state – new enemies identified as threats to the population (Jews, communists, terrorists, Muslims) establishing killing as (once more) acceptable on certain conditions, as one sub-species becomes 'other', establishing a new logic of war, signaling a destructive moment in biopower. Foucault asks:

> [w]hat in fact is racism? It is primarily a way of introducing a break into the domain of life that is under power's control: the break between what must live and what must die. The appearance within the biological continuum of a human race of races, the distinction among races, the hierarchy of races, the fact that certain races are described as good and that others, in contrast, are described as inferior: all this is a way of fragmenting the field of the biological that power controls. It is a way of separating out the groups that exist within a population (ibid., 254).

Hence, the first function of racism is to *fragment*. It enables power to 'subdivide the species it controls, into subspecies known, precisely as races' (ibid., 255). Racism thus refers to the 'caesuras within the biological continuum addressed by biopower' (ibid.). Racism's second function allows the establishment of a positive relation of the type, '[t]he very fact that you let more die will allow you to live more' (ibid.). This establishes the view, 'if you want to live, you must take more lives' (ibid.). Such a relationship was not invented by the modern state, but is essentially a relationship of war for 'in order to live, you must destroy your enemies' (ibid.). Racism thus trades on a 'biological-type relationship,' and that the 'more inferior species die out, the more abnormal individuals are eliminated, the fewer degenerates there will be in the species as a whole' (ibid.). Killing others, says Foucault, will make 'life in general healthier: healthier and happier' (ibid.).

Biopower thus allows differentiation based on threats of biology and endeavors to eliminate threats in order to improve the species.

In this sense, life justifies not only an ethics of continuance, but a justification for war, fragmentation, murder and killing, expulsion and rejection. Under the biopower mode, what Foucault calls racism develops as an ever-present possibility. Foucault articulates how war has been used as a way of enhancing one's own life at the expense of inferior others, or impure races. War has been biopower's strategy of protecting against others, of purifying and correcting anomalies. For Foucault, 'racism justifies the death-function in the economy of biopower by appealing to the principle that the death of others makes one biologically stronger insofar as one is a member of a race or a population, insofar as one is an element in a unitary living plurality' (ibid., 258).

Racism thus becomes the way the state, in the age of biopower, exercises sovereign power. Foucault takes the example of Nazism to show why 'the most murderous states are also of necessity, the most racist' (ibid.). Nazism was 'the paroxysmal development of the new power mechanisms that had been established since the eighteenth century…Controlling the random element inherent in biological process was one way of the regime's immediate objectives' (ibid., 259).

Racism is thus the way that the old sovereign right to take life is re-introduced under the era of biopower. With Nazism one gets the absolute coexistence of biopower and the sovereign right to kill (ibid., 260) as:

> Nazism alone took the play between the sovereign right to kill and the mechanisms of biopower to this paroxysmal point.… But this play is in fact inscribed in the workings of all States. In all modern States, in all capitalist States? Perhaps not. But I do think that – but this would be a whole new argument – the socialist State, socialism, is as marked by racism as the workings of the modern State, of the capitalist State.… Socialism was a racism from the outset, even in the nineteenth century (ibid., 261).

As to why Nazism arose at a particular juxtaposition of sovereign and biopower, Foucault seems not to be sure as to what precisely accounted for such aberrant tendencies, as '[t]he coexistence in political structures of large destructive mechanisms and institutions orientated to the care of individual life is somewhat puzzling. It is this rationality, and the death and life game which takes place in it, that I'd like to investigate from an historical point of view' (Foucault, 1988, 147-48). It cannot, however, be explained, as liberals are wont to do, as a consequence of the 'positive' power of the state, nor as Max Weber, Walter Benjamin, several of the Frankfurt School, or more recently, Zygmunt Bauman, would have us believe, solely on the basis of bureaucratic rationalization, or instrumental rationality. For while the specificity for the explanation for totalitarianism, or state violence, escapes any such single cause or answer, what is needed is a minute and detailed historical analysis that contemplates the full complexity of the mix of factors in their historical emergence. What Foucault invokes is a theory of affects, or combinations. As Mitchell Dean explains it, '[i]t is not merely the succession or addition of the modern powers over life to the ancient right of death but their very combination within modern states that is of significance. How these powers are combined accounts for whether they are malign or benign' (Dean 2004, 20).

Hence, it is 'the different ways in which bio-politics is combined with sovereign power [that] decide their character' (ibid.). In relation to Nazism, says Dean, it is 'the system of linkages, re-codings and re-inscriptions of sovereign notions of fatherland, territory, and blood with the new bio-political discourse of eugenics and racial hygiene that makes the unthinkable thinkable' (ibid., 20). The possibility of such monstrous juxtapositions is always present. For Foucault identifies 'governmentality which characterizes modernity as involving both sovereignty and biopower as "the intersection of two processes" – a way of managing the population using both poles' (Foucault 1991, 18-19). Traditionally, as Dean notes also, liberalism has sought to apply preventative techniques of government through two mechanisms: the idea of a self-regulating market order which in turn justifies a restriction on the scope and size of the state, and the discourse of rights, emerging from the seventeenth and eighteenth centuries.[23] If the market order is self-regulating, and nature also constitutes a 'spontaneous' order which was 'integrative' and 'self-correcting', then the state could operate as an 'umpire', or 'Night Watchman' as liberals from Adam Smith to Robert Nozick have variously expressed it. In addition to the theories of 'laissez-faire', and the self-regulating market, the discourse of natural rights, and natural law, as developed by Locke, specifying 'life, liberty and property' as God-given rights, and which no government could dislodge without jeopardizing its right to govern, and legitimating revolt by the citizenry. Foucault, says Dean (2004: 21), is open to the possibilities of a 'virtuous combination' and he 'puzzles' at the possibilities of various 'pathological' or 'virtuous' mixes.

Conclusion

In terms of constructing a future in the horizon that presents itself today, then, what prospects does positive power contain for peace and security that excludes or contains the potentials for war and fragmentation? The question is: how can positive power be rendered safe? The only answer is, I believe, a global democracy that incorporates norms for solidarity and equality and global justice and is based on a balance of power implemented at the global level, as well as new global norms of accountability and transparency. Unless people consider themselves fairly and appropriately treated, the compact for life continuance will break down. That there are prospects, in the current horizon, for state racism and pathological insurgencies cannot be denied. As Paul Hirst (2001, 2002, 2005) points out, the

23 We may of course add to Dean's list the doctrine of the separation of powers, as well as the separation of church from state.

future squeeze on global resources and instabilities associated with climate change, global poverty, and terrorism, creates distinct prospects of increased military conflict and war, as states compete for increasingly scarce resources. The future, then, is at best uncertain.

Bibliography

Agamben, G. (1999) *Potentialities* (Stanford: Stanford University Press).

—— (1998) *Homo Sacer: Sovereign Power and Bare Life* (Stanford: Stanford University Press).

Ansell-Pearson, K. (1994) *Introduction to Nietzsche as Political Thinker* (Cambridge: Cambridge University Press).

Aristotle (1905) *Politics* (trans. Jowett, B.) (Oxford: Oxford University Press).

Arneson, R.J. (2000) 'Perfectionism and Politics', *Ethics* 111 October: 3763.

Bataille, G. (2004) *On Nietzsche: The Will to Chance* (London: Continuum).

—— (1991) *Consumption*, vol. 1 of *The Accursed Share: Essays on General Economy* (New York: Zone Books).

—— (1985) *Visions of Excess: Selected Writings, 1927-1939* (ed. Stoekl, A.) (Minneapolis: University of Minnesota Press).

Canguilhem, G. (1978) *On the Normal and the Pathological* (trans. Fawcett, C.R.) (ed. Cohen, R.S.) (Boston: D. Reidel).

Dean, M. (2004) 'Four Theses on the Power of Life and Death', *Contretemps* 5 (December): 16-29.

Deleuze, G. (1993) *The Fold: Leibniz and the Baroque* (trans. Conley, T.) (Minneapolis: University of Minnesota Press).

—— (1991) *Empiricism and Subjectivity: An Essay on Hume's Theory of Human Nature* (New York: Columbia University Press).

Deleuze, G. and Guattari, F. (1994) *What is Philosophy?* (London: Verso).

Foucault, M. (2003) *Society Must Be Defended* (trans. Macey, D.) (London: Allen Lane).

—— (1998) 'Life, Experience, Science', in *Michel Foucault: Aesthetics, Method, and Epistemology*, vol. 2 of *Essential Works of Foucault, 1954-1984* (ed. Faubion, J.D.) (New York: The Penguin Press).

—— (1991) 'Governmentality', in Burchell, G., Gordon, C. and Miller, P. (eds) *The Foucault Effect: Studies in Governmentality* (Chicago: University of Chicago Press).

—— (1988) 'Technologies of the Self' in Martin, L., Gutman, H. and Hutton, P. (eds) *Technologies of the Self: A Seminar with Michel Foucault* (London: Tavistock).

—— (1978) *The History of Sexuality, Volume 1: An Introduction* (trans: Hurley, R.) (New York: Pantheon Books).

Fitzpatrick, P. (2005) 'Bare Sovereignty: Homo Sacer and the Insistence of Law', in Norris, A. (ed.) *Politics, Metaphysics and Death: Essays on Giorgio Agamben's Homo Sacer* (Durham: Duke University Press).

Grosz, E. (2004) *The Nick of Time: Politics, Evolution and the Untimely* (Durham: Duke University Press).

Habermas, J. (2003) *The Future of Human Nature* (Cambridge: Polity Press).

Hardt, M. and Negri, A. (2000) *Empire* (Cambridge: Harvard University Press).

Heidegger, M. (1993) 'The Question Concerning Technology', in Farell Krell, D. (ed.) *Basic Writings, Revised and Expanded Edition* (London: Routledge).

Hirst, P. (2005) *Space and Power: Politics, War and Architecture* (Cambridge: Polity).

—— (2002) 'Another Century of Conflict? War and the International System in the Twenty-first Century', *International Relations* 16 (3): 327-342.

—— (2001) *War and Power in the Twenty-First Century: The State, Military Conflict and the International System* (Cambridge: Polity).

Hume, D. (1978) *A Treatise on Human Nature*, 2nd edn (ed. Nidditch, P.H.) (Oxford: Clarendon Press).

—— (1970) *Dialogues Concerning Natural Religion* (ed. Pike, N.) (Indianapolis: Bobbs-Merrill).

Hunt, L.H. (1991) *Nietzsche and the Origin of Virtue* (London: Routledge).

Kraut, R. (2007) *What is Good and Why: The Ethics of Well-Being* (Cambridge: Harvard University Press).

Marks, J. (1998) *Gilles Deleuze: Vitalism and Multiplicity* (London: Pluto Press)

Morgan, A. (2007) *Adorno's Concept of Life* (London: Continuum).

Nietzsche, F. (2003) *Thus Spoke Zarathustra: A Book for Everyone and No One* (trans. Hollingdale, R.J.) (London: Penguin Press).

—— (1968) *The Will to Power* (trans. Kaufmann, W. and Hollingdale, R.J.) (New York: Vintage Books).

—— (1966) *Beyond Good and Evil* (trans. Kaufmann, W.) (New York: Random House).

Parekh, B. (1997) 'Rethinking Humanitarian Intervention', *International Political Science Review* 18(1): 49-69.

Plato (2003) *The Last Days of Socrates* (trans. Tredennick, H. and Tarrant, H.) (London: Penguin Books).

Rawls, J. (1971) *A Theory of Justice* (Oxford: Oxford University Press).

Richardson, H.S. (1990) 'The Problem of Liberalism and the Good', in Douglass, R.B., Mara, G.M. and Richardson, H.S. (eds) *Liberalism and the Good* (New York: Routledge).

Scanlon, T. (1975) 'Preference and Urgency', *Journal of Philosophy*, 72(19): 655-669.

Schmitt, C. (1985) *Political Theology: Four Chapters on the Concept of Sovereignty* (trans. Schwab, G.) (Cambridge: MIT Press).

Schnädelbach, H. (1984) *Philosophy in Germany – 1831-1933* (trans. Matthews, E.) (Cambridge: Cambridge University Press).

Chapter 3
The Exemplary Exception: Philosophical and Political Decisions in Giorgio Agamben's *Homo Sacer*

Andrew Norris

> Of all the beings that are, presumably the most difficult to think about are living creatures [*das Lebe-Wesen*], because they are in a certain way most closely akin to us, and on the other are at the same time separated [*geschieden*] from our ek-sistent essence by an abyss. (Heidegger, 'Letter on Humanism')

In *Homo Sacer: Sovereign Power and Bare Life* Giorgio Agamben draws upon metaphysics, philosophical anthropology, set theory, and the philosophy of language to advance a number of radical politico-philosophical claims. In contrast to conceptions of political community that depict it as a common 'belonging' in a shared national, ethnic, religious, or moral identity, Agamben argues that 'the original political relation is the ban' in which a mode of life is actively and continuously excluded or shut out (*ex-claudere*) from the *polis*. The decision as to what constitutes the life that is thereby taken outside of the *polis* is a sovereign decision. Sovereignty is therefore not a historically specific form of political authority that arises with modern nation-states and their conceptualization by Hobbes and Bodin, but rather the essence of the political. Similarly, biopolitics is not, as Foucault sometimes suggests, incompatible with sovereign as opposed to disciplinary power, nor is it a distinctively modern phenomenon. Instead it is the original form of politics, 'the fundamental activity of sovereign power is the production of bare life as originary political element and as threshold of articulation between nature and culture, *zoē* and *bios*.' Attending to the etymology of the word *decide*, one can understand this sovereign decision as a cut in life, one that separates real life from merely existent life, political and human life from the life of the non-human. As this cutting defines the political, the production of the inhuman – which is correlative with the production of the human – is not an activity that politics might dispense with, say in favor of the assertion of human rights. More specifically, the Nazi death camps are not a political aberration, least of all a unique event, but instead the place where politics as the sovereign decision on life most clearly reveals itself, 'today it is not the city but rather the camp that is the fundamental biopolitical paradigm of the West' (Agamben 1998a, 181). The *Lager* is a threshold in which human beings are reduced to bare life; and the torture this life suffers is nothing else but its ex-clusion from the *polis* as a distinctively human life. The bare life that is produced by this abandonment by the state is not biological life, 'not simple natural life, but life exposed to death (bare life or sacred life) is the originary political element' (ibid., 88). This is the *Muselmann* as described by Primo Levi in *If This is a Man*. One speaks of the Shoah as industrialized mass death, and of the camps as 'factories of death.' But the product of these factories is not death but, as Arendt puts it, a mode of life 'outside of life and death' (Arendt 1966, 444). If for Arendt, however, the production of *Muselmänner* is anti-political, in that the camps are spaces in which plurality is foreclosed, for Agamben it is the emergence of the essence of the political.

Such claims are difficult for political philosophy to address, as they undermine so many of its guiding assumptions. Instead of asking us to construct and evaluate different plans of action, Agamben asks us to evaluate the metaphysical structure and implications of the activity of politics as such. Instead of asking us to consider the true or proper nature of political identity, Agamben asks us to consider a threshold state of the non-identical, the liminal. And far from bringing concepts such as rights, authority, public interest, liberty, or equality more clearly into view, Agamben operates at a level of abstraction at which such concepts blur into their opposites. He takes this approach because, like Arendt, he believes that claims to justice can be made only if one understands the ground of the political upon which both justice and injustice stand. If Foucault's goal was 'to make the cultural unconscious apparent' (Foucault 1989, 71), Agamben's is that of bringing to expression the metaphysics that our history has thus far only shown. He argues that, properly understood, what that history shows us is that politics is:

> the truly fundamental structure of Western metaphysics insofar as it occupies the threshold on which the relation between the living being and the *logos* is realized. In the 'politicization' of bare life – the metaphysical task *par excellence* – the humanity of living man is decided [*si decide*]...There is politics because man is the living being who, in language, separates and opposes himself to his own bare life and, at the same time, maintains himself in relation to that bare life in an inclusive exclusion (Agamben 1998a, 8).

What is perhaps both most intriguing and most problematic about Agamben's work is that, unlike, say, that of Philippe Lacoue-Labarthe and Jean-Luc Nancy, it brings these claims about metaphysics into dialogue with a rich and specific set of quite concrete examples, including refugee camps, hospital wards, death rows, and military camps. All of these are sites where, on Agamben's account, one can perceive the metaphysical negation that allows for the affirmation of distinctively human life: bare life, *nuda vita*. One way to evaluate Agamben's claims is to consider how well they help us to describe and understand such examples. Another is to ask whether Agamben's claims are intelligible on their own account – to see, that is, whether they open themselves up to an immanent critique. This approach has a number of advantages, chief among which is that it does not demand that we simply choose whether to accept or reject Agamben's approach in a global way; instead such an approach allows us to be open to a radically different way of thinking about politics and political philosophy while at the same time maintaining some critical distance from it. In what follows I want to pursue this option by way of considering Agamben's appropriation of the early decisionist political theory of Carl Schmitt. I will argue that Agamben's acceptance of Schmitt's central claims regarding political judgment make it impossible for him to weave together his suggestive reading of examples from philosophy and political history into a mode of political thought that fulfills his own ambition of 'returning thought to its practical calling' (Agamben 1998a, 5). Agamben's project hinges upon the paradigmatic status of the camp. But on his own account, there is an isomorphism between the exception and the example or paradigm. Given his acceptance of Schmitt's analysis of the former as the product of the sovereign decision, this renders Agamben's evaluation of the camp as 'the fundamental biopolitical paradigm of the West' into a sovereign decision beyond the regulation of rule or reason. As this casts his readers as either subject or enemy, it is hard to imagine how the politics it might produce will serve as a real alternative to that which it contests.

It will be helpful to say a bit more first about Agamben's central claims and the sort of valence they have in the history of philosophy. In his insistence that the history of politics must be understood first and foremost as the history of metaphysics, Agamben clearly follows his former teacher Heidegger. But Agamben's differences from Heidegger are as important as the similarities between them. Crucial here is the fact that Heidegger does not thematize bare life or its relation to the political.[1] Indeed, he would seem to echo the inclusive exclusion that on Agamben's account produces it. Consider one of Heidegger's more political texts, his 1947 'Letter on Humanism,' in which he proposes to think 'the essence of action' (*das Wesen des Handelns*) in a more 'decisive' (*entschieden*) way than had been previously achieved. Human action – the essence of the political – is said by Heidegger to be thinking in language. Thinking does not make or cause; action is instead revelatory, it brings things out into the open. What it brings out is that human beings are related to Being in a completely different way than animal life. Animals lack language, as they have no world, '[b]ecause plants and animals are lodged in their respective environments but are never placed freely [*frei gestellt*] in the clearing of Being which alone is 'world,' they lack language.' Human beings, then, will become what they really are only in so far as they make real this distinction within themselves between their animal life and their human dwelling in the house of being.[2] Heidegger suggests that he is aware of the potential difficulties this entangles him in, but he does not directly address the problem. Instead he only adds:

1 On this point see in particular, Derrida (1989).

2 Agamben does say that for Heidegger 'man is not a living being who must abolish or transcend himself in order to become human.' But he immediately goes on to say that Heidegger's work represents 'a radicalization without precedent of the state of exception,' implying that Heidegger has not after all broken free of this demand for transcendence (Agamben 1998, 153).

> [b]ut in being denied language [plants and animals] are not thereby suspended worldlessly in their environment. Still, in this word 'environment' [*Umgebung*] converges all that is puzzling about living creatures. In its essence, language is not the utterance of an organism; nor is it the expression of a living thing… Language is the clearing-concealing advent of Being itself (Heidegger 1993, 217-230).

Without language, and yet not suspended in the absence of the clearing of Being that is world and whose advent is language, animal life is marginal life, life that only a decisive thought can distinguish from the human – which as history shows is itself all too easily collapsed into the oxymoron of the *animal rationale*. Heidegger provides a hint as to the decision this thought will make when he writes that animal life is never '*freely* placed in the clearing of Being which alone is "world."' This suggests that it will be placed there, of necessity, under coercion.[3] It is precisely the implications of this coercive, negative aspect of our relation to our own embodied life that fascinates Agamben.

Even Hannah Arendt, who sees that the camps force us to question the way we delineate the concepts of humanity and life, fails to break free of what we might term this logic of exuviation. As is well known, *The Human Condition* repeats variations of most of the gestures made by Heidegger in his letter on humanism: what has been obscured in modernity is the crucial importance to human life of action. Properly understood, action is speech; and speech is what makes possible a world. Speaking has a revelatory function, and what it reveals – in a public place that bears obvious resemblance to Heidegger's clearing of Being – is a public person, as opposed to a private individual. The achievement of such personhood is freedom. What is less obvious is that Arendt repeats Heidegger's marginalization – or, perhaps better, liminalization – of animal life. This is obscured by her seeming rejection of *Being and Time*'s analysis of being-toward-death, 'since action is the political activity par excellence [and since acting involves making a radical new beginning], natality, and not mortality, may be the central category of political, as opposed to metaphysical, thought' (Arendt 1958, 9). But this passes over the strange importance *im*mortality retains for Arendt. *The Human Condition*'s first chapter – which not coincidentally shares the title of the book – ends with a section entitled 'Eternity versus Immortality.' Here Arendt argues that while participation in the infinite is the ideal of the philosopher, immortality is that of the political actor. The first is an atemporality that is available only to the individual contemplative, who on Arendt's account experiences 'a kind of death' in thus leaving the world of men. Immortality in contrast is endurance in time. It is sought by human beings in so far as they are mortal:

---

3 Compare the discussion of man's essential violence in the earlier *Introduction to Metaphysics* (Heidegger 1959, 146ff).

> [m]en are 'the mortals,' the only mortal things in existence, because unlike animals they do not exist only as members of a species whose immortal life is guaranteed by procreation. The mortality of men lies in the fact that individual life, with a recognizable life-story from birth to death, rises out of biological life. This individual life…cuts through the circular movement of biological life (ibid., 18-19).[4]

It must do this, as 'the distinction between men and animals [in Arendt's own German translation of *The Human Condition*, "*bloßem (tierischen) Lebewesen*"] runs right through the human species itself.' Hence Arendt silently accepts the judgment of the ancient Greeks that only those 'who "prefer immortal fame to mortal things" are really human' (ibid., 18-19).[5] Noting this brings out the continuity of *The Human Condition* with the earlier *Origins of Totalitarianism*, which had argued that one of the 'decisive step[s] in the [camps'] preparation of living corpses [was] making martyrdom, for the first time in history, impossible.' Arendt cites a camp victim, '[t]o demonstrate when death can no longer be postponed' – that is, to make one's own decision on this question – 'is an attempt to give death meaning, to act beyond one's own death. In order to be successful, a gesture must have social meaning' (Arendt 1958, 451).[6] Politics – where one struggles to become a public person distinct from the private self – is not merely a sphere in which plurality is celebrated. As a sphere in which one form of life gives birth to another, it is also one in which life is placed into question, 'as if,' in Agamben's words, 'politics were the place in which life had to transform itself into good life and in which what had to be politicized were always already bare life. In Western politics, bare life has the peculiar privilege of being that whose exclusion founds the city of man' (Agamben 1998a, 7).

Agamben's *Homo Sacer* project is devoted to the justification of and elaboration upon this claim. The title of the first volume names the three moments

---

4 Recalling that this 'life-story,' as the term implies, emerges in language, compare Heidegger in *On the Way to Language*, because '[m]ortals are they who can experience death as death. Animals cannot do so. But animals cannot speak either. The essential relation between death and language flashes before us, but remains unthought' (1971, 107). These lines are cited by Agamben in the opening pages of the first volume of *Homo Sacer*.

5 Arendt (1960, 24) , *Vita Activa, oder Vom tätigen Leben* (München: Piper, 1960), 24. Arendt's German continues, '*nur die "Besten"… sind mehr als bloße Lebewesen*,' repeating the phrase that points back to Heidegger and is a probable influence upon Agamben. The more obvious source of the phrase 'mere life' is of course Benjamin's 'Critique of Violence,' and Arendt herself may have also been influenced here by her friend Benjamin's 1936 essay, 'The Storyteller,' which discusses the decline of both the thought of death and 'communicability [*Mitteilbarkeit*],' Arendt's privileged term for the analysis of political judgment – a capacity she famously describes as also being in decline. See Benjamin (1969, s. IV, X).

6 The best discussion I have seen of this aspect of Arendt is the exchange between George Kateb and Fred Dallmayr, 'Death and Politics' and 'Public or Private Freedom?' *Social Research* 54, no. 3 (Autumn 1987).

of Agamben's analysis, *Homo Sacer: Sovereign Power and Bare Life*. *Homo sacer* is a figure from Roman law, '*life that cannot be sacrificed and yet may be killed*' (ibid., 82). This life as exposure to death is what Agamben finds in the *Lager*:

> [t]he Jew living under Nazism is…a flagrant case of *homo sacer*…The truth – which is difficult for the victims to face, but which we must have the courage not to cover with sacrificial veils – is that the Jews were exterminated not in a mad and giant holocaust but exactly as Hitler had announced, as 'lice,' which is to say, as bare life (ibid., 114).

The term *holocaust* describes the destruction of European Jewry as a sacrifice, suggesting that we compare the extermination camps to holy altars upon which burned offerings are placed. It is for just this reason that Agamben rejects the use of the term as carrying with it an anti-Semitic history (Agamben 1999, 28-31). The camps of the Shoah are better understood as sites for the production of *homo sacer*, life that is, as the etymology of *sacred* suggests, both blessed and cursed, both included and excluded from the community – and ultimately both living and dead, both human and inhuman. In the '"politicization" of bare life' in which 'the humanity of living man is decided,' the threshold between the human and inhuman must be crossed, and the two distinguished. The camps are where this process is enacted most vividly, '[t]he *Muselmann*…marks the threshold between the human and the inhuman' (Agamben 1999, 55). As his title suggests, Agamben seeks to explain the production of that threshold through the concepts of sovereign power and bare life, concepts he draws, respectively, from Carl Schmitt and Walter Benjamin. I want to turn now to a discussion of the former so as to put us in a position to ask what implications Agamben's appropriation of his work might have for Agamben's own project.

Carl Schmitt presents his influential theory of sovereignty in his *Constitutional Theory* and the first volume of his *Political Theology* (Norris 2000).[7] For Schmitt, any legal system rests upon a decision that cannot itself take the form of law. Both the origin and the border of the law require a political power that exceeds legal justification, and in a state of emergency this power must re-emerge from the system of positive norms appropriate to the normal situation. The state of emergency is, however, for Schmitt only an instance of the logic of the exception, itself the expression of a spatial understanding of concepts and conceptual borders as such. Since what is within the legal system (norms and laws) is made possible (defined as being within the system) by a distinction between inside and outside that as such exceeds the limits of the set of norms and laws, no norm can make these distinctions. Hence a unified legal system requires a political decision to give it (the system, not the territory to which it is applied) borders as well as a set of fundamental values. The decision on the exception is simply the re-emergence of this border-setting power, the ability to make the decisive distinction (itself

7 My discussion of Schmitt's decisionism follows that of my article, Norris 2000.

from *distinguere*, to separate) that can be made only by a sovereign authority. This is the true force of Schmitt's infamous dictum, '[s]overeign is he who decides on the exception' (*Ausnahmezustand*). Recognizing this makes plain why Schmitt describes the concept of the sovereign decision as 'a borderline concept' (*Grenzbegriff*) that as such pertains 'to the outermost sphere' (*der äußersten Sphäre*) (Schmitt 1985, 5). Sovereignty operates at the outermost sphere; it is here, at the borderline, that it establishes and violates limits. If sovereignty decides upon its own limits, when it will and will not be called upon to emerge from behind the system of norms and laws that cloak it, its decision 'must necessarily be unlimited' (*unbegrenzte*). The sovereign is the unlimited power that makes limits – or, in other words, the ungrounded ground of the law. Schmitt's sovereign is a creature of the border, 'although he stands outside the normally valid legal system, he nevertheless belongs to it, for it is he who decides when the constitution needs to be suspended in its entirety' (Schmitt 1985, 7). But while it seems to range back and forth over it, this movement is in fact the oscillation of the border itself. Though it makes sense in one way to speak of the sovereign overstepping the limits it lays down, in a deeper sense it *is* the limit, and hence carries the limit with it in its movement as it carries itself. As Agamben notes, the exception – *die Aus-nahme* – is what is taken outside; it is the inclusive exclusion (Agamben 1998a, 18).[8] The decision and the exception it concerns are never decisively placed within or without the legal system, as they are precisely that moving border between the two.

A state of emergency is the result of the collapse of the normal order; but the normal order is only the withdrawal of the state of emergency. In Agamben's words:

> [t]he exception does not subtract itself from the rule; rather, the rule, suspending itself, gives rise to the exception and, maintaining itself in relation to the exception, first constitutes itself as a rule…The sovereign decision of the exception is the originary juridico-political structure on the basis of which what is included in the juridical order and what is excluded from it acquire their meaning' (Agamben 1998a, 18-19).

Agamben concludes from this that '[w]hat emerges in the limit figure is the radical crisis of every possibility of clearly distinguishing between membership and inclusion, between what is outside and what is inside, between exception and rule' (ibid., 25). Here the logic of borders is used to deny that borders can be confidently identified by anyone other than the sovereign, who does not identify borders so much as establish them by fiat. Having played upon a conception of the legal system as a unit defined by distinctions made between in and out, the Schmittian logic of the decision now proceeds to 'deconstruct' and hence fulfill itself by denying that

8 One could speak of the difference that makes a difference, playing upon the root of *differ* in *differre*, to carry apart. The way in which Arendt's natality remains within this compass is brought out if one reflects upon the root *bher* as carrying, bearing children.

there is a real distinction (to be made by anyone other than the sovereign) between the core and the marginal. For Schmitt, once we acknowledge that the rule gives rise to exceptions for which it cannot account, we must admit that every case can, in principle, be understood in these terms. The only alternative is to argue that exceptional cases are clearly defined as such by the rule – itself a paradoxical position. Hence Schmitt concludes that 'all law is "situational law"' (Schmitt 1985, 13).[9] As Agamben puts it, Schmitt's analysis of the sovereign shows us that 'the law is outside itself,' and that in its formalism it has *Geltung ohne Bedeutung* (Agamben 1998b, 161, 170).

Though Agamben himself has not noted this, the author of this analysis of the aporias of law also advances one of the purest expressions of the logic of exuviation discussed above: *The Concept of the Political*. Here the decisive point is the relation between the way of life protected by the polity and the life demanded of the soldiers who serve in that protection. For Schmitt, the concept of the political is defined by the criteria of friends and enemies, as the concept of the moral is defined by that of good and evil, and that of the aesthetic by beauty and ugliness. What makes friends friends and enemies enemies is something only the parties involved can recognize:

> [o]nly the actual participants can correctly recognize, understand, and judge the concrete situation and settle the extreme case of conflict. Each participant is in a position to judge [*entscheiden*] whether the adversary intends to negate his opponent's way of life and therefore must be repulsed or fought in order to preserve one's own form of existence (Schmitt 1996, 26-27).

In response to such threats the political unit has 'the right to demand from its members the readiness to die.' This is one of the most important features of the Schmittian state, as it is 'by virtue of [its] power over the physical life of men [that] the political community transcends all other associations or societies' (ibid., 46-47). Where for Hobbes the common life comes into being in the service of the individual's embodied life, Schmitt follows Hegel in decisively subordinating the latter to the former. Given his non-Hegelian refusal to describe the goods advanced by the political entity, this produces the phenomenon described by Agamben in which the political 'way of life' is defined by its negation of bare life. The citizen gives his life in resistance to 'the public enemy' because his true life is the common

9 This conclusion clearly does not necessarily follow. I do not wish to gloss over the fact that Schmitt is playing upon etymology and a particular spatial conception of sets and concepts in order to himself make distinctions his arguments do not completely justify. That said, Kant's analysis in 'Theory and Practice' would seem to suggest that, if we are not going to end up in an infinite regress, laws and rules are going to have to give out sooner or later, and find their origin in something other than yet another law or rule. Whether the non-legal *origin* of the law that is thus revealed will, as Schmitt implies, turn out to be the conceptual *foundation* of the law is yet another question.

Art von Leben (ibid., 28).[10] For Schmitt, in the absence of such a commitment life is reduced to mere life, an essentially animal existence. It is because he finds this a form of nihilism from which we need to be redeemed that Schmitt does not pursue his own suggestion that life might in itself attain a metaphysical status. He writes in *Political Romanticism*:

> [t]oday different and, indeed, mundane factors have taken the place of God: humanity, the nation, the individual, historical development, and even life for its own sake, in its complete spiritual emptiness and mere dynamic. This does not mean that the attitude is no longer metaphysical…Metaphysics is something unavoidable (Schmitt 1986, preface, 17-18).

But this suggestion is left undeveloped, and life's role in metaphysics is, in line with Agamben's analysis, that of 'an inclusive exclusion' the exuviation of which allows for the emergence of the political.[11]

The bare life that politics sloughs off is never precisely defined by Agamben. He focuses instead upon presenting examples of this 'inclusive exclusion' such as *Versuchspersonen*, Karen Quinlan, people in 'overcomas,' refugees, and so on. But his central example is the *Muselmann* of the Nazi death camps, as 'today it is not the city but rather the camp that is the fundamental biopolitical paradigm of the West.' This is a crucial claim for Agamben. It gives his work a great deal of pathos, and allows him to argue that the history of metaphysics is not an arcane subject worthy of dusty libraries, but in fact the most pressing and important ethical and political topic of our time. In reading his work, Agamben suggests, we are confronting the truth of 'the political' and of the most horrific events in modern history in a way that mere political actors never could. That one of his stated ambitions is 'to return thought to practical calling' implies that thought is now impractical, and that practice is thoughtless. Though this thoughtlessness can take many forms, they all share on Agamben's account a common essence that is exemplified by the Nazi death camps. All of politics, including liberal regimes devoted to human rights, is implicated in and *can be understood in terms of* the Shoah.[12] If this claim is not accepted, one might turn one's attention to, say, people on Texan death rows, and argue that their marginal status is an institutional rather than a metaphysical problem. Or one might argue that the common element in most

10 This is not the dominant interpretation of Schmitt. I defend it in Norris (1998).

11 To some extent this lack is made good by the suggestions of Walter Benjamin, of whose collected works in Italian Agamben is the editor. If it is Schmitt who furnishes Agamben with the basic structure of his analysis of sovereignty, it is Schmitt seen through the prism of Benjamin, whose often cited but incredibly opaque and inconclusive 1921 'Critique of Violence' introduces the concept of mere life that Agamben's work develops. Unfortunately, it is almost impossible to say what Benjamin means by this phrase.

12 This is argued most directly in the third part of *Homo Sacer*, 'The Camp as Biopolitical Paradigm of the Modern.'

of the examples listed above is the quite formal distinction between life and the good life that founds Socratic ethics and Aristotelian politics. Agamben in contrast wants to reveal the limitations of these modes of philosophical reflection upon practice by implicating them in one of the greatest catastrophes of the twentieth century. Without the claim for the paradigmatic nature of the camps, Agamben's own arguments are marginalized, and politics and law become again a matter of communities, interests, conveniences, and so on. This makes it imperative for those who find Agamben's work suggestive or compelling to ask what makes the camps and their victims the best examples of *homo sacer*, and whether the claim that they are raises problems for Agamben's analysis.

One form this question might take is asking why the camps of Stalin's Soviet Union aren't the paradigm of the political. Agamben uses the term 'camp' in a quite broad sense that suggests a deep commonality between the camps of Germany, the Soviet Union, the former Yugoslavia, and other unspecified regimes. If this is an apparent acceptance of Arendt's maligned notion of totalitarianism,[13] it is made more problematic by the fact that Agamben, unlike Arendt, does not engage in any comparative analyses that might defend the claim of a substantial commonality. Almost all of his detailed analyses are of National Socialism, with occasional reference to the former Yugoslavia, where female bodies have been the focus of a political decision to commit mass rape. It remains then an open question how his schema might apply to, say, Pol Pot's Cambodia or Mao's China, both of which go entirely unmentioned. Of course, even if the result is that Agamben's analysis is not helpful in these cases, this would imply nothing about its potential explanatory power regarding National Socialism. Agamben need not follow Arendt in attempting to give a unitary account of totalitarianism – or, for that matter, of politics. However, if he is to narrow his focus he must obviously also radically adjust his analysis.

This is not, however, the only way of asking whether Agamben is right to make the camps the paradigm of the political. One might also wonder whether the camp system can exemplify a phenomenon that includes constitutional, legally governed polities. Agamben himself emphasizes that '*the state of exception… comes to be confused with juridical rule itself*' in the Nazi state in part 'because the juridical basis for internment was not common law but *Schutzhaft*,' a kind of state of exception (Agamben 1998, 167-168). This might suggest that what is needed is the *reinstatement* of legal protection rather than a critique of law – that it is the fascist imitation of law that results in the inclusive exclusion of life, and not law itself. Such suspicions are only heightened by Agamben's reliance on the erstwhile Nazi Carl Schmitt's account of the sovereign decision. So it might be helpful to note that one legal system of unblemished merit appears to produce much the same anomaly as the Nazis' *Schutzhaft*: John Locke's account of the God-given law of nature and reason. Here I have in mind not Locke's defense of executive prerogative, though that too is surely relevant to this question, but

13 For a witty version of the many attacks on this idea, see Žižek 2001.

instead the way the logic of his argument drives Locke to allow for a horrific form of slavery even as he asserts that we are by nature free and can never consent to our own enslavement.

Locke begins the second of the *Two Treatises of Government* by identifying political power with '*a Right* of making Laws with Penalties of Death, and consequently all lesser penalties' for the preservation of property and the commonwealth 'for the Publick Good' (Locke 1963, 268). Locke grants this political power to all men in the state of nature, and argues that those who would violate these rights put themselves into a state of war with those they would subject. In judging when another has put himself in such a state of war with me, I should, according to Locke, look first to the defense of my liberty. Indeed, it is '[l]awful for a Man to *kill a Thief*, who has not in the least hurt him, nor declared any design upon his Life, any further then by the use of Force, so to get him in his Power.' 'He that in the State of Nature, *would take away the Freedom*, that belong to any one in that State, must necessarily be supposed to have a design to take away every thing else, that *Freedom* being the Foundation of all the Rest' (ibid., 279). This might be only a speculation on Locke's part as to what is likely to happen. But in fact it is closer to an identification of life with freedom. 'This Freedom from Absolute, Arbitrary Power, is so necessary to, and closely joyned with a Man's Preservation, that he cannot part with it, but by what forfeits his Preservation and Life together' (ibid., 284). This robust, normative identification of life with individual freedom is part and parcel of Locke's defense of our ability to recognize when a political ruler has put himself into a state of rebellion, and to depose him. And it sounds reassuringly far away from the bare life of the *Muselmänner*. But the hinge of freedom as life serves to open up a less familiar scene in Locke's political universe.

Because life is essentially freedom, 'a Man, not having the Power of his own life [which belongs to God], *cannot*, by Compact or his own Consent, *enslave himself* to any one' (ibid.). And yet, on precisely the same grounds, slavery is nonetheless possible. How can this be? Locke's reasoning is as follows: if someone tries to take away my freedom, he has as good as tried to kill me. Being guilty of (attempted) murder, he forfeits his life; that is, he enters a zone in which he has no power over his own life and *is in fact already dead*. As the living dead, he loses the rights and powers of the living, and may be treated as a slave, as Locke argues:

> [i]ndeed, having, by his fault, forfeited his own Life, by some Act that deserves Death; he, to whom he has forfeited it, may (when he has him in his Power) delay to take it, and make use of him to his Service, and he does him no injury by it. For, whenever he finds the hardship of his Slavery to out-weigh the value of his Life, 'tis in his Power, by resisting the Will of his Master, to draw on himself the Death he Desires (ibid.).

Locke can speak of the slave as 'drawing on himself the Death he Desires' without contradicting his claim that man does not have the right to take his own life only because he is assuming that the slave *is already dead.* Like the *Versuchspersonen* of the camps, Locke's slave lacks 'almost all the rights and expectations that we characteristically attribute to human existence, and yet [is] still biologically alive'; it thus comes 'to be situated at a limit zone between life and death, inside and outside, in which [it is] no longer anything but bare life [*nuda vita*]' (Agamben 1998, 159). Even a writer as profoundly out of temper with Agamben as Locke, and one who seeks to identify human life with a substantive vision of law-governed free activity, can become entangled in what I have termed the logic of exuviation. Indeed, it is *because* Locke is loathe to identify human beings with their bare life in an Hobbesian manner that he in the end reduces a class of people to that life.[14] If there is a moral here, it may be that simply asserting that we are not bare life and eschewing sovereign power as much as possible in favor of the rule of law will not allow us to avoid the dilemmas to which Agamben draws our attention.

But there remains a more difficult problem, one that cannot be addressed by finding parallels between Agamben's claims and those of others in the tradition because it is internal to Agamben's own analysis. As we have seen, Agamben's work concludes with the claim that 'today it is not the city but rather the camp that is the fundamental biopolitical paradigm of the West.' But *on Agamben's own terms* what does this mean? Here his reliance upon Schmitt's decisionism is crucial. Early on in *Homo Sacer* Agamben makes explicit his commitment to what I have described as the spatial and etymological understanding of logical categories when he writes, '[t]he example is truly a paradigm in the etymological sense: it is what is "shown beside," and a class can contain everything except its own paradigm,' and '[w]hat the example shows is its belonging to a class, but for this very reason the example steps out of its class in the very moment in which it exhibits and delimits it…[i]f one now asks how the rule applies to the example, the answer is not easy, since the rule applies to the example only as a normal case and obviously not as an example' (Agamben 1998, 22). This is a very particular account of what it means to be exemplary. We can easily contrast it, for instance, with the *Critique of Judgment's* enormously influential discussion of the exemplary status of genius and taste. Kant's genius 'lays down the rule' for future acts of genius by establishing a model that can be followed only by those who refrain from slavish imitation. But the rule is only demonstrated by the genius, not articulated into definite criteria. Hence Kant's reference to this rule is 'indeterminate' if not metaphoric: genius 'displays itself, not so much in the working out of a projected end in the presentation of a definite *concept*, as rather in the portrayal, or expression, of *aesthetic ideas*' (Kant 1989). Similarly, the necessity of the pleasure we take in the beautiful is *exemplary* in that it is 'a necessity of the assent of *all* to a judgment regarded as exemplifying a universal rule incapable of formulation.' The condition of this necessity is, Kant argues, the idea of a common

14 The irony of this is compounded when one observes the similarities between Locke's slave and the subject of Hobbes' 'despotical dominion.'

sense. We are 'suitors for agreement from everyone else, because we are fortified with a ground common to all,' a *sensus communis aestheticus* (ibid., 81-83). The flip side of this is that neither genius nor taste are features of determinate concepts or rule-governed acts and institutions. Neither the moral agent nor the person successfully making cognitive claims needs to be a genius or to take her guidance from exemplars as opposed to precepts. In stark contrast, Agamben makes it plain that the exceptional status of the example (as something taken outside the class in order to demonstrate that class) is a necessary feature of classes as such, be they classes of the product of artistic genius or classes of rules. 'In every logical system, just as in every social system, the relation between outside and inside, strangeness and intimacy, is this complicated.' In every case 'belonging to a class can be shown only by an example' (Agamben 1989, 22). Examples precede classes just as, for Schmitt, decisions precede norms.

I have referred to Schmitt's logic of the decision as a spatial one because it conceives of concepts in terms of groups in space with borders that need to be defined and patrolled. This is significant because if concepts are seen, following Frege, as functions, it is much less obvious that they can be understood in these terms. It is not obvious, that is, that functions have borders that are revealed by being crossed. This may help explain our sense that Agamben's is a fairly problematic account of, say, set theory. But Agamben's position not only relies upon a metaphor of boundaries that is at the very least debatable; in so doing it undermines *itself*. The clear implication of Agamben's own explanation of what makes something exemplary or paradigmatic is that in claiming a paradigmatic status for the camps he is *and can only be* making an unregulated decision that cannot be justified to his readers in a non-authoritarian manner. Since the example precedes and defines the rule, Agamben cannot appeal to an independent rule or standard to justify his claim that the camps are exemplary of anything. The determination that the camp is representative of the rule is one that is *made* and not in any substantive sense *recognized*.[15] The paradigm or example mirrors the structure of the exception: as the one is an inclusive exclusion, so is the other 'an *exclusive inclusion*.' Indeed, Agamben explicitly draws the inference that 'exception and example are correlative concepts that are ultimately indistinguishable' (Agamben 1998, 22, 21). This directly implies that the claim that something is exemplary is as much a product of a Schmitt-style decision as is the claim that something is an exception. In each case the decision is primary, and the rule derived from it. For this reason in each case the decision, in Schmitt's words, 'becomes instantly independent of argumentative substantiation and receives an autonomous value' (Schmitt 1985, 31).[16]

15 The Schmittian sovereign is *he* who decides on the exception; this decision must be made by a single person because there is no common sense amongst members of the community as to when the constitution needs to be suspended in its entirety. Hence Schmitt does not write, '[w]e are sovereign when we agree to decide upon the exception.'

16 Alain Badiou's polemic against the general use of the Shoah as the unique and privileged example of radical evil suggests another reason for this unfortunate result in

Here the contrast with the example of Kant is strong indeed. In Kant's judgments of taste, there is a 'wooing' of the assent of others who share your common sense of the matter. In Agamben, there is a decision that is imposed upon others. This difference is not noted by Steven DeCaroli in his otherwise interesting 'Visibility and History: Giorgio Agamben and the Exemplary.' Though DeCaroli refers in passing to Agamben's discussion of refugees, the sacred, and the camps, there is no specific reference to the *Homo Sacer* texts, and there is no consideration of Agamben's application of the logic of the inclusive exclusion to these political horrors. Instead the emphasis is on eighteenth century aesthetics and Renaissance humanism; ironically, it is for this very reason that DeCaroli does not see how different Agamben's analysis is from Kant's, to which he compares it. 'Unlike moral rules or normative principles,' DeCaroli writes, 'what the example promises cannot be adequately legislated and, therefore, one's response to the exemplary cannot be a simple matter of rational obedience – a mere adherence to reasonable principles' (DeCaroli 2001, 11). Nothing this mild could be said of the decision for the camps, which is far indeed from anything like Kant's common sense.[17] It should be noted that DeCaroli follows Agamben's own earlier discussions of the topic. The third chapter of Agamben's 1990 *The Coming Community*, '[t]he Example,' argues in Hegelian fashion that language involves 'an antimony of the individual and the universal,' in that language tries to capture particular things with its general terms, and in the attempt always loses their particularity. All linguistic reference involves the presentation of a particular as representative of a class and of other particulars, neither of which are *this* given particular. The example 'escapes' this antimony in that it is 'neither particular [*particolare*] nor universal [*universale*]' but:

> a singular object that *shows* its singularity [*singolarita*]. Hence the pregnancy of the Greek term, for example: *para-deigma*, that which is shown alongside… Hence the proper place of the example is always beside itself, the space in which its undeniable and unforgettable life unfolds. This life is pure linguistic life. Only life in the word is indefinable and unforgettable. Exemplary being is purely linguistic being. Exemplary is what is not defined by any property, except by

---

Agamben's case. On Badiou's account, the assertion of the exemplary status of the Shoah asserts both that it is the standard by which evil is to be judged in our time and that, as the paradigm, it is beyond such comparison with other, less radical forms of evil. 'As a result, the extermination and the Nazis are both declared unthinkable, unsayable…yet they are constantly evoked. …The measure must itself be unmeasurable, yet it must constantly be measured' (Badiou 2001, 62-63).

17 Although Agamben draws heavily upon Arendt, he shows no interest in her attempt to appropriate Kant's model of reflective aesthetic judgment for politics. I discuss the strengths and weaknesses of this attempt in Norris (1996).

> being-called. Not being-red, but being-*called*-red; not being-Jakob, but being-*called*-Jakob defines the example (Agamben 1993, 10).[18]

The exception and the decision both go unmentioned in this text, and the suggestion is left open that something like Kant's *sensus communis* allows us to recognize what '*shows* itself' as being exemplary. Indeed, the use of the language of universals, particulars, and singularities from Hegel's logic suggests that the example is a concrete universal that displays itself as such to the highest form of reason, and not merely the sovereign decision.[19] In part this reflects the fact that *The Coming Community* focuses upon the possibilities opened up by non-identical, liminal being, rather than upon the idea that the camps are where the best examples of such being is found.[20] It is only in *Homo Sacer* that Agamben relates this analysis of the example to the inclusive exclusion of the *Muselmann*, and in so doing attempts to ground an analysis of the political upon the nature of the camps. Because the nature of language alone can hardly explain the historical emergence of the camps (life in which is considerably different than 'life in the word'), Agamben appeals to a Schmittian decision. But since he remains committed to an etymological analysis of *example* (*l'esempio*) and *exception* (*l'eccezione*) in which there is an isomorphism between the exclusive inclusion and the inclusive exclusion, he is forced into the awkward position of deciding in an authoritarian fashion that politics is a matter of the decision on life as enacted in the camps.

It is one thing to suggest, as philosophers like Heidegger working in the phenomenological tradition are bound to do, that one is giving descriptions rather than arguments. It is quite another to say that the aptness or accuracy of a description is something that is appropriately determined only by a sovereign decision. To say the latter is to say that we are not returning to the 'things themselves,' but rather *constituting* them. It follows from this that if Agamben is correct about

18 I describe this discussion as Hegelian not only because Agamben's tripartite distinction between universal, particular, and individual echoes that of Hegel's logic, but also because of the obvious debt of his account of the antimony of language to the 'Sense-Certainty' chapter of the *Phenomenology*.

19 Slavoj Žižek has argued that contrasts of the sort I propose here between Schmitt and Hegel are illusory, and that Schmitt is one of 'the true heirs of Hegel' (Žižek 1999, 113). The concrete universal on Žižek's account is not a bridge crossing the gap between universal and particular opened up by the formalism of the Understanding, but a paradoxical, ungrounded and unjustified decision that some given particular embodies the universal. While there is much to be said in favor of this reading, there is also prima facie evidence against it: whatever else it may be, the *Philosophy of Right* is not *Political Theology*. For a good critique of Žižek's reading of Hegel, see, Dews 1995. On the commonalities between the Kantian and Hegelian approaches to this issue, see, Pippin 1997.

20 Agamben stated, '[t]hese pure singularities [of what in the example escapes linguistic classification] communicate only in the empty space of the example, without being tied by any common property, by any identity…[T]hey are the exemplars of the coming community' (Agamben 1993, 10-11).

the logic of politics – a claim that I have already suggested may be too broad to be sustained – he cannot be right that this logic necessarily applies to or is enacted in philosophy as well. Because if he were, his philosophical claims about the political would be the expression not of the truth of the political, but of his own sovereign decision. This makes it impossible for Agamben to offer a genuine alternative to the bloody '*nomos* of the earth' producing the potential 'biopolitical catastrophe' that he describes in such harrowing terms (Agamben 1998, 38, 188).[21] As a repetition of what it sets out to condemn, Agamben's work falls into the trap that the closing sentences of *Political Theology* claim awaits all attempts to deny the *arche* of the decision:

> [e]very claim of a decision must be evil for the anarchist, because the right emerges by itself if the immanence of life is not disturbed by such claims. This radical antithesis forces him of course to decide against the decision [*sich selbst entschieden gegen die Dezision zu entscheiden*]; and this results in the odd paradox whereby Bakunin, the greatest anarchist of the nineteenth century, had to become in theory the theologian of the antitheological and in practice the dictator of an antidictatorship (Schmitt 1985, 66).

For Agamben to escape this unwelcome paradox he would have to relax the identification he asserts between philosophy and politics. He would, in other words, have to justify a mode of evaluation that escaped the limitations he attributes to logic.[22]

21 Agamben's fourth chapter of the *State of Exception* (Agamben 2005), suggests that it is not Schmitt that he follows, but Benjamin, where the difference between the two concerns precisely the ability to decide upon the state of exception. But if that state of exception is one that cannot be decided upon, in what sense can we identify a paradigm of it? Given Agamben's argument about the relation between examples and exceptions, it would seem that it could not be identified at all.

22 The suspicion that Agamben's central claim is one made by fiat is heightened by further lacunae in his analysis of what one might term the relation between the logic of the political and the actual (or ontic) history of politics. Agamben argues that 'the link between bare life and politics…secretly governs the modern ideologies seemingly most distant from one another' (Agamben 1998, 4). Why then do they 'seem' to be so different from one another? And why is this link clearer in some modern sites – the camps – than in others, such as contemporary Britain? If contemporary Britain is essentially the same thing as a camp, why is it not a camp? More fundamentally, why is the *polis* not itself a camp? On Agamben's analysis both revolve around the unstable distinctions between life and bare life and between rule and exception. But if these distinctions are unstable in the *polis*, they are undone in the camp. The camp makes explicit what is implicit in the *polis*, and in Aristotle's reflections upon it. But what accounts for the distinction here between the implicit and the explicit, and for the significance and identity of the *modern* (cf. ibid., 1998, 6, 9, 12)? It would appear at the very least that another factor or set of factors must be at play here, such as different forms of technology and social organization, and that Agamben's analysis will

Now, it is clear that the central features of Agamben's *Homo Sacer* project are incompatible with the familiar distinction between philosophy as an arena of impartial rational argumentation and politics as one of potentially deceptive rhetoric driven by the interests of the various factions competing for power. His focus upon the first book of Aristotle's *Politics* makes this plain enough: Aristotle argues there that the *polis* is the place where citizens can realize their *telos* as language users by deliberating and deciding together what counts for them as just. Politics, that is, does the work of Socratic philosophy. And, as noted above, Agamben's characterization of the transcendence of 'mere life' by the 'good life' of the *polis* is that politics 'appears as the truly fundamental structure of Western metaphysics insofar as it occupies the threshold on which the relation between the living being and the *logos* is realized.' The *polis* is the site of the enactment of metaphysics. Consequently Agamben cannot appeal to an Aristotelian philosophical discourse wherein he might justify his claim for the paradigmatic status of the camps in a non-political (viz., non-decisionistic) way. But it remains open whether such discourse exhausts the resources of the philosophical. Agamben himself suggests a distinction within philosophy between the metaphysical and the non-metaphysical, as 'the "politicization" of bare life [is] the *metaphysical* task *par excellence*' (emphasis added). Given his close association with Heidegger and Jean-Luc Nancy, we might take the use of the word *metaphysical* here to suggest that true, non-metaphysical philosophy will be a variant of Heideggerian *Gelassenheit*. But while something like this is found in *The Coming Community*, this is not an accurate characterization of *Homo Sacer*. Moreover, what the above analysis suggests is not the need for a more poetic or poietic mode of thinking, but one that can escape the decisionist implications of Agamben's understanding of the logic of the political and still make judgments concerning what politics is and should be. This is something that the later Heidegger shies away from, and it is the return to the question of practice outside of philosophical reflection that makes Agamben's work appear as a revitalization of the Heideggerian tradition. Unfortunately, Agamben's acceptance of Schmitt's decisionism makes it impossible for his analyses to claim any general validity. Perhaps worse, it puts him in the position of deciding upon the camp victims one more time, thereby repeating the gesture of the SS in precisely the way he says we must avoid (Agamben 1999, 63-64). I conclude that if the parallels and correspondences to which Agamben's work draws our attention are to be more than suggestive – in particular, if they are to be the object of judgments that can carry any sort of authority – Agamben's own methodological commitments will have to be either radically modified or abandoned outright. This is a decidedly unwelcome conclusion for this style of political philosophy, for it implies that the very strength of its insights demands a mode of argumentation of which it is itself not yet capable.

remain incomplete until such factors are integrated into his reflections. This will require developing a set of arguments that decisively distinguish the type of decision Agamben is asking his readers to make from that he is analyzing and criticising.

Bibliography

Agamben, G. (2005) *State of Exception* (trans. Attell, K.) (Chicago: University of Chicago Press).

—— (1999) *Remnants of Auschwitz: The Witness and the Archive* (trans. Heller-Roazen, D.) (New York: Zone Books).

—— (1998a) *Homo Sacer: Sovereign Power and Bare Life* (trans. Heller-Roazen, D.) (Stanford: Stanford University Press). Italian references to the work come from *Homo Sacer: Il potere sovrano e la nuda vita* (Torino: Giulio Einaudi, 1995).

—— (1998b) 'The Messiah and the Sovereign: The Problem of Law in Walter Benjamin', in *Potentialities* (trans. and ed. Heller-Roazen, D.) (Stanford: Stanford University Press).

—— (1993) *The Coming Community* (trans. Hardt, M.) (Minneapolis: University of Minnesota Press). Italian references to the work come from *La communita che viene* (Torino: Giulio Einaudi, 1990).

Arendt, H. (1966) *The Origins of Totalitarianism* (New York: Harcourt Brace Jovanovich).

—— (1960) *Vita Activa, oder Vom tätigen Leben* (München: Piper).

—— (1958) *The Human Condition* (Chicago: University of Chicago Press).

Badiou, A. (2001) *Ethics: An Essay on the Understanding of Evil* (trans. Hallward, P.) (London: Verso).

Benjamin, W. (1969) 'The Storyteller,' in Hannah Arendt (ed.) *Illuminations* (New York: Schocken Books).

DeCaroli, S. (2001) 'Visibility and History: Giorgio Agamben and the Exemplary', *Philosophy Today* 45(5).

Derrida, J. (1989) *Of Spirit: Heidegger and the Question* (trans. Bennington, G. and Bowlby, R.) (Chicago: Chicago University Press).

Dews, P. (1995) 'The Tremor of Reflection: Slavoj Žižek's Lacanian Dialectics', in *The Limits of Disenchantment* (London: Verso).

Foucault, M. (1989) 'Rituals of Exclusion' (an interview with John Simon), in *Foucault Live* (New York: Semiotext[e]).

Kant, I. (1989) *Critique of Judgment* (trans. Meredith, J.C.) (Oxford: Clarendon Press).

Locke, J. (1963) *Two Treatises of Government* (ed. Laslett, P.) (Cambridge: Cambridge University Press).

Heidegger, M. (1993) 'Letter on Humanism', *Martin Heidegger: Basic Writings*, rev. edn (San Francisco: Harper); *Über den Humanismus* (Frankfurt: Vittorio Klostermann, 1991).

—— (1971) *On the Way to Language* (trans. Hertz, P.) (New York: Harper)

—— (1959) *Introduction to Metaphysics* (trans. Manheim, R.) (London: Yale University Press).

Norris, A. (2000) 'Carl Schmitt's Political Metaphysics: On the Secularization of the Outermost Sphere', *Theory and Event* 4(1) (Summer).

—— (1998) 'Carl Schmitt on Friends, Enemies, and the Political', *Telos* 112 (Summer).

—— (1996) 'Arendt, Kant, and the Politics of Common Sense', *Polity* 29(2) (Winter).

Pippin, R. (1997) 'Avoiding German Idealism: Kant, Hegel, and the Reflective Judgment Problem', in *Idealism as Modernism* (Cambridge: Cambridge University Press).

Schmitt, C. (1996) *The Concept of the Political* (trans. George Schwab) (Chicago: University of Chicago Press). German references are from *Der Begriff des Politischen* (München: Dunker & Humblot, 1932).

—— (1986) *Political Romanticism* (trans. Oakes, G.) (London: MIT Press).

—— (1985) *Political Theology: Four Chapters on the Concept of Sovereignty* (trans. Schwab, G.) (London: MIT Press). German references are from *Politische Theologie*, 7th ed. (Berlin: Duncker & Humblot, 1996).

Žižek, S. (2001) *Did Somebody Say Totalitarianism?* (London: Verso).

—— (1999) *The Ticklish Subject* (New York: Verso).

Chapter 4
The Value of Life: Somatic Ethics and the Spirit of Biocapital

Nikolas Rose

What is the value of life?[1] This may seem a pretentious or a philosophical question. But it is the subject of much contemporary discussion. In August 2006, England's National Institute for Clinical Excellence (NICE), which advises on medicines available on the National Heath Service (NHS) in England, ruled against two treatments for late-stage bowel cancer – Genentech's Avastin and ImClone Systems' Erbitux. Although these treatments were widely available in a number of countries, NICE declared that their use was not 'compatible with the best use of NHS resources.'[2]

NICE estimated that treatment with Avastin would cost £17,665.65 a patient, Erbitux £11,739. On average, these treatments extend the lives of those with terminal bowel cancer by five months. NICE made its judgment using a model that estimates the costs per 'quality adjusted life year' (QALY) gained, and set a 'willingness to pay' cap of £30,000 per QALY. Each of the treatments exceeded that limit. Many cancer sufferers and their supporters contested this decision. It was, they said a question of the value placed on their lives, the value of five months of life.

What, then, is the value of life? A Google search for 'the value of life' in September 2009 turned up 73,400,000 pages in 0.35 seconds. Among them, *Brainy Quote of the Day* gave us Michael de Montaigne's wise words, 'The value of life lies not in the length of days, but in the use we make of them.' But more generally, what one sees in these pages is an instructive intertwining of the ethical and the economic. Of course many of the Google hits lead to the deliberations of bioethicists. Indeed, *The Value of Life* is the title of a book by the prominent

1 This chapter draws on Rose 2006, 2007.

2 In August 2009, after a review under new rules that allow approval of more expensive drugs for terminal patients, NICE once more turned down Avastin (bevacizumab) together with three other drugs for late stage kidney cancer – Nexavar (sorafenib) and Torisel (temsirolimus) on the grounds that they were not cost effective, though it did approve Sutent (sunitinib). In June 2009, following an agreement with Merck to cut the cost of the drug by 16 per cent, NICE approved the use of a short course of Erbitux for patients whose cancer had spread to the liver on the grounds that it now offered 'value for money' for those patients.

British bioethicist John Harris. But for those of us who are not bioethicists, current debates over the value of life provide one way to explore the nature of contemporary biopolitics.

First in the Google listing was the Pope, or rather, the late Pope John Paul's encyclical letter of 1995, '*Evangelium Vitae*: On the Value and Inviolability of Human Life.' In it, the Pontiff declared the incomparable worth of the human person, and expressed concern about the increase in threats to the life of individuals and peoples, especially where life is weak and defenseless. He was particularly troubled by the new threats opened up by biomedical progress. His view was that certain sectors of the medical profession, authorized by the state, are endangering the lives of the weakest, often with the free assistance of health-care systems.

The late Pope represents only one pole of the bioethical debate that now rages over the question of whether life can be subject to judgments of value – or, whether different forms of life can or should be valued differently. Could one ever legitimately say, 'My life has no value'? Could a life be of such little value that it might be a life not worth living, a life that should be ended?

That little phrase, 'life not worthy of life,' admittedly carries chilling overtones. It evokes the German debates on euthanasia that preceded the murderous eugenic regime in Germany from 1900 to 1945, so movingly analyzed in Michael Burleigh's book *Death and Deliverance*. And yet, today, it seems we cannot avoid this issue, especially at the start or end of life – in cases of severely disabled neonates maintained on life support, or those suffering from a painful and terminal disease who wish for physician-assisted suicide.

What is important for my analysis is not the answers given, but the way the question itself is posed. Today, it is increasingly framed in terms of dignity. The UK's Voluntary Euthanasia Society, for example, recently changed its name to Dignity in Dying. The value of life here seems to exist in a kind of transactional space between the claim that existence itself has some intrinsic value, and the claim that value should attach, not to life as vitality, but to life as a subjective state – to the 'dignity' of those who live it.

Second in Google's hierarchy are the economists, for whom life *can* certainly be given a precise value. Value of life, here, is usually calculated with the classical economic measure of 'willingness to pay.'

Since there are few ways to test how much individuals are, in reality, willing to pay for their life, heath-care spending stands as the most popular proxy, in measuring the value accorded to increased longevity. One example of this calculation is evident in a paper by Robert Hall and Charles Jones, with the title 'The Value of Life and the Rise of Health Care Spending.' They point out the rise in the United States in the proportion of resources devoted to health care, '[t]he share was 5.2 percent in 1950, 9.4 percent in 1975, and 15.4 percent in 2000. Over the same period, health has improved. The life expectancy of an American born in 1950 was 68.2 years, of one born in 1975, 72.6 years, and of one born in 2000, 76.9 years.' Set the additional investment against the additional years of life, and you have a measure of the implicit value Americans attribute to life.

Others try to calculate the potential societal benefits, in financial terms, for reductions in mortality and morbidity. Kevin Murphy and Robert Topel estimate that, for the United States, 'reduced mortality from heart disease alone has increased the value of life by about $1.5 trillion per year since 1970...Even a modest 1 percent reduction in cancer mortality would be worth nearly $500 billion' (Murphy and Topel 2005).

Something similar is happening when our Google search finds the health economists who use measures like QALY to evaluate the costs of disease or the benefits of treatments: an imperfect yet seemingly necessary little technology to enable tragic choices, translating impossible moral judgments about suffering into a technical and calculable form.

Other experts estimate the value of life in terms of the money people are prepared to invest to reduce small risks of death (Viscusi 2005). The U.S. Department of Transportation, in a paper prepared just after September 11, calls this amount the 'value of a statistical life':

> [a] defined value of life has been pursued by governmental agencies here and abroad for over thirty years. It is regarded as an essential element of cost-benefit analysis to guide public policy in the areas of regulation and investment in health and safety. Some measure is necessary to ensure prudent management of public and private resources. Although saving an identifiable life is often regarded as a moral imperative on which no monetary value can be placed, *prevention of every possible accidental death would be intolerably costly in terms of both money and the quality of life*. The term 'value of a statistical life' (VSL) is widely used to emphasize that value is placed, not on a particular life, but on safety measures that reduce the statistically expected number of accidental fatalities by one (emphasis added).[3]

In a related but different economic frame, one finds the debates over the compensation given by the government to victims of disaster. When the U.S. Air Force killed and injured a number of people in bombing the Chinese Embassy in Belgrade in May 1999, the U.S. government agreed to pay $4.5 million in damages, which amounted to about $150,000 per victim. On the other hand, when a U.S. Marine jet hit aerial tramway cables in Italy in 1998, the United States gave close to $2 million to each Italian victim. Even this disparity in the value of life pales, when one learns that when a U.S. gunship attacked and strafed four villages in Afghanistan in 2003, killing 60 people, the Karzai regime offered the Afghan wedding victims about $200 on behalf of each individual killed.[4]

In the United States itself, the next of kin of each person who died in the September 11 attacks received some $2 million, sparking an angry debate in the United States about the respective compensation to the victims of Hurricanes Rita

---

3 See, http://ostpxweb.dot.gov/policy/EconStrat/treatmentoflife.htm#1.

4 See, http://www.cursor.org/stories/afghandead.htm.

and Katrina, and to the families of troops who have died in Iraq. Life, it seems, can be given a monetary value in compensation for its loss, yet that valuation depends upon the citizenship of those who have lost it, and the financial and political resources of those who contest that loss.

The lawyers came third in Google's listings. A host of papers dealing with the value of life consider the ways in which the courts measure compensation in wrongful death suits, where relatives sue doctors or others to recover damages from someone they hold responsible for a death. This is a fertile market for lawyers in the United States, judging from the numerous pages posted by law firms encouraging individuals to make such claims.

However, in the United States at least, such claim making has taken a different turn – in the form of claims for wrongful birth or wrongful life. Willy and Cynthia Fields won damages of $1.7 million for the wrongful birth of their severely handicapped daughter Jade, on the basis that their doctor failed to pick up the signs of abnormality (in an ultrasound scan of the foetus) that would have prompted them to have an abortion.[5] This was a wrongful birth case, in which *parents* take an action against a medical practitioner for failing to uncover information in genetic screening or counselling that would have enabled the mother to have her pregnancy terminated. Perhaps wrongful life cases are even more telling, for here the damaged, disabled, or terminally ill *child*, through his or her legal representatives, sues for having been allowed to be born – for example, a child with Tay-Sachs, condemned to a short life filled with suffering before an inevitable death. In effect, the child is claiming to have been damaged by having been allowed to live at all – for being condemned to a life not worth living. Of course, these cases are about raising money, for lawyers, for parents, for children; sometimes they are merely routes to obtaining the resources necessary to provide care. But they show something about our contested politics of life.

On the one hand, then, all human life has a value beyond price, and every life is of equal value. And yet we know that in practice, some forms of life are judged more valuable than others. Every session of genetic counselling, every act of amniocentesis, and perhaps even every piece of cosmetic surgery embodies just such a premise: some forms of life, some ways of living, are worth more than others, and sometimes people are willing to pay for them. Every actuarial calculation for an insurance premium, every decision about health-care provision, is also based on such a presupposition.

My Google search did not really capture a fourth dimension – that of capital. By this, I mean the practice of expressing the value of a life – of an individual, a family, a lineage, a nation, a population, a race, a species or a diversity of species – in terms of genetic or human capital.

The phrase 'genetic capital' was, perhaps, first used by modern-day proponents of eugenics, such as the authors of *The Bell Curve*, who drew on the more respectable use of the notion in evolutionary biology (Hernstein and Murray

5 See, http://www.cbsnews.com/stories/2003/06/19/60minutes/main559472.shtml.

1994). Some transhumanists have now taken up the phrase to argue for a new kind of eugenics for improving the genetic capital of the nation.

Sarah Franklin has suggested that it was first in the area of stockbreeding that the idea of genetic capital took shape – the capital that was not so much in each member of the flock but in the heritable characteristics of the lineage (Ritvo 1996). The idea of a kind of value inherent in the hereditary quality of one's stock originated before modern genetics, but in its modern form one can see it in an invitation issued by the Kansas-based Decatur Beef Alliance in 2000:

> [t]he Alliance gives progressive cattlemen a way to cash in on their genetic capital and their management expertise…Any cattleman with superior genetic cattle meeting the [defined] live animal specifications…can get involved (Decatur Beef Alliance 2000).

In a different dimension, the idea of genetic, or biological, capital has now become central to the language of those seeking to protect the planet and its biodiversity. Thus, in January 2006, *The Hindu Times* reported S. Kannaiyan, chairman of the National Biodiversity Authority of India, as saying, '[b]iodiversity represents the very foundation of human existence; yet, by our heedless actions, we are eroding this biological capital at an alarming rate.'[6]

The idea of genetic capital resonates with that of human capital, which has emerged in the writings of Chicago School economists such as Gary Becker, for whom all choices that individuals make about matters like education or medical care are seen as investments in their own human capital. The notion of human capital links to the ways in which, in advanced liberal ethics, each individual is urged to live his or her life as a kind of enterprise to maximize lifestyle or potential, to become a kind of entrepreneur of oneself and one's family.

What is one to make of this intertwining of economic and ethical concerns, these complicated relations among different registers of value? What can it tell us, if anything, about contemporary biopolitics?

Certainly the practice of medicine has become infused with these ways of thinking about the value of life.[7] Belief in the value of a healthy life, and of one's right to control and shape that life, has become central to the ethical self-management of many individuals and families, and underpins many challenges to the paternalistic power that doctors exercised over their patients. Attempts to 'empower' the recipients of medical care, to emphasize 'active citizenship,' and to transform patients into 'consumers' were underpinned, in part, by the hope that each individual would act to protect and enhance the value of their own life and that of their family, because they were committed to a secular value of health.

---

6 See, http://www.thehindu.com/2006/01/16/stories/2006011600810200.htm.

7 Richard Horton, editor of the influential medical journal, *The Lancet*, provides an overview of some of the key issues in Horton (2004).

From another direction, the practice of medicine has become saturated with issues of financial value. This phenomenon is evident, not just in the growth of private health insurance and the commoditization of health it entails, but also in the regulation of prescriptions or reimbursements for medical activity by health management organizations (HMOs) and National Health Services. As we have seen, these organizations base many judgments on criteria of value for money, and the costs and benefits of different forms of medical intervention captured in measures such as the QALY.

Further, medical knowledge, indeed medical truth itself, has become subject to intense capitalization. Basic and applied biological research – whether conducted in biotech companies or in universities – has become bound up with the generation of intellectual property, and illness and health have become major fields for corporate activity. This is largely because contemporary molecular biomedicine requires the investment of resources over long periods – for equipment, laboratories, clinical trials, and regulatory compliance – before it can achieve a return. Increasingly, such investment comes from venture capital provided to private corporations, who also seek to raise funds on the stock market. Hence, biomedicine has become subject to all the exigencies of capitalization, such as the obligations of profit and the demands of shareholder value.[8]

A path-dependent perspective on biomedical truth is necessary here. Biotech companies do not merely apply or market scientific discoveries: the pharmaceutical industry has been central to research on neurochemistry, the biotech industry to research on cloning, and genomic corporations to the sequencing of the human genome.[9] In contemporary biomedicine, the laboratory, the factory, and the stock market are interlinked. Where funds are required to generate candidates for truth in biomedicine, and where the allocation of such funds depends upon a calculation of financial return, commercial investment shapes the very direction, organization, problem space, and solution effects of biomedicine as well as the basic biology

8 Once more it is necessary to stress that there is nothing novel in itself in close relations between industrial corporations and the development of scientific research, outside and inside universities. The image of scientific knowledge as developing within the sequestered space of the university laboratory, funded by public moneys, detached from commercial imperatives, mobilized only by Mertonian norms of disinterestedness applies, if at all, only to a few disciplines during an exceptional period in the mid-twentieth century. Novelty, today, lies in the particular configuration taking shape around the life sciences.

9 I have argued elsewhere that images of the development of scientific disciplines that portray a path from the laboratory to society, described in the language of 'application,' are misleading, especially in those domains that have what Michel Foucault termed a 'low epistemological threshold.' The psychological sciences, for example, were 'disciplined' around their fields of application – in industry, the schoolroom, the military, the courtroom – and only later established in the university, see Rose 1985. In particular, the impact of military priorities and funding should not be underestimated, in even the most apparently theoretical of disciplines such as mathematics.

that supports it. In an era in which biotech enterprises such as Genentech proclaim that they are 'in business for life', biopolitics has become bioeconomics.[10]

Catherine Waldby initially proposed the term 'biovalue' to characterize the ways that bodies and tissues derived from the dead are redeployed to enhance the health and vitality of the living (Waldby 2000). A similar idea is developed by the Organization for Economic Cooperation and Development in its 'foresight' exercise to explore the potential of economic activity that 'captures the latent value in biological processes.' More generally, we can use the term to refer to the many ways in which qualities or capacities inherent in vitality have become a potential source for the production of value.

We should not overstate the novelty of these developments. Humans long ago put the vital properties of the natural world into service, with the domestication of animals and plants. They turned these properties into technologies when they, for example, harnessed the milk-producing capacities of cows and the silk-producing capacities of silkworms for the generation of biovalue.[11] Contemporary projects to embody human desires and aspirations within living entities – organisms, organs, cells, molecules – in order to extract a surplus – be it food, health, or capital – can be traced to these early events.

Yet something has changed. The very emergence of the language of bioeconomics brings into existence a new space for thought and action. The bioeconomy has appeared as a space to be mapped, managed, and understood; it needs to be conceptualized as a set of processes and relations that can be known and theorized, that can become the target of programs that seek to increase the power of nations or corporations by acting within and upon that economy.

The normalization of the term 'biocapital' is one indicator of this new turn. March 2005 saw the third annual conference of BioCapital Europe in Amsterdam – an event for pharmaceutical and biotech companies across Europe.[12] In Australia, around the same time, the state of Queensland established a AU$100 million biocapital fund to

10 The collection edited by Sarah Franklin and Margaret Lock made significant advances in our understanding of biocapital, pointing to the new hybrids of knowledge, technology, and life involved in patenting, sequencing, mapping, marketing, purifying, branding, marketing, and publicizing new life forms: these studies contributed to my own less ethnographic approach to these issues, see Franklin and Lock 2003a; Franklin 2006.

11 In Volume 3 of *Capital,* Marx points to the significance of the capitalization of cattle and sheep breeding in enabling capital to become an independent and dominant force in agriculture. Franklin argues that the cloning of Dolly the sheep – made possible by the investment of venture capital in the hope of creating transgenic 'bioreactor' sheep to produce marketable enzymes for treating human diseases – binds the oldest definitions of capital as 'stock' to the newest forms that it takes in contemporary biocapital. Human aspirations become literally 'embodied' in living capitalizable entities; see Waldby (2000).

12 The conferences of BioCapital Europe enable biotech companies to present themselves to venture capitalists, institutions, and biotech and pharmaceutical companies, looking for investment opportunities within the biotechnology market. See, www.biocapitaleurope.com.

establish globally enduring biobusinesses. In May 2005, BioSpace, a leading online information source for the biotech and pharmaceutical industry, published the fifth edition of *BioCapital*, which showcases a variety of biopharmaceutical companies located within the Mid-Atlantic region; it includes an interactive BioCapital Hotbed map that also highlights research institutes, nonprofit organizations, and universities within the area.[13] Moreover, 'biocapital' is used in the title of numerous investment and consultancy organizations worldwide. Marxists and post-Marxists may disagree about whether biocapitalism is a novel mode of production, but they cannot dispute the existence and significance of *biocapital* as a way of thinking and acting.

Projects to govern the bioeconomy sometimes involve surprising alliances between political authorities and promissory capitalism.[14] A number of 'strong state' bioeconomies – most famously illustrated in Iceland and Sweden – decided to license private companies to undertake the genetic sequencing of their populations and to combine this with publicly held genealogical and medical records, in the hope that they would be able to identify the genomic bases of common complex disorders. In the case of deCODE in Iceland these hopes were not fulfilled, at least in the short term (Palsson and Rabinow 1999; Rose 2003).[15] UmanGenomics in Sweden sought to use bioethical shields to insulate itself from some of the criticisms; but it too found that its business model was not viable (Abbott 1999; Høyer 2002, 2003; Nilsson and Rose 1999; and Rosell 1991).

The 'ex-socialist state' bioeconomies, such as Lithuania and Estonia, emerged from Soviet domination with comprehensive medical and genealogical records, together with relatively stable populations and some unusually prevalent medical conditions: these seemed to provide a favorable point of entry to a future in which biotechnology would generate employment, boost industry, and promote both public and shareholder value.[16]

---

13 See http://www.biospace.com/news_story.aspx?StoryID=20035520&full=1. There are now many such Hotbed Maps, which can be found at http://www.biospace.com/biotechhotbeds.aspx. The original 1985 Biotech Bay™ Map for the San Francisco Bay Area hangs on permanent display in the Smithsonian Institution's National Museum of American History. BioCapital was first launched in 1996.

14 Franklin and Lock, in 2003b, attributed the term 'promissory capitalism' to Charis Thompson's then-unpublished work on what she termed 'the biotech mode of (re)production.' See C. Thompson, *Making Parents: The Ontological Choreography of Reproductive Technologies* (Cambridge, MA: MIT Press, 2005), especially chapter 6. The idea that speculative, risk, and venture capital depend upon issuing promissory notes against the hope of future returns has long had a central place in studies of the rise of capitalist economies. I draw on arguments made in my Clifford Barclay Memorial Lecture at the London School of Economics and Political Science in February 2005.

15 See also http://sunsite.berkeley.edu/biotech/iceland/new.html. In a press release of August 2, 2005, deCODE Genetics put a brave face on their progress but nonetheless reported losses in their second quarter. See http://www.decode.com/

16 For the Estonian Genome Project, see http://www.geenivaramu.ee/index.php?show=main&lang=eng.

Meanwhile, 'developing state' bioeconomies have turned claims about the diversity of their populations into exploitable resources. Thus, in China (which has emphasised gene testing, biobanking, and stem cells) and India (which points to the diversity of its gene pool, developed pharmaceutical industry, CROs, and 'good subjects' for trials), local and national state authorities have focused on the development of biotech as a driver of economic development, inward investment, and international competitiveness.

Many Western and other First-World economies have also stressed their potential competitive advantage in what enthusiasts like to term 'the knowledge based bioeconomy'. In 2003, the U.K. House of Commons *Trade and Industry Committee Report on Biotechnology* identified biotechnology, especially biomedicine, as a key economic driver. It estimated that, in 2002, the U.K. biotechnology industry had a market capitalization of £6.3 billion, accounting for 42 per cent of the total market capitalization of European biotechnology, with pharmaceutical biotechnology as the dominant branch.[17]

In the United States, Ernst and Young reported that the biotech sector, in 2003, was a $33.6 billion industry, with a total of 1,466 companies, 318 of which were public (Ernst and Young 2003a). It also revealed that 'in Australia…total revenues among publicly traded companies increased 38 per cent from $666 million in 2001 to $920 million in 2002. The number of…people employed in the industry jumped 24 per cent from 5,201 to 6,464.' And in Japan, the 'government anticipates the nation's biotech workforce will surge to 1 million by 2010, an enormous increase over the estimated 70,000 today. Government officials plan to double their investment in biotechnology in the next five years' (Ernst and Young 2003b).

This is not simply another case of predatory Western capitalism plundering the resources of the poor. A report of a U.K. government mission to India in 2003 was headed with a quote from then-Indian Prime Minister Atal Behari Vajpayee, '[b]iotechnology is a frontier science with a high promise for the welfare of humanity.' At that time India had 160 biotechnology companies with combined revenues of $150 million, driven by developments in the health-care sector; the industry was expected to grow to $4.5 billion by 2010 and to generate a million or more jobs.

In China, the government spent about $180 million building a biotech industry from 1996 to 2002. By December 2006 the total R&D spending in China exceeded that of Japan for the first time, and China became the world's second highest R&D investor after the US: spending by central government in 2006 reached 71.6 billion RMB, or almost $10 billion, a considerable portion of which was directed to biotechnology and biomedicine, with government funds directed to basic science, leaving the spin-out to the clinic, and the manufacturing

17 See the U.K. House of Commons Trade and Industry Committee 2003 Report on Biotechnology, at http://www.publications.parliament.uk/pa/cm200203/cmselect/cmtrdind/cmtrdind.htm

to the growing private biotech industry. And before the Hwang debacle, the Stem Cell Research Centre in South Korea had guaranteed government funding of $7.5 million for ten years.

In each region, political investment to support the development of the biotechnology sector is driven, in part, by fears of losing out in an intensively competitive global bioeconomy. Ernst and Young's *Global Biotechnology Report 2005: Beyond Borders* argues that 'from Malaysia to Michigan, governments are developing strategic plans with ambitious goals for biotech' and points out that 'the global industry raised a whopping $21.2 billion in 2004' from private capital for early-stage development.

Yet even this was not enough to meet the challenge of finding early-stage capital.[18] The global biotechnology industry's revenues grew by 17 per cent in 2004, to $54.6 billion, but it was still making net losses of $5.3 billion, and many companies seeking to raise funds from IPOs did not obtain the valuations they sought and suffered falls in share prices. Times were 'challenging,' especially in Europe and the United States, partly because of developments in regulation and legislation: the US debates over the ethics of stem cell research, and the tendency of key policymakers to 'scrutinize research agreements between academic medical centers, clinicians and biotech/pharmaceutical companies' and to question 'potential conflicts of interest' (Ernst and Young 2005, 35).

The Asian biotech sector meanwhile continues to grow aggressively (biotech companies in the region increased their top line-revenues by 36 per cent in 2004) although they too face 'challenges,' as worries over IP protection have hampered investment from Western companies, and governments and nonbiotech industrial conglomerates have to provide the capital that, in the West, would be raised in other ways (ibid., 67).

Nevertheless, the allure of biocapital remains strong. Politicians in countries across the globe continue to foster the growth of a biotech sector and to seek a niche in this global bioeconomy by emphasising the features that make them particularly attractive, whether these be genetically stable populations, a skilled and cheap labour force, or a range of significant diseases. They attempt to map the potential of this biotechnological revolution through exercises in foresight, and formulate strategies to develop it: targeted research funding, technology transfer, support for start-up and spin-out firms, tax breaks for research and development, low regulatory hurdles, and much more. These local intensifications of biocapital are linked into transnational circuits of capital, knowledge, researchers, techniques, and also material artefacts – tissues, cell lines, reagents, DNA sequences, organs, and the like.

18 And, especially in the United States, one should not neglect the 'opportunities and challenges in biodefense' following the terrorist attacks of September 11, 2001: the Department of Health and Human Services spending on biodefense increased almost fourteen-fold from 2001 to 2005, and the Bioshield Act of 2004 earmarked £5.6 billion for U.S. countermeasures against pathogens.

Such circuits of vitality are not themselves new – consider the long-standing practices of ethnobotanical collections of seeds and plants, or of the exchange of biological material and model organisms such as fruit flies, which were central to modern genetics (Balic and Cox 1996; Kohler 1994). But today, a kind of disembedding has occurred. Molecularization strips tissues, proteins, and molecules of their specific affinities – to a disease, to an organ, to an individual, to a species – and enables us to regard them as manipulable and transferable elements or units, which we can move from place to place, from organism to organism, from disease to disease, from person to person.

Vitality has been decomposed into a series of distinct and discrete objects that can be rendered visible, isolated, decomposed, stabilized, frozen, banked, stored, commoditized, accumulated, exchanged, and traded across time and space, organs and species, and diverse contexts and enterprises, in the service of bioeconomic objectives. Whether it is the transfer of genes, along with their properties (lumiscence, salt tolerance), from one species to another, the transfer of treatments from one disease to another, or the transfer of tissues, blood plasma, kidneys, and stem cells, molecularization is conferring a new mobility on the elements of life, enabling them to enter new circuits – organic, interpersonal, geographical, and financial.

And along with this 'flattening' goes another – the attempt to flatten the transnational circuits themselves, to construct one of those level playing fields, in which standardized intellectual-property regimes, forms of ethical governance, standards and regulations, and information enable distinct and widely separated economic actors to trade with one another, and yet upon which each local actor seeks to gain competitive advantage.

Max Weber famously argued that there was an 'elective affinity' between a certain religious ethic of worldly asceticism that he saw in Calvinism and the early emergence of capitalism in Europe and North America. His thesis has been the subject of extensive debate, interpretation, and empirical refutation. But it was grounded in his more profound insight that central to the ways in which human beings conduct their lives was a 'soteriology': a way of making sense of one's suffering, of finding the reasons for it, and of thinking of the means by which one might be delivered from it.

I suggest our own soteriology increasingly takes a somatic form. Human beings identify and interpret much of their unease in terms of the health, vitality, and morbidity of their bodies; they judge and act upon their soma in their attempts to make themselves not just physically better, but also to make themselves better persons. This is what I call a 'somatic ethic.'

Is there a relationship between the birth of the bioeconomy and the emergence of the living biological body as a key site for the government of individuals – as the contemporary locus for so much of our unease and discontents, as the site of hope and potential overcoming? What are the links between the modern salience of biocapital and the ethical work that human beings are doing upon themselves in the name of health, longevity, and vital existence? To address this, we need to distinguish this sense of ethics from that entailed in the idea of bioethics. Bioethics can operate as a legitimation device within the regulatory technologies of government, as they deal with highly controversial issues of life and its management (Salter and Jones 2005, 2002). Bioethics can serve to insulate researchers from criticism, and from the detailed examination of the nature and consequences of their activities, by bureaucratizing the processes whereby they obtain 'ethical clearance' for what they do. Crucially, bioethics also provides the essential ethical guarantees that enable elements – tissues, cells, eggs, sperm, embryos, body parts – to move legitimately around the circuits of biocapital so that they can be combined and recombined in settings from laboratory to clinic. Franklin coined the term 'ethical biocapital' to draw attention to the way in which biotech corporations themselves now seek to internalize these ethical considerations in their business models and their artifacts. Bioethics thus often seems to arise from an alliance between those who want or need an ethical warrant for their commercial or scientific activities – whether they be pharmaceutical companies or those whose careers depend upon research with human subjects – and those who see here a potential locus for grants, recognition, a professional vocation, and a public role – philosophers, theologians, ethicists, and others. And as some critics claim, there are certainly moments when bioethicists, and the clean bill of health they can offer, seem to be for sale: when bioethicists, in taking subsidies for their educational activities, accepting grants, and acting as consultants to biotechnology and pharmaceutical companies, may have betrayed the trust vested in them, legitimating the unacceptable at the cost of human lives (Elliot 2004).

But alongside the urge to critique, we need to attend to that which this demand for bioethics manifests. Perhaps, at the simplest level, we need to distinguish between two general senses in which the biological and the ethical are intertwined. On the one hand stand those practices and ways of thinking that might more accurately be termed 'biomorality,' whose aim is to develop principles, and promulgate codes and rules, as to how research or clinical work in biomedicine might be conducted. At a time when the somatic, the bodily, the 'bio,' have become so central to our forms of life, we should not be surprised that one response is to try to discipline these difficulties: to find some algorithms to adjudicate them, to standardize procedures for the potentially conflictual decisions concerning them. In this way, problematic issues can be transformed into technical questions: have the proper procedures been followed? Have the proper permissions been obtained? Is confidentiality assured? Has informed consent been obtained? Bioethics, here, like accountancy, legal regulation, and so forth, has indeed become an essential part of the machinery for governing the bioeconomy; for facilitating the circuits of biological material required for the generation of biocapital; and for supervising all those practices in which life itself is the object, target, and stake.

But I am more interested here in another sense in which we can think of the ethics of the bio. This concerns the ethical considerations deemed relevant by participants – not just patients and their families, but also researchers, clinicians, regulators, and even those working in the world of commerce – in their actual conduct in relation to the dilemmas they face and the judgments they must make. Many detailed ethnographies of biosocial communities demonstrate the ways in which today's biological citizens are reformulating their own answers to Kant's three famous questions: what can I know? What must I do? What may I hope? We also see this in studies of the ethos of the authorities and professionals enmeshed in contemporary vital politics, in those working in and for commercial biotechnology and pharmaceutical companies, and perhaps even in those investors whose concerns seem purely financial. While they may have their own share of cynicism, pragmatism, ambition, greed, and rivalry, they are also searching for, assembling, and inventing ways in which they might evaluate, adjudicate, and justify the decisions they must make when human vitality is at stake.

It is this sense that is closest to my notion of a somatic ethic. I use 'ethic' here to refer to ways of understanding, fashioning, and managing ourselves in the everyday conduct of our lives.[19] If our ethic has become, in key respects, somatic, this is because it is our soma – our genome, our neurotransmitters, our 'biology' – that is given salience. It is also because the authorities that articulate the rules for living now include not merely doctors and health promoters, but so many other somatic experts: genetic counsellors, support groups, projects for the public understanding of genetics, and bioethicists. And it is because the forms of knowledge that are shaping our understandings of ourselves are themselves increasingly 'biological' – medical, of course, but also coming more directly from genomics and neuroscience, in their popular presentations, their scientific elaborations, and in the hybrid forms they take within lay discourses of everyday life. Finally it is because our expectations for our lives – our hopes for salvation, for the future – are themselves shaped by considerations about the maintenance of health and the prolongation of earthly existence.

The management of health and vitality, once derided as narcissistic self-absorption, has now achieved unparalleled ethical salience. The tensions between the intensifying demand for the products of the bioeconomy – organs, embryos, pharmaceutical products, and the like in the West – and the inequities and injustices of the local and global economic, technological, and biomedical infrastructure required to support such a somatic ethic seem to me to be a constitutive feature of contemporary biopolitics – and one in which the differential value of life is very much at stake.

What I have tried to do, in a schematic and provisional manner, is to sketch the somatic ethical economy, which perhaps has an elective affinity with a certain form of capital – biocapital – and with the capitalization of life itself. To paraphrase Max Weber, we do not have to decide between a materialistic and a

---

19 I am referring to the understanding of ethics developed by Michel Foucault (1985) and Gilles Deleuze (1988). I have discussed this way of thinking about ethics and self-technologies elsewhere, see Rose (1996).

spiritualistic interpretation of these developments.[20] Somatic ethics and biocapital have been locked together since birth. For only where life itself has achieved such ethical importance, only where the technologies for maintaining and improving it can represent themselves as more than merely the corrupt pursuit of profit and personal gain, only when they can place themselves in the service of health and life, is it possible for biocapital to achieve such a hold on our economies of hope, imagination, and profit. In this sense, I suggest, somatic ethics is intrinsically linked to the 'spirit of biocapital.'

Bibliography

Abbott, A. (1999) 'Sweden Sets Ethical Standards for the Use of Genetic "Biobanks"', *Nature* 400 (July).

Balick, M.J. and Cox, P.A. (1996) *Plants, People and Culture: Science of Ethnobotany* (New York: Scientific American Library).

Decatur Beef Alliance (2000) 'An Invitation to Join the Decatur Beef Alliance,' speech, Commercial Agriculture Producer's College, Oberlin, Kans., November 14, http://agebb.missouri.edu/commag/inst/decbeef.htm.

Deleuze, G. (1988) *Foucault* (Minneapolis: University of Minnesota Press).

Elliot, C. (2004) 'When Pharma Goes to the Laundry: Public Relations and the Business of Medical Education', *Hastings Center Report* 34(5): 18-23.

Ernst & Young (2005) *Beyond Borders: Global Biotechnology Report.*

—— (2003a), *Resilience: America's Biotechnology Report.*

—— (2003b) *Beyond Borders: The Global Biotechnology Report.*

Foucault, M .(1985) *The History of Sexuality, vol. 2. The Use of Pleasure* (London: Penguin).

Franklin, S. (2006) *Dolly Mixtures* (Durham, NC: Duke University Press).

Franklin, S. and Lock, M. (2003a) (eds) *Remaking Life and Death: Toward an Anthropology of the Biosciences* (Santa Fe: School of American Research Press).

—— (2003b) 'Animation and Cessation: The Remaking of Life and Death', in Franklin S. and Lock M. (eds) *Remaking Life and Death: Toward an Anthropology of the Biosciences* (Santa Fe: Society of American Research Press).

Herrnstein R.J. and Murray, C. (1994) *The Bell Curve: Intelligence and Class Structure in American Life* (New York: Free Press).

Horton, R. (2004) *Health Wars: On the Global Front Lines of Modern Medicine* (New York: New York Review of Books).

---

20 As Max Weber himself argues in the final paragraph of *The Protestant Ethic and the Spirit of Capitalism* (Weber 1930, 183).

Høyer, K. (2003) '"Science is Really Needed That's All I Know": Informed Consent and the Non-Verbal Practices of Collecting Blood for Genetic Research in Northern Sweden', *New Genetics and Society* 22(3): 229-244.

—— (2002) 'Conflicting Notions of Personhood in Genetic Research', *Anthropology Today* 18(5): 9-13.

Kohler, R.E. (1994) *Lords of the Fly: Drosophila Genetics and the Experimental Life* (Chicago: University of Chicago Press).

Murphy, K.M. and Topel, R.H. (2005) 'The Value of Health and Longevity', NBER Working Paper 11405, June 2005, http://www.nber.org/papers/W11405.

Nilsson, A. and Rose, J. (1999) 'Sweden Takes Steps to Protect Tissue Banks', *Science* 286: 894.

Palsson, G. and Rabinow, P. (1999) 'Iceland: The Case of a National Human Genome Project', *Anthropology Today* 15(5).

Ritvo, H. (1996) 'Possessing Mother Nature: Genetic Capital in the Eighteenth Century', in Brewer, J. and Staves, S., *Early Modern Conceptions of Property* (New York: Routledge).

Rose, H. (2003) *The Commodification of Bioinformation: The Icelandic Health Sector Database* (London: Wellcome Trust).

Rose, N. (2008) 'The Value of Life: Somatic Ethics and the Spirit of Biocapital', *Daedalus* 137(1): 36-48.

—— (2006) *The Politics of Life Itself* (Princeton: Princeton University Press).

—— (1996) *Inventing our Selves: Psychology, Power, and Personhood* (New York: Cambridge University Press).

—— (1985) *The Psychological Complex: Psychology, Politics and Society in England, 1869-1939* (London: Routledge & Kegan Paul).

Rosell, S. (1991) 'Sweden's Answer to Genomics Ethics (letter),' *Nature* 401 (September 16).

Salter, B. and Jones, M. (2005) 'Biobanks and Bioethics: The Politics of Legitimation', *Journal of European Public Policy* 12(4): 710-732.

—— (2002) 'Human Genetic Technologies, European Governance and the Politics of Bioethics,' *Nature Reviews Genetics* 3(10): 808-814.

Thompson, C. (2005) *Making Parents: The Ontological Choreography of Reproductive Technologies* (Cambridge, MA: MIT Press).

Viscusi, W.K. (2005) 'The Value of Life', *New Palgrave Dictionary of Economics and the Law*, 2nd edn (Palgrave Macmillan).

Waldby, C (2000) *The Visible Human Project: Informatic Bodies and Posthuman Medicine* (New York: Routledge).

Weber, M. (1930) *The Protestant Ethic and the Spirit of Capitalism* (London: George Allen and Unwin Ltd).

Chapter 5
How We Value Life: George Bailey and the Life Not Worthy of Being Lived

Stephen Smith

Introduction

How we value life is important. The value that we place on life impacts upon those rights which we believe individuals ought to possess as well as the duties we feel that individuals owe each other. It gives us insight into the sorts of medical treatments we should expect, what care we ought to give those in need and many other concerns. When we consider the ethical thing to do, it is usually one of our first and most foundational concerns. When turning to the law, the value of individual lives involved in the decisions that we make provide us with a framework for deciding which actions we should allow and which ones we should not. Despite the importance of concerns about the value of life, no overriding conception about how best to value life has evolved. Indeed, in many ways, the debate is more polarised now than it was previously. The two sides which have emerged in the debate over the value of life have become entrenched positions and very little headway has been made in repeated discussions about the issue. If this is the case, it is worth wondering what additions can be made by continuing the discussion. Any additional contributions seem more likely to add to any entrenchment than to reduce it. That would be the case if the purpose of this chapter were to argue for one side or the other of these two positions. However, this chapter will argue that neither adequately explains the ways in which we really go about valuing life. As such, the way to resolve the debate is not to accept either of the entrenched positions but to explore other possibilities. This chapter will, therefore, provide one such method to go beyond the two standard views and construct a more inclusive viewpoint about how we value life.

Before beginning that project, however, it is necessary to put forward the two competing standard views and explore why they do not adequately address the issue. This will be done in the next section of the chapter. Once these two views have been summarised, it will be necessary to explore how and why they fail. That will require the use of an example life. One approach to that is to present a hypothetical life for consideration. For the purposes of this paper that will be insufficient as one of the claims that will be made is that the variety and complexity of life must be accounted for in any valuation of life. A new hypothetical example will not suffice for these purposes. Instead, an example chosen from cinema will provide a more fully developed example for our purposes. The character chosen as our example is George Bailey, the protagonist played by James Stewart in *It's a Wonderful Life* (dir. Frank Capra, 1946). After discussing the character of George Bailey in relation to the two standard views, it will be necessary to explore how a third competing view which is more inclusive provides a greater insight into why the life of George Bailey is as important as it is. The final section of the chapter will look at what impact this new valuation method may have for legal decisions which rely, at least to some extent, upon the valuation of life.

The Standard Views

As noted in the Introduction, there are two standard views about how we value life. They are called the Sanctity of Life position (SOL) and the Quality of Life position (QOL) (Keown 1997, 482-488; 2002, 39-51).[1] It is generally assumed that the viewpoints of individuals can be categorized under one of these two competing views. Each will be discussed in detail.

The SOL position is often associated with writers such as John Keown (1997, 2002, 2006) and John Finnis (1993). The position holds that life has an inherent or basic value. An inherent value does not mean that life has an absolute value, but that life is one of those things that John Finnis (1980, 85-90) refers to as a self-evident basic good. A basic good is something we want whatever else we might want. These are considered self-evident not because they are things that all of us will immediately agree to, but that they are foundational concepts (ibid., 69). Consequently, there are no more foundational claims prior to these goods that we can use as premises to prove the existence of these basic goods (ibid.). We can demonstrate their value in all sorts of ways but it is not possible to *prove* their value. As a direct result of this focus on the inherent value of life, the SOL position holds that it is never permissible to intentionally end the life of an innocent human being but that we need not strive officiously to keep people alive (Keown 2002, 40; 2006, 114).[2] What this means in the context of end of life care is the following. Assisted dying is not permissible but, in some circumstances, the withdrawal and

1 A third position known as vitalism is sometimes mentioned. Vitalism holds that life has an absolute value and, consequently, should not be shortened for any reason. Additionally, every effort must be made to extend life, even for a minimal amount of time. The only people who legitimately hold such a view are an Eastern religion called the Jains. It is not considered to be a viable ethical position to take and no academic has actually defended such a view (Keown 1997, Pattinson 2006). It will therefore not be discussed further.

2 The word 'innocent' deserves highlighting. Under the standard formulation of the SOL position, the word does not mean 'free from guilt' but 'has not given up the right that others ought not to kill him or her'. Those not considered innocent are those involved in armed conflict, those executed in accordance with a lawful sentence and those aggressors who are killed in self-defence.

withholding of life-sustaining treatment may be. When determining whether to remove or withhold treatment, no concern is given to the quality of the individual's life. Concern is given, however, to the value of the treatment. The treatment must satisfy the purposes of medicine which are (1) to restore the patient to a condition of health and well-functioning (or some approximation of it) and (2) if that is not possible, to palliate symptoms (ibid., 2006, 113). If the treatment does not satisfy either of these two therapeutic goals, then it is permissible to remove or fail to provide the treatment (ibid., 113-114). If the treatment does satisfy one or the other of these goals, then it should be provided. Considered in another way, the value of life under the sanctity of life position is in existence. Under such a view, life is valuable because we exist. Once we have existence, then our life has value and it does not matter what we do with that life.

This can be contrasted with the QOL position which is associated with writers such as Peter Singer (1994), John Harris (1995) and David Price (2001, 2007). The QOL position holds that there is no inherent value in life. Instead, life is valuable because it allows you to do things which are valuable (ibid., 2007, 563). Existence, then, provides no support for any claim about value. Claims about value derive from further claims about the activities, events, relationships and so on that are possible because of my existence (Singer 1994, 106-131; Harris 1995, 6-22; Price 2001, 618; 2007, 563). So, it does not matter necessarily that I am alive. What matters instead is that I am able to do things which I value and to create a life which I find valuable. Again, this has specific results for how we consider end of life decisions. Since life itself is not valuable, we determine the value of life of the individual based upon whether or not they can do those things which they do value (Harris 1995, 10-20). This means that if those opportunities are no longer possible, then it is possible for one's life to have a negative value. When this occurs, it is not only possible for the withdrawal or withholding of treatment to be permissible but also for assisted dying practices such as physician-assisted suicide or active voluntary euthanasia. In these cases, then, we can consider the statement that life is valuable because I can X, with X being whatever the individual finds to be valuable.

Two additional points are worth mentioning. Neither of these two are generally explicit within the literature, but they form two important assumptions which lie at the heart of discussions about the end of life. The first is that these two positions are mutually exclusive. One cannot logically hold both at the same time. One must choose between them. The second point is that these two are exhaustive of the field. In other words, if one wants to hold any position on the value of life, it needs to be either the SOL or QOL position. Other possibilities are not viable options.[3]

3 Again, if we consider vitalism to be a theoretically valid position, then one could hold one of three possible views. But it only adds one additional possibility. It does not add any significant number of additional choices and, it is to be remembered, no one poses vitalism as a viable perspective on the value of life.

The Life of George Bailey

With those summaries in mind, it is now possible to turn to our examination of the value of George Bailey's life from *It's a Wonderful Life* (dir. Frank Capra 1946). For those either unfamiliar with the film or those needing a reminder, it is worth setting out the plot of the film. The basic idea of the film is that an angel (Clarence) is sent down from heaven to help one individual (George) on a particular Christmas Eve when he is contemplating suicide because he believes his life to be worthless. The film can be considered to be in two parts. The first part is the events leading up to this Christmas Eve night and is largely a kind of briefing for Clarence. In order for Clarence to understand the person he is going to be trying to help, he (as well as the viewer) is shown the life of George Bailey, who is an average guy from the small town of Bedford Falls. We learn that as a child George was involved in two important events. First, at the age of 12, George saved his brother Harry from drowning in a frozen lake. As a result, George's hearing is impaired in one ear. Additionally, when he was working at the local pharmacy a few weeks later, he stopped his employer, Mr Gower, from accidentally putting poison into a child's prescription. We also learn that George from quite a young age has an interest in seeing the world, making his fortune, and doing great things like building bridges and skyscrapers. We are next shown George at about the time when his brother is graduating from high school. George has put his own plans on hold so that he can help his father run the family business, the Bailey Building and Loan, until his brother Harry is old enough to take over. However, when celebrating his brother's graduation and discussing his future with Mary Hatch (who has had a life-long crush on him), George is informed that his father has had a stroke. George puts his plans on hold to help save the Building and Loan and keep it out of the hands of the evil slumlord of Bedford Falls, a man named Mr Potter. Mr. Potter wants to end the Building and Loan's extension of loans to disadvantaged families in Bedford Falls. George urges the board of directors of the Building and Loan to refuse Mr. Potter's offer but they do so on the condition that George stays and runs the business. George reluctantly agrees and gives his money for university to his brother Harry.

George's life story then jumps ahead another four years to the time of Harry's graduation from university. As with Harry's high school graduation, George sees this one as opportunity to leave Bedford Falls as he expects Harry to return and take over the running of the Building and Loan. To everyone's surprise, though, Harry returns to Bedford Falls with a new wife whose father has offered Harry a job. Despite the fact that Harry offers to turn down the job to run the Building and Loan, George again stays in Bedford Falls and allows Harry to take the position. It is also at this time that George realizes that he has feelings for Mary. George and Mary later get married. On their way out of town to celebrate their honeymoon, however, they notice a run on the Building and Loan which will put the business in a severe financial situation. Mr. Potter again tries to buy the Building and Loan by offering its customers fifty cents on the dollar for their shares. George and Mary use the money that they have saved for their honeymoon to prevent a panic but this prevents them from going on their honeymoon. After this, George and Mary set up a housing development called Bailey Park for lower-income families in Bedford Falls (like the immigrant restaurant owner, Mr Martini). George further refuses the attempts of Mr Potter to buy him out. George and Mary also begin to raise a family. When the Second World War hits, George is unable to fight because of the problems in his ear. His brother Harry, however, becomes a fighter pilot, saves a troop transport full of soldiers by shooting down an enemy plane and is awarded the Medal of Honor.

All of this leads up the events on Christmas Eve. During the day, a banking regulator has come to inspect the Building and Loan's records. Unfortunately, George's uncle Billy has lost $8,000 which he was to deposit in the bank. Neither George nor Billy is able to find the money because, unbeknownst to Billy, he left it in a folded up newspaper which he gave to Mr Potter. George yells at his uncle and then, upon returning home, yells at Mary, his children and the teacher of his daughter Zuzu. In desperation, he turns to Mr Potter for a loan. Mr Potter not only neglects to mention that he possesses the missing money but refuses to extend George the loan and calls the police. Fleeing from the police, George hits a tree with his car, gets into a fight with the husband of Zuzu's teacher and ends up on a bridge in Bedford Falls. He decides to jump because he believes he is worth more dead than alive due to a $15,000 life insurance policy he owns.

It is at this point that Clarence truly enters the story. In order to prevent George from committing suicide, Clarence falls in the river necessitating that George save him. Once both are out of the water, George makes two important statements to Clarence. First, he says that things would be better if he was dead. When Clarence challenges him on this, George changes his mind. He instead feels as if things would be better if he had never been born. Clarence sees an opportunity and agrees to show George what Bedford Falls would be like if he had never been born. What George sees, of course, is a nightmare. Bedford Falls has been turned into a slum called Pottersville with its main street full of seedy bars and pawn shops. Mr Martini no longer owns the restaurant and Bailey Park does not exist. What is more important is what has happened to the people he knows. Mr Gower is a drunken ex-convict because George is not around to prevent him from poisoning the child. His uncle Billy has been put in an asylum. His brother died because George did not save him and his mother runs a run-down boarding house. Since Harry died as a child, the troop transport was not saved and all of the soldiers in it were killed. Other friends such as Bert the police officer, Ernie the cab driver and Violet are unhappy. Perhaps most importantly from George's point of view, Mary is a spinster librarian who, when he confronts her in an effort to get someone to remember him, does not know who George is. As a result of these events, George returns to the bridge and begs Clarence to return him to his life because he wants to live. This wish is granted, George realises he does have a wonderful life, the townspeople return the favour he did for them years ago by bailing him out financially and Clarence finally gets his wings.

Determining the Value of George's Life

It is the conversation George has with Clarence after the river which is most important for an initial assessment as to what this may indicate about the value of life. In particular, the second statement that George makes to Clarence should help with a beginning to a theory as it is the actual 'request' which is taken up by Clarence. That statement is that things would be better if George had not been born. This appears to be a statement about existence. Claiming that the world would be better if he was not and had never been in existence is a claim about whether or not he ought to be present in the first place. It does not, as a QOL valuation would expect, depend on various things which he was or was not able to do with that existence but merely trades upon the inherent value of his life in the first place. It might then seem like the film is going to take a SOL perspective about the value of life.

However, we then need to turn to Clarence's response to that claim. By this, it is not his actual verbal response which is important (at least the initial response) but his actions in allowing George to see what life would be like without him in it. Clarence does not show him what non-existence might be. Instead, he shows George an alternative reality where he is not present to do the things which he has done (and as it turns out needs to have done). We see, in other words, a nightmarish vision of Bedford Falls which is a lesser place without George in it. Not simply because George's existence matters in some way, but because George needs to be in Bedford Falls to do certain things. He needs to save his brother from drowning and prevent Mr Gower from making his mistake. He needs to be present to oppose Mr Potter and help out the numerous people that he helps. He needs to be there to build the relationships he has with Mary, his family, his friends and the townspeople of Bedford Falls. This provides us with a view about the value of life, though, that seems more consistent with a QOL perspective. They are not claims about simple existence. They are claims that the value of George's life comes from the events he has participated in, the people he has interacted with and the relationships he has formed. These are not qualities which are there because of existence but based on those things which George finds valuable. The value of life, Clarence seems to be telling him, derives not from his existence but from those things he gets to do due to that existence.

Even with that understanding about Clarence's actions, it does not seem like the movie is only making a QOL point about the value of George's life. If it was, the focus in the initial claim about existence would be misplaced. The focus on existence *per se*, however, seems quite deliberate in the film especially if we consider the surrounding circumstances. As indicated, George does not claim at first that his life has no meaning. His initial claim to Clarence is that things would be better off if he was dead. It was this claim that Clarence could have responded to and the narrative structure of the film would not necessarily have changed very much. If we consider Clarence's prime motivating factor to be showing George that his life has value so that he should want to live, this seems as easily demonstrated by utilising any number of alternate realities instead of the means that Clarence actually uses. So, he could have shown George what Bedford Falls would have been like if he died on the bridge that night. We should keep in mind that the results of such action are unlikely to be pleasant for the residents of Bedford Falls. It will, of course, be true that Bedford Falls would not fall into a slum as early as it has in the alternative reality where George does not exist, but it is probable that no one will be able to oppose Mr Potter after George's death. The Bailey Building and Loan will be subject to the accounting scandal which causes George's crisis in the first place. It does not seem likely that it would survive that crisis intact. His uncle Billy, should he manage to avoid jail as a result of the crisis, seems ill-suited to run the company and his brother does not seem likely to run the business either as he would be either still in the military or at his job working for his father-in-law. Bailey Park, then, seems destined for failure without George running the Building and Loan.[4] As a result, Mr Potter would likely be able to buy out the Building and Loan, own the whole of Bedford Falls and turn it into the slum Pottersville anyway. Nor would things be better for Mary. George himself admits to Mr Potter that he has no savings or investments outside of a life-insurance policy. If we consider other contemporaneous works of art such as the Arthur Miller play *Death of a Salesman* (1949), then it is likely that there is a suicide clause in the policy. George's suicide, then, like Willy Loman's in *Death of a Salesman*, would invalidate the policy and Mary would not receive any money from the insurance company. She would be left with whatever survives the accounting scandal at the Building and Loan, the large house she and George own (which seems to need fairly constant upkeep), and four children in addition to the normal grief that would result from the death of her husband whom she has been in love with seemingly from the age of about eight. Her life, then, seems like it would be considerably worse than it would be if George were alive. Indeed, one might argue that her life after his death is going to be at least as bad as the one that exists in the alternate reality without George. It is true that Mr Gower will not be severely harmed by George's death and his brother Harry might be all right, but a number of important characters seem like they will have lives as bad under the 'George dies' scenario as they would under the 'George doesn't exist' one.

Alternatively, Clarence could have shown George a world in which George existed but made different choices.[5] As one possibility, Clarence could have shown

4 Without being too critical of the other residents of Bedford Falls, it is worth remembering the run on the bank which happens earlier in the film. It seems doubtful, for example, that those residents who are so scared about the run on the banks and want to close down their accounts are likely to deal any more rationally with an accounting scandal at the Building and Loan.

5 It is worth noting that two of the three original scripts for the film (prior to its purchase by Frank Capra and Liberty Films) did not have Mr Potter as a character (Moiseeff 1990). Instead, the antagonist of the film is an 'evil George Bailey'. In other words, a George Bailey who existed but who had made different choices in life.

George a world in which he gets to live the life he had always wanted to live. While such a life would have included more travel and the possibility that George would have gotten to work on some of the projects like bridges and skyscrapers that he wanted, it does not mean that George's life would invariably have been better. It does not seem that he would necessarily be married to Mary in this alternative reality as he only realises his feelings for her four years after he was supposed to leave Bedford Falls. The town itself, without George's opposition to Mr Potter, is likely to fall into ruin. The Building and Loan would, most likely, fail or be bought by Mr Potter. His brother's life is not guaranteed to improve as it was George's money that allowed him to attend college in the first place. Harry's marriage and high-paying job are unlikely to happen. Bedford Falls and the people in it are likely to be drastically changed by this alternate reality and, again, not necessarily for the better. It thus also seems like it would have been a reasonable option that Clarence could have chosen to prove his point. Indeed, this seems like it may be a preferable option to the one Clarence actually takes as we are led to believe that George's childhood dreams have at least something to do with his current bitterness about his life. An exploration of an alternate life where he got everything he wanted but which still caused unhappiness for himself and the residents of Bedford Falls would have addressed that problem head on.

The claims about existence, consequently, seem to be a major focus of the theme of the movie. The problem that George faces about his existence does not merely collapse into a question about the choices that he has made. Those choices are important and it is important, of course, that George sees that they matter. But he also needs to see that it isn't just that the choices need to be made, but that he needs to be there to make them. In the end, then, his simple existence matters as much as the choices he has made throughout his life.

The movie, therefore, seems to make the following conclusions. George Bailey matters. He matters to himself, he matters to Mary, he matters to his other friends and family and he matters to the small town of Bedford Falls. The way in which he matters, though, is reasonably complex. The first part is that George Bailey must exist. Bedford Falls is a much worse place without him and the lives of those people he interacts with are lessened without that involvement. In other words, there must be *a* George Bailey in existence. The answer does not stop there, however. The town of Bedford Falls does not just need a George Bailey. It needs *this* George Bailey. A George Bailey who did not save either his brother or Mr Gower will not suffice. A George Bailey who leaves Bedford Falls to seek his fame and fortune leaving the town's residents to the mercy of Mr Potter will not suffice. A George Bailey who does not marry his wife or form the relationships he does with Bert, Ernie, Violet, Mr Martini and others will not suffice. That is why, presumably, the movie ends in the way that it does. George, after deciding he wants to live is not returned to a better life than he had. He is still in Bedford Falls with the same job and life he had previously. The accounting scandal still exists and jail time remains a possibility. Mr Potter still owns most of the town. He is still injured from his fight with Zuzu's teacher's husband and his car has still been crashed into a tree. The weather has not even changed.[6] It is important that this be the case. It is *this* life that George has decided has meaning so a change to that, even in minor ways, would be a vastly different outcome.[7]

Translating this conclusion into our standard formulations about the value of life creates significant issues because it seems like we have reached the one conclusion we appear not to be able to reach under these formulations. The conclusion of the film seems to be that George's life matters both because of some inherent value in existence and because of the things he accomplishes during that existence. In other words, both the essential valuations of the SOL position and the QOL position appear to be correct. This, however, is the one result which is supposed to be impossible under the current formulation. Those two positions are supposed to be mutually exclusive. One is not able to reach the position that both are true and still be logically consistent. Either the hugely popular critically acclaimed film is wrong about its central idea or the standard formulations have missed a vital element about the way we value life. We need only to look around in our daily lives to know that neither critical acclaim nor popularity are necessarily great indicators of logical consistency so there is nothing inherently strange about the film failing to adhere to logical consistency. On the other hand, there is nothing that requires that the philosophical formulations set forth above are any better. So, it is worthwhile seeing if we can construct a logically consistent formulation of the value of life which is consistent with the approach taken in the film. One way to accomplish that will be considered in the following section.

An Alternative Vision of the Value of Life

Taking the position taken by the film on the value of George's life as our initial starting point, the significant problem posed is this one over mutual exclusivity. An alternative vision of the value of life would therefore need to avoid this particular point. It is thus useful to examine this notion of mutual exclusivity about the value of life more closely. As stated previously, this notion that these two distinct conceptions about the value of life are mutually exclusive is never explicitly stated in the literature. Consequently, it never receives a full justification. It is undoubtedly part of the equation, however. If we look more completely at the

6 Of course, these are also all signs (along with the flower petals from Zuzu's flower that George has in his pocket) that George has returned from the alternate reality and is back in the 'real' world. Even so, they do present an emphasis on a return to George's life as it was.

7 We could compare the ending with other alternate reality movies. For example, while not contemporaneous, the first *Back to the Future* film (dir. Robert Zemeckis, 1985) provides a useful parallel. In that film, the life Marty McFly returns to after his time travel is a vastly improved one. His father is successful, Biff no longer bullies his father and Marty's life is materially better. None of those things happen to George Bailey.

literature, there is never any mention of combining the two disparate positions to come up with additional perspectives. Nor is there any acceptance that an alternative position works for some cases even if it does not work for any others. It therefore seems evident that one of the unspoken assumptions is that these positions must necessarily be mutually exclusive.[8]

If we further examine these positions, though, the fundamental assumption about mutual exclusivity does not seem to be warranted. As noted in Section II, the SOL position can be articulated in the sentence 'My life is valuable because I exist.' The QOL position can be articulated by the sentence 'My life is valuable because I can X.' There seems nothing mutually exclusive about those statements such that if the first is true the second must necessarily be false. We can test this by combining the two statements into a third statement that 'My life is valuable because I exist and because I can X.' There does not appear to be any logical inconsistency within that statement. All it does is provide two reasons as to why a life is valuable as opposed to one. As long as those two reasons are not mutually exclusive themselves so that if one is true the other is false, then there seems to be no reason why the overall statement is false. Those two reasons do not themselves seem to be mutually exclusive. Indeed, as I am sure many in the debate would note, the existence of the person is likely a necessity condition for their ability to do X. As such, we appear to have no reason to accept the position that the two conceptions of the value of life are actually mutually exclusive.

If they are not, then it is possible to create a method for valuing life which better approximates what actually happens in *It's a Wonderful Life*. In fact, such a valuation system already exists. That system was put forward by Ronald Dworkin (1994) in *Life's Dominion*. Dworkin's formulation is based upon an exploration of 'life.' He asserts there are two different ways in which we understand life and he refers to them respectively as *zoē* and *bios*. *Zoē* is life as biological processes. It is about the notion of our lives being that period of time between when we come into existence and when we die. It is, in other words, our physical or biological existence. The second, *bios*, is our lives as lived. It is what Dworkin (1994, 83) means when he refers to 'actions, decisions, motives and events that compose what we now call a biography.' The first he refers to as 'nature.' We might also call this our biological life. The second he likens to 'art' which he sees as being less obvious but no less crucial. We might also call this our biographical life. As he explains:

8 We might contest this by the assertion that John Keown (2002) sees his sanctity of life position as a 'middle ground' between the 'two extremes' of vitalism and Quality of Life. It might further be added that he accepts quality of life judgments within the context of certain end of life decisions. A closer inspection shows that this does not mean that his SOL position accepts part of the QOL position. Quality of life judgments within his SOL position are limited to concerns about the value of particular treatment options, not valuations of parts of an individual's life. It therefore does not accept any part of the QOL position. Additionally, it focuses on the inherent or basic value of life itself and is therefore an existence based method for determining the value of life.

> each developed human being is the product not just of natural creation, but also of the kind of deliberate human creative force that we honor in honoring art. A mature woman, for example, is in her personality, training, capacity, interests, ambitions, and emotions, something like a work of art because in those respects she is the product of human creative intelligence, partly that of her parents and other people, partly that of her culture, and also, through the choices she has made, her *own* creation (Dworkin 1994: 82).

This may not sound initially like it offers much help. The concept of biological life that he refers to as *zoē* does not appear to be vastly different from the notion of an inherent or basic value in life put forward by the SOL position. Nor does the concept of *bios* seem to be significantly different from the QOL position previously considered. Whether they are or not is not the issue. What is at issue is that Dworkin sees them not as mutually exclusive but as being complementary. Instead of competing ways of describing the value of life, Dworkin asserts that you need to consider both when considering how best to value to life. As he indicates:

> [t]hat combination of nature and art – two traditions of the sacred – supports the further more dramatic claim that each individual human life, on its own, can be understood as the product of both creative traditions (Dworkin 1994: 82).

From this, a new way of valuing life can emerge. When valuing lives, we consider both the inherent value that life has and we consider the additional benefit that can exist with the things we are able to do because of it. Like in *It's a Wonderful Life* when George's valuation is the important one, the valuation is done by the person him or her self. In articulating this valuation system, we might best explain it as a baseline measurement from which additional value can either add or subtract from that initial value. It is important to stress that initial value is not the point in which we consider life to have lost all value but exists at some point above that. Perhaps it can be illustrated by parallels with a mathematical formula. If we assume that the value in which life begins to lack value (the point where it is better to be dead than alive) is slightly below zero and the point in which life begins to have value is slightly above zero, then we can consider zero to be the point of neutrality where it is neither better to be alive or dead. When we begin our valuation of life using this methodology, existence has value in and of itself. So, the starting point is always above zero. This value is then modified by the biographical story we are all telling about our own lives. The things we value within that life add value to that baseline figure. Additionally important, because there may be aspects to our lives which detract from our overall value, those may reduce the baseline figure. However, it is important to note that a simple reduction in the baseline figure is not normally enough for us to conclude that our lives do not have meaning. It is only when that baseline figure is reduced to a number less that zero that we can actually claim to be better off dead than alive.

It is important to stress, however, the individual nature of this assessment. The things that are valued by a particular individual are what is important, not how we might see that evaluation. In George's case, then, it is not how Mr Potter or Mary or even Clarence views the value of the things that George has done, it is how George himself values those things which are important. These valuations, then, do not have objective measurements. They are deeply personal decisions because the things which we value are not objective.

We thus have a new method of valuing life which provides support not only for the inherent or basic value of our lives, but also which allows that basic value to be modified by the things which we do and the interactions, events, relationships and activities that we engage in. This personal valuation of our lives as a complete story which includes our existence and our biographical lives provides us with a far more compelling value about our lives as we can see from the way in which it impacts upon the life of George Bailey in *It's a Wonderful Life*.

The Benefits of this Approach

Even if this is correct and the approach that has been outlined above is a logically consistent way to value life, it does not mean that it ought to be a method which is used. It is only if this method provides benefits for the ways in which we think about the value of life that it ought to be a preferred method for deciding upon life's value. It is worthwhile, therefore, exploring what, if any, benefits there might be to this approach outside of its use in understanding *It's a Wonderful Life*. It is worth noting at the beginning two aspects of this approach which are not benefits. First, the approach outlined above is not simpler to describe than the two standard approaches. As it combines different elements into its valuation of life, this approach is necessarily more complex to describe. Unsurprisingly considering its complexity in description, this approach also lacks the simplicity of application that the two standard approaches possess. In general, then, the approach being considered here lacks simplicity. Simplicity, however, is only a benefit to approaches such as this provided that nothing is lost because of that simplicity. It is here where the new approach begins to show benefits. While it is more complex to both describe and apply, this greater benefit may provide a more accurate assessment about the ways in which we actually value life. Some evidence for this can be shown from the film we have been considering but that is not sufficient evidence on its own. However, we do have other evidence which may show the accuracy of this approach.

For an example, it is worth examining one of the seminal cases on withdrawal of treatment in the UK – *Airedale NHS Trust v. Bland* (1993).[9] The judges who made the decision in *Bland* at the High Court, Court of Appeals and House of Lords and the parties in *Bland* all made reference to the importance of the sanctity

9 *Airedale NHS Trust v. Bland* [1993] 1 All ER 821.

of life.[10] However, they all also made reference to individual factors about the quality of life which might override the sanctity of life in the particular case in front of them.[11] Additionally, some of them also commented on how Anthony Bland was alive but had 'no life' or other phrases which seemed to indicate that the judges thought that while Anthony Bland was a living human being, he was missing in some essential characteristic which defined 'a life.' Sir Stephen Brown P *stating* 'His spirit has left him and all that remains is the shell of his body,'[12] Hoffmann LJ *stating* 'His body is alive but he has no life...,'[13] and Lord Goff described Anthony Bland's condition as a 'living death.'[14] These varied statements of the judges have been criticised for being inconsistent or misunderstanding the viewpoints about the value of life which they were trying to apply (Finnis 1993, Keown 1997). If we are examining those statements using only the standard views, then the criticisms are well-founded. The views of the judges, taken as a whole, do not appear to correspond to either a true SOL perspective or a QOL one. So, if the judges were trying to utilise one of competing standard viewpoints, then they have, indeed, failed.

It is far from clear that is what the judges were actually doing. The only academic commentator noted in the judgment is, in fact, Ronald Dworkin, who is referenced in the opinion of Hoffman.[15] More importantly for our purposes, it is the book *Life's Dominion* (then only in draft form) which Hoffman states is particularly important to his thinking.[16] It is also *Life's Dominion* which sets out the views on the value of life outlined above. Hoffman, if he was following Dworkin's views on the value of life, would be approaching something much closer to the viewpoint outlined above as opposed to the two standard views articulated in Section II. Even more convincingly, the approach taken by the judges seems more consistent with this viewpoint than either of the standard views. All of the judges indicated the importance of the inherent value of life. This can be shown by their statements in support of the sanctity of life. However, the judges also argued that this notion of inherent value did not automatically resolve the case or even end the judge's inquiry. Instead, they then focused on additional factors about Anthony Bland's life which they then appear to use to modify, at least partially, that initial inherent value to life. Again, that type of approach is not consistent with the standard views. It does, however, correspond with the viewpoint articulated

10 Ibid., 830 (Sir Stephen Brown P), 835 (Sir Thomas Bingham MR), 846 (Butler-Sloss LJ), 851-852 (Hoffmann LJ), 861 (Lord Keith), 865 (Lord Goff), 878 (Lord Browne-Wilkinson).

11 Ibid., 839 (Sir Thomas Bingham MR), 846 (Butler-Sloss LJ), 851 (Hoffmann LJ), 861 (Lord Keith) 866 (Lord Goff), 878-879 (Lord Browne-Wilkinson).

12 Ibid., 832.

13 Ibid., 850.

14 Ibid., 865.

15 Ibid., 851.

16 Ibid.

above. In other words, the judges in *Bland* do not appear to be inconsistent at all. What they are doing is using a viewpoint different than the standard views, but one which is consistent with an alternative way to value life. The method proposed here, thus, provides us with an accurate analysis of what the judges appear to have actually done in at least one very important case which turned on the value of the life of the individual.

Furthermore, it is worth emphasising that the use of this new approach does not mean that the SOL position and the QOL position disappear completely. Since this new approach argues that both the inherent value of life and the value that is added due to the additional elements of a given life are used together to come up with an overall value of life, there are a number of ways that calculation can be made. The SOL and QOL positions do not disappear as a result, but instead become two points at either end of a continuum with an infinite range of possibilities between them. This new formulation provides an additional benefit as a result. One of the problems with the two standard formulations which are currently used is that they are diametrically opposed to each other. There is no possibility of a middle ground because the essential question at the heart of the debate - does existence have an inherent value - is seen as a yes or no question. There is thus no possibility of compromise because of the binary nature of that question. There is, quite simply, nothing that can be compromised so any compromise between the two sides is impossible. Additionally, due to the nature of the inquiry, it is not subject to any rational proof. One either accepts the inherent value of life (and thus presumably the SOL position) or one does not (and thus takes the QOL position). Neither side is able to win the argument because the claim over the inherent value of life is a foundational assumption at the start. This is best illustrated by looking at its role in the SOL position. As noted above, the SOL position takes the view that there is an inherent or basic value in life. How is this conclusion reached? For some, this derives from the nature of a 'basic good'. A basic good, according to John Finnis (1980, 85-90), is something we want whatever else we might want. Most importantly, though, it is not something which is provable. Instead, a basic good is something which is self-evident (Finnis 1980, 69). At best, self-evident basic goods can be demonstrated to be such, but can never be proven to be basic because there are no more foundational claims upon which we can rely on to build the argument (Finnis 1980, 69). At its heart, consequently, the fundamental difference between the SOL position and the QOL position is an unprovable assumption and, as such, the best we can hope for is understanding about the two positions. There can never be a resolution to the problem. This new formulation, however, does not require that the controversy over this assumption be solved.

It also provides an additional benefit by presenting the valuation of life in shared terminology. Our concerns are not diametrically opposed but part of a larger methodology with differences in the application. That may not sound like a tremendous improvement, but the notion of a shared basic understanding at least allows for the possibility of a progression towards a result. Consider it in the following way. Assume we have two persons who are discussing whether or not something is 'fair.' Person A holds that Situation 1 is fair but that Situation 2 is unfair. Person B holds the opposite. Through further discussion, they realise that the problem lies in the fact that Person A believes 'fair' to mean something different from Person B. Persons A and B are unlikely to be able to progress any further until they can at least agree on a number of shared elements of what 'fair' means. Otherwise, both would likely stick to their own assessment of what matters. Thus, even if they agree entirely about Situations 1 and 2, if they continue to have different assessments of fair, then no consensus will ever emerge between the two of them. On the other hand, if they can agree a shared conception of fair, then disagreements which may arise about Situations 1 and 2 can be resolved within that framework. Even if Persons A and B still cannot agree, they can at least continue the discussion on relevant grounds. This new formulation of the value of life works in a similar way. If there is acceptance that there is an inherent value to life but that value is adjusted by additional factors, then it does not guarantee that we will all reach the same valuations in the same cases. It does not even mean that we will have exactly the same method for determining those valuations. What it will help, though, is that we are all discussing similar concerns and thus can have a discussion about the relevant differences between views instead of simply asserting that our view is correct and the opposing view is not.

We thus have important benefits to the formulation presented in this chapter. First, it appears to not only fit the value of life exercise that happens in *It's a Wonderful Life* but also seems to accurately reflect exercises happening in more important situations such as the decisions made in the *Bland* case. Our methodology is therefore, at least in some cases, a good description of ways to value life and in those cases, could be used as a good predictor of possible results. Additionally, the formulation presented is more inclusive than the standard dispute between the SOL and the QOL as it not only encompasses those views but adds additional viewpoints. Furthermore, a way to resolve disputes under this formulation seems more likely than under the standard viewpoints because it avoids the fundamental assumption problem that exists between the two standard views and presents a shared understanding of some of the foundational points which should facilitate discussion.

Conclusion

In conclusion, the purpose of this chapter has been to explore a new methodology for how we value life. It has shown that the two standard formulations of how we value life – the Sanctity of Life position and the Quality of Life position – do not and cannot accurately reflect all of the ways in which we value life. In particular, this was shown through an examination of how the life of George Bailey was valued in *It's a Wonderful Life*. With that important conclusion, the chapter then focused on an alternative way to value life which better approximated the method used in the film while maintaining logical consistency. Finally, some important benefits of this approach were considered in order to show why this method should be preferred over the standard formulations. The final point we can take from this is the same one George Bailey learns in the film. Determining our lives have value may not be easy. It is a struggle because what we value is a multi-faceted and complex notion about not only ourselves but how we interact with the people, events and things around us. It causes us to examine those things we take for granted and our failures as well as our successes. Despite this, the examination is worth doing. At the very least, it shows us that even so-called 'ordinary lives' have great meaning.

Bibliography

Dworkin, R. (1994) *Life's Dominion* (New York: Vintage Books).

Finnis, J. (1993) '*Bland*: Crossing the Rubicon?', *The Law Quarterly Review* 109, 329-337.

—— (1980) *Natural Law and Natural Rights* (Oxford: Oxford University Press).

Harris, J. (1995) 'Euthanasia and the value of life', in Keown, J. (ed.) *Euthanasia Examined: Ethical Clinical and Legal Perspectives* (Cambridge: Cambridge University Press).

Keown, J. (2006) 'Restoring the sanctity of life and replacing the caricature: a reply to David Price', *Legal Studies* 26(1): 109-119.

—— (2002) *Euthanasia, Ethics and Public Policy* (Cambridge: Cambridge University Press).

—— (1997) 'Restoring moral and intellectual shape to the law after *Bland*', *The Law Quarterly Review* 113, 481-503.

Miller, A. (1949) *Death of a Salesman* (New York: Viking Penguin, Inc.).

Pattinson, S. (2006) *Medical Law and Ethics* (London: Sweet and Maxwell).

Price, D. (2007) 'My view of the sanctity of life: a rebuttal of John Keown's critique', *Legal Studies* 27(4): 549-565.

—— (2001) 'Fairly *Bland*: an alternative view of a supposed new "Death Ethic" and the BMA guidelines', *Legal Studies* 21(4): 618-643.

Singer, P. (1994) *Rethinking Life and Death: The Collapse of our Traditional Ethics* (Oxford: Oxford University Press).

Films

Back to the Future (dir. Robert Zemeckis, 1985).

It's a Wonderful Life (dir. Frank Capra, 1946).

The Making of It's a Wonderful Life (dir. Moiseeff, 1990).

PART II
The Vicissitudes of Armed Conflict and Detention

Chapter 6

The Right to Take Life: Killing and Death in Armed Conflict

Agnieszka Jachec-Neale

Killing and death in armed conflict may appear as violent and non-violent, deliberate and incidental, lawful and unlawful, principled (or rather honourable) or unchivalrous. People in armed conflict may die as a result of violations (unlawful deaths) and may die as a consequence or in the course of a lawful military conduct (including lawful killings and deaths which are not unlawful). Any discussion engaging with killing in armed conflict would necessarily touch upon consideration of two legal branches, predominantly laws of armed conflict (known as international humanitarian law, IHL) and international human rights laws (IHRL). These two regimes, although mutually complimentary, advance two systems of protection in accordance with the specific relations of the involved subjects (Droege 2008). There is an ongoing debate about how these two regimes are to be applied to armed conflict situations (Hampson 2008; Sassoli and Olson 2008; Arnold and Quènivet 2008). IHL regulates the conduct of hostilities as well as the status and relations between the parties to the conflict and of third parties (neutral and supporting either of the sides). IHRL focuses on individual rights and duties against the actions of state authorities predominantly in peacetime, but not exclusively.

Whilst both branches of law aim to protect human life, each does it through a specific legal regime. IHRL embraces the individual's right to life which obligates State authorities to ensure the protection of individuals within their jurisdictions. This is representative of a positive obligation in that States should refrain from actions which endanger individual life, even if the person does not actually die. IHL on the other hand provides a regulation on taking human life by all actors in armed conflict as one of the acts of war. IHL dictates that States take certain precautions in order to fulfil obligations to protect the lives of persons, whether combatants or civilians (for instance, civilian evacuations, and public warnings). Both branches of international law foresee a possibility that life will be lawfully taken in certain circumstances, taking into consideration factual conditions of war or peacetime. The fundamental prohibition of arbitrary deprivation of life can be found both in human rights and IHL, the essence and the scope of which the context of armed conflict cannot be examined without IHL as the most suitable framework.

This chapter therefore focuses on primary review of the laws of armed conflict and provides limited but necessary comments on the relevant human rights standards in respect of loss of life by individuals in the course of active hostilities, including the principles of distinction and proportionality. The analysis below is confined to the situation of individuals outside of effective control of the enemy and excludes cases of persons who are in the hands of the enemy or whose liberty has been restricted (deaths in detention). That issue is discussed in the chapter in this book by Susan Breau. The temporal limitation of 'active hostilities' implies that whilst the situations of established control over the territory beyond the national borders, like military occupations, will be outside of the consideration of this chapter but the period of active hostilities on parts of national territory in non-international conflicts may be relevant. This investigation will ascertain the indicators of unlawful conduct which lead to the death of individuals whether protected persons or not. First, the *prima facie* problem of the applicability of IHRL and IHL to situations of armed conflict (Hampson 2008, 552-554) will require a brief commentary.

Applicability of IHRL and IHL in Situations of Armed Conflict

It is established that both IHL and IHRL apply to armed conflict and should be taken into account in the legal consideration of the right to life within armed conflict. IHL treaties often use very similar language, notions and concepts as to those in IHRL, see for example article 3, common to all four Geneva Conventions or specifically articles 27 or 32 Geneva Convention (hereafter GC) IV,[1] article 75 of Additional Protocol I to GCs (hereafter AP I) and article 4-5 of Additional Protocol II to GCs[2] (hereafter AP II). They even mention human rights protections explicitly (e.g. article 72 API or the preamble to AP II) linking the two branches of law (ICRC Commentary, paras 2935, 4371, 4427).

At the heart of the problem are questions of how these two regimes relate to each other in armed conflicts situations (see Hampson 2008). The ICRC Commentary to the Additional Protocols to the GCs implied that in principle:

> the rules of international law on human rights, and in particular the International Covenant on Civil and Political Rights (ICCPR),[3] would be used as a point of reference to bring into focus the fundamental guarantees given in Protocol II for

1 Geneva Convention Relative to the Protection of Civilian Persons in Time of War, Aug. 12, 1949, 75 UNTS 287, 288 [GC IV].

2 Protocol Additional to the Geneva Conventions of 12 August 1949, and Relating to the Protections of Victims of International Armed Conflicts, and Protocol Additional to the Geneva Conventions of 12 August 1949, and relating to the Protection of Victims of Non-International Armed Conflicts (8 June 1977); UN Doc. A/32/144, Annex I, II (1977), reprinted in 16 ILM. 1391 (1977).

3 International Covenant on Civil and Political Rights, Art. 4 (2), G.A. Res. 2200A (XXI), 21 UN GAOR (Supp. No. 16) at 52, UN Doc. A/6316 (December 16, 1966), 999 UNTS 171, entered into force 23 March 1976.

> the way in which human beings should be treated' (ICRC Commentary, para. 4371).

It further suggested that despite being two distinct legal systems, each with its own foundations and mechanisms, the Geneva Conventions and their additional Protocols have the same purpose as the international instruments relating to human rights. The commentary concluded that human rights apply concurrently save for any potential suspensions of human rights in times of public emergency, which threatens the life of a nation and 'only insofar as it is strictly required by exigencies of the situation' (ICRC Commentary, para. 4429). It is noteworthy that IHL does not allow for suspension of its provisions in the course of derogation from the fundamental rights protecting the human person, which guarantee respect for the physical and mental integrity of the person. Under article 5 GC IV humane treatment and fair trial rights are guaranteed even in respect of individuals allegedly involved in acts hostile to the security of the state, in which they are aliens or which is an Occupying Power in the territory of their residence.

Within IHRL some provisions can be derogated from in time of public emergency which threatens the life of the nation (article 4, ICCPR), in time of war or other public emergency threatening the life of the nation (article 15, European Convention on Human Rights (ECHR)), or in time of war, public danger, or other emergency that threatens the independence or security of a state party (article 27, Inter-American Convention on Human Rights).[4] The African Charter on Human and People's Rights of 1981[5] (ACHPR) does not provide for such exclusion and the African Commission on Human and People's Rights confirmed that such derogation was not possible.[6]

The UN Human Rights Committee noted in this context that during armed conflict rules of IHL 'become applicable and help, in addition to the provisions in article 4 and article 5(1) of the Covenant, to prevent the abuse of a State's emergency powers.'[7] In respect of the rights, which can be suspended, the Committee emphasized that 'no measure derogating from the provisions of the Covenant may be inconsistent with the State party's other obligations under international law, particularly the rules of international humanitarian law.'[8] The

4 American Convention on Human Rights, 22 November 1969, OAS Treaty Series No. 36, 1144 UNTS 123.

5 African [Banjul] Charter of Human and People's Rights, Banjul, 27 June 1981; OAU Doc. CAB/LEG/67/3 rev. 5, ILM vol. 21 (1982).

6 *Comission Nationale des Droits de l'Homme et des Libertès v. Chad*, African Commission on Human and Peoples Rights, No. 74/92, Annual Activity Report 1995-1996, para. 21.

7 General Comment No. 29: *States of Emergency (article 4)*: Human Rights Committee, UN Doc. CCPR/C/21/Rev.1/Add.11, 31 August 2001 [General Comment No. 29], para. 3.

8 Ibid., paras 9, 11.

right to life, however, constitutes a part of the irreducible core of human rights, principally a non-derogable right. Article 4(2) of the Covenant explicitly excludes derogation of article 6 of the Covenant (right to life) among others.[9] Indeed, the ECHR is the only human rights treaty to allow a derogation of this right in respect of deaths resulting from lawful acts of war. However, so far, none of the States parties have used that prerogative.[10] The same protective result appears to be ultimately achieved in both regimes.

The International Court of Justice has so far provided us with only rudimentary guidance in relation to the application of the IHL and IHRL. In its Advisory Opinion of 9 July 2004[11] the Court reaffirmed that:

> the protection offered by human rights conventions does not cease in case of armed conflict, save through the effect of provisions for derogation of the kind to be found in Article 4 of the International Covenant on Civil and Political Rights. As regards the relationship between international humanitarian law and human rights law, there are thus three possible situations: some rights may be exclusively matters of international humanitarian law; others may be exclusively matters of human rights law; yet others may be matters of both these branches of international law.[12]

The Court further emphasised that human rights laws would apply in respect of acts by a state in both territories over which a State party has sovereignty and to those over which that State exercises territorial jurisdiction, for example in situations of belligerent occupation.[13] Following this line of argument, two years later the Court observed that both branches outlaw the same conduct.[14] The International Criminal Court for the former Yugoslavia (hereafter ICTY) noted that both branches are mutually complementary. However, the Court warned that 'notions developed in the field of human rights can be transposed in international humanitarian law only if they take into consideration the specificities of the latter body of law.'[15]

The position of the regional human rights bodies has not been uniform. The American Commission on Human Rights promoted a view that the provisions of IHL generally furnish victims of armed conflict with greater or more specific

---

9 Ibid., para. 7.

10 Convention for the Protection of Human Rights and Fundamental Freedoms 4 November 1950, Council of Europe, European Treaty Series No. 5. [ECHR], Article 15(2).

11 *Legal Consequences of the Construction of a Wall in the Occupied Palestinian Territory, Advisory Opinion* (9 July 2004), 2004 I.C.J. Rep. 163 [*Wall*].

12 Ibid., para. 106.

13 Ibid., para. 110.

14 Case concerning Armed Activities on the Territory of the Congo, 19 December 2005, 2005 ICJ Rep. 116 [DRC v. Uganda], para. 220.

15 *The Prosecutor v. Kunarac*, IT-96-23-T, ICTY , Judgment of 22 February 2001, paras 467, 471.

protections than the human rights guarantees,[16] which were not designed to regulate warfare but to prevent the occurrence of the violence. The American Court of Human Rights explicitly[17] and European Court of Human Rights implicitly found themselves unwilling or unable to adjudicate in consideration of laws of armed conflict, even in cases which related to ongoing non-international armed conflicts (for more comprehensive consideration see, Hampson 2008, 564). They both concluded the respective human rights conventions furnished them with the sufficient framework to pronounce judgments, particularly where the intentional and unintentional deprivation of life was a subject matter. These will be discussed in more detail below.

Right to Life – Specific Application

The general modalities of the applicability of both branches of law in situations of armed conflict remain unresolved. This chapter does not purport to set out the issue comprehensively, instead it aims to offer a brief reminder of the issues at stake and how they may affect the protection of human life in armed conflicts. In this context the International Court of Justice held:

> [t]he Court observes that the protection of the International Covenant of Civil and Political Rights does not cease in times of war, except by operation of Article 4 of the Covenant whereby certain provisions may be derogated from in a time of national emergency. Respect for the right to life is not, however, such a provision. In principle, the right not arbitrarily to be deprived of one's life applies also in hostilities. The test of what is an arbitrary deprivation of life, however, then falls to be determined by the applicable *lex specialis*, namely, the law applicable in armed conflict which is designed to regulate the conduct of hostilities. Thus whether a particular loss of life, through the use of a certain weapon in warfare, is to be considered an arbitrary deprivation of life contrary to Article 6 of the Covenant, can only be decided by reference to the law applicable in armed conflict and not deduced from the terms of the Covenant itself.[18]

This principle reads as follows: *lex specialis derogat legi generali*, which requires the more specific law to take precedence over the more general regulation. It has been principally thought to help resolve conflicts between the two norms (Pauwelyn

---

16 *Abella v. Argentina (la Tablada),* 18 November 1997, Inter-American Commission of Human Rights, Case No. 11.137, Report N° 55/97, OEA/Ser.L/V/II.95 Doc. 7 rev. at 271 [*Abella v. Argentina*] paras 159, 161.

17 *Les Palmeras v. Colombia*, 2001, Inter-American Court of Human Rights, Judgment of 6 December 2001, Ser. C, No. 90, para. 33.

18 *Advisory Opinion on the Legality of the Threat or Use of Nuclear Weapons, International Court of Justice* (ICJ), 8 July 1996, 1996 ICJ Reports [Nuclear Weapons Opinion], para. 25.

2003, 385). It remains unclear whether this is the only permitted application of this principle or whether, in the event of absence of conflict between the norms, a more specific rule should prevail (creating an order of preference) or displace the more general law (Hampson 2008, 558).

Utilising the *lex specialis* principle, the ICJ implied that there might not be complementarity between the two sets of norms mandating the protection of life, but also additionally, certain points of inconsistency. Should any of those situations arise, priority should be given to IHL. Although what this suggested hierarchy means in practice for the international and in particular human rights bodies, continues to be debated. Bearing in mind the proposition that both branches apply to the same situation in parallel, one conclusion might be that violation of arbitrary killing under IHL must be determined for the human rights body to also establish a violation of the right to life in the human rights framework. Such synergistic supposition is plausible for this particular subject-matter, even though it may be inadequate for others (Hampson 2008, 560). Understanding what constitutes arbitrary killing in view of IHL will be therefore essential to the analysis (ibid.).

Arbitrary Killing in IHL

The laws of armed conflict in principle provide two different sets of standards applicable in various types of conflicts. The above general analysis distinguished between the situations of inter-state conflicts and non-international armed conflicts (NIACs), with the latter recognising two sub-types of conflicts (Common article 3 to GCs type and AP II type). The level of protection of life will not only vary between the conflicts but also within the same conflict between the kinds of sources of law, namely between the treaty regulation and relevant customary law, a state of affairs which is particularly pronounced in non-international armed conflicts. It is noteworthy that there could be situations in which we deal with simultaneous or overlapping circumstances characterised by all types of conflicts. Particularly in the latter occurrence, one of the special characteristics of IHL becomes of crucial importance. The laws of armed conflict bind not only the warring States but also non-state actors (NSA) fighting with the State or another non-State armed group. This rule is related to the operation of the principle of equality between the belligerents, which builds-in certain legal incentives for all the parties to respect IHL in order to protect the lives of those affected by the hostilities. The subsequent paragraphs shall examine both the permissible and prohibitory norms in relation to the protection of life.

Combatants' Right to Kill

In international armed conflicts (common article 2 to GCs, article 1 AP I) the law divides persons into two categories. For these categories the principle of distinction constitutes a fundamental rule of law of international armed conflict (LOIAC) and it is enshrined in article 48 of Additional Protocol I applicable to the situations of international conflicts as a 'basic' rule:

> [i]n order to ensure respect for and protection of the civilian population and civilian objects, the Parties to the conflict shall at all times distinguish between the civilian population and combatants and between civilian objects and military objectives and accordingly shall direct their operations only against military objectives.

This basic rule of distinction has been acknowledged to constitute one of the two 'cardinal' customary principles of the law of armed conflict in the ICJ's Advisory Opinion on the Legality of the Threat or Use of Nuclear Weapons already mentioned earlier,[19] which is recognised as a cornerstone for the entire system of international humanitarian law (ICRC Commentary para. 1863). The principle is unquestionably a norm in customary IHL.

It flows from the principle that civilians and civilian population comprising of all persons who are civilian are subject to protection. AP I defines negatively civilians as those who do not belong to the following categories:

> (1) members of the armed forces of a Party to the conflict as well as members of militias or volunteer corps forming part of such armed forces;
>
> (2) members of other militias and members of other volunteer corps, including those of organized resistance movements, belonging to a Party to the conflict and operating in or outside their own territory, even if this territory is occupied, provided that such militias or volunteer corps, including such organized resistance movements, fulfil the following conditions:
>
> (a) that of being commanded by a person responsible for his subordinates;
> (b) that of having a fixed distinctive sign recognizable at a distance;
> (c) that of carrying arms openly;
> (d) that of conducting their operations in accordance with the laws and customs of war;
>
> (3) members of regular armed forces who profess allegiance to a government or an authority not recognized by the Detaining Power; and
>
> (4) inhabitants of a non-occupied territory, who on the approach of the enemy spontaneously take up arms to resist the invading forces, without having had time to form themselves into regular armed units, provided they carry arms openly and respect the laws and customs of war (article 4 A (1), (2), (3) and (6) GC III in relation to article 50 AP I).

19 *Nuclear Weapons Opinion*, para. 78.

Article 43 AP I, customary in character, further specifies that members of the armed forces consist of all organised armed forces, groups or units, which are under a command responsible to that Party for the conduct of its subordinates, are subject to an internal disciplinary system which is designed to enforce compliance with LOIAC. All the listed categories above are granted a status of combatants, *a contrario* to civilians as per rule of distinction. It is noteworthy that the status of combatants is granted exceptionally to civilians in cases of *levée en masse* as indicated in point 4 above (see also the customary in nature article 2 of Annex to Hague Convention IV).[20]

In essence, there are three groups of combatants. First, the fighting members of armed forces (in overwhelming majority), with exclusion of medical (article 13.2.a API), and religious personnel (article 65.3 API) or military personnel assigned to civil protection agencies (article 67.1(d) API). Even though medical personnel can be lightly armed for self-defence or defence of their patients, they are not considered combatants so long as they do not engage in fighting. Although they remain members of the armed forces, they are not engaged in fighting and must not be targeted but in practice they take a greater risk of being affected by hostilities because of their function and presence on the battlefield. Second, the group of individuals recognised as combatants consists of paramilitary groups incorporated into armed forces (usually under Ministry of Defence) discharging both peace (police) and war-time (military) functions, such as the Gendarmerie forces in France or the Carabinieri in Italy. Their incorporation into the armed forces should be notified to the opposing state (article 43.3 AP I).

Thirdly, article 4 GC III mentions militias in the context of combatant status prescribing four conditions to be recognised as combatants. Non-state organised militias must be organised in a way that shows hierarchy and structure allowing for accountability. They must furthermore show their arms openly and wear an emblem (a uniform or armband) visible from a distance in order to distinguishing themselves from civilians. Last but not least they must respect the laws and customs of war as a group (article 1 Annex to Hague Convention IV). Violations of rules by a few members only would not deprive the group of their respect for IHL. However, a pattern of repeated and/or widespread atrocities committed by numerous members of the militia may indicate a lack of compliance. Accordingly, during World War II the organisation known as Free French forces (French: *Forces Françaises Libres*) would clearly satisfy the test due to their organisation and subordinate structure, but the French resistance movement or partisans would not, as it did not display a sufficiently organised hierarchy. Compliance with laws and customs of war is proving the hardest to satisfy for the various militant formations in recent years. Operations of the IRA in Northern Ireland, Fedayeen Saddam militia in Iraq as well as Hezbullah forces in Lebanon show a degree of disregard

20 *Regulations concerning the Laws and Customs of War on Land*, The Hague, 18 October 1907: Annex to the Convention (IV) Respecting the Laws and Customs of War on Land, 18 October 1907 reprinted in Schindler and Toman (2004).

for the IHL (e.g. direct attacks against civilians), thereby making it impossible to consider such forces as combatants under humanitarian law. Distinction from civilians is another marker which has been challenged recently. In the initial stages of the Afghanistan engagement, Taliban forces were said to have not distinguished themselves sufficiently from the civilian population. Although the overall dress of the Taliban was similar to that of civilians in Afghanistan, they wore a distinguishing head covering. The legal condition does not require the whole special uniform to exist; a distinctive cap, or a hand band worn openly and at all times would suffice. It is worth mentioning though here that sometimes even combatants (not militia or other organised groups aspiring to be recognised as combatants) do not clearly distinguish themselves from civilians, which may have legal repercussions. Article 44 API stipulates that a combatant (so s/he is assumed already to possess that *prima facie* status) must distinguish him/herself, at the very latest, while they are engaging in an attack. Failing to do so, he/she shall forfeit combatant status (and consequently also Prisoner of War status if captured). The provision simply allows a combatant to reveal him/herself at a significantly later stage than it was accepted in the past but in the process it has increased the risk to civilians' safety. Some states, because of the controversy around this increased risk to the protection of civilians, decided to limit the application and possible scope of this Article to the situations of occupation and others regulated by article 1.4 AP I (e.g. UK's declaration of 1998).

What a state may identify as its military forces, or as part of its forces, can change during a conflict so that the militia originally not recognised as combatants can subsequently gain this status. When the militia satisfy this threshold test in conflict, its members gain a right to fight and therefore a freedom from being prosecuted for the mere act of fighting whilst they still may face any potential charges of violations of the laws and customs of war.

The status of combatant comes with both advantages and risks. Combatants have a privilege to and a right to fight. Whilst they are taking part in hostilities, they are entitled to kill other combatants or launch attacks, which may result also in potential civilian casualties. Combatants can be lawfully killed anytime and anywhere irrespective of what they are doing until they are captured and/or rendered *hors de combat* (article 41 API), when their life should be protected and respected in accordance to the requirements of Prisoners of War status (which violation would constitute a grave breach of wilful killing regulated in article 130 GC III,[21] article 8.2(b)(vi) of Rome Statute of International Criminal Court,[22] hereafter ICC Statute). Combatants considered to be military objectives can be attacked even if they pose no threat to an adversary. The law vests all combatants with equal entitlement to fire at an enemy combatant. Equality of all parties to the

---

21 Geneva Convention Relative to the Treatment to Prisoners of War, 12 August 1949, 75 UNTS. 135, 136 [GC III].

22 Rome Statute of International Criminal Court, A/CONF.183/9 of 17 July 1998, entered into force 1 July 2002 [ICC Statute].

conflict will require that all warring parties accept this increased risk of losing their lives as an understandable limitation required by the nature of armed conflict.

The 2003 intervention in Iraq saw an increase in decapitation strikes against the Iraqi leadership (Human Rights Watch 2003). Decapitation attacks are aimed at removing vital command and control infrastructure, consisting both of human structures including the top ranking commanders as well as the physical facilities. Whether or not a head of state, national leaders or other politically engaged figures shall be targeted, will depend on their status. This is assessed according to the rules presented earlier. It will have to be established whether such person is involved in the military operation and if so, to what extent. More often than not national leaders are also supreme commanders of the armed forces of the state. They are not only members of the armed forces but also exercise some operational (or even tactical) functions. Some leaders are furnished only with general strategic decision making roles or even purely representative. More practically involved individuals may be regarded as directly engaged in hostilities; on the other hand, areas of indirect involvement or oversight (e.g. intelligence agencies or Parliamentary control of military spending) should be approached with caution as it may be seen as a step beyond the established delimitation between combatants and civilians. Similar questions are being posed in respect of employees of various Private Security Companies or Private Military Companies, who are employed to perform military functions but not to fight. Assessment of their conduct and related status would depend on a number of factors including their function, their relation to the military forces, their mandate or sources of funding. All of these will be a necessary consideration for the identification of the extent of their involvement in the conflict.

An ultimate aim, which States should endeavour to accomplish during war, is to weaken the military forces of the enemy, as identified in the St Petersburg Declaration of 1868.[23] However, such weakening of the military forces should not be achieved by the arbitrary killings of combatants. If the law finds certain methods or means of warfare as unlawful, then logically the deaths resulting from such prohibited conduct should be construed as unlawful. These are deaths resulting from certain outlawed acts of the enemy, such as refusal of quarter (article 23(c) Annex to Hague Convention IV, articles 12 of GCI and GCII, article 41 API, also regarded as a customary norm – see Rule 46 of *Customary International Humanitarian Law*, hereafter CIHL), perfidy (articles 23(b)(e)(f) and 24 Annex to Hague Convention IV, articles 5(3)(f) and 37 API, Rule 65 CIHL) or using any other prohibited means or method of warfare. In particular, a fatal use of weapons causing superfluous injury or unnecessary suffering against combatants would be regarded as contrary to the law (article 23(c) Annex to Hague Convention IV, article 35(2) API, Rule 70 CIHL). This stems from the underlying principle of humanity,

23 Declaration Renouncing the Use, in Time of War, of Explosive Projectiles Under 400 Grammes Weight. St Petersburg, 29 November/11 December 1868 [St Petersburg Declaration of 1868].

which requires minimising unnecessary suffering of combatants and incidental injury to civilians in armed conflict. The ICC Statute confirms for example that use of bullets which expand (or flatten) easily in the human body, like dum-dum bullets in IACs are prohibited and deaths resulting from their use would be considered a war crime (article 8.2 (b) (xix) and see also more general provision in this context article 8.2 (b) (xx)). It is also illegal to use certain gases, substances or devices as means of warfare, which cause death through toxic or asphyxiating properties against all protected persons. In the same context of international armed conflict, the ICC Statute also asserts a war crime for the killing of persons belonging to the adverse party resulting from a perfidious conduct (article 8.2 (b) (xi)).

Perfidy is a form of deception, in which one side invites the confidence of the adversary by resorting to rely on an apparently protective status, which the adversary must respect, with an intention to betray this confidence as soon as the enemy exposes himself and loses previous military advantage. Imagine a combatant, who pretends he is wounded (or is willing to surrender) and when the enemy soldiers are approaching his position, he opens fire at them. Any deaths of the enemy soldiers resulting from this treacherous act will be unlawful. IHL unconditionally prohibits killings (or even a capture) of the adversary resulting from any perfidious acts. The events leading to the Srebrenica massacre are considered as an example of perfidious acts. The Bosnian Serb military forces, wearing stolen UN uniforms and driving UN vehicles managed to convince several Bosnian Muslim men to surrender as they would be offered UN protection. Instead, they were all killed.

Civilians

Article 50 API identifies the protective status of civilians through the operation of the principle of distinction. Civilians not engaged in the hostilities should be protected from the dangers arising from military operations (article 51.1 AP I). To this end the law secures a number of protections consisting of the precautions to be taken before and during attacks as well as prohibition of indiscriminate attacks, provisions regarding weapons choices and proportionality and responsibilities which should be taken by the defending party in order to protect the civilian populations from the hostilities (articles 51, 52, 57 and 58 AP I, in most parts established as customary norms).

As a rule, civilians, who are not directly participating in hostilities, must not be the subjects of direct attack, and any deaths resulting from a direct intentional attack on them could be construed as arbitrary killings. Article 51.2 API clearly demands that 'the civilian population as such, as well as individual civilians, shall not be the object of attack.' Article 85 of API asserts that wilfully making the civilian population or individual civilians the object of attack constitutes a grave breach of API (article 85. 3(a) API, see also article 8.2 (b) (i) of ICC Statute). Deaths occurring in the course of indiscriminate attack are also construed as arbitrary (article 85.3 (b) API). 'Indiscriminate attack' defines principally three situations of attack against military objectives, civilians or civilian objects without distinction, which:

(a) are not directed at a specific military objective;
(b) employ a method or means of combat which cannot be directed at a specific military objective; or
(c) those which employ a method or means of combat the effects of which cannot be limited (article 51.4 AP I).

Furthermore, indiscriminate attacks are also those which even if directed against legitimate military targets occur in circumstances where an attack either is executed by means and methods which treat as a single military objective a number of clearly separated and distinct military objectives within a concentration of civilian population (article 51.5(b) API) and which may be expected to cause incidental loss of civilian life, injury to civilians, damage to civilian objects, or a combination thereof, which would be excessive in relation to the concrete and direct military advantage anticipated (article 51.5 (a) API). The term 'means of combat' or 'means of warfare' generally identifies the weapons being used, while the expression 'methods of combat' generally means the way in which such weapons are used or in general employed tactics. In relation to the latter, starvation used as a method of war against civilians is regarded as unlawful (article 54 API, article 8.2. (b)(xxv) ICC Statute).

IHL regulates not only civilian deaths stemming from direct attacks but also from indirect ones if the losses are excessive in relation to the concrete and direct military advantage anticipated from the attack. This is the principle of proportionality. This implies intentional attacks against military objectives, which entail both foreseen and unintended collateral civilian casualties. The law requires the military to evaluate the undesired and desired likely consequences. If the undesired ones are excessive in proportion to the desired ones the attack cannot be carried out (article 57 API) and if carried out it will be considered indiscriminate (article 51.5 (b) API). The ICC Statute affirms responsibility both of those who direct an intentional attack against civilians and who launch an attack (so not only those who execute it but also who plan the operation) with knowledge that attack would cause excessive incidental deaths and injury to civilians or damage to civilian objects (article 8.2 (b)(iv). Both distinction and proportionality are further stressed in the precautionary measures the attacker is obliged to undertake during planning and execution of attacks. Timely verification of the targets based on the updates and multisource intelligence will be crucial. An attack must be cancelled or suspended if the previously accounted for circumstances change and by this, affect the lawfulness of the attacks (article 57 API).

Driven by the embedded principle of humanity, a requirement is given regarding the choice of employed means and methods. An attacker should take all feasible precautions with the view to avoid or to minimise incidental loss of life. If there is a choice between several military objectives yielding a similar military advantage, the attacks should be carried out against objectives possibly resulting in lesser danger to civilian lives and property. Similarly weapons in attack should be chosen with a view of avoiding or minimising incidental loss of civilian life and damage to civilian property. Attacks will be indiscriminate and thus unlawful if the means or methods of combat employed during them could not be directed against the specific military objective or the effects of which cannot be limited (article 51.4 API). Some weapons are explicitly prohibited because they are of an indiscriminate nature, for instance, nuclear or bacteriological weapons. If the weapon is not capable of being limited in terms of its impact horizontally, then its use may cause a disproportionate number of casualties, and thus be identified as illegitimate. In effect, a ban on inherently indiscriminate weapons follows logically from the proportionality requirement. In this context, use of asphyxiating gases in international armed conflicts was first outlawed as early as 1925.[24] However, it has since been questioned whether this prohibition includes non-lethal uses of gas, because the use of gas as a riot control agent is permitted in peacetime. The nature of conflict has changed and there are circumstances in which gas can be useful as a method of crowd control. Protocol III to 1980 Convention on Certain Conventional Weapons (CCW),[25] also applicable to NIACs, prohibits in all circumstances the attack on civilians through the use of incendiary weapons, and to attack any military objective located within a concentration of civilians by air-delivered incendiary weapons (article 2 CCW). Ground delivered incendiaries against non-personnel military targets are not prohibited. Incendiary weapons include weapons or munitions which are primarily designed to set fire to objects or to cause burn injury to persons through the action of flame, heat, or combination thereof. Examples of such weapons are grenades, rockets, and bombs.

In this context there has been a sharp increase in the use of white phosphorous weapons in recent conflicts. White phosphorous is a spontaneously flammable chemical used for battlefield illumination, it has been deployed in Iraq (the 'shake and bake' operations during the Fallujah battle) or by Israel in both the 2006 conflict in Lebanon and just recently in the 2009 offensive against the Hamas fighters in Gaza. Sometimes it is not the nature of the weapon, but the way it is used, which renders an indiscriminate application. Cluster weapons represent another type of this controversial means of warfare, only recently regulated by the 2008 Oslo Convention. They were used during World War II, as well as more recently in NATO operations against Serbia in 1999, for the 7 May 1999 attack on Nis airport, where due to an alleged malfunction of the weapon it missed the target, and scattered cluster munitions over a market and hospital. In Afghanistan in the

24 Protocol for the Prohibition of the Use of Asphyxiating, Poisonous or Other Gases, and of Bacteriological Methods of Warfare. Geneva, 17 June 1925.

25 Convention on Prohibitions or Restrictions on the Use of Certain Conventional Weapons Which May be Deemed to be Excessively Injurious or to Have Indiscriminate Effects, Geneva, 10 October 1980 [CCW] and Protocol III on the Prohibitions or restrictions on the Use of Incendiary Weapons, 10 October 1980.

October 2001 attack near Qala Shalter village, again due to an apparent errant bomb, the cluster bomblets were delivered in civilian areas. They were extensively used in 2003 in Iraq, and in 2006 in Southern Lebanon, and recently in the 2008 conflict in South Ossetia. Cluster weapons can create a multitude of problems for civilians, both during conflict, and even acutely afterwards, as unexploded landmines are left behind, but they cannot be regarded as indiscriminate in nature. Cluster weapons, when used in strikes against the military objectives located away from the centres of the civilian population, are capable (in their design) of being delivered only against those targets. Imagine an attack on a military base, where there are twenty military vehicles parked in a relatively defined space. Using cluster munitions in one strike would be much more effective than executing several strikes to destroy each vehicle separately. However, problems occur when such weapons are deployed against military objectives not clearly separated from the civilian population centres. The levels of damage to civilian infrastructure and that of the civilian casualties may often indicate that compliance with the proportionality principle has been put in jeopardy. The 2008 Oslo Convention introduced a total ban on the use, production and stockpiling of cluster munitions. At the time of writing this chapter 14 states have ratified the Convention and time will tell if the fully restrictive, total ban on the use of cluster munitions will be accepted by the wider international community.

The obligations in the law of targeting rest not only on those identifying the target but also on those targeted. IHL vests defending states with legal duties to protect civilians against the dangers of hostilities. These obligations require long term peacetime planning and should be feasibly implemented. Precautionary measures in defence include avoiding location of any new military objectives in densely populated areas as well as any other measures including providing shelters, enforcement of blackout, evacuation of the civilian population, emergency services, broadcasting warnings and fencing minefields (article 58 API). This protection is vital, especially to prevent cases where civilians are deliberately placed in danger.

The use of human shields, as prohibited by article 51.7 API will be particularly pertinent in this context as one must remember that the mere presence of civilians does not transform a military objective into a civilian and therefore protected object. We can identify two types of human shields, namely civilians forcefully enrolled into combat engagements (involuntary human shields) and those who volunteer to take part. Involuntary human shields, who happen to find themselves participating against their will in hostilities, need to be taken into account in the proportionality calculus by the attacker, following the requirements of general protection of civilian population. This is, however, not necessarily applicable to the individuals who volunteer to secure the military objectives. Forced contribution to the military effort may involve, among other things, acting as the messengers, transporting military equipment, cooking for troops, acting as a sniper or walking in front of the soldiers to warn the neighbours of possible military attack. Those who decide to offer themselves as shields take a risk of losing their lives during an attack, which might not be necessarily unlawful. Even more so, their conduct can be construed as direct participation in hostilities, in which circumstance the law deprives them of immunity from direct attack and they may face prosecution simply for unlawfully taking arms in addition to any potential war crimes.[26]

Direct Participants in Hostilities (DPH)

Regarding civilian persons, the extent of the protection will depend to some degree on what the civilian does or how s/he acts during hostilities. Civilian workers in military objects or working with military forces, but not performing military functions, retain civilian status, but at the same time are more exposed to being hit during an attack on military targets. Normally, loss of their lives would not be regarded as a violation of IHL.

Civilians can by their own actions lose protection from a direct attack for such time as they engage in hostilities. They do not possess a privilege or right to fight. What happens to a civilian who starts fighting? Whilst losing elements of the protection resulting from the status (immunity from attack), s/he retains his/her civilian status. Civilians only lose their status by joining the armed forces (becoming a fighting member of the armed forces). IHL uses the term 'directly (or 'actively') participating in hostilities' both in the context of international (article 51.3 PAI) and non-international armed conflicts (common article 3 to GCs and article 4.1 APII). Understanding this term will be particularly crucial in NIACs, where the concept of combatancy does not arise (although some commentators argue it does implicitly, see Gaggioli and Kolb 2007, 145).

What is meant by participation? Does selling medicine or showing sympathy to fighters constitute direct participation? How direct is direct? It seems, after a long period of debate among international experts some guidance in this respect is emerging, not without controversy. An illustration of this is the example of Bob, a civilian truck driver (Rogers 2004, 10). He drives an oil truck with fuel for the military and whilst the truck is a valid military objective, if struck and Bob ends up dead, it would not *prima facie* be an unlawful killing. However can Bob be directly targeted? If so, when? Bob decides to stop for petrol and a cup of tea in the petrol station. Can he still be targeted or only when he gets back to the truck? The example illustrates a problem otherwise known as 'farmer by day, fighter by night', describing in shorthand the revolving door syndrome. The problem is acute in cases when people are rotating in and out of direct participation in hostilities and this makes it very difficult for the armed forces to correctly assess not only the substance and degree of the individual conduct, but also to identify whether it is legal to apprehend or kill the individual.

26 *The Public Committee against Torture in Israel v. The Government of Israel*, Israeli Supreme Court HCJ 769/02, Judgment of 13 December 2006 [Targeted killings], para. 36.

The Israeli Supreme Court has implied that if a civilian is driving ammunition to a place where it will be used for the purposes of attack, he should be seen as taking a direct part in the hostilities. The court made a distinction in stating that:

> a person who collects intelligence on the army, whether on issues regarding the hostilities…or beyond those issues…a person who transports unlawful combatants to or from the place where the hostilities are taking place; a person who operates weapons which unlawful combatants use, or supervises their operation, or provides service to them, be the distance from the battlefield as it may. All those persons are performing the function of combatants. The function determines the directness of the part taken in the hostilities.
>
> However, a person who sells food or medicine to an unlawful combatant is not taking a direct part, rather an indirect part in the hostilities. The same is the case regarding a person who aids the unlawful combatants by general strategic analysis, and grants them logistical, general support, including monetary aid. The same is the case regarding a person who distributes propaganda supporting those unlawful combatants.[27]

Furthermore, the Inter-American Commission on Human Rights indicated that participation would usually include acts which by their nature or purpose are intended to cause damage to enemy personnel or materiel. It also confirmed that activity would consist of preparation, execution and return from the violent engagement.[28] The ICRC guidance concerning an interpretation of the concept of direct participants in hostilities proposes a 'conduct' (as opposed to 'membership') approach, whereby the analysed factual circumstances refers to specific acts carried out by individuals as a part of conduct of hostilities between the parties to an armed conflict (ICRC Guidance, 2009, Recommendation IV). It establishes three constitutive elements:

> a. The act must be likely to adversely affect the military operations or military capacity of a party to an armed conflict or, alternatively, to inflict death, injury, or destruction on persons or objects protected against direct attack (threshold of harm), and
> b. there must be a direct causal link between the act and the harm likely to result either from that act, or from a coordinated military operation of which that act constitutes an integral part (direct causation), and

---

27 Ibid., para. 35.

28 Inter-American Commission on Human Rights, *Third Report on Human Rights in Columbia*, 1999, available at: http://www.cidh.oas.org/countryrep/colom99en/introduction.htm [accessed on: 29 July 2009] [1999 Report on Columbia], paras 53-57.

c. the act must be specifically designed to directly cause the required threshold of harm in support of a party to the conflict and to the detriment of another (belligerent nexus) (ICRC Guidance, 2009 Recommendation V).

Specifically in regard to NIACs, the Guidance additionally introduced a notion new in legal terminology of a 'continuous combat function.' Continuous combat function apparently relates to the individuals whose continuous function it is to take a direct part in hostilities and who belong to organised armed groups which constitute the armed forces of a non-state party to the conflict (ICRC Guidance, 2009 Recommendation II). This implies reverting from the conduct approach to the membership approach, whereby membership is based on the performance of the continuous combat function, which requires lasting integration into an organised armed group acting as the armed forces of a non-State party to an armed conflict (ICRC Guidance, 2009, 27-36). It is implied that such a function can be inferred from the conclusive conduct or openly expressed through the carrying of uniforms, distinctive signs, or certain weapons. There are a number of problems with this approach. For example, how does it identify a lasting integration into armed groups and when/how does it cease? What about the issue of forceful integration into forces? Also the weapons are not specified and whether their lack of use for fighting would warrant an attack on the person. In Afghanistan or Iraq owning and carrying a weapon is not a definite sign of participation in hostilities. It remains unclear from the commentary when and how a person disassociates him/herself actively from such function, whether this would entail some kind of affirmative action for opting out or whether the passing of time in inactivity would suffice.

This discussion around the notion of direct participation is vital to the determination of the rules of targeting rebel fighters. The ICRC Commentary to article 13.3 APII dealing with the aforementioned standard of DPH, indicates that 'those who belong to armed forces or armed groups may be attacked at any time' (ICRC Commentary, para. 4789). Would this suggest that in NIACs there is an identified standard for the rebel 'combatants'? A standard which is set around membership or belonging to a rebel group or rather 'continuous combat function,' as identified in the ICRC Guidance on one hand, and on the other hand a standard for any other civilian, based on the particular conduct of the individuals? Would this ultimately aid the military to conduct their operations without uncertainty concerning whether and when they can target the enemy in NIACs and in turn, shed some more light on what would be regarded as 'arbitrary' killing in such conflicts?

Rules on Conduct of Hostilities in NIACs

As mentioned above, treaty rules in internal and non-international armed conflicts regarding broader protection of the lives of civilians are not as extensive as the ones available in inter-state wars. Common article 3 to the four Geneva Conventions of 1949 does not address conduct against persons who are directly and actively participating in armed conflict. Civilians and those who are no longer participating are protected against violence to life, including murder of all kinds (article 3.1 (a), common to the GCs). When assessing criminal responsibility the ICTY defined murder as acts or omission leading to a death of victim, committed with the intention to kill or to cause serious bodily harm, which the perpetrator should have reasonably have known might result in death.[29] It further concluded that in substance the elements of the offence of murder are similar to those which define 'wilful killing', grave breach of GCs, with an exception to the category of victims, who are under common article 3 limited to those not participating in hostilities.[30]

Article 13 of AP II stipulates a general requirement of protection of the civilian population and individual civilians against the dangers arising from military operations and includes an absolute prohibition from making them an object of attack (see also article 8.2(e) ICC Statute). In respect of the former, that implies reducing the effects of military operations which could affect protected persons, requires that safety measures are taken both by the party launching the attack, bearing in mind the means available to it, during the planning, decision and action stages of the attack, and by the party that is attacked (ICRC Commentary, paras. 4771-72). Such measures entail prohibition of indiscriminate attacks, application of a proportionality principle, and the precautionary measures in attack and in defence. This is required by the general principles relating to the protection of the civilian population, which find their origin in the principle of distinction, applicable irrespective of whether the conflict is an international or an internal one. Principles of distinction, proportionality and humanity, after all, are considered as constituting 'cardinal principles contained in the texts constituting the fabric of humanitarian law' and 'intransgressible principle[s] of customary law.'[31] However, without specified and established details of distinction between the protected civilians and unprotected persons in NIAC, the practical application of the proportionality principle in NIACs will face difficulties.

Progressively a number of treaties regulating or banning weapons, which apply in NIACs has been developed (e.g. Conventional Weapons Convention and its Protocols, Ottawa Convention on Landmines,[32] Oslo 2008 Cluster Munitions Convention).[33] The ICTY, in their rational decision in 1995, advised that a weapon

29 *Prosecutor v. Kristic*, Case No. IT-98-33, ICTY (Trial Chamber), Judgment of 2 Aug. 2001, para. 485.

30 *Prosecutor v. Kordic and Cerkez*, Case No. IT-95-14/2 (Trial Chamber), Judgment of 26 Feb.2001, para. 233, *Prosecutor v. Brdjanin*, Case No. IT-99-36-T (Trial Chamber), Judgment of 1 September 2004 para. 381.

31 *Nuclear Weapons Opinion*, paras 78-79.

32 Convention on the Prohibition of the Use, Stockpiling, Production and Transfer of Anti-Personnel Mines and on their Destruction, 18 September 1997, entered into force on 1 March 1999.

33 Convention on Cluster Munitions, adopted in Dublin on 30 May 2008, not yet in force.

which is causing superfluous injury or unnecessary suffering in IACs will do exactly the same in any other conflict – 'what is inhumane, and consequently proscribed, in international wars, cannot but be inhumane and inadmissible in civil strife.'[34] The nature of armed conflict or its type is irrelevant to the rules on weapons. They focus on the harm caused by such means. If a weapon is causing unnecessary suffering and superfluous injuries or is indiscriminate in one conflict, the same weapon is bound to cause same effects or have same properties in any other conflict. Indeed, as stated earlier, there seems to be developing a body of customary international humanitarian law applicable in non-international armed conflicts (e.g. Rules 6-24 CIHL). They could be summarised to enshrine the principle to use the minimum force required to harm the enemy, the principle of distinction and the principle of proportionality which only is applied when it is not possible to ensure the total protection of the civilian population. These rules largely mirror the customary law norms applicable in international armed conflicts, yet without addressing in much detail the practical deficiencies in the implementation of the principle of distinction and its derivatives in NIACs.

IHL and Human Rights Bodies

In the context of the protection of life, human rights bodies have dealt predominantly with cases related to internal or otherwise non-international armed conflicts. The Inter-American Commission on Human Rights in the *Plan de Sanchez Massacre* case in Guatemala in 1999,[35] as well as UN Human Rights Committee in *Camargo v. Columbia*[36] considered arbitrary killing in NIACs. Both cases engaged with IHL, with the Inter-American Commission case concerning a direct attack on civilians, not participating in hostilities by military forces of the State. The Human Rights Committee case considered an intentional attack on persons who were suspected members of a guerrilla organisation. The Commission concluded that the death of the seven victims was an arbitrary killing because they were not given an opportunity to surrender and it was not established that any of them had actually engaged in any acts of violence.[37] The Commission did not address the question of the alleged guerrilla membership or DPH as it applied a standard of capture/arrest when possible before engaging lethal force. In another case, *Abella v. Argentina,* the Commission was concerned with an attack of 42 armed persons on the military barracks located at La Tablada, which lasted approximately 30 hours and resulted

34 *The Prosecutor v. Tadic*, Case No. IT-94-1, ICTY (Appeals Chamber) Decision on the Defence Motion for Interlocutory Appeal on Jurisdiction of 2 October 1995, para. 119.

35 *Plan de Sanchez Massacre v. Guatemala*, Inter-American Court of Human Rights, Judgment of 29 April 2004 (Ser. C).

36 *Camargo v. Columbia*, 1985, Human Rights Committee, Communication No. 45/1979, UN Doc. CCPR/C/OP/1 at 112.

37 Ibid., para. 13.

in the deaths of 29 of the attackers and several state agents. During the siege, the attackers further seized a number of weapons from the arsenal located on the base, which they used to defend their positions. The case further related to the violations of law which occurred after the actual attack, and the analysis of the position of persons during the actual attack is particularly interesting. The Commission, taking the IHL concept of distinction on board, noted:

> [s]pecifically, when civilians, such as those who attacked the Tablada base, assume the role of combatants by directly taking part in fighting, whether singly or as a member of a group, they thereby become legitimate military targets. As such, they are subject to direct individualized attack to the same extent as combatants. Thus, by virtue of their hostile acts, the Tablada attackers lost the benefits of the above mentioned precautions in attack and against the effects of indiscriminate or disproportionate attacks pertaining to peaceable civilians. In contrast, these humanitarian law rules continued to apply in full force with respect to those peaceable civilians present or living in the vicinity of the La Tablada base at the time of the hostilities.[38]

The Commission recognised a full obligation of both parties to the conflict '…to conduct their military operations within the restraints and prohibitions imposed by applicable humanitarian law rules.'[39]

The European Court of Human Rights has considered cases arising from the conflict in Northern Ireland,[40] in Turkey,[41] and in Russia in the conflict in Chechnya.[42] These involved issues of indiscriminate attacks, precautions in attack, necessity and proportionality of force, or choice of weapons (see Gaggioli and Kolb, 2007, 139-143 and Quènivet, 2008, 336-352). Even though the Court might have arrived at similar results in respect of protections granted to the individuals under IHL, it always framed it solely under human rights protections, which exposed certain legal inconsistencies. These include, for example, precautions in attack and in particular warnings to the local residents. In IHL warning of an attack might be given by the military only unless the circumstances do not permit (article 57.2 API), whereas the European Court extends such obligation as requirement in all circumstances even to warnings of a probable arrival of the rebel forces

38 *Abella v. Argentina*, paras 178-179.

39 Ibid., para. 179.

40 *McCann and Others v. United Kingdom*, European Court of Human Rights, Judgment of 27 September 1995.

41 *Guleç v. Turkey*, 21593/93, European Court of Human Rights, Judgment of 27 July 1998; *Ergi v. Turkey*, 23818/94, European Court of Human Rights, Judgment of 28 July 1998.

42 *Isayeva, Yusupova and Bazayeva v. Russia,* 57947/00, 57948/00 and 57949/00, European Court of Human Rights, Judgment of 24 February 2005; *Isayeva v. Russia*, 57950/00, European Court of Human Rights, Judgment of 24 February 2005.

in an area of local population.[43] Quite apart from the practical difficulties in implementation of such obligation on state forces (security of their own forces and the successful completion of the mission being important factors), this could be seen as a disproportionate burden placed on state forces. Similarly, the Court went beyond the laws of armed conflict in requiring the state party to take all appropriate precautions in order to avoid or minimise, to the greatest extent possible, any risk to the lives of civilians caught in hostilities, including the firepower of the rebels caught in ambush.[44] IHL does not require states to assume duties related to the potential conduct of the rebel fighters.

The European Court also sometimes seems to confuse the issues clearly defined by IHL, including indiscriminate attacks with indiscriminate weapons. In laws of armed conflict, distinction also has to be made between an indiscriminate use of a weapon and the use of it, which is indiscriminate in nature. An indiscriminate weapon is defined as a weapon which strikes military objectives and civilian objects without distinction (article 51.4 API). In other words, an indiscriminate weapon would either be inherently incapable (by design) of being directed against only military objectives or which effects could not be limited, spreading the effects wide and far without distinction. As mentioned above, an attack thus may be regarded indiscriminate not only due to the potential use of an indiscriminate weapon, but also if it is not directed against a specific military objective or expected collateral damage would be excessive in light of an anticipated military advantage (as recognised by the principle of proportionality). The Court referred to the use of 'heavy combat weapons', notably 'free-falling high-explosion aviation bombs FAB-250 and FAB-500 with a damage radius exceeding 1,000 metres.' The court concluded that 'the massive use of indiscriminate weapons stands in flagrant contrast with this aim and cannot be considered compatible with the standard of care prerequisite to an operation of this kind involving the use of lethal force by state agents.' The primary aim should be to protect lives from unlawful violence.[45]

Undoubtedly, the use of such heavy weapons in the vicinity of a village or directly in the centre of it showed a number of shortcomings. A lack of care for civilian life in planning and execution of military operations against the rebel positions clearly infringed the requirements of precaution in attack. Even the choice of weapon and the way it was used may be construed as resulting in an indiscriminate attack especially when considering the principle of proportionality. However, it remains debatable whether the weapon as such was indiscriminate as per the Court's assessment. Heavy combat weapons, like FABs, perhaps not the most appropriate to use in the attack under consideration, remain capable of being directed against military objectives, if dropped against a large military base the missiles will only hit the military base (unless the weapon malfunctions and

43 *Isayeva v. Russia*, para. 187.

44 *Ergi v. Turkey*, para. 79.

45 *Isayeva v. Russia*, paras 189, 191.

goes off the projected course). Their effects can be limited to the area of their deployment. It is unlikely that under IHL, such weapons would be considered indiscriminate. As stressed before, this would not affect the overall finding of indiscriminate attack, which may still be regarded as such due to potential breaches of proportionality or precautions in attack. It remains unknown whether the European Court took these issues into consideration in light of IHL and if it did, how the Court arrived at its conclusion in regard to the deployed weapons. More likely though and keeping with the past practice the Court confined itself to analysing human rights standards. It is therefore puzzling what the Court intended when it referred to the use of indiscriminate weapons in a human rights setting.

The applications related to the 2008 conflict in South Ossetia and Georgia have been already submitted and await the determination by the Court. Seven out of over 3,300 applications submitted against Georgia have been already communicated to Georgia under the priority Rule 41 of the Rules of the Court (European Court of Human Rights, Press Release, 14 Jan. 2009). It will be interesting to see how the Court will deal with the legal assessment of facts related to deprivation of life in these circumstances, which point to concurrent existence of at least two types of conflicts, inter-state and NIACs. In particular it will be interesting to view the consideration of the cases involving killing resulting from the attacks on territory where military occupation or effective control has not been established.[46]

Conclusion

The relationship between the application of IHR and IHRL is not yet adequately established and in particular how these juxtaposed jurisdictions are to be applied to the deprivation of life in combat circumstances. In conflict situations, the right to kill (of combatants) and an obligation of the protection of life (of civilians and combatants in certain circumstances) both exist in parallel. Civilians who decide to fight forfeit this protection and from this point risk their lives. A combatant's life can be taken anytime during hostilities until they find themselves *hors de combat*. Human rights do not empower any individual (whether private or state representative or agent) or group of individuals to take the lives of others. IHRL does, however, foresee that under some permitted conditions killing of another human being would not be seen as unlawful. These two approaches differ in the

46 See in context of other Conventional rights: *Loizdou v. Turkey,* 15318/89, European Court of Human Rights, Judgment of 18 December 1996; *Bankovic and others v. Belgium and 16 other NATO States*, 52207/99, European Court of Human Rights, Grand Chamber Admissibility Decision of 12 December 2001; *Issa v. Turkey*, 31821/96, European Court of Human Rights, Admissibility Decision of 30 May 2000, Decision of Second Chamber, 16 November 2004; *Ilaşcu et al. v. Moldova and* Russia, 48787/99, European Court of Human Rights, Judgment of 8 July 2004.

personal and material scope of permissibility of action and the legal consequences stemming from going beyond permitted actions.

IHL categorises individuals in accordance to their status. Their conduct may affect the scope of the protections guaranteed by laws of armed conflict. IHRL is concerned with the conduct of specific groups of individuals, state agents and in this context, it addresses state responses to the threat from rebel forces. Questions concerning the status of persons do not arise in human rights but they do in humanitarian law. These conceptual differences could heavily influence our interpretation of the same situations by the two legal regimes, and the relation and essence of the provisions within IHL versus human rights standards should be taken into account. In other words, each specific set of rules of IHL should be appraised separately vis-à-vis IHRL.

Whether we are dealing with NIAC or IAC, both treaty and customary law must be kept in view. Consequently, if treaty law does not contain any detailed rules and the respective customary international humanitarian law provides some relevant regulation, then it should not be ignored even if the protection enshrined therein may be perceived as more limited than currently proposed by the human rights bodies (Hampson 2008, 560). Whether human rights bodies are sufficiently equipped to deal with cases triggering simultaneous application of IHL and IHRL or whether they would be willing to entertain such an application is another matter. This is only a starting point and we have not reached the finishing line. Whether it is large-scale international war or bitter civil strife, there is no armed conflict without the use of violence. The legitimacy of the violence may vary, but violence is an inevitable part of the conflicts. Placing 'limits around violence remains…one of the hardest challenges of the human condition' (Slim 2008, 295).

Bibliography

Arnold, R. and Quènivet, N. (eds) (2008) *International Humanitarian Law and Human Rights Law: Towards a New Merger in International Law* (Leiden: Brill/Martinus Nijhoff Publishers)

Droege, C. (2008) 'Elective affinities? Human rights and humanitarian law', *International Review of the Red Cross* 90(871): 501-548.

Gaggioli, G. and Kolb, R. (2007), 'A Right to Life in Armed Conflicts? The Contribution of the European Court of Human Rights', *Israel Yearbook on Human Rights* 37: 115-163.

Hampson, F.J. (2008) 'The relationship between international humanitarian law and human rights law from the perspective of a human rights treaty body', *International Review of the Red Cross* 90(871): 549-572.

Henckaerts, J.M. and Doswald-Beck, L. (eds) (2005) *Customary International Humanitarian Law*, Vol. I (Rules) with supplementary evidence in Vol. II (Practice).

Human Rights Watch (2003) *Off Target. Interpretive guidance on the notion of direct participation in hostilities under international humanitarian law* (2009) Geneva ICRC [ICRC Guidance], available at: http://www.icrc.org/web/eng/siteeng0.nsf/html/p0990?opendocument.

Pauwelyn, J. (2003) *Conflict of Norms in International Law: How WTO Law Relates to the other Rules of International Law* (Cambridge: Cambridge University Press).

Quènivet, N. (2008) *International Humanitarian Law and Human Rights Law: Towards a New Merger in International Law* edited by R. Arnold and N. Quènivet (Leiden: Brill/ Martinus Nijhoff Publishers).

Rogers, A.P.V. (2004) *Law on the Battlefield*, 2nd edn, Melland Schill Studies in International Law (Manchester: Manchester University Press).

Sandoz, Y., Swinarski, C. and Zimmermann, B. (eds) (1987) *Commentary on the Additional Protocols of 8 June 1977 to the Geneva Conventions of 12 August 1949* (Geneva and The Hague: ICRC, and Martinus Nijhoff Publishers).

Sassoli, M. and Olson, L.M. (2008) 'The relationship between international humanitarian and human rights law where it matters: admissible killing and internment of fighters in non-international armed conflicts', *International Review of the Red Cross,* Vol. 90, No. 871, 599-627.

Schindler, D. and Toman J. (eds) (2004) *The Laws of Armed Conflict* (Leiden: Martinus Nijhoff Publishers).

Slim, H. (2008) *Killing Civilians: Method, Madness and Morality in War* (London: C. Hurst & Co. Publishers Ltd).

Chapter 7
The Right to Life of Detainees in Armed Conflict

Susan Breau

Introduction

The focus of this chapter included in the part of this book entitled 'The Vicissitudes of Armed Conflict and Detention' is on those civilians and combatants who find themselves in the hands of the armed or security forces in an international or non-international armed conflict. In order to discuss the issue of the right to life of detainees in armed conflict it is necessary to discuss two separate legal regimes that overlap in these situations, the protection of human rights and international humanitarian law. It is a regrettable fact of armed conflict that persons who find themselves in the power of the enemy are in grave peril. As an example there have been many suspicious deaths of civilians in United States and United Kingdom custody in the wars in Afghanistan and Iraq (Human Rights First 2006; Shamsi 2006).[1] However, the dubious circumstances of one death involving military forces of the United Kingdom – that of Baha Mousa in Iraq – has resulted in several years of litigation in the courts of the United Kingdom and can serve as a case study of the applicability of both regimes (see also Simpson 2007).

The course of events began on 15 September 2003 when Baha Mousa, a 26-year-old civilian, working as a hotel receptionist in Basra was beaten to death while being held in detention by British soldiers on suspicion of being an insurgent. A post mortem revealed that he sustained 93 separate injuries.[2] At that time the United Kingdom military was in occupation of this southern part of Iraq which lasted from the end of hostilities in May 2003 until sovereignty was restored to an Iraqi government on 28 June 2004 (BBC News 2004). This incident resulted in two courses of action spearheaded by Baha Mousa's father, Iraqi police Colonel Daoud Mousa, to pursue legal remedies. The first was to ensure criminal

1 Human Rights First (2006) and Shamsi (2006) estimate 98 detainee deaths in US custody with allegations that 34 of these were homicides The UK Ministry of Defence's, *Aitken Report*, released 25 January 2008, indicted that under UK control there were four suspicious deaths in Iraq including Baha Mousa (his name is also spelled in certain reports as Musa, but I am relying on the jurisprudence spelling).

2 *Mazin Jumaa Gatteh Al Skeini v. the Secretary of State for Defence,* House of Lords, 2007 UKHL 26 Judgment 13 June 2007.

accountability on the part of British soldiers for the death – crimes resulting from violations of international humanitarian law, and the second to ensure that the United Kingdom would be financially responsible for the human rights abuses visited on Mr. Mousa.

Louise Doswald-Beck persuasively argues that it is generally recognised that international human rights law continues to apply during all armed conflicts alongside international humanitarian law (Doswald-Beck 2006). As a result the issue of deaths in detention engages several rules of international human rights law and international humanitarian law and violations of these rules can result in various avenues of enforcement. This chapter firstly reviews the *lex specialis* of international humanitarian law and its enforcement regime of war crimes prosecutions. Secondly, the relevant rules of human rights law and the international and domestic enforcement mechanisms under that regime are examined. Finally, this chapter will assess the effectiveness of both overlapping regimes in bringing to justice those who deprive detainees in armed conflict of their right to life. It is the position of the author of this chapter that these legal regimes can be effective in dealing with deaths in detention but there needs to be knowledge and dissemination amongst all concerned about the obligations contained within both regimes.

International Humanitarian Law Regime for Detainees

In one part of a twin-track approach, Daoud Mousa, the father of Baha Mousa sought to ensure criminal accountability for those British soldiers who took part in the beating to death of his son. Importantly to the Mousa family any chance for individual criminal accountability rested with the regime of protection for civilians contained within customary and treaty based international humanitarian law.[3] After sustained political pressure, seven British soldiers from the Queen's Lancashire Regiment were charged on 19 July 2005 with the death and abuse of Baha Mousa, charges which represented violations of international humanitarian law (Blackstock and Norton-Taylor 2005). On 19 September 2006, Corporal Donald Payne pled guilty of inhumane treatment of Mousa, becoming the first British soldier in Iraq to admit to a war crime under the United Kingdom's, International Criminal Court Act 2001 (*Daily Mail* 2006). He was later jailed for a year and dismissed from the army but he was acquitted of the charge of manslaughter. On 14 February 2007 all charges were dropped against four of the seven soldiers including those against the commanding officer, Colonel Jorge Mendonca MBE. On 13 March 2007 the remaining soldiers were acquitted but

3 1949 Geneva Convention IV Relative to the Protection of Civilian Persons in Time of War of August 12, 1949, in force 21 October 1950 (1950) 75 *UNTS* 287-417 particularly Article 4 and 1977 Protocol Additional to the Geneva Conventions of 12 August 1949, and Relating to the Protection of Victims of International Armed Conflicts, Geneva, 8 June 1977, in force 7 December 1978 (1977) 16 *ILM* 1391-1441 particularly Article 75.

senior army officers and defence lawyers criticised the court martial proceedings (Blackstock and Norton-Taylor 2007). Phil Shiner, who represented the Iraqis at the court martial, is quoted as saying that the outcome of the courts martial was a 'travesty' (*The Scotsman* 2007). However, the regime for protection of persons under international humanitarian law is complex and the results in this particular case were unfortunate but not necessarily a travesty.

The *lex specialis* of international humanitarian law has complex conditions of applicability. Firstly, it only applies when a disturbance rises to the level of an armed conflict.[4] Secondly, it is necessary to determine the type of conflict as there is a difference in treaty protections for international and non-international armed conflict and there is also an overlapping customary law regime.[5] Finally and most importantly, it is necessary to determine the status of the individual affected by the armed conflict as there is the distinction between civilians and combatants with different protections being provided for both. In the case of Iraq, there was no doubt that there was an armed conflict of an international character and the death of Baha Mousa took place during a period of occupation when many of the rules of international humanitarian law for the conflict continued to apply (see International Humanitarian Law Research Initiative 2003b; Roberts 2004). It was also evident that Baha Mousa was a civilian so that the regime of protection was that applicable to civilians.[6]

With respect to the distinction between civilians and combatants there are crucial differences in the rules of armed conflict. Combatants unlike civilians do not have an absolute right to life and they can be targeted and killed provided that they are involved in active combat and have not surrendered.[7] Once a combatant surrenders or has been rendered *hors de combat*[8] or are captured by the enemy,

4 For an analysis of this issue see S. Breau, 'The International Law Implications of the Turkish/Kurdish Conflict' in the forthcoming Volume 41 of the *Revue Belge de Droit International*.

5 The treaty protection for non-international armed conflict is limited to Common Article 3 of the Four Geneva Conventions and Additional Protocol II of 1977 to the Four Geneva Conventions which only contains limited protection but it is arguable that customary rules provide more extensive protection in non-international armed conflict.

6 The key Treaty is 1949 Geneva Convention IV Relative to the Protection of Civilian Persons in Time of War of August 12, 1949, in force 21 October 1950 (1950) 75 *UNTS* 287-417.

7 Geneva Convention (I) for the Amelioration of the Condition of the Wounded and Sick in Armed Forces in the Field. Geneva, 12 August 1949, Article 12; 'hors de combat' means generally unable to fight.

8 1977 Protocol Additional to the Geneva Conventions of 12 August 1949, and Relating to the Protection of Victims of International Armed Conflicts, Geneva, 8 June 1977, in force 7 December 1978 (1977) 16 *ILM* 1391-1441, article 41 Safeguard of an enemy hors de combat 1. A person who is recognized or who, in the circumstances, should be recognized to be hors de combat shall not be made the object of attack. 2. A person is hors de combat if: (a) he is in the power of an adverse Party; (b) he clearly expresses an

they are known as prisoners of war. The status of prisoner of war is an important one as there are a number of treaty and customary law protections for these persons. There is a detailed list provided in article 4 of Geneva Convention III of 1949 of those who are entitled to prisoner of war status, including members of an organized armed force of a party to the conflict and members of other militias, volunteer corps, or organized resistance movements – provided that they are commanded by a person responsible for his subordinates, that they have a fixed, distinctive sign recognizable at a distance, carry their arms openly and conduct their operations in accordance with the law of armed conflict.[9] Prisoner of war status is only available in an international armed conflict and Iraq fulfilled this criteria and it is conceivable that prisoners of war could be captured after active hostilities (International Humanitarian Law Research Initiative 2003a). There are various obligations associated with prisoners of war but the main obligation is that prisoners of war must be treated humanely and their persons and honour must be respected at all times.[10] There are certain acts prohibited including those which cause death or serious injury to health and any such act will constitute a war crime.[11] It was never suggested that Baha Mousa was a combatant and at all stages his death was considered a death of a civilian. However, if he had been a combatant in custody as a prisoner of war, his death would still be considered an unlawful event requiring an investigation as it would clearly be a war crime to beat to death a prisoner of war.[12]

Civilians are under special protection in the Geneva Conventions, particularly set out in Geneva Convention IV relative to the Protection of Civilian Persons in Time of War in which they have the status of protected persons.[13] This means that an occupying power has to take special care to preserve the lives and livelihood of the civilian population. Furthermore, it is a long standing rule of customary international law that the parties to a conflict must distinguish between civilian and combatants during combat operations in order to spare the civilian population and property (UK Ministry of Defence 2004, Chapter 4; Doswald-Beck and J-M Henckaerts 2005, Rules 1-6). However, it has to be emphasized that during the military phase of the conflict civilians could be killed as they are categorised as 'collateral damage' if they are found in or near a target that is a military objective

---

intention to surrender; or (c) he has been rendered unconscious or is otherwise incapacitated by wounds or sickness, and therefore is incapable of defending himself; provided that in any of these cases he abstains from any hostile act and does not attempt to escape.

9 Geneva Convention relative to the Treatment of Prisoners of War, of 12 August 1949, article 4.

10 Geneva Convention relative to the Treatment of Prisoners of War, of 12 August 1949, article 13.

11 Ibid.

12 Ibid.

13 Geneva Convention IV Relative to the Protection of Civilian Persons in Time of War of August 12, 1949, in force 21 October 1950 (1950) 75 *UNTS* 287-417 see particularly article 4 establishing the notion of protected persons.

and the test of proportionality is met (Schmitt 2007). But once a territory is occupied after the cessation of armed hostilities, as Iraq was, the occupiers including the armed forces of the United Kingdom are under a specific obligation to ensure that the security of civilians is respected.[14] Although the distinction between civilians and combatants is critical in the battlefield, where it is permissible to kill a combatant, and the cardinal rule of distinction prevails between civilians and combatants (see the chapter by Jachec-Neale in this collection), there is very little difference in the level of legal protection when either finds themselves detained by the enemy. Both types of detainees must never be tortured or killed unless trying to escape or evade capture.

The United Kingdom is also bound by Additional Protocol I to the Geneva Conventions of 1977 which has a specific detailed provision with respect to the treatment of civilians applicable to those in detention. Under the Fourth Geneva Convention protected persons are subject to imprisonment for offences intended to harm the occupying power but Additional Protocol I provides a code of conduct for those who imprison civilians.[15] The important provision is article 75 which is arguably part of customary international humanitarian law and as a customary rule is applicable in non-international and international armed conflict (Doswald-Beck and Henckaerts 2005; Hampson 2007).

Article 75 – Fundamental Guarantees

> 1. In so far as they are affected by a situation referred to in Article 1 of this Protocol, persons who are in the power of a Party to the conflict and who do not benefit from more favourable treatment under the Conventions or under this Protocol shall be treated humanely in all circumstances and shall enjoy, as a minimum, the protection provided by this Article without any adverse distinction based upon race, colour, sex, language, religion or belief, political or other opinion, national or social origin, wealth, birth or other status, or on any other similar criteria. Each Party shall respect the person, honour, convictions and religious practices of all such persons.
>
> 2. The following acts are and shall remain prohibited at any time and in any place whatsoever, whether committed by civilian or by military agents:
>
> (a) Violence to the life, health, or physical or mental well-being of persons, in particular:

14 1949 Geneva Convention IV Relative to the Protection of Civilian Persons in Time of War of August 12, 1949, in force 21 October 1950 (1950) 75 *UNTS* 287-417 particularly Section III Occupied territories which contains extensive provisions with respect to the necessities of life.

15 Ibid., articles 64-78.

(i) Murder;

(ii) Torture of all kinds, whether physical or mental;

(iii) Corporal punishment ; and

(iv) Mutilation;

(b) Outrages upon personal dignity, in particular humiliating and degrading treatment, enforced prostitution and any form of indecent assault;

(c) The taking of hostages;

(d) Collective punishments; and

(e) Threats to commit any of the foregoing acts.[16]

Therefore, within treaty and customary law, there are extensive provisions establishing protection for the right to life in detention but the next step within the purview of international humanitarian law is to ensure criminal accountability if these protections are not respected.

If either a civilian or combatant is unlawfully killed in detention, there is a system of enumeration of violations within the Geneva Conventions applicable in international armed conflict and as a result of the practice of the International Criminal Tribunal for Yugoslavia, also applicable in non-international armed conflict.[17] These are known as grave breaches of international humanitarian law which include:

i) wilful killing;

ii) torture or inhuman treatment, including biological experiments;

iii) wilfully causing great suffering or serious injury to body or health, in particular

rape;

16 1977 Protocol Additional to the Geneva Conventions of 12 August 1949, and Relating to the Protection of Victims of International Armed Conflicts, Geneva, 8 June 1977, in force 7 December 1978 (1977) 16 *ILM* 1391-1441, Article 75.

17 The International Criminal Tribunal for Yugoslavia established that violations of international humanitarian law would involve criminal responsibility in both international and non-international armed conflict see for example *Prosecutor v Tadić*, Appeals Chamber Judgment, 15 July 1999, IT-94-1-A.

d) wilful acts or omissions, in violation of international humanitarian law, which seriously endangers the physical or mental health or integrity: subjecting persons who are in the power of the adverse Party or who are interned, detained or otherwise deprived of liberty, to any medical procedure which is not indicated by the state of health of the person concerned and which is not consistent with generally accepted medical standards which would be applied under similar medical circumstances to persons who are nationals of the Party conducting the procedure and who are in no way deprived of liberty, in particular to carry out on such persons, even with their consent:

a) physical mutilations;

b) medical or scientific experiments;

c) removal of tissue or organs for transplantation.

3. Serious violations of international humanitarian law applicable in non-international armed conflicts:

i) violence to the life, health and physical or mental well-being or persons, in particular murder, as well as cruel treatment such as torture, mutilation or any form of corporal punishment;

ii) collective punishments;

iii) taking of hostages;

iv) outrages upon personal dignity, in particular humiliating and degrading treatment, rape and enforced prostitution;

xi) starvation of civilians;[18]

Nevertheless, although the grave breaches of the Geneva Convention are enumerated, the actual criminalisation of violations of international humanitarian law is left to both domestic law and international criminal law. Within international law, violations of international humanitarian law were confirmed as criminal by the Nuremberg and other International Military Tribunals following the Second World War, and further developed by the International Criminal Tribunals established through the Security Council in Yugoslavia and Rwanda and finally confirmed

18 The definition of grave breaches above is in Geneva Convention I, article 50, Geneva Convention II article 51, Geneva Convention III, article 130 and Geneva Convention IV, article 147.

in the treaty enabled International Criminal Court.[19] However, the Mousa case reveals that probably the most important enforcement mechanism for violation of the rules of international humanitarian law is domestic criminal law and the system of military law for violations of the laws and customs of war. Members of the armed forces within a domestic legal system face court martial for violations of international humanitarian law.[20]

It is within this framework we discuss those who were charged either directly or indirectly in the United Kingdom with the events that led to the death of Baha Mousa. The criminal responsibility extends not only to those who directly perpetrate the crime but also to those in command, who bear the burden of training and supervising troops under their command. This has been a long standing rule within international criminal law that those who bear the greatest responsibility should be tried.[21] The charges in the court martial hearings were as follows:

> Cpl Donald Payne – manslaughter, inhumane treatment of persons, perverting the course of justice
>
> L/Cpl Wayne Crowcroft – inhumane treatment of persons
>
> Pte Darren Fallon – inhumane treatment of persons
>
> Sgt Kelvin Stacey – actual bodily harm, alternatively assault
>
> Warrant Officer Mark Davies – negligently performing a duty
>
> Maj. Michael Peebles – negligently performing a duty
>
> Col. Jorge Mendonca (the commanding officer) – negligently performing a duty (Blackstock and Norton-Taylor 2005).

Therefore, for the critics calling this process a travesty, the major issue that emerged in this hearing was the thorny question of command responsibility. It was notable that only the junior ranks were actually charged with offences that could constitute grave breaches of international humanitarian law and the more senior officers were

---

19 Rome Statute of the International Criminal Court, 17 July 1998, see article 8, War Crimes. For a historical development, see Cassese (2008) Part 1.

20 See for example the United Kingdom Army Act 1955 Chapter 18(3) and (4) and the United Kingdom International Criminal Court Act 2001, Chapter 17 – this act confers on United Kingdom courts jurisdiction over crimes set out in the Rome Statute of the International Criminal Court.

21 See *Trial of Tomoyuki Yamashita* (United States Military Commission, Manila, 1945) 4 *Law Reports of Trials of War Criminals* 14 and the Judgement of the International Military Tribunal at Nuremberg.

merely charged with the military law offences of negligently performing a duty under the United Kingdom Army Act of 1955.[22] However, on reflection, this is not surprising. Regrettably since the Japanese war crimes trials and the conviction of General Yamishita arguably on the basis of strict liability, command responsibility has been rarely litigated and the provisions in the Rome Statute establishing the International Criminal Court are disappointing in this regard as they establish some sort of subjective test.[23] Article 28(a) of the Statute specifies that military commanders will be individually responsible for crimes committed by forces under their effective command and control if they 'either knew or, owing to the circumstances at the time, should have known that the forces were committing or about to commit such crimes.'[24] The critical issue in this case was the allegation that senior officers might have approved of so called 'conditioning techniques' that included the use of hooding and the stress position, which the human rights community has condemned as torture.[25] However, the Justice convening the court martial held that Colonel Mendonca had no case to answer at the end of the Crown's case because it was accepted by the Crown that the Colonel had been told by the officer responsible for detainees that the use of these techniques had been sanctioned by both the Brigade Intelligence and Brigade Legal Department.[26] Only after proceedings were concluded did General Sir Richard Dannatt accept that Mousa and others were 'subjected to a conditioning process that was unlawful' (Joint Committee on Human Rights 2008, para. 6). However, no senior officer at Brigade level has been held criminally accountable for either giving the orders for treatment of prisoners that was tantamount to torture or approving the technique. Nevertheless, in the actual circumstances of the trial itself, it cannot be argued that the United Kingdom court martial departed from the Rome Statute that required actual knowledge of unlawfulness. The issue may well be who should have been charged in the first place. A proper investigation of the approval of unlawful methods should have gone to the highest level of military command.

In spite of this debate of command responsibility for the conditioning process, it is clear that Baha Mousa had been subjected to ill treatment far beyond the disputed conditioning techniques, previously considered and declared to be inhuman and degrading treatment and punishment in the European Court of Human Rights

22 Army Act 1955 Chapter 18 (3) and (4) Eliz. (2) and see Simpson (2007) for a discussion of the decision to charge a negligent performance of duty rather than a more serious offence.

23 For discussion of this issue see Meloni (2007) and *Trial of Tomoyuki Yamashita* (United States Military Commission, Manila, 1945) 4 *Law Reports of Trials of War Criminals* 14.

24 Rome Statute of the International Criminal Court, article 28.

25 See, Joint Committee on Human Rights (2008), para. 5, which confirms that approval for those techniques were at the highest level.

26 Transcript of the Court Martial 13 February 2007, pp. 8, 32 and 36 as quoted in The Redress Trust (2007), and see also the Joint Committee on Human Rights (2008).

decision in *Ireland v. UK*.[27] He was clearly beaten to death. The general issue of command responsibility for training and supervision of troops seems to have been overlooked. This important point was pursued as a result of an inquiry made by the Joint Committee on Human Rights which asked 'whether the Government intends to take any further steps to revise the training, guidance and procedures for the treatment of detainees and internees' (Joint Committee on Human Rights 2008, para. 7). The Secretary of State for Defence responded that he was commissioning a review of the lessons learned from the death of Baha Mousa, which subsequently became known as the Aitken report. It concluded that:

> [t]he great majority of officers and soldiers who have served in Iraq have done so to the highest standards that the Army or the Nation might expect of them, under extraordinarily testing conditions. There is no evidence of fundamental flaws in the Army's approach to preparing for or conducting operations: we remain the envy of our allies for the professionalism of our conduct…the doctrine, training and education required to deal specifically with detained civilians has been comprehensively reviewed, …measures have been put in place to ensure that all those involved in prisoner handling or interrogation are now significantly clearer about the correct procedures…and that the procedures of the Military Criminal Justice System are fit for purpose (The Aitken Report 2008, para. 44).

This assurance of modifications to the training regimes cannot provide comfort to Police Colonel Mousa as no one has been convicted of his son's death or anyone who exercised the superior responsibility for the behaviour of the soldiers involved.

In terms of the trial of the ordinary soldiers, it has to be acknowledged that in a criminal trial which a court martial is, there must be proof beyond a reasonable doubt that someone had caused injuries resulting in death. In this case one might surmise that a culture of closing of the ranks to protect fellow soldiers resulted in a lack of accountability for the homicide. Simpson relies on the opening statements in the court martial trials that a disciplinary breach was the only appropriate way to deal with such an incident. The defence lawyers argued that the killing of Mousa took place in a.military context in which some killing is permissible, and therefore was not a war crime but a breach of discipline explained by the difficult situations in which the UK soldiers were operating (Simpson 2007, 318). Simpson also assesses General Dannatt's statement at the conclusion of the court martial that on the same date as Mousa's death, the UK had lost 12 soldiers to enemy action in Iraq and that torture and inhumane treatment might affect the UK Armed Forces' reputation and command structure and correctly disputes this type of statement stating:

---

27 *Ireland v. United Kingdom*, 5310/71, Judgment of 18 January 1978 [1978] ECHR 1.

> Mousa and his fellow victims are consigned to the margins; their terrible suffering over 36 hours in Basra becomes an 'unlawful conditioning process'. In the end, there is no direct expression of regret or sense of outrage in the General's carefully chosen statement. The killing of Mousa is understood here primarily as a breach of discipline that might have the effect of undermining discipline more broadly and diminishing the effectiveness of the UK Armed Forces (ibid., 319).

One has to agree with Simpson that the court martial seems not to have taken the death as seriously as it should have and the terrible suffering Mousa must have undergone to sustain 93 separate injuries is not addressed. It may not be quite a travesty but the result is clearly troubling from both command responsibility and the responsibility of the individual perpetrators.

Human Rights of Detainees in Armed Conflict

The second course of action was to raise the human rights obligations of the United Kingdom. In the Court of Appeal case in *Al Skeini*, Lord Justice Brooke raised the issue of the relationship between international human rights law and international humanitarian law by stating:

> [t]he reason why these issues are so important is that what is known as international humanitarian law imposes a number of unexceptional moral precepts on occupying forces ('Thou shalt not commit murder'; 'Thou shalt not be guilty of torture or other inhuman treatment,' etc) but it imposes none of the positive human rights obligations that are inherent in the ECHR. It is a far cry from the complacency of 'You must not kill but need not strive officiously to keep alive' to the obligations imposed on a member state of the Council of Europe by the case law on Articles 1 and 2 of the ECHR ('the High Contracting Parties shall secure to everyone within their jurisdiction [their] right to life').[28]

This perceptive statement reveals just how important it is to the Mousa family that the human rights obligations apply as the state that supervises the soldiers can be held accountable for failing to protect the life of Baha Mousa. As Lord Brooke asserted it was the relationship between the positive obligations contained in the ECHR and the status of an occupying force which is accepted to have sufficient authority in the territory it occupies for the purposes of international humanitarian law which is at the heart of the Mousa decisions and the issues in this chapter.[29]

28 *The Queen – on the Application of Mazin Jumaa Gatteh Al Skeini and others v. The Secretary of State for Defence and The Redress Trust,* Court of Appeal [2005] EWCA Civ 1609, para. 8.

29 Ibid., para. 11.

Human rights law provided the mechanism of enforcing violations of human rights but at the same time was dealing indirectly with violations of international humanitarian law. This is particularly important as although the senior officers were relieved of criminal responsibility, the United Kingdom could be held liable under its human rights obligation for failing to absolutely prohibit robust methods of interrogation, known in this case as 'conditioning techniques' and for failing to live up to their positive obligations to preserve and protect life. The practice in human rights law is to assess financial penalties for violation of human rights law which was also very important to the Mousa family.

Firstly within the human rights action, consideration of the meaning of the right to life is pertinent. Under what is known as the International Bill of Rights, the prohibition against the violation of the right to life can be safely argued to be a peremptory norm of public international law, known as a norm of *jus cogens* (see Rodley 2000, 202; Gormley 1985, 121). It is argued that sovereign states in their constitutional and municipal legislation should guarantee the right to life (Gormley 1985, 125). No state by its treaties or by the actions of its public officials can violate these peremptory norms. The key concept related to *jus cogens* is the notion of non-derogability. This means that a peremptory norm such as the right to life cannot be altered under any circumstances even during a state of emergency that threatens the life of a nation.[30] This would include such activities as the serious and sustained insurgency in Iraq – it would never justify civilian deaths. Gormley argues that the arbitrary killing of a single individual violates the peremptory nature of *jus cogens* (ibid., 148).

Aside from the customary nature of the prohibition and its enunciation in the Universal Declaration of Human Rights (UDHR) as the right to life, liberty and security of the person, (article 3) there are numerous widely ratified treaty provisions on the topic. Article 6 (1) of the International Covenant on Civil and Political Rights (ICCPR), article 4(3) of the American Convention on Human Rights (ACHR) and article 4 of the African Charter on Human and Peoples' Rights (ACHPR) all specify that no one may be 'arbitrarily' deprived of life.

In the case of Baha Mousa the rights engaged were those as outlined in the ECHR which are very similar to those outlined in the UDHR and the ICCPR but the crucial difference is that, under the Human Rights Act 1998, the British courts must consider the ECHR where human rights are implicated in a case. These rights are specified as:

> Article 2 Right to life
>
> Everyone's right to life shall be protected by law. No one shall be deprived of his life intentionally save in the execution of a sentence of a court following his conviction of a crime for which this penalty is provided by law.

---

30 Human Rights Committee, General Comment 29, States of Emergency (article 4), UN Doc. CCPR/C/21/Rev.1/Add.11 (2001) para. 7.

2. Deprivation of life shall not be regarded as inflicted in contravention of this article when it results from the use of force which is no more than absolutely necessary:

(a) in defence of any person from unlawful violence;

(b) in order to effect a lawful arrest or to prevent the escape of a person lawfully detained;

(c) in action lawfully taken for the purpose of quelling a riot or insurrection.

Article 3 – Prohibition of torture

No one shall be subjected to torture or to inhuman or degrading treatment or punishment.

As can be seen in article 2(2) the right to life is not absolute and there are exceptions for certain state actions. Although all human rights treaties consider the right to life as non-derogable, the ECHR makes an exception in article 15(2) for 'deaths resulting from lawful acts of war'. This exception has not been used in the numerous cases considering deaths in armed conflict.[31] However, the limitation on the right to life for affecting a lawful arrest and preventing escape of detainees could conceivably provide a justification for the deprivation of the right to life but this was distinguished in the Mousa case. The European Court of Human Rights has established a firm body of jurisprudence on the protection of the right to life, as the case of *Khashiyev and Akayeva v. Russia* demonstrates. The Court stated:[32]

1. The Court reiterates that Article 2, which safeguards the right to life and sets out those circumstances in which deprivation of life may be justified, ranks as one of the most fundamental provisions in the Convention, to which no derogation is permitted. Together with Article 3, it also enshrines one of the basic values of the democratic societies making up the Council of Europe. The circumstances in which deprivation of life may be justified must therefore be strictly construed. The object and purpose of the Convention as an instrument for the protection of individual human beings also requires that Article 2 be interpreted and applied so as to make its safeguards practical and effective (*McCann and Others v. the*

31 See for example *Isayeva v. Russia* where the court found a violation of Article 2 on the basis of the use of a weapon in a populated area, outside wartime and without prior evacuation of civilians. See *Case of Isayeva, Yusupova and Bazayeva v. Russia* (Application nos. 57947/00, 57948/00 and 57949/00), 24 February 2005.

32 *Case of Khashiyev and Akayeva v. Russia* (Application nos. 57942/00 and 57945/00), 24 February 2005.

United Kingdom judgment of 27 September 1995, Series A no. 324, §§ 146-147).

2. In the light of the importance of the protection afforded by Article 2, the Court must subject deprivations of life to the most careful scrutiny, taking into consideration not only the actions of state agents but also all the surrounding circumstances (see, amongst other authorities, *Avsar v. Turkey*, no. 25657/94, § 391, ECHR 2001).

3. Where the events in issue lie wholly, or in large part, within the exclusive knowledge of the authorities, as in the case of persons within their control in detention, strong presumptions of fact will arise in respect of injuries and death occurring during that detention. Indeed, the burden of proof may be regarded as resting on the authorities to provide a satisfactory and convincing explanation[33]

This is an extremely important decision as it confirms that in the case of deaths in detention, the onus shifts to the detaining power to explain how the death occurred lawfully, something that would be impossible in the circumstances of the death of Baha Mousa.

It should also be noted that the protection of the right to life is also included in many domestic constitutional provisions including the Canadian Charter of Rights and Freedoms. The United Kingdom Human Rights Act of 1998 'brought home' the provisions of the ECHR including the right to life which empowers British courts to consider violations of human rights by public officials.[34]

It should also be noted that the prohibition against torture is a norm of *jus cogens* and it can never be derogated from even in states of emergency.[35] In a critical case in the UK House of Lords, Lord Bingham held that the prohibition against torture imposed on states obligations towards all other members of the international community and therefore, there would be a claim to compliance on the part of all states (even if the torture took place elsewhere). He also confirmed that the prohibition against torture had acquired the status of a peremptory norm of customary international law and was one of the most fundamental standards of the international community. Lord Bingham held there was a duty on states to reject the

33 Cases cited in judgment: *Salman v. Turkey* [GC], no. 21986/93, § 100, ECHR 2000-VII; *Çakici v. Turkey* [GC], no. 23657/94, § 85, ECHR 1999-IV; *Ertak v. Turkey,* no. 20764/92, § 32, ECHR 2000-V, and *Timurtaş v. Turkey*, no. 23531/94, § 82, ECHR 2000-VI.

34 Human Rights Act 1998, 1998 Chapter 42. Preamble and see *The Queen – on the Application of Mazin Jumaa Gatteh Al Skeini and others v. The Secretary of State for Defence and The Redress Trust,* Court of Appeal [2005] EWCA Civ 1609 para. 7.

35 House of Lords, *A (FC) and others (FC) (Appellants) v. Secretary of State for the Home Department (Respondent)*, 8 December 2005.

fruits of torture inflicted in breach of international law.[36] In an important argument relevant to the death of Baha Mousa from torture, Lord Bingham summarized the common law position stating '[i]t is, I think, clear that from its very earliest days the common law of England set its face firmly against the use of torture.'[37]

In spite of these clear prohibitions, the treaty provisions are enforceable in various guises. The International Covenant is enforced by the Human Rights Committee which reviews country reports and issues views on individual complaints from citizens of countries that have ratified the first additional protocol to the Covenant. The Inter American Court and the European Court of Human Rights issues orders which can include financial penalties and costs. This will soon be the case for the African Court of Human Rights when it is up and running. In human rights litigation it is important to note that the complaint is brought against the state for not protecting the rights of individuals in detention.

To find the United Kingdom responsible for violation of its treaty obligations was by no means a straightforward exercise as one of the most controversial issues in international human rights law is the issue of extraterritoriality. Does a nation's human rights obligation apply when the nation is involved in an armed conflict elsewhere? The death of Baha Mousa and five other Iraqi civilians led to a serious consideration of the applicability of the ECHR to the situation of the British occupation in Iraq and the litigation of this issue resulted in one of the most important human rights cases arising from the war. The case of *Mazin Jumaa Gatteh Al Skeini v. the Secretary of State for Defence* worked its way from the Divisional Court, through the Court of Appeal to the House of Lords.[38] This case was brought on behalf of six Iraqi civilians who were killed during the occupation of Iraq. Amongst the claimants was Police Colonel Daoud Mousa. It was argued that these provisions under the ECHR, articles 2 (the right to life) and 3 (the prohibition against torture and inhuman and degrading treatment or punishment) were breached by the United Kingdom and that the government should hold an independent inquiry to determine responsibility for these deaths.

The other five victims besides Baha Mousa had died allegedly while under British control but not while in British custody and at each level the court agreed with the Government position that the UK while in occupation did not have the required degree of control for the ECHR to apply. The details of the deaths in

36 Ibid.

37 Ibid., para. 11.

38 *Mazin Jumaa Gatteh Al Skeini v. the Secretary of State for Defence,* House of Lords, 2007 UKHL 26 and *The Queen – on the Application of Mazin Jumaa Gatteh Al Skeini and others v. The Secretary of State for Defence and The Redress Trust,* Court of Appeal [2005] EWCA Civ 1609 and *The Queen – on the Application of Mazin Jumaa Gatteh Al Skeini and others v. The Secretary of State for Defence and The Redress Trust Intervener,* High Court of Justice, Queen's Bench [2004] EWHC 2911 (Admin) (all three judgments are well worth reviewing) .

custody as outlined by Lord Bingham in the House of Lords decision were as follows:

> Case 1
>
> Mr Hazim Jum'aa Gatteh Al-Skeini was shot dead on 4 August 2003 by a member of a British military patrol in Basra. The claimant is his brother. Very different accounts of the incident have been given by the claimant and his witnesses on one side and British military witnesses on the other.
>
> Case 2
>
> Mr Muhammad Abdul Ridha Salim was fatally wounded on 6 November 2003 when British troops raided a house in Basra where he was. He received medical attention but died on 7 November 2003. The claimant is his widow. There is again a radical divergence between the respective parties' accounts of this incident.
>
> Case 3
>
> Mrs Hannan Mahaibas Sadde Shmailawi was shot and fatally wounded on 10 November 2003 in the Institute of Education in Basra. On the British military account she was shot unintentionally during an exchange of fire between a British patrol and a number of gunmen. The claimant is the widower of the deceased, who accepts that the shooting of his wife was not intentional. It appears that she may have been a very unfortunate bystander, and the Secretary of State does not accept that the fatal shot was fired by a British soldier rather than a gunman.
>
> Case 4
>
> Mr Waleed Sayay Muzban was shot and fatally injured on the night of 24 August 2003 in Basra. He was driving a people-carrier when he was shot, and he died the next day. The shooting occurred when a British military patrol was, on its account, carrying out a perimeter check and the vehicle, having initially stopped, was driven away and appeared to represent a threat. The claimant is the brother of the deceased.
>
> Case 5
>
> Mr Raid Hadi Sabir Al Musawi was shot and fatally wounded by a member of a British military patrol in Basra on 26 August 2003. He died nine weeks later, on 6 November 2003. The claimant is his mother. The parties' respective accounts of what happened, as in the first case (which, on the facts, it resembles), are radically divergent.

Case 6

> Mr Baha Mousa was employed as a receptionist at a hotel in Basra and was working there on the morning of 14 September 2003 when British troops entered the hotel. He was seized and detained and taken to a British military base in Basra. At the base he was brutally beaten by British troops. He died of the injuries so inflicted during the night of 15 September 2003. The claimant is the father of the deceased, and is a colonel in the Basra police. This deceased, unlike the others, was killed by British troops when held as a prisoner in a British military detention unit. This is the limited basis upon which the Divisional Court held that this case falls within the scope of the Convention, and this is the basis upon which the Secretary of State accepts that finding.[39]

Regrettably, at every level in this pivotal case, it was only the killing of Baha Mousa that was declared to be within the jurisdiction of the European Convention of Human Rights. The High Court ruled that the Human Rights Act and the European Convention of Human Rights applied in the cases of persons detained in British military prisons. Even more importantly, the Court stated that the United Kingdom had failed to fulfil its obligations under articles 2 and 3 of the European Convention. Furthermore, it declared that the United Kingdom failed to conduct an independent investigation. Regrettably to many human rights scholars the Court ruled that the ECHR could not apply outside of Europe even where a State Party had effective control of a territory.[40] This would seem to contradict the most recent case from the European Court of Human Rights, the case of *Issa v. Turkey* which found that where effective control exists, the ECHR could apply outside the borders of the Council of Europe.[41]

At the second level, the Court of Appeal upheld the High Court ruling that the Human Rights Act and the European Convention of Human Rights only applied to Mr Mousa's case due to the fact that he came within the authority and control of the British forces in Iraq. However, the court went a step further and held the law applied not only to persons in British prisons but to persons whose liberty had been restricted by British forces. This meant that this case was closer to the *Issa* decision as the protection of the ECHR could extend to territory outside Europe where a state was found to be in effective control of a territory and persons were stopped by military forces. It further agreed that the protections offered by the ECHR included a positive obligation under article 2 and 3 to conduct an

39 *Mazin Jumaa Gatteh Al Skeini v. the Secretary of State for Defence*, House of Lords, 2007 UKHL 26 para. 6, per Lord Bingham.

40 *The Queen – on the Application of Mazin Jumaa Gatteh Al Skeini and others v. The Secretary of State for Defence and The Redress Trust Intervener*, High Court of Justice, Queen's Bench [2004] EWHC 2911.

41 *Issa and others v. Turkey,* European Court of Human Rights, Application no. 31821/96, 16 November 2004.

independent investigation. The Court of Appeal pointed out that the difficulty in the investigation of this death in custody was because the investigation was not independent as it was conducted by the military chain of command.[42] Judge Sedley got to the heart of the matter when he stated:

> I share the view of both the Divisional Court and the other members of this court that there would be something amiss if a prisoner in a British military prison, to which it is now accepted that the European Convention on Human Rights applied because it lay within the UK's jurisdiction, had nevertheless no protection under legislation which was designed specifically to afford redress in our domestic courts for violations by the British state of people's Convention rights.[43]

Once again the remaining five cases were not successful. The Court held that the victims had not had their liberty restricted nor did the United Kingdom exercise effective control over the territory in Southern Iraq where the deaths took place. These Court decisions were consistent with the previous European Court of Human Rights decision in *Bankovic v. Belgium*, which held on a narrow jurisdictional issue that those NATO powers bound by the European Convention of Human Rights did not extend to scrutinize the actions during the aerial bombardment of territory outside of the Council of Europe.[44]

Significantly for the Mousa family on 13 June 2007 in the House of Lords, the Law Lords upheld the lower court ruling that UK human rights laws did apply to Mousa because he was in actual British custody in Iraq. Therefore, according to Baroness Hale, the United Kingdom 'would be answerable in Strasbourg for the conduct of the British army while Mr. Mousa was detained'.[45] This ruling paved the way for a public inquiry. Finally on 14 May 2008 the Ministry of Defence (hereafter MOD) announced an inquiry into Mousa's death. The case stands for the proposition that the right to life applies during armed conflict and that a power that detains another national is bound by its own human rights obligations.

As a result of this extensive litigation, the Secretary of State for Defence announced that there would be a public inquiry into the death of Baha Mousa, in a written statement given in Parliament on 14 May 2008. He described Mousa's death as a disturbing incident: not just because a man died in the custody of British soldiers but because an investigation by the Royal Military Police and a subsequent Court Martial highlighted further important questions that needed to be answered.

---

42 *The Queen – on the Application of Mazin Jumaa Gatteh Al Skeini and others v. The Secretary of State for Defence and The Redress Trust*, Court of Appeal [2005] EWCA Civ 1609.

43 Ibid., para. 182.

44 *Bankovic v. Belgium et al.* App. No. 52207/99, ECtHR (2001), available at 41 ILM 517.

45 Ibid., para. 88.

The legal basis for the inquiry is provided under the Inquiries Act 2005 and it is being chaired by the Right Honourable Sir William Gage, a retired Court of Appeal judge. His terms of reference are:

> [t]o investigate and report on the circumstances surrounding the death of Baha Mousa and the treatment of those detained with him, taking account of the investigations which have already taken place, in particular where responsibility lay for approving the practice of conditioning detainees by any members of the 1st Battalion, The Queen's Lancashire Regiment in Iraq in 2003, and to make recommendations.[46]

The results of this inquiry should hopefully shed further light on the facts of the death and the human rights obligations of the British armed forces should be carefully considered. It will be this inquiry that will assign responsibility to the United Kingdom if violations of the right to life or prohibition against torture are found. This case, then, is far from concluded but at least an avenue for accountability has been established.

The Relationship between the Two Regimes and their Efficacy

At first glance it may seem that neither of the regimes of international humanitarian law and international human rights law have been particularly effective in addressing the unlawful death of Baha Mousa. But that is perhaps an unsophisticated response. Firstly, although there were acquittals in the courts martial, British soldiers were being held to account domestically for the violations of the *lex specialis* of international humanitarian law. It is important to note that as with every violation of criminal law, proof would be beyond a reasonable doubt and that criminal liability for the murder with the culture of military silence would be difficult. As Rowe states:

> [i]n the course of this process, the eventual outcome may look quite different from the way in which it looked at the initial stages of an investigation. This is hardly surprising since civilian criminal proceedings may share similar problems. These can include difficulties with the identification of soldiers, their victims, the investigation of alleged crime scenes, the bringing to the court of witnesses, translation, disputes over testimony (particularly where the motive to lie may be strong), the possible need to offer immunity from prosecution for potential military prosecution witnesses and the ability to prove a case against an individual (Rowe 2008).

46 Taken from the web site established for the inquiry. See, www.bahamousainquiry.org.

The determination of human rights violations is comparatively complex. The issue of jurisdiction was a very contentious one, but at the Court of Appeal and the House of Lords level the government acknowledged their possible liability with respect to Baha Mousa. However, it seems a false distinction to only apply jurisdiction to those in physical custody rather than in a situation of occupation. It seems incongruous that a military regime can be responsible for similar human rights guarantees under international humanitarian law but not under human rights law. One could argue that this is not a Bankovic situation, as the British Army was clearly in occupation and should have been able to secure the area. It will remain an area of great controversy. But at least for those in detention, the British government will have to ensure human rights obligations are adhered to no matter where the person is detained. The right to life and freedom from torture are non-derogable rights and no situation no matter how dire, can be an excuse for using torture.

The two regimes if they work in tandem effectively provide criminal accountability for the perpetrators and financial penalties for a country who fails to provide adequate human rights monitoring. The standard as set out by the European Court of Human Rights in many cases provides for an almost strict liability test, so that even if the political environment in the country discourages such conduct there will be accountability if it occurs as the onus shifts to the state officials to explain the circumstances of the death. In this case it has been reported that the Ministry of Defence paid 'the bulk' of £2.8 million to the Mousa family (*The Times* 2008a). This was after Des Browne the Secretary of State for Defence admitted in the House of Commons 'substantive breaches' of the parts of the European Convention on Human Rights which protect the right to life and prohibit torture (*The Times* 2008b). Therefore, the course of action to establish jurisdiction over five years eventually resulted in a substantial payment to raise Baha Mousa's surviving children (his wife had died previously of a tumour). However, it did emerge in the reporting that Police Colonel Mousa was highly critical that only one solider had been convicted of a charge relating to his son's death (*The Times* 2008a).

In spite of two legal regimes in place to protect detainees and a large body of case law on the subject, persons continue to be in mortal peril while in detention. Unless there is consistent and vigorous enforcement both against the perpetrator and the state responsible for the human rights violation these deaths will continue to occur. There is another crucial body of international law that brings violations of both international human rights law and international humanitarian law into sharp focus. State responsibility is a core concept of customary international law (Brownlie 1998, 79). The traditional notion of state responsibility was that if a state violated an international obligation under a treaty or a rule of customary international law it owed an international responsibility for such a violation (Crawford 2002, 241). Traditional state responsibility focused on bilateral relations between states and not on the community of states. State responsibility was divided into two branches. The first consisted of primary rules of international law, those customary and treaty rules that governed the conduct of states. The second branch set out the rules establishing the conditions on when breach of the primary rules might have occurred and the legal consequences of such breaches (ibid., 243). The formula for a claim of state responsibility involved three aspects: a call for preventive measures, a claim for the punishment of those responsible and a demand for payment of compensation (Brownlie 1983, 26).

On 28 January 2002 the General Assembly passed Resolution 56/83 with an annex attached on the Responsibility of States for internationally wrongful acts. The operative paragraph of the resolution states:

> [*t*]*akes note* of the articles on responsibility of States for internationally wrongful acts, presented by the International Law Commission, the text of which is annexed to the present resolution, and commends them to the attention of Governments without prejudice to the question of their future adoption or other appropriate action.[47]

These articles do not constitute a multilateral convention but a resolution recommending these articles to states. Nevertheless, the resolution is very significant as these articles in some parts are reflective of customary law and other articles could evolve into customary law, even if no further codification takes place. These Articles of State Responsibility commended to the international community contain a special provision on violation of peremptory norms of *jus cogens*. This provision states:

> Article 40 states:
>
> 1. This chapter applies to the international responsibility which is entailed by a serious breach by a State of an obligation arising under a peremptory norm of general international law.
>
> 2. A breach of such an obligation is serious if it involves a gross or systematic failure by the responsible State to fulfil its obligation.

The Articles also outline the consequences of such a breach. Article 41 states:

> 1. States shall cooperate to bring to an end through lawful means any serious breach within the meaning of article 40.
>
> 2. No State shall recognize as lawful a situation created by a serious breach within the meaning of article 40, nor render aid or assistance in maintaining the situation.

47 GA Res. 56/83, 28 January 2002, para. 3.

> 3. This article is without prejudice to the other consequences referred to in this part and to such further consequences that a breach to which this chapter applies may entail under international law.[48]

The violation of the right to life and the prohibition against torture are just such norms. Graefrath argued that after the Second World War state responsibility had undergone a transformation. It was not just about obligations to make reparations for damages and 'through recognition of *jus cogens* rules a universal legal basis for ensuring and developing peaceful international co-operation among States of difference social orders comes into existence' (Graefrath 1984, 28). He stated that:

> [s]tate responsibility can no longer be understood as a civil law like obligation to make reparation. It can no longer be oriented or restricted to protection of foreign capital interests. It rather serves for stabilization and enforcement of rules agreed upon between equal subjects (ibid., 29).

It is in the consequences of serious breaches of obligations under peremptory norms that we find a departure from ordinary state responsibility. The first important factor is that all other states can take action. This arises from the often quoted *Barcelona Traction* decision that:

> [a]n essential distinction should be drawn between the obligations of a State towards the international community as a whole, and those arising vis-à-vis another State in the field of diplomatic protection. By their very nature the former are the concern of all States. In view of the importance of the rights involved, all States can be held to have a legal interest in their protection, they are obligations *erga omnes*.[49]

All other states are entitled to: (a) invoke the aggravated responsibility by bringing their claim to the notice of the state, (b) demand cessation of the wrong, (c) claim reparation on behalf of the victims, (d) bring the matter to competent international bodies such as the UN or regional organizations, (e) if that international organisation took no action then states could take *peaceful* countermeasures on an individual basis and finally; (f) to resort to collective self-defence in the case of aggression subject to the request or consent of the victim of the aggression (Cassese 2005, 275-277). Article 41 does not specify the form this international cooperation should take. It could be organized under the auspices of the United Nations but it also could be 'non-institutionalized

48 On 28 January 2002 the General Assembly passed Resolution 56/83 with an annex attached on the Responsibility of States for internationally wrongful acts. GA Res. 56/83, 28 January 2002.

49 *Barcelona Traction case, ICJ Reports* 1970, para. 33.

cooperation' (Crawford 2002, 1-60, 249). Article 41(2) obligates other states not to recognize as lawful a situation created by a serious breach nor render aid or assistance to that state.

It must be evident that these articles do not open the door for an argument for a specific responsibility to act to protect citizens of other nations. The first reason was that these articles only cover secondary rules of state responsibility and do not set out primary rules for responsibilities of states. The second reason is that even the drafters of these articles acknowledge that aggravated state responsibility was not a doctrine in customary international law. In his commentaries to the Draft Articles, James Crawford recognizes that paragraph 1 may not be part of general international law but could constitute a progressive development of the law (ibid., 249). There may be future development of 'a more elaborate regime of consequences entailed by such breaches' (ibid., 253). The movement in international law had been from 'sovereignty to obligation' and from 'immunity to accountability' (Crawford 2001, 307, 309). However, Graefrath argued with respect to international crimes that '[a] relationship of responsibility arises entitling all States and the Organization of the United Nations to take appropriate measures to stop the violation of international law and to remedy the consequences caused' (Graefrath 1984, 58).

It can be argued then that the United Kingdom in breaching these peremptory norms of public international law had an obligation not only to compensate the Mousa family but to ensure that this type of 'conditioning technique' ceased forthwith. From the fact of compensation being paid to the Mousa family and the establishment of a public inquiry it seems that there has been an acknowledgement that the United Kingdom fell below the standard required for treatment of detainees in international law and the situation is being addressed.

It seems therefore, that there is another international law regime besides international human rights law and international humanitarian law that can be invoked when a state violates the most important rules of international law and that is the regime of state responsibility and articles 40 and 41 of the Draft Articles of State Responsibility. Certainly the international community has been informed through the efforts of non-governmental organisations that serious violations have taken place in the wars in Afghanistan and Iraq and that a state's treaty and customary obligations are not to be ignored. This might in future be an important avenue to address these issues when a state is unable or unwilling to address its violations.

Conclusion

The murder of Baha Mousa in Iraq is just one of many deaths in detention that continue to take place in areas of international and non-international armed conflict covering large parts of the globe. The difficulty during the current crisis with the threat of terrorist attacks is that these deaths are often tacitly excused on the grounds of national security. A further difficulty is that too often in the enforcement of the international humanitarian law, it is the direct perpetrator that is brought to justice and the command structure and the country escapes on both jurisdictional issues and a lack of clarity concerning the issue of command responsibility. The case law that developed in the Nuremberg and other military tribunals established subsequent to the Second World War that attached responsibility for massive violations of human rights to the highest level of military and government command seems to be fading into obscurity. A country attempts to evade its responsibility on the basis of the lack of extra territorial effect of human rights obligations, a view not assisted by the case of *Bankovic v. Belgium et al.* in the European Court of Human Rights. The House of Lords in the Mousa case has finally confirmed extra territorial applicability of human rights but only in situations of detention during occupation. The phenomenon of unlawful death while in custody during an armed conflict or in peacetime engages domestic responsibility but if that state is unwilling or unable to protect their civilian or military populations then it is the international community that must assume this obligation to combat violations of peremptory norms of international law as set out in the Articles of State Responsibility. This part of international law is just beginning to be developed and it remains to be seen how the global community will respond to systematic and pervasive violations of the rights of detainees in armed conflict.

Bibliography

BBC News (2004), *US Hands back power in Iraq*, 28 June.

Blackstock, C. and Norton-Taylor, R. (2007) 'Colonel and three of his men cleared over abuse of detained Iraqis', *The Guardian,* 15 February.

—— (2005) 'Britons face Iraq war crime trials', *The Guardian*, 20 July.

Brownlie, I. (1998) *The Rule of Law in International Affairs: International Law at the Fiftieth Anniversary of the United Nations* (The Hague: Kluwer Law).

—— (1983) *System of the Law of Nations State Responsibility (Part 1)* (Oxford: Clarendon Press).

Cassese, A. (2008) *International Criminal Law*, 2nd edn (Oxford: Oxford University Press).

—— (2005) *International Law*, 2nd edn (Oxford: Oxford University Press).

Crawford, J. (2002) *The International Law Commission's Articles on State Responsibility: Introduction, Text and Commentaries* (Cambridge: Cambridge University Press).

—— (2001) 'The Earl A. Snyder Lecture in International Law: Responsibility to the International Community as a Whole', 8 *Ind. J. Global Leg. Stud.* 303.

Daily Mail (2006) 'Corporal Pleads Guilty to Iraq War Crimes Charges', *The Daily Mail*, 19 September.

Doswald-Beck, L. (2006) 'The Right to Life in Armed Conflict: Does International Humanitarian Law Provide all the Answers?', *International Review of the Red Cross* 881.

Doswald-Beck, L. and Henckaerts, J-M. (2005) *Customary International Humanitarian Law* (Cambridge: Cambridge University Press).

Graefrath, B. (1984) 'Responsibility and Damages Caused: Relationship between Responsibility and Damages', 185 *Recueil des cours* 9.

Gormley, P.W. (1985) 'The Right to Life and the Rule of Non-derogability: Peremptory Norms of *Jus Cogens*', in Ramcharan, R.G. *The Right to Life in International Law* (Dordrecht: Martinus Nijhoff).

Hampson, F. (2007) 'Fundamental Guarantees', in Wilmshurst, E. and Breau, S. (eds) *Perspectives on the ICRC Study on Customary International Humanitarian Law* (Cambridge: Cambridge University Press).

Human Rights First (2006) *By the Numbers: Findings of Detainee Abuse and Accountability Project*, New York, April.

International Humanitarian Law Research Initiative (2003a), 'On the Status and Treatment of POW's', Policy Brief 3427, 25 March 2003, found at http://www.ihlresearch.org/iraq/pdfs/briefing3461.pdf.

—— (2003b), 'Military Occupation of Iraq: I. Application of IHL and the Maintenance of Law and Order', Policy Brief 3423, 14 April, found at www.ihlresearch.org/iraq/pdfs/briefing3423.pdf.

Joint Committee on Human Rights (2008), United Kingdom House of Commons and House of Lords, Twenty-Eighth Report, 15 July.

Meloni, C. (2007) 'Command Responsibility', 5 *Journal of International Criminal Justice* 619.

Roberts, A. (2004) 'The End of Occupation in Iraq, International Humanitarian Law Research Initiative', Policy Brief 3461, found at http://www.ihlresearch.org/iraq/pdfs/briefing3461.pdf.

Rodley, N. (2000) *The Treatment of Prisoners under International Law*, 2nd edn (Oxford: Oxford University Press).

Rowe, P. (2008) 'Military Misconduct during International Armed Operations: 'Bad Apples' or Systematic Failures', 13 *Journal of Conflict and Security Law* 165.

Schmitt, M. (2007) 'The Law of Targeting', in Wilmshurst, E. and Breau, S. (eds) *Perspectives on the ICRC Study on Customary International Humanitarian Law* (Cambridge: Cambridge University Press).

Shamsi, H. (2006) *Command Responsibility Detainee Deaths in US Custody in Iraq and Afghanistan*, Human Rights First, New York, February.

Simpson, G. (2007) 'The death of Baha Mousa', 8 *Melbourne Journal of International Law* 311.

The Aitken Report (2008) Ministry of Defence, published 25 January, accessed at http://www.mod.uk/NR/rdonlyres/7AC894D3-1430-4AD1-911F-8210C3342CC5/0/aitken_rep.pdf.

The Redress Trust (2007) *UK Army in Iraq: Time to Come Clean on Civilian Torture* (Redress Trust: London, October),

The Scotsman (2007) 'Judge clears British officers of allowing Iraqi prisoner abuse', 13 March.

The Times (2008a) 'MOD to pay £3 million in compensation to Iraqi torture victims', 11 July.

—— (2008b) 'MOD Faces unlimited payout after admitted abuse in Baha Musa Death, 27 March'.

UK Ministry of Defence (2004) *The Manual of the Law of Armed Conflict* (Oxford: Oxford University Press).

Chapter 8
At the Hands of the State: When Arrest and Imprisonment Prove Fatal

Caroline Fournet

> We were guards, our job was to guard the prisoners, we couldn't just let them escape [...] if we'd opened the doors, there would have been chaos. How could we have restored order? It happened so fast, it was snowing...the bombs...the flames...there were flames all over the village, then the screaming began and got worse and worse...and if they'd all come rushing out, we couldn't just let them escape. We couldn't, we were *responsible* for them! (Hanna Schmitz, *The Reader*[1])

These terrible words were pronounced by Hanna Schmitz, the central character of the critically acclaimed fiction film *The Reader*, as she stood trial for brutally causing the death of 300 Jewish women by leaving them in a locked church which was bombed during the evacuation of a camp. Albeit fictitious, these words resound, in all their horror and abjection, as a powerful reminder of what may go on behind barbed wires and prison walls. This reminder must nonetheless be expressly moderated and contextualized in so far as it is obviously not the purpose of the present work to even suggest that contemporary detention facilities, with all the problems they might face and the questions they might raise with respect to human rights law, could ever be equated with Nazi concentration camps. Equally rejected here is the incongruous and revolting idea that today's prison officers could ever be compared with Nazi camp guards. Still, this quote – although an extract from a fiction film – remains very much realistic and, in its interesting recognition of the responsibility of prison guards over the individuals placed in detention and under their custody, precisely reflects the issue the following analysis proposes to explore.

Death following arrest and imprisonment is, perhaps unsurprisingly, a contentious issue which is too often met with social indifference and state tacit approval. The situation of detainees and their vulnerability while in the hands of state agents seem to generate little interest among public opinion as arrest and detention generally vehicle the idea of guilt. Simultaneously, state authorities appear to be less than willing to fully investigate such deaths.

Yet, respect for human rights – including human dignity, the right to physical integrity and the right to life – transcends penitentiary walls and applies to all

1 Quote pronounced by Hanna Schmitz, fictional character in the film *The Reader*, directed by Stephen Daldry (2008). The emphasis is added here, although it does respect the intonation used by the actress.

human beings, including detainees. The following analysis accordingly proposes to review states' international law obligations – notably under the Convention for the Protection of Human Rights and Fundamental Freedoms (ECHR)[2] – and, via this lens, to assess the steps taken by the United Kingdom's authorities to comply with such duties, notably in terms of conditions of detention, investigation into cases of deaths following arrest and detention, and adequate information to the families of the victims. This jurisprudential assessment notwithstanding, the present work will also consider recent statistics as to the number of deaths occurring while individuals are held in custody, comparing the situation in the United Kingdom with France. This will enable a conclusion as to the role law could and should play, not only in the repression of the individuals responsible for the deaths of individuals placed in detention, but also in the prevention of such occurrences, whether self-inflicted or not.

Physical Integrity at Risk

Issues surrounding detention are usually analyzed from the standpoint of the right to liberty and security, as protected by article 5 of the ECHR, which, as unequivocally explained by the European Court of Human Rights in *Engel and others* v *The Netherlands*, contemplates:

> individual liberty in its classic sense, that is to say the physical liberty of the person. Its aim is to ensure that no one should be dispossessed of this liberty in an arbitrary fashion. As pointed out by the Government and the Commission, it does not concern mere restrictions upon liberty of movement (Article 2 of Protocol no. 4). This is clear both from the use of the terms "deprived of his liberty", "arrest" and "detention", which appear also in paragraphs 2 to 5, and from a comparison between Article 5 and the other normative provisions of the Convention and its Protocols.[3]

Nonetheless, while the importance of article 5 is beyond doubt, having been labelled by the European Court of Human Rights itself as 'too important in a "democratic society" within the meaning of the Convention',[4] an analysis of deaths in detention and their impact on both law and society falls outside the scope of application of article 5, which exclusively deals with arbitrary deprivations of liberty, thus

2 The almost exclusive focus of the present work on the ECHR is due to the extremely sophisticated case law elaborated by the Strasbourg institutions on the issue of detention.

3 *Engel and others* v *The Netherlands*, Application no. 5100/71; 5101/71; 5102/71; 5354/72; 5370/72, 8 June 1976, para. 58.

4 *De Wilde, Ooms and Versyp* v *Belgium* ('Vagrancy'), Application no. 2832/66; 2835/66; 2899/66, 18 June 1971, para. 65.

leaving aside the risks posed by the prison environment to the physical integrity of detainees.

The Council of Europe and Conditions of Detention

More relevant here is the other favoured field of analysis of matters related to detention, namely, the prohibition of torture and other forms of ill-treatment, as encapsulated in article 3 of the ECHR in the following terms: '[n]o one shall be subjected to torture or to inhuman or degrading treatment or punishment.' Although this disposition prohibits in an absolute way torture and inhuman or degrading treatment or punishment, which negate the dignity inherent to the human being, and although the Convention makes the right not to be subjected to such treatments non-derogable, even in times of war or of public emergency threatening the life of the nation,[5] it must also be noted that, unlike other instruments of protection of human rights, the ECHR contains no specific disposition as to the treatment of detainees.[6] Yet, thanks to a clever construction on the part of the Strasbourg institutions, this absolute prohibition of torture became a central element of European human rights law, applicable to everyone, at all times and in all places, and a key component of the 'common heritage' of the European countries mentioned in the Preamble of the Convention. Through its case law, the European Court of Human Rights have continuously affirmed and confirmed that the right not to be subjected to treatments contrary to human dignity is an inalienable attribute of the human being, based on common values shared by all cultural heritages and social systems. As the Court has repeatedly recalled:

> [t]his absolute prohibition of torture and of inhuman or degrading treatment or punishment under the terms of the Convention shows that article 3 enshrines one of the most fundamental values of the democratic societies making up the Council of Europe.[7]

Most interestingly, the conventional omission of conditions of detention has not prevented the Court from successfully developing the most sophisticated jurisprudence on the prohibition of torture and of inhuman or degrading treatment or punishment with respect to detainees. And indeed, in order to ensure the

---

5 See ECHR article 15.

6 See, however, article 10 (1), of the International Covenant on Civil and Political Rights which states that 'All persons deprived of their liberty shall be treated with humanity and with respect for the inherent dignity of the human person.' See also article 5(2), of the Inter-American Convention on Human Rights, which provides that: 'All persons deprived of their liberty shall be treated with respect for the inherent dignity of the human person.'

7 *Soering* v *United Kingdom*, Application no. 14038/88, 7 July 1989, Series A-161, para. 88.

effectiveness of the prohibition of ill-treatment, the European Commission of Human Rights and the Court have both boldly forced an interpretation of article 3 so as to elaborate specific criteria of construction, thereby extending its applicability to areas not explicitly covered by the conventional scope of protection, and notably to conditions of detention. Very early on the European Commission of Human Rights affirmed that detention did not deprive the individual of the rights and freedoms guaranteed by the Convention.[8] Faced with the absence of an express provision within the Convention, the Commission analyzed conditions of detention by reference to the prohibition of torture and found that 'issues may arise under Article 3 in relation to any lawful sentence of imprisonment as regards the manner of its execution and its length.'[9] Benefiting from this daring interpretation and dynamic construction of article 3 of the ECHR, conditions of detention have given rise to an elaborate and comprehensive series of principles, jurisprudentially created and based on a case-by-case approach. In particular, resort to the relative appreciation of each instance has permitted a judicial evaluation of the seriousness of the acts as well as an assessment of whether the threshold of gravity and severity of the ill-treatment is considered to have been reached. According to a now well-established case law:

> ill-treatment must attain a minimum level of severity if it is to fall within the scope of Article 3. The assessment of this minimum is, in the nature of things, relative; it depends on all the circumstances of the case, such as the duration of the treatment, its physical or mental effects and, in some cases, the sex, age and state of health of the victim, etc.[10]

In other words, the Strasbourg institutions will systematically review both objective and subjective parameters so as to appreciate conditions of detention and evaluate the severity of the ill-treatment. In particular, they will always give due consideration to the length of the detainee's isolation in order to assess its lawfulness. In its *Kötalla* decision, the Commission had settled the case law on the matter when it had unambiguously found that: '[n]evertheless, issues may arise under Article 3 in relation to any lawful sentence of imprisonment as regards the manner of its execution and its length.'[11] Far from limiting itself to the consideration of objective factors, the European Court of Human Rights unequivocally held in *Soering* that in its view:

8 *Ilse Koch* v *Federal Republic of Germany*, Application no. 1270/61, 8 March 1962, p. 127.

9 *Kotälla* v *The Netherlands*, Application no. 7994/77, 6 May 1978, p. 240.

10 *Ireland* v. *United Kingdom*, Application no. 5310/71, 18 January 1978, Series A-25, para. 162.

11 *Kotälla* v *The Netherlands*, *supra* note 9, p. 240.

> having regard to the very long period of time spent on death row in such extreme conditions, with the ever present and mounting anguish of awaiting execution of the death penalty, and to the personal circumstances of the applicant, especially his age and mental state at the time of the offence, the applicant's extradition to the United States would expose him to a real risk of treatment going beyond the threshold set by Article 3.[12]

The Court thereby justified, and in a sense legitimized and legalized, its overview of such subjective indicators. For instance, the Strasbourg institutions have not hesitated to take into account the state of health of the detainee, the maintenance in detention of an individual potentially constituting inhuman treatment if the detention seriously compromises his or her health.[13] On that matter however, it is worth noting that the controversial question of the age of the detainee has been treated in a more restrictive fashion, as illustrated by the *Papon* case, in which the Court observed that none of the member states of the Council of Europe had an upper age limit for detention. While it did not exclude the possibility that the detention of an elderly person over a lengthy period of time might, in certain circumstances, raise an issue under article 3 of the Convention, it held that, considering the applicant's general state of health and his conditions of detention, his treatment had not reached the level of severity required to trigger the application of article 3.[14]

Even more subjective perhaps is the question of the humiliation caused by the ill-treatment, which the Strasbourg institutions have reviewed in certain instances so as to assess the severity of the treatment or punishment. As the Court explained in its *Tyrer* judgment:

> in order for a punishment to be 'degrading' and in breach of Article 3, the humiliation or debasement involved must attain a particular level and must in any event be other than that usual element of humiliation referred to in the preceding subparagraph. The assessment is, in the nature of things, relative: it depends on all the circumstances of the case and, in particular, on the nature and context of the punishment itself and the manner and method of its execution.[15]

---

12 *Soering* v *United Kingdom*, *supra* note 7, para. 111.

13 See, for example, *Bonnechaux* v *Switzerland*, Application no. 8224/78, European Commission on Human Rights, 5 December 1978 (a detention for 35 months of a 74-year-old man, with diabetes and a heart condition, would constitute inhuman treatment); *Chartier* v *Italy*, Application no. 9044/80, European Commission on Human Rights, 8 December 1982 (29 years of imprisonment for a man with severe hereditary obesity could potentially amount to inhuman treatment. The Commission went as far as to declare that all appropriate steps were to be taken to diminish the effects of the detention on the individual and to even consider putting an end to the detention).

14 *Papon* v *France*, Application no. 64666/01, 7 June 2001.

15 *Tyrer* v *United Kingdom*, Application No. 5856/72, 25 April 1978, para. 30.

Although the Court further clarified that 'it may well suffice that the victim is humiliated in his own eyes, even if not in the eyes of others,'[16] it nonetheless expressly limited its understanding of humiliation as a treatment contrary to article 3 by specifying that:

> a person may be humiliated by the mere fact of being criminally convicted. However, what is relevant for the purposes of Article 3 (art. 3) is that he should be humiliated not simply by his conviction but by the execution of the punishment which is imposed on him. In fact, in most if not all cases this may be one of the effects of judicial punishment, involving as it does unwilling subjection to the demands of the penal system. [...] It would be absurd to hold that judicial punishment generally, by reason of its usual and perhaps almost inevitable element of humiliation, is 'degrading' within the meaning of Article 3. Some further criterion must be read into the text. Indeed, Article 3, by expressly prohibiting 'inhuman' and 'degrading' punishment, implies that there is a distinction between such punishment and punishment in general.[17]

In other words, judicial punishment will only be inhuman or degrading, and thus contrary to the prohibition of torture and other forms of ill-treatment, if the humiliation or the suffering incurred by this punishment goes beyond the normal and usual humiliation or suffering caused by judicial punishment or sentencing. As held by the Court in its *Soering* judgment:

> [i]n order for a punishment or treatment associated with it to be 'inhuman' or 'degrading', the suffering or humiliation involved must in any event go beyond that inevitable element of suffering or humiliation connected with a given form of legitimate punishment (see the Tyrer judgment). In this connection, account is to be taken not only of the physical pain experienced but also, where there is a considerable delay before execution of the punishment, of the sentenced person's mental anguish of anticipating the violence he is to have inflicted on him.[18]

To contravene article 3 of the Convention, conditions of detention must therefore reach a certain level of humiliation or debasement greater than the degree of humiliation or debasement usually incurred by a prison sentence. A reasoning which arguably leaves the door open for complete subjectivity and legal uncertainty as the appreciation of humiliation and debasement is very much personal and relative. Yet, what the Court undoubtedly highlighted here is that applications dealing with unavoidable consequences of detention, with the usual disciplinary sanctions, with suspension of privileges, or with measures of house arrest, will

16 Ibid., para. 32.

17 Ibid., para. 30.

18 *Soering* v *United Kingdom*, *supra* note 7, para. 100.

be inadmissible and that it is therefore only in abnormal circumstances that the Strasbourg institutions will review and scrutinize the conditions of detention in relation with article 3.[19]

The Council of Europe and State Sovereignty: Police Brutalities and the Requirements of Justice

There is little doubt that insults, brutalities or cruelties inflicted on individuals placed under the authority of the penitentiary personnel or of the military or police forces raise a problem of proof. To try and bypass this issue, the Strasbourg Commission initially opted for recourse to the criterion of the proof "beyond all reasonable doubt" and was extremely strict in its examination of evidentiary elements. Yet, the *Tomasi* case marked a clear shift in the case law as the Commission greatly softened its position so as to consider brutalities perpetrated by the police as inhuman or degrading treatment, and as the Court subsequently upheld its findings.[20] And indeed, the Strasbourg institutions here enacted a real presumption of causality, considering as established, in the absence of proof or of contrary explanation by the state, the allegations of the applicant.[21] If this might have been seen as stretching the rules of evidence and as holding the risk to trivialize the notion of torture and inhuman or degrading treatment, even a brief look at the facts of the case overwhelmingly reveals the outmost gravity of the ill-treatment, thus reducing critics to silence. As alleged by the applicant in this case:

> [h]is body had borne marks which had only one origin, the ill-treatment inflicted on him for a period of forty odd hours by some of the police-officers responsible for his interrogation: he had been slapped, kicked, punched and given forearm blows, made to stand for long periods and without support, hands handcuffed

19 As the Commission explained in the *McFeely et al.* case, where the applicants had started a 'dirt strike' in order to obtain the status of political detainees, material conditions of detention will only amount to degrading treatment if two elements are present: an objective element (conditions of detention degrading in themselves, which was the case here: dirt, no hygiene, etc.) and a subjective element (i.e. a willingness to humiliate the detainee, which was here lacking as such conditions were self-imposed). As a result, the Commission did not find a violation of article 3. See *McFeely, Nugent, Hunter and Campbell* v *United Kingdom*, Application no. 317/78, 15 May 1980. In its *Kalashnikov* judgment, the European Court of Human Rights found a violation of article 3 (degrading treatment) based only on the conditions of detention and despite a lack of intent on the part of the state agents to humiliate the applicant. In this instancc, thc applicant had been subjected to years of imprisonment in extremely small – and overcrowded – cells. See *Kalashnikov* v *Russia*, Application no. 47095/99, 15 July 2002.

20 *Tomasi* v *France*, Application no. 12850/87, decision on the admissibility of the application, 13 March 1990; *Tomasi* v *France*, Application no. 12850/87, 27 August 1992.

21 *Tomasi* v *France*, European Court of Human Rights, *supra* note 20, paras 108-111.

> behind the back; he had been spat upon, made to stand naked in front of an open window, deprived of food, threatened with a firearm and so on.[22]

The Court thankfully seized this opportunity to reiterate the absolute protection which is to be granted to the physical integrity of the human being, unequivocally stating that:

> [t]he requirements of the investigation and the undeniable difficulties inherent in the fight against crime, particularly with regard to terrorism, cannot result in limits being placed on the protection to be afforded in respect of the physical integrity of individuals.[23]

If the *Tomasi* case was received with understandable shock in France, insofar as it shed some dark light on the functioning of the self-proclaimed land of human rights, this instance was, sadly, not isolated. A few years later, the European Court of Human Rights, sitting in Grand Chamber, qualified as torture the treatment endured by M. Selmouni at the hands of French police officers. Here also, a look at the facts of the case unquestionably attests of the extreme seriousness of the ill-treatment. In his criminal complaint lodged at the domestic level, the applicant indeed alleged that he had been the victim of:

> assault occasioning actual bodily harm resulting in total unfitness for work for more than eight days; assault and wounding with a weapon (namely a baseball bat); indecent assault; assault occasioning permanent disability (namely the loss of an eye); and rape aided and abetted by two or more accomplices, all of which offences were committed between 25 and 29 November 1991 by police officers in the performance of their duties.[24]

Although it considered that the rape had not been proved, the Grand Chamber was, however, satisfied that the other facts were to be considered as established.[25] Far from merely highlighting the unforgivable behaviour of these police officers, the *Selmouni* judgment also unveiled the appalling functioning of French justice, so much so that the Grand Chamber decided to bend the admissibility rule on the exhaustion of domestic remedies, finding that, in this instance, such exhaustion had been made impossible.[26] It is true that this was not a revolutionary finding insofar as the European Court of Human Rights had reached a similar conclusion in *Aksoy* v *Turkey*, a case in which the applicant complained of the following ill-treatment, qualified by the Court as torture:

22 Ibid., para. 108.
23 Ibid., para. 115.
24 *Selmouni* v *France*, Application no. 25803/94, 28 July 1999, para. 28.
25 Ibid., paras 82-90.
26 Ibid., paras 74-81.

> [a]ccording to the applicant, on the second day of his detention he was stripped naked, his hands were tied behind his back and he was strung up by his arms in the form of torture known as 'Palestinian hanging.' While he was hanging, the police connected electrodes to his genitals and threw water over him while they electrocuted him. He was kept blindfolded during this torture, which continued for approximately thirty-five minutes. During the next two days, he was allegedly beaten repeatedly at intervals of two hours or half an hour, without being suspended. The torture continued for four days, the first two being very intensive.[27]

Where *Aksoy* and *Selmouni* are at least evolutionary is in the extension of this softening of the admissibility criteria to individual and occasional cases of violence by police forces. Until then, the availability of domestic remedies had solely been reviewed in instances involving an organizational use of violence against individuals placed in detention. In *Ireland* v *UK*,[28] the European Court of Human Rights had indeed already established that the existence of a pre-established plan of inflicted violence, of 'an administrative practice' of ill-treatment, was in itself an indication of the admissibility of the application. According to the Court, such practice could be defined in the following way:

> A practice incompatible with the Convention consists of an accumulation of identical or analogous breaches which are sufficiently numerous and inter-connected to amount not merely to isolated incidents or exceptions but to a pattern or system; a practice does not of itself constitute a violation separate from such breaches.
>
> It is inconceivable that the higher authorities of a State should be, or at least should be entitled to be, unaware of the existence of such a practice. Furthermore, under the Convention those authorities are strictly liable for the conduct of their subordinates; they are under a duty to impose their will on subordinates and cannot shelter behind their inability to ensure that it is respected.[29]

Furthermore, in the eyes of the Court, the existence of such 'administrative practice', implying both a repetition of acts contrary to the Convention and an official tolerance for the acts committed, is to be taken so seriously that, in practice, it excludes the application of the principle according to which all domestic remedies have to be exhausted, this exhaustion of remedies being made impossible by the official tolerance as regards the prohibited acts. In other words, with its *Aksoy* and *Selmouni* decisions, the Court reaffirmed the gravity of allegations of ill-treatments

---

27 *Aksoy* v *Turkey*, Application no. 21987/93, 18 December 1996, para. 14. See also paras 51-57.

28 *Ireland* v *United Kingdom*, Application no. 5310/71, 18 January 1978.

29 Ibid., para. 159.

in detention and reinforced the obligation of the state to adequately provide for an effective remedy, the failure to do so implying a substitution of the Strasbourg institutions to the domestic ones and thus a loss of state sovereignty.

The dispersion of state sovereignty undoubtedly reflects the seriousness with which the European Court of Human Rights is willing to consider the respect for the human rights of individuals placed in detention. And indeed, ill-treatments constitute an inadmissible assault on the physical integrity of the individual and could easily provoke the death of the victim. In this sense, there is an unavoidable link between the prohibition of torture and inhuman or degrading treatment on one hand and the right to life on the other.

This overlap between freedom from torture and right to life had in fact been indirectly acknowledged by the Court when it did not at this time feel it could consider the issue of death penalty under the ambit of the right to life, and so it chose to rule on the death row phenomenon – an inevitable corollary of capital punishment – using article 3 of the Convention, holding that:

> in the Court's view, having regard to the very long period of time spent on death row in such extreme conditions, with the ever present and mounting anguish of awaiting execution of the death penalty, and to the personal circumstances of the applicant, especially his age and mental state at the time of the offence, the applicant's extradition to the United States would expose him to a real risk of treatment going beyond the threshold set by Article 3.[30]

It is worth recalling here that article 2 of the Convention, on the right to life, expressly provides that, '[n]o one shall be deprived of his life intentionally save in the execution of a sentence of a court following his conviction of a crime for which this penalty is provided by law' and thus, *prima facie*, permits resort to the death penalty.[31] For a detailed consideration of this point see Yorke, this collection.

Life Endangered: The Vulnerability of Detainees

As already mentioned in the introduction of the present analysis, the right to life of detainees remains an issue which, if not totally forgotten, is generally bypassed in the social arena and it must be observed – and simultaneously regretted – that this indifference has, although only to a certain extent, also been met in the scholarly

30 *Soering* v *United Kingdom*, *supra* note 7, para. 111.

31 If, in its original and initial version the Convention does not abolish the death penalty, it must be pointed out that, since then, however, both Protocol No. 6 and Protocol No. 13 came into force, thereby abolishing death penalty in all circumstances. Furthermore, it is now the policy of the Council of Europe to require that all new Member States abolish capital punishment as a condition of their admission into the organization. For case law, see *Öcalan* v *Turkey*, Application no. 46221/99, 12 May 2005.

legal sphere. This is all the most surprising as the right to life is duly considered as one of the most fundamental human rights, protected by all human rights law instruments. The European Convention on Human Rights thus provides in its article 2 that:

> 1. Everyone's right to life shall be protected by law. No one shall be deprived of his life intentionally save in the execution of a sentence of a court following his conviction of a crime for which this penalty is provided by law.
> 2. Deprivation of life shall not be regarded as inflicted in contravention of this article when it results from the use of force which is no more than absolutely necessary:
>   a. in defence of any person from unlawful violence;
>   b. in order to effect a lawful arrest or to prevent the escape of a person lawfully detained;
>   c. in action lawfully taken for the purpose of quelling a riot or insurrection.

In spite of the express recognition in article 15 of the same Convention that there shall be 'no derogation from article 2, except in respect of deaths resulting from lawful acts of war', the right to life is not labelled in absolute terms. And indeed, the aim of article 2 is to protect the individual against any arbitrary deprivation of life by the state, not to guarantee an unconditional right to life.

This limitation notwithstanding, what is crucial for the purposes of the present analysis is that article 2 unequivocally specifies that 'everyone' has the right to life, thus expressly protecting all individuals not only against arbitrary death but also against all attack against their physical integrity which would put their life at risk. The indiscriminate scope of application of article 2 undoubtedly covers all individuals, including detainees. As recognized in *L.C.B* v *United Kingdom*,[32] 'the first sentence of article 2 (1) enjoins the State not only to refrain from the intentional and unlawful taking of life, but also to take appropriate steps to safeguard the lives of those within its jurisdiction'.[33]

In *Osman* v *United Kingdom*,[34] arguably responding to an educational ambition aimed at Member States, the European Court of Human Rights – sitting as a Grand Chamber – recalled its *L.C.B* decision and further listed the positive obligations of the state under article 2 of the Convention in the following terms:

> [i]t is common ground that the State's obligation in this respect extends beyond its primary duty to secure the right to life by putting in place effective criminal-

32 *L.C.B* v *United Kingdom,* Application no. 14/1997/798/1001, 9 June 1998.

33 Ibid., para. 36. See also *Öneryildiz* v *Turkey,* Application no. 48939/99, 30 November 2004, in which the Grand Chamber even found that the obligation to take appropriate steps to safeguard the lives of those within the State's jurisdiction 'must be construed as applying in the context of any activity, whether public or not, in which the right to life may be at stake', para. 71.

34 *Osman* v *United Kingdom*, Application no. 87/1997/871/1083, 28 October 1998.

> law provisions to deter the commission of offences against the person backed up by law-enforcement machinery for the prevention, suppression and sanctioning of breaches of such provisions. It is thus accepted by those appearing before the Court that Article 2 of the Convention may also imply in certain well-defined circumstances a *positive obligation on the authorities to take preventive operational measures to protect an individual* whose life is at risk from the criminal acts of another individual.[35]
>
> For the Court, and bearing in mind the difficulties involved in policing modern societies, the unpredictability of human conduct and the operational choices which must be made in terms of priorities and resources, such an obligation must be interpreted in a way which does not impose an impossible or disproportionate burden on the authorities. Accordingly, not every claimed risk to life can entail for the authorities a Convention requirement to take operational measures to prevent that risk from materialising. Another relevant consideration is the need to ensure that the police exercise their powers to control and prevent crime in a manner which fully respects the due process and other guarantees which legitimately place restraints on the scope of their action to investigate crime and bring offenders to justice, including the guarantees contained in Articles 5 and 8 of the Convention.[36]

What has subsequently been termed 'the *Osman* obligation' namely, the obligation to take preventive operational measures to protect an individual whose life is at risk (see Harris, O'Boyle and Warbrick 2009, 44), also applies to individuals placed in detention. This 'highly desirable extension of *Osman*' recognizes the vulnerability of detainees 'as prisoners obviously have limited abilities to protect themselves' (Mowbray 2007, 118). In other words, '[t]he state must take reasonable measures to protect detained persons in real and immediate danger of life-threatening attacks from other detainees of which the authorities knew or ought to have known'(Harris, O'Boyle and Warbrick 2009, 45). According to the European Court of Human Rights' case law, article 2 contains a two-fold obligation for the state: not only must the state refrain from intentionally inflicting death (the negative application of article 2), it must also take all appropriate measures to protect life – and this obligation arguably finds itself heightened precisely when the individuals are at the hands of state agents or, in other words, in detention (the positive application of article 2). This increase in the state's obligation is a rather logical consequence of the custody under which individuals in detention are placed. What applies in private law is here simply transposed to penitentiary matters.

Practically speaking, this means that, should death occur, the state has the obligation and the responsibility to effectively investigate and to adequately inform the families of the individuals detained and deceased. Interestingly, the

35 Ibid., para. 115. Emphasis added.

36 Ibid., para. 116.

state bears this responsibility even in cases where the death remains uncertain. For instance, in *Timurtas* v *Turkey*,[37] the European Court of Human Rights found a violation of article 2 where the applicant's son had been arrested more than six years before, where there had been no news of him during this period and where the Government had been unable to provide any explanation or disclose any information on what had happened to him. The Court unequivocally pointed to the 'lethargy displayed by the investigating authorities'[38] and expressed the state's obligations in the following terms:

> [i]t notes the length of time it took before an official investigation got under way and before statements from witnesses were obtained, the inadequate questions put to the witnesses and the manner in which relevant information was ignored and subsequently denied by the investigating authorities. The Court is in particular struck by the fact that it was not until two years after the applicant's son had been taken into detention that enquiries were made of the gendarmes in Şırnak.[39]

The same duty to investigate and inform the family of the detainees also applies – unsurprisingly – in the case of confirmed deaths in custody, as evidenced by the existence of a dead physical corpse. In *Salman* v *Turkey*,[40] the Court unequivocally recalled that 'the mere fact that the authorities were informed of the death in custody of Agit Salman gave rise *ipso facto* to an obligation under article 2 to carry out an effective investigation into the circumstances surrounding the death'.[41] It further held that:

> [i]n the light of the importance of the protection afforded by Article 2, the Court must subject deprivations of life to the most careful scrutiny, taking into consideration not only the actions of State agents but also all the surrounding circumstances. Persons in custody are in a vulnerable position and the authorities are under a duty to protect them. Consequently, where an individual is taken into police custody in good health and is found to be injured on release, it is incumbent on the State to provide a plausible explanation of how those injuries were caused...*The obligation on the authorities to account for the treatment of an individual in custody is particularly stringent where that individual dies* (emphasis added).[42]

---

37 *Timurtas* v *Turkey*, Application no. 23531/94, 13 June 2000.

38 Ibid., para. 89.

39 Ibid.

40 *Salman* v *Turkey*, Application no. 21986/93, 27 June 2000.

41 Ibid., para. 105. The Court also referred to *mutatis mutandis*, the *Ergi* v *Turkey* judgment of 28 July 1998, *Reports* 1998-IV, p. 1778, s. 82, and the Yaşa judgment, p. 2438, s. 100.

42 *Salman* v *Turkey*, *supra* note 43, para. 99.

While in this particular instance there was clear evidence that the death had been effectively caused by state agents, thus explaining the 'obligation on the authorities to *account* for the treatment' of the individual in custody, the obligation of the state to investigate cases of deaths in custody and to adequately inform the families of the victim exists regardless of the existence or not of a proactive role played by state agents in the occurrence of these deaths. Put differently, the state will also have the obligation to adequately investigate cases of suicides in detention.

Interestingly for the purposes of the present analysis, the United Kingdom didn't escape scrutiny and, in the *Keenan* case,[43] although concluding to a non-violation of article 2, the European Court of Human Rights was given the opportunity to recall that:

> [i]n the context of prisoners, the Court has already emphasised in previous cases that persons in custody are in a vulnerable position and that the authorities are under a duty to protect them. It is incumbent on the State to account for any injuries suffered in custody, which obligation is particularly stringent where that individual dies (see, for example, *Salman v. Turkey* [GC], no. 21986/93, § 99, ECHR 2000-VII). It may be noted that this need for scrutiny is acknowledged in the domestic law of England and Wales, where inquests are automatically held concerning the deaths of persons in prison and where the domestic courts have imposed a duty of care on the prison authorities in respect of those in their custody.[44]

In its subsequent *Jordan* judgment,[45] the Court further specified that the state was also under an obligation to *effectively* inquire into cases of deaths in custody and thus elaborated a list of criteria testing the effectiveness of the investigation, criteria which are worth reproducing here:

> The obligation to protect the right to life under Article 2 of the Convention …also requires by implication that there should be some form of effective official investigation when individuals have been killed as a result of the use of force…The essential purpose of such investigation is *to secure the effective implementation of the domestic laws* which protect the right to life and, in those cases involving State agents or bodies, to ensure their accountability for deaths occurring under their responsibility. What form of investigation will achieve those purposes may vary in different circumstances. However, whatever mode is employed, *the authorities must act of their own motion*, once the matter has come to their attention. They cannot leave it to the initiative of the next of kin

43 *Keenan* v *United Kingdom*, Application no. 27229/95, 3 April 2001.

44 Ibid., para. 91. See also *Edwards* v *United Kingdom*, Application no. 46477/99, 14 March 2002, para. 56.

45 *Jordan* v *United Kingdom*, Application no. 24746/94, 4 May 2001.

either to lodge a formal complaint or to take responsibility for the conduct of any investigative procedures.

For an investigation into alleged unlawful killing by State agents to be effective, it may generally be regarded as necessary for the persons responsible for and carrying out the investigation to be *independent* from those implicated in the events…This means not only a lack of hierarchical or institutional connection but also a practical independence.

The investigation must also be effective in the sense that it is capable of leading to a *determination of whether the force used in such cases was or was not justified* in the circumstances…and to *the identification and punishment of those responsible*…This is not an obligation of result, but of means…

A requirement of *promptness and reasonable expedition* is implicit in this context…

For the same reasons, there must be a *sufficient element of public scrutiny* of the investigation or its results to secure accountability in practice as well as in theory. The degree of public scrutiny required may well vary from case to case. In all cases, however, the *next-of-kin of the victim must be involved* in the procedure to the extent necessary to safeguard his or her legitimate interests (emphasis added).[46]

State initiative, independence, ability to determine the legality of the use of force and the identity and punishment of those responsible, promptness, transparency and family involvement are thus a set of criteria which investigations into deaths while in state custody have to comply with so as to be in line with human rights law. In *Edwards* v *United Kingdom*, the Court further indicated that article 2 placed a positive duty on the state to investigate following any death in state custody, whether or not involving agents of the state and recalled that, to satisfy the requirements of article 2, such investigation had to be effective.[47]

Far from remaining dead letter, the principles erected in Strasbourg were rather swiftly internalized at the domestic level when the House of Lords concurred with the European judges in the *Zahid Mubarek* case.[48] The facts of this instance are worth recalling here as they do shed an interesting – to say the least – light on the failures of prison authorities to adequately prevent deaths in custody and appropriately protect inmates. In this case, after having been found guilty of stealing razors and interfering with a motor vehicle, the victim had been sent to

46 Ibid., paras 105-109.

47 *Edwards* v *United Kingdom*, *supra* note 44.

48 *Regina* v *Secretary of State for the Home Department* (Respondent) *ex parte Amin* (FC) (Appellant), [2003] UKHL 51, [2004] HRLR 3.

Feltham Young Offenders Institute. A few hours before his release, he was battered with a table leg by his cellmate, Robert Stewart, well-known for his anti-social and racist behaviour. Zahid Mubarek died seven days later from his injuries. As Robert Stewart was charged with murder, the inquiry rapidly confirmed that he was a psychopath with racist tendencies. When the case came before the House of Lords, the Law Lords expressly pointed to the prison failings and requested that an inquiry into the death be held as 'a systemic failure to protect the lives of persons detained in custody may well call for even more anxious consideration and raise even more intractable problems'.[49] For Lord Steyn, 'the investigation of cases of negligence resulting in the death of prisoners may often be more complex and may require more elaborate investigation. Systemic failures also affect more prisoners'.[50] And in the words of Lord Hope:

> failures by the prison service which lead to a prisoner's death at the hands of another prisoner are no less demanding of investigation, and of 'the widest exposure possible', than lethal acts which state agents have deliberately perpetrated. Indeed there is a strong case for saying that an even more rigorous investigation is needed if those who are responsible for such failures are to be identified and made accountable and the right to life is to be protected by subjecting the system itself to effective public scrutiny.[51]

More recently, the United Kingdom's obligations with respect to detainees came again to the judicial forefront in the *Al-Skeini* case,[52] following the death of Baha Mousa, who was previously tortured and ill-treated by British troops – while in British custody, at a British-run detention facility in Iraq in September 2003. As explained by Lord Bingham of Cornhill:

> [t]he case of the sixth death, that of Mr Baha Mousa, differs from the other cases insofar as '[t]his deceased, unlike the others, was killed by British troops when held as a prisoner in a British military detention unit. This is the limited basis upon which the Divisional Court held that this case falls within the scope of the Convention, and this is the basis upon which the Secretary of State accepts that finding.'[53]

---

49 Ibid., *Per* Lord Bingham, [2003] UKHL 51, para. 21.

50 Ibid., para. 50.

51 Ibid., para. 62.

52 *Al-Skeini and others* (Respondents) v *Secretary of State for Defence* (Appellant), *Al-Skeini and others* (Appellants) v *Secretary of State for Defence* (Respondent), (Consolidated Appeals), 13 June 2007 [2007] UKHL 26.

53 Ibid.

Exploring the arduous issue of the potential extra-territoriality of human rights law, the Law Lords heavily and extensively relied on the *Banković* decision on admissibility,[54] in which the Strasbourg Court famously ruled that:

> Article 1 of the Convention must be considered to reflect this ordinary and essentially territorial notion of jurisdiction, other bases of jurisdiction being exceptional and requiring special justification in the particular circumstances of each case.[55]

And that:

> The Court's obligation, in this respect, is to have regard to the special character of the Convention as a constitutional instrument of *European* public order for the protection of individual human beings and its role, as set out in Article 19 of the Convention, is to ensure the observance of *the engagements undertaken* by the Contracting Parties (the above-cited Loizidou judgment (*preliminary objections*), at § 93). It is therefore difficult to contend that a failure to accept the extra-territorial jurisdiction of the respondent States would fall foul of the Convention's *ordre public* objective, which itself underlines the essentially regional vocation of the Convention system, or of Article 19 of the Convention which does not shed any particular light on the territorial ambit of that system…
>
> In short, the Convention is a multi-lateral treaty operating, subject to Article 56 of the Convention, in *an essentially regional context* and notably in the legal space (*espace juridique*) of the Contracting States...The Convention was not designed to be applied throughout the world, even in respect of the conduct of Contracting States. Accordingly, the desirability of avoiding a gap or vacuum in human rights' protection has so far been relied on by the Court in favour of establishing jurisdiction only when the territory in question was one that, but for the specific circumstances, would normally be covered by the Convention (emphasis added).[56]

Following the *Banković* precedent, the Law Lords ultimately concluded that the European Convention on Human Rights did not apply in the area of Iraq controlled by British forces, except in the very limited circumstances of British-run military prisons, thus remitting the Baha Mousa's case to the Divisional Court. While the *Al-Skeini* decision undoubtedly raises serious questions of jurisdiction and legal

---

54 *Banković and Others* v *Belgium and 16 Other Contracting States*, Application no. 52207/99, Decision as to the admissibility, 12 December 2001. For an in-depth analysis of the judgment, see, Happold 2003, 77-90.

55 Ibid., para. 61.

56 Ibid., para. 80. Footnote omitted.

reasoning as well as of legal qualification of military detention facilities,[57] the interesting point to note here is that, by recognizing the applicability of human rights law to the case of Baha Mousa, the Law Lords paved the way for a public inquiry into his death. An inquiry which opened in July 2009, and thus complied with the obligations laid down in Strasbourg.

Self-inflicted Deaths: Legal Oblivion, Academic Silence, Political Motivation, and a Diseased Penitentiary System

As the above-mentioned case law highlights, judicial instances do not seem to differentiate between cases of self-inflicted deaths in custody and other occurrences of deaths in custody. In other words, the law of human rights does not operate a distinction between suicides and other cases of deaths in detention. As previously exemplified, in all instances of death, the state finds itself under the exact same obligation to effectively investigate and adequately inform the family of the deceased and there is thus no specific legal appreciation of cases of suicide.

This global and indiscriminate legal and judicial approach to death in custody is arguably not a problem *per se*. What is questionable, however, is the almost total disregard of legal doctrine for the cases of self-inflicted deaths. While assaults on physical integrity and on the life of detainees by state agents are regularly commented upon and legally analyzed, cases of suicides in custody generally fail to attract the interest of legal scholars. As a result, the issue of self-inflicted deaths in detention remains very much the focus of sociologists[58] and journalists.

This is to be highly regretted as, the psychological and social dimension of suicide notwithstanding,[59] it seems that self-inflicted death should also be analyzed from a legal viewpoint, not only to inform the debate on whether there is – or should be – an individual right to end one's own life but also, and more critically for the purposes of the present analysis, to fully review conditions of detention. To address the causes of suicide would indeed mean to question the very function of the penitentiary administration. Consequently, the current failure of the legal doctrine to explore the occurrences of suicides in detention prevents it from adequately assessing the way in which prisons operate.

A legal analysis of self-inflicted deaths in prison custody would arguably face the obstacle generated by the fact that these constitute a variable data, which may fluctuate over time. For instance, the statistics for England and Wales for 2008 show that the number of suicides in prison was at its lowest since 1995 and digesting the numbers from a legal perspective might prove an arduous task. Yet, these statistics

57 For an analysis of this decision, see for example, Lewis 2007; Thienel 2008.

58 See in particular Dear 2006; Liebling 1992; Towl, Snow and McHugh 2000.

59 For an examination of 'the impact of a death in prison custody on the different groups who are likely to be affected namely family and friends, other prisoners, and staff', see, Snow and McHugh 2000, 135-155.

seem to indicate that the Prison Service is willing to respect its obligation 'to protect the public by holding those committed by the courts in a safe, decent and healthy environment' (Snow and McHugh 2000, 135). As explained by Michael Spurr, Director of Operations of the Prison Service:

> [t]he Prison Service has been pursuing a vigorous programme to reduce self-inflicted deaths over a number of years. The programme includes support from specially trained "listeners" (fellow prisoners) and the development of safe cells where ligature points and other means to self-harm are, as far as possible, designed out.[60]

Whether the evolution regarding deaths in detention in England and Wales is marking a real shift into the law and practice, so much so that it should serve as a model for other jurisdictions to follow, or if it is a purely cosmetic change, remains to be seen. What is certain, however, is the fact that the statistics for England and Wales stand in sharp contrast with those recently making press headlines in France.

Ironically, perhaps easier to analyze from a legal perspective is the reverse situation, where the number of suicides in prison would have undergone a dramatic increase, thus revealing an intrinsic failure within the penitentiary system and arguably pointing out the violations of human rights law norms and obligations. Far from being a hypothetical suggestion, this is in fact currently the situation faced by France where the number of deaths in custody has reached a peak. As reported in the newspaper *Le Monde* in March 2009 (Seelow 2009), there had already been 28 suicides in French prisons since the start of 2009, which is to say one death every three days (Le Monde 2009a). As of August 2009, this number had increased to 81, according to official governmental sources, and 92, according to non-governmental organisations (Guichard and Lévêque 2009).[61]

The interest these dramatic statistics have generated in the media has not only forced the executive into taking some form of action and responsibility, it has also lifted the veil on unbearable and appalling conditions of detention, in total contravention with human rights standards, which undoubtedly heavily participate in driving some detainees to commit the irreparable. In particular, the overcrowding of French prisons came under the limelight (see Herzog-Evans 2009), as it was revealed that the average density of prisons and detention facilities is currently 136 per cent, a shocking situation – to say the least – which, astonishingly, has yet to be adequately taken into account, let alone fixed.

---

60 Available at: http://www.unafei.or.jp/english/pdf/PDF_rms/no67/03_Mr.Spurr__pp. 48-60.pdf

61 Half of the detainees who committed suicide were still awaiting trial, even though they only represent 28 per cent of the prison population. The suicide rate among defendants is thus twice as high as that of the individuals condemned (Guichard and Lévêque 2009).

As mentioned above, there was some form of official reaction, notably under the form of a legal reform of the penitentiary system – a new law having been approved by the *Sénat* in March 2009 – but the governmental propositions remain rather timid and all but revolutionary. Symptomatic of this cautious attitude is the fact that the law in question seems to establish individual imprisonment as a principle to be complied with – save in exceptional circumstances – somehow omitting the fact that such a principle exists in French law since 1875 but has so far failed to be properly implemented. Perhaps more interestingly, the legal reform also contemplates and develops other repressive measures such as house arrest and control orders.

It is, however, doubtful that such steps will be sufficient to truly remedy the extreme seriousness of the situation. And indeed, the legal reform notwithstanding, its efficiency has yet to be proven in practice as the number of suicides has not ceased to increase, even since the adoption of the law. It thus seems that it will take more than the adoption of random legal rules to adequately fight against the terrible statistics, and this is probably where the lack of legal academic analysis can cruelly be felt.

So far, the absence of scholarly legal expertise has indeed enabled the government to continuously deny the existence of a link between the overcrowding of prison cells and the number of suicides. This is not to say that there was no governmental response to the high rate of self-inflicted deaths in custody, and notably a proposal to set up an individualized and personalized monitoring of each detainee, to offer specific training to penitentiary staff, to improve the reception of new detainees, to maintain a close association with the detainees' families, to exclusively use tear-proof sheets and blankets as well as non-flammable mattresses and even to organize a tutoring system among detainees (Le Monde 2009b). While such measures can only be welcomed, they nonetheless appear more like emergency patches to solve a situation so grave and severe that it will certainly take more than a re-arranging of the bed linen to solve it (Bekmezian 2009).

The reluctance of French officials to properly look into the matter of the overcrowding of prisons fails, however, to be surprising. There is indeed little doubt that the fight against terrorism and the alleged need for increased security have provided a great incentive – like in most democracies – to bend human rights law and to breach the right to liberty (Jolly 2009). The very well documented fight against terrorism, which has been greatly commented upon and criticized in legal scholarship (Gearty 2008; Lowe 2005; Von Schorlemer 2003), has indeed enabled the government to justify human rights restrictions as well as a rise in the number of arrests and detention. Yet, while this situation has been meticulously studied, the doctrine failed to further its scrutiny into the consequences of this focus on security. In a way, what is more astonishing is not so much the willingness of the French government to avoid bringing up the issue – a politically motivated attitude, albeit evidently questionable – but the disinterest of the legal scholarship to globally analyze and dissect the full range of effects of the fight against terrorism, and not only the increase in the number of arrests and detentions. The doctrinal analysis indeed seems to stop at the denunciation of unlawful arrests and detention and to refrain from looking into the resulting overcrowding of prison cells, which in turn most certainly participated in – if not heavily contributed to – the high rate of self-inflicted deaths in prison. If this vicious circle was academically drawn, it would undoubtedly highlight the slippery slope taken by the French democracy to fight against terrorism to the detriment of human rights law and it would constitute a first step towards forcing the French government into re-establishing individual human rights as a priority on its agenda.

Unless and until it is officially recognized that the dramatic number of suicides in custody is the most dramatic and visible symptom of a terminally-ill penitentiary system, infected from within by appalling sanitary conditions and overcrowding, the disease will simply remain uncured. It is submitted here that this official acknowledgment, required to pave the way for drastic and efficient measures, will only be made possible through academic intervention. Scholarly legal analysis would indeed be crucial for identifying the cause of the disease, and thus in establishing a diagnosis, in researching different methods of treatment, notably through a comparative analysis with other jurisdictions, and in ultimately greatly informing legal reform, thus contributing to provide an effective and efficient remedy. It is well and truly about time that suicides in prison become a juridical focus and the seriousness of the French case dramatically calls for close academic attention, not only to help solve this particular situation but also to once again warn against the dangers of increased security: all in the name of liberty.

Bibliography

Bekmezian, H. (2009) 'Suicide en prison: les syndicats doutent de l'efficacité des mesures', *Le Monde* 19 August.

Dear, G.E. (ed.) (2006) *Preventing Suicide and Other Self-Harm in Prison* (Basingstoke: Palgrave Macmillan).

Gearty, C. (2008) *Essays on Human Rights and Terrorism: Comparative Approaches To Civil Liberties in Asia, the EU and North America* (London: Cameron May).

Guichard, M. and Lévêque, T. (2009) 'Michèle Alliot-Marie promet d'agir contre les suicides en prison', *Le Monde* 18 August, available at: http://www.lemonde.fr.

Happold, M. (2003) 'Bankovic v Belgium and the Territorial Scope of the European Convention on Human Rights', *Human Rights Law Review* 3:1, 77-90.

Harris, D.J., O'Boyle, M. and Warbrick, C. (2009) *Harris, O'Boyle & Warbrick Law of the European Convention on Human Rights*, 2nd edn (Oxford: Oxford University Press).

Herzog-Evans, M. (2009) 'Prisons: On légifère trop et de manière incohérente', *Le Monde* 2 March, available at: http://www.lemonde.fr.

Jolly, P. (2009) '"On paie l'obsession sécuritaire" – Entretien avec le Dr Louis Albrand, auteur d'un récent rapport sur le suicide carcéral', *Le Monde* 18 August available at: http://www.lemonde.fr.

Le Monde (2009a), 'Associations et ministère de la justice divergent sur le nombre de suicides en prison', *Le Monde* 7 August available at: http://www.lemonde.fr

—— (2009b), 'Une honte – Editorial', *Le Monde* 19 August.

Lowe, V. (2005), 'Clear and Present Danger': Responses to Terrorism, *ICLQ* 54, 185-196.

Lewis, J. (2007) 'The European Ceiling on Human Rights', *Public Law* 720-47.

Liebling, A. (1992), *Suicides in Prison* (Oxford: Routledge).

Mowbray, A. (2007) *Cases and Materials on the European Convention on Human Rights*, 2nd Edition (Oxford: Oxford University Press).

Seelow, S. (2009) 'Prison: un suicide sur deux n'avait pas encore été jugé', *Le Monde* 19 March, available at: http://www.lemonde.fr.

Snow, L. and McHugh, M. (2000) 'The Aftermath of a Death in Prison Custody, in Towl, G., Snow, L. and McHugh, M. (eds).

Towl, G., Snow, L. and McHugh, M. (eds) (2000) *Suicide in Prisons*, *with a foreword by Martin Narey* (Oxford: Blackwell Publishers).

Thienel, T. (2008) 'The ECHR in Iraq – The Judgment of the House of Lords', in *R (Al-Skeini) v. Secretary of State for Defence*, *Journal of International Criminal Justice* 6, 115-126.

Von Schorlemer, S. (2003) 'Human Rights: Substantive and Institutional Implications of the War Against Terrorism', *EJIL* 14, 265-282.

PART III
The Denunciation of the Death Penalty

Chapter 9
International Criminal Justice and the Death Penalty

Steven Freeland

Introduction – Differing Approaches to International Crimes

On 2 September 1988, Jean-Paul Akayesu, the former Bourgemestre of Taba Commune in Rwanda, was convicted of genocide by the Trial Chamber of the International Criminal Tribunal for Rwanda (ICTR)[1] as a consequence of his actions during 1994, it having been proven beyond reasonable doubt that he had the requisite intention to 'destroy' the Tutsis (*dolis specialis)*.[2] This was the first time that an international criminal Tribunal had considered the meaning of the crime of genocide – the definition of which had been drawn from the 1948 Genocide Convention[3] – and the first conviction at the international level for this crime. At the time, the Trial Chamber described the crime of genocide as the 'crime of crimes'.[4]

In addition, Akayesu was found guilty of other serious crimes, including one count of direct and public incitement to commit genocide and seven counts of crimes against humanity. In passing sentence one month later, the Trial Chamber imposed a notional life imprisonment against three of the convictions, and various prison sentences of either 10 or 15 years in relation to each of the others. In the end, the Trial Chamber ruled that all of these sentences should be served concurrently and that Akayesu should therefore receive 'a single sentence of life imprisonment'.[5] This

---

1 International Criminal Tribunal for the Prosecution of Persons Responsible for Genocide and Other Serious Violations of International Humanitarian Law Committed in the Territory of Rwanda and Rwandan Citizens Responsible for Genocide and Other Such Violations Committed in the Territory of Neighbouring States, between 1 January 1994 and 31 December 1994 (ICTR).

2 Judgement, *Prosecutor v. Jean-Paul Akayesu*, Case No. ICTR-96-4-T, Trial Chamber, 2 September 1998.

3 Convention on the Prevention and Punishment of the Crime of Genocide, 78 UNTS 277 (1948 Genocide Convention).

4 Judgement, *Prosecutor v. Jean-Paul Akayesu*, Case No. ICTR-96-4-T, Trial Chamber, 2 September 1998, paragraph 16.

5 Sentence, *Prosecutor v. Jean-Paul Akayesu*, Case No. ICTR-96-4-T, Trial Chamber, 2 October 1998.

was consistent with the powers of the ICTR in relation to sentence and punishment, which are as follows:[6]

> [t]he penalty imposed by the Trial Chamber shall be limited to imprisonment.

It is interesting to compare the *Akayesu* decision and sentence with the position at the trials that had taken place before the Nuremberg[7] and Tokyo[8] Military Tribunals some five decades earlier. The Charter of the Nuremberg Military Tribunal[9] – which did not define or incorporate the crime of genocide, but still related to other very serious crimes[10] – empowered that Tribunal to pass sentence as follows:[11]

> [t]he Tribunal shall have the right to impose upon a Defendant, on conviction, death or such other punishment as shall be determined by it to be just.

---

6 Statute of the International Criminal Tribunal for the Prosecution of Persons Responsible for Genocide and Other Serious Violations of International Humanitarian Law Committed in the Territory of Rwanda and Rwandan Citizens Responsible for Genocide and Other Such Violations Committed in the Territory of Neighbouring States, between 1 January 1994 and 31 December 1994, 33 ILM 1598 (ICTR Statute), article 23(1).

7 International Military Tribunal for the trial of the German major war criminals at Nuremberg (Nuremberg Military Tribunal).

8 International Military Tribunal for the trial of the major war criminals in the Far East (Tokyo Military Tribunal).

9 Charter of the Nuremberg International Military Tribunal, annexed to the 1945 London Agreement for the Establishment of an International Military Tribunal, 8 August 1945, 82 UNTS 279 (Nuremberg Military Tribunal Charter).

10 Article 6 of the Nuremberg Military Tribunal Charter specifies the crimes for which the Nuremberg Military Tribunal had jurisdiction:

'(a) Crimes Against Peace: namely, planning, preparation, initiation or waging of a war of aggression, or a war in violation of international treaties, agreements or assurances, or participation in a common plan or conspiracy for the accomplishment of any of the foregoing;

(b) War Crimes: namely, violations of the laws or customs of war. Such violations shall include, but not be limited to, murder, ill-treatment or deportation to slave labor or for any other purpose of civilian population of or in occupied territory, murder or ill-treatment of prisoners of war or persons on the seas, killing of hostages, plunder of public or private property, wanton destruction of cities, towns or villages, or devastation not justified by military necessity;

(c) Crimes Against Humanity: namely, murder, extermination, enslavement, deportation, and other inhumane acts committed against any civilian population, before or during the war; or persecutions on political, racial or religious grounds in execution of or in connection with any crime within the jurisdiction of the Tribunal, whether or not in violation of the domestic law of the country where perpetrated.'

11 Nuremberg Military Tribunal Charter, article 27.

Indeed, the Nuremberg Military Tribunal imposed a sentence of death by hanging on 12 defendants at the main trial. Of these 12 defendants, two were in fact not hanged – Hermann Göring committed suicide the night before the execution and Martin Bormann was tried and sentenced *in absentia*. However, the death penalty was carried out on the remaining 10 defendants who had been given that sentence.

Article 27 of the Charter of the Tokyo Military Tribunal[12] was identical in terms to the provision of the Nuremberg Military Tribunal Charter referred to above, and thus gave the Tokyo Military Tribunal the same sentencing powers. Seven defendants were sentenced to death by hanging by the Tokyo Military Tribunal, the sentence being carried out in December 1948, one month after the completion of the trials.

Consequently, if one were to compare the sentences handed down by the Nuremberg and Tokyo Military Tribunals with the much more recent decision and sentencing in *Akayesu*, it can be concluded that the attitude towards the death penalty within the context of the development of international criminal justice has changed. As indicated by these examples, the recently established international criminal Tribunals have more limited sentencing powers than was the case at the time of the Nuremberg and Tokyo Military Tribunals, and are as a result unable to impose a death sentence. This chapter describes how and why the death penalty now no longer features as a characteristic of international criminal justice.

An Evolving Process of the 'Internationalization of Justice'

The differing approaches taken in the *Akayesu* case on the one hand and the Nuremberg and Tokyo Military Tribunal trials on the other, as to what might represent an appropriate sentence for those convicted of the most serious international crimes, are one aspect of a broader evolution of the nature of international criminal justice that has taken place over the twentieth century, and more particularly over the past 60 years. This process of what might be described as the 'internationalization of justice' has seen some failed attempts, remarkable successes, long periods of inaction and, more recently, the establishment of a range of different mechanisms designed to enforce still evolving concepts of justice.

Towards the end of the twentieth century, and leading into the current decade, this process has seen significant development, culminating (thus far at least), in the establishment, as from 1 July 2002, of the world's first ever permanent international criminal court, the International Criminal Court (ICC). A brief chronology of this process of internationalization is set out below.

---

12 Charter of the International Military Tribunal for the trial of the major war criminals in the Far East, 19 January 1946, 1589 TIAS 3 (Tokyo Military Tribunal Charter).

Prior to the Second World War

Even before the Nuremberg and Tokyo Military Tribunal trials, there had been earlier (unsuccessful) attempts to establish mechanisms of international criminal justice. Once victory by the Allied and Associated Powers seemed likely during the First World War, they began to publicly call for the punishment of war criminals. For example, it was reported in *The Times* (London) and *The New York Times* (New York) in October 1918 that the French Government, in response to a request by the Germans for an armistice, had declared that:

> [c]onduct which is equally contrary to international law and the fundamental principles of all human civilization will not go unpunished … the authors and directors of these crimes will be held responsible morally, judicially, and financially (cited in Jørgensen 2000, 5).

At the conclusion of the First World War, the Treaty of Versailles[13] included an article providing for the prosecution of 'persons accused of having committed acts in violation of the laws and customs of war'.[14] More specifically, the Allied and Associated Powers publicly arraigned William II of Hohenzollern, formerly the German Emperor (Kaiser), 'for a supreme offence against international morality and the sanctity of treaties'.[15] The Treaty of Versailles provided for a special international Tribunal to be constituted, comprising Judges from the United States of America, Great Britain, France, Italy and Japan, to try the Emperor. The proposed Tribunal had the following sentencing powers, which undoubtedly would have included the death penalty:[16]

> [i]n its decision the tribunal will be guided by the highest motives of international policy, with a view to vindicating the solemn obligations of international undertakings and the validity of international morality. It will be its duty to fix the punishment which it considers should be imposed.

---

13 Treaty of Peace between the Allied and Associated Powers and Germany, 112 BFSP 317 (Treaty of Versailles).

14 Treaty of Versailles, article 228.

15 Treaty of Versailles, article 227. On the first day of the First World War, the German Emperor had reportedly written in a letter to the Austrian Emperor:

'Everything must be drowned in fire and blood. It is essential to kill men and women, children and old men, not to leave standing a single house or a single tree. By these terrorist methods, the only methods capable of frightening such a degenerate people as the French, the war will be ended in less than two months: while if I take considerations of humanity into account, the war will last several years': see Jørgensen 2000, 4, and the corresponding footnote.

16 Treaty of Versailles, article 227.

However, by the time the Treaty of Versailles was in force, the Emperor had already sought refuge in The Netherlands, which did not agree to surrender him for prosecution, on the basis that that country regarded itself as a 'land of refuge for the vanquished in international conflicts' (Jørgensen 2000, 7). A trial *in absentia* was considered to be futile and, as a result, the international Tribunal was not established and the proposed trial never took place. The Emperor remained in The Netherlands until his death in 1941.

The Treaty of Versailles also envisaged the establishment of other military Tribunals. Pursuant to article 228 of the Treaty, the German Government was deemed to have expressly recognized the right of the Allied and Associated Powers to bring persons accused of having committed acts in violation of the laws and customs of war before their own military Tribunals. Persons found guilty by those Tribunals would be 'sentenced to punishments laid down by law', once again including the death penalty. Despite the terms of the Treaty, however, the German leadership did not accept this provision in practice, and eventually a compromise was reached by which the Germans themselves would try alleged war criminals. However, as that process developed, it became increasingly clear to the Allied and Associated Powers that these trials fell far below their expectations, and the sentences that were imposed were, in their opinion, grossly inadequate.[17]

In 1920, the Treaty of Sèvres,[18] which covered the terms of peace reached with Turkey, provided for war crimes trials to be held in relation to certain events, including not only the deaths of either Allied soldiers or civilians in occupied territories, but also those of many thousands of Armenians that had taken place under the Ottoman Empire.[19] However the Treaty of Sèvres was never ratified by Turkey and never came into force. It was subsequently 'replaced' (Schabas 2001, 4) in 1923 by the Treaty of Lausanne, which contained a 'Declaration of Amnesty'

17 Between 23 May and 16 July 1921, a number of German War Crimes Trials were conducted under German national law in the Leipzig Criminal Senate of the Imperial Court of Germany. The Allied countries had prepared an initial list of some 900 persons to be tried by that court, which was over time reduced to about 40 individuals. In the end, 12 men were tried, with six being convicted. However, the conduct of these trials was 'very different from the trials expected by the public after the Armistice of 11th November 1918' (Mullins 1921, 23). The sentences delivered by the seven German Judges were widely regarded as being too lenient in the circumstances, and those who had been on trial were considered in Germany as being war heroes. As a result, in the following year, the Allied countries demanded that the Leipzig trials should not continue and that Germans accused of war crimes should instead be tried before an international Tribunal to be established under the Treaty of Versailles. As noted above, this Tribunal never came into existence.

18 1920 UKTS 11.

19 Article 230 of the Treaty of Sèvres provided for the establishment of a Tribunal to try persons responsible for 'massacres committed during the continuance of the state of war on territory which formed part of the Turkish Empire on August 1, 1914'.

for all such offences that had been committed between 1 August 1914 and 20 November 1922.[20]

In 1937, a treaty was adopted by the League of Nations that envisaged the establishment of an international criminal court.[21] However, this instrument was not widely supported and also never came into force. Thus, despite some attempts to do so, at the commencement, and during the course of the Second World War, there was yet to be established any international judicial mechanism that could prosecute those persons charged with having committed war crimes.

The Period Immediately Following the Second World War

This situation changed markedly following the end of the Second World War. As noted, international Military Tribunals were established by the victorious powers in Nuremberg and Tokyo. The agreement to establish these Tribunals as a mechanism to try senior military and political leaders from the defeated German and Japanese war-time regimes respectively only came late in the peace. The Allies, with the exception of the United States, had initially been of the opinion that an international judicial process was not appropriate for this purpose. This was only partially due to the fact that such an approach was unprecedented; it also stemmed from their more 'extreme' views as to how such persons should be brought to account. The British Government had, for example, instituted a formal policy of 'summary execution' of enemy leaders in 1943, which remained in place until the end of the war (Overy 2003, 3-4).

In the end, however, the viewpoint of the United States prevailed – that a public and (largely) transparent international judicial process was the most appropriate mechanism to deal with such persons – and these Military Tribunals were established with a mandate and procedural framework that largely reflected 'Western notions of justice' (ibid., 4). As noted above, an important element in this mechanism was that the death penalty could be imposed. Certainly, without this inclusion (which was not seriously questioned by any of the Allies), there would not have been any agreement to establish these Military Tribunals.

Undoubtedly, during the course of the various trials that ensued before these Military Tribunals, a number of difficult legal issues arose. This was not surprising, given that this was, up until this point, an untested form of criminal justice. It was, for example, asserted by the accused at Nuremberg that the law had been made 'on the run' to fit the actions of those brought before the Military Tribunals, and that their respective mandates offended fundamental principles relating to the rights of an accused. Although the establishment of these Military Tribunals represented a very significant advancement on previous methods of dealing with

20 Treaty of Lausanne Between Principal Allied and Associated Powers and Turkey, 28 LNTS 11.

21 Convention for the Creation of an International Criminal Court, LN Doc C.547(I).M.384(I).1937.V.

crimes committed during hostilities, these assertions were not without some justification.[22]

Indeed, as the trials at the Nuremberg and Tokyo Military Tribunals demonstrated, the international regulation of international crimes is typically developed *in reaction to* rather than in anticipation of horrendous events. As a practical matter, this may sometimes necessitate the adaptation of principles to meet particular situations. This suggests that international criminal courts can work within the *nullum crimen sine lege* (legality) principle[23] whilst, at the same time, refining and elaborating upon 'by way of legal construction, *existing* rules' (Cassese 2003, 149). While this may be a necessary *modus operandi* of the judicial mechanisms of international justice, particularly given the very complex and unique factual situations with which they often deal, it does have its dangers, even the more so if the relevant Tribunal were to have the power to impose a sentence of death.

In December 1946, the United Nations General Assembly affirmed 'the principles of international law recognized by the Charter of the Nürnberg Tribunal and the judgment of the Tribunal' and directed the United Nations International Law Commission (ILC) to formulate those principles for the purposes of codification.[24] The 'Nuremberg Principles' were adopted by the ILC and presented to the United Nations General Assembly in 1950.[25] They were soon considered to reflect customary international law.

---

22 For example, the act of waging an aggressive war had, up until that time, never been defined as a crime in international law. The defendants at the Nuremberg Military Tribunal trials argued that the *ex post facto* punishment of such 'new' crimes in the Nuremberg Military Tribunal Charter violated the *nullum crimen sine lege* principle, which, although not specified in the Nuremberg Charter, had by this time already emerged an overarching principle of many domestic jurisdictions. Although it must be noted that such assertions were not dealt with in an entirely conclusive or satisfactory manner by the Judges of the Nuremberg Military Tribunal, it was generally recognized that those crimes for which the defendants in Nuremberg and Tokyo were charged and convicted were actions that did, in fact, offend the values of the international community.

23 The legality principle is expressed in article 15(1) of the International Covenant on Civil ad Political Rights, 993 UNTS 3 (ICCPR), in the following terms:

'No one shall be held guilty of any criminal offence on account of any act or omission which did not constitute a criminal offence, under national or international law, at the time when it was committed'.

24 United Nations General Assembly Resolution 95(I) (11 December 1946) on the Affirmation of the Principles of International Law Recognized by the Charter of the Nürnberg Tribunal. The ILC was established following the adoption by the United Nations General Assembly of Resolution 174 (II) (21 November 1947) on the Establishment of an International Law Commission, which approved the Statute of the International Law Commission (ILC Statute). Article 1(1) of the ILC Statute provides that '[t]he International Law Commission shall have for its object the promotion of the progressive development of international law and its codification.'

25 See *inter alia* United Nations General Assembly Resolution 488 (V) (12 December 1950) on the Formulation of the Nürnberg Principles.

These principles confirmed the notion of individual criminal responsibility for the commission of crimes under international law, even where national law does not prescribe a penalty for such actions (International Law Commission 1950, Principle II). The notion of a crime under international law was therefore to be regarded as different from, and not dependent upon, specific provisions of national criminal law or any particular characteristic of a State or region. Moreover, it was apparent that those actions that constituted an international crime were not limited to the crimes that were within the specific jurisdiction of the Nuremberg and Tokyo Military Tribunals. Already in its first session in 1946, the United Nations General Assembly had affirmed that 'genocide is a crime under international law'; this being before the crime itself had been formally defined.[26]

Indeed, the Nuremberg Military Tribunal had observed that individual criminal responsibility for the actions in respect of which it was imposing judgment stemmed from the commission of acts that represented a breach of those standards imposed at the international level, and that:[27]

> international law imposes duties and liabilities upon individuals as well as upon States has long been recognized…Crimes against international law are committed by men, not by abstract entities, and only by punishing individuals who commit such crimes can the provisions of international law be enforced.

While there have, of course, been many criticisms of the Nuremberg and Tokyo Military Tribunal processes as simply representing 'victors' justice', this conception of certain 'international' crimes as being (by definition) a part of international law has not been contested and represents an important part of international (criminal) law. For example, over 50 years after the judgment of the Nuremberg Military Tribunal, Lord Browne-Wilkinson of the British House of Lords noted in the *Pinochet* case that:[28]

---

26 United Nations General Assembly Resolution 96(I) (11 December 1946) on the Crime of Genocide, paragraph 4. This Resolution (at paragraphs 1, 2 and 4) referred to genocide as 'a denial of the right of existence of entire human groups', irrespective of whether the actions were 'committed on religious, racial, political or any other grounds'. In the end, the definition of genocide in the 1948 Genocide Convention does not include a 'political' group, but does include 'national' and 'ethnical' groups.

27 'International Military Tribunal (Nuremberg) Judgment and Sentences' (1947) 41 *American Journal of International Law* 172, 221.

28 *R v. Bow Street Metropolitan Magistrate and others, Ex Parte* Pinochet Ugarte (Amnesty International and others intervening) (No 3) (1999) 2 All ER 897 (HL), 898. In fact, it is widely agreed that the international crime of *piracy jure gentium* had been recognized by the maritime States of the world 'since time immemorial': *Attorney-General of the Government of Israel v Eichmann* (1961) 36 ILR 5, paragraph 13. See also, Harris 2004, 266.

> [s]ince the Nazi atrocities and the Nuremberg trials, international law has recognised a number of offences as being international crimes.

An Era of Impunity

Despite the (generally) positive steps made by the Nuremberg (in particular) and Tokyo Military Tribunals regarding the formulation of principles of international criminal law and the development of a process of judicial accountability at the international level, it would take almost 50 years until the next formative stage in the development of international criminal justice was to take place.

Before then, there had been some suggestions in the early 1950s that a permanent international criminal court should be established (Crawford 2003, 109-110), either as a separate institution, or as part of a treaty regime focused on particular crimes. In the aftermath of the horrors of the Second World War, a landmark treaty, the 1948 Genocide Convention, was finalized, which, as noted above, provided for the first time a codified definition of the crime of genocide.[29] Article 6 of that instrument provided as follows:[30]

> [p]ersons charged with genocide or any of the other acts enumerated in article III shall be tried by a competent tribunal of the State in the territory of which the act was committed, or by such international penal tribunal as may have jurisdiction with respect to those Contracting Parties which shall have accepted its jurisdiction.

In the same resolution in which it approved the text of the 1948 Genocide Convention, the United Nations General Assembly expressed the view that, over time, there would evolve an 'increasing need of an international judicial organ for the trial of certain crimes under international law'.[31] Accordingly, it invited the ILC to:[32]

---

29 Article 2 of the 1948 Genocide Convention defines genocide as follows:

'… any of the following acts committed with intent to destroy, in whole or in part, a national, ethnical, racial or religious group, as such:

(a) Killing members of the group;

(b) Causing serious bodily or mental harm to members of the group;

(c) Deliberately inflicting on the group conditions of life calculated to bring about its physical destruction in whole or in part;

(d) Imposing measures intended to prevent births within the group;

(e) Forcibly transferring children of the group to another group.'

30 1948 Genocide Convention, article 6.

31 United Nations General Assembly Resolution 260 (III) B (9 December 1948) on the Prevention and Punishment of the Crime of Genocide: Study by the International Law Commission of the Question of an International Criminal Jurisdiction, paragraph 2.

32 United Nations General Assembly Resolution 260 (III) B (9 December 1948) on the Prevention and Punishment of the Crime of Genocide: Study by the International Law

> study the desirability and possibility of establishing an international judicial organ for the trial of persons charged with genocide or other crimes over which jurisdiction will be conferred upon that organ by international conventions.

Acting on this invitation, the ILC quickly concluded that the establishment of an international court to try persons charged with genocide or other crimes of similar gravity was both desirable and possible. The United Nations General Assembly then established a committee to prepare proposals relating to the establishment of such a court.[33] The committee prepared draft statutes in 1951 and again in 1953.

During the course of finalizing its drafts, the ILC engaged in lengthy discussions about the nature of any penalties associated with a conviction for the commission of an international crime. Although there was some divergence of opinion as to the precise wording of a possible provision on penalties to be included in the draft statute, and indeed whether a maximum penalty should be expressly specified at all, there was general agreement that the proposed court should have the power to impose the death penalty in appropriate circumstances. Indeed, among the views expressed, it was argued that the omission of a reference to penalties would be a 'retrograde step' in comparison to the Nuremberg Military Tribunal Charter;[34] that 'the crimes concerned were so serious that death would not be too severe a punishment for them';[35] and that failure on the part of the ILC to prescribe the death penalty 'would suggest that it disapproved of the penalties imposed by the [Nuremberg Military] Tribunal'.[36]

Indeed, one ILC Member even went so far as to suggest that, in conformity with the expressed desire that States themselves also take all appropriate measures to prosecute those persons alleged to have committed international crimes, those States that did not have, or had recently abolished the death penalty in their domestic laws (for example, Brazil) would willingly (re)incorporate that penalty

Commission of the Question of an International Criminal Jurisdiction, paragraph 3.

33 United Nations General Assembly Resolution 489 (V) (12 December 1950) on International Criminal Jurisdiction, paragraph 1. The committee was initially comprised of representatives of 17 States – Australia, Brazil, China, Cuba, Denmark, Egypt, France, India, Iran, Israel, The Netherlands, Pakistan, Peru, Syria, the United Kingdom of Great Britain and Northern Ireland, the United States of America and Uruguay.

34 ILC Member Ricardo J. Alfaro (Panama), [1951] Vol. I, *Yearbook of the International Law Commission*, 'The Draft Code of Offences Against the Peace and Security of Mankind', p. 254, paragraph 107.

35 ILC Member J.P.A. François (The Netherlands), [1951] Vol. I, *Yearbook of the International Law Commission*, 'The Draft Code of Offences Against the Peace and Security of Mankind', p. 252, paragraph 90.

36 ILC Member Mr François (The Netherlands), [1951] Vol. I, *Yearbook of the International Law Commission*, 'The Draft Code of Offences Against the Peace and Security of Mankind', p. 255, paragraph 142.

into its national legislation for these crimes, 'for philosophical reasons connected with the concept of educative or corrective penalties'.[37]

Although it had been making considerable progress in its work, the United Nations General Assembly suddenly stepped in to instruct the ILC to indefinitely halt all work on the drafting of a statute for a proposed permanent international criminal court.[38] The spectre of *Realpolitik* had emerged, with the onset of the Cold War making it impossible for the international community to find the common will to build upon the foundations laid by the Nuremberg and Tokyo Military Tribunal processes. There were also other very strong political forces at work, as States sought to cling to the principle of 'non-intervention', as specified in article 2(7) of the United Nations Charter.[39]

Instead, over the ensuing decades, an era of 'impunity for the perpetrators of these [international] crimes'[40] took hold, which would not be challenged to any significant degree until after the fall of the Berlin Wall in November 1989. During this period, atrocities took place in countries around the globe – including in the Soviet Union, Uganda, Nigeria, Argentina, Bangladesh, East Timor, Algeria, Cambodia and Iraq to name but a few. However, these crimes were for all intents and purposes neither investigated, let alone punished, by a court of law.

Indeed, it has been estimated that approximately 170 million people were killed during the period 1945 to 1990, with little if any accountability (Bassiouni 1998; Freeland 2006, 11). In certain respects, it was as if the principles that had emerged from the Nuremberg Military Tribunal process, as well as the 1948 Genocide Convention, were treated as ends unto themselves – sitting on the shelf – with little tangible action to address the commission of such crimes in a practical sense.

There were only a few relatively minor steps taken in this regard by the international community during this lengthy period of (virtual) inaction. A treaty was finalized specifying that statutory limitations under national law were inappropriate and should not be applicable to war crimes and crimes against humanity, which were described as 'among the gravest crimes in international

37 ILC Member Gilberto Amado (Brazil), [1951], Vol. I *Yearbook of the International Law Commission*, 'The Draft Code of Offences Against the Peace and Security of Mankind', p. 253, paragraph 103.

38 See United Nations General Assembly Resolution 897 (IX) (4 December 1954) on the Draft Code of Offences Against the Peace and Security of Mankind, paragraph 3; United Nations General Assembly Resolution 898 (IX) (14 December 1954) on the International Criminal Jurisdiction, paragraph 2.

39 1 UNTS 16; 59 Stat.1031 (United Nations Charter). Article 2(7) of the United Nations Charter provides *inter alia* as follows:

'Nothing contained in the present Charter shall authorize the United Nations to intervene in matters which are essentially within the domestic jurisdiction of any state or shall require the Members to submit such matters to settlement under the present Charter'.

40 Rome Statute of the International Criminal Court, 2187 UNTS 3 (Rome Statute), preambular paragraph 5.

law'.[41] Yet, there was an almost total lack of political will by most countries to prosecute, within their respective national court systems, individuals suspected of committing such crimes over more than four decades.

The prosecution and subsequent conviction of Otto Adolf Eichmann by the Israeli District Court in 1961[42] (affirmed by the Israeli Supreme Court in the following year)[43] was one of the very few exceptions to this failure to act. Following the dismissal of his appeal, the death sentence by hanging imposed on Eichmann was carried out on 31 May 1962. After his death, Eichmann's body was cremated and his ashes scattered in international waters, so as to ensure that there could be no future memorial to his life and that no State would serve as his final resting place. Despite the fact that it still remains legal under Israeli national law to impose a death sentence for 'exceptional crimes',[44] this has been the only civil execution ever carried out in that country, which has a general policy of not instituting the death penalty.

Another example (of sorts) of an attempt during this period to prosecute those alleged to have committed international crimes followed the fall of the Khmer Rouge regime in Cambodia in 1979. The genocide carried out by that regime in the period 1975-1979 represents one of the most cataclysmic events that the Asian region, if not the world, has ever experienced. By most estimates, almost two million people, representing over 20 per cent of the total population of the country at the time, died directly as a result of the four year reign of terror.[45]

Following its invasion of Cambodia, the Vietnamese authorities established a revolutionary people's tribunal, which in 1979 tried, convicted and imposed a death sentence on Khmer Rouge leader Pol Pot and his deputy Prime Minister. However, this judicial process and the subsequent sentence of death had not been preceded by any semblance of due process (for example, the 'trial' was held *in absentia*) and was not recognized internationally as a credible trial. In any event, the accused were by that time already safely in Thailand, where their protection was also supported by both China and the United States, thus rendering futile any attempt to have them extradited back to Cambodia. As noted below, it would not be until the beginning of the twenty-first century that a mechanism of international justice would be established to investigate and prosecute the 'killing fields' of Cambodia.

---

41 Convention on the Non-Applicability of Statutory Limitations to War Crimes and Crimes against Humanity, 8 ILM 68, preambular paragraph 4.

42 *Attorney-General of the Government of Israel v Eichmann* (1961) 36 ILR 5. Eichmann was prosecuted under Israeli law (the 1951 Nazi and Nazi Collaborators (Punishment) Law) for war crimes, crimes against the Jewish people (the definition of which was modeled on the definition of genocide in the 1948 Genocide Convention) and crimes against humanity.

43 *Eichmann v Attorney-General of the Government of Israel* (1962) 36 ILR 277.

44 Amnesty International website, 'Abolitionist and Retentionist Countries' <http://www.amnesty.org/en /death-penalty/abolitionist-and-retentionist-countries>

45 Yale University, 'Cambodian Genocide Program' <www.yale.edu/cgp>

In 1987, Klaus Barbie, who had been the head of the Gestapo in Lyons from November 1942 to August 1943 and was known as the 'Butcher of Lyons', was convicted by the Rhone *Cour d'assises* of 17 counts of crimes against humanity. His appeal was dismissed by the French Court of Cassation.[46] By the time that he was charged and convicted, the death penalty was no longer available under French national law[47] and Barbie was sentenced to life imprisonment. He died of leukaemia four years later.

Apart from these isolated examples, however, there was a singular lack of credible action on the part of national jurisdictions to deal with the perpetrators of serious crimes and, coupled with the fact that the prevailing geopolitical climate had meant that there were also no international mechanisms of criminal justice in existence, this led to an acknowledgement by the United Nations General Assembly in 1970 that:[48]

> many war criminals and persons who have committed crimes against humanity are continuing to take refuge in the territories of certain States and are enjoying protection.

Shortly afterwards, an attempt was, in fact, made to at least create the legal framework for the establishment of a new mechanism of international justice during this otherwise period of inaction. In 1973, a treaty was concluded that dealt with the crime of apartheid.[49] According to one commentator, the 1973 Apartheid Convention categorized apartheid as 'a separate and special phenomenon, confined essentially to southern Africa' (Crawford 2003, 123). However, this instrument did again raise the possibility that an international criminal Tribunal might be established. In similar wording to article 6 of the 1948 Genocide Convention, article V of the 1973 Apartheid Convention provided as follows:[50]

> [p]ersons charged with the acts enumerated in article II of the present Convention may be tried by a competent tribunal of any State Party to the Convention which may acquire jurisdiction over the person of the accused or by an international

46 *Féderation National des Déportées et Internés Résistants et Patriots and Others v. Barbie* 100 ILR 330.

47 France had abolished the death penalty for all crimes within its national law in 1981: Amnesty International website, 'Abolitionist and Retentionist Countries' <http://www.amnesty.org/en/death-penalty/abolitionist-and-retentionist-countries>

48 United Nations General Assembly Resolution 2712 (XXV) (9 December 1970) on the Question of the Punishment of War Criminals and of Persons who have Committed Crimes against Humanity, paragraph 1.

49 International Convention on the Suppression and Punishment of the Crime of Apartheid, 1015 UNTS 243 (1973 Apartheid Convention).

50 1973 Apartheid Convention, article V.

> penal tribunal having jurisdiction with respect to those States Parties which shall have accepted its jurisdiction.

The 1973 Apartheid Convention also affirmed that international criminal responsibility was to apply to individuals, members of organizations and institutions and representatives of the State.[51] In 1980, the *Ad Hoc* Working Group of Experts on South Africa for the United Nations Commission of Human Rights commissioned various legal experts to prepare a draft statute for this proposed Tribunal (Jørgensen 2000, 45). It was not, however, contemplated that the death penalty would apply to this proposed Tribunal. The draft statute was eventually approved by the *Ad Hoc* Working Group[52] but, as was the case with its proposed predecessor under the 1948 Genocide Convention, no such Tribunal was established under the 1973 Apartheid Convention.

A New Era of International Justice – the 1990s and Beyond

In fact, it was not until the shackles of the Cold War were loosened in the early 1990s, and the United Nations Security Council was then able to play a more active role in addressing international crimes, albeit *after* the fact, that the world finally saw a renewed and much more concerted effort to create a system of international criminal Tribunals. Faced with the genocides in both Rwanda and in the former Yugoslavia – each of which took place 'under the watch of the [United Nations] Security Council and United Nations peacekeepers'[53] – the United Nations Security Council, acting under its powers pursuant to Chapter VII of the United Nations Charter,[54] eventually

51 1973 Apartheid Convention, article III.

52 See 'Report of M.C. Bassiouni to the *Ad Hoc* Working Group of Experts on South Africa for the Commission of Human Rights', *Study on ways and means of insuring the implementation of International instruments such as the International Convention on the Suppression and Punishment of the Crime of Apartheid, including the establishment of the international jurisdiction envisaged by the Convention*, 19 January 1981, UN Doc E/CN/4/1426.

53 United Nations General Assembly, 'Implementing the responsibility to protect: Report of the Secretary-General' (12 January 2009) UN Doc A/63/677, paragraph 5.

54 Chapter VII of the United Nations Charter (articles 39-51) gives the United Nations Security Council certain powers 'with respect to Threats to the Peace, Breaches of the Peace, and Acts of Aggression': United Nations Charter, chapter VII, title. This was the first time that these powers had been used to establish *ad hoc* international criminal Tribunals. In early cases before each of the *ad hoc* Tribunals, it had been argued that they were established unlawfully by the United Nations Security Council. In both cases, these claims were dismissed: see Decision on Defence Motion for Interlocutory Appeal on Jurisdiction, *Prosecutor v Duško Tadić*, Case No. IT-94-1, Appeals Chamber, 2 October 1995: Decision on the Defence Motion on Jurisdiction, *Prosecutor v. Joseph Kanyabashi*, Case No. ICTR-96-15-T, Trial Chamber II, 18 June 1997.

agreed to establish two *ad hoc* Tribunals to prosecute the perpetrators of serious crimes committed during those conflicts.[55]

The establishment of these *ad hoc* Tribunals was a significant and highly symbolic development. As noted above, it had been almost 50 years since the Nuremberg and Tokyo Military Tribunals had been created. Apart from the judgments of those two Military Tribunals and the rare national trial, there had been virtually no jurisprudence relating to the application of international law principles to the commission of international crimes. There was a clear recognition that such crimes existed in international law – however, there was, understandably, only limited expertise in the area of international criminal law. For all intents and purposes, there had been no 'practice' of international criminal law for two generations.

Moreover, difficult decisions had to be taken as to the scope of their respective jurisdiction, logistical issues such as location, staffing and financing for these *ad hoc* Tribunals (England 2001, 943) as well as their procedural arrangements, which would, ultimately, represent an 'amalgam' of common law and civil law principles (Podgers 1996, 58).[56] At the time that they were created, no-one could be entirely sure how the first international criminal Tribunals to be established for five decades would fare and what would flow from their activities, and from the activities of any other subsequent international Tribunals.

No doubt conscious of the arguments raised by the accused before the Nuremberg Military Tribunal in relation to the *nullum crimen sine lege* principle, the then Secretary-General of the United Nations, Kofi Annan, in reporting on the establishment of the ICTY, expressed the widely held view that this new Tribunal would only be concerned with the prosecution of those crimes that were 'doubtless part of customary international law.'[57] Like the Nuremberg and Tokyo Military Tribunals, both of these *ad hoc* Tribunals were created and mandated by way of a Statute,[58] with the crimes within the jurisdiction of each

55 These are the International Criminal Tribunal for the Former Yugoslavia (ICTY), which was formally established pursuant to United Nations Security Council Resolution 827 (25 May 1993) on the Tribunal (Former Yugoslavia), and the ICTR.

56 Podgers quotes Judge Gabrielle Kirk McDonald in Decision on the Prosecutor's Motion Requesting Protective Measures for Victims and Witnesses, *Prosecutor v Duško Tadić*, Case No. IT-94-1, Trial Chamber, 10 August 1995, paragraph 22. This amalgam of principles has, at times, lead to significant differences in the approach taken by some Judges from common law as opposed to those from civil law backgrounds, particularly in the early days of these Tribunals: see, for example, the Separate Opinion of Judge Stephen in the same case. For a discussion of the application of this amalgam of principles in the procedural practice of the *ad hoc* Tribunals, see, Freeland 2001, 260.

57 United Nations Security Council, 'Report of the Secretary-General Pursuant to Paragraph 2 of Security Council Resolution 808' (3 May 1993), paragraphs 33-35.

58 These were the Statute of the International Tribunal for the Prosecution of Persons Responsible for Serious Violations of International Humanitarian Law Committed in the

Tribunal clearly specified,[59] as were their respective temporal and geographic jurisdictions.[60]

Also similar to the Nuremberg Military Tribunal Charter and Tokyo Military Tribunal Charter, the ICTY Statute and ICTR Statute specify the penalties that each of the *ad hoc* Tribunals is able to impose.[61] As noted above, this does not include the death penalty. Instead, the ICTY and ICTR Statutes both specify that the sentences that either of the Tribunals could impose were limited to 'imprisonment', as well as some possible additional sanctions in appropriate circumstances.[62]

The decision to exclude any power to impose the death penalty within the terms of the ICTY and ICTR Statutes was not, however, unanimous. In drafting the relevant Statutes, it was regarded as important to specify that each Tribunal should take cognizance of the relevant national sentencing practices when imposing sentences, among other things so as to assuage concerns regarding the application of the principle of legality (see Cryer et al. 2007, 394).

In the ICTR Statute, for example, the Tribunal is directed that:[63]

> [i]n determining the terms of imprisonment, the Trial Chambers shall have recourse to the general practice regarding prison sentences in the courts of Rwanda.

Territory of the Former Yugoslavia since 1991, 32 ILM 1159 (ICTY Statute) and the ICTR Statute respectively.

59 The crimes for which the ICTY has jurisdiction are Grave breaches of the Geneva Conventions of 1949 (ICTY Statute, article 2), Violations of the laws or customs of war (ICTY Statute, article 3), Genocide (ICTY Statute, article 4) and Crimes against humanity (ICTY Statute, article 5). The crimes for which the ICTR has jurisdiction are Genocide (ICTR Statute, article 2), Crimes against humanity (ICTR Statute, article 3) and Violations of Article 3 Common to the Geneva Conventions and of Additional Protocol II (ICTR Statute, article 4).

60 The territorial jurisdiction of the ICTY is 'the territory of the former Socialist Federal Republic of Yugoslavia, including its land surface, airspace and territorial waters' and its temporal jurisdiction 'extend[s] to a period beginning on 1 January 1991': ICTY Statute, article 8. The territorial jurisdiction of the ICTR is 'the territory of Rwanda including its land surface and airspace as well as…the territory of neighbouring States in respect of serious violations of international humanitarian law committed by Rwandan citizens' and its temporal jurisdiction 'extend[s] to a period beginning on 1 January 1994 and ending on 31 December 1994': ICTR Statute, article 7.

61 See ICTY Statute, article 24 and ICTR Statute, article 23.

62 For example, article 24(3) of the ICTY Statute provides that:

'[i]n addition to imprisonment, the Trial Chambers may order the return of any property and proceeds acquired by criminal conduct, including by means of duress, to their rightful owners.' See also ICTR Statute, article 23 (3).

63 ICTR Statute, article 23(1).

A similar provision (referring to the general practice in the Former Yugoslavia) is found in the ICTY Statute.[64] Despite the reference in these provisions to the relevant national sentencing practices, however, the *ad hoc* Tribunals have concluded that they are not actually bound by those practices, although they must 'consider' them.[65]

In the case of the ICTR, there was one point of radical departure between the sentences permissible in the international Tribunal and Rwanda's own domestic laws. At the time that the ICTR Statute was finalized – and also at the time of the conviction and subsequent sentencing of Jean-Paul Akayesu – the national courts of Rwanda had the power to impose a sentence of death.[66] At the time that the United Nations Security Council was voting on the Resolution by which the ICTR was to be established,[67] Rwanda was (coincidentally) a non-permanent member of the Council. The vote at the United Nations Security Council to establish the ICTR was 14 in favour and one (Rwanda) against.

Ironically, therefore, although it was in favour of the creation of an international criminal Tribunal to examine the atrocities that had taken place in its territory during 1994 and to prosecute the perpetrators of those crimes – indeed, the Rwandan Government had called for the establishment of an international Tribunal

64 ICTY Statute, article 24(1).

65 In Judgement, *Prosecutor v. Radislav Kristić*, Case No. IT-98-33-A, App. Ch., 19 April 2004, the Appeals Chamber of the ICTY, quoting with approval the conclusion of the ICTY Trial Chamber in Judgement, *Prosecutor v. Dragoljub Kunarac and others*, Case Nos. IT-96-23-T and IT-96-23/1-T, 22 February 2001 (at paragraph 829), confirmed that (at paragraph 260):

'[a]lthough the Trial Chamber is not bound to apply the sentencing practice of the former Yugoslavia, what is required certainly goes beyond merely reciting the relevant criminal code provisions of the former Yugoslavia. Should they diverge, care should be taken to explain the sentence to be imposed with reference to the sentencing practice of the former Yugoslavia, especially where international law provides no guidance for a particular sentencing practice. The Trial Chamber notes that, because very important underlying differences often exist between national prosecutions and prosecutions in this jurisdiction, the nature, scope and the scale of the offences tried before the International Tribunal do not allow for an automatic application of the sentencing practices of the former Yugoslavia.'

66 Rwanda only abolished the death penalty for all crimes within its national law in 2007: Amnesty International website, 'Abolitionist and Retentionist Countries' <http://www.amnesty.org/en/death-penalty/abolitionist-and-retentionist-countries>. By contrast, the death penalty was abolished in most of the republics of the Former Yugoslavia (apart from Bosnia and Herzegovina) by a constitutional amendment in 1977: see Judgement, *Prosecutor v. Dragoljub Kunarac and others*, Case Nos. IT-96-23-T and IT-96-23/1-T, 22 February 2001, paragraph 831. In fact, the ICTY has found that the (subsequent) abolition of the death penalty also in Bosnia and Herzegovina was a factor to be taken into account when imposing a prison sentence: see Sentencing Judgement, *Prosecutor v. Ivica Rajić*, Case No. IT-95-12-S, Trial Chamber I, 8 May 2006, paragraphs 175-6.

67 United Nations Security Council Resolution 955 (8 November 1994) on the establishment of an International Tribunal and adoption of the Statute of the Tribunal.

as quickly as possible – Rwanda was opposed to the powers of the Tribunal itself. This was for a number of reasons, but among the most significant was its view that the death penalty should be an integral part of any system of justice to be established to deal with the genocide that had taken place.

Notwithstanding these concerns, however, by the time that these new Tribunals were to be established, international human rights standards restricting the use of the death penalty had developed, and the legal context relating to sentences for international crimes had thus changed significantly from the position that prevailed in the period immediately following the Second World War (see below).

In the 15 years since the establishment of the *ad hoc* Tribunals, a number of other international/internationalized criminal Tribunals have also been established to prosecute the perpetrators of international crimes.[68] None of these allow for the imposition of the death penalty.[69] The establishment of all of these Tribunals, as well as the ICC itself, and the broad extent of their collective jurisdictional reach, represent a continuation of the ongoing process of the internationalization of criminal justice – incorporating the establishment of formal international mechanisms to apply and enforce existing universal norms of international criminal law, as well as those that will develop in the future.

Each of these developments therefore reflects a remarkable turnaround in terms of accountability. Whereas, for example, Heads of State would have once regarded themselves as above the law, the process that was begun by the *ad hoc* Tribunals and has since continued indicates that this is no longer the case. This has seen former leaders such as the former Yugoslavia's Slobodan Milosevic, Chile's Augusto Pinochet, Liberia's Charles Taylor, Rwanda's Jean Kambanda, Peru's Alberto Fujimori, Iraq's Saddam Hussein and Chad's Hissène Habré[70] all face legal accountability in some form relating to their (alleged) crimes.

---

68 These include The Special Court for Sierra Leone, The Extraordinary Chambers for Cambodia, The Serious Crimes Panels for Timor-Leste and, most recently, The Special Tribunal for Lebanon. Even more recently, there has even been a suggestion to establish another international Tribunal to try those persons currently detained at Guantánamo Bay, see Mettraux 2009, and (once again) in relation to the violence that took place in East Timor in 1999, see Vaswani 2009.

69 In the case of the Special Tribunal for Lebanon, for example, Lebanese criminal law will be applied by the Tribunal, subject to the exclusion of penalties such as death penalty and forced labor, which are otherwise applicable under the Lebanese law, Instead, article 24(1) of the Statute of the Special Tribunal for Lebanon provides that the Tribunal has the following sentencing powers: 'The Trial Chamber shall impose upon a convicted person imprisonment for life or for a specified number of years.' In relation to Lebanese domestic law, in 2008, the Minister of Justice submitted a draft law proposing that the death penalty be abolished, see Amnesty International 2009, 9.

70 On 19 February 2009, Belgium instituted proceedings before the International Court of Justice against Senegal, on the grounds that a dispute exists 'between the Kingdom of Belgium and the Republic of Senegal regarding Senegal's compliance with its obligation to prosecute' the former President of Chad, Hissène Habré, 'or to extradite him to Belgium

More recently, in early 2009, the ICC issued an arrest warrant for President Omar Al Bashir for his alleged responsibility for crimes against humanity and war crimes in relation to the situation in Sudan.[71] This represents the first time that the ICC has indicted a sitting Head of State and marks an important step forward in the activities of the Court.

While each of these processes have had and will have varying degrees of 'success', the point to note is that it would have been unthinkable even 15 years ago that Heads of State such as these would ever have faced trial in a public forum. What this process has demonstrated is that, despite the flaws inherent in any system of international criminal justice, those suspected of bearing the greatest responsibility for serious crimes can be made accountable pursuant to principles derived from international law, under which it is not necessary (or appropriate) to impose a death penalty in order for this to be the case.

This has continued with the establishment of the ICC, which also does not have the power to impose a death sentence. Following years of debate and negotiation, involving work by the ILC and others in the drafting of a proposed treaty, the United Nations General Assembly convened the United Nations Diplomatic Conference of Plenipotentiaries on the Establishment of an International Criminal Court (1998 Rome Conference), which was to be held from 15 June to 17 July 1998, 'with a view to finalizing and adopting a convention on the establishment of an international criminal court'.[72]

The 1998 Rome Conference was attended by delegations from over 160 States, 30 Intergovernmental Organizations and 230 Non-Governmental Organizations. At the beginning of those four weeks in Rome, several complex questions remained to be agreed. As a result, the discussions during the 1998 Rome Conference were at times tortured and acrimonious, not the least because many of the States represented there had not participated in the preliminary drafting and negotiation sessions and were thus confronted with a detailed draft perhaps even for the first time (Kalivretakis 2001, 697-698). Right up until the final vote at the 1998 Rome Conference, there remained a number of significant issues – particularly in relation to the extent of the Court's proposed jurisdiction and its relationship with the United Nations Security Council – with which some States had great difficulty.

for the purposes of criminal proceedings': International Court of Justice, 'Belgium institutes proceedings against Senegal and requests the Court to indicate provisional measures' (Press Release, 19 February 2009), <http://www.icjcij.org/docket/files/144/15052. pdf?PHPSESS ID=662d101b508c0ff67b1fcafb724d112f>.

71 Decision on the Prosecution's Application for a Warrant of Arrest against Omar Hassan Ahmad Al Bashir, *The Prosecutor v. Omar Hassan Ahmad Al Bashir ('Omar Al Bashir')*, Case No. ICC-02/05-01/09, Pre-Trial Chamber I, 4 March 2009.

72 United Nations General Assembly Resolution 52/160 (15 December 1997) on the Establishment of an International Criminal Court, paragraph 3.

In the end, however, the 1998 Rome Conference agreed on the final terms of the Rome Statute, albeit not unanimously.[73]

As events at the 1998 Rome Conference and subsequently have illustrated, the establishment of the first permanent international criminal court was as political an event as it was significant in the evolution of international criminal justice. The negotiating States, as well as the other stakeholders at the 1998 Rome Conference, represented a multitude of differing views as to how the Court should be structured. There were significant divisions among the participating delegations in a number of important areas. The final terms of the Rome Statute were, in many respects, the result of an 'enduring tension inherent in multilateral negotiations between sovereignty and universality' (McCormack and Robertson 1999, 636), which by necessity required a 'solution' based upon political compromise. Indeed, compromise was needed on all sides in order that the Rome Statute could be presented as a 'marketable' instrument to the conference delegates. Such is the nature of multilateralism, which seeks to be broadly inclusive, rather than representing the prevailing views of one or two States above all others.

In relation to the appropriate penalty to be included in the Rome Statute, in line with the development of the *ad hoc* Tribunals and the other mechanisms of international justice established since the 1990s, the view prevailed at the 1998 Rome Conference that the death penalty should not be included. Once again, however, this was not unanimous, with the issue remaining quite controversial. Some States claimed that inclusion of the death penalty was an essential element in establishing the credibility of the Court (Cryer et al. 2007, 394) and that it would promote the deterrence aspects of the Court's operation as a way of 'contribut[ing] to the prevention of such [international] crimes'.[74] Other States asserted at the 1998 Rome Conference that if the Rome Statute were to be considered as 'representative' of all systems, it should include the death penalty.

In the end, however, predominantly at the insistence of European States, the decision was taken that, despite the undoubted *sui generis* nature of the ICC (as being the first *permanent* institution), the Rome Statute should reflect the trend adopted in the other contemporary mechanisms of international criminal justice on this issue. Article 77(1) of the Rome Statute, which is headed 'Applicable Penalties', thus provides that the ICC may impose one of the following penalties on a convicted person:[75]

---

73 Of those represented at the 1998 Rome Conference, 120 States voted to adopt the Rome Statute. There were 21 abstentions and seven States – China, Iraq, Israel, Libya, Qatar, Yemen and the United States of America – voted against the resolution. For details of the 1998 Rome Conference, see the website of the Conference at <http://www.un.org/icc/index.htm>.

74 Rome Statute, preambular paragraph 5.

75 Rome Statute, article 77(1). In addition, article 77(2) provides that:

'In addition to imprisonment, the Court may order:

(a) A fine under the criteria provided for in the Rules of Procedure and Evidence;

> (a) Imprisonment for a specified number of years, which may not exceed a maximum of 30 years; or
>
> (b) A term of life imprisonment when justified by the extreme gravity of the crime and the individual circumstances of the convicted person.

However, given the need to find a compromise in order to finalize the terms of the Rome Statute, an additional provision in the instrument makes it clear that its terms do not 'prejudice' punishment under national law. Consequently, article 80 of the Rome Statute, which is headed 'Non-prejudice to national application of penalties and national laws', provides as follows:

> Nothing in this Part affects the application by States of penalties prescribed by their national law, nor the law of States which do not provide for penalties prescribed in this Part.

Nonetheless, there is no doubt that the Rome Statute excludes the death penalty. It is clear, therefore, that this has now become, and remains a fundamental characteristic of international criminal justice, unlike the time of the Nuremberg and Tokyo Military Tribunals. This has not deterred some States that still retain the death penalty (for example, Japan) from becoming States Parties to the Rome Statute.

Contrast with National Criminal Justice?

It should be noted, however, that this process of internationalization through the establishment of mechanisms of international justice does not necessarily equate to a 'harmonization' of existing *national* criminal law principles,[76] including in relation to the death penalty. Rather, this internationalization of justice recognizes that there are certain norms of *international* criminal law that transcend national boundaries and, like fundamental human rights norms, these are regarded as

(b) A forfeiture of proceeds, property and assets derived directly or indirectly from that crime, without prejudice to the rights of bona fide third parties.'

Moreover, the Court is also empowered to 'make an order directly against a convicted person specifying appropriate reparations to, or in respect of, victims, including restitution, compensation and rehabilitation': Rome Statute, article 77(2). In appropriate circumstances, these reparations may be made through a Trust Fund established pursuant to article 79 of the Rome Statute.

76 Having said this, there is certainly an argument to suggest that, by its very nature, criminal law is an appropriate area of law to be the subject of a gradual process of harmonization. This issue is, for example, the subject of much debate in the broader context of European integration within the European Union. There is much conjecture, however, as to what 'harmonization' means (and should mean) in this context: see, for example, Klip, 2006, 109-153.

universal in acceptance and thus should be universal in application. These are particularly reflected in the nature of the specific international crimes that exist, as well as those principles that regulate and protect the rights of all stakeholders – the accused, witnesses, victims – in any trial arising from the alleged commission of such crimes. It also extends to the prohibition of the death penalty under *international* criminal justice.

By contrast, the specific domestic criminal laws – including its punishment regime – of any one State will depend, at least to a certain degree, on that country's history, culture, political system and values and, as such, remain the exclusive domain of each State. In terms of the death penalty, the potential for a divergence of approach between international and national justice systems with respect to the appropriate sentence for a person convicted of an international crime(s) still remains. Although there is clearly an undeniable trend towards the abolition of the death penalty worldwide, as at the end of 2008, there were still 59 countries that retained the death penalty (Amnesty International 2009a, 8). The potential exists for a differentiation of approach towards the death penalty between the system of international criminal justice and some national criminal justice systems. In this regard, it is perhaps instructive to consider two examples as to how this dichotomy has manifested itself and (in the latter case), how international criminal justice may play a role in 'shifting' national law on the issue of the death penalty.

The Trial of Saddam Hussein

The different approach between international criminal justice and some national criminal justice systems in relation to the death penalty was starkly demonstrated by the trial of former Iraqi President Saddam Hussein. When he was captured in late 2003, there was much international discussion as to what would be the most appropriate way to bring Saddam to justice. Many commentators called for the establishment of an international Tribunal, which like the others that had been established over the previous decade, would not have had the power to impose a death penalty. It was argued by those advocating this approach that it would be impossible for him to receive a fair trial in Iraq in the prevailing circumstances and, in any event, that it would be difficult to identify sufficient suitably qualified judges, prosecutors and administrators within Iraq who had not themselves in some way been personally affected by events during the Saddam regime.

In the end, however, an Iraqi Court – The Iraqi High Criminal Tribunal – was established to hear the trials. Unfortunately, that Court lacked several fundamental protections to which accused are entitled under both international human rights law and the procedural standards that had been established under the system of international criminal justice that had emerged over the preceding decade. One startling example, among many, of the shortcomings of the Iraqi national system was the fact that there was no requirement of guilt to be proven 'beyond reasonable doubt'. Rather, it was sufficient that the Court was 'satisfied' on the evidence that an accused is guilty.

Equally troubling was the fact that both the Dujail and Genocide trials before this Court were marked by governmental interference (including the replacement of some Judges seen as being too lenient towards Saddam), the murder of several defence lawyers, the involvement of inexperienced Judges, chaotic scenes within the court room, allegations of bribery of, and perjury by Prosecution witnesses, allegations of forgery of Prosecution evidence and allegations of torture made by the accused.

These are more than theoretical problems and of particular concern given that the Court did have the power to order the death penalty. Although the Coalition Provisional Authority had imposed a moratorium on the death penalty in Iraq in July 2003, this was reinstated for certain crimes by the Interim Government in August 2004 and was applicable under Iraqi national law at the time of the trial of Saddam. The powers of the Iraqi High Criminal Tribunal included the following:[77]

> [t]he penalties that shall be imposed by the Tribunal shall be those prescribed by Iraqi law (especially Law Number 111 of 1969 of the Iraqi Criminal Code), save that for the purposes of this Tribunal, sentences of life imprisonment shall mean the remaining natural life of the person.

The Trial Chamber of the Iraqi High Criminal Tribunal imposed the death penalty on Saddam Hussein and two associates in relation to crimes against humanity committed against the people of the town of Dujail, following a failed assassination attempt there in 1982. Saddam was executed by hanging in late 2006, amid morbid and chaotic scenes. In fact, footage of his execution was soon circulating over the internet.

As a result of the flawed processes involved in his trial, an important opportunity was missed. The Saddam trial simply failed to promote reconciliation in Iraq. The circumstances leading up to, and including, the death sentence significantly undermined the credibility and potential for positive consequences that might otherwise have possibly stemmed from the trial of the former dictator. Instead, what it demonstrated was that, unlike the process that was actually implemented, if international criminal justice is to make an important contribution to peace, then it must respect the rule of law and ensure the rights of the accused, so as to limit any suggestions that it simply represents 'victors justice'.

Interaction between the ICTR and the Rwandan Criminal Justice System

As noted above, the *ad hoc* international criminal Tribunals were the first such courts established for almost 50 years. In terms of accountability, the ICTY and ICTR appear to have made quite significant progress, at least in terms of numbers of persons prosecuted for (allegedly) having committed such crimes. As at 11

77 Statute of the High Criminal Tribunal, article 24(a).

February 2009, there have been a total of 236 persons indicted by and surrendered to these two Tribunals (ICTY 161, ICTR 75), with proceedings concluded against 157 of these (ICTY 116, ICTR 41) and proceedings ongoing in relation to another 61 (ICTY 45, ICTR 16).[78]

Nevertheless, these Tribunals were set up as 'UN subsidiary organs' (Sarooshi 1999, 389) in response to specific events and were always intended to have a limited life-span. Given the complex factual background to these cases and the difficulties associated with investigation – often while hostilities have been ongoing – this form of international judicial process has come at a considerable cost. Some commentators estimate that (up until 2006) this may have been as much as US$4.5 billion (Roper and Barria 2006), although this probably overstates the true position.[79]

Irrespective of the correct figure, however, there can be no doubt that the high cost associated with these *ad hoc* Tribunals was an important factor leading to the articulation of their respective 'Completion Strategies' by the United Nations Security Council, which confirmed that the activities of these Tribunals was ultimately to come to an end.[80] This was driven not only by cost considerations, but also by the fact that the establishment of the permanent court, the ICC, had by this time come to fruition and that the closing down of the *ad hoc* Tribunals might help to avoid what some States saw as an expensive 'proliferation' of international criminal judicial bodies.

Consequently, the United Nations Security Council set out the proposed terms of these Completion Strategies for the ICTY and ICTR. These (originally) envisaged that all investigations will have been completed by the end of 2004, all

78 See ICTY Website, <http://www.icty.org/sections/TheCases/KeyFigures> and ICTR Website, <http://69.94.11.53/default.htm>. A number of other persons have either had their indictments withdrawn and were released immediately, were transferred to national jurisdiction for trial, or died before the conclusion of proceedings.

79 In the period 1993 to 2008-2009, the 'Regular Budget' of the ICTY (which has been the more expensive of the two *ad hoc* Tribunals) has been calculated at approximately US$1.7 billion: ICTY Website, 'The Cost of Justice' <http://www.icty.org/sid/325>.

80 See United Nations Security Council Resolution 1503 (28 August 2003) UN Doc S/Res/1503 on the International Criminal Tribunal for the former Yugoslavia and International Criminal Tribunal for Rwanda, which refers in preambular paragraph 7 to the 'ICTY Completion Strategy' and in preambular paragraph 8 to the 'ICTR Completion Strategy'. Paragraph 3 of United Nations Security Council Resolution 1534 (26 March 2004) UN Doc S/Res/1534 on the International Criminal Tribunal for the former Yugoslavia and International Criminal Tribunal for Rwanda emphasizes the 'importance' of each of the *ad hoc* Tribunals implementing their respective Completion Strategies and calls upon the Tribunals to 'plan and act accordingly'. However, it remains to be seen whether the *ad hoc* Tribunals will be able to adhere to the timetable specified in their respective Completion Strategies for the completion of their work.

trial activities at first instance by the end of 2008, and that the work of each of the Tribunals will be completed in 2010.[81]

As part of the implementation of these plans, additional procedures have been put in place within the framework of both the ICTY Statute and the ICTR Statute to more easily allow for the transfer of indictees and detainees from those *international* courts to *national* courts, where they could then be tried within an appropriate national criminal justice system for their alleged crimes. The *ad hoc* Tribunals have, of course, always had concurrent jurisdiction with national courts, although they have operated under a principle of 'primacy' of jurisdiction.[82] However, additional provisions were incorporated into their respective Rules of Evidence and Procedure (RPE) to establish more specific guidelines for the transfer of cases back to national courts.

It is in this regard that the issue of the death penalty was also of relevance. Given the exclusion of the death penalty from these newly established mechanisms of international justice, it would have been inconceivable that the Judges – who are responsible for drafting the RPE of these two Tribunals – would have allowed for the transfer of persons who, but for the Completion Strategy, would have been prosecuted within the international system, to national jurisdictions where they could potentially be subject to the death penalty.

This was, of course, of particular relevance to indictees before the ICTR, given that the Rwandan national courts did, at the time, have the power to impose a sentence of death. Indeed, of the first 150 trials conducted under Rwandan domestic law for crimes committed during the genocide of 1994, some estimates are that approximately 40 per cent resulted in the imposition of a death sentence.

---

81 With the arrest of one of its most sought after indictees, Radovan Karadzic, only in 2008, it is uncertain as to precisely when the ICTY will be in a position to formally conclude its trials. Karadzic's first appearance before the Tribunal was on 31 July 2008 and his case is still at the pre-trial stage. For the background to the proceedings against Karadzic, see the ICTY website, 'Case Information Sheet', <http://www.icty.org/x/cases/karadzic/cis/en/cis_karadzic_en.pdf> (accessed 31 August 2009).

82 Article 9(1) of the ICTY Statute stipulates that the ICTY and national courts have 'concurrent jurisdiction'. However, article 9(2) expressly grants the ICTY 'primacy over national courts' and that, '[a]t any stage of the procedure, [it] may formally request national courts to defer' to its competence. The Appeals Chamber of the ICTY confirmed the legitimacy of its primacy in Decision on Defence Motion for Interlocutory Appeal on Jurisdiction, *Prosecutor v Duško Tadić*, Case No. IT-94-1, Appeals Chamber, 2 October 1995, paragraphs 49-64. Article 8(1) of the ICTR Statute also specifies that the ICTR and national courts have 'concurrent jurisdiction'. However, article 8(2) of the ICTR Statute is expressed in broader terms than its counterpart in the ICTY Statute, specifying that the ICTR has 'primacy over the national courts of *all States*' (emphasis added). It has been suggested that this wording in the ICTR Statute, which was drafted subsequent to the ICTY Statute, reflected a broader consensus at that time among the United Nations Security Council as to the concept of primacy, see Brown 1998, 402.

As a result, although not based on any express legal powers within the ICTR Statute, Rule 11 *bis* (A) of the ICTR RPE allows the ICTR to refer indictments currently before it to another (national) court in the following circumstances:

> (A) If an indictment has been confirmed, whether or not the accused is in the custody of the Tribunal, the President may designate a Trial Chamber which shall determine whether the case should be referred to the authorities of a State:
>
> (i) in whose territory the crime was committed; or
>
> (ii) in which the accused was arrested; or
>
> (iii) having jurisdiction and being willing and adequately prepared to accept such a case,
>
> so that those authorities should forthwith refer the case to the appropriate court for trial within that State.

The terms of Rule 11 *bis* (A) of the ICTY RPE are broadly similar.[83] Both Rules also make it clear, however, that an indicted person cannot be transferred to a jurisdiction where the death penalty may be imposed. The ICTY RPE provide as follows:[84]

> (B) The Referral Bench may order such referral *proprio motu* or at the request of the Prosecutor, after having given to the Prosecutor and, where applicable, the accused, the opportunity to be heard and after being satisfied that the accused will receive a fair trial and *that the death penalty will not be imposed or carried out*.
>
> (C) In determining whether to refer the case in accordance with paragraph (A), the Referral Bench shall, in accordance with Security Council resolution 1534 (2004), consider the gravity of the crimes charged and the level of responsibility of the accused.

Likewise, the ICTR RPE provides:[85]

---

83 The chapeau of Rule 11 *bis* (A) of the ICTY RPE provides as follows:

'(A) After an indictment has been confirmed and prior to the commencement of trial, irrespective of whether or not the accused is in the custody of the Tribunal, the President may appoint a bench of three Permanent Judges selected from the Trial Chambers (hereinafter referred to as the "Referral Bench"), which solely and exclusively shall determine whether the case should be referred to the authorities of a State'.

84 ICTY RPE, Rule 11 *bis* (B) and (C) (emphasis added).

85 ICTR RPE, Rule 11 *bis* (C) (emphasis added).

> (C) In determining whether to refer the case in accordance with paragraph (A), the Trial Chamber shall satisfy itself that the accused will receive a fair trial in the courts of the State concerned and *that the death penalty will not be imposed or carried out.*

While the restriction on the death penalty was not a particularly contentious issue in relation to possible transfers to the national courts of the respective countries that formerly comprised the Federal Republic of Yugoslavia, it was, not surprisingly, highly controversial in the case of Rwanda. As noted above, Rwanda did maintain the death penalty within its national laws at the time that the ICTR Completion Strategy was being formulated and was concerned that it would not be able to exercise jurisdiction over (at least some) of those whom it regarded as the main perpetrators of the 1994 genocide.

It particularly objected to the possibility that the 'leaders' of the genocide, prosecuted before the ICTR or before the courts of another country, would escape the death penalty, while 'lower-level' perpetrators, who faced the courts in Rwanda, would be sentenced to death. At the time, one official was quoted as saying that this perceived 'mismatch' of justice 'is not conducive to national reconciliation on Rwanda' (Morris 1997).

Yet, for as long as Rwanda retained the death penalty within its domestic laws, this restriction effectively meant that no person could ever be transferred by the ICTR to face trial there. Given the relatively slow pace with which the ICTR was proceeding at the time (it has, in recent times, become more effective, particularly with the appointment by the United Nations Security Council of *ad litem* Judges to sit on a specific trial(s) at both of the *ad hoc* Tribunals), this has prompted other countries to seek to try indictees from the ICTR, although this has prompted further strong criticism from the Rwandan Government (BBC 2006).

However, this process of transferring cases has itself not always been a smooth process, particularly with respect to the ICTR. In *Bagaragaza*,[86] the accused had been charged with three counts: 'conspiracy to commit genocide, genocide and complicity in genocide in the alternative', under an indictment issued by the ICTR in July 2005. Subsequently, both the Prosecutor and the Defence in that case argued that the trial of the accused should be transferred to Norway, which was prepared to allow the trial to be conducted there in accordance with its national criminal laws. Had that request been successful and the accused transferred to Norway for trial, he would have been charged as an accessory to homicide or for negligent homicide under Norwegian law and, if found guilty, would have faced a maximum of 21 years imprisonment.

In these circumstances, Trial Chamber III of the ICTR refused to transfer the trial under Rule 11 *bis*, concluding that Norway did not have jurisdiction

86 Decision on the Prosecution Motion for Referral to the Kingdom of Norway: Rule 11 *bis* of the Rules of Evidence and Procedure, *Prosecutor v. Michel Bagaragaza*, Case No. ICTR-2005-86-R11 *bis*, Trial Chamber III, 19 May 2006.

(*ratione materiae*) over the crimes as charged in the confirmed ICTR indictment. In addition, the Chamber noted that the crimes alleged in the indictment were significantly different (higher) in terms of gravity from the crime of homicide under the national laws of Norway. According to the website of the ICTR the accused Bagaragaza is still awaiting trial.[87]

Nonetheless, the virtual exclusion of the Rwandan national court system from prosecuting those initially indicted by the ICTR was an important reason why Rwanda ultimately agreed in 2007 to abolish the death penalty within its national laws. In this way, it overcame one of the preconditions for a transfer of the trial of ICTR indictees to its national system under Rule 11 *bis* (C). However, to date no ICTR indictee has yet had his/her trial transferred to Rwanda, and it is thought that this may result from concerns about the other precondition – whether such an accused would receive a fair trial in that country.

In this regard, it is relevant to note that, as recently as April 2009, the UK High Court allowed an appeal by four Rwandan nationals against an order that they be extradited to Rwanda to face trial there for various alleged crimes arising from the events of 1994. The maximum penalty that these accused would have faced in Rwanda was life imprisonment, since the death penalty had already been abolished in that country by the time of this case. Yet, the UK Court still decided that they should not be extradited to Rwanda to be tried within the national criminal justice system of that country. In handing down its reasons for ruling against extradition, the Court made some strong observations about the state of the criminal justice system in Rwanda, including the following comments:[88]

> We certainly cannot sanction extradition as a means of encouraging the Rwandan authorities to redouble their efforts to achieve a justice system that guarantees due process. That might serve a political aspiration, but would amount to denial of legal principle.
>
> (…)
>
> We have reached a firm conclusion as to the gravity of the problems that would face these appellants as regards witnesses if they were returned for trial in Rwanda. Those very problems do not promise well for the judiciary's impartiality and independence. The general evidence as to the nature of the Rwandan polity offers no better promise. When one adds all the particular evidence we have described touching the justice system, we are driven to conclude that if these

87 ICTR Website, Status of Cases' <http://69.94.11.53/ENGLISH/cases/status.htm> (accessed 27 August 2009).

88 *Vincent Brown aka Vincent Bajinja, Charles Munyaneza, Emmanuel Nteziryayo and Celestin Ugirashebuja v. The Government of Rwanda and The Secretary of State for the Home Department* [2009] EWHC 770 (Admin), paragraphs 120, 121 (Case No: CO/6247/2008, 8 April 2009).

> appellants were returned there would be a real risk that they would suffer a flagrant denial of justice.

It seems that, at least up until the present time, there is still a perceived 'mismatch' between the standards of international criminal justice and those of the Rwandan justice system, even though one of the initial 'sticking points', the retention of the death penalty within national law, is no longer one of those areas of concern.

Reasons for the Move Away from the Death Penalty under International Criminal Justice

The exclusion of the death penalty from the structure of the newly created era of international criminal justice that has emerged since the 1990s has come about for a number of reasons. Some of these are briefly raised below:

Emerging Human Rights Standards

As noted above, initially in response to the horrors that took place during the Second World War, a detailed framework of formalized human rights standards has developed over the past 60 years. In 1948, a fundamental document, the Universal Declaration of Human Rights, was adopted by the United Nations General Assembly.[89] Article 3 of the UDHR provides that:

> [e]veryone has the right to life, liberty and security of person.

Building upon article 3 of the UDHR, both the 1950 European Convention on Human Rights (ECHR)[90] and the 1966 ICCPR confirm the existence of a legal 'right to life' in a binding conventional form.[91] However, in relation to the use of the death penalty, both of these instruments only impose restrictions, but do not abolish it. For example, article 6(2) of the ICCPR provides that:[92]

---

89 United Nations General Assembly Resolution 217A (III) (10 December 1948) on the Universal Declaration of Human Rights (UDHR).

90 European Convention for the Protection of Human Rights and Fundamental Freedoms, 213 UNTS 221 (ECHR).

91 See ECHR, article 2 and ICCPR, article 6. Article 2(1) of the ECHR provides as follows:

'Right to Life

1. Everyone's right to life shall be protected by law. No one shall be deprived of his life intentionally save in the execution of a sentence of a court following his conviction of a crime for which this penalty is provided by law.'

92 The remainder of article 6 of the ICCPR provides as follows:

'1. Every human being has the inherent right to life. This right shall be protected by law. No one shall be arbitrarily deprived of his life.

> [i]n countries which have not abolished the death penalty, sentence of death may be imposed only for the most serious crimes in accordance with the law in force at the time of the commission of the crime and not contrary to the provisions of the present Covenant and to the Convention on the Prevention and Punishment of the Crime of Genocide. This penalty can only be carried out pursuant to a final judgement rendered by a competent court.

Over time, the restrictions in these instruments that related to the death penalty were strengthened. Pursuant to optional protocols in 1983[93] and 1989[94] respectively,

---

(…)

3. When deprivation of life constitutes the crime of genocide, it is understood that nothing in this article shall authorize any State Party to the present Covenant to derogate in any way from any obligation assumed under the provisions of the Convention on the Prevention and Punishment of the Crime of Genocide.

4. Anyone sentenced to death shall have the right to seek pardon or commutation of the sentence. Amnesty, pardon or commutation of the sentence of death may be granted in all cases.

5. Sentence of death shall not be imposed for crimes committed by persons below eighteen years of age and shall not be carried out on pregnant women.

6. Nothing in this article shall be invoked to delay or to prevent the abolition of capital punishment by any State Party to the present Covenant.'

93 Protocol No. 6 to the ECHR provides as follows:

'Article 1 – Abolition of the Death Penalty

The death penalty shall be abolished. No-one shall be condemned to such penalty or executed.

Article 2 – Death penalty in time of war

A State may make provision in its law for the death penalty in respect of acts committed in time of war or of imminent threat of war; such penalty shall be applied only in the instances laid down in the law and in accordance with its provisions. The State shall communicate to the Secretary General of the Council of Europe the relevant provisions of that law.'

94 The 1989 Second Optional Protocol to the ICCPR provides as follows:

'The States Parties to the present Protocol,

Believing that abolition of the death penalty contributes to enhancement of human dignity and progressive development of human rights,

(…)

Convinced that all measures of abolition of the death penalty should be considered as progress in the enjoyment of the right to life,

Desirous to undertake hereby an international commitment to abolish the death penalty,

Have agreed as follows:

Article 1

1. No one within the jurisdiction of a State Party to the present Protocol shall be executed.

2. Each State Party shall take all necessary measures to abolish the death penalty within its jurisdiction.

Article 2

it was provided that the death penalty could only be imposed 'in time of war'. Subsequently, a further protocol to the ECHR in 2002 banned the use of the death penalty 'in all circumstances'.[95]

Changing Societal Values and a Trend towards Abolition at the National Level

In addition, the attitude of general civil society over the past 60 years has changed with respect to the death penalty, a phenomenon that has seen a broader movement towards an abolitionist approach to the death sentence in many national jurisdictions.[96] This trend continues to the present day. For example, according to Amnesty International, by 1977, only 16 countries had abolished the death penalty for all crimes. As of December 2008, that figure stood at 92 and 'more than two thirds of the countries in the world ha[ve] abolished the death penalty in law or practice'. In 2009, for example, both Togo and Burundi abolished the death penalty and other African countries such as Mali are currently in the process of reviewing their laws with a view to removing the penalty (Amnesty International 2009b).

In these circumstances, it would no longer acceptable for the international community to establish an international criminal Tribunal with the power to impose the death penalty. In practical terms, even before the establishment of the *ad hoc* Tribunals, there would have been insufficient political support for the establishment by the United Nations of mechanisms of international justice that could impose such a penalty, notwithstanding the serious nature of the crimes that were to be investigated and prosecuted.

Indeed, just a few years earlier, the United Nations General Assembly had, by majority vote, adopted the Second Optional Protocol to the ICCPR,[97] and it therefore would have been inconceivable for the United Nations to then support the

---

1. No reservation is admissible to the present Protocol, except for a reservation made at the time of ratification or accession that provides for the application of the death penalty in time of war pursuant to a conviction for a most serious crime of a military nature committed during wartime.'

95 Protocol No. 13 to the ECHR provides as follows:

'The member States of the Council of Europe signatory hereto,

(…)

Being resolved to take the final step in order to abolish the death penalty in all circumstances,

Have agreed as follows:

Article 1 – Abolition of the death penalty

The death penalty shall be abolished. No one shall be condemned to such penalty or executed.'

96 Amnesty International website, 'Figures on the death penalty' <http://www.amnesty.org/en/death penalty/numbers>

97 See United Nations General Assembly Resolution 44/128 (15 December 1989) on Elaboration of a 2nd Optional Protocol to the International Covenant on Civil and Political Rights Aiming at the Abolition of the Death Penalty. It should be noted, however, that this

establishment of a Tribunal that would permit the death penalty, at the same time that it was actively opposing it on these other fronts. In similar vein, there would no doubt have been considerable reluctance among many countries – particularly those that were already opposed to the death penalty – to cooperate with, or surrender people to an international Tribunal that could impose such a sentence.

The United Nations General Assembly continues to raise the issue of the death penalty. In 2007, it called upon States (this was reaffirmed again in 2008)[98] that still retained the death penalty:[99]

> (*c*) [t]o progressively restrict the use of the death penalty and reduce the number of offences for which it may be imposed;
>
> (*d*) [t]o establish a moratorium on executions with a view to abolishing the death penalty.

This is not, however, the same as suggesting that the death penalty is now unlawful under customary international law. Such arguments continue to be raised (Amnesty International 2009a, 7), with the main propositions being that the death penalty violates the right to life (but see above) and/or the prohibition of cruel and unusual or inhuman treatment or punishment.[100] With respect to the latter prohibition, it is true that the 'death row phenomena' had in 1989 already been held by the European Court of Human Rights to represent a breach in particular circumstances,[101] but this does not relate to the death penalty *per se*.

Indeed, if one were to apply the classic description of what constitutes a rule of customary international law, as stated by the International Court of Justice in the *North Sea Continental Shelf Cases*,[102] it would be quite clear that the argument that the death penalty is illegal is unlikely to prevail. The Court confirmed that

---

Resolution was not adopted unanimously – the vote was 59 in favour, 29 abstentions and 48 against.

98 United Nations General Assembly Resolution 63/168 (18 December 2007) on a Moratorium on the use of the death penalty.

99 United Nations General Assembly Resolution 62/149 (18 December 2007) on a Moratorium on the use of the death penalty, paragraphs 2(c) and (d).

100 See, for example, article 7 of the ICCPR which provides *inter alia* that:

'[n]o one shall be subjected to torture or to cruel, inhuman or degrading treatment or punishment'.

101 See *Soering v. United Kingdom* (1989) 11 EHRR 439. In this case, the Court was considering article 3 of the ECHR.

102 See *North Sea Continental Shelf Cases (Federal Republic of Germany v. Denmark and Federal Republic of Germany v. The Netherlands)* (Judgment) [1969] ICJ Rep 3, paragraph 77. There have, of course, been earlier definitions of international custom, some dating back to early international law treatises, see, Ochoa 2007, 122 and the references in the corresponding footnote; and see, Falstrom 2007, for a detailed description of the work of Alberico Gentili (1552-1608), an early international lawyer who published a series of

customary international law evolves over time[103] and is derived from sufficient (in the circumstances) evidence of both the 'settled practice' of States, as well as *opinio juris* ('recognition as law'), which it described as:[104]

> a belief that this practice is rendered obligatory by the existence of a rule of law requiring it.

As such, the traditional view of customary international law is that it encompasses an objective element, as well as a subjective or 'psychological' element (Koppe 2006, 166). Much has been written about these two elements and how they should be properly formulated,[105] which is also relevant to the process by which they may

---

books in which he prescribed ten principal rules relating to the application of international law, which also related to the development of principles of custom.

103 There has, however, been at least one generally accepted instance of what some commentators refer to as 'instant' customary law. In October 1957, the Soviet Union launched Sputnik I into outer space. This was the first man-made object to orbit the earth. Almost immediately, important principles of the international law of outer space were born – in particular the so-called 'non-appropriation' and 'freedom' principles, subsequently reflected in articles I and II of the Treaty on Principles Governing the Activities of States in the Exploration and Use of Outer Space, including the Moon and Other Celestial Bodies, 610 UNTS 205, which respectively provide *inter alia* that '[o]uter space … shall be free for exploration and use by all States … and there shall be free access to all areas of celestial bodies' (article 1) and '[o]uter space … is not subject to national appropriation by claim of sovereignty, by means of use or occupation, or by any other means' (article 2). As Judge Lachs of the International Court of Justice has observed:

'[t]he first instruments that men sent into outer space traversed the air space of States and circled above them in outer space, yet the launching States sought no permission, nor did the other States protest. This is how the freedom of movement into outer space, and in it, came to be *established and recognised as law within a remarkably short period of time*': *North Sea Continental Shelf Cases (Federal Republic of Germany v. Denmark and Federal Republic of Germany v. The Netherlands)* (Dissenting Opinion of Judge Lachs) [1969] ICJ Rep 3, 230 (emphasis added).

104 *North Sea Continental Shelf Cases (Federal Republic of Germany v. Denmark and Federal Republic of Germany v. The Netherlands)* (Judgment) [1969] ICJ Rep 3, paragraph 77.

105 For example, in 1987, a group of United States international lawyers produced the Restatement of the Law: Third Restatement of U.S. Foreign Relations Law, Volume 2 (1987), 165, in which (at ss 102(2)) they define customary international law as the law that 'results from a general and consistent practice of states followed by them from a sense of legal obligation'. This description has subsequently been regarded by some commentators as accurately specifying the necessary prerequisites for the formation of customary international law: see, for example, Cash 2007, 592.

be adduced in relation to a specific customary rule. As noted by the International Court of Justice:[106]

> [i]t is of course axiomatic that the material of customary international law is to be looked for primarily in the actual practice and *opinio juris* of States.

When one looks to the actual practice of States, certainly, as noted above, there are many countries that have abolished the death penalty, and there are a number of international instruments that also reflect this abolitionist approach. Yet, it is undeniable that many countries still retain, and use the death penalty. Amnesty International has estimated that, in 2008, at least 2,390 people were known to have been executed in 25 countries and that at least 8,864 people were sentenced to death in 52 countries around the world. In the light of this, it would be very difficult to argue successfully that either necessary element for the establishment of a principle of customary international law would be satisfied.

Rather, as noted earlier, there is an undeniable trend towards abolition, so that the illegality of the death penalty might more accurately be described as an 'emerging norm' of international law. It is this trend itself that was one of the reasons that the death penalty was not incorporated into the structure of international criminal justice that has developed since the 1990s. The exclusion of the death penalty from the Statutes establishing the mechanisms of international criminal justice certainly does give further momentum to the developing nature of this norm. However, we are simply not there as yet as far as being definitive as to the illegality of the death penalty under customary international law.

The Need for Resources – Both Financial and Otherwise

As noted above in relation to the *ad hoc* Tribunals, the mechanisms of international justice are expensive to establish and maintain. By their very nature, they typically involve long, difficult investigations and lengthy (certainly in comparison to most trials under national legal systems) trials. These international Courts and Tribunals are largely reliant on funding from other countries. If they were to have the power to impose the death penalty, it would be difficult, if not impossible, to obtain funding from countries that are opposed to and/or have abolished the death penalty.

Similarly, it would be difficult to attract international Judges from countries that have abolished the death penalty. It seems that, at least in those countries, there is a solid consensus among Judges on the issue. Naturally, however, such concerns do not arise where trials are held within national criminal justice systems – such as Iraq – before local Judges only.

---

106 *Continental Shelf (Libyan Arab Jamahiriya v. Malta)* (Judgment) [1985] ICJ Rep 13, paragraph 27.

Avoiding Perception of 'Victor's Justice' – the Need for a Fair Trial

One of the overwhelmingly important aspects to any system of justice – including the international criminal justice system – is the need for a fair trial. Not only does this represent a fundamental principle of human rights law,[107] it also contributes significantly to the effectiveness of the justice system itself. The mechanisms of international criminal justice that have been established over the past 15 years have incorporated important 'minimum guarantees' for the accused.[108] Of course, given the unique nature of trials that take place before the international Tribunals and Courts, there may sometimes be the need for a degree of flexibility of approach in order to meet the demands of the circumstances before the Judges.

---

107 See, for example, ICCPR, article 14.

108 See, for example, article 67 of the Rome Statute, which provides as follows:

'Rights of the accused

1. In the determination of any charge, the accused shall be entitled to a public hearing, having regard to the provisions of this Statute, to a fair hearing conducted impartially, and to the following minimum guarantees, in full equality:

(a) To be informed promptly and in detail of the nature, cause and content of the charge, in a language which the accused fully understands and speaks;

(b) To have adequate time and facilities for the preparation of the defence and to communicate freely with counsel of the accused's choosing in confidence;

(c) To be tried without undue delay;

(d) Subject to article 63, paragraph 2, to be present at the trial, to conduct the defence in person or through legal assistance of the accused's choosing, to be informed, if the accused does not have legal assistance, of this right and to have legal assistance assigned by the Court in any case where the interests of justice so require, and without payment if the accused lacks sufficient means to pay for it;

(e) To examine, or have examined, the witnesses against him or her and to obtain the attendance and examination of witnesses on his or her behalf under the same conditions as witnesses against him or her. The accused shall also be entitled to raise defences and to present other evidence admissible under this Statute;

(f) To have, free of any cost, the assistance of a competent interpreter and such translations as are necessary to meet the requirements of fairness, if any of the proceedings of or documents presented to the Court are not in a language which the accused fully understands and speaks;

(g) Not to be compelled to testify or to confess guilt and to remain silent, without such silence being a consideration in the determination of guilt or innocence;

(h) To make an unsworn oral or written statement in his or her defence; and

(i) Not to have imposed on him or her any reversal of the burden of proof or any onus of rebuttal.

2. In addition to any other disclosure provided for in this Statute, the Prosecutor shall, as soon as practicable, disclose to the defence evidence in the Prosecutor's possession or control which he or she believes shows or tends to show the innocence of the accused, or to mitigate the guilt of the accused, or which may affect the credibility of prosecution evidence. In case of doubt as to the application of this paragraph, the Court shall decide.'

Yet, the fairness of the trial represents a fundamental element of human rights law as it is applied to this system of internationalized criminal justice. Indeed, one of the primary justifications of the system of internationalized criminal justice is that it ensures a fair trial for all accused – even those accused of the most heinous of crimes – so that the credibility of the process will itself reinforce the importance of the decision of the relevant Tribunal or Court, as well as the historical record that arises from the evidence presented. This absence of any potential for the death penalty also adds to the perception that it is not 'victor's justice', and further contributes to the overall fairness of the proceedings, both in reality and perception.

Concluding Remarks

As this chapter seeks to demonstrate, there has been a marked shift in approach regarding the death penalty in the process of internationalization of criminal justice that has taken place since the 1990s, when compared to the first international attempts to implement a system of criminal justice in the years immediately following the conclusion of the Second World War. None of the mechanisms of international criminal justice that have been established over the past 15 years have the power to impose the death penalty. Instead, the maximum sentence is usually life imprisonment. This is notwithstanding the fact that these Tribunals typically have jurisdiction over what are generally regarded as the most serious crimes – those reflecting 'unimaginable atrocities that deeply shock the conscience of humanity'.[109]

There are a number of possible reasons why this change of attitude has occurred. These represent a mixture of what might be called 'micro' reasons – for example, the need to garner sufficient financial support for these mechanisms from as wide a range of States as possible – as well as 'macro' reasons, which reflect the broader movement 'towards global abolition of the death penalty' at the national level (Amnesty International 2009, 11). Yet, it has been argued that the death penalty *per se* has not yet reached the point of being illegal at customary international law, although there is clearly momentum moving towards that end result.

In this regard, the structure of these mechanisms of international justice can also play a role. The Rwandan experience represents an interesting example of this. It is apparent that, the structure of the ICTR – both in terms of not having the power to impose the death sentence, and also in terms of its inability to transfer indictees to countries that retain the death penalty – had an influential impact on the eventual decision by the Rwandan Government to abolish that sentence under its domestic law.

In similar vein, The Special Court for Sierra Leone, whose seat is in that country,[110] does not have the power to impose the death penalty, even though,

109 Rome Statute, preambular paragraph 2.

110 However, the trial of the former President of Liberia, Charles Taylor, before that Court is actually taking place at the premises of the ICC in The Hague. This is due

conversely, that penalty is still legal under the domestic laws of Sierra Leone. It is to be hoped that this may give added impetus towards moves in that country to ultimately abolish the death penalty.

This certainly seems to be the case with respect to Lebanon; once again, an international Tribunal, The Special Tribunal for Lebanon, has been established and, unlike the domestic law of that country, does not have the power to impose the death penalty. As noted above, there are currently moves being made towards the abolition of that sentence under the national law of Lebanon.

These developments towards abolition are more than coincidental. There is a relationship between a country's direct exposure to the approach taken under international criminal justice, and the ongoing development of its own national criminal justice system in terms of abolishing the death penalty. This does not work quickly, nor all the time, but the signs are there that there is a 'cause and effect'. In this way, the internationalization of criminal justice might also be seen as a way of 'persuading' countries to acknowledge the irreversible momentum towards universal abolition of the death penalty.

Bibliography

Amnesty International (2009a) *Death Sentences and Executions in 2008* (March)

— (2009b) 28:3 *Human Rights Defender* 19.

Bassiouni, M.C. (1998) 'Introduction to the Symposium: The Normative Framework of International Humanitarian Law: Overlaps, Gaps and Ambiguities', 8 *Transnational Law and Contemporary Problems* 199.

BBC (2006) *Rwandan Anger at Suspect Transfer*, BBC News, 16 February.

Brown, B.S. (1998) 'Primacy or Complementarity: Reconciling the Jurisdiction of National Courts and International Criminal Tribunals', 23 *The Yale Journal of International Law* 391.

Cash, H. (2007) 'Security Council Resolution 1593 and Conflicting Principles of International Law: How the Future of the International Criminal Court is at Stake', 45 *Brandeis Law Journal* 573.

Cassese, A. (2003) *International Criminal Law* (Oxford: Oxford University Press).

Crawford, J. (2003) 'The Drafting of the Rome Statute', in Sands, P. (ed.), *From Nuremberg to The Hague: The Future of International Criminal Justice* (Cambridge: Cambridge University Press).

Cryer, R., Friman, H., Robinson, D., and Wilmshurst, E. (2007) *An Introduction to International Criminal Law and Procedure* (Cambridge: Cambridge University Press).

---

to concerns about regional security, had the trial been held in Sierra Leone. Taylor was transferred to The Hague on 30 June 2006.

England, J.F. (2001) 'The Response of the United States to the International Criminal Court: Rejection, Ratification or Something Else?', 18 *Arizona Journal of International and Comparative Law* 3, 941.

Falstrom, D.Z. (2007) 'Can International Law Survive the 21st Century? Yes, with Patience, Persistence and a Peek at the Past', 8 *San Diego International Law Journal* 291.

Freeland, S. (2006) 'Saddam trial underlines need to take tough stand on genocide', *The Canberra Times* (Canberra) 29 August.

—— (2001) 'Commentary on Decision on Prosecutor's Appeal on Admissibility of Evidence, *Prosecutor v Zlatko Aleksovski*', in Klip, A. and Sluiter, G. (eds) *Annotated Leading Cases of International Criminal Tribunals, Volume III, The International Criminal Tribunal for the Former Yugoslavia, 1997-1999* (Antwerp: Intersentia).

Harris, D.J. (2004) *Cases and Materials on International Law* 6th edn (Sweet and Maxwell).

International Law Commission (1950) 'Principles of International Law Recognized in the Charter of the Nürnberg Tribunal and in the Judgment of the Tribunal', 2 *Yearbook of the International Law Commission* 374.

Jørgensen, N.H.B. (2000) *The Responsibility of States for International Crimes* (Oxford: Oxford University Press).

Kalivretakis, E.I. (2001) 'Are Nuclear Weapons Above the Law? A Look at the International Criminal Court and the Prohibited Weapons Category', 15 *Emory International Law Review* 683.

Klip, A. (2006) 'European Integration and Harmonisation and Criminal Law', in Curtin, D.M. et al. (eds) *European Integration and Law* (Antwerp: Intersentia).

Koppe, E.V. (2006) *The Use of Nuclear Weapons and the Protection of the Environment During International Armed Conflict* (Oxford: Hart Publishing).

McCormack, T. and Robertson, S. (1999) 'Jurisdictional Aspects of the Rome Statute for the New International Criminal Court', 23 *Melbourne University Law Review* 635.

Mettraux, G. (2009) 'A Nuremberg for Guantánamo', *The New York Times*, 19 August.

Morris, M.H. (1997) 'The Trials of Concurrent Jurisdiction: The Case of Rwanda – Justice in the Wake of Genocide', *American Diplomacy* <http://www.unc.edu>

Mullins, C. (1921) *The Leipzig Trials: An Account of the War Criminals' Trials and a Study of German Mentality* (London: H.F. & G. Witherby).

Ochoa, C. (2007) 'The Individual and Customary International Law Formation', 48 *Virginia Journal of International Law* 119.

Overy, R. (2003) 'The Nuremberg Trials: International Law in the Making', in Sands, P. (ed), *From Nuremberg to The Hague: The Future of International Criminal Justice* (Cambridge: Cambridge University Press).

Podgers, J. (1996) 'The World Cries for Justice', *American Bar Association Journal* 52.

Roper, S.D. and Barria, L.A. (2006) *Designing Criminal Tribunals – Sovereignty and International Concerns in the Protection of Human Rights* (Aldershot: Ashgate Publishing).

Sarooshi, D. (1999) 'The Statute of the International Criminal Court', 48 *International and Comparative Law Quarterly* 387.

Schabas, W.A. (2001) *An Introduction to the International Criminal Court* (Cambridge: Cambridge University Press).

Vaswani, K. (2009) 'Still no justice in East Timor', *BBC News*, 27 August.

Chapter 10

The Right to Life and Abolition of the Death Penalty in the Council of Europe

Jon Yorke[1]

Introduction

Article 2(1) of the European Convention on Human Rights 1950 (ECHR) states '[e]veryone's right to life shall be protected by law. No one shall be deprived of his life intentionally save in the execution of a sentence of a court following his conviction of a crime for which this penalty is provided by law.'[2] Although, as A.H. Robertson noted, the text was 'careful to protect the legality of capital punishment,' (Robertson 1965, 205) from the early life of the Council of Europe there were stalwart parliamentarians who would not allow the human rights organisation to completely reject the anti-death penalty sentiments which had emerged from the Enlightenment.[3] Over the proceeding 30 years, the Council held numerous debates and gradually the arguments against the punishment solidified and instruments were adopted for restriction and abolition. The first regional curtailment of the punishment occurred in 1983, when article 1 of Protocol No. 6 to the ECHR provides for the removal of the death penalty in times of peace, but article 2 concedes that states may 'make provision in its law for the death penalty in respect of acts committed in time of war or of imminent threat of war.'[4] More debates followed as the wartime exception proved problematical and so the abolitionist discourse became more complex with techniques employed to encourage regional abolitionism which would be extended to the new member states from Central and Eastern European countries post-1994. Then in 2002, Protocol No. 13 to the ECHR

1 This chapter is an expanded version of an article in the *European Law Review*, vol. 34. No. 2. April 2009, and it has benefited from discussions and insights from; Günter Schirmer, Michelle Lafferty, Paul Harvey, Luis Arroyo, Antonio Muños Aunion, Panos Koutrakos and Andrew Williams.

2 Convention for the Protection of Human Rights and Fundamental Freedoms, CETS No. 5 (1953).

3 The Enlightenment humanist Cesare Beccaria, and his principled position against the sovereign possessing a 'right' of the death penalty, is frequently referred to during the debates on the punishment within the Council of Europe (for example, see, Ancel 1962, 2; Council of Europe 1980a, 2).

4 Protocol No. 6 to the Convention for the protection of human rights and fundamental freedoms concerning the abolition of the death penalty, Strasbourg, 28 April 1983.

was adopted and article 1 decrees that in all circumstances, '[t]he death penalty shall be abolished. No one shall be condemned to such penalty or executed.'[5]

With such clear wording it would appear that the denunciation of the punishment is now incontrovertible. However, the problem of the punishment has not completely gone away, as although both Protocols provide for 'abolition,' neither specifically amend the text of ECHR article 2(1). Thus the question remains as to whether the resultant juxtaposition of the provisions furnishes a coherent discourse on abolition and the right to life, and whether a satisfactory human rights position can be identified. If it can be, the amendment of article 2(1) is not of immediate necessity. But if an ambiguity, or ambivalence, is present then amendment should still be viewed as an exigent human rights quest. The analysis which follows questions whether the Council of Europe has adequately resolved the interpretive difficulties.

To isolate the right to life and attempt to provide an interpretation of what it means is no easy task. There is consistent academic opinion concerning the difficulties associated with identifying the parameters of the right, as in 1968 Hugo Bedau remarked that 'the salient fact about this right is the considerable disagreement over its scope, form and status' (Bedau 1968, 550). Then in the 1980s and 1990s the Association of International Consultants on Human Rights investigated the right to life and identified the expanding and varying boundaries of the right (Association of International Consultants on Human Rights 1992, 3). More recently James Griffin has observed that this right does not have a 'clear boundary' because what 'starts off as the least problematic of rights becomes, on reflection, distinctly problematic,' (Griffin 2008, 213) and placing such observations within the specific context of the ECHR, Torkel Opsahl affirmed, 'Article 2 of the Convention and the context in which it operates will show that what at first seemed simple may have problematic points' (Opsahl 1993, 207). To investigate the interpretive problem is to firstly engage with the drafting of the ECHR, then the complicated past-half century dialogue between the Parliamentary Assembly and the Committee of Ministers. Secondly, it is necessary to analyse the European Commission of Human Rights and European Court of Human Rights' interpretation of the instruments which have emerged from this dialogue. Several questions arise which require analysis including: what was the role of each Council organ in the initial evolution of the abolitionist discourse? How has the Council approached the question of the amendment of article 2(1)? Are all the organs unified or are there differences of opinion on the appropriate way to further the abolitionist agenda?

5 Protocol No. 13 to the Convention for the protection of human rights and fundamental freedoms concerning the abolition of the death penalty in all circumstances, Vilnius, 3 May 2002.

The Drafting of the Convention and the Right to Life

One of the first projects the Council undertook was to formulate the ECHR to mandate human rights. To achieve this the Committee on Legal and Administrative Questions was established in 1949 and Sir David Maxwell-Fyfe was appointed as chairman and Pierre-Henri Teitgen as *rapporteur*. During the initial quorum of the drafting meetings, Teitgen took the floor and identified the intrinsic value of the Statute of the Council of Europe[6] articles 1 and 3 to the proceedings (Council of Europe 1976, vol. I, 38, 290). Article 1 states:

> [t]he aim of the Council of Europe is to achieve a greater unity between its members for the purpose of safeguarding and realising the ideals and principles which are their *common heritage* and to facilitate their economic and social progress (emphasis added).

and article 3 states:

> [e]very member of the Council of Europe must accept the *principles of the rule of law* and of the enjoyment by all persons within its jurisdiction of human rights and fundamental freedoms, and collaborate sincerely and effectively in the realisation of the Council (emphasis added).

Teitgen argued that these two Statute articles provided the guiding legislative framework which Maxwell-Fyfe approved (ibid., 114).[7] Hence the Statute article 1 identification of a European 'common heritage' and article 3 promotion of the 'rule of law' provided an important tool for the drafting of the Convention text. The article 1 search for a 'common heritage' of the Council was identified as a desired aim within the Statute Preamble. The second paragraph makes reference to 'spiritual and moral values which are the common heritage of their peoples,' and that 'although heterogeneous in many respects…they have a certain tradition of history and civilisation which is common to all of them.'[8] This notion of a common heritage has been recognised by the European human rights scholars, Steven Greer (2006, 15-16) and Alastair Mowbray (2007, 2)[9] to be part of the core principles

6 Statute of the Council of Europe, CETS 001 (1949)

7 Furthermore, Mr Jaquet, a French representative, identified the importance of the two articles, 134; and article 1 was specifically mentioned in a Committee questionnaire, 156, and Mr Wold, the representative from Norway, discussed the binding nature of article 3 on the drafting process, in (ibid., vol. II, 170).

8 Preambles to treaties often reveal the political objectives of the contracting parties as, J.G. Merrills and A.H. Robertson stated it is 'useful for locating the political obligations that follow in a historical context,' (Merrills and Robertson 2001, 1).

9 Alastair Mowbray has also stated that the 'major aim of the Council of Europe was to achieve greater unity between the Member States' (Mowbray 2007, 2).

which underpinned the Council's creation. However, a detailed discussion of the meaning of 'common heritage' was not possible due to time constraints, and so the drafters sought a basic, restricted, articulation of rights (Weil 1963, 28). It is clear from the outset that the various drafting discussions could not accommodate all the necessary investigations to scrutinise fully how government policies and actions would affect each human right. A triage process was adopted to produce the Convention in an expedient manner. Teitgen stated:

> [w]e should need years of mutual understanding, study, and collective experiments, even to attempt after many years, with any hope of success, to formulate a complete and general definition of all the freedoms and all the rights which Europe should confer on the Europeans. Let us therefore discard for the moment this desirable *maximum*. Failing this, however, let us be content with the *minimum* which we can achieve in a very short period, and which consists in defining the seven, eight or ten fundamental freedoms that are essential for a democratic way of life and which our countries should guarantee to all their people. It should be possible to achieve a common definition of these (emphasis added) (Council of Europe 1976, vol. I, 44).

Maxwell-Fyfe affirmed that the Convention was needed to come into 'existence reasonably soon,' (ibid., 116) and Teitgen further emphasised 'the current year is the critical year…we should do what we consider to be our duty towards Europe quickly, and we hope, effectively' (ibid., 58-60). However, the speed of the drafting debates did not allow for all the aspects of the rights to be discussed, and this included the compatibility of the right to life with the application of the death penalty.

Article 2(1) and the Death Penalty

From the very beginning of the drafting debates there was a conflict of opinion on how they should approach the question of the right to life. The civil lawyers argued for an *enumeration* of rights, but the common law lawyers stated that a *definition* of the extent of the right was necessary. Elizabeth Wicks stated that this 'disagreement may be in part a legacy of the different approaches to the common law and civil law systems' (Wicks 2000, 439), and A.H. Robertson argued that the civil lawyers:

> were content to incorporate these words textually in the draft Convention. The common lawyers, on the other hand, thought that a statement of the 'right to life,' necessitated a statement of the circumstances in which someone may be legally deprived of his life (Robertson 1950).

The debate resulted in a stalemate and two Convention drafts were then submitted to the Secretariat General (Council of Europe 1976, vol. III).[10] Draft Alternative A presented an enumeration of rights (ibid., 312), and Draft Alternative B provided a definition of rights (ibid., 320).[11] The Universal Declaration of Human Rights 1948 (UDHR)[12] was used as a template of the rights which they thought appropriate to discuss in the initial drafting quorum. Teitgen opened the first session and set out what he believed to be the most important rights for debate, and borrowing from the UDHR, identified ten initial 'rights.'[13] The first proscribed 'right' was to 'ensure... security of the person, in accordance with Articles 3-5, and 8 of the United Nations Declaration' (Council of Europe 1976, vol. I, 296). Concerning the 'right to life,' UDHR article 3 stated, '[e]veryone has the right to life, liberty and security of the person' but this was interpreted as not prohibiting the death penalty.

In Teitgen's enumeration of rights, he did not explicitly use the words 'right to life,' the 'death penalty' or 'capital punishment.' But concerning the possibility of the punishment, what occurred within the debates was a gradual move away from the enumeration of the right to life, to a definition of when the state may legally impose executions. This shift in emphasis was predominantly guided by the delegates from the United Kingdom, and Wicks argues that the different drafting negotiators were 'in no doubt about the strength of the feeling on the part of the United Kingdom,' and that the precise definitions were an 'essential prerequisite to any Convention' (Wicks 2000, 440). What was achieved was that the member state right to choose whether or not to impose the death penalty, instead of being *implied* within the Convention text, was to be explicitly mandated.

10 For the issue of the different drafting techniques, the Secretariat General stated, '[a]s regards the substance of the collective guarantee, the Assembly and its Legal Committee were faced with two problems: 1) the enumeration of the rights to be guaranteed, the list of rights to be covered by the guarantee system; 2) the definition of those rights in terms of extent and content, both nationally and internationally,' in the *Preparatory Report by the Secretariat General concerning a preliminary draft convention to provide a collective guarantee of human rights* (Council of Europe 1976 vol. III, 6).

11 Council of Europe 1976 vol. IV, 16, states, 'the Committee decided to submit both texts to the Committee of Ministers, without indicating its preference, since it was not able to decide unanimously in favour of one or other of these systems.'

12 GA Res. 217 A (III), UN Doc. A/810; A/RES/62/149, 76th Plenary Session, 18 December 2007.

13 The ten rights were taken from the Universal Declaration of Human Rights. They were: a) security of the person; b) immunity from all arrest, detention or arbitrary exile; c) exemption from all slavery and servitude, and from all forced labour of discriminatory nature; d) freedom of speech and in general of the expression of opinion; e) freedom of religious belief, practice and teaching; f) freedom of association and meeting; g) natural rights appertaining to marriage, paternity and the family; h) inviolability of domicile; i) equality before the law; j) protection against all discrimination based on religion, race, national origin, profession of political opinion or other opinion (Council of Europe 1976, vol. I, 160).

The text first evolved towards a definition when the European Movement worded their Draft European Convention on Human Rights, article 1 as, '[e]very state party to this Convention shall guarantee to all persons within its territory the following rights: a) Security of life and limb...'[14] 'Security' did not yet represent a 'right' to life, but merely, that the government should *secure* the life of its citizens. Then in the United Nations drafting debates of the International Covenant on Civil and Political Rights, on 4 January 1950, the Secretary General received a report from the governments of Australia, Denmark, France, Lebanon and the United Kingdom. This report recommended that the article on the right to life should include a textual explanation which more clearly defined the administration of the death penalty. The United Kingdom government presented this UN report to the Convention drafting meeting as a Working Paper. The provisions concerning the death penalty stated:

1. No one shall be deprived of his life intentionally.
2. There shall be no exception to this rule save where death results in those States where capital punishment is lawful, from the execution of such a penalty in accordance with the sentence of a court.[15]

The United Kingdom proposal was an attempt to define when the right to life can be restricted and began to establish the parameters for state application of the punishment. The proposal can be read as identifying that the *language* of human rights should encompass an explicit mandate legitimising the state's choice over the use of the punishment. Furthermore, the declaration 'in those States where capital punishment is lawful,' endorsed the death penalty as ultimately a municipal issue. The United Kingdom therefore confirmed that any new human rights discourse in 1950 could not override the state's monopoly over the domestic legislation of capital crimes. Following further drafting discussions, this specific phrasing was modified by a subsequent United Kingdom proposal. However, the purpose of maintaining municipal authority remained unchanged as it stated:

> [t]he Government of the United Kingdom desire that the Convention, which the present Committee have been asked to draft, should contain certain articles which appear in the text of the latest draft of the United Nations Convention of Human Rights...Article 5 of the latest version of the United Nations draft Covenant refers *to punishment of offenders including deprivation of life.* If the

14 Draft European Convention on Human Rights, Convention for the collective protection of individual rights and democratic liberties by the states, Members of the Council of Europe, and for the establishment of a European Court of Human Rights to ensure the observance of the Convention, prepared by the European Movement (see, Council of Europe 1976, vol. I, 296).

15 Annex II of the Report of the Commission (E/1371), cited in ibid., vol. III, 158.

> Committee should desire to include this article in the proposed new Convention, the United Kingdom desire that the text of it should be as follows:
>
> 1) No one shall be deprived of his life intentionally save in the execution of the sentence of a court following his conviction of a crime for which his penalty is defined by law (emphasis added) (Council of Europe 1976, vol. III, 186).

This new proposal confirmed the sovereign state's right to legislate capital crimes, but it removed the words 'capital punishment' and 'death' from the specific Convention draft. These words which were formally adequate descriptions identifying the punishment and its consequence were substituted. The *travaux préparatoires* do not explain why the phrases were changed and there are no specific records of any debates on whether the application of the death penalty was inconsistent with the formation of the Convention text. Torkel Opsahl noted that the 'United Kingdom proposal was not opposed and there are no signs that restrictions nor limitations on its use were intended or even discussed' (Opsahl 1993, 217). All we have is the tabled proposal and then the amended proposal. He further stated, '[i]f there was any discussion of what was intended [concerning the death penalty] the published *travaux préparatoires* reveal little of it' (ibid., 208; see also, Ramcharan 1985a, 57-61). J.E.S. Fawcett has also confirmed 'there is almost no reported discussion on the drafts' (Fawcett 1987, 34).

What the *travaux préparatoires* do chronicle are numerous side-comments related to the death penalty. These comments included the execution of the Greek philosopher, Socrates, discussed by Mr. Maccus, the Greek representative at the first session of the Consultative Assembly (Council of Europe 1976, vol. I, 108). At the presentation of questions concerning Teitgen's original report, what the *rapporteur* meant by 'security of person' was not debated or whether an execution violated this 'security' (ibid., 106). In the same debate the Turkish representative, Mr Düsünsel, questioned the validity of 'so-called popular courts condemning to death and executing deputies' and stated that this was a 'travesty of justice'(ibid., vol. II, 30). But these comments were not picked up as essential for formulating any specific debate on whether the death penalty was a possible violation of the text.

There are also no specific discussions dealing with the scope of the death penalty. In theory, even under the new Convention system of human rights, the punishment could be applied to any crimes which were legislated as a 'capital crime.' A.W. Brian Simpson argued, within his authoritative study on the Convention, that article 2(1) 'had nothing to say as to what crimes could be capitally punished' (Simpson 2004, 876). The drafters did not mention the mandatory or discretionary application of the punishment or whether it was appropriate for an appeals process to be guaranteed or whether capital laws could be retroactively applied.[16] Also no mention was made

16 Although following the retroactive application of the Nuremburg Charter in the sentencing of the defendants at the Nuremburg Tribunal, it cannot be stated that at this time the Convention would prevent retroactively applied death sentences (see, Kelsen 1947).

of whether human rights prohibit any specific execution method, including the guillotine, gas chamber, hanging or shooting. There was also no mention of whether clemency petitions should be guaranteed (Weil 1963, 46).

Furthermore, the subsequent 14 proposals to amend article 2 did not challenge the member state right of the death penalty (Council of Europe 1976, vol. III, 190). Only four proposals considered article 2 generally but did not refer to the punishment.[17] In the subsequent proposed drafts of the Convention text there were only small amendments shifting the right to life from a position of article number 3 to number 2, and whether it should be all one sentence or include a subsection. The final wording of article 2(1) is essentially the same mandate as provided in the final United Kingdom proposal. What is added is the right to life at the beginning of the article, and the word 'defined' is replaced with 'provided' by law. Both adjectives appear to provide the same result as they confirm that a capital crime must be legislated in the civil codes and statutes, or be developed through the common law of member states. It also provides that the death penalty must be 'provided by law,' and that a 'court' only has competence to pass such a sentence. If these provisions were met, at this moment in European history the death penalty was an acceptable punishment by virtue of the specific wording of article 2(1).

The Dialogue Between the Parliamentary Assembly and the Committee of Ministers

1950-1982: Uncertainties and Frictions

In reviewing the early work of the Council of Europe, Frank Dowrick stated that the various 'organs of the Council of Europe [were] very much alive to the need to revise and extend the basic doctrine of human rights' (Dowrick 1974, 616). From its early stage, there were those within the Council who displayed a firm dissatisfaction that the 'basic doctrine' preserved the death penalty within Convention article 2(1), and in 1958 various subordinate committees were created to investigate the problematical human rights issues of the time. One of these committees was the European Committee on Crime Problems which in turn established sub-committees including the Sub-Committee on the Death Penalty (Ancel 1962, 3; 1967; Krüger 2004).[18] The Sub-Committee agreed that the death penalty was a problem (Robertson 1961, 159-60), and so in 1961 Marc Ancel led a study compiling information on member state implementation or rejection of

17 Luxembourg (A 783); Ireland (A 778) Ireland and Turkey (A 776) and Italy (A 786), see, Index of Amendments Proposed (Doc A 795), see Council of Europe 1976, vol. III, 198.

18 Hans Christian Krüger stated, 'barely four years after the entry into force of the Convention, there was a move at expert level of the Council of Europe to study the problem of capital punishment in Europe' (Krüger 2004, 87).

the punishment. A quantitative analysis was provided of member state practices focusing upon judicial and administrative practice, sociological and criminological factors, proposed legislative reform and crime policy. Ancel did not seek to extend the investigations to formulate a human rights perspective. He stated that the purpose was to focus on the implementation of criminal law, and other aspects of the punishment were 'outside the scope of the study' (Ancel 1962, 3). As a result the early initiatives did not demonstrate how human rights arguments could be formulated to tackle the punishment, and so by 1966, only four years after the publication of the Ancel report, the Committee decided to cease the investigations (Schabas 2002, 280).

Then in 1973, Astrid Bergegren, a Swedish parliamentarian, presented a Motion for a resolution on the abolition of capital punishment.[19] This first specific proposition calling for the Parliamentary Assembly to renounce the death penalty relied upon theories of utilitarianism and humanism, and stated, *inter alia*, that capital punishment is irrevocable,[20] that the punishment does not possess any special deterrent quality,[21] that the use of the punishment for retribution is no longer representative of a civilised society,[22] and consequently, called for abolition in all member states and for the Assembly to develop initiatives to achieve this penological change.[23] However, Bergegren's motion did not find favour within the Assembly and it was sent back to the Committee on Legal Affairs where it was stalled. Then, a newly appointed *rapporteur*, Bertil Lidgard, reignited the debates and presented a report. After lengthy discussions at several meetings in January 1975, the Committee on Legal Affairs evaded the issue when it decided 'not to submit the report to the Parliamentary Assembly' (Council of Europe 1980a).[24] But some parliamentarians refused to back-down and in April 1975, the *rapporteur* presented an unpublished report identifying that the 'debate on the death penalty ought [to be carried on]. Attention should be drawn to various new developments as well as certain familiar arguments which militate strongly in favour of the abolition cause' (ibid., 3). This stalwart effort was stonewalled by the Committee on Legal Affairs in 1976, and it stated that the question of the death penalty should be 'deferred' (ibid.). So Lidgard resigned as *rapporteur* (Council of Europe 1980b, 86).[25]

19 Motion for a resolution on the abolition of capital punishment (Doc. 3297), Committee on Legal Affairs, 8th Sitting, 18 May 1973.

20 Ibid., point 2.

21 Ibid., point 3.

22 Ibid., point 4.

23 Ibid., points 8-9.

24 Unpublished Report submitted to the Committee on Legal Affairs in 1975, cited in, Council of Europe 1980a, 2.

25 During the debates, Mr Grieve of the United Kingdom revealed the *rapporteur's* emotion when he described Bertil Lidgard as 'sorrowful' after the Committee on Legal Affairs voted against the report (Council of Europe, 1980b, 86).

However, this was not the end. In 1978 the European Ministers of Justice considered the issue at their Conference held in Copenhagen,[26] and the Austrian Minister of Justice, Christian Broda, championed Resolution No. 4 which recommended that the Committee of Ministers 'refer questions concerning the death penalty to the appropriate Council of Europe bodies for study as part of the Council's work programme.'[27] After further examination, the Ministers of Justice reiterated their position and were more pointed declaring, 'Article 2 of the European Convention on Human Rights does not adequately reflect the situation actually attained with regard to the death penalty in Europe.' They suggested that the Parliamentary Assembly 'study the possibilities for the elaboration of new and appropriate European standards concerning abolition of the death penalty.'[28] Carl Lidbom, the next Committee on Legal Affairs *rapporteur*, firmly grasped the abolitionist mantel and authored a pioneering report in 1980 (Council of Europe 1980a). He forcefully explained to the Assembly that 'there is no doubt that abolition of capital punishment is one of the most controversial topics we can tackle, and at the same time one of the most important subjects for an organisation whose calling is to further liberty and human rights' (Council of Europe 1980b, 52).[29] The published records of the drafting debates on the report in the Parliamentary Assembly reveal a similar outline of the anti-death penalty arguments put forward by Bergegren in 1973. Numerous parliamentarians accepted the prominence of the discourse which led to *de facto* abolition of the death penalty within Western European member states by 1981, including the punishment's lack of special deterrent effect,[30] the renunciation of retribution and the *lex talionis*,[31] the probability that innocent people have been and will be executed,[32] that the

26 European Ministers of Justice, 11th Conference (Copenhagen, 21-22 June, 1978).

27 Resolution No. 4 of the 11th Conference of European Ministers of Justice on the death penalty, Copenhagen (21-22 June 1978).

28 European Ministers of Justice, 12th Conference (Luxembourg, 20-21 May, 1980).

29 Mr Koehl of France agreed when he stated that the 'abolition of capital punishment is…one of the greatest issues of our time' (Council of Europe 1980b, 84).

30 As argued by Mr Lidbom of Sweden, 53; Mr Flanagan of Ireland, 56; Mr Stoffelen of the Netherlands, 60; Mr Meier of Switzerland, 60-61; Mr Bacelar of Portugal, 62; Mrs Hawlicek of Austria, 63; Mr Reddemann of the Federal Republic of Germany, 65; Mr Batliner of Liechtenstein, 66; Mrs Aasen of Norway, 67; Mr Bardens of the Federal Republic of Germany, 74; Mr Beith of the United Kingdom, 80; Mr Belin of France, 84; Mr Koehl of France, 84 (ibid.).

31 As argued by Mr Lidbom of Sweden, 53; Mr Aksoy of Turkey, 57; Mrs Hawlicek of Austria, 63; Mr Batliner of Liechtenstein, 66; Mrs Aasen of Norway, 67 (ibid.).

32 As argued by Mr Lidbom of Sweden, 53; Mr Mercier of France, 55; Mr Flanagan, 56; Mr Stoffelen of the Netherlands, 60; Mr Meier of Switzerland, 61; Mrs Hawlicek of Austria, 63; Mrs Aasen of Norway, 67; Mr Urwin of the United Kingdom, 69 (ibid.).

punishment brutalizes society,[33] but the methods of execution by hanging and guillotine were not debated.

Lidbom restricted the abolition strategy to times of peace because he thought it 'realistic to proceed by stages' (Council of Europe 1980a, 5). He held the view that the death penalty should be abolished because it was barbaric, but he maintained that 'it is an illusion to believe that in the present state of the world we can put an end to barbarism in times of war. Unfortunately times of war are, by definition, times of barbarism and cruelty' (ibid.). So in peacetime, the death penalty was no longer to be seen as an exclusive issue for the state and a centralised challenge to the sovereign's monopoly over the death penalty in peacetime was beginning to be formulated. Mr Ruperez Rubio of Spain declared, 'we believe that nobody in this world should have a monopoly or claim the right to put an end to the life of others, not even the state' (Council of Europe 1980b, 71). The renunciation of this sovereign state right was then affirmed through recourse to the individual's right to life. As Mrs Lindquist of Sweden reasoned, '[i]f we really mean what we say, we cannot deprive human beings of the most fundamental human right, namely, the right to life' (ibid., 65) and Mrs Meier of Switzerland affirmed, 'we set the right to life in the first place on the list of human rights because without this all other rights are meaningless' (ibid., 61).

These arguments were used as the basis for the Parliamentary Assembly's adoption of Resolution 727 which called for abolition in peacetime,[34] and Recommendation 891 to the Committee of Ministers to 'amend Article 2 of the European Convention on Human Rights.'[35] As Lidbom stated, '[l]egally speaking… the European Convention on Human Rights does not preclude capital punishment. Article 2 even allows it *expressis verbis*' (Council of Europe 1980a, 13) and so this was the central legislative problem to be rectified. Lidbom attempted to map out the amendment process when he identified, '[a]ny decision to amend the Convention can be taken solely by the Committee of Ministers of the Council of Europe' (Council of Europe 1980b). But a conflict of opinion arose as to whether it was appropriate for the Parliamentary Assembly to endorse such a provision. It may have been useful if the political debate had considered the Statute of the Council of Europe, article 15(a), as it identifies that with the recommendation of the Parliamentary Assembly:

> or on its own initiative, the Committee of Ministers shall consider the action required to further the aim of the Council of Europe, including the conclusion

33 As argued by Mr Lidbom of Sweden, 54; Mr Stoffelen of the Netherlands, 60 (ibid.).

34 Resolution 727 (1980) on the abolition of capital punishment, text adopted by the Parliamentary Assembly (3rd sitting), 22 April 1980.

35 Recommendation 891 (1980) on the abolition of capital punishment, text adopted by the Parliamentary Assembly on 22 April 1980 (2nd and 3rd Sittings), point 3.

> of conventions or agreements and the adoption by governments of a common policy with regards to particular matters.[36]

But the debate did not consider this mandated action, and Mr Grieve of the United Kingdom, the Chairman of the Committee on Legal Affairs, argued that the Committee of Ministers could not change the Convention text, but only draft an additional protocol, 'which would require the consent of every one of the…countries that make up our Assembly' (ibid., 87). It was then argued that the Parliamentary Assembly could not recommend this amendment mechanism and so the proposals should be rejected. In essence, Mr Grieve and others sought to elevate state sovereignty and renounce any perceived centralised encroachment upon the right of the death penalty. As Mr Smith of the United Kingdom argued, '[i]t is up to each individual country at the end of the day to make its own decision' (ibid., 58) that the states themselves should grapple with the penological questions and the Parliamentary Assembly 'should stop interfering' (ibid., 59).[37] Mr Grieve continued:

> in the end it is for each country to decide what is right for its own society and whether a reserved power which, after all, has been kept by nearly all human societies since the beginning of time, should be withdrawn. I respectfully suggest that it is not for this Assembly to say that countries that still believe that it is right to retain that power are wrong (ibid., 87).[38]

These propositions maintained that the member state sovereign right of the punishment was not evanescent. But such impaired political logic did not deter the majority of the Parliamentary Assembly as it adopted the report, resolution and recommendation. Hence, Lidbom's initiatives should be seen as a significant moment in the history of the Parliamentary Assembly's formulation of a human rights discourse against the punishment. In many ways, the time was now ripe to make such an argument, as, in Western Europe in 1980, France was the only country who would be likely to impose executions in peacetime.[39] In this geo-political region, Denmark[40] had removed the death penalty from its statutes for ordinary criminal offences in peacetime in 1933, and so had (West) Germany (who

---

36 For more information on the roles of the Committee of Ministers and the Parliamentary Assembly on the drafting of legislation, see Polakiewicz 1999; Benoît-Rohmer and Klebes 2005.

37 This position was supported by Mr Karamollaoglu of Turkey (Council of Europe 1980b, 68).

38 See also, Mr Michel of Belgium, 58-59; Mr Banks of the United Kingdom, 78-79; Mr Beith of the United Kingdom, 80-81; Mr Michel of Belgium, 59 (ibid.).

39 France abolished the death penalty in 1981, and Belgium still had the punishment on its statute books but had not executed anyone since 1950.

40 Denmark had administered the death penalty for wartime offences in 1950.

abolished the punishment for all crimes in 1949, and East Germany had done so in 1978), Italy (1947), the Netherlands (1870), Norway (1905), Portugal (1978), Spain (1976), Sweden (1921), and the United Kingdom (suspended in 1965, and confirmed in 1969).

The Parliamentary Assembly had a strong political basis to approach the Committee of Ministers and request that it formulate these principles of abolitionism within new legislation.[41] Then in 1981 the Committee of Ministers gave direction to the Steering Committee for Human Rights to prepare 'a draft additional protocol to the European Convention on Human Rights abolishing the death penalty in peacetime' (Council of Europe 1983, 5). William Schabas notes that in 1982 the Parliamentary Assembly asked the Committee of Ministers for a progress report, and they indicated that the European Committee on Crime Problems and the Steering Committee for Human Rights had been instructed to draw up the protocol, and the joint committees were of the opinion that a protocol would be a 'possible solution' (Schabas 2002, 286). For the first time a substantial meeting-of-the-minds occurred between the Committee of Ministers and the Parliamentary Assembly on what would become Protocol No. 6. This would create the first regional human rights treaty to call for a restriction of the death penalty to wartime application.

The Impact of Protocol No. 6

The 'possible solution' quickly became reality. Protocol No. 6 was adopted in 1983, and it mandated a restriction of the *prima facie* unconfined scope of Convention article 2(1) through formulating abolition of the death penalty in peacetime. As such this Protocol provided an opportunity for abolitionist member states to confirm their commitment to a centralised regional instrument, and at the same time establish an ideological platform from which the Council of Europe could encourage those member states which had not yet restricted the death penalty to do so. The Commentary on Protocol No. 6, article 1 states that the article should be read in conjunction with article 2 and that the two articles 'affirm the principle of abolition of the death penalty' (Council of Europe 1983, 6). However, the mechanism which the Protocol utilised was not specifically a 'human rights' mandate to reduce the punishment, but a centralised affirmation of an already existent state practice. But Protocol No. 6 did provide the genesis for a regional principle of European constitutionalism and should be seen as the first time that the Convention human rights discourse attempted to reflect, and influence, member state public law on the punishment. The Council had for the first time attempted to rectify the inadequate position created by the inability of the drafters of the Convention to deal with the relationship of state sovereignty and the punishment: as through article 2(1) they had conceded too much ground on the state's side and not enough to the human rights of the individual. Of course, the

41 Resolution 727 (1980); Recommendation 891 (1980); Council of Europe 1980a.

state may decide not to impose a death penalty in wartime but article 2(1) allowed the possibility of the punishment to remain in the state's arsenal.

Even though Protocol No. 6 reflected the position of Western European governments post-1981, the dark shadow of state sovereignty lingered as some states were reluctant to sign and ratify a document which would symbolise an acceptance that this anti-death penalty position was evolving into a regional public law norm (Rosen and Journey 1993, 166-169; Bae 2007, 1-12). By 1989, of the then 22 member states, 14 had ratified Protocol No. 6, including Austria (1984), Denmark (1983), France (1986), Germany (1989), Iceland (1987), Italy (1988), Luxembourg (1985), Netherlands (1986), Norway (1988), Portugal (1986), San Marino (1989), Spain (1985), Sweden (1984), Switzerland (1987). However, there were still eight member states which had not posted their ratifications at that time including Belgium, Cyprus, Greece, Ireland, Liechtenstein, Malta, Turkey and the United Kingdom.[42] This displayed insecurity on the part of these members in relinquishing their monopoly to decide whether or not to impose the death penalty. The lack of majority ratifications revealed that even though the centralising of the discourse reflected what the states had already decided individually, some were cautious about the process facilitated through Protocol No. 6. The regional codification was perhaps thought more significant than individual states renouncing the punishment by themselves and remaining separate and autonomous in their decision making.

A comparative example can be seen from a resolution adopted in the European Community. In 1985 the European Commission spoke against the reluctance of some member states to sign and ratify Protocol No. 6.[43] Of the 12 member states of the European Community in 1985, the Resolution noted that Ireland and the United Kingdom had not signed the Protocol,[44] and Belgium, Germany, Greece, Italy, the Netherlands and Portugal, had not posted their ratifications.[45] Point 3 states that the European Parliament '[e]xpresses its misgivings over the delay,' and Preamble E noted a regret that 'the procedures for the ratification...are being carried out very slowly, which might be considered as an expression of some hesitation on the part of those States over being bound by an international undertaking to abolish the death penalty.'[46] Hence, the 1980s can be seen as a significant, but not yet general, member state acceptance of the evolving Convention human rights discourse.

42 Belgium ratified Protocol No. 6 in 1998, as did Greece (1998), Ireland (1994), Liechtenstein (1990), Malta (1991), Turkey (2003), and the United Kingdom (1999).

43 Resolution on the abolition of the death penalty and the accession to the Sixth Protocol to the Convention for the Protection of Human Rights and Fundamental Freedoms, Doc. A2-167/85, OJ, C 36, 17/2/1986.

44 Ibid., Point 1.

45 Ibid., Point 3.

46 Ibid., Preamble E.

The Drafting of Protocol No. 13

Following the Vienna Summit in 1993 and the adoption of the Vienna Declaration,[47] greater emphasis was placed upon the development of policies to intensify abolitionism for all circumstances and thus strengthen the regional position. Roger Hood described the Vienna Summit's condition of acceptance of the Convention system as the 'most important political decision' (Hood 2004, 16) for the furtherance of human rights. Only one year after the Vienna Declaration, Hans Göran Franck, the new *rapporteur* to the Committee on Legal Affairs, took the opportunity and inspired further change (Franck 2003, 64). He authored a report which focused upon clearing up the existing capital laws within member states, as at this time although the Western member states had removed the death penalty for ordinary crimes, Protocol No. 6 still had not been signed and ratified by all of them (Council of Europe 1994).[48] Franck argued that a 'control mechanism' should be set up under the Secretary General to analyse the remaining retentionist member state's capital laws. He advised 'all states whose legislation still provides for the death penalty to set up a commission as soon as possible in their country with a view to abolishing capital punishment' (ibid., paragraph 6(ii)(a)).

A regionalised abolition position would lay the foundation for the expectation that new member states should follow suit and so a draft resolution was included in the report (ibid., paragraphs 5-6 of the appended draft resolution). In 1994, Resolution 1044 was adopted which stated that the 'willingness to ratify the protocol be made a prerequisite for membership,'[49] and to bolster the Resolution, Recommendation 1246 was sent to the Committee of Ministers inviting it to implement the outlined provisions.[50] In its interim reply, the Committee of Ministers noted that it would examine the Parliamentary Assembly's recommendations, and also emphasised that it would encourage 'member states which have not abolished the death penalty to operate de facto or de jure a moratorium on the execution of death sentences' (Council of Europe 1996b). The Committee of Ministers had been nuanced in its response to the Parliamentary Assembly and it began to promote the initiation of moratoriums as a kind of political middle-ground between the role of the sovereign member states in abolition and the radical expansion of the human rights boundaries by the Assembly. Danny Nicol noted this intricate legislative friction and argued that the Parliamentary Assembly was more 'enthusiastic' in

47 Vienna Declaration, Decl-09.10.93E, 9 October 1993.

48 These countries are listed here and the ratification dates are in brackets: Belgium (1998), Estonia (1998), Greece (1998), Ireland (1994), Romania (1994), Russia (still to ratify), Slovenia (1994), and United Kingdom (1999).

49 Resolution 1044 (1994) on the abolition of capital punishment, text adopted by the Parliamentary Assembly on 4 October 1994 (25th sitting), para. 6.

50 Recommendation 1246 (1994) on the abolition of capital punishment, text adopted by the Parliamentary Assembly on 4 October 1994 (25th sitting).

its legislative transcriptions and the Committee of Ministers displayed a more 'cautious' approach (Nicol 2005, 154).

Consequently, a difficult dialogue resulted between the Parliamentary Assembly and the Committee of Ministers. The Committee did not initially deal with the 1994 provisions and so in 1996 the Assembly adopted a further Recommendation calling on the Committee to respond.[51] It welcomed the Committee's encouragement of moratoria, but regretted it had 'not yet taken any action on the most important proposals.'[52] The Assembly was not satisfied with the Committee dragging its feet on the new protocol, and called for complete abolition and a greater monitoring of member states which imposed the punishment. Following its preference of moratoria over explicit calls for signature and ratification of Protocol No. 6, the Committee instructed the Rapporteur Group on Human Rights to examine both Recommendations with a view to proposing a draft reply (Council of Europe 1997a). The Assembly was again dissatisfied as it viewed the Committee's actions as another stalling tactic, but the determined efforts of the Assembly finally forced their hand. In 1997, the Committee put forward an interim reply to Recommendation 1302 (see, Council of Europe 1997a; 1997b; 1997c) stating that it 'fully shares the concern voiced by the Parliamentary Assembly,' but equanimously explained that the 'parliaments and governments share responsibility regarding the abolition of the death penalty,' and that the Committee:

> considers that the process of monitoring compliance with commitments accepted by *member States of the Council of Europe can contribute, in a spirit of dialogue and co-operation*, to the process of putting an end to capital punishment. It also considers that the Parliamentary Assembly has an important role to play in this regard (emphasis added) (Council of Europe 1997b, Point D).

This may be read as the Committee of Ministers attempting to distance itself as the final arbiter to determine the Parliamentary Assembly's stream of recommendations. The Committee demonstrated that it sought to share the burden with the national parliaments, and identified the importance of 'dialogue' for this abolition process. It emphasised that the Parliamentary Assembly played a crucial role in this dialogue, but this was stating nothing new to the Assembly: it already possessed an acute sense of the importance of its work. So this manoeuvre by the Committee appears to indicate that there was a heavy uncertainty on how to balance a new protocol and the possibility of amending article 2(1), with the impact of this process on the sovereign member states (see Türmen 2005, 57). It appears that 'dialogue' was the buffer for remedying any difficulties. However, the Assembly displayed no

---

51 Recommendation 1302 (1996) on the abolition of the death penalty in Europe, text adopted by the Parliamentary Assembly on 28 June 1996 (24th Sitting). This Recommendation was adopted following the Report on the abolition of the death penalty in Europe (Council of Europe 1996a).

52 Ibid., Recommendation 1302 (1996), para. 2.

uncertainty, or ambivalence, and boldly reaffirmed its position in Resolution 1097 which stated:

> the Assembly reminds applicant states to the Council of Europe that the willingness to sign and ratify Protocol No. 6 to the European Convention on Human Rights and to introduce a moratorium upon accession *has become a prerequisite for membership* of the Council of Europe on the part of the Assembly (emphasis added).[53]

Clearly the Assembly did not want to wait any longer for specific affirmation from the Committee on the reach of its abolitionist agenda, and therefore developed its own membership criteria. The language had markedly shifted from the Resolution 1044 invitation that states display a 'willingness' to adopt the specified penal changes, to a position that it has become 'a prerequisite for membership' under Resolution 1097. The Assembly was not acquiescing with the legislative mire created by the Committee, it sought to map out new boundaries for the human rights discourse against the punishment. In the battle for abolition in all circumstances the Assembly was leading the way and the Committee then, again, felt compelled to reaffirm its nuanced position stating that it 'considers that the priority is to obtain and maintain moratoria on executions, to be consolidated by complete abolition of the death penalty' (Council of Europe 1997a). Even though the Committee had the fundamental responsibility as the 'legislator in this field,' (Council of Europe 1998) it still did not simply endorse the Assembly's position, and shifted the deliberations to the Second Summit held in Strasbourg on 10-11 October 1997.[54] It sidestepped the call to require prospective member states to ratify Protocol No. 6, and reemphasised instead the 'maintenance, in the meantime, of existing moratoria of executions in Europe.'[55] But this prevarication was not the end, as the European Ministerial Conference on Human Rights held in Rome on 3-4 November 2000 changed the legislative tide.[56] A further Resolution was drafted inviting the Committee of Ministers to adopt a 'new additional protocol to the Convention which would exclude the possibility of maintaining the death penalty in respect of acts committed in time of war or of imminent threat of war.'[57]

53 Resolution 1097 (1996) on the abolition of the death penalty in Europe, text adopted by the Parliamentary Assembly on 28 June 1996 (24th Sitting), para. 6.

54 Second Summit of Heads of State and Government of the Council of Europe, Strasbourg, 10-11 October, 1997: Final Declaration.

55 Ibid.

56 For the draft documents see, Steering Committee for Human Rights, 49th Meeting, 3-6 October 2000, CDDH (2000) 025 Addendum, Strasbourg, 11 October 2000; and for the adopted text, see, Proceedings: European Ministerial Conference on Human Rights and Commemorative Ceremony of the 50th Anniversary of the European Convention on Human Rights, Rome, 3-4 November 2000.

57 European Ministerial Conference, Paragraph 14 (ii) of Resolution IIB (2000).

The Foreign Ministers produced a Declaration for a European Death Penalty-Free Area, which identified that the achievement of abolition of all member states was 'our common goal.'[58] This was not quite the same as specifically stating that the Committee would formulate a protocol in order to abolish the death penalty in wartime, or that, even, article 2(1) would be amended. Resolution II was then adopted at the Ministerial Conference and the section on the death penalty, *inter alia*, invited member states to consider the possibility of the abolition of the death penalty in all circumstances, which would in effect make abolition a condition of membership.[59] This was a departure from the singular focus on moratoria as a stepping stone to abolition. However, the wording of the Draft Declaration was restricted as it stated that the Committee of Ministers considered, 'the signing and the ratification of Protocol No. 6 by all member states [is] highly advisable.'[60] Making ratification a 'highly advisable' position, as opposed to a 'prerequisite for membership,' was a tentative step in the Parliamentary Assembly's direction. The subsequent text did not simply state that member states should ratify Protocol No. 6, but requested that the 'member states ratify as soon as possible, if they have not yet done so, Protocol No. 6 and in the meantime, respect the moratoria on executions.'[61] Again this was not a specific affirmation of the Parliamentary Assembly's position. However, the Committee of Ministers should be viewed as providing a certain freedom, and discretion, to the Assembly. The Committee was not opposing the Assembly's prerequisites for future member states, but it did not plainly endorse them either. As a result, the Committee's promotion of moratoria can be seen as a minimal requirement and the Assembly's position provided a higher human rights threshold.

Then in 2001, the Rapporteur Group on Human Rights submitted to the Committee of Ministers the Draft Protocol for the abolition of the death penalty in all circumstances.[62] The text called for complete abolition but, as with Protocol No. 6, there were no provisions specifically amending article 2(1). It considered and accepted the Draft Protocol, and it was then presented with an Explanatory

58 Declaration 'For a Death Penalty-Free Area' adopted by the Committee of Ministers, 9th November 2000, 107th Session.

59 Proceedings, Resolution II: B. Abolition of the death penalty in times of war and times of peace, para. 14(ii) 'invites the Committee of Ministers to consider the feasibility of a new additional protocol to the Convention, which would exclude the possibility of maintaining the death penalty in respect of acts committed in time of war or imminent threat of war.'

60 Draft Declaration on the European Death Penalty-Free Area, CM(2000)163 (Restricted) 27 October 2000, 728th meeting, 30 October 2000, para. 5.

61 Declaration 'For a European Death Penalty-Free Area,' para. 4.

62 Draft Protocol No. 13 to the Convention for the Protection of Human Rights and Fundamental Freedoms, concerning the abolition of the death penalty in all circumstances, Ministers' Deputies Meeting (773rd meeting) 21 November 2001.

Report to the Assembly for opinion.[63] In her Explanatory Memorandum to the Draft Protocol, Renate Wohlwend, the next *rapporteur* to the Committee on Legal Affairs, reiterated that the unsatisfactory situation of article 2(1) remained under the draft and that amendment was required to match 'theory with reality.'[64] Wohlwend proposed a seemingly reasonable legislative mechanism to remedy the deficiency when she argued that a provision should be included in the new protocol according to which:

> [w]hen this Protocol has come into force in all States Parties to the Convention, the second sentence of Article 2 paragraph 1 of the Convention shall be replaced with the text of Article 1 of this Protocol, and in the first sentence of Article 47 of the Convention, after the words 'provision of the Convention' the words 'except for Article 2, paragraph 1' shall be added.[65]

Wohlwend argued that Protocol No. 13 was a great opportunity for textual abolition. She proposed that, when universal ratification occurs, the member states should be viewed as signalling a collective affirmation of amendment to the article.[66] A legislative mechanism would fall into place which alters the specific text by deleting the second sentence and inserting the replacement wording, '[t]he death penalty shall be abolished. No one shall be condemned to such penalty or executed.' However, the Committee of Ministers, in the final drafting of Protocol No. 13, did not include Wohlwend's provisions and so the perplexed *rapporteur* strongly questioned:

> are we then going to draw up another (the third!) Protocol on the same subject – the abolition of the death penalty – in order to at long last amend Article 2 of the Convention itself? In treaty law, this is a very inelegant solution…I would suggest a 'hybrid' Protocol, which starts out as an additional Protocol, and becomes an amending Protocol when it has entered into force in all State Parties to the Convention.[67]

---

63 European Convention on Human Rights – Draft Protocol No. 13 on abolition of the death penalty in all circumstances, Parliamentary Assembly, Doc. 9291, 14 December 2001.

64 Explanatory Memorandum, by Mrs Renate Wohlwend, *rapporteur*, point, 1, in Draft Protocol to the European Convention on Human Rights concerning the abolition of the death penalty in all circumstances, Doc. 9316, 15 January 2002.

65 Opinion No. 233 (2002), Draft Protocol to the European Convention on Human Rights concerning the abolition of the death penalty in all circumstances, 1st Sitting, Assembly Debate, 21 January 2002, paras 5-6.

66 See, Explanatory Memorandum, paras 1-12.

67 Ibid., para. 9-10.

This unimpeachable approach of constructing a hybrid protocol was not followed by the Committee of Ministers as they would not 'think the unthinkable,'[68] and the exchange of opinions between the Assembly and the Committee on the status of article 2(1) reveals the frustration that was present at this time. Indeed, Wohlwend's exclamation of the need for 'the third!' protocol, and sighing 'at long last,' exposes the historical tensions between the Parliamentary Assembly and the Committee of Ministers. Following this exchange, the Assembly's efforts were again thwarted, and, in response to Wohlwend, the Rapporteur Group on Human Rights stated:

> [w]ith regards to the Assembly's Opinion the Group, whilst welcoming its strong political support for such a protocol, came to the conclusion that it was not advisable to accede to the Recommendation...In the Group's view such an amendment would present only limited interest given that the purported legal effect in respect of Article 2, ECHR will in practice also be achieved through an additional protocol. Furthermore, the amendment could, in the opinion of the [Rapporteur Group on Human Rights], give rise to some legal questions, not least with regard to territorial declarations and reservations, extending beyond the scope of the consideration of the protocol itself, which could delay unduly the adoption of this important text (Council of Europe 2002, sixth unnumbered paragraph).

The Rapporteur Group on Human Rights were advancing complex legal arguments but displayed a notable ambivalence in that it recognised the importance of abolition in all circumstances, and at the same time allowed for the preservation of the punishment in the text of article 2(1). However, the Group was of the opinion that Protocol No. 13 would provide amendment by implication, and that the 'purported legal effect' will be achieved 'in practice.' But such an interpretation seems to be irreconcilable with Protocol No. 13, article 5 on the relationship of the protocol with the Convention as it stated that the 'Protocol shall be regarded as additional articles to the Convention,' and not that it amends the Convention. Also, the final Protocol Commentary on article 5, confusingly states:

> [a]s an additional Protocol, it does not, as far as the Parties to the Protocol are concerned, supersede Article 2 of the Convention, since the first sentence of paragraph 1 and the whole of paragraph 2 of that article still remain valid...It is clear that the second sentence of paragraph 1 is no longer applicable in respect of the States Parties to this Protocol.[69]

---

68 Ibid., para. 2.

69 Protocol No. 13 to the Convention for the protection of human rights and fundamental freedoms, concerning the abolition of the death penalty in all circumstances, Commentary on the provisions of the Protocol, Article 5: Relationship to the Convention.

Although the Commentary endorsed the inapplicability of the second sentence of article 2(1), the Protocol nevertheless preserved the possibility of the death penalty within the main text of the Convention. The Committee allowed this complex human rights position because of some undisclosed 'legal questions,' and again the issue of state sovereignty raised its ugly head. The Group considered two reasons which, in their view, rendered amendment unnecessary, and both related to the preservation of member state's opinions. Firstly, it presumed that the amendment would only be of 'limited interest' to the signatories, and secondly, that the proposal may attract unwanted considerations of 'territorial declarations and reservations.' However, territorial considerations have been a central factor of the sovereignty of European states since their legal articulation following the Treaty of Westphalia in 1648, and the *travaux préparatoires* reveal that the sovereignty issue was hegemonic within the 1949-50 drafting debates of the Convention and can be seen as directly contributing to the preservation of the death penalty within article 2(1). So the importance of the recognition of state issues should not have been underestimated. Indeed the death penalty has an intricate genealogy which reveals that the punishment has been considered within the annals of European history to be an essential element of sovereign power (for example see, Foucault 1976; Spierenburg 1984; Whitman 2003). And although the vast majority of member states have ratified Protocol No. 13,[70] the preservation of the text of article 2(1) still, theoretically at least, allows such power to be legitimately applied. This was the result of the Committee endorsing the Group's opinions over the Parliamentary Assembly's analysis of the final wording of Protocol No. 13, and as with Protocol No. 6, we see the manifestation of a political middle-way.

The Interpretation of Article 2(1)

The Preamble to Protocol No. 13 states that 'everyone's right to life is a basic value in a democratic society and that the abolition of the death penalty is essential for the protection of this right.' The right to life is stated twice in the Preamble, although not in the Protocol articles, and reminiscent of the internal conflict detailed above, Convention article 2(1) is not specifically referred to. The important question remains as to why article 2(1) was not amended if the right to life is such an intrinsic aspect of the Protocol? The Explanatory Report point 1 refers to the European Court of Human Rights' judgment in *Streletz, Kessler and Krenz v. Germany*, which held that the right to life is 'an inalienable attribute of human beings,' and that this right possesses 'supreme value in the international hierarchy of human rights.'[71] Nowhere is it stated that 'life' itself is inalienable, only that it is an 'inalienable attribute.' An attribute is an aspect of something and

70 See below for the ratification process.

71 *Streletz, Kessler and Krenz v. Germany*, Application Nos. 34044/96; 35532/97; 44801/98, 22 March 2001, paras, 72, 85, 87 and 94.

not the essence of it, and here we see the root issue. Can the right to life be used as an *end* to eradicate the sovereign use of the death penalty, or is it only a *means* with which to challenge the punishment? The case-law that attempts to provide an answer to this fundamental question is considered below.

1957-1983: The Literal Endorsement of Article 2(1)

The early decisions of the European Commission of Human Rights and the European Court of Human Rights suggest that the judicial bodies accepted the textual affirmation of the death penalty in article 2(1). In 1957, the European Commission of Human Rights considered *Greece v. United Kingdom*,[72] and a special Sub-Committee of the Commission was established with an investigatory mandate restricted to scrutinising the emergency situation of the British colonial control in Cyprus (Holland 1998, 133).[73] The punishment was indirectly affirmed as the fundamental issue it determined was that the British government had legitimately used its powers of derogation under Convention article 15, and in derogation the death penalty had been implemented. Article 2(1) appeared to legitimise the colonial use of the death penalty in legally mandated capital crimes, and following the emergency in 1956, Regulations 52, 53, 53A and 53B considerably extended its scope and introduced the mandatory application of the punishment in terrorist cases.[74] These draconian laws were applied to administer the executions of two Cypriots, Andreas Demetriou on 10th May 1956 and Evagoras Pallikarides on 14th March 1957. Demetriou was found guilty of wounding, and Pallikarides, who was only 18 years old, was arrested in December 1955 when an army patrol came across an armed EOKA group making its way to their winter hide-out. Pallikarides's companions escaped but he surrendered without resistance and following a trial was executed.[75] Nancy Crawshaw observed concerning the two executions of Demetriou and Pallikarides, that in the former case under normal criminal law he would have been liable for only a maximum sentence of life imprisonment, and in the later case no severe charges would have been possible (Crawshaw 1978, 232-3). The *Second Cyprus Case* was to consider the

72 Council of Europe, *Application by the Government of the Kingdom of Greece, lodged against the Government of the United Kingdom of Great Britain and Northern Ireland*, Application No. 176/56, *Application of the European Convention of Human Rights and Fundamental Freedoms to the Island of Cyprus*, *Report of the European Commission of Human Rights*, Doc. No. A 42.048 (Article 31 of the Convention) (Strasbourg, 26 September, 1958), in Robertson et al. 1959, 48-49.

73 For a detailed analysis of the two cases brought by Greece against the United Kingdom, see Simpson 2004, 924-1052.

74 Supplement to Cyprus Gazette, No. 4001 (22 November 1956), cited in Simpson 1996, 658, fn. 264. David Pannick argued that the mandatory death penalty is 'neither fair nor reasonable, and lacks the procedural safeguards demanded by the rule of law' (Pannick 1983, 114).

75 *Times of Cyprus*, 14 March 1957, cited in Holland 1998, 173.

specific allegations of human rights violations. There was an outcry by the Greek government against the application of the death penalty, and although article 2(1) allows for the use of the punishment, it had not eradicated the problems presented by its application. However, after many legal petitions by the British government which argued against judicial scrutiny, the case was discontinued (see, Simpson 2004, 924-1052; Robertson 1959, 48-49).

Following this, the next cases to consider the death penalty were in the early 1980s where there was further judicial acceptance of the punishment. In *Deweer v. Belgium*, the Court noted in an *obiter* statement that the 'Convention permits under certain conditions some very serious forms of treatment, such as the death penalty,'[76] and in *Kirkwood v. United Kingdom*,[77] the United Kingdom government had argued that extradition circumstances where the person transferred would face a capital trial could not violate article 2(1).[78] The Commission stated that 'the provisions of Article 2(1) of the Convention...expressly recognises the ending of life through the death penalty following appropriate criminal conviction.'[79] *Deweer* and *Kirkwood* endorsed a literal application of the text of article 2(1), but this was not the only interpretative mechanism open to the Court at this time. In *Tyrer v. United Kingdom*,[80] the Court held that the *Convention* must not be viewed in a vacuum because the document is a 'living instrument,' which 'should be interpreted in the light of present day conditions.'[81] By the time of *Deweer* in 1980, only France would be seen to possibly apply the death penalty, and four years later in *Kirkwood* every Western European state had renounced the punishment for peacetime offences. Hence, an evolution of municipal law was occurring within Western Europe, but at the time it was not considered to be constitutive of a uniform 'present day condition.' In fact, the *Kirkwood* decision would mark the beginning of a judicial reluctance to apply the living instrument doctrine to specifically amend the text of article 2(1).

---

76 *Deweer v. Belgium*, Application No. 6903/75, 27 February 1980, para. 53.

77 *Kirkwood v. United Kingdom*, Application No. 10479/83, 12 March 1984. In *Amekrane v. United Kingdom*, Application No. 5961/72, 19 July 1974, the United Kingdom reached a friendly settlement with Mrs Amekrane, as it had extradited her husband back to Morocco for a capital crime and he was executed.

78 *Kirkwood v. United Kingdom*, Application No. 10479/83, 12 March 1984, para. 183-184.

79 Ibid., paras 188, 190.

80 *Tyrer v. United Kingdom*, Application Nos 5856/72; 5775/72, 14 December 1976.

81 Ibid., para. 31. Furthermore, it should be noted that the Court should interpret the *Convention* and any bilateral or multilateral treaties following the rules in the Vienna Convention on the Law of Treaties, 1969, articles 31-33, which call for *inter alia* interpretation in 'good faith in accordance with the ordinary meaning to be given to the terms of the treaty in their context and in the light of its object and purpose.' Although the Vienna Convention was not specifically referred to in *Deweer*, *Kirkwood* or *Soering*, the Court appears to have followed the 'ordinary meaning' of article 2(1).

The Interpretation of Protocol No. 6

The judicial interpretation evolved following the adoption of Protocol No. 6 and the introduction of the possible prohibition against the death penalty in peacetime. In 1989 the Commission considered the application of article 2(1) to extradition proceedings in *Soering v. the United Kingdom*.[82] Hans Soering was detained in the United Kingdom and the Virginian government requested his extradition to stand trial for capital murder. The Commission considered that Soering was only 18 at the time of the purported crime, that he suffered from the mental condition *folie à deux*, and the extreme conditions of death row in the State of Virginia were enhanced by prolonged incarceration of up to eight years. However, the Commission relied on the interpretation of article 2(1) that it established in *Kirkwood*, and held that Soering could be extradited to face a capital trial. The Commission did not venture to apply any evolutive interpretation to move away from the *Kirkwood* decision, but on appeal to the European Court of Human Rights, the question arose as to how article 2(1) was to be interpreted against Protocol No. 6.[83] The Court considered the issue at length and stated:

> [s]ubsequent practice in national penal policy, in the form of a generalised abolition of capital punishment, could be taken as establishing the agreement of the Contracting States to abrogate the exception provided for under Article 2(1)...However, Protocol No. 6, as a subsequent written agreement, shows that the intention of the Contracting Parties as recently as 1983 was to adopt the normal method of amendment of the text in order to introduce a new obligation to abolish capital punishment in time of peace and, what is more, to do so by an optional instrument allowing each State to choose the moment when to undertake such an agreement.[84]

The political debates and jurisprudence concerning article 2(1) reveals that the *locus* of the authority to dictate the final decision of whether or not to apply the death penalty manifests through a three-layered political process of Committee of Ministers legislating protocols and then the acceptance or rejection of the provisions of the protocols by the member states, and finally the Court's adjudication on the state signature and ratification process. As the dialogue between the Committee of Ministers and Parliamentary Assembly displayed, it is a sensitive political project to engage the sovereign state in relinquishing such an historically legitimised right, even when it was just applied in wartime. In his 1980 report for the Parliamentary

82 *Soering v. the United Kingdom*, Application No. 14038/88, 19 January 1989.

83 *Soering v. the United Kingdom*, Application No. 14038/88, 7 July 1989, para. 103. The then 13 ratifying states were: Austria, Denmark, France, Germany, Iceland, Italy, Luxembourg, the Netherlands, Norway, Portugal, San Marino, Spain, Sweden, Switzerland.

84 Ibid.

Assembly, Carl Lidbom had stated that it was the Committee of Ministers who could only provide for the possibility of the amendment of the Convention text itself (Council of Europe 1980a, 22), and *Soering* agreed that this legislative offering is then accepted or rejected by the member state governments. Alastair Mowbray has cogently observed that the Court was careful to display a legitimate basis for its decision and this is why it gave prominence to the actions of the states and adopted a 'limitation on the use of the "living instrument" doctrine' (Mowbray 2005, 66). But Judge De Meyer held the view that the *Soering* Court should have gone further and he stated in his concurring opinion that:

> [t]he second sentence of Article 2(1) of the Convention was adopted nearly forty years ago, in particular historical circumstances, shortly after the Second World War. In so far as it still may seem to permit, under certain conditions, capital punishment in times of peace, it does not reflect the contemporary situation, and is now overridden by the development of legal conscience and practice.[85]

Judge De Meyer's concurring opinion is more strongly worded than the majority's and it echoed the determined Parliamentary Assembly resolutions and recommendations. In effect, he was arguing that the member states had over a 39 year period, arrived at a better understanding of the penal issues concerning the death penalty. George Letsas views the importance of member states endeavouring to develop 'better' legislation as he argues 'it is not enough to there being a different understanding evolved, this understanding must also be better, i.e., towards the truth of the substantive protected right' (Letsas 2007, 79; see also, Foucault 1976, 73). Even though the *Soering* Court did not hold that the member states had agreed to amend article 2(1), it is evident that the states were formulating a collective understanding of more effective and humane penal policy. Judge De Meyer thought that there had been a significant ideological shift, but whilst the Court did observe this development, it did not see that it had a judicial function in furthering this new penal perspective through specific textual amendment. It delineated what was happening in 1989, and as Mowbray observed, left any subsequent advances to the member states (Mowbray 2005, 66).

The juxtaposition of article 2(1) with Protocol No. 6 did not provide the only interpretive difficulty. A further issue was presented by the balancing of article 2(1) with article 3, which prohibits *inter alia* inhuman punishment. *Kirkwood* first considered this intricate question and held that there was a 'certain disharmony between Articles 2 and 3 of the Convention,' resulting in the death penalty not being denounced as it stated '[w]hereas Article 3 prohibits all forms of inhuman and degrading treatment and punishment without qualification of any kind, the right to life is not protected in an absolute manner. Article 2(1) expressly envisages the possibility of imposing the death penalty.'[86] The Commission established a

85 Ibid., para. 51.

86 *Kirkwood*, 190.

rule concerning the parameters of the right to life and what this seems to mean in a practical sense is that there will be some (unspecified) circumstances where the death penalty was not considered to be an article 3 violation. As such, the Commission was demonstrating that there were pragmatic issues to this evolving discourse with which the Assembly had not adequately engaged and which it had not resolved. The *Soering* Court then persisted with this reasoning and affirmed that, with the presence of article 2(1), 'Article 3 cannot be interpreted as generally prohibiting the death penalty.'[87] William Schabas has observed that the Court viewed this interpretive conundrum as a 'matter for the States parties to resolve by amendment to the Convention and not something to be tackled by the judiciary' (Schabas 1996, 9). Protocol No. 13 would provide a significant opportunity for this specific amendment procedure.

The Interpretation of Protocol No. 13

In 2002 the Chamber of the European Court of Human Rights considered *Öcalan v. Turkey*.[88] Turkey had imposed a death sentence on Abdullah Öcalan, the leader of the PKK (Kurdistan Worker's Party),[89] for the Kurdish uprisings aimed at destroying the 'integrity of the Turkish state' (Trilsh and Rüth 2006, 180; see also, Sherlock 2001; Schabas 2002, 277-279). This was the first case to come before the Chamber which involved a member state's application of the death penalty within its municipal territory.[90] Following the ratifications of Protocol No. 6 and Protocol No. 13, it was argued for the applicant that the practice of the Contracting States in this area can be taken as establishing an agreement to abrogate the exception provided for in the second sentence of article 2(1). The Chamber noted the Parliamentary Assembly's Opinion on the Draft Protocol No. 13, and engaged with the dialogue between the Parliamentary Assembly and the Committee of Ministers on the amendment of article 2(1). However, it adopted the *Soering* reasoning that the normal method of Convention amendment is through state practice in signing and ratifying optional protocols,[91] and asked 'whether it is necessary to await [complete] ratification of Protocol No. 6…before concluding that the death penalty exception in Article 2 has been significantly modified.'[92] It

87 *Soering*, paras 103-104.

88 *Öcalan v. Turkey* [C] Application No. 46221/99, 12 March 2003.

89 For an outline of the history of the Kurdistan Worker's Party see, Chiapetta 2001, and for a review of the legal and political polices adopted by Turkey in an attempt to join the European Union, see Kanarek, 2003.

90 Sir Sydney Kentridge, one of the lawyers for Abdullah Öcalan, pointed out in his opening statement, 'this is one of the most significant and high-profile cases ever to come before the European Court of Human Rights…it is a case in which the passing and proposed implementation of the death penalty within a signatory state has resulted in litigation before the court', cited in Wells 2003, 9.

91 *Öcalan* [C] para. 191.

92 Ibid., para. 196.

thought it was, and consequently it looked for member state unanimity to enable it to present an interpretation that article 2(1) had been amended. The Chamber then applied this interpretive methodology to Protocol No. 13 and held:

> [i]n expressing this view, the Court is aware of the opening for signature Protocol 13 which provides an indication that the Contracting States have chosen the traditional method of amendment of the text of the Convention in pursuit of their policy of abolition. However this Protocol seeks to extend the prohibition by providing for the abolition of the death penalty in all circumstances – that is to say both in times of peace and in times of war. This final step toward complete abolition of the death penalty can be seen as a confirmation of the abolitionist trend established by the practice of the Contracting States. It does not necessarily run counter to the view that Article 2 has been amended in so far as it permits the death penalty in times of peace.[93]

The Chamber does identify a development towards possible amendment, but ultimately its language is imprecise and does not say simply and categorically, that article 2(1) *is* amended. Mowbray observed that the Chamber 'would not unequivocally rule that the State's contemporary practice had modified Article 2(1),' (Mowbray 2005, 67) and this decision outlines the fact that the development of abolition in member states, 'could,' and 'can,' but 'does not necessarily run counter' to the signalling to 'abrogate' article 2(1). The Chamber explained that 'it can' be said that the death penalty is 'unacceptable' in peacetime, and so, if article 2(1) is now interpreted judicially to be amended to reflect this specific prohibition, this does not mean that there is a textual change. The Chamber held that the ratifications of Protocol No. 13 did not yet create a *per se* rule for member states, as by the date of the judgment (12 March 2003), only eight countries had posted their ratifications, which were: Bulgaria, Croatia, Cyprus, Denmark, Liechtenstein, Malta, Switzerland and the Ukraine. The Partly Dissenting Opinion of Judge Türmen furthers the argument when he stated that the specific amendment 'would require clear evidence over and above the uniform amendment of penal policy in favour of abolition. Such evidence is, however, lacking.'[94] The Judge then affirmed that it is for the states to specifically decide, and, in his opinion, Protocol No. 13 only strengthened Protocol No. 6, and it did not directly provide textual amendment as:

> [i]n reality there is no basis for the view that this new Protocol represents the treaty confirmation of any previous agreement between the States to complete abrogation – only partially achieved in Protocol No. 6 – of the exception contained in Article 2(1). Against such a clear background, the conclusion reached in the judgment that the exception in Article 2(1) is abrogated is not

93 Ibid., para. 197.

94 *Öcalan* [C] Partly Dissenting Opinion of Judge Türmen.

> tenable. Accordingly, Article 2(1) must still be read as permitting the imposition of the death penalty.[95]

Judge Türmen is correct in his literal application of the current text of article 2(1), but he has not given enough judicial credence to the practical application of Protocol No. 6 and Protocol No. 13 and that in reality there is a current abolition position in practice. It also appears that Judge Türmen is not completely clear on his interpretation of the majority judgment, as it does not specifically state that article 2(1) *is* abrogated, only that it 'could,' and 'can,' not that it *does*.[96] However, this decision identifies a theoretical loophole, as, even with the presence of Protocol No. 6 and Protocol No. 13, the death penalty is still possible pursuant to the text of article 2(1). By implication, this judicial reasoning severely questions the Rapporteur Group on Human Rights' position on the extent of Protocol No. 13 as detailed above. It appears that the lack of express reference to article 2(1) is the 'clear evidence' which Judge Türmen required, but which the Group had mistakenly thought was not necessary. Furthermore, he made reference to the Preamble, noting that 'the final step'[97] has not yet been taken. But it is difficult to see how the final step could be taken if the Committee does not legislate for this possibility. The Committee must open the door and then it will be for the states to step in.

The *Öcalan* Chamber judgment was appealed to the Grand Chamber, and it stated that the applicant asked it to take its jurisprudence 'a stage further by concluding that the States had, by their practice, abrogated the exception set out in the second sentence of Article 2(1).'[98] This confirms that the Chamber had not abrogated article 2(1) and Öcalan was trying to persuade the Grand Chamber to adopt an 'evolutive' interpretation of the Convention, and in effect create European policy. But echoing *Kirkwood*, the Grand Chamber held that, 'if Article 2 is to be read as permitting capital punishment, notwithstanding the almost universal abolition of the death penalty in Europe, Article 3 cannot be interpreted as prohibiting the death penalty since that would nullify the clear wording of Article 2(1).'[99] This displays the difficulty the Grand Chamber had in dealing with the *prima facie* theoretical loop-hole left by Protocol No. 13 and so, following the Chamber, it deferred the question to the practice of the member states.[100] It appears that the Grand Chamber is waiting for unanimity, as by the time of the Grand

95 *Öcalan* [C] para. 70.

96 Ibid., para. 196.

97 Ibid., Partly Dissenting Opinion of Judge Türmen.

98 *Öcalan v. Turkey*, Application No. 46221/99, Grand Chamber Judgment [GC], 12 May 2005, para. 175.

99 Ibid., para. 162.

100 Ibid., para, 164. With regards to article 3, the Court has evolved its interpretation to hold that on death row the prison conditions should not be constructed to infringe 'human dignity,' see *Poltoratskiy v. Ukraine*, Application no. 38812/97, 29 April 2003, para. 132.

Chamber judgment, 16 member states had not posted their ratifications,[101] and as of March 2010, Armenia, Azerbaijan, Latvia and Poland, have not posted their ratifications, and Azerbaijan and Russia, are the only Council member states who have not signed the Protocol. The majority clearly thought that the ratifications of these countries is required, but such implementation of judicial restraint did not find favour from all on the Court, as a Partly Concurring, Partly Dissenting, Opinion from Judge Garlicki displays. He stated:

> [t]oday the Court, while agreeing that 'it can be said that capital punishment in peacetime has come to be regarded as an unacceptable…form of punishment which is no longer permissible under Article 2,' seems to be convinced that there is no room for the death penalty even in the original text of the Convention. But, at the same time, it has chosen not to express that position in a universally binding manner. In my opinion, there are some arguments suggesting that the Court could and should have gone further in this case.[102]

The judge then cited the Opinion of the Parliamentary Assembly and could not give, in his mind, 'a good reason' why the Court did not follow the Opinion as he held that the Court did have jurisdictional competence.[103] He stated, '[t]he only problem is: who shall have the power to declare, in a binding manner, that such modification has taken place? So this is a problem not of substance, but of jurisdiction (competence).'[104] In effect, Judge Garlicki was asking, *where does the authority to amendment lie*? And he further stated, 'I am not convinced by the majority's replication of the *Soering* approach. I do not think that there are any legal obstacles to this Court's taking a decision with respect to the nature of capital punishment.'[105] If Judge Garlicki had considered Lidbom's 1980 report and the subsequent Parliamentary Assembly recommendations to the Committee of Ministers, he would have been able to identify the apparent prominent legislative position of the Committee of Ministers. It would have been useful if Judge Garlicki had distinguished the observation that the Committee of Ministers is the only Council organ which can offer the specific amendment of the text of the Convention. In 1980, Lidbom had pointed out that the amendment authority resided within the Committee, and the Grand Chamber's judgment displayed an acceptance of this amendment mechanism. It appears that the current Council of Europe three-layered process for amendment still holds strong. If this is correct,

---

101 See, *Öcalan* [GC] para, 164, the 16 member states who had not posted their ratifications were: Albania, Armenia, Azerbaijan, France, Italy, Latvia, Luxembourg, Moldova, Monaco, Netherlands, Norway, Poland, Russia, Slovakia, Spain, and Turkey.

102 *Öcalan* [GC] Partly Concurring, Partly Dissenting Opinion of Judge Garlicki, para. 2.

103 Ibid., paras 3-7.

104 Ibid., para. 3.

105 Ibid., para. 5.

the European Court of Human Rights must adhere to the wording of the Protocol. In this case, neither Protocol No. 6 nor Protocol No. 13 expressly amends article 2(1), so it would appear that, in strict literal application, the Grand Chamber did not have jurisdiction at this time.

The European Court of Human Rights has considered cases post-*Öcalan* and, although specific amendment has not occurred, an evolution of the jurisprudence has been apparent. Peter Hodgkinson had predicted in 2000 that the 'Court will probably be obliged to go beyond the principles laid down in the Soering judgment' (Hodgkinson 2000, 630) and Mirja Trilsh and Alexandra Rüth note that in *Öcalan* the 'Court's interpretation of Article 2 was…too narrow' (Trilsh and Rüth 2006, 182). Post *Öcalan*, the Court has not reconsidered its decisions of the complicated balancing of the textual amendment of article 2(1) with Protocol No. 13, because no other member state has sought to directly impose the death penalty. But it has considered the parameters of the right to life of condemned prisoners during moratoriums and in extradition circumstances where a suspect may be transferred by a member state to a receiving state to face a capital charge (Yorke 2004). In between the two *Öcalan* judgments, the Court considered *G.B. v. Bulgaria*,[106] where the applicant was convicted and sentenced to death in 1989. Then a moratorium was put in place and Bulgaria abolished the death penalty in 1998 and ratified Protocol No. 6 in 1999. No article 2(1) violation was held, and this reasoning was followed in *Iorgov v. Bulgaria*.[107] In *Mamatkulov and Askarov v. Turkey*,[108] the Court held unanimously that in extradition circumstances, if a death penalty would be applied then there is a violation of article 3 under *Soering*, and so it does not need to consider the case under article 2(1).[109] This decision was handed down in February 2005, and two months later in *Shamayev and 12 others v. Georgia and Russia*,[110] the Court confirmed that extradition would not expose the applicants to a real risk of extra-judicial execution, contrary to article 2(1).

Then, in November 2005 the Court modified its jurisprudence. *Bader and others v. Sweden*,[111] concerned the deportation of a suspect to Syria with the possibility of facing a capital trial. The Court considered that article 2(1) may be implicated if a member state deports an alien who has suffered or risks suffering a flagrant denial of a fair trial in the receiving state, the outcome of which was or

---

106 *G.B. v. Bulgaria*, Application No. 42346/98, 11 March 2004.

107 *Iorgov v. Bulgaria*, Application No. 40653/98, 11 March 2004.

108 *Mamatkulov and Askarov v. Turkey* Applications Nos 46827/99 and 46951/99, 4 February 2005, were the assurances that the death penalty are sufficient, article 2 is not violated. See also, *S.R. v. Sweden*, Application No. 62806/00, 23 April 2002; *Ismaili v. Germany*, Application No. 58128/00, 15 March 2001; *Bahaddar v. the Netherlands* (145/1996/764/965) 19 February 1998, paras 75-78.

109 *Mamatkulov and Askarov*, para. 78.

110 *Shamayev and 12 others v. Georgia and Russia*, Application No. 36378/02, 12 April 2005.

111 *Bader and others v. Sweden*, Application No. 13284/04, 8 November 2005.

is likely to be the death penalty.'[112] It found that 'the deportation of the applicants to Syria, if implemented, would give rise to [a violation of article 2].'[113] As such, the Court was extending its jurisprudence on the right to life and the death penalty, and it now declared that there are some circumstances where an execution does not have to take place to initiate an article 2(1) violation. Only the potential of an execution is required, and the determining factor in this case was the possibility of an arbitrary deprivation of life. Judge Cabral Barreto stated in his concurring opinion that this was the first time 'the Court has plainly stated that the extradition or deportation of a person to a country where he or she risks an unfair trial followed by capital punishment will violate Article 2 of the Convention.'[114]

Conclusion

The essential question for the amendment of article 2(1) is to determine whether an alteration of the text would provide clarity for the abolitionist position. The answer to this question is not as simple as it first may appear to be, and the debates between the Committee and Assembly, and the uncomfortable jurisprudence of the Court, represent this fact. It is perhaps true that this question can only be answered with the benefit of hindsight, and if this is the case, the abolition of the death penalty in the Council of Europe should be viewed as an on-going legal and political project, and not exclusively determined by the event of amendment. If the current mechanisms through Protocol No. 6 and Protocol No. 13 keep the death penalty at bay, then amendment would not appear to be necessary. But this is not to forget that in 1957, Albert Camus argued, 'in the unified Europe of the future the solemn abolition of the death penalty ought to be the first article of the European Code we all hope for' (Camus 1988, 230)[115] and this abolitionist cry has been echoed in the Parliamentary Assembly. Wohlwend has explained that the fulfilment of this goal is constantly on the parliamentarian's hearts as she stated '[i]t is taking a long time to bring about abolition of the death penalty,' and revealed 'the anxieties felt by the Assembly...remain.'[116] Furthermore, in 2006 René van der Linden, the President of the Parliamentary Assembly, declared '[c]apital punishment must be

112 Ibid., para. 42.

113 Ibid., para. 48.

114 See also the decisions in, *Koktysh v. Ukraine*, Application No. 43707/07, 10 December 2009; and *Al-Saadoon and Mufdhi v. the United Kingdom*, Application No. 61498/08, 2 March 2010.

115 Renate Wohlwend noted that Camus's phrase was quoted in some reports presented to the Parliamentary Assembly, and that some parliamentarians recited it in debates, see, Wohlwend 2004, 84.

116 Position of the Parliamentary Assembly as regards the Council of Europe member and observer states which have not abolished the death penalty, Doc. 10911, 21 April 2006, paras 1, 49-50.

totally removed once and for all from the legislation of all countries which strive to uphold democracy, the rule of law and human rights' (Council of Europe 2006).

The anxieties felt by these contemporary parliamentarians reveal the constant fight in which human rights is engaged against the sovereign power to implement the death penalty. They are attempting to ensure that municipal law no longer, and never in the future, reflects the possibility of the punishment. It is the stalwart proposition that law does *not* have to reach its lethal potential to rule situations and promote legitimate governmental action. At the moment, Protocol No. 6 and Protocol No. 13 constitute hegemonic advances towards total abolition, and in the current practice of the member states, textual amendment will perhaps not alter the abolitionist position. However, the danger may arise if states begin to want to pull out of Protocol No. 6 and Protocol No. 13, as Andrew Clapham has observed, 'we cannot absolutely discount the possibility that states may in the future try to denounce [the Protocols]' (Clapham 2003, 483). If this happens, the current text of article 2(1) may provide a legal loophole for rogue states to implement the death penalty. As such, in order to provide a uniform expression of abolitionism it still appears necessary to do away with the second sentence of this problematical provision.

Bibliography

Ancel, M. (1967) 'The Problem of the Death Penalty', in Sellin, T. (ed.) *Capital Punishment* (New York: Harper and Row).

—— (1962) *The Death Penalty in European Countries* (Strasbourg: Council of Europe Press).

Association of International Consultants on Human Rights (1992) *The Right to Life Forty Years After the Adoption of the Universal Declaration of Human Rights: Evolution of the Concept, Norms and Case-Law* (Genève: CID: Association of International Consultants on Human Rights).

Bae, S. (2007) *When the State no Longer Kills: International Human Rights Norms and Abolition of the Death Penalty* (New York: State University of New York Press).

Bedau, H. (1968) 'The Right to Life', *The Monist*, 550.

Benoît-Rohmer, F. and Klebes, H. (2005) *Council of Europe Law: Towards a pan-European Legal Area* (Strasbourg: Council of Europe Publishing).

Camus, A. (1988) 'Reflections on the Guillotine', in, *Resistance, Rebellion, and Death* (trans. J. O'Brien) (New York: Vintage Press).

Chiapetta, H. (2001) 'Rome, 11/15/1998: Extradition or Political Asylum for the Kurdistan Worker's Party Leader Abdullah Öcalan', *13 Pace Int'l L. Rev 117.*

Clapham, A. (2003) 'Symbiosis in International Human Rights Law: The Öcalan Case and the Evolving Law on the Death Sentence', *JICJ* 1, 475.

Council of Europe (2006) 'Capital punishment must be totally removed once and for all from the legislation of all countries which strive to uphold democracy, the rule of law and human rights', Press Release, Strasbourg, 10 October 2006.

—— (2004) *Death Penalty – Beyond Abolition* (Strasbourg: Council of Europe Publishing).

—— (2002) Reference Documents: 4.5 European Convention on Human Rights, Draft Protocol No. 13 on the abolition of the death penalty in all circumstances, Ministers' Deputies Meeting (784th Meeting), 21 February.

—— (1998) Abolition of capital punishment, reply to Recommendation 1246 (1994); Abolition of the death penalty in Europe, reply to Recommendation 1302 (1996), adopted, 16th April 1998 at the 628th meeting of the Minister's Deputies, Doc 8079, 21 April.

—— (1997a) Notes on the Agenda; Reference Documents, 628/4.6, Abolition of the death penalty in Europe: Draft Reply to Recommendation 1246 (1994) and 1302 (1996) of the Parliamentary Assembly, 555th meeting (January 1996) and 588th meeting (April).

—— (1997b) Reply to Recommendation 1246 (1994) and 1302 (1996) of the Parliamentary Assembly, 555th meeting (January 1996) and 588th meeting (April).

—— (1997c) Interim Reply to Recommendation 1302 (1996), Abolition of the death penalty in Europe, Communication from the Committee of Ministers, Doc 7798, 15 April 1997, adopted 9 April 1997, 588th Meeting of the Minister's Deputies.

—— (1996a) Report on the abolition of the death penalty in Europe, Doc. 7589, text adopted by the Parliamentary Assembly on 28 June 1996 (24th sitting).

—— (1996b) Interim reply to Recommendation 1246 (1994) on the abolition of capital punishment, Doc. 7466, adopted on 22 January.

—— (1994) Report on the abolition of capital punishment, Doc. 7145, 15 September.

—— (1980a) Report on the abolition of capital punishment, Doc 4509 (2nd and 3rd sittings) 22 April.

——(1983) 'Introduction', Explanatory Report on Protocol No. 6 to the Convention for the Protection of Human Rights and Fundamental Freedoms concerning the Abolition of the Death Penalty (Strasbourg: Council of Europe Publishing).

—— (1980b) Parliamentary Assembly, Official Report of Debates (32nd Ordinary Session), 'Abolition of capital punishment, Debate on the report of the Committee on Legal Affairs', 2nd and 3rd Sittings, 22 April).

—— (1976) *Collected Edition of the 'Travaux Préparatoires' of the European Convention on Human Rights, vols I-V* (The Hague: Martinus Nijhoff).

Crawshaw, N. (1978) *The Cyprus Revolt: An Account of the Struggle for Union with Greece* (London: George Allen & Unwin).

Dowrick, F.E. (1974) 'Juristic Activity in the Council of Europe: 25th Year', 23 *ICLQ* 3, 610.

Fawcett, J.E.S. (1987) *The Application of the European Convention on Human Rights* (Oxford: Clarendon Press).
Foucault, M. (1976) *Discipline and Punish: The Birth of the Prison* (London: Penguin).
Franck, H.G. (2003) *The Barbaric Punishment: Abolishing the Death Penalty* (ed. W.A. Schabas) (The Hague: Martinus Nijhoff).
Greer, S. (2006) *The European Convention on Human Rights: Achievements, Problems and Prospects* (Cambridge: Cambridge University Press).
Griffin, J. (2008) *On Human Rights* (Oxford: Oxford University Press).
Hodgkinson, P. (2000) 'Europe – A Death Penalty Free Zone: Commentary and Critique of Abolitionist Strategies', 26 *Ohio NUL Rev*. 625
Holland, R. (1998) *Britain and the Revolt in Cyprus, 1954-1959* (Oxford: Clarendon Press).
Hood, R. (2004) 'Introduction: The Importance of Abolishing the Death Penalty', in Council of Europe, *The Death Penalty – Beyond Abolition*.
Kanarek, D. (2003) 'Turkey and the European Union: The Path to Accession', 9 *Colum. J. Eur. L*. 457.
Kelsen, H. (1947) 'Will the Judgment in the Nuremburg Trial Constitute a Precedent in International Law?' 1 *Int L Q*. 153.
Krüger, H.C. (2004) 'Protocol No. 6 to the European Convention on Human Rights', in Council of Europe, *Death Penalty – Beyond Abolition*.
Letsas, G. (2007) *A Theory of Interpretation of the European Convention on Human Rights* (Oxford: Oxford University Press).
Merrills, J.G. and Robertson, A.H. (2001), *Human Rights in Europe: A Study of the European Convention on Human Rights*, 4th edn (Manchester: Manchester University Press).
Mowbray, A. (2007) *Cases and Materials on the European Convention on Human Rights*, 2nd edn (Oxford: Oxford University Press).
—— (2005) 'The Creativity of the European Court of Human Rights', *H.R.L. Rev.* 5(2), 57-79.
Nicol, D. (2005) 'Original intent and the European Convention on Human Rights', *P.L.* 152.
Opsahl, T. (1993) 'The Right to Life', in Macdonald, R.St.J. et al. (eds) *The European System for the Protection of Human Rights* (Dordrecht: Martinus Nijhoff).
Pannick, D. (1983) *Judicial Review of the Death Penalty* (London: Duckworth).
Polakiewicz, J (1999) *Treaty Making in the Council of Europe* (Strasbourg: Council of Europe Publishing).
Ramcharan, B.G. (ed.) (1985a) *The Right to Life in International Law* (Dordrecht: Martinus Nijhoff).
—— (1985b) 'Introduction', in Ramcharan, B.G. (ed.) *The Right to Life in International Law.*
Robertson, A.H. (1959) et al. (ed.) *European Commission on Human Rights: Documents and Decisions 1955-1956-1957* (The Hague: Martinus Nijhoff).

Robertson, A.H. (1965) 'The Contribution of the Council of Europe to the Development of International Law', 59 *Am. Soc'y Int'l L. Proc.* 201.
—— (1961) 'The Legal Work of the Council of Europe', 1 *I.C.L.Q.* 1, 143.
—— (1950) 'The European Convention for the Protection of Human Rights', *B.Y.I.L.*145, p. 151.
Rosen S. and Journey, S. (1993) 'Abolition of the Death Penalty: An Emerging Norm of International Law', *Hamline J. Pub. L. & Pol'y* 163.
Schabas, W.A. (2002) *The Abolition of the Death Penalty in International Law*, 3rd edn (Cambridge: Cambridge University Press).
—— (1996) *The Death Penalty as Cruel Treatment and Torture: Capital Punishment in the World's Courts* (Boston: Northeastern University Press).
Sherlock, A. (2001) Case Comment: *Öcalan v. Turkey* (46221/99) (unreported, December 14, 2000), *E.L. Rev.* 133.
Simpson, A.W.B. (2004) *Human Rights and the End of Empire: Britain and the Genesis of the European Convention* (Oxford: Oxford University Press).
—— (1996) 'Round Up the Usual Suspects: The Legacy of British Colonialism and the European Convention on Human Rights', 41 *Loy. L. Rev.* 629.
Spierenburg, P. (1984) *The Spectacle of Suffering: Executions and the Evolution of Repression* (Cambridge: Cambridge University Press).
Trilsh, M. and Rüth, A. (2006) Case Comment: *Öcalan v. Turkey* 100 *A.J.I.L.* 180
Türmen, R. (2005) 'Right to Life (Article 2)', *Bulletin des Droits de L'Homme*, No. 11/12.
Weil, G. (1963) *The European Convention on Human Rights: Background, Development and Prospects* (Leyden: Sythoff).
Wells, C. (2003) 'Human Rights in Turkey: Death by State Hanging', 9 *Amicus Journal* 8.
Whitman, J.Q. (2003) *Harsh Justice: Criminal Punishment and the Widening Divide between America and Europe* (New York: Oxford University Press).
Wicks, E. (2000) 'The United Kingdom Government's Perception of the European Convention on Human Rights at the Time of Entry', *P.L.* 438.
Wohlwend, R. (2004) 'The Role of the Council of Europe's Parliamentary Assembly', in Council of Europe, *Death Penalty – Beyond Abolition*.
Yorke, J. (2004) 'Europe's Judicial Inquiry in Extradition Cases: Closing the Door on the Death Penalty', *E.L. Rev.* 29(4), 546.

Chapter 11
The Death Penalty and Russia

Bill Bowring

Introduction

As a result of the judgment in *Öcalan v Turkey*[1] the use of the death penalty has effectively been prohibited in the whole of the territory of the Council of Europe, with its 47 states and over 811 million inhabitants. When Russia joined the Council of Europe in 1996 it entered into an obligation to ratify Protocol No. 6 to the European Convention on Human Rights (ECHR), prohibiting the death penalty, within three years. President Yeltsin moved swiftly to impose a moratorium on executions (BBC 1999) – in Russia, by firing squad. Russia signed the Protocol on 16 April 1997.[2] Yet Russia is the only remaining Council of Europe member state to have failed, 13 years on, so far to ratify Protocol No. 6.

In the *Öcalan v Turkey* case the Grand Chamber agreed with the Chamber's view:

> [e]qually the Court observes that the legal position as regards the death penalty has undergone a considerable evolution since *Soering* was decided. The *de facto* abolition noted in that case in respect of twenty-two Contracting States in 1989 has developed into a *de jure* abolition in forty-three of the forty-four Contracting States and a moratorium in the remaining State that has not yet abolished the penalty, namely Russia. This almost complete abandonment of the death penalty in times of peace in Europe is reflected in the fact that all the Contracting States have signed Protocol No. 6 and forty-one States have ratified it, that is to say, all except Turkey, Armenia and Russia. It is further reflected in the policy of the Council of Europe, which requires that new member States undertake to abolish capital punishment as a condition of their admission into the organisation. As a result of these developments the territories encompassed by the member States of the Council of Europe have become a zone free of capital punishment.[3]

Since then, Armenia ratified the Protocol on 29 September 2003, and Turkey ratified on 12 November 2003. Russia now stands alone.

1 *Öcalan v Turkey*, Application no. 46221/99, 12 May 2005.

2 See the Council of Europe's chart of signatures and ratifications at http://conventions.coe.int/Treaty/Commun/ChercheSig.asp?NT=114&CM=8&DF=18/09/2009&CL=ENG.

3 *Öcalan v Turkey*, para. 163.

The Russian Constitution of 1993 does not prohibit the death penalty, but provides, in Article 20, that every citizen threatened with the death penalty has the right to a jury trial. All 83 regions of Russia now have trial by jury, since the coming into force of the Criminal Procedural Code of 2002, with the exception of Chechnya. In 1999, the Constitutional Court of the Russian Federation ruled that the death penalty cannot be imposed in Russia until jury trial is guaranteed in every part of Russia. Jury trial should have come into force for Chechnya on 1 January 2007, but at the last moment the State Duma intervened to delay jury trial until 1 January 2010.

At the time of writing the issue has once again become prominent in the Russian media and public discussion (Taratuta and Zygar 2009), especially in view of the fact that in a few months it will be lawful to execute convicted criminals in Russia, as I show in more detail below. As in many countries of the world, the death penalty is enormously popular. But, as I report below, the death penalty is now effectively abolished.

If Russia had restored the death penalty, it would have joined an illustrious group of states which between them execute some 1,500 persons a year. In September 2009 *Russian Newsweek* provided for its readers the following table of 15 states, in order of executions carried out:

State	Executions	Sentences	Methods	In public?
China	1,718	7,003	Firing squad, lethal injection	Yes
Iran	346	No data	Firing squad, hanging, stoning	Yes
Saudi Arabia	102	No data	Beheading, firing squad, stoning	Yes
USA	37	111	Lethal injection, electric chair, firing squad, gas, hanging	No
Pakistan	36	236	Hanging, stoning	Yes
Iraq	34	285	Hanging	No
Vietnam	19	59	Firing squad	No
Afghanistan	17	131	Firing squad, hanging	No
North Korea	15	No data	Firing squad, hanging	Yes
Japan	15	27	Hanging	No
Yemen	13	No data	Firing squad	Yes
Indonesia	10	10	Firing squad	No
Libya	8	No data	Firing squad, hanging	No
Bangladesh	5	185	Hanging	No
Belarus	4	1	Firing squad	No

In this chapter I first explore the religious and philosophical arguments for and against the death penalty in Russia. Second, I explain the curious trajectory of the death penalty in Tsarist Russia, followed thirdly by the USSR. Fourth, I chart the halting progress which has been made in post-Communist Russia. Fifth, I examine the current tensions between Russia and the Council of Europe. Finally, I conclude by bringing matters up to date and offering a tentative diagnosis.

Religious, Political and Philosophical Issues

The Christian religion (indeed, any religion) ought to be incompatible with the death penalty, and Communism would seem in theory to be the type of society able to dispense with it. But the debate concerning abolition or retention has taken some surprising turns in Russia. Will Adams has described (Adams 1970) a tradition of Russian hostility to the death penalty, which was exemplified by a passage from the Testament of the Grand Prince of Kiev, Vladimir Monomakh, in 1125, '[d]o not kill anyone, either guilty or not, nor do you order to kill. Do not destroy a Christian soul, even in case death is well deserved.' Adams points out that capital punishment did not reappear in Russian codes until the end of the fourteenth century, although the Mongol-Tatars brought the death penalty as part of their rule in the meantime (Adams 1970, 575, citing Vernadsky 1947).

The eighteenth century was the formative period for the development of Russian law. The great work of Cesare Beccaria, *On Crimes and Punishments*, first published in 1764, had a powerful impact in the Tsarist Russia of that period and later, as T. Cizova shows in an extraordinary work of scholarship (Cizova 1962). Beccaria focused on torture, mitigation of penalties, and capital punishment. His argument against the death penalty was that it was unnecessary for the protection of society. In defence of his argument Beccaria cited the fact that in Russia the death penalty had been abolished and that this had not led to an increase in crime (Cizova 1962, 388), and almost one third of Catherine II's *Nakaz* of 1766 came directly from Beccaria's *On Crimes and Punishments*. Catherine had received, through d'Alembert, a copy of the French translation of Beccaria's book (Cizova 1962, 392); a Russian translation did not appear until 1803. Beccaria's ideas had decisive influence on the leaders of the Decembrist uprising of 1825. According to Cizova, 'they were the first intellectual group who fearlessly brought Beccaria's arguments to their logical conclusion in the framework of Russian reality' (Cizova 1962, 404).

Beccaria also strongly influenced those who drafted the laws which made up the Great Reforms of Aleksandr II in 1864. Cizova (1962) states:

> [o]n 20 November 1864, law reform was introduced and, reading the *Sudebnyye Ustavy*, one realises that their creators adhered to the rules laid down in *On Crimes and Punishments*. It was not a coincidence that the man who contributed most to the compilation of the Ustavy, S. I. Zarudnyy, published in 1879 a new translation of Beccaria and compared it to Chapter X of Catherine's *Nakaz* (ibid., 407).

The last edition of Beccaria's work in Russia appeared at an extraordinarily unpropitious time (Cizova 1962). It was done:

> by the well-known Russian jurist, Professor M. M. Isayev in 1939. It was published in Moscow by the then people's commissariat of justice. It is prefaced by an essay; terse in style, scholarly and comprehensive in its content… One cannot help wondering at the fact that the new translation and edition of the work which passionately defended the dignity and the rights of the individual was being prepared at the very time when the people of the Soviet Union experienced injustice and arbitrariness on a scale unparalleled in the whole of Russian history (ibid., 408).

It is an ineluctable feature of Russian history that the achievements of the liberals and 'Westernisers' are balanced if not overwhelmed not only by 'Slavophile' intellectuals, but especially by the Russian Orthodox Church. According to Mikhail Gernet (1913), 'many facts bear witness to the welcoming attitude of the higher echelons of the Russian Orthodox clergy.' This was especially the case in the aftermath of the 1905 Revolution. Reasonably reliable contemporary sources show that between 2000 and 3000 persons were executed in the period 1905 to 1908.[4] Stephen Wheatcroft (2002; and Ohr 2004) has argued in an analysis of the crackdown following 1905, with an upsurge in mass executions, that 'it is here, in the reversal of this liberal trend in the post-1905 period, that we can see the roots of the monstrous developments that were to come during the First World War, Civil War, collectivisation and the Ezhovshchina.' The liberal trend in question was that of Aleksandr II, who, in the aftermath of Russian defeat in the Crimean War, abolished serfdom in 1861 and in 1864, in his great legal reforms, instituted an independent judiciary as well as jury trials (Bowring 2009).

Gernet (1913) cites amongst others the fact that at the session of the State Council on 27 June 1906 the Protodeacon (*protoierei*) T.I. Butkevich made a long speech in favour of the death penalty, although he held himself out as a dedicated opponent of spilling even one drop of blood. But, he said, there were special political moments when the use of the 'exclusive measure' was necessary. Turning his attention to the opinions against the death penalty, he said 'those commentaries on the teachings of the New Testament which say the Evangelists had a direct condemnation of the death penalty are too bold… I find no such condemnation.' He was inclined to think that the death penalty was not the most severe punishment. He had seen one of the cells in the old Shlisselburg Fortress and 'was horrified at the human cruelty… I do not have the spirit to ask you, dear statesmen, what is worse for the human being: the momentary death penalty or many years of confinement in the Shlisselburg Fortress.'

Another Protodeacon, E. A-ov, wrote in the journal 'Christian Teachings' at great length, discussing various texts of holy writers, and hotly defended the death

4 See http://www.law.edu.ru/script/cntSource.asp?cntID=100066404.

penalty. What was interesting for Gernet was the tone, quite unbecoming to a spiritual person, in which the article was written. Thus, 'in the name of love of humanity' this holy man was ready to advise the authorities to seize the noose and 'use it for the preparation of a forgotten but none the less in some cases effective means for making some of those who have been led astray understand.' He found that it was not popular conscience in the State Duma which uttered the decisive sentence of execution, but the 'sad inability to think things out of those Duma *neveglasov* (heathens – an archaic word) who after what the unforgettable Lyapkin-Tyapkins[5] thought up for themselves, with their own wisdom get to the creation of the world.' In fact, Gernet observed that there were relatively few protests against the death penalty by the clergy. Some of those who protested were held responsible by the higher spiritual leadership. Thus, five priests from Kharkov and one from Tiflis (Tbilisi) were condemned for protesting against the death penalty.

The Russian Communists were equally contradictory in their approach. In his essential study of 'The Soviet Union and the Death Penalty', Ger van den Berg (1983) was anxious to show that the foundation for the bloodthirsty excesses of the Soviet period was provided by Karl Marx himself. The youthful Marx is cited by him as saying in 1849 'We are merciless and we do not ask for mercy for us. When it is our turn, we will not conceal the terror behind the hypocritical phrases' (van den Berg 1983, 154). The English translation of Marx's article in the final issue of the *Neue Rheinische Zeitung* (Marx 1849) is rather different:

> [d]id we therefore have to advance our social republican tendency only in the "last pieces" of the *Neue Rheinische Zeitung*? Did you not read our articles about the June revolution, and was not the essence of the June revolution the essence of our paper?
>
> Why then your hypocritical phrases, your attempt to find an impossible pretext?
>
> We have no compassion and we ask no compassion from you. When our turn comes, we shall not make excuses for the terror. But the royal terrorists, the terrorists by the grace of God and the law, are in practice brutal, disdainful, and mean, in theory cowardly, secretive, and deceitful, and in both respects disreputable.

Will Adams (1970, 578) cites a rather different passage, from an article written by Marx in 1853 for the *New-York Daily Tribune,* '[i]t would be very difficult, if not altogether impossible, to establish any principle upon which the justice or expediency of capital punishment could be founded, in a society glorying in

5 Lyapkin-Tyapkin – a vindictive judge, one of Nikolai Gogol's satirical inventions in *Dead Souls* (Gogol 2004).

its civilization.' Robert Bohm (2008) has provided a detailed analysis of Marx's article, drawing out its implications for the debate concerning the death penalty.

Lenin opposed the death penalty prior to the Bolshevik revolution for reasons broadly similar to this expressed by Marx. In July 1917 (Lenin 1977) he wrote, '[i]nstead of liberty, the old tyranny is coming back. The death penalty is being introduced for the soldiers at the front.' However, in the conditions of intervention and civil war after 1917, Lenin (1971) wrote differently, '[s]o long as martial law introduced on the railways by the Council of Defence continues, the district transport departments of the Cheka are to be given the right to apply capital punishment to persons found guilty of bribery, theft of freights and railway material, and systematic abuse on the part of officials.' And in 1920 (Lenin 1965) he explained that the death penalty had been reintroduced strictly for reasons of expediency, and that it was his firm intention to renounce it again as soon as possible. He argued that his sincerity had been proved by the facts:

> [w]e were forced to use terror in response to the terror employed by the Entente, when the mighty powers of the world flung their hordes against us, stopping at nothing. We could not have lasted two days had we not replied to these attempts of officers and whiteguards in a merciless fashion. This meant the use of terror, but this was forced on us by the terrorist methods of the Entente. But as soon as we had gained a decisive victory, even before the end of the war, immediately after the capture of Rostov, we renounced capital punishment, and have therefore proved that we intend to carry out our own programme as we had promised. We say that the use of violence arises from the need to crush the exploiters, the landowners and capitalists. When this is accomplished we shall renounce all extraordinary measures. We have proved this in practice. And I think, I hope, and I am confident that the All-Russia Central Executive Committee will unanimously endorse this measure of the Council of People's Commissars and will implement it in such a way that it will be impossible to apply the death penalty in Russia.

Of course, he died in 1924, and the real terror began.

Tsarist Russia

Donald Barry and Eric Williams (1997, 232) have pointed out that capital punishment has been part of Russian law throughout most of the country's history. Mikhail Gernet (1913) explained that in seventeenth century Russia about 60 articles of the *Ulozheniye* (Code) of 1649 provided for various forms of the death penalty. But in practice alternative penalties were often imposed. In the sixteenth and seventeenth centuries the death penalty was prescribed for unlawful picking of crops, sale of prohibited goods, purchase of fur without payment of excise, inaccurate weighing of salt when affixing excise duty, helping to hide deserting soldiers, and many religious and state crimes.

The Empress Elizabeth abolished the death penalty in 1735, but abolition was short-lived (Mikhlin 1997). Gernet (1913) explained that an example of the total abolition of the death penalty in legislation was given to Russians when in 1744 the Empress Elizabeth decreed that all death sentences should be submitted to her for reconsideration. On 30 September 1754 the Senate decreed that the death penalty be abolished and replaced by a life sentence of imprisonment with hard labour, and branding the offender on the forehead with the word 'thief' and cutting off the tip of the nose. This decree was based on the Royal instruction of 29 March 1753, replacing the death sentence by hard labour. According to Adams (1970, 576) Elizabeth exiled rather than executing her opponents, and '[o]n this basis, Russia could claim to be the first European country in the modern era to abolish capital punishment, although abolition was never complete de facto.' However, Gernet (1913) pointed out, later judicial practice interpreted this decree as not abolishing the death penalty for all crimes and therefore death sentences were handed down and carried out, for example, in 1764, 1771, 1775 and on other occasions.

As Barry and Williams (1997, 232) observe, several other Russian rulers instituted moratoriums or near moratoriums on executions for parts of their reign, while leaving the legal provisions permitting the death penalty untouched. Catherine's *Nakaz* of 1767 (drawing as it did on Beccaria) contained strong hostility to capital punishment (Adams 1970, 576). Adams also points out that the death penalty did not reappear in Russia's ordinary criminal legislation until the Speransky codification of 1833. Offences such as murder and rape were not capital. And the many executions following 1905 were not based on the criminal code, but were the product of military courts and codes, and extraordinary decrees.

During the late Tsarist period leading scholars, on the basis of analysis of international research and practice, began to argue against the death penalty (Kistyakovsky 1896). They were joined by literary giants such as Radishchev, Dostoevsky and Tolstoy (Adams 1970, 577).

The Communist Period

Officially, the death penalty was restored by a decree of 5 September 1918 'On Red Terror',[6] although the first death sentence by a Soviet court had already been pronounced on 21 June 1918 by the Supreme Tribunal of the Russian Socialist Federation of Soviet Republics (RSFSR) in the case of Aleksei Shchastny, the Admiral of the Baltic Fleet (van den Berg 1983, 155). However, on 17 January 1920, in keeping with Lenin's arguments mentioned above, the Soviet state once again declared the death penalty abolished.[7] And abolition applied only to the

6 *SU RSFSR* 1918 No.65, item 710.

7 *SU RSFSR* 1920 No. 4-5, item 22.

ordinary courts, since military and revolutionary tribunal could still sentence to death. However, with the Polish advance on Ukraine, capital punishment was again restored.

The RSFSR Criminal Code of 24 May 1922[8] provided for the death penalty for political, military and some economic crimes. The new Code enacted in 1926[9] also included the death penalty as 'an exceptional measure for the protection of the worker's state… until its abolition.'[10] Stalin consolidated his power following Lenin's death in 1924, and in 1927 began his campaign of collectivisation, which, combined with his policy of 'liquidation of the kulaks (richer peasants)' led inexorably to the great famine of 1932-33 in which many millions died, not executed, but from starvation. From 7 August 1932 the collectivisation campaign extended the use of the death penalty to cases of theft of property from trains, ships and collective farms (*kolzhozy*).[11]

Van den Berg (1983, 158) identifies a third period in the history of the death penalty in the USSR, the period from 1934 until Stalin's death. In 1934, the penalty was imposed in peacetime on theft of weapons, murder committed by servicemen under aggravating circumstances, and treason. The death penalty could not be imposed on people under 18. Precise information as to the numbers of people killed in the purges of 1937-38 is not available, but as many as one million may have been executed. In 1947 the death penalty was abolished in peacetime,[12] but it was revived again in 1950, but only for certain crimes against the state.[13] It appears that at the time of Stalin's death very few executions were taking place (van den Berg 1983, 159).

There was a dramatic change in 1954, when a decree of 30 April 1954 imposed the death penalty for intentional homicide under aggravating circumstances.[14] According to van den Berg, the reason for this dramatic change was its demand by public opinion. The reason was the closing by Beria of a number of prison camps, releasing large numbers of hardened criminals, followed by a steep rise in the rate of serious crime. This has been dramatised in the film *Cold Summer of 1953* (Aleksandr Proshkin). However, the *Principles for Criminal Legislation of the USSR and the Union Republics* promulgated on 25 December 1958[15] retained the death penalty as an 'exceptional measure of punishment until its complete abolition,' for certain crimes against the state, some military crimes, and aggravated intentional murder. In 1961-62 economic crimes and some other specified crimes

8 *SU RSFSR* 1922 No. 15, item 153.
9 *SU RSFSR* 1926 No. 80, item 600.
10 Article 21 of the 1926 Code.
11 *SZ SSSR,* 1932, No. 62, item 360.
12 *Ved SSSR,* 1947, No. 17.
13 *Ved SSSR*, 1950, No. 3.
14 *Ved SSSR,* 1954, No. 11, item 221.
15 *Ved SSSR,* 1959, No. 1, item 12.

attracted the death penalty, and in 1973 hijacking became a capital crime (van den Berg 1983, 159).

William Cary Quillin wrote a few years later (1977) in terms which indicated that there were many similarities between the USA and USSR in the attitude to the death penalty, with an equally small prospect of abolition. By the time van den Berg composed his article, in 1983 (the year this author first visited the USSR), the death penalty in peace time was possible (van den Berg, 1983, 160) for 17 crimes:

Political crimes	Criminal Code
Treason	Article 64
Espionage	Article 65
Terrorist acts against a public official or representative of a foreign state	Articles 66, 67
Sabotage	Article 68
The crimes above committed by an organised group	Article 72
The crimes above committed against another workers' state	Article 73
Banditry	Article 77
Action disrupting the work of prison camps	Article 77-1
Economic crimes	
Counterfeiting	Article 87
Speculation in currency, speculation as a business	Article 88
Stealing of state property on an especially large scale	Article 93-1
Taking of bribes by an official under certain circumstances	Article 173
Crimes against the person	
Intentional homicide under aggravating circumstances	Article 102
Rape under certain circumstances	Article 117
Killing a police officer or people's guard	Article 191-2
Hijacking an aircraft with grave consequences	Article 213-2
Military crimes	
Intentional homicide, in conjunction with resisting a superior, by a person subject to military service	Article 240

According to van den Berg (1983, 162), at a conservative estimate, about 2,000 death sentences were pronounced each year during the 1960s and 1970s, although only one third were actually carried out. Andrei Sakharov (1975, 43) estimated in 1975 that between 700 and 1,000 criminals were shot each year. In one well known case, Yuri Sokolov, the manager of the most prestigious food store in Moscow, Gastronom No.1 in Gorky Street, was arrested in April 1983 on charges of corruption, and shot in July 1984.[16]

16 http://www.time.com/time/magazine/article/0,9171,926717,00.html.

The Post-Soviet Period

By 1997, when Barry and Williams (1997) published their study, attitudes had changed substantially. In 1987, in the context of Gorbachov's *glasnost* and *perestroika*, a substantial public debate began in the mass media. By 1989 it was possible for the leading official law journal, *Soviet State and Law* to publish a translation of a chapter from the Amnesty International book *When the State Kills: The Death Penalty and the Human Rights Issue* (Kelina, 1989; Barry and Williams, 1997, 234, n.11).

A new draft of the USSR Principles of Criminal Legislation which appeared in 1988 had six rather than 17 capital crimes, and when the Principles were finally adopted in July 1991, just a few months before the USSR ceased to exist, there were five capital crimes: treason, premeditated murder under aggravating circumstances, rape of a minor under aggravating circumstances, child kidnapping resulting in particularly grave circumstances, and especially grave crimes against the peace and security of mankind.[17] However, the RSFSR chose not to follow the USSR, and in December 1991 legislated[18] that three of the economic crimes (illegal currency operations, theft of state property, and bribery) should cease to be capital offences, but leaving counterfeiting as a capital crime until its removal as a offence carrying the death penalty in 1994[19] (Barry and Williams 1997, 235).

Until 1992 pardons and commutation of sentences were within the jurisdiction of the Presidium of the RSFSR Supreme Soviet, and then by a Supreme Soviet Clemency Commission. When in 1991, for the first time in its history, the RSFSR elected a president, Boris Yeltsin, he was given authority over pardons.[20] On 12 January 1992, very shortly after the collapse of the USSR, President Yeltsin decreed the creation of a Clemency (*pomilovaniye*) Commission within the President's Administration. This body, composed of 15 members and led by the well-known writer Anatoly Pristavkin, met once a week, and reviewed between 100 and 150 cases (Barry and Williams 1997, 237). Of these some 7 to 10 were capital cases. The Commission then made a recommendation to the President, who would write 'agree' or 'don't agree' on the draft.

However, as Robert Kushen (1993) points out, the fractured and dynamic political situation of the time, when President Yeltsin's future was in doubt, made any substantive reform or abolition highly unlikely. Nevertheless, abolition remained a longer term goal of the reformers. The new Constitution of the Russian Federation, adopted by referendum in December 1993 following Yeltsin's 'constitutional coup d'etat,' contained the following Article 20:

1. Each person shall have the right to life.

---

17 *Ved SSSR*, 1991, No.30, item 82, article 40.

18 *Rossiiskaya Gazeta* 25 December 1991, p. 6.

19 *Rossiiskaya Gazeta* 7 July 1994, p. 3.

20 RSFSR Law of 24 April 1991, *Sovetskaya Rossiya* 20 April 1991, p. 1.

2. The death penalty, until its abolition, may be prescribed by federal law as an exceptional penalty for particularly grave crimes against life with the granting to the accused of the right to have the case heard by a court with the participation of jurors.

A new Criminal Code of the Russian Federation was not enacted until May 1996, and came into force on 1 January 1997 (Naumov 1997).[21] This contained just five capital crimes: premeditated murder under aggravating circumstances; murder or attempted murder of a state or pubic official; murder or attempted murder of a law enforcement officer; and genocide. The offences against minors had gone, as well as crimes against peace and security of mankind. Article 59 provides:

1. The death penalty as an exceptional measure of punishment may be established only for exceptionally grave crimes which are life threatening.
2. The death penalty is not imposed upon women, nor upon persons who committed the crime prior to 18 years of age, nor upon men who had reached the age of 65 at the time of sentencing.
3. When clemency is granted, the death penalty may be replaced by life imprisonment or imprisonment for a term of 25 years.

Barry and Williams (1997, 239-242) provided an analysis of the numbers of executions carried out from 1985, when death penalty data, albeit containing discrepancies, began to be released. There was a significant drop in the numbers executed in the USSR, from 770 in 1985, to 526 in 1986, 344 in 1987, 271 in 1988, 276 in 1989, and 195 in 1990. Numbers granted clemency varied from 20 in 1985 to 72 in 1988. The Russian Federation is of course smaller than the USSR, but from 1989 the statistics show that 93 persons were executed in 1989, 76 in 1990, 59 (or 15 according to the Clemency Commission – see Pristavkin 1997) in 1991, 18 (or 1) in 1993, 4 in 1993, 19 in 1994, 86 in 1995 and 56 in 1996.

Amnesty International (1997) estimated that 140 persons were executed in Russia in 1996, the year Russia joined the Council of Europe. Anatoly Pristavkin (1997, 5; Barry and Williams 1997, 241) wrote that the Council of Europe considered the total of 16 executions reported to its officials unacceptably high. When Pristavkin explained that the true number was 86, he was told that had this been known, Russia would never have been admitted.

The sudden increase in the number of executions in 1995-1996 is striking. In the same period there are practically no instances of clemency. According to Barry and Williams (1997: 242) Yeltsin was responsible for a harsher policy following the murder of the famous journalist Vladislav Listyev, and was influenced by senior law enforcement officials for whom 'an act of clemency is equivalent to weakening the struggle against crime' (Pristavkin 1997, 5). And a study published

21 Translation into English by the OSCE Legislationline at http://www.legislationline.org/documents/section/criminal-codes/country/7.

in early 1995 based on reputable polling showed that 25 per cent of respondents wanted an expansion of the death penalty; 37 per cent preferred retaining the death penalty as contained in the USSR Criminal Code; and only 15 per cent advocated moving gradually to its abolition (Levada 1995; Barry and Williams 1997, 251, n.62). Of course, Russia is not the only country in which a large majority of the population is in favour of the death penalty.

Obligations Undertaken on Joining the Council of Europe

At a ceremony held in Strasbourg on 28 February 1996, to mark Russia's entry into the Council of Europe, the Russian Foreign Minister signed the ECHR and other Council of Europe treaties. He did this pursuant to the obligations accepted by Russia, set out in Parliamentary Assembly of the Council of Europe (PACE) Opinion 193(1996) of 25 January 1996 (Glotov 1996, 82-89). In February 1998 the Duma once again voted overwhelmingly to ratify the ECHR, and it entered into force for Russia on 1 November 1998. In this way, Russia fulfilled one of the most important commitments which it made on accession to the Council of Europe. The PACE Opinion contained a long list of obligations. Russia has satisfied a number of them, including transfer of the penitentiary system from the Ministry of the Interior to the Ministry of Justice, in 1998, and enactment of new judicial procedural laws, as well as ratification of most of the important Council of Europe treaties (see for more detail Bowring 1997 and 2000). However, a very important obligation was:

> to sign within one year and ratify within three years from the time of accession, Protocol No. 6 to the European Convention on Human Rights on the abolition of the death penalty in time of peace, and to put into place a moratorium on executions with effect from the day of accession.

Accordingly, and as noted above, Russia signed Protocol No. 6 on 16 April 1997. It should be noted that as a matter of international law, enshrined in the 1969 UN Vienna Convention on the Law of Treaties,[22] a state which has signed a treaty is prohibited, pending ratification, from acting in such a way as to violate the substance of the treaty it has signed. On 16 May 1996 President Yeltsin issued a Decree[23] 'On the gradual curtailing of the application of the death penalty in connection with the admission of Russia to the Council of Europe' (Barry and Williams 1997, 244). Barry and Williams (1997, 245) observe that the decree had four substantive provisions. It:

22 At http://untreaty.un.org/ilc/texts/instruments/english/conventions/1_1_1969.pdf.

23 Decree No.724 (16 May 1996).

1. charged the Russian government within one month to prepare the draft of a law ratifying Protocol No. 6.
2. recommended that both houses of parliament speed up the process for amending the criminal legislation.
3. instructed the Ministry of Internal Affairs to submit within three months proposals for the facilities for life imprisonment, in accordance with UN standards.
4. recommended that the Prosecutor General increase supervision over the implementation of laws on conditions under which capital prisoners are held.

It was unfortunate that the very first sentence of the Decree referred to Council of Europe 'recommendations,' when it was perfectly clear that Russia had entered into an obligation on joining. Furthermore, the parliament was not called upon to eliminate capital punishment, but only to curtail it. According to Pristavkin (1996, 10; Barry and Williams 1997, 245, n.45), a paragraph instituting a moratorium was dropped from the draft of the Decree following 'intense pressure from officials of the Office of the Prosecutor General, the Ministry of the Interior and the Russian Supreme Court.' Moreover, the Decree was promulgated only a few weeks before the presidential elections, in which he was seeking a second term, against a very strong challenge from the Communist Party.

A further indication of the discrepancy between Russia's expressions of good faith towards the Council of Europe and the reality was the enactment in 1996 of the new Criminal Code, noted above, which came into force on 1 January 1997, and which contained several offences attracting the death penalty, several of them new. On 2 August 1996 Yeltsin announced an unofficial moratorium on executions. A typical response was that of Vladimir Guliev (1996):

> [l]iberals, in our opinion, completely ignore Russian sociocultural "background." Among us there has always existed an extremely significant number of people who are not deterred from committing murder either by prison or in particular by labor colonies…And the succession of wars and cruel repressions [that we have experienced] has lowered catastrophically the value of the human personality, of life itself.…And this applies even more so to present Russia.

Catherine Merridale (1996, 16) supported this view:

> Russian attitudes to death and to the value of life have probably been affected, in the medium term, by repeated exposure to unmourned, unvalued death. What others have described as the brutalization of society may have some applicability to Russia, though distinctions need to be made between those directly exposed to violence and those who experienced it at second hand or as children.

In March 1997 the Duma refused to ratify Protocol No. 6, and also refused to enact a law on moratorium. At the same time the Clemency Commission simply stopped sending cases to the President, so executions ceased for that reason if no other (Barry and Williams 1997, 247). In August 1999 the Russian Government once more submitted Protocol No. 6 to the Duma for ratification. This met a similar fate. However, the matter was resolved indirectly when, in February 1999, the Federal Constitutional Court held[24] that in order for the death penalty to be applied in Russia, the accused must in every part of Russia have the right to a trial by jury. At that time trial by jury existed in only 9 of 89 regions of Russia. Igor Petrukhin, a leading expert on criminal law and procedure, was one of many scholars and experts to call for full abolition (Petrukhin 1999). Following a detailed legal analysis, he concluded:

> [t]he death penalty breeds cruelty in society and nourishes the illusion that crime can only be resolved through measures of horror. It is impossible to fight cruelty with cruelty.

And Sergei Pashin, who was the driving force behind the reintroduction of trial by jury in Russia, described the desire to restore the death penalty as 'disgraceful atavism' (Pashin 2001). His close colleague Sergei Vitsin, a member of the Clemency Commission, wrote (1999) '[t]here has now appeared in Russia a great historical chance once and for all to rid ourselves of the punishment which brings disgrace to our country. This is necessary for our own benefit, and not that of other countries or the Council of Europe. The impermissible retention of the death penalty "in a society" as Karl Marx once wrote "which plumes itself on its own civilisation".'

Will the Death Penalty Return to Russia?

Russia has not executed an accused since 1999. But the Criminal Procedural Code of 2001 extended jury trial to the whole of Russia except Chechnya, where it should have been introduced not later than 1 January 2007. This would then, of course, triggered the automatic restoration of the death penalty, following the judgment of the Constitutional Court referred to above.

However, on 15 November 2006 the State Duma adopted at first reading a draft law which changes the date for introduction of jury trials in Chechnya from 1 January 2007 to 1 January 2010.[25] The (good) reason they gave was that lists of potential jurors must be compiled by municipalities, which do not yet exist in Chechnya. On 27 December 2006, the draft law was signed by the President; and

24 Decision of 2 February 1999, No. 3-P, *Rossiskaya Gazeta*, 10 February 1999, English summary in Venice Commission, Bulletin on Constitutional Case-Law, Edition 1999-1, pp. 96-98.

25 http://prima-news.ru/eng/news/2006/11/17/37095.html.

it was published in the Russian Gazette and came into force on 31 December 2006, in the nick of time.[26] So Russia had only until 1 January 2010 before the death penalty would automatically have become available once more.

This extraordinary delay in abolishing the death penalty has not gone unnoticed in Strasbourg. On 10 December 2006 the Council of Europe Commissioner for Human Rights, Thomas Hammarberg, expressed his regret that Russia is the only European state where the death penalty has yet to be abolished, despite Russia's promise to ban it ten years ago. For this reason, and, for example, because of deep concern regarding new amending legislation on NGOs, he announced that the Council of Europe is not planning to wrap up its monitoring mission in Russia.[27] Russia has been lobbying hard for an end to monitoring.

However, as Roger Hood points out (2008), on 18 December 2007 at the United Nations General Assembly Russia voted with 103 other states for a resolution calling for a moratorium on the use of the death penalty with a view to its abolition. All the other former Soviet states except Belarus, which as the table above shows retains the death penalty, were in support; and Belarus abstained rather than opposing. There was renewed speculation that the death penalty will indeed return to Russia. The Beslan school siege tragedy led to renewed calls for restoration. On 9 September 2004 the influential Governor of Kemerovo Oblast, Aman Tuleev, demanded that parliamentarians reintroduce capital punishment for terrorist offences. He was joined by the then Deputy Speaker of the State Duma, the leader of the nationalist Liberal Democrat party, Vladimir Zhirinovsky.[28]

However, Nikolai Petrov of the Moscow Carnegie Centre has been quoted as saying, '[t]he time to revise Russia's foreign policy concept may not have come, but there have been lots of signals suggesting the need to improve relations with European structures. Reintroducing the death penalty would directly contradict all the signals President Dmitry Medvedev has been sending' (Oliphant 2009). And on Wednesday 9 September 2009 President Medvedev sent a strong signal, when his spokeswoman Natalia Timakova denied that reintroducing the death penalty was even under discussion (ibid.), apparently in direct response to the Newsweek article referred to above (Taratuta and Zygar 2009).

Conclusion – and a Happy Ending?

Sociologists joke that the current opinion poll rating of capital punishment in Russia is, at 80 per cent, even higher than that of Vladimir Putin. The former Deputy Chairman of the Constitutional Court and renowned law reformer, Tamara Morshchakova, said that '[o]ur parliamentary deputies suffer from dependence on populism. They say that society does not want to abolish the death penalty. So

26 http://www.demokratia.ru/archive-ru/2007/obzor_zakonov_109.zip.

27 http://www.accessmylibrary.com/coms2/summary_0286-28873633_ITM.

28 http://www.newsru.com/russia/09sep2004/tuleev.html.

what? In no country in the world does society want to abolish the death penalty. Even in England, in that ethical old democracy. But there society is not asked' (Taratuta and Zygar 2009). At the root of the continuing debate is a perplexing paradox. Mikhail Margelov (2006) wrote, '…the will of the Russian people is bewildering. They have no trust in punitive bodies yet two-thirds of the population want the death penalty, that is, they are ready to entrust to these bodies the right to decide who must live and who must die. The average Russian seems to be more inclined to act on his conviction rather than on the rational assessment of possible consequences.'

Russia is often portrayed as a primitive and bloodthirsty society, ruled by the authoritarian governments it deserves. Yet, as has been shown in this chapter, Russia was the first European state to abolish the death penalty in the eighteenth century, if not permanently, and throughout its contemporary history there has been an engaged and informed debate on the question of abolition. There have now been no executions for more than a decade, and the present political leadership has shown no desire for the restoration of capital punishment.

There appears to be a happy ending to this tale. At the time of finalising this chapter, the Russian Constitutional Court has once again appeared as a *deus ex machina*, and may well have secured an almost final abolition of the death penalty in Russia. Following a request from the Supreme Court of the Russian Federation, and with unprecedented speed, on 19 November 2009 the Constitutional Court handed down its Decision (*Opredeleniye*), clarifying its Resolution (*Postanovleniye*) of 2 February 1999 referred to above.[29] The Decision ruled that the death penalty may not be re-introduced even when trial by jury becomes available in the whole of the Federation, including Chechnya. The basis for the decision is very significant. The Court noted that Russia signed Protocol 6 to the ECHR on 16 April 1997, and is therefore obliged, by virtue of Article 18 of the *Vienna Convention on the Law of Treaties* 1969[30] 'to refrain from acts which would defeat the object and purpose' of the Protocol. Thus, the moratorium presently in place continues until ratification by Russia of the Protocol. As the commentator Anna Zakatnova pointed out,[31] three judges (out of 19), Sergei Kazantsev, Mikhail Kleandrov and Yurii Rudkin voted against the Decision, and the Court's Chairman, Valerii Zorkin, could not predict what the Russian parliament would do in the future. But Judge Kononov, one of the majority of judges who voted in favour, insisted that the Constitutional Court had not exceeded its jurisdiction, and that the effective abolition of the death penalty in Russia is irreversible.

---

29 Published in the official *Rossiiskaya Gazeta* on 27 November 2009, at http://www.rg.ru/2009/11/27/postanovlenie-ks-dok.html (accessed on 12 January 2010).

30 http://untreaty.un.org/ilc/texts/instruments/english/conventions/1_1_1969.pdf (accessed on 12 January 2010).

31 In *Rossiiskaya Gazeta* 20 November 2009 at http://www.rg.ru/2009/11/20/kazn.html (accessed on 12 January 2010).

Celebration of the Constitutional Court's decision was swiftly tempered by disturbing news. On 2 December 2009 Judge Kononov and his colleague Judge Yaroslavtsev, both of them leading advocates of human rights on the Court, were forced to resign their positions – Kononov from the Court, and Yaroslavtsev as the Court's representative o the Council of Judges – following public criticism by them of political control of the judiciary in Russia.[32]

Ten years have passed since Russia signed Protocol 6, and there is no sign that the State Duma will enact legislation for ratification. But in order to restore the death penalty Russia would be obliged to leave the Council of Europe, a step it is presently unlikely to take. But, as always, the future of the rule of law in Russia is clouded by uncertainty.

Bibiography

Adams, W. (1970) 'Capital Punishment in Imperial and Soviet Criminal Law', 18 *American Journal of Comparative Law* 575.

Amnesty International (1997) *Torture in Russia* (April) at http://www.amnesty.org/en/library/info/EUR46/007/1997.

Barry, D. and Williams, E. (1997) 'Russia's Death Penalty Dilemmas', 8 *Criminal Law Forum* 231-258.

BBC (1999) 'Russia suspends death penalty Tuesday', February 2, at http://news.bbc.co.uk/2/hi/europe/270713.

Bohm, R. (2008) 'Karl Marx and the Death Penalty', 16 *Critical Criminology* 285.

Bowring, B. (2009) 'Russia and Human Rights: Incompatible Opposites?', 1 *Göttingen Journal of International Law* 257.

—— (2005) 'Russia in a Common European Legal Space. Developing effective remedies for the violations of rights by public bodies: compliance with the European Convention on Human Rights', in Hober, K. (ed.) *The Uppsala Yearbook of East European Law 2004* (London: Wildy, Simmonds and Hill), 89-116.

—— (2000) 'Russia's accession to the Council of Europe and human rights: four years on', 4 *European Human Rights Law Review* 362-379.

—— (1997) 'Russia's Accession to the Council of Europe and Human Rights: Compliance or Cross-Purposes?', 6 *European Human Rights Law Review* 628. This has been translated into Russian, and appears in *Rossiiskii Byulleten po Prava Cheloveka* (Russian Bulletin on Human Rights) Issue 10 1998, 12.

32 In Russian in the daily *Kommersant* at www.kommersant.ru/doc.aspx?DocsID=1284828 (accessed on: 12 January 2010); and see Nikolaus von Twickel '2 Senior Judges Quit After Criticism', *The Moscow Times* 3 December 2009.

—— (1995) 'Human Rights in Russia: A Discourse of Emancipation or Just Another Mirage?', in Pogany, I. (ed.) *Human Rights in Eastern Europe* (London: Edward Elgar), 87.

Cizova, T. (1962) 'Beccaria in Russia', 40 *The Slavonic and East European Review* 384.

Fawn, R. (2001) 'Death Penalty as Democratisation: Is the Council of Europe Hanging Itself?', 8 *Democratization* 69.

Foinitskiy, I. (2001) *Otsenka smertnoi kazni* (Evaluation of the death penalty) *Ucheniye o nakazanii* (Studies on punishments) Moscow (1989), (2001) at http://deathpenalty.narod.ru/nauka/foini.htm.

Gernet, M.N. (1913) *Smertnaya kazn i obshchestvennoye mneniye* (The death penalty and public opinion)' in Gernet, N., *Smertnaya kazn* [The death penalty] 1913 at http://deathpenalty.narod.ru/nauka/gernet.htm.

Glotov, S.A. (1996) *Pravo Soveta Evropi i Rossii* [The Law of the Council of Europe and Russia] (Krasnodar).

Gogol, N. (2004) *Dead Souls*, trans. Robert Maguire (London: Penguin Classics).

Guliev, V. (1996) *Moratorii na smertnuyu kazn'prezhdevremenen* [The moratorium on the death penalty is premature] *Nezavisimaya Gazeta*, 21 December.

Hood, R. (2008) 'Russia and its death penalty', *Open Democracy*, 1 October at http://www.opendemocracy.net/article/russia-theme/russia-and-its-death-penalty.

Ivashko, S. (2001) 'Duma Discusses Abolishment of Death Penalty', 10 December at www.gazeta.ru.

Kelina, S. (1989) *Kogda ubivaet goisudarstvo: Sertnaya kazn protiv prav cheloveka* no.12 *Sovetskoye Gosudarstvoi Pravo* 127.

Kistyakovsky, A.F. (1896) *Issledovaniye o smertnoi kazni* [Research on the death penalty[Chapter 2, at http://deathpenalty.narod.ru/nauka/kist.htm.

Kolokolov, N. (1998) *Smertnaya kazn glazami sudi* (The death penalty through the eyes of judges) *Rossiiskaya Yustitsiya* No.7 1998, at http://deathpenalty.narod.ru/nauka/kolok.htm.

Kovalev, N. (2008) 'Trial by Jury in Russian Military Courts No. 8', *The Journal of Power Institutions in Post-Soviet Societies* 2.

Kushen, R. (1993) 'The death penalty and the crisis of criminal justice in Russia', v.19 n.2 *Brooklyn Journal of International Law* pp. 523-581.

Kvashis, V.E. and G.-I. Albrecht *Kuda idyot smertnaya kazn?* [Where is the death penalty going?)] n. 6 (2001) *Pravo i Politika* at http://deathpenalty.narod.ru/nauka/kuda.zip.

Kvashis, V.E. (2008) *Smertnaya kazn. Mirovoye tendentsii, problemy i perspektivi* [The death penalty. World tendencies, problems and perspectives] (Moscow: Yurait).

Lenin, V. (1977) 'Lessons of the Revolution' written at the end of July 1917, published on 12 and 13 September (30 and 31 August), 1917, in the newspaper *Rabochy* Nos. 8 and 9, Lenin Collected Works, Progress Publishers, 1977,

Moscow, Volume 25, 227-243, at http://www.marxists.org/archive/lenin/works/1917/sep/06.htm.

—— (1971) Draft Decision for the Council of Defence on Regulating Relations Between the Vecheka, the Railway Cheka and the Commissariat for Railways and a Letter to the Members of the Council of Defence, 28 February 1919, First published in 1933 in *Lenin Miscellany XXIV*, Lenin *Collected Works*, 2nd English Edition, Progress Publishers, 1971, Moscow, Volume 42, 127b-129a, at http://www.marx.org/archive/lenin/works/1919/feb/28.htm.

—— (1965) Report On The Work Of The All-Russia Central Executive Committee And The Council Of People's Commissars Delivered At The First Session Of The All-Russia Central Executive Committee, Seventh Convocation, 2 February 1920, Brief reports published on 3 February 1920 in *Pravda* No. 23 and in *Izvestia* No. 23; Lenin's *Collected Works*, 4th English Edition, Progress Publishers, Moscow, 1965, Volume 30, 315-336, at http://www.marx.org/archive/lenin/works/1920/feb/02.htm.

Levada, Y. (1995) 'The Soviet Man Five Years Later: 1989-1994 (Preliminary Results of a Comparative Study)' *Sevodnya* 24 January 10.

Levintova, E. (2003) 'Government-Affiliated Intellectuals, Official Discourse and Public Opinion in Post-Communist Societies (Russia and Poland)' Prepared for delivery at the 2003 Annual Meeting of the American Political Science Association, at http://apsa03_proceeding_63043.pdf.

Malko, A. V. (1998) 'The death penalty: contemporary problems', 1 *Pravovedeniye* at http://deathpenalty.narod.ru/nauka/malko.htm.

Margelov, M. (2006) 'The Specter of Capital Punishment in Russia', *Russia in Global Affairs* 1, January–March 2006 at http://www.eng.globalaffairs.ru/numbers/14/1006.html.

Marx, K. (1853) 'Capital Punishment' *New-York Daily Tribune*, 17-18 February at http://www.marxists.org/archive/marx/works/1853/02/18.htm.

—— (1849) 'Suppression of the *Neue Rheinische Zeitung*' *Neue Rheinische Zeitung No. 301* final issue 19 May 1849, at http://www.marxists.org/archive/marx/works/1849/05/19c.htm.

Merridale, C. (1996) 'Death and Memory in Modern Russia', 42 *History Workshop Journal* 1.

Mikhlin A.S. (2002) *Pozhizhnennoye lisheniye svobody kak vid ugolovnovo nakazaniya* [Life imprisonment as a form of criminal punishment] *Rossiiskaya Ustitsiya* No.5, http://deathpenalty.narod.ru/nauka/pls.htm.

—— (1997) 'Sposoby primeneniia smertnoi kazni: istoriia i sovremennost' [Ways of introducing the death penalty: history and the present day], *Gosudarstvo i Pravo* (State and Law) No. 1, 72.

Naumov, A. (1997) 'The New Russian Criminal Code as a Reflection of Ongoing Reforms', 8 *Criminal Law Forum*.

Ohr, N.H. [2004] Review of Wheatcroft, http://www.h-net.org/reviews/showrev.php?id=9524.

Oliphant, R. (2009) 'Capital Offences', *Russia Profile* 10 September at http://www.russiaprofile.org/page.php?pageid=Politics&articleid=a1252609152.

Pashin, S. (2001) *O prirode smertnoi kazni* [On the nature of the death penalty] No. 14 Index on Censorship, at http://deathpenalty.narod.ru/nauka/Pashin.htm

Petrukhin, I. (1999) *Pravo na zhzin i smertnaya kazn* [The right to life and the death penalty] No. 5 *Obshchestvenniye nauki i sovremennosti* at http://deathpenalty.narod.ru/nauka/pravon.htm.

Pozdnov, M. (2002) *O sudebnikh oshibkakh* [On miscarriages of justice], at http://deathpenalty.narod.ru/nauka/errors.htm.

Pristavkin, A. (1997) *Kaznit? Milovat?* [Execute? Pardon?] No. 4 *Yuridicheskii Vestnik* 5.

—— (1996) *Kommentarii* [Commentary on the President's Decree of 16 May]. 6 *Rossiiskaya Yustitsiya*.

Quillin, W.C. (1997) 'The Death Penalty in the Soviet Union', 5 *American Journal of Criminal Law* 225.

Radelet, M. and Marian, B. (2000) 'The Changing Nature of Death Penalty Debates', 26 *Annual Review of Sociology* 43.

Ritter, K. (2000) 'The Russian death penalty dilemmas: Square pegs and round holes', 32 *Case Western Reserve Journal of International Law* 129.

Sakharov, A. (1975) *My Country and the World* (New York: Knopf).

Taratuta, Y. and Zygar, M. (2009) *Smertniye kozyn* [Death machinations] – this is a play on words, since "death penalty" in Russian is "*smertniye kazn*" – *Russian Newsweek* 7-12 September, at http://www.runewsweek.ru/country/30122/.

Van den Berg, G. (1983) 'The Soviet Union and the Death Penalty', 35 *Soviet Studies* 154.

Vernadsky, G. (1947) *Medieval Russian Laws* (New York: Columbia University Press).

Vitsin, S. (1999) *Vremya kaznit v Rossii zakonchilos?* [The time of the death penalty in Russia has come to an end?] No. 3 *Rossiiskaya Yustitsiya*, at http://deathpenalty.narod.ru/nauka/vicin.htm.

Wheatcroft, S.G. (2002) 'The Crisis of the Late Tsarist Penal System', in Wheatcroft, S.G. (ed.) *Challenging Traditional Views of Russian History.* (Basingstoke: Palgrave Macmillan).

Zhiltsov, S.V. (2002) *Ponyatiye smertnoi kazni* [The concept of the death penalty], in Zhiltsov, S.V. *Smertnaya kazn v istorii Rossii* [The death penalty in the history of Russia] 24.

PART IV
Medical Countenance at the End of Life

Chapter 12
Assisted Suicide, Voluntary Euthanasia, and the Right to Life

David Benatar

Introduction

One of the few significant freedoms still not legally accorded to people even in liberal democracies is the freedom either to obtain assistance from others in taking one's own life or to be actively and voluntarily euthanazed by those willing to help one. While liberal societies accord competent adults extensive freedom to *lead* their lives in the ways they choose, all but a handful of such societies deny people freedom to obtain assistance to *end* their lives.

There is, to be sure, more freedom to end one's life now than there was before. Many countries that previously criminalized suicide itself, prosecuting those who made unsuccessful attempts or penalizing the estates or bodily remains of successful suicides, no longer prohibit suicide per se. However, with the exception of very few states, it remains a crime to assist others in suicide or to perform euthanasia on humans.

The legal freedom to kill oneself without the assistance of others is often insufficient for the same sort of reason that a freedom to treat oneself medically is often insufficient. Some of us are sometimes capable of medicating ourselves. We have a headache and thus we ingest a tablet that brings relief. We incur a minor cut, which we disinfect and then perhaps plaster. However, we are not expected to diagnose more complicated or serious ailments or to decide, unaided, which therapies to pursue. The reason is obvious. Most people lack the requisite training to diagnose and to treat effectively, and the consequence of prohibiting others from helping them would be that people would be much worse off.

Something similar can be said of those who want to die. While many people who find that their lives have reached an intolerably low quality *could* kill themselves unaided, they would run the risk, if acting without assistance, of either dying painfully or gruesomely or of botching the attempt. In any of these cases they would be worse off than if they had been able to secure professional assistance. Moreover, there are some people who simply *cannot* kill themselves unaided. There are others who cannot kill themselves even with assistance, as they are so paralyzed that they are unable to perform any action that will bring about their deaths.[1] The people in the last category, if they are to die when they want to die, will need to have others kill them in an act of voluntary euthanasia.

The observation that a legal freedom to kill oneself unaided is often insufficient for a person to attain the death he[2] prefers is not intended to show, by itself, that assisted suicide[3] and voluntary euthanasia are morally justifiable. Instead, it is intended only to ward off the claim that there is no need to allow assisted suicide or euthanasia, on the grounds that people currently, at least in some places, have the option to kill themselves without the threat of criminal or civil response.

Reference has now been made to suicide, assisted suicide and to voluntary euthanasia. While there are obviously some differences between each of these categories, they also have some elements in common. In speaking about suicide, whether assisted or otherwise, I shall restrict my attention to those cases where the person killing himself is competent to decide whether continued life is in his interests because it is these cases that are worthy of consideration alongside *voluntary* euthanasia. What these cases of suicide and assisted suicide have in common with voluntary euthanasia is that in all three situations the person who dies is competent to and does genuinely consent to his or her own death. The difference between them is that whereas in suicide, whether assisted or not, the person who dies is the same person as the one who kills, in euthanasia the person who dies is somebody other than the person who kills. Suicide is the killing of the self, whereas euthanasia is the killing of or by another, but always for the sake of the person who is killed.

In speaking about suicide and voluntary euthanasia I have described them as instances of *killing*. Although one could bring about one's own or another's death passively, my focus in this paper will be on killing, or actively bringing about people's death. This is because most of the controversy pertains to killing rather than to letting die.

Many people fail to recognize that there are two distinct moral questions one can ask about assisted suicide and euthanasia. The one is whether these practices

---

1 Where they are permitted to refuse nutrition, they could choose to die of dehydration or starvation, but again that is clearly a worse way to die than a more speedy method.

2 Although I shall sometimes also use the female pronoun I shall, for convenience, sometimes use only the male pronoun. For an explanation why this is not sexist, see Benatar 2005.

3 It is common in the literature to refer to 'Physician Assisted Suicide' (PAS). I eschew this convention for two reasons. First, 'Physician' is used in the American sense and thus means 'doctor,' and thus the phrase refers to 'Doctor Assisted Suicide.' Elsewhere in the English-speaking world, physicians are what the Americans call 'Internists.' The term 'Physician Assisted Suicide' is thus either potentially misleading outside of America or assumes that everybody must accommodate to American usage. Second, while the assistance of doctors is often what is needed, on account of their expertise, I do not want to preclude the possibility that assistance could sometimes come from somebody other than a doctor.

are morally acceptable, while the other is whether they ought (morally) to be legal.[4] These two questions are often either confused or the answer to the one is thought to entail the answer to the other. Thus, some people think that if the practices are immoral they ought also to be illegal, and if they are morally permissible then they ought to be legal. It is possible, however, to answer the two questions differently.

One could think that while assisted suicide and euthanasia are immoral they ought not to be illegal. To make sense of this, consider the view, widespread in liberal democracies, that saying certain things may be immoral but ought nonetheless to be legally permitted. One possible justification for such a view is that it is not the state's business to interfere with the freedom of its competent adult citizens (except where they wrongfully harm others), even if what they are doing either is or is thought to be immoral.

Similarly, one could think that while assisted suicide and euthanasia are morally permissible, they ought nonetheless to be illegal. One common justification for such a view, which I shall discuss later, is that legalizing permissible instances of euthanasia or assisted suicide would soon lead to the performance of impermissible instances. On this view, although euthanasia may sometimes be permissible, legalizing it would be a bad public policy.

Although the two questions – whether euthanasia is morally acceptable and whether it should be legal – are distinct, the arguments I shall advance in this chapter will be relevant to both. More specifically, I intend to argue for affirmative answers to both these questions. I shall do so by focusing, at least in the first instance, on the right to life. I shall argue that a reasonable interpretation of such a right is sufficient to show that assisted suicide and voluntary euthanasia are morally permissible, and that there is no need to postulate a *separate* right to die in order to reach this conclusion. Although, in certain circumstances, I also endorse *non-voluntary* euthanasia – that is, euthanasia of beings that are not competent to make a judgement for themselves – I shall not argue for that here. Towards the end of the chapter, I shall consider and reject arguments for the view that even if assisted suicide and voluntary euthanasia are morally permissible they ought nonetheless to be illegal.

The Right to Life

Opponents of assisted suicide and euthanasia, who are often also opponents of abortion, frequently support their conclusions by appealing to a right to life. The assumption, it seems, is that if somebody has a right to life then it is wrong to kill him. Perhaps it is also thought that because a right is a 'trumping' moral principle,

---

4 The latter question should, in turn, be distinguished from a third question – whether assisted suicide or voluntary euthanasia *is* legal in a given jurisdiction. This third question is obviously a legal question rather than a philosophical one, and I shall not consider it here.

it cannot be overridden by other moral considerations that defenders of assisted suicide, euthanasia and abortion might advance.

Although attributing a right to life to foetuses is a contentious matter, the attribution of such a right to competent adults is widely accepted. Indeed, it is so widely accepted, both by opponents and proponents of assisted suicide and voluntary euthanasia that it cannot be what divides those on different sides of this issue. Instead the debate is often characterized as being over whether in addition to a right to life people also have a right to die. I plan to show, however, that there is no need to postulate a right to die in order to defend assisted suicide and voluntary euthanasia. I shall argue that if we understand the right to life in the most plausible way, we find that the attribution of a right to life to a competent adult entails the moral permissibility of assisted suicide and, if that is not possible, voluntary euthanasia.

The phrase 'a right to life' is ambiguous between 'a right not to be killed' and 'a right to have one's life saved'. Interpreted in the former way it is a *negative* right (a right *not* to be treated in a certain way), while interpreted in the latter way it is a *positive* right (a right *to* be treated in a certain way). It is entirely possible, of course, that people have both a negative and a positive right to life. However, both because the attribution of a positive right to life is more controversial and because discussing it does not add anything to discussion of the right not to be killed, I shall focus only on the negative right.

The right not to be killed is, at the very least, a *claim* on others not to kill the bearer of the right. In other words it is, minimally, what Wesley Hohfeld (1919) called a 'claim right'. If the right in question is a moral right, then the claim is a moral one. If the right is a legal one, then the claim is correspondingly a legal one. The right not to be killed can, and often is, *both* a moral and a legal right. The claim right has a correlative duty – the duty (whether moral or legal, or both) not to kill the right-bearer.

With regard to assisted suicide and voluntary euthanasia the crucial question about the right not to be killed is whether it can be waived. The right not to be killed obligates others not to kill the right-bearer. However, if the right-bearer is entitled to waive his right, then he is entitled to release others from their duty not to kill him. Another way of putting the question is to ask whether the right not to be killed, consists not only of a *claim* that others not kill one, but also a *power*[5] to alter the moral or jural relations in such a way that a specific person in specific circumstances may be released, by the right-bearer, from his duty. Obviously, if a right not to be killed included the power to waive the right, then the right not to be killed would not preclude assisted suicide and voluntary euthanasia. Indeed such a power would positively permit these practices.

Before I argue that the negative right to life is most plausibly understood as including this power, I want to clarify what a right waiving is and is not. Waiving a right sometimes involves its loss. If, for example, one (unconditionally) releases

5 This term is also Wesley Hohfeld's.

somebody from a debt owed to one, then one no longer has a claim against that person for what was owed. Waiving one's right here involves losing it. However, waiving a right need not always involve its loss. If one invites guests to one's home, one waives, for the duration of the visit, one's right that those people not enter one's home. One does not thereby lose one's right. One could re-assert it and ask the guests to leave if one so chose. Moreover, even for the duration of one's guests' visit, the right remains in full effect against everybody other than one's guests.

Given this, it is apparent that even if a right not to be killed is what some call 'inalienable' – a right that may not be given up – it could still be waived.[6] One could grant a specific person at a specific time permission to kill one in a specific way. One could withdraw that permission at any time until one lost the ability to do so. The method of killing would be restricted in accordance with one's directive. Through all this, everybody else would remain under a duty not to kill one.

Why should we understand the right to life as including the power to waive the right? The answer lies in the moral basis of the right. The justification for a right to life lies in the importance that continued life ordinarily has. The right protects against others violating our very strong and valid interests in continuing to live. Now, although continued life is *ordinarily* in our interests, it is not *always* so. The quality of one's life can be so bad that one reasonably judges death to be less bad than continuing to live in one's condition.

We need not agree on how bad life must get before continued life ceases to be in one's interests. Indeed, part of the point of assisted suicide and voluntary euthanasia is that decisions about whether the quality of a competent person's life is bearable or unbearable are largely left up to that person. I say 'largely' rather than 'entirely' because once second parties are involved in one's death, as is the case in both assisted suicide and euthanasia, the perspective of those second parties is also relevant. One person cannot be expected to kill another if he lacks adequate reason to see the death as being in the interests of the person who is killed. The issue for second-party involvement is not merely whether the death is in the interests of the person who dies, but whether it is sufficiently clearly so that the second party acts reasonably in providing assistance. I shall say more about this later, but all we need agree upon here is that it *does* sometimes get so bad that a second party could reasonably see that continued life was no longer in that person's interests. And it seems to me that one cannot reasonably deny that life does sometimes get this bad for at least some people.

Consider, for example, those people who face unremitting excruciating pain. Opponents of assisted suicide and voluntary euthanasia often respond to such cases by noting that in such cases there is always an alternative to death – palliation. Although there are parts of the world where people do not have access to the medication that can relieve their pain, the claim is true for many people. However, the assumption here is that life in the palliated state is worth continuing.

6 That is, unless one takes 'inalienable' to mean 'unwaivable'.

Some people may accept this for themselves. For others, however, the costs of sedation or analgesia – lingering in a state of minimal consciousness, which has no pleasures and in which one must be subject, even if only obliviously, to ongoing indignities – may be worse than death.[7]

Similarly, we can consider other conditions, which even if not excruciatingly painful (in the literal sense) nonetheless cause immense suffering. For example, there are people who are unable to move any of their limbs or, in still worse cases, anything other than their eyelids. They are bowel and bladder incontinent, must be turned regularly in an effort to avoid bedsores, and can breathe only with the assistance of machines. There are others who endure horribly disfiguring diseases or injuries. They have severe burns over much of their bodies, they suffer from some ulcerating condition, or the only treatment for a cancer is to undergo surgery that mutilates their faces, for example.

It is obtuse to insist either that there are not (many) people in such conditions or that everybody with such conditions must judge continued life of this kind to be preferable to death. Perhaps opponents of assisted suicide and euthanasia believe that their own lives would be worth continuing in such situations. Even if they are correct that this is what they would believe if they actually found themselves in such situations, it is immensely arrogant to think that everybody else must be bound by their own preferences or judgements in such cases.

John Keown, arguably one of the most sophisticated opponents of euthanasia, rejects the idea that 'life can lose its worth so as to make death a benefit' (Keown 2002, 39). This is because he maintains humans possess 'an intrinsic dignity [that] grounds the principle that one must never intentionally kill an innocent human being' (Keown 2002, 40). In its religious form, this is the sanctity of life doctrine, according to which, 'human life is created in the image of God and is, therefore, possessed of an intrinsic dignity which entitles it to protection from unjust attack' (Keown 2002, 40). In its non-religious form, human dignity is grounded upon 'that radical capacity, inherent in human nature, which normally results in the development of rational abilities such as understanding and choice' (Keown 2002, 40).[8]

---

7 Empirical studies from those jurisdictions in which voluntary active euthanasia or assisted suicide are practised show that many people who elect to die, do so not (simply) because of pain but because of other impoverishments in their quality of life, including loss of autonomy and an inability to participate in activities which make life enjoyable. See, for example: Kissane, Street, and Nitschke 1998; Chin, Hedberg, Higginson, and Fleming 1999; Ganzini, Nelson, Schmidt, Kraemer, Delroit, and Lee 2000; Sullivan, Hedberg, and Fleming 2000.

8 Actually Dr Keown says this about both the religious and the non-religious form of the argument. The problem with that, however, is that it need not be the case that being created in God's image is the same as having the capacity for the rational abilities of understanding and choice. If it is, then it is unclear what work is being done, in the religious form, by the claim that humans are created in the divine image. However, it makes no

These views face many problems. First, it is unclear whether the claims are true. Whether or not humans are created in God's image is at least as controversial as the euthanasia question and thus is an unpromising means to resolving the latter. Nor is it clear that humans have dignity on account of their rational nature. There are many humans – infants and those who are seriously mentally disabled – whose understanding and ability to choose is less than that of many animals. Dr Keown's response to those cases is to distinguish between a capacity and an ability. He says that one might have the capacity to learn Swahili but not (now) have the ability to speak it. Now, while it is true that normal human infants do have the capacity to learn any languages, it is not true that those who are seriously mentally disabled have that capacity. Although it is true that but for their disability they would have the capacity, it is equally true that but for the nature of their brains, squirrels would also have the capacity. Both conditions are actually immutable and it is not clear why the fact that one is a deviation from normal species functioning and the other is not, entails that one has the relevant capacity and the other does not.

Second, even if humans were created in God's image or had the rational capacities of understanding and choice, this would not entail that their lives cannot be so bad that it is no longer in their interests to continue living, or that it is always wrong to kill them. Indeed, one could argue that somebody's being created in God's image makes it especially important to spare that person life under horrific conditions. Similarly, one could argue that it is precisely because somebody has the capacity for understanding and choice, that he can understand the nature of his condition and choose whether or not he wants to continue living. Curiously, Dr Keown extends the inviolability principle only to *innocent* humans, and seems to allow for the capital punishment of those convicted of a sufficiently serious crime. But surely even guilty humans are created in God's image and have the rational capacities of understanding and choice? Indeed, if they lacked the latter capacities, punishment would be inappropriate (at least on a retributivist view). Thus, if we may sometimes kill rational beings purportedly created in the divine image, why may we not make a similar exception for those who are suffering unbearably? While the latter, unlike the former, may be 'innocent', the relevance of this is merely stipulated by opponents of euthanasia and certainly does not follow from the notion that humans are rational beings created in the divine image.

In defending the claim that human life is inviolable against the claim that life is valuable only when of a sufficient quality, Dr Keown tendentiously says that those defending the latter view distinguish between 'worthwhile' and 'worthless' *patients* (Keown 2002, 47). This, he says, stands in contrast to the 'sanctity/inviolability of life' view's distinction between 'worthwhile' and 'worthless' *treatments*. But those of us who think that a life can be of so poor a quality that it is not worth continuing do not think that this is because the *patient* (whether oneself or another) with such a life is worthless. Indeed, if one thought that the *person* were worthless one would

difference to what I shall say if one views the sanctity of life view making both claims and the non-religious version only one of the claims.

not care whether he or she continued to endure horrid conditions. Why worry about worthless beings? Recognizing the value of a person is not incompatible with recognizing that that person's life may have ceased to be in that person's interests.

Dr Keown's position is not strengthened by claiming that 'human life is not only an *instrumental* good, a necessary precondition of thinking or doing, but a *basic* good, a fundamental basis of human flourishing' (Keown 2002, 41). The problem is that life is not only a fundamental basis of human flourishing, but also a fundamental basis of human floundering. One cannot languish without living. Perhaps, then, we cannot say categorically whether life is a basic good, but rather only that its status as such depends upon whether it is the basis of flourishing or of its opposite. And if this is thought to sound too much like instrumental value and that we *can* categorically classify life as a basic good because it *usually* is the basis of human flourishing, then it is unclear why its being a basic good entails that that basic good may not be sacrificed when it *is* the basis of floundering.

Once we recognize that life could become so bad that continued life is no longer in one's interests, we must recognize that a right not to be killed can outlive its moral purpose – to protect an individual's important interests. If a right to life does not include a power to waive the right then instead of the right serving the interests of the right-bearer it becomes the right-bearer's master. And the worse the quality of life is, the more cruel a master it is.

Those who would deny that the right to life includes a power to waive a claim that one not be killed seem committed to treating the right to life very differently from other rights, where we routinely recognize the right-bearer's power to waive his claim. If, for example, one could not waive one's property claims, one could never lend, sell or give one's property away. Similarly, if one could never waive one's right to bodily integrity, one could never grant a surgeon permission to operate on one. Just as a negative right to property or to bodily integrity would become an oppressive principle if one could never waive it, so the same can be said of a right to life that the bearer has no power to waive.

This does not entail that the waiving of a right is sufficient to justify a second party's acting in accordance with the waiving. In other words, we are not morally entitled to do to others *whatever* they voluntarily consent to. If a person consents to my harming him, there is something presumptively problematic about my acting on this. But the kind of case we are considering here is one in which a person's voluntary consent to his death *benefits* rather than harms him.

Now it might be suggested that in arguing that a right to life must be liable to waiving if it is to serve the interests of its bearer, I have implicitly presupposed a particular view of rights. According to this view, known variably as the Interest or Benefit theory, rights essentially protect interests. In one way my argument does indeed presuppose this theory because I have said that the power element in the right is explained with reference to the right-bearer's *interest*. At the same time, however, my argument is not liable to criticism from those holding the opposing view, namely the Choice or Will theory, which maintains that rights essentially protect choices. This is because the permissibility of assisted suicide and voluntary euthanasia would be even easier to derive from a right to life if it were conceived in accordance with the Choice theory. Instead of the power to waive the right being derivative from the interests of the right-bearer, the Choice theory makes the power basic. The right consists in the power to choose whether or not others may kill one. I happen to think that the Interest theory is preferable, but those who reject this view in favour of the Choice theory cannot reject assisted suicide and voluntary euthanasia on the grounds that I have presupposed a contested view of rights. Had I accepted the opposing, Choice view, the argument for assisted suicide and voluntary euthanasia would have been even easier.

Beyond the Right to Life

Next it may be suggested that my argument presupposes that one has a right to life. Once the implications of such a right for assisted suicide and voluntary euthanasia are made clear, opponents of these practices might reconsider the notion of a right to life, preferring to eschew it. This is not a promising line of argument. Irrespective of whether one thinks that people have a (waivable) right to life, one is going to be hard-pressed to explain why it is wrong to (help) bring about the death of somebody whose quality of life has deteriorated to the point that his life is not worth continuing. In other words, the argument for assisted suicide and voluntary euthanasia can be recast without reference to rights. The argument might be formulated as follows:

1. Sometimes the quality of somebody's life is so bad that the life is not worth continuing.
2. When somebody's life is not worth continuing, it is better (or less bad) for him if his life were to end.
3. Sometimes there are no countervailing moral considerations that are sufficiently strong to override such a person's interest in ending his life.
4. When one's life is not worth continuing and there are no overriding reasons why one should nonetheless not end one's life, it is permissible to kill oneself.
5. Sometimes to ensure one's own death without making one's life still worse, the assistance of others is necessary (or preferable).
6. When it is permissible to end one's own life for one's own sake, but one needs the assistance of others, it is permissible to obtain or for others to provide such assistance.
7. Therefore, it is sometimes permissible to obtain assistance in ending one's life or to provide such assistance to those who need it.

I argued earlier for the first and fifth premises. The second premise is analytically true. To say that one's life is not worth continuing is to say that death would be preferable to continued existence. The third and sixth premises are the ones to which opponents of assisted suicide and voluntary euthanasia are most likely to object. However, the objections are not promising.

Those rejecting the third premise must show that countervailing moral considerations *always* override such a person's interest in ending his life. This is a highly implausible claim. Many people try to defend it by saying either that life has sanctity or that it is inviolable. It implies that no matter how bad the quality of a life is and no matter how little benefit its continuation brings others, there is always some stronger moral consideration that outweighs this and requires the suffering person to continue existing. This amounts to a (negative) *duty* to live – a duty never to kill oneself or to allow others to do so. But such a duty is much harder to defend than is a right to life, which I have suggested permits assisted suicide and voluntary euthanasia. The view that life has sanctity or is inviolable is one common way to defend a duty to live, but I have already argued that such a view fails.

Objections to the sixth premise are also likely to fail. It may well be true that we are not *always* warranted in helping others to do things that they are themselves permitted to do. For example, it is arguably impermissible for doctors to help people sacrifice themselves *for the benefit of others* (by, for example, transplanting the heart of a perfectly healthy willing donor into somebody else). However, it is very difficult to see how it would be impermissible to help somebody spare *himself* unspeakable harm when, all things considered, there was no moral reason for him to endure it. Now those who object to the sixth premise might argue that even when there are no moral considerations that override an individual's interest in killing himself there may be moral considerations that override somebody else's helping him. I am willing to grant that there could sometimes be such considerations. However, those wishing to object to the sixth premise need to show that there are *always* overriding reasons not to help others to end their own lives. But this is as implausible as the objection to the third premise. It implies that no matter how bad the quality of a life is and no matter how little benefit its continuation brings others there is *always* some stronger moral consideration not to help him end his life. It is hard to see how this could be the case, at least if we are speaking about the morality of individual acts of assisted suicide or euthanasia. However, if the objection is not to the morality of individual instances of assisted suicide or euthanasia but rather to morality of legalizing them, then the objection is not as flimsy and requires further investigation. I turn now to consider a number of reasons that have been advanced against legalizing assisted suicide and euthanasia.

Concerns about Legalizing Assisted Suicide and Voluntary Euthanasia

I have argued so far that assisted suicide and voluntary euthanasia are sometimes morally permissible. It is highly implausible to think that in *every* instance in which somebody's continued life is worse than death for him there is some stronger moral consideration not to help him end his life. However, when we think about law or public policy we need to think not of individual acts but of groups of acts. This is because the rules or laws must apply to sets of acts. Thus, for example, there may be some small set of individuals who could and would drive as safely at somewhat higher speeds as most people do at somewhat lower speeds. Yet, when determining the appropriate speed limit, the regulations must be concerned not with what would be a safe speed for some or other individual, but rather with what would be a safe speed for the great mass of drivers. Of course, when making laws we can pay attention to exceptional cases. For example, we can exempt ambulances, fire trucks and police vans from adhering to the speed limit when they are responding to an emergency. There is good reason to grant these exemptions and it is relatively easy to determine when such exemptions apply. Other kinds of exemptions would be much harder to grant. We cannot easily and reliably determine the optimum speed for each individual driver and then set a personal speed limit for each driver, thereby allowing more skilful drivers the right to drive faster. Thus the focus when judging what law would be morally appropriate is different from when judging the morality of individual actions.

A number of critics of assisted suicide and voluntary euthanasia have argued that even if these practices are sometimes morally permissible, legalizing them would be morally unacceptable. It is usually the case that those who think they would be illegal also think they are immoral and I suspect that the arguments that these practices ought to be illegal are actually often attempts to enforce a particular moral view. Nevertheless, because it is possible to think that a practice ought to be legally prohibited even if it is morally permissible, we should consider, on their merits, the arguments for making assisted suicide and voluntary euthanasia illegal.

The Slippery Slope Argument

Arguably the most common line of reasoning for this conclusion is a slippery slope argument. According to this argument, although a given act of assisted suicide or voluntary euthanasia may not be wrong in itself, legalizing such practices will lead to the performance of actions that are wrong. Therefore, the argument concludes, these practices should not be legalized.

A slippery slope of this kind is certainly a possibility and one to which one ought to be sensitive. However, because it is so much easier to assert rather than to demonstrate the existence of a slippery slope, we need to greet claims of its presence with a great deal of caution. If we are to evaluate the argument, we need to be clear about what precisely it is. The first problem in clarifying the argument, as it pertains to assisted suicide and voluntary euthanasia, is that there are many versions of it.

Versions of the argument differ both regarding the probability of the outcome and the seriousness of the outcome. In its most deterministic forms, the claim in the premise is that taking the first step, inevitably leads to the undesirable end.[9] On the less deterministic, but more unusual versions, a weaker claim is made – that the first step only *may* or (at most) probably will lead to the unacceptable actions. Regarding the seriousness of the outcome, the more extreme versions claim that the bottom of the slope is catastrophic, while more moderate versions claim only that it is bad (or very bad).

The worse the outcome and the greater its probability the stronger the reason we have to avoid stepping onto the 'slippery slope.' However, the worse and more inevitable the bad outcome is alleged to be the less plausible the claim is. The claim that legalizing assisted suicide and voluntary euthanasia will lead to mass murder, for example, is less plausible than the claim that it will lead only to some sporadic abuses. Similarly, the claim that one of these outcomes is an inevitable consequence of legalizing assisted suicide or voluntary euthanasia is less plausible than the claim that legalizing these practices merely *might* have such a result. In other words, the more likely the claim is true the less forceful it is, and the more forceful it is the less likely it is to be true.

There are some who have claimed that legalizing euthanasia leads to mass murder. Those who make this claim note that the Nazis started their killing with a euthanasia programme and ended with genocide. This, however, is very misleading. The Nazi's was a 'euthanasia' programme in name only. Such euphemisms were typical Nazi fare and the acts of euthanasia they carried out were in fact attempts to rid the Reich of people who were deemed unable to contribute to it. It is quite unsurprising then, that one mass killing programme should have led to another more ambitious one. Moreover, it is quite clear that those few jurisdictions where assisted suicide and voluntary euthanasia have been practised have not slipped into genocide.

This is probably why more thoughtful opponents of assisted suicide and voluntary euthanasia claim that legalizing these practices will lead to less drastic, but nonetheless bad consequences. These practices are legal in only a few jurisdictions. The most notable examples are Switzerland and the especially the Netherlands,[10] which are the two (modern) jurisdictions in which assisted suicide or euthanasia have been legal for the longest.[11] Has there been a slippery slope in such places?

9 A common distinction in the literature is between *logical* and *empirical* slippery slopes. I have primarily empirical slippery slopes in mind here, but a comparable point could be made about logical ones, where the claim is that accepting X logically entails Y.

10 For reviews of the Dutch practices see, for example: van der Maas, van der Wal, Haverkate, de Graaff, Kester, Onwuteaka-Philipsen et al. 1996; van der Wal, van der Maas, Bosma, Onwuteaka-Philipsen, Willems, Haverkate et al. 1996.

11 Other places where it is legal include Belgium and the state of Oregon. It was also briefly legal in Australia's Northern Territory. For further information on assisted suicide or voluntary euthanasia in these contexts see the following: Deliens, Mortier et al. 2000; Mortier, Deliens et al. 2000; Chin, Hedberg et al. 1999; Ganzini, Nelson et al. 2000;

Although there is some debate about the facts, what divides opponents and proponents of legalization are primarily differing *interpretations* of the facts, either because they have different definitions of 'euthanasia' or because they have different evaluations of what has happened. However, it is clear that the law has become more permissive. In the Netherlands, for example, it has become permissible under some circumstances to assist the suicide of people who are suffering from severe mental anguish even though they have no bodily illness. The Netherlands now also allows *non*-voluntary euthanasia – euthanasia of those who lack the competence to decide whether their lives are worth continuing.

Opponents of legalization take this to be evidence of a slippery slope. However, it is a slippery slope[12] only if what is now permitted should not be permitted. Yet many proponents of legalization think that it is entirely appropriate that Dutch law has liberalized in the way it has.

To understand this point more clearly, imagine a defender of Apartheid in the 1960s employing a slippery slope argument against eliminating some item of so-called 'petty' Apartheid, such as separate entrances to the post office. He might argue that if we permit people of different races to use the same entrance to the post office this will lead, by a series of steps, to complete racial integration. Opponents of Apartheid could agree that some initial liberalizing step would indeed make it more likely that 'white' racists will adapt and realize that some next step is not so bad and then, eventually, lead to the complete dismantling of Apartheid. Indeed, many advances – in the abolition of slavery, the improved status of women, the protection of animals – have involved gradual changes. The ultimate goal cannot be achieved all at once and thus one makes what progress one can in the hope that further progress will follow.

The above example is not intended to be tendentious. Whether it is a good analogy for the legal changes pertaining to euthanasia in the Netherlands depends on whether one thinks that the Netherlands has progressed or regressed with regard to euthanasia. But that is exactly my point. It is not sufficient for opponents of legalization to show that the law has become steadily more tolerant of euthanasia. They must also show that what is now permitted is morally undesirable.[13] Assuming that my earlier arguments are sound, they are unlikely to be able to make this case.

First, nothing in my defence of assisted suicide or voluntary euthanasia assumes that what can make one's continued life worse than death must be some physical condition. One premise of my argument is that the quality of one's life

---

Sullivan, Hedberg, and Fleming 2000; Ganzini, Harvath et al. 2002; Singer 1995; Kissane, Street, and Nitschke 1998.

12 I am reserving the term 'slippery slopes' to refer to dangerous declines. Although there can be slopes to better places, as I shall now show, that is not what opponents of assisted suicide and euthanasia mean when they caution that legalization will lead us down a slippery slope.

13 One must also show that the first step could not be taken without the later, undesirable steps (very likely) being taken.

can be so bad that continued life is not in one's interests. It is hard to see why only physical conditions could make one's life that bad. To suggest that it is only physical conditions is to underestimate just how bad mental anguish can be. Nor will it do to say that mental anguish is always irrational. Thus even where it can be cured chemically, that may come at a cost that a person reasonably deems to be unacceptable.[14] In this way, mental anguish is not relevantly different from physical pain, which I said, often can be controlled but only at a cost that the person concerned deems to be unacceptable.

Second, just as the continued life of a competent person can be worse than death, so can the life of an incompetent being be that bad. Many people recognize this in the case of animals, but it is equally true of incompetent humans (because they are liable to the same conditions). Nor is it any more plausible to suggest in the case of non-voluntary euthanasia than it is in the case of voluntary considerations, that countervailing considerations *always* outweigh the suffering being's interest in ceasing to exist. To be sure, non-voluntary euthanasia does raise issues that do not arise in the case of assisted suicide and voluntary euthanasia. Whereas decisions about the quality of a competent person's life can be left largely to that person, decisions about the quality of incompetent beings' lives have to be taken by others. Making such decisions for others is clearly very difficult but there is no alternative. Never terminating the life of an incompetent being, no matter how poor its quality, is also a decision – a decision to allow suffering to continue. The appropriate response to a difficult decision is to make it as well as possible rather than to pretend that it need not be made. I shall not say here how such decisions should be made as my focus is on assisted suicide and *voluntary* euthanasia. I have mentioned non-voluntary euthanasia only to note that many of us take it to be both a morally acceptable implication of the defence of voluntary euthanasia.

If opponents of legalizing assisted suicide and voluntary euthanasia are unable to show that legalizing these practices will eventually lead to the legalizing of other practices that should remain prohibited, they could offer a still more moderate version of the slippery slope argument. They could argue that permitting assisted suicide and voluntary euthanasia will lead to instances of abuse. This is a more moderate claim because instead of saying that more and more kinds of euthanasia will be legally permitted, it claims only that there will be some instances of abuse.

However, this argument is also problematic. First, as far as I know, nobody advancing it has even considered whether, let alone shown that, there are more instances of inappropriate euthanasia when euthanasia is legal than when it is illegal.[15] Yet that is exactly what one needs to show in order to demonstrate that

14 See Benatar (2010).

15 Opponents of euthanasia have noted that the incidence of euthanasia in the Netherlands, for example, has increased. However, this is to be expected in just the way that the number of people taking advantage of a new drug or surgical procedure is likely to increase as it becomes more familiar. In any event, what opponents of euthanasia need

legalizing euthanasia leads to (more) abuse (than not legalizing it). We know that there are instances of euthanasia even in jurisdictions where it is legally prohibited. Some of these instances are morally justified, but it is highly unlikely that all are. Yet when euthanasia is illegal the abuses may well be better hidden than when it is legal. This is because people are less likely to report performing euthanasia where it is illegal, and this in turn is either because they fear repercussions or because the illegality of the practice has led to a level of self-deception about what is and is not euthanasia.

However, even if we grant that there is more abuse if some instances of assisted suicide and voluntary active euthanasia are permitted, there is a second problem. Many things we do and should permit are abused. There probably is more abuse of cars and of *prescription* drugs than there would be if these were illegal, yet it would not be appropriate to prohibit the prescription drugs that so many people need. Even cars should not be prohibited because in the current context doing so would create considerable hardship and constitute an undue violation of people's freedom without comparable benefit. We can and should regulate these, which is why prescription drugs require a *prescription* and why cars require roadworthy certificates and licensing. There may also be scope for increasing restrictions to prevent abuse. However, it would be inappropriate to ban these and other things outright on the grounds that some people will abuse them. If we are to violate people's freedom we need to have very good reasons for doing so. The fact that some small number of other people will abuse the freedom because they are unwilling or unable to comply with clear regulations is not an adequate reason. This is especially so when the freedom is a very important one. The freedom to obtain medication for one's ailments is such a freedom. So is the freedom to end one's life when it becomes unbearable to continue. Those who think that *any* innocent deaths resulting from abuses of a freedom are sufficient to remove the freedom will have to prohibit automotive transport, building construction and many sports, to name but a few activities that result in the deaths of many innocents each year.

The 'Compromise of Voluntariness' Argument

I turn now to a second kind of argument that those opposed to legalizing assisted suicide and voluntary euthanasia may want to advance. They might argue that assisted suicide and 'voluntary' euthanasia ought to be illegal because the voluntariness of decisions to die will almost always, or at least very often, be dubious. This sort of argument does not deny that voluntary deaths are permissible. It denies only that voluntariness is a condition that can ordinarily be met in the sort of circumstances in which people consider euthanasia or assisted suicide. For that reason, it might be argued, these practices ought to be legally impermissible.

---

to show is not that the incidence of euthanasia is increasing but rather that the incidence of inappropriate euthanasia is increasing.

One version of such an argument claims that when people want to die on account of some terrible condition they have, the decision is very often not fully voluntary but is rather the result of clouded thinking induced by the pain, suffering or other negative features of the condition. According to this argument they are 'coerced' by their circumstances. Thus, even if there are some people who make the decision voluntarily, assisted suicide and voluntary euthanasia should not be legalized.

What this objection gets right is the obvious fact that the suffering leads to the decision to die. Were it not for their condition, these people would not want to die. But this does not entail that the voluntariness of the decision is routinely compromised. Although the person would not want to die in its absence, the suffering, far from being an impediment to a voluntary decision, could be a very rational basis for the decision. It is because of the unfortunate condition that continued life is no longer judged to be in the person's interests. This is not to deny that *some* people who want to die lack the capacity to make a truly voluntary choice. The same, of course, is true of some people who do *not* want to die. Instead, we cannot assume, because many people who are suffering want to die, that their decision to die is usually not truly voluntary. We must distinguish assessments of voluntariness or competence from the decision to die (or to live), and to recognize that a decision cannot be judged to be insufficiently voluntary just because it is a decision to die.

Another, more compelling, version of the 'compromise of voluntariness' argument suggests that although we might initially be able to distinguish voluntary from involuntary requests for euthanasia or assisted suicide, legalising these practices would lead to a situation in which they became commonplace. In such a society, it might be argued, an expectation might arise that people in certain circumstances will ask to die. People will internalize this expectation and then request euthanasia even if that is not their 'true' preference.

A helpful analogy to present this argument as charitably as possible is that of duelling. In a society in which duelling is an accepted practice, people are much more likely to challenge others to duels and those who are challenged are much more likely to accept the challenge. This is not accidental. Clearly the social acceptance of duelling plays an important role in the formation of people's preferences and choices regarding duelling. When those in duelling societies offer and accept duelling challenges, this is very likely attributable in large part to their social milieu. And even those who have not internalized the social expectations will nonetheless be aware of and liable to them. Failure to accept a duel in a duelling society leads to the sort of ostracism that people in those societies cannot ignore. The result is that whether somebody offers or accepts a duel depends in large part on whether he lives in a society that accepts duelling.

It might be argued that something similar would happen if we were to legalize assisted suicide and voluntary euthanasia. Once it became a legal option, more people would come to want it. And those who did not come to want it might feel pressure to request the ending of their lives if they became a burden on their families or other caregivers.

There is an important lesson to be learnt from this objection, but the objection itself fails to provide adequate reason for prohibiting assisted suicide and voluntary euthanasia. First, although it is true that many of our preferences are, to a significant extent, a product of our social context, it is far from clear that for this reason these preferences should not be respected.[16] If it were otherwise, then the implications would reach far beyond preferences for ending one's life in intolerable circumstances. Consider, for example, the preference religious people have to practise their particular religion. It is no coincidence that the overwhelming majority of such people were either reared in that religion or had connections to it. Their background plays a significant part in the formulation of their preference. If, for that reason, it need not be respected as the preference of an autonomous person, then we would be permitted to override people's religious preferences much more often than liberal principles actually permit. If those preferences, notwithstanding the influences that shape them, are deemed sufficiently voluntary, then the same should be said of preferences to die.

Second, it is not clear that the social acceptance of euthanasia does impose pressures analogous to that of a duel in a duel-accepting society. The legalization of assisted suicide and euthanasia allows those who want to make use of these options to do so, but it also allows those moral and religious groups or individuals who reject them to condemn them. In a society characterized by plural views on euthanasia, those not wanting to be part of such practices have moral space into which they can withdraw.[17] They are not like dishonoured duel decliners. The experience in those jurisdictions where assisted suicide or voluntary euthanasia is permitted bears this out. The proportion of people requesting active termination of their lives is small.[18]

---

16 I can imagine a species much more sophisticated than our own. The members of this species form preferences much more autonomously than we do. They are not as influenced by their context as we are. They have much greater capacity to imagine alternative scenarios and to consider them as real options. Ordinary humans would appear as mentally disabled to such a species. Perhaps in such a society, the preferences of ordinary humans would be less worthy of respect and more readily overridden by those much more advanced than us. However, we do not live amidst such beings and thus paternalistic overriding of our preferences by suitably more sophisticated beings is not possible.

17 Similar freedom is not accorded those who want assistance in ending their lives but find themselves in a society that prohibits euthanasia.

18 Although the opponents and proponents of euthanasia have very different readings of the figures, none of the estimates makes euthanasia even nearly so prevalent that it would be reasonable to think those preferring not to die would feel they were in even a large minority. Moreover, it is interesting that in the Netherlands only a minority of those who requested assistance in killing themselves were provided with that assistance. This, like other evidence from the Netherlands, bespeaks (although, of course, does not prove) a cautiousness that is incompatible with a societal perception that there is a duty for the old infirm to die.

Third, there is an important disanalogy between duelling and euthanasia. The costs of abandoning duelling are zero – at least in the long run, because alternative, more satisfactory ways of settling disputes become available. By contrast, the costs of prohibiting euthanasia are immense. Those who want such an end to their lives and are denied this option are condemned to endure lives they find unbearable and thus to suffer immense harm. Any concern about possible dangers of legalizing assisted suicide and voluntary euthanasia has to be balanced against the very serious and assured costs of prohibiting it.

Finally, none of the foregoing responses entail that we should be unconcerned about the possibility of people feeling pressured into requesting (assistance in) the termination of their lives. However, the appropriate response to those concerns, given the great costs of prohibiting assisted suicide and voluntary euthanasia, is to build robust safeguards into the legislation that legalizes these practices. Such legislation can protect not only against this pitfall, but also against others. No safeguard can be one hundred percent effective, but to expect perfect protection against error or abuse is to set the bar too high. We do not expect it in any other area and thus we should not expect it here.

Conclusion

I have argued that not only is a right to life compatible with assisted suicide and voluntary euthanasia, but that such a right, appropriately understood, actually entails the moral permissibility of these practices. I showed that there is no necessity to postulate a *distinct* right to die. The permissibility of obtaining assistance in one's suicide or of being euthanazed by willing others could be expressed in terms of a right to die, but such a right is entirely derivative from a right to life.

I have also argued that assisted suicide and voluntary euthanasia ought to be legally permissible. The interest in terminating one's own life when it is not worth continuing, as well as the interest in determining when one's own life is not worth continuing are very strong interests. They are at least as important as our interests in freedom of speech, religion, association and movement, for example. If these interests are to be overridden, there needs to be excellent reason for doing so. Although there may be some cases where there is sufficient reason, there are not good reasons for a blanket legal prohibition on assisted suicide and euthanasia.

Although I differentiated assisted suicide from euthanasia descriptively, my *normative* discussion has not distinguished between them. This is because they are morally very similar. However, there are reasons to prefer assisted suicide to voluntary euthanasia. First, it is arguably psychologically a little more difficult to take one's own life, even with assistance, than to have somebody do the deed on one's behalf. For this reason, requiring those who want their lives to end to perform the final act that ends their lives provides additional assurance that these people really want to die. It is an additional hurdle or safeguard. Second, taking somebody else's life, even when it is in that person's interests, may be a greater psychological burden than assisting somebody to kill himself. It is obviously preferable, all things being equal, if the suffering person can be helped without the imposition of the greater cost on the one who helps.

That said, the advantage of assisted suicide over voluntary euthanasia is a modest one, and there will be circumstances, such as advance motor neurone disease, where assisted suicide is not possible because the suffering person is unable to kill himself, even with assistance. In such circumstances, voluntary euthanasia is preferable to assisted suicide simply because suicide is not possible. Another reason why euthanasia is morally permissible and should be legally permitted is that it may actually prevent premature suicides. Some people elect to kill themselves earlier than they would prefer because they want to guarantee that they do not degenerate to the point that they can no longer kill themselves and there is nobody either to assist them or to terminate their lives for them. Providing people with the assurance that they can be assisted in killing themselves or euthanazed if they are unable to kill themselves even with assistance, will minimize the number of people who fear being forced to endure the unbearable and who therefore kill themselves before their lives have ceased to be worth continuing.

With the exception of expressing a preference for assisted suicide over voluntary euthanasia where the former is possible, I have not said anything about the precise circumstances in which these practices are morally permissible and in which they should be legal. This has been largely to focus discussion on the key area of dispute – whether these practices are *ever* morally permissible and should *ever* be legally permissible. I have argued for affirmative answers. Once that is granted, there can be discussion about how bad one's life needs to be in order for its termination (by self or others) to be morally or legally permissible. This is a topic for another occasion.[19]

References

Benatar, D. (2010), 'Suicide: A Qualified Defence', in J. Stacey Taylor (ed.) *The Ethics and Metaphysics of Death: New Essays* (New York: Oxford University Press.

—— (2005) 'Sexist language: alternatives to the alternatives', *Public Affairs Quarterly* 19(1), 1-9.

Chin, A.E., Hedberg, K., Higginson, G.K. and Fleming, D.W. (1999) 'Legalized physician-assisted suicide in Oregon – the first year's experience', *New England Journal of Medicine* 340(7), 577-583.

Deliens, L., Mortier, F. et al. (2000) 'End-of-life decisions in medical practice in Flanders, Belgium: a nationwide survey', *The Lancet* 356, 1806-1811.

19 See Benatar (2010).

Ganzini, L., Harvath, T.A. et al. (2002) 'Experience of Oregon nurses and social workers with hospice patients who requested assistance with suicide', *New England Journal of Medicine* 347(8), 582-588.

Ganzini, L., Nelson, H., Schmidt, T.A., Kraemer, D.F., Delroit, M.A. and Lee, M.A. (2000) 'Physicians' experiences with the Oregon Death with Dignity Act', *New England Journal of Medicine* 342(8), 557-563.

Hohfeld, W.N. (1919) *Fundamental Legal Conceptions as Applied in Judicial Reasoning* (New Haven: Yale University Press).

Keown, J. (2002) *Euthanasia, Ethics and Public Policy: An Argument Against Legalisation* (Cambridge: Cambridge University Press).

Kissane, D.W., Street, A. and Nitschke, P. (1998) 'Seven deaths in Darwin: case studies under the Rights of the Terminally Ill Act', Northern Territory, Australia. *The Lancet* 352, 1097-1102.

Mortier, F., Deliens, L. et al. (2000) 'End-of-life decisions of physicians in the city of Hasselt (Flanders, Belgium)', *Bioethics* 14(3), 254-267.

Singer, P. (1995) 'The legalisation of voluntary euthanasia in the Northern Territory'. *Bioethics*, 9(5), 419-436.

Sullivan, A.D., Hedberg, K. and Fleming, D.W. (2000) 'Legalized physician-assisted suicide in Oregon – the second year', *New England Journal of Medicine* 342(8), 598-604.

Van der Maas, P.J., van der Wal, G., Haverkate, I., de Graaff, C.L.M., Kester, J.G.C., Onwuteaka-Philipsen, B.D. et al. (1996) 'Euthanasia, physician-assisted suicide, and other medical practices involving the end of life in the Netherlands, 1990-1995', *New England Journal of Medicine* 335, 1699-1705.

Van der Wal, G., van der Maas, P.J., Bosma, J.M., Onwuteaka-Philipsen, B.D., Willems, D.L., Haverkate, I. et al. (1996) 'Evaluation of the notification procedure for physician-assisted death in the Netherlands', *New England Journal of Medicine* 335, 1706-11.

Chapter 13
Positive and Negative Obligations under the Right to Life in English Medical Law: Letting Patients Die

Elizabeth Wicks

The right to life is a fundamental human right, protected, *inter alia*, in article 2 European Convention on Human Rights (ECHR) and in English domestic law through Sections 3, 4 and 6 of the Human Rights Act 1998. How is this right implemented within the context of healthcare when countless patients die every day? Is the right infringed by a medical decision to withdraw life-sustaining treatment, or by a decision to ease a patient to an early death as an act of mercy? What about the common practice of termination of pregnancy, or the rare practice of separating conjoined twins? Does a patient's refusal of life-sustaining medical treatment engage the right? And how do any of these decisions fare in a modern world in which funding for medical treatment is limited? This chapter will consider these issues against a backdrop of the two relevant obligations (one negative; one positive) imposed by the right to life.

Negative Obligation: No one Shall be Deprived of his Life Intentionally

The General Obligation

Article 2 ECHR protects the right to life and at its core is a prohibition of the intentional deprivation of life. This is not an absolute prohibition, and the second paragraph of the article identifies some sweeping exceptions in the context of the prevention of crime, but in other contexts, including healthcare, the prohibition on intentionally depriving a person of their life is absolute. The importance of the right to life within the terms of the Convention was made very clear in *McCann v United Kingdom*[1] when the Court confirmed that article 2 is 'one of the most fundamental provisions in the Convention' and that 'its provisions must be strictly construed.'[2] The core obligation in article 2, the prohibition of the intentional deprivation of life, most obviously has application where an agent of the state uses

1 *McCann v. United Kingdom* [1995] Series A, No. 324; 21 E.H.R.R. 97.

2 Ibid., para. 147.

lethal force against an individual. The bulk of the Convention caselaw under article 2 has been focused upon these extreme situations. However, article 2's prohibition of the intentional deprivation of life extends much further than a requirement that police officers or members of the armed forces use lethal force in a proportionate manner. It also requires that there be a more general prohibition on the taking of human life. Thus an important aspect of the article 2 obligation upon states will be the need for domestic legal systems to impose criminal sanctions upon the deprivation of human life. This will require an effective policing system to seek to prevent the criminal deprivation of life, a legal prohibition on criminal activities resulting in the deprivation of life, and sufficient punishment of those individuals convicted of such offences, whether they are agents of the state or not.

In England and Wales, the criminal prohibition on the taking of life focuses upon the two offences of murder and manslaughter. Murder is any act that causes the death of another where the intention is to kill or cause grievous bodily harm, and it carries a mandatory sentence of life imprisonment. Manslaughter covers a disparate range of killings, including where death results from an unlawful and dangerous act of the defendant, or where the defendant was subjectively reckless as to death or grievous bodily harm or grossly negligent as to death. (There are also specific offences such as infanticide and causing death by dangerous driving that are designed to apply to the taking of life in specific circumstances.) There has been some dissatisfaction in recent years with this traditional system, due both to the breadth of the range of activities encompassed by the offence of manslaughter, and the false equality implied by a mandatory life sentence for all intentional killings (see, for example, the Law Commission for England and Wales 2006). The latter issue is one of particular concern in the medical law context because it can operate harshly against a so-called mercy killer. If a doctor (or a relative) causes the death of a terminally ill patient in order to end that patient's suffering, he or she will face a charge of murder and a punishment, if convicted, of life imprisonment. While there are a variety of defences available, including general defences such as insanity, and specific 'partial defences' to murder which reduce the prohibited behaviour to manslaughter (such as provocation, diminished responsibility and a half-completed suicide pact), these will have limited applicability to a mercy-killing, especially if performed by a medical professional rather than grief-stricken relatives who may be able to avail themselves of the partial defence of diminished responsibility. In addition to the criminal prohibition of killing, English law prohibits assisting a suicide in Section 2(1) Suicide Act 1961. The criminal prohibitions on taking human life in English law are, of course, backed up by a policing and criminal justice system, as well as by the civil law which further regulates the taking of life in the context of negligent deaths or the award of compensation to the deceased's relatives. English law seems unambiguous, therefore, in protecting the right to life's prohibition of intentional deprivation of life, including in the medical context.

However, the apparent strictness of English law in prohibiting all forms of causing or assisting death is undermined (or mitigated, depending upon one's viewpoint) in the medical context by prosecuting and sentencing discretion, as well as by generally sympathetic juries. For example, in *R v Cox*,[3] a doctor was charged with attempted murder after injecting an elderly patient suffering from rheumatoid arthritis with potassium chloride (which was potentially fatal and had no pain-relieving functions) after the patient expressed a wish to die. The charge was one of attempt even though the patient had died, because the body had been cremated before suspicion arose and cause of death was impossible to determine. This introduced sentencing discretion because it avoids the mandatory life sentence for murder and provides the judge with a variety of other sentencing options. On trial for attempted murder, the doctor was found guilty but was not imprisoned, with the judge instead exercising leniency to give him only a 12 month suspended sentence. Dr Cox's profession was even more lenient and the General Medical Council did not strike him off the medical register. Dr Cox was, therefore, able to continue to practice medicine despite being convicted of attempting to murder one of his patients. As I have argued elsewhere, this result sends a mixed message concerning the taking of human life in this context, '[t]he mixed messages sent by the *Cox* case reflects the general uncertainty of society, divided on whether assisting a patient to die in order to relieve his or her suffering is heroic or criminal. At present the message seems to be that it is both' (Wicks 2007, 255).

In addition to the sentencing discretion apparent in the *Cox* case, there are other means by which a doctor who kills his patient might be treated sympathetically by the criminal justice system. The famous case of *R v Adams*[4] reveals two such means. Dr Adams had given an incurably, but not terminally, ill patient increasing doses of opiates leading to her death. He was charged with murder but acquitted, even though he benefited substantially from the patient's will and had lied on the death certificate. One factor contributing to his acquittal is the fact that juries tend to be sympathetic to doctors accused of killing their patients. Very few doctors have been convicted of murder. Infamous exceptions such as Harold Shipman show how extreme a case must be before a jury will convict. Furthermore, the development and application of a doctrine of double effect has provided juries with the framework needed in order to excuse a doctor of criminal liability for causing the death of a patient when he acts with good intentions. In *Adams*, the judge, Devlin J, confirmed that a doctor 'is entitled to relieve pain and suffering even if the measures he takes may incidentally shorten life.' This has subsequently been approved by the House of Lords in *Airedale NHS Trust v Bland*.[5] The doctrine of double effect has been the subject of much academic criticism because it enables two doctors who prescribe equally lethal pills to a patient to be treated in two entirely different ways depending upon the pill prescribed. If the pills have a pain-relieving function, as in *Adams*, a doctor may avail himself of the doctrine of double effect even if he prescribes a lethal dose. However, if the pills do not have

3 *R v. Cox* (1992) 12 BMLR 38.

4 *R v. Adams* [1957] Crim L.R. 365.

5 *Airedale NHS Trust v. Bland* [1993] AC 789.

any pain-relieving functions, as in *Cox*, the doctor has no available defence. Thus, the doctrine of double effect has been described as 'a curtain behind which judges can allow moral judgements to influence the conclusion as to the physician's legal culpability' (Ost 2005, 358). The acquittal of Dr Adams and the conviction of Dr Cox, in respect of very similar acts, are not conducive to transparent and consistent law in this area and raise some doubts about English law's implementation of the requirements of the right to life.

So far we have seen that English law prohibits all forms of positive assistance in causing death, except where death results from the provision of pain-relieving pills prescribed primarily to relieve pain (and subject to some reservations about the enforcement of the law against the medical profession). There are, however, a couple of possible exceptions to this general prohibition. One concerns the widespread killing of foetuses, especially at the latter stages of pregnancy when, arguably, they enjoy protection of the right to life. First, however, we will look at the most blatant exception to the prohibition on doctors causing death by a positive act: the authorisation of the separation operation in the conjoined twins' case.

Killing Mary: The Conflicting Rights Exception

Re A (children) (conjoined twins: surgical separation)[6] presented a very difficult dilemma to the British courts. The twins, named Jodie and Mary by the court, had been born conjoined. Mary was the weaker twin, with a poorly developed brain, an abnormal heart and scarcely any functional lung tissue. The only reason she survived after birth was because her sister Jodie's heart was pumping blood through both of their bodies. Unfortunately, the extra effort required for this task by Jodie's heart would soon lead to Jodie suffering heart failure. When this happened, within an estimated three to six months, both twins would die. An operation to separate the twins would save Jodie's life, but would simultaneously and inevitably cause Mary's death. The question facing the Court of Appeal judges in this case was whether they could, and should, authorise the separation operation, knowing that to do so would be to authorise the killing of Mary. A further question that is of direct concern to us is whether to do so would violate the right to life's prohibition of intentional deprivation of life.

Ward LJ undertook a balancing exercise between the rights and interests of each twin. He began by putting both girls' right to life into a set of scales, while acknowledging that '[t]he universality of the right to life demands that the *right* to life be treated as equal. The intrinsic value of their human life is equal. So the right of each goes into the scales and the scales remain in balance.'[7] It is important to note here that the judge is particularly emphasising that the right to life of each twin is equal, not that the life of each twin is equal, and is thereby

6 *Re A (children)(conjoined twins: surgical separation)* [2000] 4 All E.R. 961.

7 Ibid., 1010.

leaving some scope for the development of an argument that the lives of each twin may not deserve equal protection. The development of this argument began with a recognition that, when deciding on the best interests of each twin, 'it is legitimate to have regard to the actual condition of each twin' and 'to bear in mind the actual quality of life each child enjoys and may be able to enjoy.'[8] Immediately, therefore, we can see that, despite declaring that the rights to life of Jodie and Mary are equal, it is regarded as legitimate by Ward LJ to take into account their respective physical conditions and quality of life, which inevitably means that Jodie is placed at an advantage over Mary. This advantage is then compounded by the taking into account of issues of life expectancy. While Jodie has good prospects for a relatively normal life after the separation, Mary's death within a few months is inevitable. Mary was, therefore, described as 'designated for death.'[9] Such a concept presents significant difficulties in the context of the right to life. First, it assumes that we can be certain about the timing and circumstances of a future death, whereas in reality there is often a crucial lack of certainty about such issues. Secondly, there are ethical difficulties in a determination that a life that is soon to end is of less value than one which will continue. Often the last days and hours of a person's life may be the most valuable of all, while in a case such as Mary her impending death is a defining feature of her life. It should not be used as a reason for negating the inherent value of that life. Finally, and most fundamentally, we are all designated for death from the moment we are born. In order for such a factor to have legal relevance, a line would have to be drawn to distinguish the cases in which our designation for death becomes a relevant factor from those in which it is not, and any such line will be no more than arbitrary. For example, is a designation for death relevant if an individual has only one day to live, or one month, or one year? The designated for death argument must be rejected as a means of reducing the protection afforded by the right to life. We are all designated for death and the imminence of an expected death is not a sufficient reason for abandoning legal and ethical protection for that life

Even though the designated for death argument cannot be regarded as reducing Mary's protection under the right to life, it may be possible to identify a slightly different argument that may help us to decide whether the doctors should be authorised to kill Mary in order to save Jodie. This is the argument that the existing threat of the twins' conjoined nature will inevitably kill at least one person and therefore the doctors may be justified in intervening in order to deflect that threat from both Jodie and Mary towards Mary alone. This would ensure a net gain in human life: one death rather than two. This does not mean that Mary loses her right to life but rather that a conflict of rights to life may be resolved in a manner that ensures a net gain in human life. It is vital in this context to regard the twins' conjoined nature as an existing threat which threatens both twins. Regrettably, Ward LJ implied a rather different situation when he emotively

8 Ibid.

9 Ibid.

described Mary as posing a threat to her sister, 'Mary may have a right to life, but she has little right to be alive. She is alive because and only because, to put it bluntly, but none the less accurately, she sucks the lifeblood of Jodie and she sucks the lifeblood out of Jodie.'[10] The implication here seems to be that Mary is not entitled to a full right to life because she is a threat (albeit an innocent threat) to Jodie and therefore has forfeited her right to life. The judgments in *Re A* certainly imply a moral distinction between Mary and Jodie that enables them to deny practical effect to Mary's right to life. David Gurnham (2003) argues that, by relying upon metaphors of threat, the judges distinguish Mary's moral position from that of Jodie. They are not treated as two individuals born into a dire situation, but rather as one individual threatening the life of another. While the judges do not explicitly deny Mary a right to life in a theoretical sense, as Gurnham argues 'through their rhetoric of aggression, threat and dependence, they make it clear that she is beyond the right's practical limit' (Gurnham 2003, 30). Ward LJ, for example, describes Mary's 'parasitic living' and claims that, if Jodie could speak, she would say, '[s]top it, Mary, you're killing me.'[11] Ward LJ says that Mary would have no answer to that, but it is entirely likely that Mary would respond by saying, 'stop what? I'm not doing anything.' This implication that Mary is threatening her sister is regrettable. Both twins were born into the unfortunate situation in which they had now found themselves; Mary had not attached herself to Jodie and she was not 'sucking the lifeblood' out of her. Rather, both twins were attached to each other and both were threatened by that attachment.

The Court of Appeal's reasoning for favouring Jodie's right to life over Mary's is fundamentally flawed. Mary should not be excluded from the practical effect of her right to life, to which the Court unanimously agrees she is entitled. Similarly, any attempt to sidestep the consequences of killing Mary should be avoided: state interference, by means of an operation to separate the twins, will prima facie be a violation of Mary's right to life. However, where an existing threat to life is merely diverted so as to achieve a net gain in human life it is arguable that the state does not violate the right to life by so acting, provided that this can be achieved without violating the rights of the person who is to die, particularly by treating her as a mere object or means to an end (as, for example, by killing a potential organ donor in order to save other lives). In the case of the conjoined twins, a tragic choice between lives had to be made and it was clear that both twins would soon die without an intervention; reasonably certain that Jodie could be saved by such an intervention; and possible to divert the lethal threat posed by the twins' conjoined nature from its current burden upon Jodie's heart to a new burden of lack of blood for Mary. In these circumstances, this was the best solution in terms of the right to life, for it saved Jodie's life.

10 Ibid.

11 Ibid.

Killing the Unborn: The Foetal Right to Life Exception

The conjoined twins case of *Re A* was unique in explicitly authorising the causation of death by a medical professional. There is another group of patients, however, whose deaths are caused with apparent impunity: the unborn. Given that the right to life prohibits the intentional deprivation of life, and given that this is exactly what a termination of pregnancy entails, this section will seek to address two questions. First, it will be necessary to determine whether a foetus enjoys the protection of the right to life. Secondly, and a question too often overlooked, it is then essential to investigate the requirements of the right to life in the context of a foetus residing within another human being's body.

The fundamental question of when life begins has no easy answer, even within the limited context of the right to life. In legal terms, neither English law nor the ECHR is unambiguous on when the right to life begins. While there is English case law establishing that a foetus has no legal rights until birth, there is also extensive judicial and statutory protection for the foetus, including by means of the offence of procuring a miscarriage and the restrictive defences to that in the abortion context. At the European level, *Vo v France*[12] was the latest in a long line of cases where the crucial issue of whether the right to life extends to a foetus has been sidestepped by the Strasbourg institutions. Ethically the question is no less challenging, but it will be argued here that a viable foetus does indeed enjoy the protection of the right to life. There is nothing inherent within the right to life, as defined in article 2 or elsewhere, that excludes a foetus. However, pre-viability the foetus arguably lacks the basic integrative function as a living organism that, by analogy with the end of life, we may regard as crucial. (This argument is developed more fully in my forthcoming book *The Right to Life and Conflicting Interests*.) The right to life ceases to provide protection at the stage at which a human being dies. The definition of death, again a legally and ethically complex issue, focuses on hypoxia: a lack of oxygen to the cells of the body resulting in their gradual death. Because the cells of the body die at different rates, and complete death of them all may take a considerable time, it is not appropriate to wait for the death of every cell in the body before declaring that the human being has died. Rather, it is the death of the living organism as a whole that is crucial and that depends upon integrative action between the organs of the body. It is the life of the organism which matters, not its living component parts, and thus it is the permanent destruction of that integrative organism which signifies the end of the organism's life. The crucial factor at the end of life tends to be the fact that integrative action between the organs of the body is governed by the brain and so once the brain is dead, the whole organism can be regarded as dead also. But it is important when considering the beginning of life to note that integrative action between the organs of the body also requires sufficiently developed lungs to supply oxygen to the major organs. And this will only begin to occur at the stage

12 *Vo v. France* (2005) 10 E.H.R.R. 12.

of viability. Indeed, the main factor that determines whether a foetus is viable or not is whether the lungs are sufficiently developed so as to enable the baby to breathe (with mechanical assistance, if necessary), as was demonstrated by the case of *C v S*.[13] At present, in developed countries where neonatal intensive care is available, viability stands at about 22 weeks. Even after this stage, the chances of long term survival are slim but, with medical assistance, the baby's body has the potential to function effectively. Until the lungs are sufficiently developed to enable the supply of oxygen to the other organs (with assistance if necessary), the body cannot be regarded as capable of functioning as an integrated organism. Before viability, therefore, the foetus cannot benefit from the protection of the right to life. This does not mean that a pre-viability foetus should not have some degree of legal and ethical protection. Ronald Dworkin (1994) produces one potential, if controversial, argument for this when he draws a distinction between derivative and detached objections to abortion. From viability onwards, however, there is no obvious reason to exclude the foetus from the protection afforded to all other living human organisms.

If we accept, for the purposes of this chapter, that a viable foetus has a right to life, how do we then resolve the issue of a conflict with the rights of the mother? Is the English law's approach to this conflict, in which access to abortion is restricted by the law and yet some viable foetuses are killed as the result of an abortion, justifiable? The key to this issue is not the resolution of a conflict of rights but rather a definition of the boundaries of a right to life. While the right not to be killed is at the core of the right to life, it does not encompass a right to demand every assistance necessary in order to remain alive. In line with the positive obligations inherent in the right to life, discussed below, the state will have a duty to take reasonable steps to preserve the lives of those in its jurisdiction, including viable foetuses, but does this include compelling a pregnant woman to continue her pregnancy when to so do involves a violation of that person's bodily integrity? Judith Thomson's famous violinist example illustrates the reasonable boundaries of a right to life (Thomson 1971). She described a hypothetical case of a woman who awakes to find that a world-class violinist has been attached to her kidneys in order to preserve his life. Most people admit that there would be no obligation upon the woman to permit the violinist to stay attached to her, even on a temporary basis, despite the violinist having an equal right to life. There is no question of choosing to favour the woman's right to life over that of the violinist; instead the focus is upon what is required by the right to life. Thomson argues that it does not include a right to all assistance necessary in order to preserve life if otherwise there would be no right to such a thing. So, as there is not generally a right to use another person's kidneys, this right does not suddenly appear merely because it is necessary in order to preserve the violinist's life. The same principle can be applied to pregnancy: there is not generally a right to use another's body for sustenance and thus no reason why the foetus should acquire such a right merely

13 *C v. S* [1987] 1 All E.R. 1230.

because it is necessary for its survival. In Thomson's words, 'having a right to life does not guarantee having either a right to be given the use of or a right to be allowed continued use of another person's body – even if one needs it for life itself' (Thomson 1971). This approach suggests that the legality of abortion, even of a viable foetus, does not necessarily amount to an infringement of the foetus' right to life.

This is a controversial conclusion, however, and many commentators have sought to distinguish pregnancy from the violinist example by means of what is usually referred to as the responsibility objection to Thomson's argument. This is the argument that 'ordinary, non-rape, pregnancies are crucially disanalagous' to the violinist example because the pregnant woman must take some responsibility for the joining of her body with that of the foetus (Silverstein 1987, 104). In all cases of pregnancy, other than those resulting from rape, the pregnant woman partook of voluntary behaviour which she knew, or should have known, held a risk of resulting in pregnancy. It is argued, therefore, that the woman has acquired some degree of responsibility for ensuring the survival of the foetus, given that it is (at least partly) her actions that have resulted in its current situation. There are problems with the responsibility argument, however. For example, it distinguishes pregnancies resulting from rape from all other pregnancies and yet from the perspective of the foetus – and it is the foetus' right to life that is in issue here – whether it came into existence from rape should have no impact on its rights. It makes no sense to assert that viable foetuses have a right not to be killed, except if their conception arose from rape, as the entity is the same and should bear no responsibility for the acts of its father. Further difficulties with the responsibility objection include the difficulty in holding a pregnant woman responsible, not only for the fact that the foetus exists but also, crucially, for the fact that, given that it exists, it needs the use of her body. As Silverstein points out, there is no alternative for the woman that would have avoided that outcome: the foetus could not both exist and not need her body (Silverstein 1987, 108). Nothing the woman has done, or can bear responsibility for, has caused this reliance upon her body.

For a number of reasons, the responsibility objection to Thomson's argument appears to be flawed. It fails to convincingly counter the argument that a foetal right to life, as with the post-birth right to life, does not entail a right to all assistance necessary to preserve life. A foetal right to life does not, therefore, entail a right to remain within, and using, its mother's body. What exactly does this mean? It does not give the foetus' mother, or anyone else, the right to kill it. While there may be no obligation on the pregnant woman to permit the foetus to continue to use her body to preserve its life, all that she can do is to ask for the foetus to be removed (as the woman in Thomson's example is entitled to ask for the violinist to be removed). From the state's perspective, therefore, it is not an infringement of the right to life if the law permits the abortion of a viable foetus. On the basis of the argument above, that the foetus only acquires a right to life once it is viable, then the woman's desire to terminate the pregnancy may not result in the death of the foetus. This raises the key distinction between killing and letting die, as applicable to the viable foetus as it is to the living patient. Once viable, the foetus has a right to life and must not be killed but its mother is not obligated to continue the pregnancy until full term. In practice, this means that after viability only so-called extractive abortions, during which the foetus is removed from the woman while alive and intact, can be regarded as consistent with the foetus' right to life. In many requested terminations after viability, the woman will wish the child to survive. The pregnancy may need to be terminated prematurely for the woman's health or life and a healthy child remains the desired outcome. Sections 1(1)(b) and (c) of the Abortion Act 1967 (as amended by the Human Fertilisation and Embryology Act 1990) present no ethical difficulties in this regard. However, late abortions under Section 1(1)(d) will be more problematic. If a foetal abnormality is discovered after viability, and with many abnormalities this is inevitable, the abortion will take place at a stage where the foetus has a right to life and should not, under the argument developed here, be killed. In some such cases, the foetus may not survive after being extracted from the woman, even though it is past the stage of viability, because of the severity of its abnormalities. But what if the foetus can survive and the mother wishes it not to do so? In this situation, the viable foetus should not be killed at the request of its mother (although it is conceivable that it may be in the foetus' own interests to die and this possibility raises quality of life considerations, discussed below). What is crucial is that a viable foetus, even though it has a right not to be killed, cannot depend upon a continued violation of another person's bodily integrity. The right to life never guarantees to anyone that their life will be preserved.

Positive Obligations: Doing all that is Reasonably Expected in Order to Preserve Life

The General Positive Obligation

Under article 2 ECHR, the right to life extends far beyond a negative duty on the state not to kill. It encompasses both a requirement to establish effective investigations into deaths (which is not of relevance to this discussion) and a positive obligation to preserve human life. First hinted at in *L.C.B. v United Kingdom*,[14] it was the case of *Osman v United Kingdom*[15] in which the extent of the obligation became clear. In the context of a failure on the part of the police to prevent a death, the Court held that article 2(1) 'enjoins the state not only to refrain from the intentional and unlawful taking of life, but also to take appropriate steps to safeguard the lives of those within its jurisdiction.'[16] This duty was said to require effective criminal law provisions, backed up by law-enforcement machinery, and the obligation

14 *L.C.B. v. United Kingdom* (1998) 27 E.H.R.R. 212; Reps 1998-III.

15 *Osman v. United Kingdom* (1998) 29 E.H.R.R. 245; Reps 1998-III.

16 Ibid., para. 115.

may even require preventive operational measures to protect an individual whose life is at risk from the criminal acts of another individual. Of wider significance, the Court established an important principle that state authorities must do all that could reasonably be expected of them to avoid a real and immediate risk to life of which they have or ought to have knowledge.[17] However, the positive obligation identified in *Osman* was subjected to extensive limitations. First, the Court emphasised that any such obligation must be interpreted in a way which does not impose an impossible or disproportionate burden on the authorities. This limitation was imposed by the Court due to the 'difficulties involved in policing modern societies, the unpredictability of human conduct and the operational choices which must be made in terms of priorities and resources.'[18] Significantly, the Court also held that the positive obligation on the police to safeguard lives is subject to the requirements of due process. This included the requirements implied within the Convention by the right to liberty (article 5) and the right to respect for private life (article 8). Thus the Court recognised that the positive aspect of the right to life must be balanced with both competing public interests, such as public resources, and also with conflicting Convention rights, including autonomy. Both factors will be very relevant to the question of letting patients die.

Since *Osman*, the positive obligation inherent in article 2 has been applied in a variety of contexts, including safeguarding the public from the possibility of a lethal explosion at a hazardous waste site,[19] the lack of an effective criminal law regime in a region of the state,[20] and obligations placed upon prison authorities to safeguard the lives of detainees.[21] It is in the latter context in which it was first confirmed that the positive obligation to preserve life includes the provision of timely and adequate medical care.[22] In *Cyprus v Turkey*,[23] the Court observed that 'an issue may arise under Article 2 of the Convention where it is shown that the authorities of a contracting state put an individual's life at risk through the denial of health care which they have undertaken to make available to the population generally.' In this case, the Court left open the question of whether article 2 'may impose an obligation on a contracting state to make available a certain standard of health care.'[24] That question remains open but in *Calvelli & Cigliou v Italy*[25] it was confirmed that article 2 requires regulations compelling hospitals in the public health sphere to adopt appropriate measures to protect patients' lives (although

17 Ibid., para. 116.
18 Ibid., para. 116.
19 See, *Öneryildiz v Turkey* (2005) 41 E.H.R.R. 20.
20 See, *Mahmut Kaya v Turkey*, [2000] ECHR 129.
21 See, *Paul and Audrey Edwards v United Kingdom* (2002) 35 E.H.R.R. 19.
22 See, *Augvelova v Bulgaria* (Judgment of 13 June 2002).
23 See, *Cyprus v. Turkey*, ECHR 2001-IV.
24 Ibid., para. 219.
25 *Calvelli & Cigliou v Italy*, ECHR 2002-I.

a death caused by medical negligence will not necessarily require a criminal conviction).

The right to life thus imposes a duty upon the state to do all that can be reasonably expected of it to preserve life when there is a known risk to life that is real and immediate. This duty is mirrored within English law by the significant exception to the general act/omission distinction that in general relieves us of any obligation to be a good Samaritan. The exception, of course, is the duty of care owed to patients by their doctors and other medical professionals. This duty ensures that there is an obligation to act in the best interests of the patient and failure to do so may result in legal liability if harm to the patient is caused as a result. There is, however, a clear mismatch here. While the obligation on the state under the right to life is to take reasonable steps to preserve life, the legal obligation upon doctors under English medical law is to treat a patient in his or her best interests, a duty backed up (or perhaps undermined) by criminal prohibitions on actively causing death. What happens if preserving life and acting in the patient's best interests are not compatible? Is there sufficient flexibility in the 'reasonable' restriction to the positive obligation under the right to life to justify a decision to allow a patient to die (in circumstances where life could be preserved, at least for a time)?

Withdrawal of Life-Sustaining Treatment: The Quality of Life Exception

In English medical law, the withdrawal of life-sustaining medical treatment is a relatively common occurrence and case law at the highest level has confirmed the legality of this. The withdrawal of medical treatment that is essential for the continuation of life undoubtedly raises issues under the right to life. We have just seen that a state is obligated to take reasonable steps in order to preserve the life of those within its jurisdiction. What life-saving measures will be reasonable will depend on all the circumstances and, as discussed above, both the public interest and the rights of the individual will be relevant considerations. Extensive and intrusive life-saving measures may not always be reasonable. The cases that often present most difficulty, however, are those where the life-sustaining assistance needed is something as simple as the provision of hydration and nutrition. In *Airedale NHS Trust v Bland,* the House of Lords authorised the withdrawal of artificial hydration and nutrition from a patient diagnosed with PVS because the continued provision of such treatment was held to be no longer in the patient's best interests. The legacy of this landmark case continues to reverberate many years later. Although the judges were careful to avoid expressly holding that death may be in a patient's best interests, this appears to be the regrettable implication. Lord Goff explained that 'the question is not whether it is in the best interests of the patient that he should die. The question is whether it is in the best interests of the patient that his life should be prolonged by the continuance of this form of medical treatment or care.'[26] As nobody can live for long without food and water,

26 *Bland*, 869.

a finding that this treatment was no longer in the patient's best interests inevitably meant that death would be, by implication, the preferred solution. To complicate the issue further, some of the judges considering Bland's situation instinctively felt that he no longer had any interests of any kind. Lord Keith explained the difficulty of ascribing any interests to Anthony Bland:

> [i]n the case of a permanently insensate being, who if continuing to live would never experience the slightest actual discomfort, it is difficult, if not impossible, to make any relevant comparison between continued existence and the absence of it. It is, however, perhaps permissible to say that to an individual with no cognitive capacity whatever, and no prospect of ever recovering any such capacity in this world, it must be a matter of complete indifference whether he lives or dies.[27]

When Lord Mustill concluded that Bland had 'no interests of any kind,'[28] including in being kept alive, he overlooked the personal interests inherent in the right to life. There are two (perhaps related) explanations for ignoring Bland's right to life. First, many commentators regard rights as attaching only to persons rather than to all human beings. If Bland is not a person, due to his lack of mental capacity, or self-awareness, for example, then he would not benefit from the protection of the right to life (Singer 1995). Whatever the merits and demerits of the personhood argument in general, it is flawed in the context of human rights law. The essence of a human right is that it applies to all humans, equally. While that may be aspirational in many parts of the world, and even in England at times, it represents the cornerstone of the body of law. No living human being will be excluded *ex officio* from the protection of human rights law. This brings us to the second explanation for Bland's exclusion from the right to life: that he is not, despite appearances, a living human being. There are some hints in the court judgments that this patient was not regarded as truly alive and could thus be regarded as bereft of interests. For example, Bland was described as existing in 'a twilight world'[29] and in a 'living death.'[30] Hoffmann LJ in the Court of Appeal also stated that 'the very concept of having a life has no meaning in relation to Anthony Bland. He is alive but has no life at all.'[31] If Bland had no life, how could he be protected by a right to life? This approach is also fatally flawed, however. In law (and, many would say, in morality as well) Bland was alive. (For an opposing view, see McMahan 1998 and Lizza 2006.) Because Bland was alive, he had a variety of interests, some of which may have conflicted with each other. He had interests, for example, in not being abused or assaulted or left in unsanitary conditions. If Bland were dumped

27 Ibid., 860-861.
28 Ibid., 894.
29 Ibid., 842, per Butler-Sloss LJ.
30 Ibid., 865, per Lord Goff.
31 Ibid., 853.

on the pavement outside the hospital, would that not be against his interests? It seems clear that, from a human rights perspective, Anthony Bland retained both interests and rights in how he was treated and that his loss of both competence and consciousness did not detract from this. Furthermore, the interests that Bland retained were potentially conflicting interests which should have been unpicked and balanced by the court. This was especially important because of the extremely vulnerable position in which he found himself, in which there was no possibility of him being able to defend his own rights or interests. The message from the *Bland* judgments that a PVS patient has no interest in being alive or in dying; in being subjected to futile treatment or in being deprived of food and water, is both legally and ethically objectionable. The duties owed to Anthony Bland by the state under his right to life were not properly assessed.

Subsequent cases have assumed the difficult task of attempting to reconcile the *Bland* case with the obligations under a right to life. In *NHS Trust A v M; NHS Trust B v H*,[32] involving two patients diagnosed as in a PVS condition, Dame Butler-Sloss considered in some detail whether article 2 ECHR was consistent with the withdrawal of artificial nutrition and hydration (ANH) from a patient in PVS, but arguably failed to achieve more than a superficial analysis of the demands of the right to life in this context. When considering the positive obligation to preserve life under article 2, Dame Butler-Sloss held that the positive obligation is discharged if a decision to withdraw life-sustaining treatment is taken in the patient's best interests and supported by a responsible body of medical opinion. In other words, the domestic best interests test was read into the terms of article 2. This is problematic because it suggests that everyone's right to life must be protected by law under article 2 only until the continuation of that life is no longer in the person's own interests. The best interests test is not expressed within the text of article 2 and has not been expressly read into it by the Strasbourg institutions. The implication that article 2 requires that everyone's right to life be protected by law only until the continuation of that life is no longer in the person's own interests, suggests the rejection of the sanctity of life principle to be replaced by an acknowledgement that death may sometimes be preferable to life. Such an approach has some merit, but its adoption in the *NHS Trust* case, with little ethical justification, merely sidesteps a detailed analysis of the key issue of whether article 2 seeks to uphold the sanctity of life in a relatively strict form or whether it represents the idea that life has mainly instrumental value. This latter argument gains some support from the location of article 2 in a human rights convention primarily concerned with upholding an individual's rights to self-determination within a democratic society. But the failure to even acknowledge this question undermines Dame Butler-Sloss's conclusion. For this reason, the *NHS Trusts* case's reconciliation of the *Bland* principles with article 2 is unconvincing.

The conclusion in the *NHS Trusts* case that the principles governing the treatment of PVS patients stemming from *Bland* present no human rights difficulties

32 *NHS Trust A v M; NHS Trust B v H* [2001] 2 WLR 942.

is overly simplistic because it fails to adequately investigate the complex dilemmas presented by the patient whose life no longer has much, if any, value. What is needed is a more meaningful balancing exercise that takes into account the varied rights and interests of the patient concerned. On the one hand, lies the principle of the sanctity of life. This ethically complex principle is the subject of much debate in the academic literature. In *Bland*, Lord Hoffmann recognised both the religious origin of the concept and its more recent secular application:

> [w]e have a strong feeling that there is an intrinsic value in human life, irrespective of whether it is valuable to the person concerned or indeed to anyone else. Those who adhere to religious faiths which believe in the sanctity of all God's creation and in particular that human life was created in the image of God himself will have no difficulty with the concept of the intrinsic value of human life. But even those without any religious belief think in the same way.[33]

This secular belief in the sanctity of human life is particularly important in the context of the modern right to life. Contemporary human rights law is based upon the concept that all humans are equal and are entitled to protection of their life, dignity, liberty and freedoms. All humans are treated as valuable and deserving of respect under human rights law and this contributes to the idea of human life as sacred. It is clear, however, that the sanctity of life cannot be an absolute principle. Both self-determination and dignity of the person are potentially conflicting principles which may outweigh the sanctity of life in certain circumstances. Thus, on the other side of the balancing scales, we can place the dignity and self-determination interests of the patient. For a patient in PVS, self-determination is unlikely to be an issue, unless the patient has previously expressed wishes that are relevant. Even if that is not the case, the patient retains an interest in personal dignity; in relief of suffering; avoidance of humiliation or bodily harm. To complicate the issue, the very fact that such interests endure also strengthens the weight of the other side of the scales: the value in that patient's life must be increased because of the rights and interests retained by the patient. Nevertheless, an irreversibly comatose life is of very limited value (both to the individual and to society) and it may be outweighed by the need to reduce the suffering caused by the artificial intervention necessary to ensure continuation of life.

There are also other factors that will be of relevance to this balancing exercise: distress caused to others, the use of limited public resources, the message sent to wider society by either the continued treatment or lingering death of such a patient. While these factors could never justify the infringement of the right to life in terms of the prohibition of the intentional deprivation of life by the state, they may be relevant to the assessment of what steps of positive assistance are reasonable in the circumstances. The most important factor, however, will be the overall quality of life of the patient. Some inherent value in human life will remain, even if that life

33 *Bland*, 851.

is of an irreversibly comatose nature, but most intrinsic value will have ceased. At the same time, human dignity will be challenged by the dire condition in which the patient is surviving and perhaps (although not inevitably) that type of survival may be contrary to the previous wishes and desires for life of the patient. It should not be forgotten that the withdrawal of food and water may also amount to an infringement of human dignity, but it may be that its finite duration elevates it over continued treatment for an indefinite period. The patient in PVS is not bereft of rights and interests, as the case law regrettably implies, but rather it is the very continuance of these rights and interests that may justify the state withdrawing life-sustaining treatment and ceasing to take positive steps to preserve that patient's life. For a patient in PVS, individual autonomy is not a key factor but in respect of other patients this value becomes fundamental.

Refusal of Life-Sustaining Treatment: The Autonomy Exception

While it is relatively easy to accept that human life has some inherent value, the question arises of to whom is that life of value? Is it valuable only to the individual who is enjoying that life? If so, individual autonomy will be of crucial importance and it may be that it is an individual's desire for respect for his or her own life that provides the inherent value in that life. Furthermore, if life is legally protected in deference to the individual's wish for respect for that life, then the protection would logically cease when an autonomous choice is made to bring the life to an end. On the other hand, it might be argued that there is also a broader societal benefit in the protection of human life and that it is thus a matter of public interest. This would suggest that an individual's autonomous choice to end his or her life is not necessarily the decisive factor in determining whether legal protection for that life should continue. There is, undoubtedly, some merit in the argument that the state has an interest in the lives of its citizens, not least because a human life has the potential to make a significant contribution to the society in which it lives. However, each human life, despite its contributions to society and state, is also a unique individual whose autonomous choices are what sustain that life. Therefore, the state's duty under the right to life to preserve human life must take into account the autonomous choices of the living entity.

One difficulty with the implementation of a right of autonomy in the medico-legal context is the question of whether an autonomous choice has to be rational in order to be deserving of respect. Some commentators, such as Julian Savulescu (1994), argue that our autonomous actions are only those which are based upon rational desires. In practice, when a patient refuses life-sustaining medical treatment, the decision may be challenged on the basis that the patient lacks mental competence, not because of any independent evidence of mental illness, but merely because the decision to refuse treatment appears to be irrational and thus might be evidence in itself that the patient's capacity to make decisions is currently impaired. Such an approach can most famously be seen in the series of cases in which a pregnant woman refused a caesarean section delivery against medical advice.

While the higher courts have criticised any first instance judge who overrules the refusal of consent without finding that the woman lacks competence (as in *St George's Healthcare NHS Trust v S*[34]), judges facing emergency applications have invariably allowed the operation to go ahead. The implication (from cases such as *Re S*,[35] *Rochdale Healthcare NHS Trust v C*,[36] *Re MB*[37] and *St George's*) that an irrational refusal of treatment is surreptitiously regarded as evidence of a lack of competence by the courts, as well as by doctors, is hard to avoid. This is problematic because the choice of the patient is not being respected; a freedom to agree with medical advice is not a freedom to choose.

Recent emphasis in the right to die debate also frequently falls into the trap of incorporating rationality considerations into protection of autonomy. Increasing recognition that there may exist some good reasons for preferring death to the alternative, such as unbearable pain, continues to regard rationality as a key factor. For example, Battin recognises a recent move 'from the recently predominant view that there is *no* good reason for suicide (and hence that all suicide is irrational or insane) to the view that there is after all one adequate reason for suicide: extreme and irremediable pain in terminal illness' (Battin 1994, 198-199). This only raises the question, however, of why autonomous choice, in the context of choosing death, is subjected to tests of rationality. While there may indeed be some rational reasons for choosing to die, such as terminal illness, and many other irrational reasons for making this choice, the rationality of a choice should not affect the manner in which we treat the autonomous choice. Thankfully, both English medical law and the ECHR confirm that autonomy is not subject to a rationality limitation, even if the message has not yet reached all doctors and judges.

Refusals of medical treatment have not traditionally been regarded as suicide attempts, even when the treatment is essential in order to preserve life. It is not clear, however, how this distinction can be justified. There seems to be no sound reason for distinguishing a refusal of life-sustaining medical treatment from a person who takes an overdose of pills or jumps from a bridge if in all cases death is the clearly intended outcome. Again, the rationality of the choice should not be relevant, and so the fact that a terminally ill patient may be making an objectively more reasonable choice than the typical suicide should not affect the law's treatment of it. The explanation for the purported distinction is not hard to discern, however. If a patient who refuses life-sustaining medical treatment is attempting suicide, then a doctor who helps him or her will be assisting a suicide. And assisted suicide remains a criminal offence in English law. So, for example, when Ms B was permitted, in line with well-established English medical law principles, to refuse consent to the continuation of artificial ventilation, it was categorically stated by the judge that she was not committing suicide, and that the doctors who

34 *St George's Healthcare NHS Trust* [1998] 3 All E.R. 673.

35 *Re S (adult: refusal of medical treatment)* [1992] 4 All E.R. 673.

36 *Rochdale Healthcare NHS Trust v C* [1997] 1 FCR 274.

37 *Re MB* [1997] 8 Med LR 217.

turned off the ventilator would not be guilty of a criminal offence (see *Re B*).[38] Much has been written about the distinction (or lack of it) between the case of Ms B and that of Dianne Pretty who was refused permission to commit suicide with the assistance of her husband (see *Pretty v. United Kingdom*).[39] The intentions of both women are identical: to choose death as a preferable alternative to their current state of living, and the cases should not be distinguished on that basis. This does not mean that the requests to die should be treated identically by the courts. A much more convincing and pertinent distinction, that arguably justifies the different outcomes in the two cases, is that the doctors were committing a battery upon Ms B by subjecting her to artificial ventilation against her wishes. Such a blatant infringement of physical integrity must negate any general rules against actions that assist a person to commit suicide.

In general, English law is strongly opposed to such assistance. The Suicide Act 1961, which abrogated the offence of suicide, created a new statutory offence of assisted suicide in Section 2(1) which states that 'A person who aids, abets, counsels or procures the suicide of another or an attempt by another to commit suicide, shall be liable on conviction on indictment to imprisonment for a term not exceeding 14 years.' This is an unusual offence because it imposes criminal liability for assisting an act that is not in itself unlawful. It is said to be justified by the law's strict rejection of any third party involvement in causing death. It is clear, however, that the offence of assisted suicide not only prohibits active involvement in the ending of life but also in persuading another person to end their life.[40] It is the justifiable concern that vulnerable persons, especially the elderly, will be bullied into ending their lives that provides the strongest principled need for the offence of assisted suicide, and in this way the offence serves an important goal under the right to life by protecting the lives of vulnerable persons in society. Of course, the offence may also prevent the exercise of autonomy where a person wants to die but needs assistance to do so, as was the case with Dianne Pretty.

The European Court of Human Rights has confirmed that the right to respect for private life protected under article 8 ECHR is engaged by the prohibition of assisted suicide and thus the offence of assisted suicide is recognised as infringing the autonomy of persons who want to commit suicide but are unable to do so unaided. However, both the European Court and the House of Lords regard this as a permissible interference with the right to respect for private life because, under article 8(2), it is necessary in a democratic society in order to protect the rights of others, namely those vulnerable members of society who might be pressured into ending their lives in the absence of an offence of assisted suicide. The 'clear risks of abuse' in any relaxation of the prohibition on assisted suicide mean that

38 *Re B (adult: refusal of medical treatment)* [2002] 2 All E.R. 449.

39 See, *R (on the application of Pretty) v. Director of Public Prosecutions* [2002] 1 All E.R. 1; *Pretty v. United Kingdom* (2002) 35 E.H.R.R. 1.

40 See, *AG v. Able* [1984] QB 795.

the Strasbourg Court is happy for each state to assess this issue in its own way.[41] The UK's approach, although not regarded as essential under the Convention, was found to be consistent with it: '[i]t does not appear to be arbitrary to the Court for the law to reflect the importance of the right to life, by prohibiting assisted suicide while providing for a system of enforcement and adjudication which allows due regard to be given in each particular case to the public interest in bringing a prosecution, as well as to the fair and proper requirements of retribution and deterrence.'[42] Procedural safeguards are therefore essential for any offence of assisted suicide but states are under no obligation to provide or permit assistance in committing suicide, regardless of the wishes of the person wanting to die. It is arguable that a limited exception to this general prohibition could be justified to cover cases such as Dianne Pretty's. It may be justifiable, in order to protect a particularly strong autonomy interest, to permit physician-assisted suicide in tightly defined circumstances, including only where there is unbearable suffering and the patient is unable to take his or her own life unaided. This argument may also draw support from quality of life considerations. The combined weight of the principles of autonomy and quality of life present a strong conflicting interest to the state's positive obligations to preserve life under the right to life. It is worth noting, however, that the argument that the right to life protects autonomous choices as to how to die was categorically rejected by both the House of Lords and the European Court of Human Rights.

The state's positive obligation to take reasonable steps to preserve life under article 2 does not, therefore, require the provision of assistance to commit suicide. Does it require that persons who can end their lives unaided are free to do so? In other words, does the individual interest in autonomy outweigh the general obligation to preserve life? Despite a long history of religious condemnation of suicide, it was decriminalised in the 1961 Suicide Act. Perhaps surprisingly, the protection of autonomous choices was not an express reason for this legislative intervention. Lord Bingham has explained that:

> [s]uicide itself (and with it attempted suicide) was decriminalised because recognition of the common law offence was not thought to act as a deterrent, because it cast an unwarranted stigma on innocent members of the suicide's family and because it led to the distasteful result that patients recovering in hospital from a failed suicide attempt were prosecuted, in effect for their lack of success.[43]

So, suicide was decriminalised because criminalising it was not an effective deterrent and the punishment, either directly of someone who has failed in a suicide attempt, or indirectly of the family of one who has succeeded, was increasingly seen to be

---

41 *Pretty v. United Kingdom*, para. 74.

42 Ibid., para. 76.

43 *R (on the application of Pretty) v. Director of Public Prosecutions*, para. 35.

distasteful. The absence of autonomy from the list of justifications for the legalisation of suicide reflects the strongly held opinion that suicide remains something to be prevented and condemned, even if it no longer attracts legal culpability. While there have been some academic attempts to recognise a 'right to suicide' (such as Battin 1994), the British courts have been adamant that there is no such right. For example, Lord Bingham explained in *Pretty* that 'while the 1961 Act abrogated the rule of law whereby it was a crime for a person to commit (or attempt to commit) suicide, it conferred no right on anyone to do so' and justified his conclusion by noting that the 1961 Act creates an offence of assisting suicide which demonstrates that the 'policy of the law remained firmly adverse to suicide.'[44] While this is undoubtedly a correct reading of the implications of the 1961 Act, it is not the end of the issue because committing suicide may (sometimes, not always, as not all suicide attempts will be made by individuals capable of making a competent choice) be a manifestation of autonomy, and this is a right protected in various ways in English law. It has been accepted, at both domestic and ECHR level, that the right of autonomy under article 8 ECHR applies to choices as to how and when to die, as well as to choices of how to live. In a statement expressly approved by the European Court of Human Rights, Lord Hope stated in respect of Dianne Pretty that '[t]he way she chooses to pass the closing moments of her life is part of the act of living, and she has a right to ask that this too must be respected.'[45] The Strasbourg Court has also made clear that when the state intervenes in such a way as to prevent by law an individual 'exercising her choice to avoid what she considers will be an undignified and distressing end to her life,' this may constitute an interference with article 8.[46] Suicide may thus be an exercise of autonomy that serves as a limitation upon the state's positive obligation to protect life. It will be important, however, that the exercise of autonomy is unambiguous. If the patient is not mentally competent to make an autonomous choice, the state should take reasonable steps to prevent suicide (and the reasonableness will be effected by the infringement of the other rights of the patient inherent in the steps necessary to preserve life). In addition, if there is no clear intention to die, the state should strive to protect individuals from their own recklessness or unthinking behaviour that may unwittingly result in death. But where a wish to die is the result of self-reflection, and this is highly likely to be the case where the person wishing to die is a patient in hospital, then the right to life does not obligate (and the right to respect for private life does not permit) the prevention of the exercise of an autonomous choice to reject life-sustaining medical treatment in order to die.

Failure to Fund Treatment: The Limited Resources Exception

The positive obligation to take appropriate steps to safeguard life where there is a real and immediate risk to life would seem to impose a duty on the state to provide

44 Ibid.

45 Ibid., para. 100.

46 *Pretty v. United Kingdom*, para. 67.

life-saving medical treatment to patients in need. However, when outlining this positive obligation, the European Court of Human Rights explicitly recognised the need to balance public resources and held that the obligation to safeguard lives 'must be interpreted in a way which does not impose an impossible or disproportionate burden on the authorities.'[47] This is a particularly crucial restraint in the context of a public healthcare system, and one that has been at the core of domestic judicial reasoning on any purported right to treatment. The first judicial recognition of the issue of limited resources came in the 1980 case of *R v Secretary of State for Health, West Midlands Regional Health Authority and Birmingham Area Health Authority, ex parte Hincks*[48] when the Court of Appeal held that the statutory duty of the Secretary of State to promote and provide a free and comprehensive health service (under the National Health Service Act 1977) is subject to the need to take into account the financial resources available. Later cases soon revealed that the sticky topic of limited resources would act as a restraint upon all judicial intervention into allocation of resource issues. In *R v Secretary of State for Social Services, ex parte Walker*,[49] Sir John Donaldson MR said that, '[i]t is not for this court, or indeed any court, to substitute its own judgment for the judgment of those who are responsible for the allocation of resources' and in *R v Cambridge District Health Authority, ex parte B*, the Court of Appeal recognised that '[d]ifficult and agonising judgments have to be made as to how a limited budget is best allocated to the maximum advantage of the maximum number of patients' and '[t]hat is not a judgment which the court can make.'[50] In this latter case, Laws J, at first instance, had emphasised the patient's right to life and held that this required, at the very least, an explanation from the health authority as to the conflicting priorities which had led it to refuse potentially life-saving treatment: '[w]here the question is whether the life of a 10-year-old child might be saved, by however slim a chance, the responsible Authority must...do more than toll the bell of tight resources. They must explain the priorities that have led them to decline to fund the treatment.' This seems to be a reasonable requirement to ensure that the authorities comply with the obligation under the right to life to take reasonable steps to preserve life. It will be difficult for a court to assess the reasonableness of the refusal to fund potentially life-saving treatment unless it has information about the context in which the decision was reached. The Court of Appeal in *ex parte B* found such a requirement to be unrealistic but the alternative of an abdication of responsibility for the decision entirely is problematic given the importance of ensuring that state authorities meet the more onerous positive obligations inherent in the right to life.

---

47 *Osman*, para. 116.

48 *R v Secretary of State for Health, West Midlands Regional Health Authority and Birmingham Area Health Authority, ex parte Hincks* [1980] 1 BMLR 93.

49 *R v Secretary of State for Social Services, ex parte Walker* [1987] 3 BMLR 32.

50 *R v Cambridge District Health Authority, ex parte B* [1995] 2 All E.R. 129 (CA), 137, per Sir Thomas Bingham MR.

The case of *R (on the application of Burke) v General Medical Council* (2005)[51] provided a clear opportunity for the courts to consider whether a patient has a right to receive life-sustaining medical treatment (in this case, artificial nutrition and hydration). The right to life would be a strong foundation for the building of such a right. However, the Court of Appeal appeared to hold that there was no right to treatment:

> [a]utonomy and the right of self-determination do not entitle the patient to insist on receiving a particular medical treatment regardless of the nature of the treatment. Insofar as a doctor has a legal obligation to provide treatment this cannot be founded simply upon the fact that the patient demands it. The source of the duty lies elsewhere.[52]

This statement does not preclude a right to treatment, however; it merely asserts that any such right is not dependent upon a patient's expression of autonomy. The fact that a patient has no right to demand treatment does not impact upon the question of whether the state's obligations under the right to life require the provision of such treatment. The Court of Appeal is clearly correct to describe the source of the doctor's duty to treat a patient as residing in the legal requirement that a doctor treat in the best interests of the patient. To omit to do so leaves a doctor open to a charge of murder or manslaughter should the patient die from the lack of treatment. And if, as in the case of Mr Burke, a patient requests ANH, the request will not be the source of the doctor's duty to provide it, but will merely 'underscore' that duty[53]. However, the Court of Appeal also held that article 2 ECHR's protection of the right to life would be infringed if life-sustaining treatment is withdrawn contrary to a competent patient's wishes.[54] These two principles, when coupled together, seem to indicate a limited right to treatment under the right to life in English law. This is because, on the one hand, a patient cannot demand treatment and a doctor has no legal obligation to provide it unless it is regarded as clinically indicated. On the other hand, the withdrawal of life-sustaining treatment against a competent patient's wishes violates his or her right to life. Thus, as the Court of Appeal confirmed,[55] the provision of life-sustaining treatment such as ANH will always be clinically indicated – or in other words, regarded as in the best interests of the patient – if a patient who is still competent wants to continue to live. A patient in this (admittedly rare) situation – competent but needing ANH to live – has a right to receive that treatment, because a withdrawal of it will violate his or her right to life. From the perspective of article 2 this suggests that the positive obligation to take reasonable steps to preserve life includes the provision of ANH

51 *R (on the application of Burke) v General Medical Council* (2005) 3 WLR 1132.
52 Ibid., para. 31.
53 Ibid., para. 32.
54 Ibid., para. 39.
55 Ibid., para. 53.

to a competent patient wanting to live. If the patient is not competent, a different view on whether delaying death is in his or her best interests may legitimately be taken, and if a competent patient refuses ANH, then it must be withdrawn. But for the competent patient, requiring ANH to live, and wishing to receive it, the right to life requires its provision. It is doubtful that a limited resource argument would succeed in this context. This is, in part, because ANH is a special form of life-sustaining treatment. Indeed, it is arguable whether it is medical treatment at all. It was held to be so by the House of Lords in *Airedale NHS Trust v Bland*[56] but this was largely in order that it could be withdrawn and, as Keown has queried poignantly, '[t]he question in such a case is why the pouring of food down the tube constitutes medical treatment. What is it supposed to be treating?' (Keown 1997, 491). In *Burke*, the Court of Appeal does not address this issue at all but merely assumes, in line with the House of Lords precedent, that ANH is treatment. It could be argued that the provision of food for patients unable to feed themselves is a basic expectation within an affluent society, rather than an extraordinary means of preserving life, and thus is far more likely to fall within a state's positive obligations to preserve life. It is certainly easier to enforce an obligation to provide ANH than a much more costly obligation to provide a particular drug or operation. So, both in terms of the ease of implementation, and the expectation of what is a reasonable intervention to preserve life, the provision of ANH is a unique form of medical care. The provision of basic care such as food and water to a patient who otherwise requires no medical intervention to support life is an obligation entirely fitting for an affluent state such as the UK within the context of international and domestic obligations to preserve life, subject to the possible exceptions (as argued above) imposed by either the autonomous wishes of a competent patient or the poor quality of life of an incompetent patient.

In respect of more expensive, or intrusive medical treatment, the issue of cost comes to the fore in any reasonableness equation. The National Institute for Clinical Excellence (NICE) has the unenviable job of making appraisals of new medical technologies, a task that it performs by applying the quality adjusted life year (QALY) mechanism. This is a controversial approach to the allocation of finite healthcare resources. A numerical value is placed on the quality of an individual's life and this is then multiplied by his expected lifespan. Most obviously this approach discriminates against the elderly and the disabled due to their shorter life expectancy and/or lower quality of life, but it is objectionable on more general terms as well. The QALY approach does not value life itself but rather quality adjusted life years and thus it does not prioritise the saving of as many lives as possible. Under the right to life, equality of protection is vital. Everyone's life should be protected by the law, regardless of life expectancy, quality of life, or the conflicting needs of healthier or younger individuals. On the other hand, we know that not all lives can reasonably be saved. In addition to the need to ensure a balance between the preservation of life and quality of life and/or autonomy

56 *Airedale NHS Trust v Bland*, [1993] AC 789.

considerations, there needs to be a recognition that, in the real world, healthcare rationing is a fact of life. Every new, potentially life-saving, treatment approved by NICE will cost other lives. As the right to life legally obligates states to do all that is reasonable to preserve the lives of its citizens, a body such as NICE has a vital function to perform but issues of the greater good of society (i.e. the maximisation of 'life years' throughout a community) should not detract from the need to protect each individual's right to life. The giving of many life years to a few at the expense of a few life years to many will arguably not be a reasonable allocation of finite resources in the context of the state's positive obligations to protect individuals under the right to life.

Conclusion

This whirlwind tour through English medical law has highlighted the disparate range of circumstances in which patients are allowed to die by their doctors (and indirectly by the state). While the right to life offers fundamental protection for human life, it has to operate within the real world in which we will all die and some inevitably sooner rather than later. In other contexts, such as policing or criminal justice, the right can and should be enforced relatively harshly. While the use of lethal force by an agent of the state may occasionally be necessary and proportionate, these situations will be extremely rare. In the healthcare context, however, the loss of human life is a common occurrence and although it is important that medical staff strive to preserve human life for as long as possible, there are weighty conflicting interests that will justify the cessation of life-saving measures. As has been discussed, issues of a poor quality of life, individual autonomy and limited resources may all, either alone or in conjunction with each other, justify the withdrawal or withholding of potentially life-sustaining treatment. The right to life is far less forgiving of positive acts that cause death, even within the healthcare context. Only in circumstances where the rights of others are directly engaged (such as in respect of a foetus or a conjoined twin) may a patient be subjected to an intervention that will cause death. The act/omission distinction is a highly controversial one in English medical law, and elsewhere, but its application is unavoidable within the terms of the right to life. There are two crucial obligations upon states (and, under the HRA, public authorities) under the right to life – the prohibition on intentional deprivation of life and the duty to take reasonable steps to preserve life – and while one of them is, in most circumstances, protected in absolute terms, the other is conditional upon a reasonableness calculation. While some may be uncomfortable with such a distinction, its application in the healthcare context confirms our instinctive feeling that patients should be treated in a manner that will ensure the preservation of their lives until that objective is no longer a reasonable or proportionate goal. That is why Anthony Bland could legitimately be allowed to die by the withdrawal of ANH by his doctors but remained legally protected from a police officer's gun. The right to life in this context is less about preserving life in all circumstances and more about the need for a sufficiently compelling justification before the legal protection for life can be overridden.

Bibliography

Battin, M. (1994) *The Least Worst Death: Essays in Bioethics on the End of Life* (Oxford: Oxford University Press).

Dworkin, R. (1994) *Life's Dominion: An Argument about Abortion and Euthanasia* (London: HarperCollins).

Gurnham, D. (2003) 'Kantian Principle and the Right to Life in Legal Judgement: The Case of the Conjoined Twins', *King's College Law Journal*, 14, 21.

Keown, J. (1997) 'Restoring Moral and Intellectual Shape to the Law after *Bland*', *Law Quarterly Review* 113, 481.

Law Commission for England and Wales (2006) 'Murder, Manslaughter and Infanticide', London: Law Com. No. 304.

Lizza, J.P. (2006) *Persons, Humanity and the Definition of Death* (Baltimore: Johns Hopkins University Press).

McMahan, J. (1998) 'Brain Death, Cortical Death and Persistent Vegetative State', in *Companion to Bioethics*, edited by Kuhse, H. and Singer, P. (Oxford: Blackwell).

Ost, S. (2005) 'Euthanasia and the Defence of Necessity: Advocating a More Appropriate Legal Response', *Criminal Law Review* 355.

Palmer, H. (1957) 'Dr Adams' Trial for Murder', *Criminal Law Review* 365.

Price, D. (1997) 'Euthanasia, Pain Relief and Double Effect', *Legal Studies* 17, 323.

Savulescu, J. (1994) 'Rational Desires of the Limitation of Life-Sustaining Treatment', *Bioethics*, 8, 191.

Silverstein, H.S. (1987) 'On a Woman's "Responsibility" for the Fetus', *Social Theory and Practice* 13, 103.

Singer, P. (1995) *Rethinking Life and Death: The Collapse of our Traditional Ethics* (Oxford: Oxford University Press).

Thomson, J.J. (1971) 'A Defence of Abortion', *Philosophy and Public Affairs* 1, 47.

Thomson, J.J. (1986) *Rights, Restitution and Risk: Essays in Moral Theory*, edited by Parent, W. (Cambridge: Harvard University Press).

Wicks, E. (2010) *The Right to Life and Conflicting Interests* (Oxford: Oxford University Press).

—— (2007) *Human Rights and Healthcare* (Oxford: Hart Publishing).

Williams, G. (2001) 'The Principle of Double Effect and Terminal Sedation', *Medical Law Review* 9, 41.

Chapter 14
Conjoined Twins: Separation as Lethal Mutilation

Helen Watt

Introduction

The harrowing case of *Re A (Children)*, conjoined twins separated in the knowledge that one would die, has relevance to many other areas of medical ethics and ethics of homicide. In what follows, I will leave aside questions concerning the extent of parents' rights to refuse consent to operations on their children. I will focus on the question whether separating conjoined twins, where one twin will die as a result, is justified in any situation, with or without the parents' consent. Such operations are extremely rare; however, they help us to focus on moral principles which apply in other situations where the interests of two subjects are thought to be in conflict.

The Body and the Person

The suggestion was sometimes made in regard to *Re A*[1] that there was only one child to consider. For example, a surgeon who had himself separated conjoined twins claimed that 'Mary' in *Re A* was not a human being but a tumour (Roberts 2000, 12).[2] As such, she could be excised from 'Jodie' with no qualms – at least as far as 'Mary' was concerned. Clearly, this claim raises fundamental questions concerning who should count as a human being or person when assessing claims of harm.

The word 'person' is notoriously defined in different ways. If by 'person' – or '*human* person' – we mean a *human moral subject* then this subject is, we normally assume, the *human being*: the living human organism. We are bodily beings, not purely spiritual beings or series of thoughts. We all experience ourselves as bodily beings at times when we are conscious. We also know that there are times when we go on existing despite not being conscious – for example, when we are asleep or in a coma. At such times, we retain our rights to bodily immunity, despite the possibility of waking with few or no memories of our past life. Even the interest in retaining

---

1 *Re A (Children) (Conjoined Twins: Medical Treatment) (No.1)*, [2001] Fam. Law 16 (High Court Decision); [2001] 2 W.L.R. 480 (Court of Appeal Decision).

2 Keith Roberts opposed the operation, in view of what he saw as Jodie's poor prospects and the parents' refusal of consent.

memories and at least our better character traits is an interest ascribable to the living human being who may lose them. The human moral subject is not reducible to his or her experiences, which come and go; rather, it is the underlying bodily being who is the stakeholder here.

In identifying human beings or human bodily subjects, we need to bear in mind that human bodies do not all look the same. Even healthy bodies go through major changes as they grow and develop. Disabled bodies also look different from the kind of bodies to which we are accustomed. We need to go back to the concept of an organism – a living, self-organizing whole – to count how many human subjects were present in the case of *Re A*. It was clear from the physical behaviour attributed to Jodie and Mary that there were two separate systems of self-organization, despite some overlap in the parts controlled by each system. (Here I am referring not so much to the activity of two separate brains (Sheldon and Wilkinson 1997, 152) as to self-organization from two separate sources, however this was achieved.) In contrast, where a baby is born with (for example) an extra leg, this leg is clearly not a part of an alternative self-organizing system. Rather, it is simply an abnormal part of the baby from whom it is protruding. Excising the leg poses no moral problem in principle, whereas excising a twin poses obvious problems concerning his/her interests and rights.

Conjoined Twins and Disability

If separation of conjoined twins is (as I will argue) morally wrong in some cases, this is not because being conjoined is a harmless variation on the norm. This does not seem true of *any* case of conjoined twins, let alone a case where twins will die within months if left as they are. A condition affecting two people which leads to the death of both will either be or involve some pathology. Although Mary was, of course, dependant for life on remaining conjoined, it was surely a pathological feature of Mary that she was so dependant.

To say this is not, of course, to say that being conjoined cannot have positive aspects. It is notable that adult conjoined twins refuse to be separated, in all or almost all cases, and are adamant that their situation is in many ways good (Dreger 1998). They refuse to be separated even to save their lives where one twin has died – presumably because they recoil from such a violent divorce from a much-loved brother or sister. In general, conjoined twins appear to be emotionally as well as physically close, despite having what are often very different personalities. However, there is nothing new in something bad in itself – a state of functional impairment – having positive effects in terms of human relations. As with other good effects of bad things, this should not necessarily prevent us from combating the bad thing itself, by attempting to treat the condition where authorised to do so.[3]

---

3 There are social benefits, as well as harms, attached to separation which need to be acknowledged: were it not for the trauma and/or danger often involved in separation,

To return to the case of infant conjoined twins who will die within months unless they are separated, is this a pathological condition which is worse than death? Should we agree with Polly Toynbee of the *Guardian*, who described conjoined twins as 'fascinatingly horrible freaks of nature'? (Toynbee 2000, 23). Or with Mr Justice Johnson of the High Court, who said that prolonging Mary's life would be 'very seriously to her disadvantage'?[4] Or with Lord Justice Walker of the Appeal Court, who suggested that Mary would gain from separation in acquiring 'bodily integrity,' even in death?[5]

This way of thinking of conjoined twins is surely misconceived. Being conjoined is a disability – but not a fate worse than death. The suggestion that a conjoined twin should be given a more normal-looking body at the cost of her life represents a new low point in the way we see disabled people. What would we say about an operation to straighten the spine of someone with osteoporosis which would kill the patient if it 'worked'? How would that be in the patient's interests? To reduce a patient who is still functioning – though in a precarious and anomalous way – to a non-functional corpse is not a healing intervention on that patient but an act of mutilation. If able-bodied people are unable to tolerate the structure and appearance of disabled people, disabled people should not be made to pay with their lives.

The Value of Life

'But' (it might be objected) 'someone with osteoporosis is – or may be – a rational, self-conscious person. Such a person can tell us what value she herself places on life. In contrast, Mary was, perhaps, only minimally conscious, and was certainly not rational, nor expected to become so. How can life in a state of minimal consciousness have any real value? How can any state have value for anyone if she is unable to prefer it? Even if Mary was not the gainer from the operation to separate the twins, was she in any way the loser?'

There is, I think, a serious though common confusion here between *having* an interest and *taking* an interest, which are two quite different things. It is often the case that what is in our interest is something in which we *take* no interest (Grisez, Boyle and Finnis 1987).[6] As a suicidal person, I might *take* no interest in life or the good things life can contain; this does not, however, mean I *have* no interest in life and those other good things. There is not a reliable link between what is good for us and what we happen to prefer. There are 'human goods' (as they are sometimes called) which are objectively in my interest, but in which I may not

---

preferring to remain conjoined might not seem an entirely healthy preference.

4 *Central Manchester Healthcare Trust v Mr and Mrs A and Re A Child (by her guardian ad litem, the Official Solicitor)*, Judgement, p. 5.

5 Judgement, Section 34.

6 See also Oderberg 2000, 40-45; Chappell 1998; Coope 2006.

take an interest. If someone injures me when I am an infant, so that I am severely brain-damaged, my interest in my own healthy future has been unjustly thwarted. This is despite the fact that, as an infant, I lack the concept of my healthy future and do not in any way desire it. In the same way, if someone kills me as an infant, I am deprived of my entire future on earth, whether healthy or otherwise. Of course, in the second case, I do not continue to exist as a living human being in a state of deprivation. Nonetheless, there is a benefit – the benefit of my future life – which I could have enjoyed, and do not.

'But' (my critic might reply) 'even admitting that we have objective interests in a *healthy* future, do we have objective interests in a short, semi-conscious life? What is good about such a life? We may have interests of which we are unaware – health, friendship and so on – but do they include life *per se*?'

It is difficult to demonstrate the goodness of *any* basic, non-instrumental 'human good' – whether life, knowledge, friendship or anything else. On one plausible account of human flourishing, our knowledge of what fulfils us and those like us is directly apprehended, not derived from other things we know (Grisez, Boyle and Finnis 1987, 101-102, 111). Be that as it may, it is surely part of what it means to be an organism that one has certain biological interests, including the interest in survival. If this is true of lower organisms, it is true in a much richer sense of human beings, whose presence in the world carries with it the meaning and value of the kind of being they are. Mary was a member of the rational human species: her interests in the range of 'human goods' were those of her species. Even if most of these interests were doomed to be thwarted in Mary's lifetime, this did not mean that her existence itself was a bad or worthless thing. Nor did her life become that of a lower animal as soon as she was mentally disabled;[7] rather, she remained a member of the rational human kind, with all the dignity that brings. The presence of Mary in the world – in whatever state of health – was something good, not something bad. We are not respecting a disabled human being if we see her life as having no value, or value of a subhuman kind.

Respect for Life

But what, we might ask, was the practical import of Mary's interest in life? Jodie too had interests in life and other goods; moreover, her interests could be promoted much further than those of her sister. Just because life retains a certain value, even in a highly damaged state, this does not mean we should go to all possible lengths to promote or safeguard that value. The good of life must compete with other goods, and with life in other people, when it comes (for example) to allocating resources. If Jodie and Mary had been in competition for some scarce medical

---

7 An odd result of this would be that a cure of the condition, if discovered, would not be in the interest of the 'subhuman' patient but would create a new individual – who would again be destroyed if his or her condition then deteriorated.

treatment, it would not have been wrong to give the treatment to the twin who could benefit more.[8]

No-one is urging a vitalist pursuit of life for one person, at any cost to other people's lives and well-being. Respect for life does not involve this kind of monomaniac pursuit (see, for example, Keown 1997). What it does involve is respect for certain *negative* rights people have: rights that other people *not* make certain choices to affect their bodily integrity. These rights are not in *conflict* with positive rights, such as rights to life-saving treatment. Rather, the *scope* of positive rights is limited by negative rights and by other factors. Any attempt to promote someone's welfare must be compatible with respect for the negative rights of that person and others. There is, first of all, the right not to have one's life deliberately shortened, by act or by omission. This right has traditionally been ascribed to all innocent human beings. However, there are other negative rights concerning bodily integrity[9] which are less often mentioned. We will come to these shortly.

Unjust Aggression

The view that Mary's life had no value was, in fact, rejected by the main Appeal Court judge, Lord Justice Ward.[10] However, Ward approved the separation, which he saw as a form of quasi self-defence of Jodie from Mary. Ward used the example of a six-year-old child who is shooting other children with a gun: would it not be right to kill such a child?[11]

Morally, lethal force can indeed be used against an unjust aggressor, and it is not necessary to intend death, as opposed to sufficient force/harm to thwart the attack. However, it is less clear that lethal force is justified where the person threatening one's life has no intention to do so. If a two-year-old child is about to set a bomb off, may I shoot her through the head? There is surely a difference between true aggression and simply posing a threat. The relevant difference is not culpability (after all, an enemy soldier may be acting in good faith) but rather intention to harm. While the six-year-old to whom the judge referred is, at least, trying to harm others, Mary was not trying to harm Jodie. Rather, she found herself doing harm to Jodie through no choice of her own, just as Jodie earlier found herself doing harm to Mary. Both twins were harmed by their growing together, and neither chose this harm, for herself or her sister.

---

8 I am assuming here that neither twin has a prior claim on the treatment – for example, because she is already receiving it; see Sulmasy and Sugarman 1994.

9 These rights, too, are involved in respect for life in the broad sense, if health – a person's physical well-being – is an aspect of life – a person's being itself.

10 *Re A*, Section IV (7.5), 187.

11 Ibid., Section V (7.7), 203.

Principle of Double Effect

One startling aspect of the Appeal Court judgement was the statement that the doctors were intending to kill Mary, but were justified in doing so.[12] There was, indeed, some legal basis for saying that since Mary's death was foreseen as certain, it could be regarded as intended.[13] Clearly, however, it is not in fact the case that we intend everything we foresee as certain. We do not intend, in walking down the road, to wear down the soles of our shoes. Not only is it factually not the case that we intend everything we foresee as certain, but this fact has moral implications.

The *principle of double effect*, according to which it makes a difference morally whether we intend a bad result or merely foresee it, is crucial both in medicine and in life.[14] Sometimes we do or refrain from doing something where we know that some bad result will follow. A classic example – more common in books than in real life medicine – is giving morphine to a terminal patient with the aim of treating pain, while foreseeing that the patient's life will or may be shortened thereby. If killing the patient is no part of our plan, and if the bad effect is in proportion to the good we are achieving for the patient, the treatment can be morally defended.

Another example is that of *withholding* treatment from a patient in order to treat someone else. It is not murder to withhold a treatment knowing that this will shorten life if our aim is not to do this or any other harm,[15] but to allocate resources elsewhere. Not only is this not murder, but it may be fully justified and, perhaps, morally required, depending on the circumstances. If giving the treatment would be unfair to someone who has a prior claim, then it may be withheld for that reason, without intending death.

The principle of double effect was in fact discussed repeatedly in relation to *Re A*. Some commentators defended separation on the grounds that death was not intended. And indeed, Mary's death may not have been intended as part of the plan to save Jodie. On the face of it, Jodie did not benefit from the fact that Mary died. There were some token efforts made to revive Mary after separation, though these efforts predictably did not succeed.[16] If they had succeeded, however, separation would have benefited Jodie no less.

---

12 Ibid., Section V (4.1), 198.

13 *R. v. Woollin* [1999] 1 A.C. 82, 91A.

14 See Finnis 1991; Gormally 1994, 48-50; Garcia 1997; Watt 2004.

15 The central case of murder is intentional killing, by act or by omission. However, there are 'penumbra' cases of murder where this intention is absent (see Finnis 1991, 49, 60-1; Gormally 1994, 38-39, 49-50). These include the intentional removal of vital organs, and other cases where someone does, without excuse, what foreseeably results in loss of life. Thus the person who blows up a plane to get the insurance is morally (and legally) guilty of murder, despite the fact that his intention may not have been to cause deaths.

16 Note that where successful 'stage two' procedures are not possible, this can radically change the nature of a 'stage one' procedure (compare a Caesarian section where the woman can be stitched up successfully, and one where she cannot – say, because she is too ill or the facilities are not available).

Mutilation

There is no reason to say that separation required an intention to kill Mary. This does not, however, mean that separation involved no other wrongful intention. For the principle of double effect to apply, it must be the case that nothing we *do* intend is morally unjustified. Take the case of a heart transplant where the donor is alive. Even if the donor's *death* is not intended – is in no way part of our plan – what we *do* intend with regard to the donor is an immediate change to his body of a kind I will call *mutilation*. By this I mean an effect known to constitute a serious, permanent, non-therapeutic effect, whether or not intended precisely as harmful, or as causing loss of function.

It may be objected that in Mary's case we were not removing her organs. However, this is not required for mutilation, as the following example will show. Imagine that a doctor experiments on a baby who is terminally ill, and fully anaesthetized, in a way he knows will do the baby no good, but serious and permanent harm (see Watt 2004). For example, he cuts into her body, looks at her organs, and operates on those organs. Surely what the doctor does is morally wrong, even if neither death nor bodily harm forms any part of his intention. Even if many future patients could benefit from cutting into this patient's body, the doctor is violating bodily integrity in a way which cannot be defended.

Yet this is almost what the doctors were doing in the case of Jodie and Mary. They cut into Mary, inflicting a wound from which she would not recover. They looked at Mary's organs, and made harmful changes to her body. True, this operation benefited not unknown people in the future, but a known person who was unwittingly endangered by the person whose body was invaded. In that respect, the operation was preferable to the 'opportunistic' involving of someone (the research subject) not already involved in the situation (Quinn 1993, 186). However, unless we are to defend the killing of toddlers who are about to set off landmines, for example, the difference between the operations, though real, is not sufficient to justify separation.

It is worth noting that the harm to Mary was not limited to causing her death. Mary was certainly killed by the cutting of what seems to have been her – as well as Jodie's – aorta. Though the site could have been biased towards Jodie, if still a part of Mary, remarks made by one of the surgeons after the operation suggest that it was not. But in any event, whether or not the aorta was shared at the point it was cut, the bodily integrity of Mary had already been assaulted by the earlier procedures.

Thought Experiments

The fact that separation involved an invasion of Mary's bodily integrity was not acknowledged in some of the examples used in Court to defend separation. To cut a rope to free a mountain climber from his dangling companion is not a mutilating bodily invasion of the person who will die. Any effect on that person's bodily integrity could and should be outside our plan in cutting the rope and releasing the other climber. The impact of the fall on the victim will not advance our goals, and most agents will not even be tempted to include it in their plans.[17] The same is true of pushing someone off a lifeboat he is threatening to swamp, or off a rope ladder where he is blocking the way of escape for other people. The right to remain in a place of temporary safety is a more conditional right than the right not to have one's body invaded in a foreseeably, seriously and exclusively harmful way. Even non-invasive interventions on one's body which do irreparable harm are mutilation – at least if they would harm, to some extent, any human being.

Perhaps the best example used in Court to defend separation was that of a dying accident victim who is moved, at the cost of his life, to rescue someone trapped underneath. Here we could be intending a change to the dying person's body itself (for example, to the way in which the limbs were positioned) and not just a change to the body's overall location. However, this would be a non-invasive intervention, of a kind which would do no harm – even temporary harm – to someone who was not in the dying person's condition. It would have been more to the point to imagine that we *cut through* the dying person's body to get to the person underneath, since this is an invasive procedure, and would seriously harm even a healthy human being.

Separation and Intention

Included in the operation to separate Jodie and Mary were interventions on what was agreed to be Mary's body only: exploratory procedures carried out on Mary's organs. Other interventions were performed on parts shared by Jodie and Mary – for example, the cutting apart of shared skin. What should we say about these interventions? If we intend to cut apart two bodies, we are intending an immediate change to the bodies which we cut apart. We are intending that our incision separate Body A from Body B, and Body B from Body A. The immediate effect on both bodies must be justified as fair to both parties. For Mary, this effect was mutilation – in the sense of a loss of bodily integrity – which was not, I am claiming, fair to her. Indeed, there is even more of a reason to oppose the cutting of the aorta, for example, since arguably, the intention was not just to invade the aorta, but to stop it functioning in Mary.

Even if we could somehow restrict our intentions to invading Jodie's body – though we knew the part invaded was also Mary's body – this would still be mutilation. Here it may be helpful to look at the example of theft. It is theft if I intentionally appropriate what I know belongs to two people, if one person has

17 The question of what we intend is an empirical question, though it can be psychologically difficult not to intend things one knows have a close causal and/or logical connection with what we are seeking to achieve, see Garcia 1997, 164-166.

given me permission while the other has refused it. In the same way, it is mutilation if I intentionally invade what I know is a part shared by two people, if this will benefit only one person, and do the other permanent harm.

For me to be a thief, it is not necessary that I intentionally take property *because* it belongs to someone else. It is enough if I intentionally take property – without an excuse – which I *know* belongs to someone else. Again, with murder, if I intentionally kill what I know to be an innocent human being, it is not necessary that I intentionally kill that human being *because* he is innocent.[18] Here it may be added that while there are various excuses for appropriating objects, the same cannot be said of intentionally killing or mutilating innocent human beings. Human welfare is immediately affected by such interventions, in a way which is morally conclusive.

While intention is certainly essential to identify any human action, we should not over-specify the intention needed to put an action in some moral class. Or rather, it may be not so much the intention – long or short-term – as the intention-foresight combination that is morally decisive, whatever the benefits at stake. Not all side-effects are 'mere' side-effects, of a kind that intended effects, such as long-term effects, could in principle outweigh.

Conclusion

What, then, can we learn from *Re A* in the way of principles for action? Doctors should not merely avoid deliberate killing – although they should certainly do that – but should otherwise respect the lives and bodies of those on whom they intervene. It is unacceptable to invade the body of a patient if this will do the patient no good,[19] but only serious and permanent harm. This applies whether or not there are two patients physically linked in some way (for example, it would be wrong to do a lethally-harmful caesarean on a dying pregnant woman, even to save her unborn child).[20] Surgery is not about mutilating people in the course of helping others: negative rights to life and bodily integrity must always be respected.[21]

18 Such an intention – to kill a human being precisely because he is innocent – does, however, seem a more heinous crime than the standard case of murder.

19 The good referred to is the prevention of mental or physical dysfunction. 'Relationship' goods, such as the survival of a sibling, cannot justify major damage to a person's psychophysical well-being. Moreover, even if Jodie was physically benefited by the operation, there is a 'social' sense in which one is harmed, not benefited, by the exploitation of a sibling on one's behalf.

20 For other obstetric implications of this principle, see Watt 2004, 242-247. The boundaries between the pregnant woman and her unborn child, despite one body being entirely inside the other, are, in fact, clearer than the boundaries between conjoined twins, at least if we treat the placenta as a temporary organ of the foetus.

21 J.L.A. Garcia observes that sometimes two things will be so connected that intending one will be vicious for similar reasons to intending the other (Garcia 1997, 165-

In this as in any other field, it is not enough to have a good end: we also need to have a good means. A means can be disqualified in various ways, including by side-effects linked to our short-term intention of a kind which are morally decisive.[22] In *Re A*, there were two patients, each of whom had the right to immunity from harmful bodily invasions. Cutting into Mary, in a way which did her only serious permanent harm, was a bad means to the good end of saving her twin sister's life.

Bibliography

Chappell, T.D.J. (1998) *Understanding Human Goods: A Theory of Ethics* (Edinburgh: Edinburgh University Press).

Coope, C. (2006) *Worth and Welfare in the Controvery over Abortion* (Basingstoke: Palgrave Macmillan).

Dreger, A.D. (1998) 'The Limits of Individuality: Ritual and Sacrifice in the Lives and Medical Treatment of Conjoined Twins', 29 (1) *Stud. Hist. Phil. & Biomed. Sci.* 1.

Finnis, J. (1991) 'Intention and Side-effects', in Frey, R. and Morris, C. (eds) *Liability and Responsibility: Essays in Law and Morals* (Cambridge: Cambridge University Press)

Garcia, J.L.A. (1997) 'Intentions in Medical Ethics', in Oderberg, D. and Laing, J. (eds) *Human Lives: Critical Essays on Consequentialist Bioethics* (Basingstoke: Palgrave Macmillan).

Gormally, L. (1994) (ed.) *Euthanasia, Clinical Practice and the Law* (London: Linacre Centre).

Grisez, G., Boyle, J. and Finnis, J. (1987) 'Practical Principles, Moral Truth, and Ultimate Ends', 32 *American Journal of Jurisprudence* 99.

Keown, J (1997) 'Restoring Moral and Intellectual Shape to the Law after *Bland*', 113 *LQR* 481.

Oderberg, D.S. (2000) *Moral Theory: A Non-Consequentialist Approach* (Oxford: Blackwell).

Quinn, W. (1993) 'Actions, Intentions, and Consequences: The Doctrine of Double Effect', in Quinn, W. *Morality and Action* (Cambridge: Cambridge University Press).

167). Life and bodily integrity (that is, the absence of internal effects of a certain kind) would seem to have this kind of close connection as components of human well-being.

22 Of course, side-effects which are not in themselves morally decisive (for example, the causing of short-term harms) may nonetheless be serious enough to outweigh the benefits of acting in a certain situation. Moreover, some 'means' to our long-term goal may not be intended, but merely (as it happens) causally necessary to achieve our goal – in which case our action will again not be justified, despite all our good intentions. This is, however, a separate issue.

Roberts, K. (2000) 'As a Surgeon, I believe Jodie and Mary Should be Allowed to Die', *Daily Mail*, 15 September.

Sheldon, S. and Wilkinson, S. (1997) 'Conjoined Twins: The Legality and Ethics of Sacrifice', 5 *Med.L.R.* 152.

Sulmasy, D.P. and Sugarman, J. (1994) 'Are Withholding and Withdrawing Therapy Morally Equivalent?', 20 *Journal of Ethics and Medicine* 218.

Toynbee, P. (2000) 'Two into One', *Guardian*, 8 September.

Watt, H. (2004) 'Beyond Double Effect', in Oderberg, D.S. and Chappell, T. (eds) *Human Values: New Essays on Ethics and Natural Law* (Basingstoke: Palgrave Macmillan).

PART V
Access to Medical Treatment and the Preservation of (New) Life

Chapter 15
Access to Medicines and the Right to (Cultural) Life

Johanna Gibson

Introduction

Access to information and the right to participate in the benefits of scientific research and progress are instrumental in the achievement of high standards of health. This is important in terms of the goods available to individuals, including access to quality medicines. But it is also critical that individuals have access to adequate information delivered in a culturally relevant and meaningful context. Indeed, the significant relationship between development, poverty and health is crucial to understand in the broader context for health, including the right to development[1] and the right to cultural life.[2] The relationship between the cultural life of scientific research and progress and the human right to health is arguably fundamental, yet it receives perhaps less attention in the context of access to medicines than the more explicit negotiations of the right to the highest attainable standard of health.[3] Furthermore, the delivery of the right to development rests upon cultural participation and health as essential components of development itself. For these reasons, it is not merely related to but rather it is critical to the characterisation of the right to health to examine the relationship with development and culture. In the context of debates in intellectual property protection and commercialisation, this chapter considers the right to access quality medicines as an element of the right to cultural life, including the right to participate in the benefits of scientific research.

The discourse on rights indicates a certain dichotomy between natural or 'moral' rights and economic rights. The latter is attended by more robust implementation and enforcement, premised and articulated upon binding legal statute. With the effects of globalisation on legal systems and trading environments, economic rights become perhaps prioritised or interpreted as the totality of legal rights and indeed the 'whole picture' with respect to models for innovation (including

1 UN General Assembly. Resolution 41/128 Declaration on the Right to Development. A/RES/41/128. 4 December 1986.

2 International Covenant on Economic Social and Cultural Rights (ICESCR), article 15.

3 ICESCR, article 12.

pharmaceutical innovation). Indeed, the democratisation of the public sphere is premised upon relationships in private property, upon the recognition and exercise of proprietary rights, and so the 'morality' of the legal system is rendered somewhat ancillary. Privileged discourses of 'freedom' and 'rights' come to be attached to private property and, as such, a principal authority is conferred upon the value of 'property,' including that prescribed by the intellectual property system.

Of critical importance to ensuring the access of individuals to public health, including the necessary opportunities for social well-being, development and cultural participation, is the communication of human rights principles within commercial systems: 'human rights institutionalize the communicative conditions for a reasonable political will-formation' (Habermas 2001, 117). Indeed, what is at stake is not the rendering of certain frameworks, like the patent system, as ethical frameworks, but rather it is the intervention of moral rationalism within legal discourse and towards sustaining its legitimacy. While the economic intellectual property system may be seen to allow for the privateering of the private sphere, it is necessary to examine the way in which the moral principles of the private sphere can be invigorating and legitimating forces in a functioning economic system, '[human rights] are constitutive for the legal order as a whole and to this extent determine a framework within which normal legislation must be conducted' (ibid., 1998, 190). Therefore, as well as noting the basis in human rights for ensuring an individual's right to health and access to health care opportunities, it is necessary in the present discussion to consider further the circumstances by which to achieve the right to health, including cultural and political circumstances in accessibility and acceptability of health care.

The Cultural Basis for Health

The cultural and physical health and well-being of the individual underpins the full realisation of the right to cultural life, comprising the individual's access to the public sphere and to the institutions within that sphere, including the institution of medicine and health care. The ongoing cultural and legitimate constitution of that institution's normative and legal order indicates the role of access (more properly, the role of use) by the individual and the collective in its maintenance and reproduction.

The right to health, being a broad inclusive right to the circumstances necessary for physical as well as social and mental well-being, is fulfilled where there is meaningful access to and availability of health care goods and services.[4] Thus, the full realisation of the right to health includes fulfilment of the underlying cultural,

4 ICESCR article 12; Committee on Economic Social and Cultural Rights (CESCR). General Comment No 14 (2000). The right to the highest attainable standard of health (article 12 of the International Covenant on Economic, Social and Cultural Rights, 22nd Session. E/C.12/2000/4. 11 August 2000.

social and political determinants relevant to health. Not only is health thus a condition of fuller participation in cultural life, but also cultural participation and access to the benefits of cultural and intellectual life, persist as predetermining conditions of the fulfillment of the right to health. Therefore, the present discussion concentrates on the examination of this relationship between culture and health, in the context of the wider scholarship on the right to health and the relationship between health and development. If obligations to the fulfilment of individual rights with respect to health are met, then arguably this is the mechanism by which to overcome individual life chances. Robust protection of rights would provide the opportunity to access health and autonomy over the conduct of one's own life. Thus, rights must necessarily secure both the democratisation of the public sphere, ensuring access to the institution of health, and the morality and legitimacy of judgments and participation within that sphere (ibid., 1997, 111).[5]

Jürgen Habermas explains that a democratic and political public sphere will be one where there is access to the necessary opportunities for participation and development (ibid., 1997, 367). These are the necessary circumstances for the integrity of the individual, '[s]ocialized individuals could not maintain themselves as subjects at all if they did not find support in the relationships of reciprocal recognition articulated in cultural traditions and stabilized in legitimate orders – and vice versa' (ibid., 80). That is, cultural and knowledge exchange reproduces individual integrity and control that may be guaranteed through access to production (that is, access to consumption of knowledge) and indeed reproduces the lifeworld itself (ibid., 2001. 152). Again, the access to knowledge is critical to health not only in the immediate context of access to medicines but also in terms of the broader well-being and integrity of the individual. From the perspective of the patent as a private proprietary right, the relationship between property and the public sphere comes to the fore. If private property rights suggest the participation in the public sphere (the democratisation of the public sphere) then it is only when genuine accessibility is achieved that the right to health can be understood as fully realised. And as a component of the right to cultural life, this accessibility to the services, goods and information necessary to health is not merely a personal interest but also an important aspect of the broader social benefit, '[o]nly the rights of political participation ground the citizen's reflexive, self-referential legal standing. Negative liberties and social entitlements, on the contrary, can be paternalistically bestowed…Historically speaking, liberal rights crystallized around the social position of the private property owner' (ibid., 1997, 78).

5 Habermas explains that there 'are two tasks the required system of rights is supposed to solve. It should institutionalize the communicative framework for a rational political will-formation, and it should ensure the very medium in which alone this will-formation can express itself as the common will of freely associated legal persons' (Habermas 1997, 111).

Indeed, health arguably has become less a condition of biology and more a condition of social status,[6] that is, the 'life chances' of the particular individual:

> [i]t is the most elemental economic fact that the way in which the disposition over material property is distributed among a plurality of people, meeting competitively in the market for the purpose of exchange, in itself creates specific life chances ... the kind of chance in the *market* is the decisive moment which presents a common condition for the individual's fate (Weber 1968, 927-928).[7]

Representative of an economic and social class, life chances manifest in the opportunities for access to and possession of goods (ibid., 927). These life chances therefore administer not only the individual's access to medicines but also the research agenda into diseases affecting certain populations and regions, in that the latter will be dominated by considerations of the profitability of markets. The ability to use creative material, to access medicines and to access educational material are all key issues demonstrating the conflict between the ordinary lives of citizens and the commercial system of intellectual property. The critical articulating factor is therefore access.

Health and the Right to Culture

Despite the central and critical role of the individual's and the community's socio-economic and cultural conditions, the right to culture nevertheless has received considerably less attention in the context of health debates. Indeed its role in relation to the right to health is somewhat marginalised in the debates, some going as far as suggesting that it is ancillary to the right to health.[8] However, arguably its relevance in this area is much more significant and indeed it is an interpretive framework for the right to health itself. Article 15 of the ICESCR provides for the right to culture, broadly speaking:

> 1. The States Parties to the present Covenant recognize the right of everyone:
>   (a) To take part in cultural life;
>   (b) To enjoy the benefits of scientific progress and its applications;
>   (c) To benefit from the protection of the moral and material interests resulting from any scientific, literary or artistic production of which he is the author.

6 The 2008 WHO Report of the Commission on Social Determinants of Health (CSDH) reports on the inequities of access to health care as determined by social status rather than biological or physical environmental vulnerabilities to which a particular group may be subject. See, CSDH 2008.

7 Weber develops the concept of life chances in *Economy and Society*, particularly Volume III. See, Weber 1968.

8 For instance, see the discussion in Hestermeyer 2007, 112.

2. The steps to be taken by the States Parties to the present Covenant to achieve the full realization of this right shall include those necessary for the conservation, the development and the diffusion of science and culture.

3. The States Parties to the present Covenant undertake to respect the freedom indispensable for scientific research and creativity activity.

4. The States Parties to the present Covenant recognize the benefits to be derived from the encouragement and development of international contacts and co-operation in the scientific and cultural fields.[9]

The broader entitlements and freedoms within this right are importantly relevant to providing for equal opportunities for all citizens to take part in cultural life[10] and enjoy the benefits of scientific progress,[11] regardless of individual life chances. Significantly, this would indicate the right to access the benefits of medical research and development, including medicines. Further, it would also indicate the need for attention to possible obstacles to incentives to scientific research that may be posed by excessive intrusion of intellectual property monopolies.[12]

On the greater relevance of article 15 to the right to health, the General Comment No. 16 on the implementation of article 3[13] is important. Article 3 concerns equality of access for men and women to economic, social and cultural rights:

> [t]he States Parties to the present Covenant undertake to ensure the equal right of men and women to the enjoyment of all economic, social and cultural rights set forth in the present Covenant.[14]

The significance of this right is that it is a 'non-derogable standard for compliance with the obligations of States parties as set out in Articles 6 through 15 of ICESCR'[15]

9 ICESCR, article 15.

10 Article 15.1(a).

11 Article 15.1(b).

12 For instance, consider the specific nature of patents for gene-related inventions, where the classical interpretation of patent protection may preclude further commercialisation of products for other uses based on the same gene sequence, and the relevance of purpose-bound protection in these areas. See further, Gibson 2009, particularly chapters 2 and 6.

13 CESCR. General Comment No. 16 (2005). The equal right of men and women to the enjoyment of all economic, social and cultural rights (art 3 of the International Covenant on Economic, Social and Cultural Rights). E/C.12/2005/4. 11 August 2005.

14 ICESCR, article 3.

15 CESCR. General Comment No 16(2005). The equal right of men and women to the enjoyment of all economic, social and cultural rights (article 3 of the International Covenant on Economic, Social and Cultural Rights). E/C.12/2005/4. 11 August 2005, para. 17.

and is of particular relevance to the access to health care and information in many developing countries. Further, the General Comment's approach to the eradication of discrimination and the promotion of equality of opportunities for all individuals to access economic, social and cultural rights is important. In particular, it takes account of discrimination both within the law and in a broader social context, citing failure to address the total context for the realisation of economic, social and cultural rights being a violation of those rights:

> [t]he principle of equality between men and women is fundamental to the enjoyment of each of the specific rights enumerated in the Covenant. Failure to ensure formal and substantive equality in the enjoyment of any of these rights constitutes a violation of that right. Elimination of de jure as well as de facto discrimination is required for the equal enjoyment of economic, social and cultural rights. Failure to adopt, implement and monitor effects of laws, policies and programmes to eliminate de jure and de facto discrimination with respect to each of the rights enumerated in rights 6 to 15 of the Covenant constitutes a violation of those rights.[16]

In May 2008, during its 40th Session, the CESCR organised a Day of General Discussion (DGD) on the right to take part in cultural life (article 15.1(a)). A DGD is a public meeting open to international UN institutions, governments, intergovernmental organisations, non-governmental organisations (NGO) and civil society. The meeting on article 15.1(a) structured discussions around four themes: the definition of cultural life within the human rights framework; analysing the right to cultural life itself and access to that right; exploring and identifying the interaction between the right to cultural life and other universal human rights; and the individual and collective character of the right. The last theme is particularly relevant in the context of discussions throughout this book of the need to interpret the full realisation of human rights through participation in the public sphere as an important aspect of the social formation of human collectives. In a background paper to the DGD, Elissavet Stamatopoulou, Chief of the Secretariat of the Permanent Forum on Indigenous Issues (PFII) welcomed the DGD, describing the right to participate as a neglected human right (Stamatopoulou 2008, 2).

Contributions by participants explored explicitly the link between the right to cultural life and the right to health. The International Commission of Jurists argued that health is in fact an aspect of cultural life, acknowledging the importance of cultural acceptability and relevance in the implementation and realisation of human rights throughout the work of the CESCR:

16 CESCR. General Comment No 16(2005). The equal right of men and women to the enjoyment of all economic, social and cultural rights (article 3 of the International Covenant on Economic, Social and Cultural Rights). E/C.12/2005/4. 11 August 2005, para. 41.

> [t]he right to participate in cultural life is closely connected with many other human rights. Some other human rights are particularly significant for the right to participate in cultural life … However, the exercise of many other human rights also entails cultural components, relevant to assess the enjoyment of the right to take part in cultural life. The Committee on Economic, Social and Cultural Rights has adequately captured this concept in several of its General Comments referred to specific economic and social rights, through the notion of 'acceptability,' 'cultural adequacy' or 'cultural appropriateness.' The Committee has employed this notion to define the normative requirements of other rights set forth by the International Covenant on Economic, Social and Cultural Rights (ICESCR) – such as the right to adequate housing, the right to adequate food, the right to the highest attainable standard of health and the right to water. This, in turn, implies that *food, housing, health and water can be, inter alia, significant components of cultural life* (emphasis added) (International Commission of Jurists 2008, 2).

Indeed, towards achieving accessibility to the right, article 15.1(a) should be interpreted with respect for cultural relevance and acceptability. In particular, in the context of traditional medical knowledge, the right to cultural life is significant not only in terms of access to participate and practise traditional knowledge, but also in terms of achieving relevant protection for the holders of that knowledge, pursuant to article 15.1(c). Traditional medicine is a particularly significant public health resource for many communities and regions in the world (WHO 2008). With respect to medical research and public health, both the transfer of traditional medical knowledge in research and development as well as its cultural and social relevance to adequate health care in many regions raise the issue of the right to culture as it interacts with health.

A broader understanding of the importance of cultural specificity and relevance in delivering health care therefore will offer insight into the efficacy of primary health care. Indeed, sharing of benefits, delivery of public health care and access to medicines in traditional and indigenous communities directly implicates the importance of culture to medicine and medical systems. As well as the question of access to medicines in broader populations in developing countries, associated prevention and treatment must be prepared and available within a respected and trusted infrastructure, which includes cooperation with traditional healers. The World Health Organization (WHO) traditional medicine strategy 2002-2005 outlines its main objectives with respect to traditional medicine, including the integration of traditional medicine in national health systems,[17] implementation of international standards and clinical guidelines and the facilitation of knowledge transfer (ibid., 2002).

---

17 Traditional medicine is also an important aspect of the full realisation of article 12 of the ICESCR. See CESCR. General Comment No 14 (2000). The right to the highest attainable standard of health (article 12 of the International Covenant on Economic, Social and Cultural Rights. 22nd Session. E/C.12/2000/4. 11 August 2000, para. 27.

Current intergovernmental discussions towards the equitable management and benefit sharing of traditional knowledge and genetic resources are also immediately relevant to health and access to medicines in the community concerned.[18] In particular, the critical social and cultural dimension to medicine and medical practice in many indigenous and traditional communities is significant to delivering culturally-relevant and effective health care (such as through collaborations between western and traditional practitioners) as well as fulfilling the cultural participation of the groups involved. Furthermore, the potential research and commercial value in genetic resources and associated traditional knowledge indicates the importance of developmental concerns in the context of the realisation of the right to health and the creation of frameworks within which to manage medicinal products and knowledge. Realisation of the right to health not only underpins development, but also the right to development and culture emerge as determining factors for health.

The Right to Development

The UN General Assembly adopted the Declaration on the Right to Development, by Resolution 41/128, in its 41st Session, 1986.[19] Article 1.1 declares the right to development to be an inalienable human right:

> [t]he right to development is an inalienable human right by virtue of which every human person and all peoples are entitled to participate in, contribute to, and enjoy economic, social, cultural and political development, in which all human rights and fundamental freedoms can be fully realized.[20]

This character of the right to development is articulated with respect to health in article 8. Article 8.1 provides for health as one of the underlying determinants for the full realisation of the right to development:

> [s]tates should undertake, at the national level, all necessary measures for the realization of the right to development and shall ensure, inter alia, equality of opportunity for all in their access to basic resources, education, health services, food, housing, employment and the fair distribution of income.[21]

---

18 In particular, see the documents of the World Intellectual Property Organization (WIPO) Intergovernmental Committee in Intellectual Property and Genetic Resources, Traditional Knowledge and Folklore. For a full discussion of the cultural and legal conflicts between traditional knowledge and intellectual property frameworks, the work of WIPO and international initiatives towards protection, see Gibson 2005.

19 UN General Assembly. Resolution 41/128 Declaration on the Right to Development. A/RES/41/128. 4 December 1986.

20 Ibid., para. 1.1.

21 Ibid., para. 8.1.

In effect, the fulfilment of the right to development necessarily addresses the life chances of all citizens and provides for opportunities for all individuals to these fundamental human rights. As such, the Declaration also provides that the right to development necessarily supports the right to self-determination in article 1.2, including the right to sovereignty over genetic resources:

> [t]he human right to development also implies the full realization of the right of peoples to self-determination, which includes, subject to the relevant provisions of both International Covenants on Human Rights, the exercise of their inalienable right to full sovereignty over all the natural wealth and resources.

Importantly, beyond the primary nature attributed to the value of property in democratic systems, the right to development and its implication of the right of self-determination articulate democracy upon principles of the collective. This is significant not only for human rights discourse but also for the social and political dimension of individual human rights as safeguarding the individual's opportunities to participate in the public sphere: 'States should encourage popular participation in all spheres as an important factor in development and in the full realization of all human rights.'[22]

This resonates with earlier examinations of the importance of the individual's life chances and access to the public sphere. Habermas emphasises the communicative value of the law and the legitimating force of addressing the circumstances for that social cohesion. In other words, in addressing not only access, in terms of availability, but also use in terms of genuine participation, 'governmental authority derives from the power produced communicatively in the civic practice of self-determination, and it finds its legitimation in the fact that it protects this practice by institutionalizing public liberty' (Habermas 1997, 270). The right to development articulates this 'use' of the public sphere as an inalienable human right and characterises the value of the fulfillment of that right to the social collective:

> development is a comprehensive economic, social, cultural and political process, which aims at the constant improvement of the well-being of the entire population and of all individuals on the basis of their active, free and meaningful participation in development and in the fair distribution of benefits resulting therefrom … everyone is entitled to a social and international order in which the rights and freedoms set forth in that Declaration can be fully realized.[23]

In 1993, the World Conference on Human Rights considered the right to development at length and adopted by consensus of the 171 Member States the

22 Ibid., para. 8.2.

23 Ibid., Preamble. See further, para. 2.

Vienna Declaration and Programme of Action.[24] Paragraph 10 of the Declaration 'reaffirms the right to development, as established in the Declaration on the Right to Development, as a universal and inalienable right and an integral part of fundamental human rights.'[25] Indeed, the right to development is inextricably and necessarily implicated in the realisation of fundamental human rights,[26] including the human right to health[27] and freedoms and entitlements contained within that human right. This includes access to benefits of scientific research and development as part of the meaningful fulfillment of the right to development, arguably incorporating access to medicinal products. Paragraph 11 provides that:

> [e]veryone has the right to enjoy the benefits of scientific progress and its applications. The World Conference on Human Rights notes that certain advances, notably in the biomedical and life sciences as well as in information technology, may have potentially adverse consequences for the integrity, dignity and human rights of the individual, and calls for international cooperation to ensure that human rights and dignity are fully respected in this area of universal concern.[28]

The Vienna Declaration reaffirms the right of self-determination of all peoples in Paragraph 2 and explains its basis for the free pursuit of economic, social and cultural development.[29] This is related to Paragraph 20, which calls for the facilitation of indigenous peoples' full social, political and cultural participation:

> [t]he World Conference on Human Rights recognizes the inherent dignity and the unique contribution of indigenous people to the development and plurality of society and strongly reaffirms the commitment of the international community to their economic, social and cultural well-being and their enjoyment of the fruits of sustainable development. States should ensure the full and free participation of indigenous people in all aspects of society, in particular in matters of concern to them.

---

24 World Conference on Human Rights. Vienna Declaration and Programme of Action. A/CONF.157/23. 12 July 1993.

25 Ibid., para. 10. See further para. 72 which declares that the right, as established in the Declaration on the Right to Development, must be implemented and realised. Further, the Declaration recommends the participation of civil society and NGOs in normative developments and cooperation with State Actors (Paragraph 38; Paragraph 73) and notes the necessary cooperation between actors in the field of development (Part C), compatible with the principles of cooperation for achievement of the MDGs. The relevance of civil society activity is considered further in Part IV: Access.

26 Ibid., para. 74.

27 Ibid., para. 31.

28 Ibid., para. 11.

29 Ibid., para. 2.

Again, the link between development and access to the public sphere is instrumental and fundamental to the full realisation of human rights, with self-determination being a critical mechanism through which to achieve development. The Vienna Declaration 'recommends that priority be given to national and international action to promote democracy, development and human rights'[30] and thus 'reaffirms that the universal and inalienable right to development, as established in the Declaration on the Right to Development, must be implemented and realized.'[31]

The open-ended Working Group on Development was established by the Commission on Human Rights by Resolution 1998/72[32] and the UN Economic and Social Council (ECOSOC) Decision 1998/269[33] to monitor and review progress on the implementation of the right at national and international levels for an initial period of three years. Pursuant to Commission on Human Rights Resolution 2004/7, the high-level task force on the implementation of the right to development was established. The high-level task force is a group of five experts nominated by the Chairperson of the Working Group, mandated by the Working Group to examine particular issues with respect to its objectives and subsequently provide technical expertise to the Working Group in its recommendations on implementation.

The first meeting of the high-level task force was held in December 2004 with the mandate to examine two aspects of implementation: obstacles and challenges to the Millennium Development Goals (MDGs)[34] in the context of the right to development; and national and international social impact assessments in trade and development. MDG 6 (to combat HIV/AIDS, malaria and other diseases) includes access to medicines as one of its explicit targets towards achieving this goal.[35]

30 Ibid., para. 66.

31 Ibid., para. 72.

32 Commission on Human Rights. Resolution 1998/72. The Right to Development.

33 ECOSOC. Decision 1998/269. The Right to Development.

34 At the 2000 UN Millennium Summit 189 UN Member States and at least 23 international organisations agreed to the Millennium Declaration (UN General Assembly. Resolution 55/2. UN Millennium Declaration. 51st Session General Assembly, 18 September 2000). The Millennium Declaration establishes a set of eight development goals to be achieved by 2015. These goals, known as the MDGs, include: the eradication of extreme poverty and hunger; the facilitation of universal access to and participation in primary education; the promotion of gender equality; the alleviation of child mortality; improve maternal health; the escalation of the campaign against HIV/AIDS, malaria and other diseases; ensure environmental sustainability; and the development of global partnerships towards development. Within each goal certain targets have been established to indicate progress towards achievement of the development programme. See further the discussion of the Millennium Development Goals (MDGs) and the targets defined within the eight MDGs in, Gibson 2009, particularly chapter 3.

35 This target includes the achievement of universal access to HIV/AIDS treatment by 2010 and securing access to antiretroviral drugs for a proportion of the population with advanced HIV infection.

MDG 8 (to develop a global partnership for development) includes the target to provide for access to affordable essential medicines for developing countries, by working in cooperation with pharmaceutical companies.

In its final report[36] the task force identified 'a holistic view of human rights' as underlying the Declaration on the Right to Development and agreed a series of 12 recommendations regarding implementation of the MDGs, including the recommendation to the Working Group to map the progress of the MDGs against existing human rights instruments.[37] The second session considered MDG 8 in particular (global partnership for development) and agreed upon criteria for its periodic evaluation, which were subsequently adopted by the Working Group. The progress of these criteria was considered in the third session in 2007 and at the fourth session in 2008 these criteria and the progress of their application were reviewed and revised.

The fourth session deals at length with MDG 8 (develop a global partnership for development) and in particular Target 17 (access to affordable essential drugs in developing countries) which comes within the global partnership goal.[38] Importantly, this target demonstrates the inextricable relationship between health and development, the link being explicit not only in the agreement on this Target but also in the commentary on the relevant achievement of the MDGs. Towards advancing progress on Target 17, the task force has resolved to conduct two working sessions: the first concerned with procurement and pricing, including multilateral frameworks and public-private initiatives; and second to deal with trade-related aspects of intellectual property rights under the World Trade Organization (WTO) system and the bilateral system of free trade agreements (FTA):

> [t]he task force proposes to examine the role of key multilateral and public-private initiatives in implementing Target 17 relating to access to affordable essential drugs in developing countries. This dialogue would involve partnerships focused on procurement and pricing as well as on trade-related aspects of intellectual property protection in the WTO and bilateral and regional free trade agreements involving relevant institutions.[39]

---

36 Commission on Human Rights. 61st Session. Review of Progress in the Promotion and Implementation of the Right to Development: Consideration of the Report of the High-Level Task Force on the Implementation of the Right to Development. Report of the high-level task force on the implementation of the right to development. E/CN.4/2005/WG.18/2. 24 January 2005.

37 Report of the high-level task force on the implementation of the right to development. E/CN.4/2005/WG.18/2. 24 January 2005. Paragraph 45.

38 A full list of the goals and the targets comprising each goal in the Annex to the Road map towards the implementation of the United Nations Millennium Declaration, UN General Assembly, 56th Session, 6 September 2001 (A/56/326).

39 Human Rights Council. 8th Session. Report of the high-level task force on the implementation of the right to development in its fourth session. A/HRC/8/WG.2/TF/2. 31

Similarly, the task force recommends work with the WHO and other relevant institutions towards the advancement of MDG Target 17, acknowledging the importance of the UN Special Rapporteur's draft Human Rights Guidelines for Pharmaceutical Companies in relation to Access to Medicines.[40]

The World Health Organization

At the Ninth Session of the open-ended Working Group, held in Geneva in August 2008, the Working Group mandated the task force to 'give priority to the issue of access to essential medicines in developing countries (Target 8.E)'[41] and to do so through a review of the work of the WHO Intergovernmental Working Group on Public Health, Innovation and Intellectual Property (IGWG). The IGWG was established in 2006 by resolution WHA 59.24[42] at the 59th World Health Assembly (WHA) of the WHO. The IGWG was given a mandate to develop and prepare a global strategy and work programme, with particular regard to the special issues for developing countries.

Following the report of the IGWG, at the 61st WHA in 2008 the meeting adopted the Global Strategy and Plan of Action by resolution,[43] reaffirming the right to health as a fundamental right and prioritising the importance of addressing the health needs of developing countries in the research and development agenda of developed countries. Furthermore, the promotion of research and development is understood to include not only support to governments in the development of national programmes, but also the promotion of accessibility to research benefits in order to build capacity and innovation in developing countries. Mechanisms by which to achieve this advocated in the global strategy include open-source methods and the identification of incentives and barriers to research and development, including intellectual property.[44] Access to knowledge and technology is

January 2008. Paragraph 85(a).

40 UN Special Rapporteur on the right of everyone to the enjoyment of the highest attainable standard of physical and mental health. *Human Rights Guidelines for Pharmaceutical Companies in relation to Access to Medicines*. Draft for Consultation. 19 September 2007.

41 Human Rights Council. Report of the Working Group on the Right to Development on its Ninth Session. A/HRC/9/17. 4 September 2008.

42 WHA. Resolution WHA59.24. Public health, innovation, essential health research and intellectual property rights: towards a global strategy and plan of action. 27 May 2006.

43 WHA. Resolution WHA61.21. Global strategy and plan of action on public health, innovation and intellectual property. 24 May 2008: Element 1.

44 Element 2 of the Global Strategy and Plan of Action includes 'promoting upstream research and product development in developing countries' a component of which includes the support of scientific research capacity and discovery including, 'where feasible and

emphasised throughout the strategy and includes mechanisms both within the intellectual property system (such as patent pools[45]) and through competition to improve availability and accessibility of products.

In establishing the IGWG, Resolution WHA 59.24 emphasizes critical issues in global health in the context of the freedom to participate in the cultural life of the community and characterises the broader context in which the right to health is realised, also reflected in the global strategy ultimately adopted by the WHA. This broader context includes concerns related to pricing and access to medicines and the need for new models and initiatives to encourage and promote innovation. This is an important articulation of the interaction between various human rights and the critical question of social, cultural and political access.[46] In this context, the resolution links questions of access and public health to the underlying determinants for public health, including the commercial environment in that the WHA urges Member States:

1. to make global health and medicines a priority sector, to take determined action to emphasize priorities in research and development addressed to the needs of patients, especially those in resource-poor settings, and to harness collaborative research and development initiatives involving disease-endemic countries;
2. to consider the recommendations of the report and to contribute actively to the development of a global strategy and plan of action, and to take an active part, working with the Secretariat and international partners, in providing support for essential medical research and development;

---

appropriate, voluntary open-source methods,' Global Strategy and Plan of Action on Public Health, Innovation and Intellectual Property, adopted at the 59th Session of the World Health Assembly by Resolution WHA61.21, 24 May 2008.

45 A patent pool is a consortium of at least two companies agreeing to cross-license patents relating to a particular technology, often introduced as a measure between competitors to avoid infringement and litigation. Therefore, a patent pool can also create a monopoly over certain technology if competitors cooperate in such a way (and cross-license rather than sue for infringement or revocation of weak patents). As a result, competition issues can become very important when a large consortium or 'cartel' is formed. As a business model, patent pools are not new but have been relevant throughout the modern patent system. More recently, patent pooling has been advocated as a mechanism to promote generic competition in markets for essential medicines, thus lowering prices and also promoting access to research resources for ongoing drug development and improvement (addressing both issues of cost and production). In particular, the patent pool is advocated as an incentive and mechanism by which to stimulate innovation, simplifying the legal obstacles to access and pooling 'expertise' and establishing global norms in collective management and open competition.

46 WHA. Resolution WHA59.24. Public health, innovation, essential health research and intellectual property rights: towards a global strategy and plan of action. 27 May 2006: Preamble.

3. to work to ensure that progress in basic science and biomedicine is translated into improved, safe and affordable health products – drugs, vaccines and diagnostics – to respond to all patients' and clients' needs, especially those living in poverty, taking into account the critical role of gender, and to ensure that capacity is strengthened to support rapid delivery of essential medicines to people;
4. to encourage trade agreements to take into account the flexibilities contained in the Agreement on Trade-Related Aspects of Intellectual Property Rights and recognized by the Doha Ministerial Declaration on the TRIPS Agreement[47] and Public Health.[48]

The holistic approach to human rights advocated throughout the documents on development indicates that the right to culture should be considered in the context of intellectual property and health. Indeed, it is through the interrogation of human rights frameworks that the cultural life of patents is becoming particularly clear.

Intellectual Property and the Right to Cultural Life

The relationship between cultural relevance and legitimacy becomes clearer in this context. Legitimacy is derived from a system that is actually meaningful to the development of national industry and technical expertise, as distinct from the illegitimacy of a system that appears to promote external interests over and above those subjects to which the law is to apply. In this way, local expertise and consultation is crucial to the implementation of law so as to motivate legitimacy and promote national interests. Thus, there is a clear relationship between use and the creation of a beneficial interest in the resources and benefits of scientific and medical research and development; that is, in the full realisation of an individual's right to cultural participation or cultural life. In the context of access to the benefits of scientific research, that use necessitates the safeguarding of the beneficial enjoyment of scientific research as distinct from any legal rights created in those benefits through intellectual property systems.

This central value of use is critical to questions of morality in the application and exercise of patent law. When examining the concept of use in patent rights, not only the scope of the patent (the legal rights in the invention) but also the accessibility for users (the beneficial interests in the invention) will be manifest. This characterisation of use is furthermore critical to an appreciation of the cultural life of patents and provides a foundation for maintaining access to the beneficial interest in the invention, on behalf of the whole of society. In other words, the exercise of the legal rights in the patent should therefore be subject to obligations

47 The WTO Agreement on Trade-Related Aspects of Intellectual Property Rights (TRIPS).

48 WHA. Resolution WHA59.24. Public health, innovation, essential health research and intellectual property rights: towards a global strategy and plan of action, para. 2.

to the beneficial interests in the patent. Following this argument, failure to fulfil the equitable interests may thus compromise the ability to enjoy the legal rights. The invention is, in other words, held in trust – that is, both legal and equitable interests are held in the one property. This forms the basis of modern personal equitable obligations to deal with property for the benefit of another class of persons (that is, a beneficial interest other than the legal interest of the owners) – a type of 'Global Medicines Trust.'[49]

Thus, while the goods comprising the resources necessary to the realisation of the right to health might incorporate private property interests (in the form of the patent), the knowledge contained within those goods might be seen as held in equitable trust to which all are entitled as beneficiaries under article 15.1(b) of the ICESCR. Therefore, although the private property holder has certain legal rights to the invention defined within the patent, the invention itself is a public good. In principle, this can be interpreted as a beneficial interest in the invention held by each individual. In other words, there are two simultaneous interests in an invention – one is the legal interest defined by the patent; the other is the equitable interest in the invention as a public good.

Where the rights in the patent interfere with the beneficial interest in the public good to such an extent that the human right to health and to enjoy the applications of scientific research are compromised, then it must be possible to address this. That is, where the exercise of those rights begins to pose real and material obstacles to the capacity of governments to fulfil the right to health, then there may be a right against the 'trustee.' This human rights qualification on the exercise of trade-related intellectual property rights is found not only in instruments towards the interpretation and application of the right to health (OHCHR/UNAIDS 2006, 48, para. 52), but also in instruments concerning the full implementation of the right to development[50] and in the TRIPS Agreement itself. Article 8 provides:

1. Members may, in formulating or amending their laws and regulations, adopt measures necessary to protect public health and nutrition, and to promote the public interest in sectors of vital importance to their socio-economic and technological development, provided that such measures are consistent with the provisions of this Agreement.
2. Appropriate measures, provided that they are consistent with the provisions of this Agreement, may be needed to prevent the abuse of intellectual property rights by

49 This concept is dealt with in greater detail in Gibson 2009.

50 Commission on Human Rights. 61st Session. Review of Progress in the Promotion and Implementation of the Right to Development: Consideration of the Report of the High-Level Task Force on the Implementation of the Right to Development. Report of the high-level task force on the implementation of the right to development. E/CN.4/2005/WG.18/2. 24 January 2005: Paragraph 45. See further Human Rights Council. 8th Session. Report of the high-level task force on the implementation of the right to development in its fourth session. A/HRC/8/WG.2/TF/2. 31 January 2008, para. 85(a).

right holders or the resort to practices which unreasonably restrain trade or adversely affect the international transfer of technology.[51]

Indeed, it is contended in this chapter that the law itself already recognises this beneficial interest of the public in the invention in the form of provisions for compulsory licensing. While the limitations imposed upon compulsory licensing by the TRIPS Agreement[52] have been criticised,[53] arguably the public health amendment to TRIPS goes a significant way to redress this.[54] That is, where the beneficial interest is obstructed by the exercise of the legal interest, the balance is addressed by compulsory licensing. The central value of the trust, as it were, is that of use. Use not only constitutes the possessory relationship to knowledge, but also is the mechanism by which to fulfil the trust. That is, use constrains the legal rights; use contains the equitable interests.

Despite the 'crisis' in access and the creation of limitations on the benefits of these institutions, intellectual property and medicine and health care themselves are arguably, importantly and necessarily public goods rendered excludable by specific technical, but not consensual, intrusions. Therefore, the patent system takes non-excludable knowledge and produces an excludable good (as an alternative to protecting one's invention by secrecy). It creates, therefore, legal rights in the invention that subsist alongside beneficial interests in the diffusion of that technology. Access to these institutions therefore underlies an individual's right to cultural life, not only in terms of the accessibility to the benefits of those institutions but also in terms of the use of those benefits for all regardless of individual life chances. Similarly, as a public good, the research and development that inputs into the institution of medicine and health care comprises not only the economic functioning of that institution but also the cultural life. Therefore, the cultural life of patents comprises not only the research culture that produces the resources of the institution of medicine, but also the ethical oversight for medicines (including both the ethical context for patents and the regulatory framework for medicines).

51 TRIPS, article 8.

52 Article 31.

53 In relation to pharmaceuticals see, Bass 2002; and generally, see, de Carvalho NP 2005, 147-54; Correa 1999.

54 Article 31 *bis* (the public health amendment) implements the Decision on Paragraph 6 of the Doha Declaration, waiving the obligations of TRIPS members to manufacture under a compulsory licence for the domestic market only, as provided under article 31(f). Without this waiver, article 31(f) posed a significant limit to the amount of generic product that could be exported when manufactured under a compulsory licence. Because of the limitation to the domestic market, this restriction limits the possible supply to countries unable to manufacture under compulsory licence themselves in times of national emergency. The Decision made it possible, within the terms set out in the Decision itself, for any member country to export generic product made under a compulsory licence.

Therefore if private property rights suggest the participation in the public sphere (the democratisation of the public sphere) then it is only when genuine accessibility is achieved that the right to health can be understood to be fully realised. And as a component of the right to cultural life, this accessibility to the services, goods and information necessary to health is not merely a personal interest but an important aspect of the broader social benefit: 'Only the rights of political participation ground the citizen's reflexive, self-referential legal standing. Negative liberties and social entitlements, on the contrary, can be paternalistically bestowed…Historically speaking, liberal rights crystallized around the social position of the private property owner' (Habermas 1997, 78).

Use, in this context, generates the relationship of possession in the sense of historical relationships to land. During the period of feudal law, land could not be devised by will.[55] Rather, it was held in strict feudal incidents of tenure whereby relationships to land were constructed in a hierarchy of obligations between vassals and lords. The 'use' was developed in order to overcome the rule as to divestiture by will. In this way, use constitutes 'ownership' and authority with respect to the land. This is of particular interest in the context of the contemporary model of western democracy modeled on private property rights. That is, use, in the fuller sense, appropriates this proprietary language and is part of the underlying mechanism for realisation of the right to cultural life. The right to cultural life incorporates participation through use.

Conclusion

The right to health is importantly and meaningfully an element of the full realisation of the right to cultural participation – not only in terms of the access to the benefits of scientific research[56] but also in the broader sense of the right to cultural life.[57] Incorporating both physical and mental well-being, the definition of health not only includes cultural identity but also relies upon attention to cultural diversity in its very interpretation and realisation, as embodied in the element of 'acceptability.'[58] Therefore, the full realisation of the right to health derives from more than mere entitlement to access. It necessarily comprises the four principles of the right, which arguably constitute the fuller concept of 'use.' Importantly, participating in this public sphere and within this logic of the proprietary model of democracy and freedom, fulfilling use also fulfils the basis for 'possession'

55 See further the discussion in Gray and Gray 2005, 92. For greater detail see Simpson 1986.

56 ICESCR article 15.1(b).

57 ICESCR article 15.1(a).

58 CESCR. General Comment No 14 (2000). The right to the highest attainable standard of health (article 12 of the International Covenant on Economic, Social and Cultural Rights. 22nd Session. E/C.12/2000/4. 11 August 2000. Paragraph 12.

in a sense of meaningful and accessible use and benefit. The opportunity to use accounts for differences in life chances and addresses the genuine value upon which the western model of democracy is articulated. Use thus fulfils 'ownership,' that is, the political participation of individuals regardless of individual life chances. Meaningful access to medicines is fundamentally a question of the right to life.

Bibliography

Bass, N.A. (2002) 'Implications of the TRIPS Agreement for Developing Countries: Pharmaceutical Patent Laws in Brazil and South Africa in the 21st Century', 34 *George Washington Law Review* 191.

de Carvalho, N.P. (2005) *The TRIPS Regime of Patent Rights* (The Hague: Kluwer Law International).

Correa, C. (1999) *Intellectual Property Rights, the WTO and Developing Countries: The TRIPS Agreement and Policy Options* (London: Zed Books).

CSDH (2008) *Closing the Gap in a Generation: Health Equity through Action on the Social Determinants of Health* (Geneva: World Health Organization).

Gibson, J. (2009) *Intellectual Property, Medicine and Health: Current Debates* (Farnham: Ashgate Publishing).

—— (2005) *Community Resources: Intellectual Property, International Trade and Protection of Traditional Knowledge* (Aldershot: Ashgate Publishing).

Gray, K. and Gray, S.F. (2005) *Elements of Land Law* (Oxford: Oxford University Press).

Habermas, J. (2001) *The Postnational Constellation: Political Essays* (trans. and ed. Pensky, M.) (Cambridge: Polity Press).

—— (1998) *The Inclusion of the Other: Studies in Political Theory* (trans. Cronin, C. and de Greiff, P.) (Cambridge: Polity Press).

—— (1997) *Between Facts and Norms: Contributions to a Discourse Theory of Law and Democracy* (trans. Rehg, W.) (Cambridge: Polity Press).

Hestermeyer, H. (2007) *Human Rights and the WTO: The Case of Patents and Access to Medicines* (Oxford: Oxford University Press).

International Commission of Jurists (2008). Background Paper. Day of General Discussion on the right to take part in cultural life (article 15(1)(a) of the Covenant). E/C.12/40/9. 9 May.

OHCHR/UNAIDS (2006) *International Guidelines on HIV/AIDS and Human Rights* (Geneva: WHO).

Simpson, A.W.B. (1986) *A History of The Land Law*, 2nd edn (Oxford: Oxford University Press).

Stamatopoulou, E. (2008). 'The right to take part in cultural life'. Background Paper. Day of General Discussion on the right to take part in cultural life (article 15(1)(a) of the Covenant). E/C.12/40/9. 9 May.

Weber, M. (1968) *Economy and Society: An Outline of Interpretive Sociology*, in Roth, G. and Wittich, C. (eds) (New York: Bedminster Publishers).
WHO (2008) Fact sheet No. 134. Traditional Medicine, December (Geneva: WHO).
—— (2002) *Traditional Medicine Strategy 2002-2005* (Geneva: WHO).

Chapter 16
Assessing Vitality: Infertility and 'Good Life' in Urban China

Ayo Wahlberg

Introduction

On one of Beijing's many university campuses, a small ad was posted on a notice board some time in the spring of 2007:

> [a]n infertile couple is seeking an ovum. The desired egg donor should be: aged 20 to 29 years old, with at least an undergraduate diploma, no family medical history, good looking, regardless of marriage status. The reward will be above ten thousand yuan.

The advertiser was the father of a 42-year-old woman who had been diagnosed with dysfunctional ovaries. Her doctor had said that the only way to overcome this was 'if good quality donated eggs could be found.' When asked, the father told doctors that the reason he preferred advertising for eggs on campus rather than getting them through the hospital was because he could see the donor in person 'to make sure she is healthy and good looking' (BIONET 2007, 4). While the commercialised sale of ova and sperm is forbidden by law in China, like in many other countries there is a chronic shortage of donors, leading this family to directly solicit potential donors.[1]

It is only twenty years since the first successful *in vitro* fertilised (IVF) pregnancy culminated in a live birth at the Peking University Third Hospital in Beijing's Haidian district. Zheng Mengzhu was born in March 1988 after her 39 year-old mother had undergone IVF treatment led by Prof. Zhang Lizhu who recently recalled at a celebration marking Mengzhu's 20th birthday that 'her parents had been trying for nearly twenty years to have a child' (Xinhua 2008). Since then, the demand for and provision of assisted reproductive technologies (ART) to involuntarily childless couples has risen rapidly. In Beijing alone, by 2005 an estimated 10,000 couples had sought treatment for infertility with over 3,000 IVF babies born (*China Daily* 2005). The Reproductive and Genetic Hospital CITIC-Xiangya in Hunan province has consistently increased the number of IVF cycles it

1 In this case, the advertisement was taken down and the father was informed that it is illegal to solicit donors in this manner.

provides annually from 2,000 in 2003 to over 10,000 in 2009. Throughout China, the rapid uptake of assisted reproductive technologies (ART) in the 1990s meant that by the turn of the millennium, over 200 hospitals and health centres were thought to be providing ART treatment to a growing proportion of China's infertile couples. When the Ministry of Health introduced new regulations stipulating standards and requiring all clinics providing ART to apply for a license in 2001, the number of ART clinics fell to 88 although it has since climbed back up to over 100 (Yu 2007).

As Handwerker (2002) has noted, these developments have taken place in exactly the same period that family planning policies and practices in China have firmly pursued goals of restriction and prevention (see also Greenhalgh and Winckler 2005).

> [a]fter 30 years of efforts, exponential population growth has been effectively controlled, and some 300 million births have been prevented. Under undeveloped economic circumstances and in a relatively short period of time, the country has realized a remarkably low birth rate (Zhao Bingli, Vice Minister of the State Family Planning Commission cited in Hu 2002).

This control has been achieved through strict limits on the number of children a couple can give birth to (popularly referred to as the 'one-child' or 'one-and-a-half child'[2] policy) and, more controversially, also through genetic counselling and sterilisation campaigns. These latter practices have attracted considerable international attention with a number of scholars describing them as eugenic efforts to improve the quality of the population, in particular by preventing births of 'inferior quality' (Handwerker 2002; MacLeod and Clarke 1998; *Nature* 1994).

In much of hitherto social studies of infertility and involuntary childlessness there has been important focus on the often devastating personal, social and ideological consequences of involuntary childlessness and/or infertility treatment – their *lived experience*. There has also been focus on the social and ethical implications of new reproductive technologies as they trouble nature/culture boundaries and reconfigure patterns and understandings of kinship. With an initial concentration of studies in those Western countries in which new reproductive technologies originated (especially the United Kingdom and America) (Arditti et al. 1984; McNeil et al. 1990; Strathern 1992; Franklin 1997; Becker 1997; Throsby 2004; Thompson 2005), more recently social scientists have shifted empirical focus to African (Inhorn 1994, 1996), Asian (Bharadawaj 2003) and Latin American (Roberts 2006) countries, not least as a way of 'countering the predominant Western view of infertility as a yuppie complaint of little concern to the rest of the purportedly overpopulated developing world' (Inhorn and van Balen

2 In some rural areas, families are allowed to have a second child if their first-born was a girl, while in urban areas couples where both are single children will be allowed to have two children.

2002, 7). Indeed, infertility and involuntary childlessness are considered by many as an unrecognised or at the very most under-recognised public health problem in 'high fertility' countries 'where children are highly desired, parenthood is culturally mandatory [and] infertility is a socially unacceptable condition, leading most infertile couples on a relentless "quest for conception" that may eventually involve resort to new reproductive technologies' (Inhorn 2003, 1838; see also Evens 2004). In such socio-cultural contexts, Inhorn and van Balen argue, 'infertile people's suffering is often exacerbated' (Inhorn and van Balen 2002, 6).

One such country, according to Lisa Handwerker (1995; 1998; 2002), is China. Following ethnographic studies at a number of infertility clinics in Beijing, she has argued that China's 'birth policy aimed at reducing births has ironically led to the further stigmatization of infertile women' as the pressures to have 'one child' have intensified (Handwerker 2002, 310). One of her informants explains, 'I am sure the pressure to have children in China is greater than in any other country...I feel so much pressure because of the mandatory birth certificate which provides me with permission to have a child. I have had to turn in my certificate the last three years because I couldn't have a child. I felt terrible. Here they give you permission and then you can't even give birth' (in Handwerker 2002, 302).

In this chapter, I shift empirical focus away from ethnographic description of the lived experience of involuntary childlessness among expectant couples. Indeed, the ways in which infertility is seen to affect the lives of involuntarily childless couples is part of the problem space that I will be examining. Neither will I seek to trace out social and ethical implications of the increasing use of new reproductive technologies in China. Instead, my focus will be on the multiple forms of life at stake in the practice of assisted reproduction in urban China today – through *in vitro* fertilisation (IVF), artificial insemination by donor (AID), intrauterine insemination (IUI) or intracytoplasmic sperm injection (ICSI) – as a way to situate these practices in terms of the concepts, norms, objects and telos that make them at once desirable and problematic. My primary questions will be: if reproductive technologies are used to improve life, then what kind of life is it that is seen to hold such innate potential for improvability? And related to this, what kind of a problem is infertility/involuntary childlessness (and its treatment) in urban China?

To answer this question, I will focus on how different forms of life organise the ways in which infertility and assisted reproductive technologies are thought about and practiced in four IVF clinics and associated sperm banks located in Beijing and Changsha. I will further contextualise these practices in broader debates about assisted reproductive technologies among academics, policymakers and clinicians. While it is clear that assisted reproductive technologies in urban China are assemblages of practices aimed at (though not always successful in) improving human *life* (*shēng*), this is not a singular kind of life, rather it is life that is at once biological and social, cellular and psychological, individual and collective. What is more, it is improvable in an equally plural although not necessarily compatible way.

Historically, debates around vitality, vitalism, vital forces and vital principles have concerned living cellular organisms and whether or not 'mechanistic' physical and chemical sciences are able to account for their innate tendencies, exigencies, potentialities and propensities to adapt and survive (Canguilhem 1994; Greco 2005). Yet, when it comes to *human* life, vitality is not solely a matter of bodies, organisms, cells, biological processes and their pathologies. It is also about individual thriving, flourishing and fulfilling of human potentialities as opposed to suffering, languishing and stagnation. It is about collective relationalities, socialities and connections and how these can be upset, disturbed, stabilised or transformed. And if we are to investigate how assisted reproductive technologies in urban China are used to try to improve life, we must pay attention to how these multiple forms of life that comprise human vitality co-circulate and interact.

The aim of the chapter, then, is not to evaluate the personal consequences, ethical propriety or social effects of infertility and ART practices in urban China today. Instead it is to investigate the interlinkages between certain concepts of 'quality' and the very practical and normative assessments of 'good life' that they make possible (cf. Canguilhem 1989). As we will see, different forms of the concept of 'quality' (such as 质量 *zhìliàng* and 素质 *sùzhì*) are central in efforts to both map out and intervene upon human life in IVF clinics in urban China. The importance of such studies which map out interactions between 'ways of knowing' and 'ways of doing' lies in what might be described as an empirical clarification of the conditions or terms of normativity that make certain practices (e.g. infertility counselling, grading embryo quality, screening gamete donors) appear suitable for attaining particular ends (e.g. better 'quality of life' for involuntarily childless couples, improved 'population quality,' or ensuring 'good quality' donor sperm for recipients). To understand how certain ways of evaluating, assessing and judging what constitutes (a) good life come to be stabilised and contested in the context of ART, it is crucial to map out the terms of their normativity.

The empirical data for this paper has been gathered during several visits to four IVF clinics (three in Beijing and one in Changsha) and two sperm banks (also in Beijing and Changsha) in 2007-2008, during which time I had the opportunity to meet, speak with and interview fertility doctors, embryologists, nurses and lab technicians. Material has also been collated from two workshops and one conference on the topics of reproductive and regenerative medicine held in Beijing, Shanghai and Changsha in the period April 2007 to April 2008 as part of the European Commission-funded BIONET project, all of which were attended by leading fertility experts and clinicians in China. The analysis is based on interviews as well as documents including national regulations on ART in China, informed consent forms from IVF clinics and sperm banks, leaflets and materials provided to patients/donors at the clinics and banks, scientific articles by embryologists and other fertility experts in China as well as various national media articles on infertility in China. My working language has been English and I have therefore relied on assistance for interpretation and translation while in Beijing and Changsha as well as on personal communication with a number of fertility experts in China with all the limitations that this entails. The analysis cannot and should not be generalised to China as a nation since it pertains the provision of ART in a very limited urban context. Nevertheless, the chapter does circumscribe and present some key concepts and practices which currently inform debates and deliberations about what constitutes good life in assisted reproduction in China.

Burdened Life – The Problem of Infertility/Involuntary Childlessness

On any given weekday, the third floor of the Reproductive and Genetic Hospital in Changsha is thronging with people. Most of them are couples in search of answers as to why they are unable to conceive a child, but there are also landlords hawking rooms to rent for those who have travelled from afar. Many of the couples have already tried cheaper options, such as traditional Chinese medicine, and some have borrowed large sums of money to help pay for modern treatment (costing around RMB 25-30,000 or €2,600-3,100 for one IVF cycle), which can leave them in debt for years to come.

As one of the largest and most sought after in China, the Reproductive and Genetic Hospital organises introductory lectures for patients on Mondays, delivered with the help of a microphone, laptop and projector to standing-room-only audiences. Many of the couples present have 'made their excuses' to be there. According to Liu Wei who counsels patients undergoing artificial insemination by donor (AID) this is because 'infertility is a big taboo, especially in China. It can be a source of great embarrassment and shame for couples, and many of our patients will not even confide in close family members. It is a large burden for them'.

Herein lies the problem of infertility – it is a problem that must be remedied insofar as it leads to *burdened lives*. Just as was the case in the United Kingdom where IVF techniques originated in the 1970s, assisted reproductive technologies were not embraced by all when introduced to China in the 1980s. Handwerker (2002, 302-4) has shown how a number of doctors were sceptical if not disapproving of techniques to treat infertility in the context of a 'population explosion' that government authorities were actively trying to get under control: why treat infertility when hospitals were otherwise busy performing abortions in the name of population control? Proponents and pioneers of IVF in China parried by pointing out that in this logic one might just as well ask 'why bother to treat diseases? Why help the disabled? Why cure the wounded and save the dying?' (ibid., 303).

The rapid growth in availability of IVF treatment in China since the early 1980s attests to which side 'won' the debate.[3] Nonetheless, the debate does raise the important question of just what is being treated when assisted reproductive treatments are prescribed. To begin with, the causes of infertility (and subsequent

3 It is, however, noteworthy that health insurance schemes in China do not reimburse IVF treatment.

involuntary childlessness) are most often clinically localised in anatomical and biological pathology (e.g. tubular blockages, ovulation disorders, poor egg quality, endometriosis, azospermia). Yet, these pathologies are usually not life-threatening.[4] As suggested in the standard definition of infertility – inability to become pregnant after 1-2 years of unprotected intercourse – it is not a biological ability to survive (生存 *shēngcún*) but rather a physiological inability to reproduce that is the problem. Endometriosis, tubular blockages, azospermia, etc. are pathologies primarily because they deny reproduction not survival. So, in an instrumental sense, the objective of infertility treatment is to overcome biological obstacles to reproduction using assisted reproductive technologies such as *in vitro* fertilisation and embryo transfer, intrauterine insemination or intra cytoplasmic sperm injection. However, technologically overcoming biological obstacles is a therapeutic means rather than therapeutic objective.

To unpack this further we have to understand how distinctions are maintained between having a biological[5] condition (infertility) and living with it (involuntary childlessness). As put by, Xiao Shuiyuan of the Central South University in Changsha, 'surely a majority of infertility has a biological origin, however suffering with infertility is not only a biological problem, but also a psychosocial process' (Xiao 2008). Infertility – or any other condition for that matter – is not just something one has, it is also something one *lives with*.

In China, infertility experts, clinicians, nurses and commentators very often describe living with infertility in existential terms of a burdened life infused by suffering, unhappiness and stigma. For example, Qiao Jie, head of the Reproductive Medicine Centre at the Peking University Third Hospital, refers to it as the 'heavy psychological burden (心理负担 *xīnlǐ fùdàn*)' of infertility which 'most often falls on the woman' (Qiao 2007). Indeed, when speaking with doctors, embryologists and nurses about assisted reproduction in China, on almost every occasion the point was made that the burden of infertility was *particularly* devastating in China because of a complex mix of cultural, regulatory, socio-economic and psychological pressures, which are all seen to contribute to the stigmatisation of infertile couples (especially women) as in some sense 'incomplete,' 'insufficient' or even 'immoral.'

Culturally, a virtue of 'filial piety' (孝 *xiào*) – an obligation to honour and respect one's parents and ancestors as well as to extend the life of one's ancestors indefinitely through patrilineal birth[6] – is invoked in accounts of the pressures that

4 Which is NOT to say, of course, that such biological pathologies cannot cause considerable bodily pain and discomfort for some patients. And in some cases, infertility can be a consequence of an otherwise life-threatening disease or condition.

5 In an unspecified percentage of cases, biological causes for infertility are not found (see Inhorn and van Balen 2002).

6 The origin of this virtue is traced to a passage from chapter 26 in the *Mencius* in which Mèng Zǐ (a 4th century BC Confucian philosopher) is cited as proclaiming that, '[t]here are three things which are unfilial, and to have no posterity is the greatest of them.'

involuntarily childless couples face. It is, for example, no coincidence that the advertisement requesting ovum donors with which this paper began was placed by the father of an infertile woman. Qiu Renzong, a bioethicist at the Chinese Academy of Social Sciences, argues that today:

> [l]iving in a Confucian pro-natalist society, couples known as infertile are always under grave psychological and social pressure. They will always ask themselves 'what is wrong with me?' They may be stigmatized in the community. Especially for women, everything depends on if she can deliver a boy. As a result, they will make every effort to treat their infertility (Qiu 2007).

This stigmatization is intensified, according to Xiao, by notions of an incomplete life ('life is meaningless without a child'), immorality ('infertility might be perceived as a punishment on the couple, for example, for having been unfilial'), insufficiency ('to be seen as a "hen who cannot lay eggs" can be a source of great shame for women'), matrimonial failure ('to have a child is considered to be a primary purpose of marriage') as well as uncertainness about later life ('economic and emotional support from children and grandchildren is important in a country that doesn't have a modern social security system') (Xiao 2008; see also Handwerker 1995). This latter point is considered especially pressing in the context of China's 'one-child' policy as parents will in many cases be dependent on their only child and his/her spouse in old age. All of these socio-culturally intensified 'shortcomings' are described by infertility experts in China as elements of *living with infertility*. It is no surprise then that Qiu lists individual unhappiness, disharmony in families, stigmatization of especially women, domestic violence and divorce as some of the distressing social implications of infertility in contemporary China (Qiu 2007).

Recently, such expert discourse about the impact of infertility on involuntarily childless couples has been supplemented by questionnaire-based research among infertile couples in China. At the Reproductive and Genetic Hospital in Changsha, medical staff and psychologists have carried out questionnaire research among infertile couples measuring their levels of depression, anxiety and life satisfaction using standardised rating scales, documenting 'feelings of guilt,' 'fear of divorce' and 'psychological burdens.' And Lau et al. (2008) have interviewed 192 infertile couples using quality of life scales, concluding that pressures resulting from infertility are associated with 'lowered quality of life.'[7]

---

7 These analyses fit well with accounts of the impact of involuntary childlessness in many other countries. For example, in a global review, Emily MacDonald Evens summarises that, 'documented consequences include: anxiety, depression, lowered life satisfaction, frustration, grief, fear, guilt, helplessness, reduced job performance, marital duress, dissolution and abandonment; economic hardship, loss of social status, social stigma, social isolation and alienation, community ostracism, [and] physical violence' (Evens 2004, 10).

We can see then how it is burdened life rather than pathological life *per se* that assisted reproductive technologies are called upon to redress in urban China today. It is a form of life located not in a cellular but a subjective realm where experience rather than biological regulation is at stake. This is why, even though most infertility treatments aim at overcoming those anatomical and biological pathologies that are diagnosed as hindering unassisted reproduction, Xiao suggests that 'improving the quality of life [*shēnghuó zhìliàng* 生活质量] of the couple and the family should be considered the *primary purpose* of treatment' (Xiao 2008, emphasis added). And Lu Guangxiu, Head of the Reproductive and Genetic Hospital in Changsha argues that the importance of assisted reproductive technologies is that they can '*remove the agony* of those who are unable to reproduce, by *realizing their desire* of having a healthy child' (emphasis added). Biological treatments (IVF, ICSI, IUI, AID) are a means to the end of improving a couple's and family's quality of life by eliminating their agony and suffering.

How should we understand this therapeutic objective of improving quality of life? According to social psychologist Liu Li at the Beijing Normal University 'quality of life' as a concept is relatively new in China. And, just as has been the case in so-called advanced industrial countries of the West (Armstrong and Caldwell 2004; Wahlberg 2007), Liu argues that its emergence can be linked to the ambivalences of modernisation:

> China has been undergoing a massive and rapid transition towards a market economy since the early 1980s. The social change is associated with the emergence of public discourse and communication about quality of life. The transition towards modernisation engenders the paradoxes of public concern with the 'good life': improvement in material wealth goes hand in hand with environmental degradation; greater freedom links up with social alienation; increased opportunities blend with insecurities and uncertainties; modern lifestyles confront the traditional way of life (Liu 2006, 218).

In Mandarin, there are three common ways of conveying a concept of 'quality of life': *shēngcún zhìliàng* (生存质量), *shēngmìng zhìliàng* (生命質量) and *shēnghuó zhìliàng* (生活质量), where *shēngcún* denotes the minimum requirements for life (to exist, to survive), *shēngmìng* refers to life as a vital force and *shēnghuó* conveys a sense of life as an activity (being alive, living, working). And so, in Chinese terminology, one might distinguish between physiological and health-related forms of quality of life on the one hand and a more social form of quality of life on the other. When it comes to the therapeutic objective of infertility treatment, as we saw, Xiao argues that it is the improvement of *shēnghuó zhìliàng* (生活质量) of the couple and the family that is at stake. In this latter sense, the concept of 'quality' (质量 *zhìliàng*) relates to the social experience of those couples and families who are living with infertility/involuntary childlessness. The assumption is that living a childless life for a married couple is vastly inferior to living life with a child for the cultural, psychological and socio-economic reasons discussed above. It is the well-being of couples and families that is at stake.

To summarise, biological pathologies notwithstanding, it is 'burdened life' – living with infertility – that is considered the primary vital problem to be redressed through ART. And Chen Gui'an, a clinician at the Reproductive Medicine Centre of the Third Hospital in Beijing argues that one should not underestimate the impact that childlessness can have just because this impact is not life-threatening:

> [c]ancer will deprive the patient of his life although nobody wishes that to happen. This is similar to the case of those who cannot conceive a child…They are deprived of being mothers, which is a matter of regret for the whole family (Peking University Third Hospital 2003).

A Beijing newspaper concurs, 'slowly but surely, women in China are realizing there is hope out there and they do not have to helplessly suffer the intense stigma of being childless in a society that places supreme importance on having children' (*China Daily* 2005). Good life is a life with child.

Pathological Life – Biology and the Quest for (Superior) Conception

A good deal has been written and studied about China's new generation of so-called 'little emperors' (謏皇帝 *xiǎo huángdì*), a 100-million-strong demographic of only children that is concentrated in urban areas where stricter limits on the number of children allowed per family are in force (Falbo and Poston 1993; Jun 2000; Wang et al. 2002). Some suggest that the 'one child policy' has effectively produced a generation (born in the 1980s) of children who are 'self-centred, narrow-minded, and incapable of accepting criticism' (Yang Xiaosheng cited in Chandler 2004), while others highlight the 'unimaginable stress' and 'subjective burden' faced by these singletons on whose shoulders rest all of their parents' expectations and future care, not to mention their own feelings of indebtedness to their parents (Zhan 2002, 267).

At the same time, scholars have also highlighted a concurrent late twentieth century emphasis on conceiving and raising a 'superior' or 'quality child' (healthy, intelligent, talented) as encapsulated in slogans like *yōushēng, yōuyù, yōujiāo* (优生, 优育, 优教) which translates as 'superior birth, superior childrearing, superior education' (Greenhalgh and Winckler 2005; Murphy 2004; Zhao 1986). It is suggested that the exclusive focus of a family's hopes and desires on their single child has resulted in an intensely competitive climate for children, which has become entwined in the new materialism and commercialism attributed to the economic reforms of the late 1980s and early 1990s. What is more, a much debated 'cultural' preference for a son, facilitated by increasing availability of ultrasound technologies and selective abortion, is blamed for having exacerbated

China's gender imbalance such that an estimated 118 boys are born for every 100 girls in China today (Handwerker 2002; Blanchard 2007; Döring 2008).

Involuntarily childless couples who seek reproductive assistance are, of course, in many ways outside such debates since they are, in the first place, trying to get pregnant, let alone give birth to, raise or educate a 'superior' child of any particular sex. Nevertheless, such preferences play an important part in ART practices. We can see this in the ways in which the quality of couples, their gametes and (if required) their gamete donors are assessed in the ART treatment process. Indeed, assisted reproduction is a process saturated with normative assessments of vitality at every step.

To begin with, the science of fertility treatment is reliant on evaluative concepts of 'quality', for example in diagnoses of 'poor sperm quality' (精子质量差 *jīngzǐ zhìliàng chā*) and 'poor quality eggs' (卵子质量差 *luǎnzǐ zhìliàng chā*) or in decisions about which 'excellent quality embryos' (优质胚胎 *yōuzhì pēitāi*) should be implanted. Couples attending their first consultation at the PUMC ART Unit are given plenty of information and lifestyle advice about how to optimise their chances of achieving pregnancy. Advice includes recommendations for traditional Chinese medicine (acupuncture and herbal tonics) for both men and women as a way to enhance their vitality and thereby increase the likelihood of reproductive success. At the Reproductive and Genetic Hospital in Changsha, nurses make it clear to prospective patients that traditional remedies can be good, but only before ART treatment commences after which only those forms of medication prescribed by clinicians should be taken in order to avoid any unnecessary risks from possible drug interactions.

But perhaps more importantly, in each of the fertility clinics visited, there was a firm emphasis on lifestyle advice concerning both physical and psychological preparations for fertility treatment. Men are encouraged to refrain from alcohol, nicotine, caffeine, and, in Changsha, also betel nut chewing in the lead up to IVF cycles in order to ensure 'excellent quality sperm' (优质精子 *yōuzhì jīngzǐ*). Women are similarly encouraged to refrain from stimulants and to eat a balanced and nutritious diet as a way to ensure 'high quality eggs' (卵子质量高 *luǎnzǐ zhìliàng gāo*). They are also advised to exercise in moderation – 'not too strenuously, do not lift more than 20 pounds of weight; walking or swimming are very good training methods' (RGH 2007). Just as important is advice about ensuring the best possible psychological support for women. In Changsha, couples were informed by nurses that 'we actively seek the support of family members, in particular the husband's care and attention…, you must eliminate discomfort and enhance self-confidence' (RGH 2007). All of this advice is aimed at ensuring the best possible conditions for undergoing fertility treatment, for optimising a couple's biological, psychological and social conditions for reproduction.

Part of the psychological preparation is to inform couples about the treatment process itself, in particular as a means of clarifying uncertainties and dispelling possible misconceptions. Infertility treatment is by its very nature an uncertain process which doctors point out will often contribute to stress and depressed moods. For example, sperm quality is graded according to criteria of motility, morphology, density, fructose level and pH level. It is not only the number of sperm in a sample that is assessed but also whether microscopic observations of sperm show them to have an 'oval form,' 'good forward movement' and 'smooth contours'. Spectroscopy techniques can also be used to identify and sort out sperm cells with DNA damage before *in vitro* fertilisation is carried out. In China, as elsewhere, there are some who argue that using low quality sperm for ICSI (intra-cytoplasmic sperm injection where single sperm cells are injected directly into an egg) IVF treatment will have a deleterious effect on the future child:

> sperm injection technology, is likely to use low-quality sperm... This 'inferior quality' (劣质 *lièzhì*) sperm carries large amounts of bad genes and when it combines with the egg it is difficult to ensure that future generations do not inherit their genetic flaws (Jia 2001).

Consequently, at the Jiaen Hospital in Beijing (specialists in using modern ICSI technologies) sufferers of male infertility are told that even if they have poor sperm quality, they may still be able to have their own genetically-related offspring and that according to the latest science low sperm quality does not mean that resulting offspring will be of 'low quality.'

Table 16.1 Embryo grading system used at PUMC

卵裂球期胚胎，首先记录细胞数，然后根据以下标准评定质量级别：

第一级	Grade 1	分裂球均匀，大小相等，没有碎片。
第二级	Grade 2	分裂球均匀，碎片在20%之内。或者分裂球不均匀。
第三级	Grade 3	碎片 20%～50%。
第四级	Grade 4	碎片在 50% 以上。

(After the assessment of the cell number and morphology, cleavage stage embryos are graded as follows:

Grade 1 embryo: no fragmentation with equal sized homogenous blastomeres

Grade 2 embryo: <20% fragmentation with equal or unequal sized homogenous blastomeres

Grade 3 embryo: 20%–50% fragmentation with unequal sized blastomeres

Grade 4 embryo: >50% fragmentation with unequal sized blastomeres)

Similarly, it is standard practice in IVF treatment to grade the quality of embryos as a means of selecting which embryos to implant using morphological criteria in order to increase the likelihood for successful pregnancies (see also Svendsen and Koch 2008; Wahlberg 2008). Embryos are visually evaluated according to number of fragments, size of cells, 'roundness', 'clarity' and 'symmetry' after which they are given scores (see Table 16.1 and Figure 16.1).

Regulations in China permit the implantation of two embryos for women under 35 and 3 embryos for women over 35. Patients are routinely informed of how many successfully fertilised embryos they have following IVF as well as whether they are of good or bad quality. In Changsha, upon showing a picture of an excellent quality embryo on a large screen, nurses reassure prospective patients 'don't worry if your embryos aren't this beautiful, this is a perfect one; it does not mean that your chances are less' (RGH 2007). And embryologist Sun Zheng-yi at the PUMC ART Unit emphasises that 'it is important for us to emphasise that the quality of an embryo does not tell you anything about the quality of the child – some good quality embryos do not come to term just as bad quality embryos can result in a healthy child' (Sun 2007).

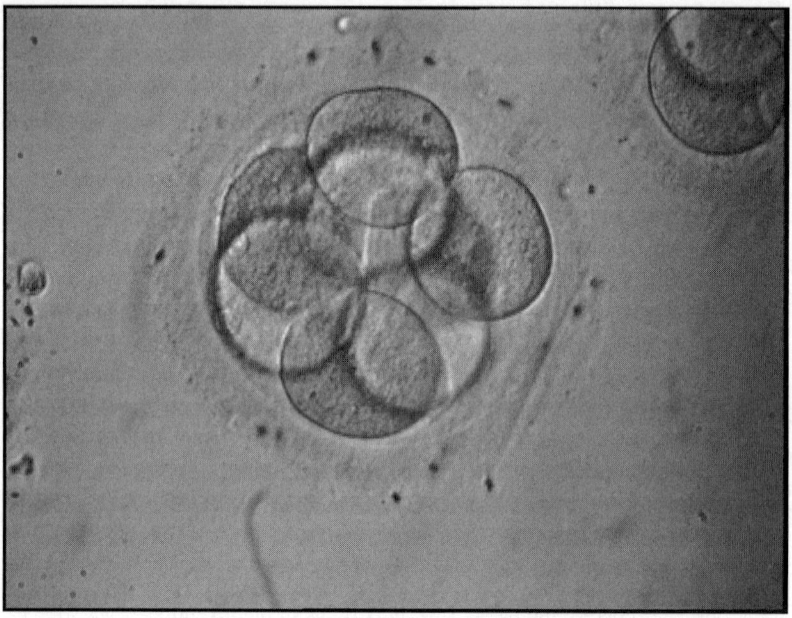

Figure 16.1 An 'excellent quality' embryo (*yōuzhì pēitāi*)

This point is also underscored in informed consent forms where patients are reminded that if they achieve pregnancy through fertility treatment, then their chances of having an unhealthy or disabled child are the same as for those couples who conceive without assistance. At the Reproductive and Genetic Hospital in Changsha, upon signing informed consent forms, couples receiving assisted insemination agree that: 'we also know even in normal people there will be some rate of babies born with deficiency in body or intellect (about 4%) and that this can also happen following artificial insemination, the doctor cannot control that, thus we understand and also agree that the reproductive centre's doctors have no responsibility for any deficiencies in offspring resulting from Artificial Insemination' (RGH 2007). Doctors do, however, acknowledge the 'heavy pressure (from society, family, work and economic fields)' for couples to have a 'healthy child' (健康的小孩 *jiànkāng de xiǎohái*) (RGH 2007).

In this context, the concept of quality refers to the biological characteristics of gametes and embryos which are analysed in morphological, quantitative and chemical terms. Good life (as observed and measured in living gametes, zygotes, blastocysts and embryos) is that which will improve (although never guarantee) an infertile couple's chances of having a child. And the aim of assessing biological quality is to ensure the best possible biological conditions for achieving a pregnancy – whether a gamete or embryo is of good or bad quality is directly related to its projected ability to secure a viable pregnancy and not to the 'quality' or traits of the future offspring. Developments in preimplantation genetic diagnosis (PGD) techniques have further cemented this point as embryos which are morphologically assessed to be of 'excellent quality' can at the same time be diagnosed as genetically 'tainted,' for example by a particular single gene disorder (see Franklin and Roberts 2006). In genetic terms, good life is that which is not tainted by genetic errors known to cause certain 'serious diseases' such as cystic fibrosis and thalassemia (see Wahlberg 2009). Morphological and genetic assessments of embryo quality do not necessarily gel.

There is a further important way in which biological quality is assessed, namely through selective screening of those persons from whom gametes originate. Partner selection of course inevitably entails some kind of 'screening' – a process in which individuals and family members are seen to have varying degrees of input. Socio-economic status, education level, medical history, family lineages, ethnic background, etc. may all be scrutinised in partner 'screening' processes. Since ART can only be offered to married couples in China, partner selection has already taken place prior to treatment. Nevertheless, at a Beijing workshop on reproductive technologies held in April 2007 an unusual case was discussed where although 'Mr X's sperm meets the standard of AIH [Artificial Insemination by Husband]… the wife considered her husband bad looking and not smart and her mother-in-law also worried that his mental retardation might affect her grandchild, [hence] both Mr X's mother and wife strongly asked for AID (Artificial Insemination by Donor)' (BIONET 2007). In this case biological sperm quality assessment standards were not compatible with Mr X's wife's and mother's assessment of his 'quality' or stock.

For some couples, fertility treatment is not biologically possible without an egg or sperm donor. As is the case in many other countries, there is a chronic shortage of gamete donors in China leading to waiting lists of up to two years. By law, egg donation is only allowed by women undergoing infertility treatment and only if more than 15 oocytes are retrieved following stimulation. In Changsha, the waiting list for oocyte donors stands at 500 while only around 30 couples per year are offered donor oocytes. For those couples in need of egg donors there is not much choice but to accept that which becomes available. There are many more sperm donors, although still not nearly enough. In Shanghai, Dr Li Zheng of the Shanghai Municipality Human Sperm Bank explained in late 2004 that while it had 8,000 sperm samples at the time, some 200,000 were needed, 'Chinese men are usually reluctant to donate sperm, or even to talk about it, perhaps due to our conservative social traditions. That's why I expect that a sperm shortage will always exist in China' (cited in Mao 2004).

Shortages notwithstanding, assessing the quality of potential donors is a key part of donor-assisted fertility treatment. We saw earlier how a father, as a way of socially-vetting potential oocyte donors, advertised for women 'aged 20 to 29 years old, with at least an undergraduate diploma, no family medical history, good looking.' Similarly, before the Ministry of Health's new regulations covering the practice and administration of gamete donation were introduced in 2001, a so-called 'Prominent Persons' Sperm Bank' was established in Sichuan Province (Xinhua 1999). The bank only accepted donations from men who held positions as Associate Professors or above, since such persons were considered to be very attractive to those who needed a donor. Today, such specialised sperm banks are not permitted under law as donors are screened according to biological criteria (chromosome tests, sexually transmitted diseases, sperm quality, family medical history, personal medical history, blood type) (P.R. China 2001). Nevertheless, university campuses remain the primary sites of donor recruitment.

Those couples in need of a donor are provided with a limited amount of social and biological information about potential donors including:

- blood type
- race (90 per cent of Chinese are Han, but there are also 55 minority ethnic groups)
- physique (high, middle, low)
- height and weight
- shape of face (round, square or triangular)
- skin colour (yellow with some white or yellow with some black)
- eyelid form (single or double)
- educational level (Bachelor, Masters, Doctor)
- special hobbies

We can see then how determining what a 'good quality' egg or sperm is in the case of gamete donation is not only a biological task but also one of social evaluation (albeit as a proxy for biological evaluation). Good life here relates to the 'stock' and perhaps also 'pedigree' of a gamete donor – are the physical and social qualities of a donor 'good enough' for a recipient? The assumption is that an individual's traits will be transmitted to offspring through his/her gametes and therefore 'bad' traits (e.g. genetic diseases, chromosomal abnormalities, low intelligence,[8] etc.) should be screened out while 'good' traits (e.g. high intelligence, 'good looks', good physique, etc.) should be screened in during donor recruitment.

Finally, it should be noted that for those involuntarily childless couples who are lucky enough to achieve a viable pregnancy with the help of different kinds of ART (roughly one-third), the quest no longer only concerns having a successful birth, but also a superior birth (优生 *yōushēng*) with the help of pregnancy nutrition advice, 'foetal education' (胎教 *tāijiāo*) programmes aimed at nurturing foetuses throughout pregnancy, as well as standard prenatal screening and healthcare. Indeed, prenatal diagnoses of a 'serious disease' or malformation in assisted pregnancies can be among the most devastating since getting pregnant in the first place has most likely been an arduous, perhaps unrepeatable, task. While no statistics are available, in both Beijing and Changsha doctors noted that although some patients choose to avoid prenatal screening (because of worries about possible post-screening abortion), if prenatal screening does result in a diagnosis of, for example, Down's syndrome or congenital malformation, IVF couples will 'usually choose to have an abortion.'

In short, it is no straightforward task to assess biological quality. This is in large part because there are different objectives at stake: to improve a couple's chance of conceiving; to promote the transmission of certain traits; to prevent the transmission of other traits; and ultimately to ensure the birth of a healthy (if not 'superior') child. It is therefore the vitality of couples, gametes/embryos and a future child that is simultaneously at stake. In these cases it is not so much human life that is being improved, rather the pathologies and hurdles blocking not only reproduction itself but also the birth of a 'healthy child' are to be overcome using ART techniques (including fertility treatment, genetic diagnosis and other forms of prenatal testing/screening), psychological counselling and foetal education programmes. It is an individual's or couple's 'biological lot' that is to be technologically overcome as a means to improve their quality of life, which as we saw earlier, is the therapeutic objective of infertility treatment. Every successful assisted birth is, in a sense, a victory over the 'bad life' (inferior quality sperm, bad quality embryos, tubular blockages, endometriosis, etc.) that would otherwise prevent it.

Weak Life – Improving Population Quality (提高人口素质 tígāo rénkǒu sùzhì)

When potential donors recruited from nearby university campuses arrive at the premises of the State-authorised sperm bank of the Xiangya Medical College

8 Apparently indicated by insufficient education as universities are the primary sites of donor recruitment.

in Changsha (China's largest with some 40,000 samples in storage), the first information they receive is printed on an A4 sheet:

> The Changsha Human Sperm Bank Welcomes You
>
> Dear student,
>
> How are you! We are the hospital staff responsible for advising you. As is well known, recently, more and more infertile couples have not received treatment in time bringing great sadness to many families. We call on our university friends to help in this regard…
>
> Donating sperm is like donating blood, both are in the service of the people. In order to understand how you can contribute please read the following points:
>
> 1. Donating can bring happiness to many infertility patients and help scientific research. Donating sperm is not only altruistic it can also improve the Chinese people's (中华民族 *zhonghuá mínzú*) quality (素质 *sùzhì*). Since you are university students you are of very high quality (素质高 *sùzhì gāo*) so if you join this project we will reach this goal quicker.
>
> 2. Our hospital is a standard hospital belonging to Xiangya Medical College, so it can provide those students who are considering donating free medical tests covering chromosome, blood, microorganism and whole body examinations. In order to assure the quality of sperm, and thereby ensure superior birth (优生 *yōushēng*), every donor should have a systematized body examination, free of charge… (Hunan Sperm Bank 2008)

Greenhalgh and Winckler have argued that when it comes to reproductive politics in China, if 'during the long 1980s [1979-1993], the dominant norm promoted by the state was one of quantity…in the 1990s and early 2000s…the enhancement of population "quality", has become increasingly central to the politics of population' (2005, 215, 217). It was also during this time that the term *rénkŏu zhìliàng* was gradually replaced by *rénkŏu sùzhì* in official and popular discussions about 'population quality' as the meaning of *sùzhì* ('inner quality') was transferred from things to persons (Bakken 1999, 60; Fong 2007; Kipnis 2006). Many scholars have pointed to the contemporary pervasiveness of the *sùzhì* concept in China as a kind of spontaneous ideology as it permeates not just official population strategies and policies but also everyday practice through popular media, consumer goods, pharmacies, etc. (Kipnis 2007; Murphy 2004; Anagnost 2004). This is not to say that questions of quantity have become any less pressing, rather that in more recent years questions of quality have become equally important at the bio-political level of managing the population as reflected in a slogan seen on one family planning billboard hanging in Beijing in 2007, 'control population quantity, raise population quality' (控制人口数量，提高人口素质 *kòngzhì rénkǒu shùliàng, tígāo rénkǒu sùzhì*).

We have already seen how individualised norms of quality are used to assess the vitality of prospective parents, donors, gametes, embryos or foetuses in the sections above. How do they differ from this notion of 'population quality' (人口素质 *rénkǒu sùzhì*)? Most importantly, as always in matters of population, *rénkǒu sùzhì* concerns an aggregated collective, which is to say 'population' as an entity, object or body in its own right that can be mapped out in terms of fertility, mortality, morbidity, literacy, and/or productivity rates and measured against norms of wealth, health and/or quality. With *rénkǒu sùzhì*, it is the inner quality of such an aggregated collective rather than an individual person or biological sample that is at stake.[9]

At the same time, however, just as one can distinguish between a subjective form of quality of life of individuals and the biological quality of their gametes or embryos, so too can one at the collective level distinguish between 'superior childrearing' (优育 *yōuyù*) and 'superior education' (优教 *yōujiāo*) on the one hand, and 'superior birth' (优生 *yōushēng*) on the other. The former two concern pedagogical and educational efforts to improve 'spiritual civilization' (精神文明 *jīngshén wénmíng*) through the 'raising of people's political consciousness and moral standards… as well as raising the level of the general knowledge of the people' (Hu Yaobang cited in Bakken 1999, 55). That is to say, improving the quality of the population in this sense requires *post-natal* cultivation of the physical, intellectual and moral qualities of the people through education and training programmes such as the 'education for quality' (素质教育 *sùzhì jiàoyù*) campaign introduced by the national government in the 1990s (Murphy 2004).[10] *Sùzhì*, in this sense, is therefore something to be acquired, cultivated and improved through education, training, awareness raising and other forms of spiritual advancement.

Yōushēng (superior birth), on the other hand, concerns *pre-natal* biomedical and educational efforts aimed at ensuring healthy births by preventing the transmission of 'serious hereditary diseases' through general medical advice, genetic counselling and by encouraging healthy pregnancies through foetal education (胎教 *tāijiāo*) programmes (Dikötter 1998). It is these latter forms of improving population quality by promoting *yōushēng* that I will focus on here.

In December 1993, the Chinese government proposed a draft bill on 'Superior birth and health protection' (优生保健 *yōushēng bǎojiàn*). In part as a response to international reactions which dubbed it China's 'Eugenics law' (Nature 1994), the law was revised, renamed 'Law on Maternal and Infant Healthcare' and subsequently passed in October 1994 with primary aims of 'ensuring the health of

9 Which of course does not mean that this concept cannot have subjectifying effects as it circulates and comes to inform patterns of self constitution and interpellation.

10 A number of scholars have discussed this 'spiritual' aspect of *rénkǒu sùzhì* in the English-language social science literature (Anagnost 1995; Bakken 1999; Fong 2007; Greenhalgh and Winckler 2005; Kipnis 2006).

mothers and infants and improving the quality of the newborn population' (P.R. China 1994: article 1).

This raises questions of just how the quality of the newborn population can improve (or deteriorate) as well as for what reasons it should be improved. What is it that is 'better' in this context after *rénkǒu sùzhì* has been improved? And for the purposes of this paper, how does infertility treatment (which must 'obey national population and family-planning legislation and policies' (P.R. China 2003: B.1)) contribute (or detract) from this objective? We find part of an answer to this question in a controversy that played out in China's Heilongjiang province in 2005. The 1994 law on Maternal and Infant Healthcare had made it obligatory for all couples to undergo a premarital medical examination 'to see whether [the male or female] suffer from any disease that may have an adverse effect on marriage and child-bearing' (P.R. China 1994, articles 7 and 10), keeping also in mind that China's marriage law from 1980 had prohibited marriage 'if either the man or the woman is suffering from any disease that is regarded by medical science as rendering a person unfit for marriage' (P.R. China 2001, article 7). Also controversial have been articles 16 and 18 which concern genetic counselling for married couples of childbearing age and pre-natal screening of foetuses for pregnant women respectively.

What links articles 10, 16 and 18 in the Maternal and Infant Healthcare Law (1994) is an objective to prevent the transmission of defects and genetic diseases 'of a serious nature' to future offspring with the help of pre-marital, pre-conception and pre-natal medical examinations and related counselling. Unmarried couples found to be suffering from 'certain genetic diseases of a serious nature which are considered to be inappropriate for child-bearing from a medical point of view' were given permission to marry only if they consent to 'long-term contraceptive measures or performance of ligation operations' rendering them 'unable to bear children' (P.R. China 1994, article 10). Married couples of 'childbearing age' found to be suffering from a 'genetic disease of a serious nature' were to be given 'medical advice, according to which the said couple shall take corresponding measures' (article 16). And finally, pregnant women who, following prenatal diagnosis, were found to be carrying a foetus 'suffering from a genetic disease of a serious nature' or 'a defect of a serious nature' were to be given 'medical advice on a termination of gestation…subject to the consent and signing of the person per se' (articles 18 and 19).

In 2003, premarital medical examinations were made voluntary in connection with an adjustment of China's Marriage laws. Moreover, couples would have to pay for such examinations. As a direct result the proportion of couples who underwent premarital examination reportedly 'plummeted from 68 percent in 2002 to 3 percent in 2005' (*China Daily* 2007). This prompted Zhao Shaohua of the All-China Women's Federation to warn that 'if the rate of premarital medical examinations continues to decrease so sharply…the quality of the population will be seriously affected' (cited in Chen 2005). And a report written by the State Council's National Working Committee on Children and Women in 2007 argued that the dramatic drop in premarital medical checkups explained why 'the rate of newborns with congenital defects has risen from 11 per thousand in 2002 to 14 per thousand in 2005' (*China Daily* 2007). This was the very same form of epidemiological reasoning that had led health administrators in Heilongjiang to re-introduce compulsory premarital medical checkups in July 2005 – a deterioration of *rénkǒu sùzhì* had to be stopped. An editorial in the *Nanguo Morning Post* summarised their arguments:

> [p]remarital physical examinations have a direct bearing on the happiness of newly-weds and the health of their newborn children. They affect the future of the nation and the overall health of the entire population (*Nanguo Morning Post* 2005).

What this suggests is that to understand the biological norms contained within the concept of *rénkǒu sùzhì* that allow for assessments of population quality, it is necessary to unpack what is meant by defects and genetic diseases of a 'serious nature.' For, it is these diseases and defects that are considered to negatively impact on or lower population quality if biologically transmitted to offspring through reproduction, and, conversely, preventing their transmission is seen by some as a way of improving the quality of the newborn population as it helps to separate out 'the unhealthy genes of our country's gene pool' (Zhu Hong cited in Dikötter 1998, 140).

It is important to note, in this connection, that there is currently no consensus in China (or any other country for that matter) on what constitutes a 'serious disease.'[11] Before the national law on Maternal and Infant Healthcare came into force in 1995, a number of individual provinces in China had especially emphasised 'mental diseases' (精神病 *jīngshénbìng*) in their definitions of 'serious hereditary disease', thus listing psychosis, mental deficiency and mental retardation as inappropriate for childbearing on the grounds that persons suffering from such conditions were likely to transmit these conditions through reproduction and were not able to look after themselves, let alone any children (Kristof 1991). According to the law, the criteria for determining which diseases and defects are serious are that they 'may totally or partially deprive the victim of the ability to live independently' and are 'medically considered inappropriate for reproduction' (article 38).

When it comes to *rénkǒu sùzhì* in a biological sense, 'good life' is that which animates a healthy, vibrant and strong collective free of persons suffering from genetic diseases of a serious nature, congenital defects of a serious nature, target infectious diseases as well as so-called 'relevant mental diseases'. And although *rénkǒu sùzhì* is often used to refer to China's population as a whole, it can also be used to parcel out and break down this national aggregation into sub-populations which can subsequently be ranked according to their *sùzhì*. Those born with a

11 For in depth discussions on what constitutes a 'serious disease' in the United Kingdom context, see Wahlberg (2009).

'serious disease', 'congenital defect' or 'relevant mental disease' are considered of 'low quality' compared to *yōushēng* newborns (see Kohrman 2005).[12]

Debates and regulations concerning population quality are relevant to ART clinics since they are required by Ministry of Health regulations to 'obey national population and family-planning legislation and policies' (P.R. China 2003: B.1). That is to say, there are instances where clinics are forbidden from providing fertility treatment to a couple. Some of these instances are administrative, i.e. if a couple is unable to provide the hospital with a copy of their ID documents, marriage certificate as well as an original copy of their so-called 'qualification for pregnancy certificate' that confirms they are allowed to have a child in accordance with family planning laws.[13] And since premarital checkups have become voluntary the Regulation on Assisted Reproductive Technology stipulates that treatment cannot be provided in situations where the 'wife or husband has a severe mental disease, genitourinary system inflammation or sexually transmitted diseases' and/or where 'in accordance with the Law on Maternal and Infant Healthcare, the couple have serious diseases considered inappropriate for conception and PGD' (P.R. China 2003, 1.C.2). In situations concerning the former, treatment may be offered once the wife or husband has overcome the illness, whereas in the latter, treatment cannot be offered to the couple in question. Treatment can only be offered to those persons who are 'qualified under national population regulations' (P.R. China 2003, D.1).

And so, in the context of ART 'raising population quality' (*tígāo rénkǒu sùzhì*) refers to practices which promote 'superior birth' (优生 *yōushēng*) by screening involuntarily childless couples, gamete donors and foetuses in order to prevent the transmission of certain 'serious hereditary diseases' and to minimise the risk of 'serious congenital defects.' Yet, there are also instances where ART is seen to negatively impact population quality, for example, by those who suggest that using 'inferior quality' sperm to fertilise eggs through ICSI technology may perpetuate 'genetic flaws' – 'harmful sperm development can adversely affect the quality of the population: foetal deformities, premature births, stillbirths and birth defects may all be related to sperm' (Zhao 2008; also Jia 2001). Indeed, as we saw, 'high quality' (*sùzhì gāo*) donors at the Xiangya Medical College sperm bank are told that they will actively contribute to efforts aimed at improving population quality.

Finally, it should be pointed out that concerns have been raised that rising infertility in China is itself a sign of declining population quality – delayed marriages (as couples focus on careers first), declining sperm quality (believed to be resulting from environmental pollution and lifestyle changes), sexually transmitted diseases (related to growing sexual promiscuity) and multiple induced

12 Similarly, in spiritual terms rural and migrant populations are described by some as being of 'low quality' (*sùzhì dī*) in comparison to 'high quality' (*sùzhì gāo*) urban dwellers who are considered more 'cultivated' and 'civilised' (Anagnost 2004).

13 These requirements also disqualify single women, unmarried women and lesbian couples from ART treatment in China.

abortions (related to sex selective practices as well as pre-marital sex) are all seen to be contributing to rising infertility rates in a modernising China. 'With environmental and lifestyle changes, the incidence of infertility is increasing… According to preliminary estimates, infertility affects about 5-8 percent of couples of childbearing age in China, so this is a very large group' (Peking University Third Hospital 2003).

Conclusions

In this paper, I have asked what forms of life are being improved by assisted reproductive technologies and for what benefit? Through this analysis I have shown how different concepts of 'quality' allow for the normative assessments of vitality that make ART suitable for efforts to improve the vitality of involuntarily childless couples, the future child as well as the population. What has become clear through the analysis is that multiple forms of life co-circulate when assisted reproductive technologies are mobilised to mitigate the burdened lives of involuntarily childless couples by helping them to overcome those biological pathologies diagnosed as denying them (healthy) offspring.

I have suggested that it is the concept of 'quality' (精子 *zhì*, 素质 *sùzhì*, 质量 *zhìliàng*) that makes normative assessment and evaluation of 'good life' practicable in infertility treatment. Yet in the context of ART in urban China I have argued there are different forms of life at stake in such assessments: it is an improvement of the quality of life of involuntarily childless couples (and their families) that is the key therapeutic objective of ART techniques which in turn are reliant on morphological, genetic and social techniques of grading donor/gamete/embryo quality as means not only of securing a viable pregnancy and live birth, but as far as possible also a 'superior birth' which can contribute to an overall national project of raising population quality. This neat equation is, however, beset with hurdles, side effects and, all too often, human tragedies. When a couple's *in vitro* fertilised embryos are peered at through a microscope in order to grade them they are invested through and through by a multiplicity not only of human lives (the potential human life in each embryo, the involuntarily childless couples' lives, their families' lives) but also of forms of life (social and biological, individual and collective, cellular and psychological, genetic and morphological, genomic and demographic).

When new forms of treatment are introduced, the goal is to improve people's lives. Such objectives must of course be subject to scrutiny and much research has been and continues to be carried out to determine whether assisted reproductive technologies do indeed improve the lives of involuntarily childless couples (e.g. what of those many couples for whom ART fails?). The task of this chapter however, has not been to determine *whether* ART improves the lives of involuntarily childless couples in urban China, but rather to empirically clarify what forms of life are at stake in ART practices. In doing so, I have shown how biological and social norms of good life intertwine, as well as how individual and collective life are implicated in the practice of ART.

Acknowledgements

Research for this article was made possible by the European Commission Sixth Framework Programme funded BIONET project (http://www.bionet-china.org/). I would in particular like to thank Lu Guangxiu, He Jing, Cong Yali, Li Rong, Zhai Xiaomei and Zhou Mengmeng for their assistance and support during my stays in China. For detailed critique and feedback on earlier versions of the paper my thanks to Qiu Renzong, Margaret Sleeboom-Faulkner and Klaus Høyer.

References

Anagnost, A. (1995) 'A Surfeit of Bodies: Population and the Rationality of the State in Post-Mao China', in F.D. Ginsburg and Rayna Rapp (eds) *Conceiving the New World Order: The Global Politics of Reproduction* (Berkeley: University of California Press), 22-41.

Anagnost, A. (2004) 'The Corporeal Politics of Quality (*Suzhi*)', *Public Culture* 16(2): 189-208.

Arditti, R., Klein, R. and Minden, S. (eds) (1984) *Test-tube Women: What Future for Motherhood?* (London: Pandora Press).

Armstrong, D. and Caldwell, D. (2004) 'Origins of the Concept of Quality of Life in Health Care: A Rhetorical Solution to a Political Problem', *Social Theory and Health* 2/4: 361-371.

Bakken, B. (1999) *The Exemplary Society: Human Improvement, Social Control, and the Dangers of Modernity in China* (Oxford; New York: Oxford University Press).

Bharadawaj, A. (2003) 'Why Adoption is Not an Option in India: The Visibility of Infertility, the Secrecy of Donor Insemination, and Other Cultural Complexities', *Social Science and Medicine* 56: 1867-1880.

Becker, G. (1997) *Healing the Infertile Family: Strengthening your Relationship in the Search for Parenthood* (Berkeley: University of California Press).

BIONET (2007) '1st Workshop Report: Informed Consent in Reproductive Genetics and Stem Cell Technology and the Role of Ethical Review Boards', *Ethical Governance of Biological and Biomedical Research: Chinese-European Co-operation* available at: http://www.bionet-china.org/pdfs/BIONET_1st_Workshop_Report.pdf.

BIONET (2007) 'Cases for Discussion – Assisted Reproductive Technologies', *Workshop on informed consent in reproductive genetics and stem cell technology and the role of Ethical Review Boards*, Beijing: 1-5 April 2007.

Blanchard, B. (2007) 'Gender Imbalance in China Could Take 15 Years to Correct', *The Guardian* 24 January.

Canguilhem, G. (1989) *The Normal and the Pathological* (New York: Zone Books).

Canguilhem, G. (1994) *A Vital Rationalist* (New York: Zone Books).

Chandler, C. (2004) 'Little Emperors', *Fortune Magazine*, 4 October.

Chen, Q. (2005) 'Keeping Policy-making Process Transparent', *China Daily*, 14 September, 4.

China Daily (2005) 'Fertility Industry Takes Off in China', *China Daily*, 30 March.

China Daily (2007) 'Birth defects rise as checkups slide', *China Daily*, 21 May, 3.

China.org.cn (2001) 'Interview – Gestational Surrogacy Banned in China', <http://www.china.org.cn/english/2001/Jun/15215.htm> accessed on 5 July.

Denmark (2006) 'Bekendtgørelse af lov om kunstig befrugtning i forbindelse med lægelig behandling, diagnostik og forskning m.v [Fertilization Act]', Interior and Health Ministry, LBK no. 923, 4 September.

Dikötter, F. (1998) *Imperfect Conceptions: Medical Knowledge, Birth Defects and Eugenics in China* (London: Hurst and Co.).

Döring, O. (2008) 'What's in a Choice? Ethical, Cultural and Social Dimension of Sex Selection in China', *Human Ontogenetics* 2(1), 2008: 11-24.

Evens, E. McDonald (2004) *A Global Perspective on Infertility: An Under Recognized Public Health Issue* (Carolina Papers International Health: University of North Carolina at Chapel Hill).

Falbo, T. and Poston, D.L. (1993) 'The Academic, Personality, and Physical Outcomes of Only Children in China', *Child Development* 64/1: 18-35.

Fong, V. (2007) 'Morality, Cosmopolitanism, or Academic Attainment? Discourses on "Quality" and Urban Chinese-only-Children's Claims to Ideal Personhood', *City and Society* 19/1: 86-113.

Franklin, S. (1997) *Embodied Progress: A Cultural Account of Assisted Conception* (London; New York: Routledge).

Franklin, S. and Roberts, C. (2006) *Born and Made: An Ethnography of Preimplantation Genetic Diagnosis* (Princeton: Princeton University Press).

Greco, M. (2005) 'On the Vitality of Vitalism', *Theory, Culture, Society* 22(1): 15-27.

Greenhalgh, S. and Winckler, E.A. (2005) *Governing China's Population: From Leninist to Neoliberal Biopolitics* (Stanford: Stanford University Press; [London: Eurospan distributor]).

Handwerker, L. (1995). 'The Hen that Can't Lay an Egg (*bu chia dan de mu ji*): Conceptions of Female Infertility in Modern China', in J. Urla, and J. Terry (eds) *Deviant Bodies* (Bloomington: Indiana University Press), pp. 358-386.

Handwerker, L. (1998). 'The Consequences of Modernity for Childless Women in China: Medicalization and Resistance', in M. Lock, and P.A. Kaufert (eds) *Pragmatic Women and Body Politics*. (Cambridge: Cambridge University Press) pp. 178-205.

Handwerker, L. (2002) 'The Politics of Making Modern Babies in China: Reproductive Technologies and the "New" Eugenics', in M. Inhorn and F. van Balen (eds) *Infertility Around the Globe: New Thinking on Childlessness, Gender, and Reproductive Technologies* (San Diego: University of California Press).

He, F.F. (2007) 'Personal communication', 24 September.

HFEA (2005) 'Welfare of the Child and the Assessment of those Seeking Treatment' (London: Human Fertilisation and Embryology Authority, CH(05)04, 2 November).

Hu, H. (2002) 'Family Planning Law and China's Birth Control Situation', in *China.org.cn* (Beijing).

Hunan Sperm Bank (2008) 'Information Leaflet for Donors', in Human Sperm Bank of Hunan, Changsha, P.R. China.

Inhorn, M.C. (1994) *Quest for Conception: Gender, Infertility, and Egyptian Medical Traditions* (Philadelphia: University of Pennsylvania Press).

Inhorn, M.C. (1996) *Infertility and Patriarchy: The Cultural Politics of Gender and Family Life in Egypt* (Philadelphia: University of Pennsylvania Press).

Inhorn, M.C. (2003) 'Global Infertility and the Globalization of New Reproductive Technologies: Illustrations from Egypt', *Social Science and Medicine*, 56: 1837-1851.

Inhorn, M.C. and F. van Balen (eds) (2002). *Infertility Around the Globe: New Thinking on Childlessness, Gender, and Reproductive Technologies* (Berkeley: University of California Press).

Jia, X-H. (2001) 'The Choice of Life and Life Choices', *Science and Technology Daily* http://www.people.com.cn/GB/kejiao/42/155/20011224/633758.html: accessed on 10 June 2008.

Jun, Jing (2000) *Feeding China's Little Emperors: Food, Children, and Social Change* (Stanford: Stanford University Press).

Kipnis, A. (2006) 'Suzhi: A Keyword Approach', *The China Quarterly* 186: 295-313.

Kipnis, A. (2007) 'Neoliberalism Reified: *Suzhi* Discourse and Tropes of Neoliberalism in the People's Republic of China', *Journal of the Royal Anthropological Institute* 13: 383-400.

Kristof, N.D. (1991) 'Some Chinese Provinces Forcing Sterilization of Retarded Couples', *The New York Times*, 15 August.

Kohrman, M. (2005) *Bodies of Difference: Experiences of Disability and Institutional Advocacy in the Making of Modern China* (Berkeley: University of California Press).

Lau J.T., Wang Q., Cheng Y., Kim, J.H., Yang, X., Tsui, H.Y. (2008) 'Infertility-Related Perceptions and Responses and Their Associations With Quality of Life Among Rural Chinese Infertile Couples', *Journal of Sex and Marital Therapy* 34(3): 248-267.

Liu, L. (2006) 'Quality of Life as a Social Representation in China: A Qualitative Study', *Social Indicators Research* 75: 217-240.

Liu, W. (2007) 'Personal communication', 13 November, Changsha.

MacLeod, P. and Clarke, F.F. (1998) 'Forget Cloning Sheep and Pay Attention to China', *Canadian Medical Association Journal* 159/2: 153-155.

Mao, X.(1998) 'Chinese Geneticists' Views of Ethical Issues in Genetic Testing and Screening: Evidence for Eugenics in China', *American Journal of Human Genetics* 63: 688-695.

McNeil, M., Varcoe, I. and Yearley, S. (eds) (1990) *The New Reproductive Technologies* (London: Macmillan).

Monga, M., Alexandrescu, B., Katz, S., Stein, M. and Ganiats, T. (2004) 'Impact of Infertility on Quality of Life, Marital Adjustment, and Sexual Function', *Urology* 63/1: 126-130.

Murphy, R. (2004) 'Turning Peasants into Modern Chinese Citizens: "Population Quality" Discourse, Demographic Transition and Primary Education', *The China Quarterly* 177: 1-20.

Nanguo Morning Post (2005) 'Free Premarital Check-up', 24 July, 4.

Nature (1994) 'China's Misconception of Eugenics', *Nature* 367: 1-2.

P.R. China (1994) 'Law on Maternal and Infant Health Care', in Tenth Meeting of the Standing Committee of the Eighth National People's Congress, 27 October 1994.

P.R. China (2001) 'Marriage Law', in 1980 – amended according to the Decision on Amending the Marriage Law of the People's Republic of China made at the 21st meeting of the Standing Committee of the Ninth National People's Congress, 28 April 2001.

P.R. China, Ministry of Health (2001) 'Human sperm bank basic standards and technology criteria', in: as approved by the Ministry of Health, P.R. China.

P.R. China, Ministry of Health (2003) 'Ethical Principles for Human Assisted Reproductive Technology and Sperm Banks', in: Issued and revised by the Ministry of Health, P.R. China, July 2003.

P.R. China, Ministry of Health (2003) 'Regulation on Assisted Reproductive Technology', in: Issued and revised by the Ministry of Health, P.R. China, July 2003.

Peking University Third Hospital (2003) 'Reproductive medicine and assisted reproductive technology international seminar report', available at: http://www.bysy.edu.cn/bysy/dept/fu/meeting1.htm (Beijing: Reproductive Medicine Centre, March 2003).

Post, T. (1994) 'Quality Not Quantity: China: A New Population Law Tries To Weed Out "Inferior' Births"', *Newsweek*, 28 November.

Qiao, J. (2007) 'Informed Consent in Clinical Practice Ethical Dilemmas', *Workshop on informed consent in reproductive genetics and stem cell technology and the role of Ethical Review Boards*, Beijing: 1-5 April.

Qing, M. (2004) 'Coming to the Rescue', *Shanghai Star*, 14 October.

Qiu, R. (1996) 'Does Eugenics Exist in China? Ethical Issues in China's Law on Maternal and Infant Healthcare', presented at meeting of HUGO Ethical Committee in San Francisco, USA: 25 November.

Qiu, R. (2001) 'Sociocultural Dimensions of Infertility and Assisted Reproduction in the Far East', *Current Practices and Controversies in Assisted Reproduction* Report of a meeting on "Medical, Ethical and Social Aspects of Assisted Reproduction" WHO Headquarters, Geneva, Switzerland: 17-21 September.

Qiu, R. (2007) 'Philosophical Concept of Reproduction and its Cultural Transformation with Technology Advancement', *Workshop on informed consent in reproductive genetics and stem cell technology and the role of Ethical Review Boards*, Beijing: 1-5 April.

Qiu, R. and Dikötter, F. (1999) 'Is China's Law Eugenic?' *The UNESCO Courier* September: 30-31.

RGH (2007) 'Informed Consent Form Artificial Insemination (AI)' (Reproductive and Genetic Hospital of CITIC-Xiangya, Changsha), P.R. China.

RGH (2007) *Introduction Lecture for IVF Patients* (Reproductive and Genetic Hospital Changsha, 12 November 2007).

Roberts, E. (2006) 'God's Laboratory: Religious Rationalities and Modernity in Ecuadorian *in vitro* Fertilization', *Culture, Medicine and Psychiatry* 30: 507-536.

Strathern, M. (1992) *Reproducing the Future: Essays on Anthropology, Kinship and the New Reproductive Technologies* (Manchester: Manchester University Press).

Svendsen, M.N. and Koch, L. (2008) 'Unpacking the "Spare Embryo"', *Social Studies of Science* 38(1): 93-110.

Sun, Z. (2007) Personal communication, 26 September 2007.

Thompson, C. (2005) *Making Parents: The Ontological Choreography of Reproductive Technologies* (Cambridge, MA: MIT Press).

Throsby, K. (2004) *When IVF Fails: Feminism, Infertility and the Negotiation of Normality* (Basingstoke: Palgrave Macmillan).

Valentine, D.P. (1986) 'Psychological Impact of Infertility: Identifying Issues and Needs.' *Social Work in Health Care* 11/4: 61-69.

Wahlberg, A. (2007) 'Measuring Progress – Calculating the Life of Nations', *Distinktion – Scandinavian Journal of Social Theory* 14: 65-82.

Wahlberg, A. (2008) 'Reproductive Medicine and the Concept of "Quality"', *Clinical Ethics* 3(4): 189-193.

Wahlberg, A. (2009) 'Serious Disease as Kinds of Living', in Bauer, S. and Wahlberg, A. (eds) *Contested Categories: Life Sciences in Society* (Farnham: Ashgate), pp. 89-112.

Wang, W., Du, W.Y., Liu, P., Liu, J.H. and Wang, Y.H. (2002) 'Five-factor Personality Measures in Chinese University Students: Effects of One-child Policy?' *Psychiatry Research* 109/1: 37-44.

Xiao, S. (2008) 'Suffering with Assisted Reproduction: Clinical and Ethical Concerns', *BIONET Conference on ethical governance of reproductive technologies, therapeutic stem cells and stem cell banks* Changsha: 1-3 April.

Xinhua (1999) 'China's 1st Notables' Sperm Bank Opens', *Xinhua News Agency* (Beijing).

Xinhua (2008) 'China's First "Test-Tube Baby" Celebrates Her 20th Birthday', *Women of China* (http://www.womenofchina.cn/news/Updates_on_Women/201827.jsp: accessed on 10 March.

Yu, X. (2007) 'Personal communication', Deputy Chief, Bureau for Science and Education, Ministry of Health, 8 November.

Zhan, H. (2002) 'Chinese Caregiving Burden and the Future Burden of Elder Care in Life-course Perspective', *International Journal of Aging and Human Development* 54/4: 267-290.

Zhao, Y. (1986) *Yousheng, Youyu, Youjiao* (Beijing: Renmin Weisheng Chubanshe).

Zhao, Z. (2008) 'Experts Say: Serious Sperm Problem, in 60 Years, 62% decline', *Global Times – Life Times [环球时报 – 生命时报]* (http://health.sohu.com/20080729/n258448484.shtml: accessed on 30 July.

Chapter 17

Illiberal Biopolitics and 'Embryonic Life': The Governance of Human Embryonic Stem Cell Research in China

Kerstin Klein

Introduction

In China, biotechnology and the life sciences have become a matter of national importance. In his opening address at the 4th National Congress for Science and Technology on 9 January 2006, President Hu Jintao stated that 'biotechnology is the priority of high-tech industries by which China will try to catch up with the developed countries' (as cited in Chen et al. 2007). 'Catching up' is no longer the sole motive of China's national science policy though. While science and technology (S&T) have played a key role in the achievement of national development in all of the reform era since the late 1970s, the Communist Party of China (CPC) has now much greater ambitions for the not too distant future. In 2006, the State Council implemented a new 15-year *National Middle- and Long Term Science and Technology Plan* (2006-2020) that envisions China to innovate independently from the developed world ('indigenous innovation') by 2020. In the same year, the release of the *China Modernization Report* of the Chinese Academy of Science (CAS) marks an even more programmatic vision for the next 50 years. By 2050, it states, China will have established itself as a world leading power in science (CAS 2006).

Since Hu Jintao took office in 2002, the CPC has stipulated *scientific development* (kexue fazhanguan) as its new official guiding ideology. Although scientific development is promoted as a sustainable and people-centered concept, it foremost seeks to combine the utilization of S&T with human resources to boost social and economic development.[1] There is general agreement that talent base is a central factor of a nation's economic growth (Simon and Cao 2009).

1 Hu first presented the new concept during an inspection trip to Jiangxi Province in September 2003, where he also gave an extensive explanation of scientific development,'[i]t is necessary to solidly adopt the scientific development concept of coordinated development, all-round development, and sustainable development, [and to] actively explore a new development path that conforms to reality, further improves the socialist market economic structure, combines intensified efforts to readjust structure with the promotion of rural development, combines efforts to bring into play the role of science and technology with

The size, quality, and utilization of human resources influence a country's level of technological capability as well as its future trajectory. The term 'human resources in science and technology' is an internationally shared key indicator for assessing a nation's technological strength, and China's leaders have now also identified the importance of human resources and to develop a talent pool that will determine the nature of China's competitive positioning in the coming years (e.g., ibid.; Hoffman 2006). Under the premises of 'scientific development' and 'independent innovation,' the population is called upon to become an 'innovation-oriented society,' and China's Vice Minister of the National Population and Family Planning Commission has made the new direction of utilizing human resources for innovation clear. In a speech at the UN, he pointed out that 'regarding talent resources as the No. 1 resource for socioeconomic development' is a core strategy to enhance national development and innovation in China (Guoqiang 2004).

In China's race to the top, the country still falls far behind in many scientific and technological fields though, and the central government therefore targets specific selected areas with the potential to compete successfully internationally. Human embryonic stem cell research (hESCR) is one such area, because cautious stem cell policies and the ongoing controversy in large parts of the developed world offer unprecedented research and commercialization opportunities for China. In contrast to the controversy elsewhere, in China the government and bioethics experts pertain an official view according to which China has a cultural environment with far fewer moral obstacles to the use of human embryos in stem cell research than many other nations have (e.g., Qiu 2004; Yang 2004). In this sense, bioethicists suggest that due to Confucian moral philosophy Chinese have no moral qualms in China about using human embryos in stem cell research. As personhood can only be acquired through social practice, according to Confucian teachings, human value evolves out from an individual's social relations with society, the family or other groups, but it cannot be acquired before birth.[2] It is also often said that the principle of *ren* (humaneness) weighs higher than the concern for unborn life. Medicine as the 'art of ren' is seen to be committed to treating patients and helping or doing good to them more than protecting unborn life that has not yet acquired personhood. It is not at all clear though, whether the majority of the one-party state's peculiarly silent public does indeed represent this uniform view, or whether beliefs and attitudes about the moral status of human embryos diverge from the official view. Cong Yali (2008) for instance acknowledges that a fraction of people believe that an embryo is already a full human life, in the sense of a person. There are in fact also some Chinese scientists and scholars,

efforts to bring into play the advantages of human resources' (as quoted in Fewsmith 2004).

2 This does not mean though that human embryos can be used without restrictions. In line with the established standard in more liberal regulatory frameworks that allows research with human embryos up to 14 days of development, Chinese national law also accepts this gradualist view of human embryos.

as Wang (2003, 2006) points out, who object that hESCR should be forbidden, because it violates human dignity and is a big challenge to human life. Eventually, Cong also points at a reason why there is not more debate on this issue in China, 'objectively speaking, in Chinese society, we do not yet have an atmosphere that would encourage discussing the moral status of the human embryo and foetus.' As official discourse outperforms other viewpoints, the field is invested heavily with considerable public resources supported by liberal policies.

In the following, it will be shown how under the premises of 'scientific development' the 'population' and human embryos are harnessed as 'experimental' resources for national development through scientific progress. In order to develop this argument, the chapter will draw on Michel Foucault's theory of biopolitics (Foucault 1978). This theory sketches out how, historically in the liberal West, population has become a central domain of government. What is different about this new power, as noted in the *History of Sexuality* (ibid.), is that it utilizes life not by killing it but by investing it 'through and through'. The structure of the chapter is as follows: first, the theory of biopolitics will be made available in the Chinese non-liberal context and in relation to human embryos. Second, it will present the national stem cell program in terms of how it has evolved and how it is funded. Third, it will be shown how in the interplay of contemporary guiding principles, policies and medical practice the population is turned into human capital, and how in this context human embryos are turned into 'experimental' resources for stem cell research. Lastly, it will be argued how the governance of the national stem cell program in the one-party state exemplifies a particular type of illiberal biopolitics. It will be suggested how such a concept may usefully be employed in the present-day study of regulatory practices and the control of life and populations in illiberal states in relation to biotechnology and the life sciences. By doing so, it hopes to make a contribution to an emergent literature in the field of comparative science and technology studies (STS) on the governance of science in new Asian science powers. As such, it also attempts to develop an analytical framework for the study of science and technology in illiberal states, an area which STS has largely neglected to date.

Biopolitics and 'Embryonic Life' in China

In the eighteenth century, Michel Foucault (1978, 2003, 2008) pointed out, power underwent a transformation from power as sovereignty to a new form of power, *biopower*. Biopower takes on two different forms: a *disciplinary power* and a *regulatory control* of life or, as the latter is also called, 'biopolitics.' Sovereign power, essentially, is a 'right of seizure: of things, time, bodies, and ultimately life itself' (Foucault 1978). It prohibits, confiscates or destroys what sovereign power declares illegitimate. In contrast to this older juridical form of power, biopower regulates subjects through numerous and diverse techniques to achieve the 'disciplining' of individuals and a 'regulatory control' of the 'population.'

While disciplinary power targets the individual to increase the capability and strength of his body and to maximize its utility, *biopolitics* targets the 'population' as a whole and as a 'species body.' What was radically new in this shift was that 'life and its mechanisms,' the body and the population, all have moved into the realm of politics and strategic calculation. As Foucault (1978) notes, 'for the first time in history, no doubt, biological existence was reflected in political existence' (ibid.). This new 'biopolitics of the population' takes account of and manages birth and death rates, illness, public hygiene and other anomalies. Biopolitics has facilitated new regulatory mechanisms whose function it is to forecast, make statistical estimates and make overall measures of the population as a whole, with the purpose to intervene at the level of collective phenomena. These mechanisms, in turn, bring about new guidelines and recommendations that prescribe norms, adjust anomalies to an equilibrium and maintain an average among the 'general population.'

Foucault has located the 'birth' of biopolitics in European modernity and the liberal state (Foucault 2008). As a period, this modernity was characterized by the formation of the nation state, the Industrial Revolution, capitalism and liberalism, as well as a competitive battle between nations in need of vital and resourceful populations (Rabinow and Rose 2006). Foucault has been criticized by many for leaving entirely blank the question of biopolitical practices on bodies and populations outside the liberal Western nation state. For James Clifford (1988) for instance, Foucault was 'scrupulously ethnocentric,' and Ann Laura Stoler (1995) asks how biopolitics can be used in the colonies and colonial bodies. According to her, his genealogy of nineteenth century bourgeois identity is not only bound to the geographical parameters of Europe, but it is also 'deeply rooted in a self-referential western culture.' With Stoler, it therefore needs to be asked whether and how biopolitics can be used in the time, geography and culture of the 'other' and in this instance the People's Republic of China (PRC). One answer has been that the former colonies can be studied as experimental spaces and laboratories of Western liberalism's modernity (e.g., Stoler 1995).

Evidence that it is possible to make out a regulatory control of life in China that seeks to improve the 'quality' of the population can be found in Foucault's own work. As Foucault situated the 'threshold of biological modernity' at the point where political strategies are concerned with the existence of the species *per se*, recent developments in the life sciences and biotechnology in China suggest that this threshold is now also far behind in the PRC. The implementation of a Protection of Human Genetic Resources Act (1998) by the Chinese Human Genetic Resources Management Office, which was jointly established by the Chinese Ministry of Health (MOH) and the Ministry of Science and Technology (MOST), is one instance of a regulatory control of the population that targets its biological existence and its well-being. The act seeks to protect the human genetic resources of the population from exploitation by foreign researchers. In order to do so it restricts the export of human genetic material out of China and reserves all claims for benefits derived from international biomedical research using Chinese resources. With this act, the population, as a 'species body,' has become the stakes, and 'nationalization' of the biological has been achieved as well.

Others have already used biopolitics in China in relation to the governance of the population under the one-child policy. It has been acknowledged that ever since the foundation of the PRC in 1949, the size and composition of the population have been a central object of power in the building of the Socialist state (e.g., Greenhalgh and Winckler 2005; Sigley 1996). Under the one-child policy, which controls the size of the population, but by doing so is also concerned with its 'quality' (Sigley 1996), Greenhalgh and Winckler have made out a shift in the late stage of the policy, as a transformation from 'Leninist' to more 'neo-liberal biopolitics'. In the last decade, they argue, the regime has drastically shifted its 'hard' Leninist methods of birth planning toward 'softer' neo-liberal approaches, which involve new and more indirect forms of regulation by the state and more self-regulation by citizens themselves.

Life and *population* are key terminology of biopolitics, but since Foucault lectured on biopolitics, technical advances in the life sciences have altered our understanding and the meaning of what 'life' is (see also Dillon 2007). As Dillon has put it (2007), 'the life that biopower takes as its referent object of power, a life that Foucault first interrogated in the form of population, has been transformed by the history of the twentieth century.' As Foucault's life predated the time of modern biotechnology's full impact after the mid-1980s, there are no direct references in his work to transformations of life in the age of molecular biology. He has, however, made use of a notion that purposely or not envisages bioscience's new capabilities to create 'life' and extract biovalue and vitality at the level of cells, genes and molecules. According to Foucault, it is an *excess of biopower*, 'when it becomes technologically and politically possible for man not only to manage life but to make it proliferate, to create living matter, to build the monster,' as 'this formidable extension of biopower … will put it beyond all human sovereignty' (Foucault 2003, 254).

Today, the 'molecular vision of life' (Kay 1994) has changed what 'life itself' (Rose 2007) is, or was. We can access it in altogether new ways, at the level of molecules, stem cells and genes, and we can do this *in-vitro* or *ex vivo* as well as *in-vivo*. We have technical possibilities at hand to engineer and enhance it to our desires, and we can create it, e.g. by the means of IVF, research cloning (somatic cell nuclear transfer, SCNT), synthetic biology, etc. As these new technologies have 'transformed the western understanding of what it is to be a living thing,' Dillon and Lobo-Guerrero (2009) have stated, two transformations have taken place. One, in what it is to be a 'living thing,' and the other is a transformation of life into 'value,' into commodity and capital. This challenges us to rethink what notions like life and population mean and what they encompass, and the important point to make, as Dillon and Lobo-Guerrero have said it, is that this has changed our 'bio-political imaginary of species-being' and of 'life.'

In this sense, stem cell research has changed our 'imaginary of life' (ibid.) as well. For human embryos have become so precious to the advancement of stem cell science, they have gained a new role in science and society for the life-like qualities that they possess and the prospects that they offer for curing medical conditions and improving public health. In the public debate about stem cell research, human embryos have also obtained a new moral status in society. They are envisaged as moral entities requiring whatever form of protection by the law against their misuse by science and medicine. In a new way, human embryos are being re-imagined in relation to the continuum of human life. The constitution of embryos in society and the law has been taken into account in social science perspectives on e.g. 'embryonic personhood' (Cussins 1996), 'embryonic citizenship' (Holc 2004) and 'embryonic nationhood' (Metzler 2007) which illustrate that the subject's position and the power of technologies, as Cussins has pointed out, are negotiated together. In other words, they demarcate a 'co-construction' of subjects (the embryo) and technology (ibid.). As the 'life' that biopower takes as its reference point has been transformed by the life sciences, as noted by Dillon (2007) earlier on, the life that biopolitics embraces as the object of its exercise is now also that of its emergent form, human embryos. Henceforth, the use of the term *embryonic life* identifies that human embryos have also become objects of biopolitical practices of the state. While this analytical strategy does not depart from a specific standpoint in the moral controversy about hESCR and the question whether human embryos are 'persons' or not, it seeks, however, to open up, analytically, the regulatory control of life to the molecular level of human embryos.

One instructive place to search for the co-construction of embryonic personhood is what Sarah Franklin (2006) has termed the 'IVF-stem cell interface', the gateway between the infertility clinic and the stem cell lab. Here, as Cussins (ibid.) shows, the embryo outside the body is subject to political and juridical control. During the fertilization and development of embryos in the lab, developmental details are recorded which are used to separate 'good' from 'bad' embryos, to tell apart which embryos should be transferred to the patient's uterus, which embryos should be frozen, and which ones can be treated as 'waste.' Segregating embryos in this way is a biopolitical management of the embryo population in the IVF clinic. Some embryos are disposed as 'waste,' because they are considered as 'bad embryos,' others are frozen because they are deemed 'good embryos' viable of potentially becoming future citizens, and yet others, both good and bad spare embryos[3] (Svendsen and Koch 2008), are delivered to the stem cell lab to be utilized in science and medicine. Developmental criteria used in this process justify the exemption of certain embryos from the moral and legal status that applies to embryos as potential human lives and future citizens. When the egg does not fertilize, when

3 Svendsen and Koch demonstrate that the category of 'waste embryos' is a blurred concept, because there is no straight-forward set of criteria for defining which embryos are waste or not. As this is constantly negotiated by IVF lab-technicians who are caught in the middle of the reproductive and the 'research trail,' the necessity to deliver viable embryos to the stem cell lab often means that this category recurrently also includes surplus 'good' quality embryos.

it fails to develop 'normally,' or when it has been created in excess, it is removed from the 'reproductive trail' that leads back to the uterus. Its ontological bond is then cut (Cussins 1996), and leaving this trail relaxes the legal, moral, parental and political properties of those embryos. The lab is penetrated by numerous extensive legislative and bureaucratic technical standards, inscribing every embryo and prescribing reproducible success rates (ibid.), which determine whether embryos are granted the right to actualize their 'potency' (Gomez-Lobo 2005)[4] to become future citizens. The other alternative is that they have to leave the reproductive trail of the uterus either to be disposed of as waste or enter the 'research trail' where they will be killed and 'transformed into medicine,' as Svendsen and Koch (2008) have termed it.

In the way that scientific advances in the life sciences have changed our understanding of what 'life' is, stem cell research has also changed the way how 'population' is regulated, controlled and utilized. The need of stem cell scientists to obtain more embryos and the framing of stem cell science as an urgent matter of national survival is a form of regulatory intervention into 'life' including its emergent form and the 'population' including its emergent form as embryo population. In the way that not yet or 'not to be' actualized future citizens, 'good' and 'bad' embryos, may or may not become parts of the population body but resources for stem cell research, they are objects of governmental technologies, regulatory control and intervention. While the population delivers their reproductive assets as resources potentially for both trails, it is these 'fetal citizens' (Holc 2004) on which the advancement of stem cell science depends.

China's National Stem Cell Program

As noted in the introduction, biotechnology and the life sciences are centre-stage in the CPC's endeavor to climb to the top league. In China, biotechnology was first mentioned as a focal point of science policy in the earliest stage of China's reform program, when it was driven by a feeling of urgency to 'catch up' with the Western world and scientific developments in the field of molecular biology that China had missed out on in the Mao era, when Lysenkoism and the Cultural Revolution halted classical genetics in China for several decades (Schneider 2003). In the opening

4 In response to a debate with Mary Mahowald, Gomez-Lobo's (2005) argument is part of the debate about the biological 'potentiality' of human embryos to become persons. This argument emphasizes that in the appropriate cytoplasmic environment, the biological program contained in the genome sets off the development to become a male or female adult. In response to Mary Mahowald's objection to differentiate the potentiality argument in two senses, namely potentiality and actualization (as active potency), Lobo-Gomez (2005) argues that both *in-vitro* and *in-vivo* embryos inhere the same potency, precisely because infertility treatment is based on the assumption of active potency present in the embryos selected for implantation.

ceremony of the National Science Conference on 18 March 1978, Deng Xiaoping declared the new role of S&T, 'without the rapid development of S&T, there can be no rapid development of the country' (Deng 1978). A 'Four Modernizations' policy[5] implemented as China's new state science policy by the 11th National Party Congress' Central Committee in December 1978 targeted agriculture, industry, national defence and science and technology (S&T) as key areas of national modernization. Another visionary pillar of the Dengist era was the *National High-Tech Research and Development Program* (863 Program) implemented in 1986. The program highlights the priority of applied research with the purpose of commercialization and clinical application.[6] Initiated by four scientists, Deng was convinced that if China does not want to fall behind the West, chief investments in research and development (R&D) were necessary in order to accelerate high-tech development and to realize the 'Four Modernisations.'[7] With the launch of the program, biotechnology was assigned the role of a key technology, initially with a particular emphasis on high-tech medicines and vaccines, protein engineering and gene therapy.

When the first significant breakthroughs in the field of hESCR made headlines in the US in 1998, China had already gained the infrastructure and technical ability to jump on that bandwagon. Chinese scientists were therefore in a position to achieve early successes in the advancement of the field. Only three years after Gearhart and Thompson created the world's first stem cell lines from human embryos, a team of Chinese researchers led by Xu Ling claimed that it too had successfully isolated and grown hESC's (U.S. Embassy Beijing Report 2001). In the same year, Chinese scientists at Huashan Hospital, a part of Shanghai's Fudan University, carried out the first clinical trial with adult stem cells to treat patients with traumatic brain malfunction. Other early successes comprised the cloning of pulsating heart cells (cardiomyocites) from human embryonic stem cells,[8] and in 2003 Huizhen Sheng's team at Shanghai Second Medical University successfully extracted stem cells from embryos by fusing adult human stem cells with specially

5 The 'Four Modernisations' Program was in fact already first introduced in 1975 by Zhou Enlai at the 4th National People's Congress and was one of his last public acts. After Zhou's death in 1976 and Mao's soon thereafter, Deng Xiaoping took up Zhou's programmatic concept and started the new reform era.

6 It defines R&D priority areas in ca. 20 different subjects identified as having the most significant impact on enhancing overall national strength. Subjects reach across six high-tech priority fields in the civil sector, such as IT, biotechnology and advanced agricultural technology, advanced materials technology, advanced manufacturing and automation technology, energy technology as well as resource and environment technology. 863 stands for 86 as the year and 3 for the month (March) of that year of the release of the program. See the website of MOST's 863 Program, on, www.most.gov.cn/eng/programmes1/index.htm (accessed: 25 June 2009).

7 The four scientists who proposed the plan were Wang Daheng, Wang Ganchang, Yang Jiachi, and Chen Fangyun.

8 The collaborative work was published as Boheler, et al. (2002, 189-201).

prepared rabbit eggs. In the same year, Guangxiu Lu's team at Xiangya Medical College cloned human embryos to the blastocyst stage.

Today, the bulk of research is funded directly by MOST and predominantly in the form of two dedicated national long-term research initiatives, one for applied and the other for basic research. The first major S&T funding program is the already mentioned 863 Program, and the other one is the 1997 'National Basic Research Program' (973 Program). Even in this second program, however, China retains the major direction of its science policy. By emphasizing 'strategic' basic research, the 973 Program seeks to further overcome the perceived bias of scientists toward basic research over application.[9] Another major goal of the program is to give project leaders more flexibility, by making it easier for them to employ top scientists from home or abroad and to attract outstanding overseas Chinese to return home to serve the motherland. Under the 973 Program, stem cell research has become a priority area within health biotechnology. As stated on the program's website, stem cell-related projects are currently funded under the general heading of 'Population and Health' and 'Synthesis and Frontier Research', with each supported project receiving an average of Yuan 20-30 million (US$2.6-3.9 million). According to the latest available figures, it is estimated that between 300-400 trained PhD researchers are working on all types of stem cells in approximately 30 separate institutions (Normile and Mann 2005). There are about seven highly advanced stem cell labs in China's five major city stem cell centres in Beijing, Shanghai, Tianjin, Changsha and Guangzhou (Murray and Sparr 2006). China's top national centres of excellence in stem cell research are Beijing University's Stem Cell Research Centre and the Institute of Zoology at CAS, the Centre for Developmental Biology at Xinhua Hospital in Shanghai, and Xiangya Medical College in Changsha. Each of these laboratories is run by a top-calibre scientist, some of which returned home under the provisions of the 973 Program's returnee program (see also Global Watch Mission 2005).[10]

In October 1992, the 14th National Congress of the CPC officially gave China the name of a 'socialist market economy,' but despite of capitalist reforms and marketization of the economy, China is still run by the command institution of the five-year-plan. The major S&T funding initiatives distribute their monies through these plans. Precise total spending figures for stem cell research are hard to come by, but Murray and Sparr (2006) estimate that between 2000 and 2005 the MOST provided about Yuan 100 million (roughly US$12 million) to each of the two major S&T projects. Monies are also pumped into stem cell labs and projects by a variety of other public bodies, such as the Chinese Academy of Sciences and the National Natural Science. City and provincial governments as well as universities

9 For more details on the 973 Program, see the website of the National Basic Research Initiative, on www. 973.gov.cn/English/Index.aspx.

10 Li Lingsong is heading Beijing University's Stem-Cell Research Centre, Zhou Qi is directing the Institute of Zoology, Shenghui Zhen is running the Centre for Developmental Biology at Xinhua Hospital, and Lu Guangxiu is the director of Xiangya Medical College.

themselves also invest into research and development. Under the tenth five-year plan, Murray and Sparr estimate that this could have made up for another Yuan 100 million, so that total funding of stem cell research between 2000 and 2005 was roughly US$ 38 million. In this period, annual investment into both forms of stem cell research, embryonic and adult, were therefore between US$ 4-10 million.[11]

Under the current eleventh five-year plan (2006-2010), investment in research has been forecast to accelerate by perhaps up to 70 per cent. The UK Stem Cell Initiative (2005) in the Pattison Report estimates that under the current plan stem cell research spending will soar up to somewhere between US$ 61 million and US$ 245 million (ca. US$145 million to US$580 million based on 'purchasing power parity'). Due to concealment of data, the countless number of national and local research and funding initiatives and the conversion of the inland value of the Chinese currency as opposed to its formal exchange rate (purchasing power parity), it is impossible to present more exact figures of total funding under the current five-year plan. Even the minimal estimate seems impressive though, and China's investment into stem cell research is held as a concern by at least some Western scientists (e.g., Global Watch Mission 2005, UK Stem Cell Initiative 2005). Yet others have also questioned whether China is already able to compete successfully in terms of its expenditure for stem cell research, as other countries have also started to pour monies into the field (Murray and Sparr 2006). Chinese government funding, both central and municipal, is outspent for instance by the budgets of some US states and the UK.[12] Even though money goes further in China (in the sense of the relative value of the US dollar in terms of purchasing power parity), where salaries are lower and technical equipment is cheaper, the differences in resources could still make up for a strong dissimilarity.

A whole novelty in the People's Republic, private capital and private sector research form another pillar of China's S&T policy in the reform era. A review of the National High-Tech Program as early as 1988 drew attention to the centralized, top-down nature of Chinese research institutions and also identified a lack of commercial incentives as a major obstacle to the translation of research into marketable products. The review further promoted the non-state sector, and Chinese researchers were encouraged to set up their own enterprises and to establish American-type public-private partnerships (Segal 2003). A key policy

11 See the UK Stem Cell Initiative's country profile for China, on its website: www.advisorybodies.doh.gov.uk/uksci/global/china.htm.

12 In the US for instance, the State of California alone has allocated a budget of US$3 billion to fund stem-cell research related projects in Californian research institutions in the period between 2004 and 2014. Around the same time, other US states have also announced their stimulus packages: New Jersey for instance has claimed to invest US$380 million in a state stem cell centre, and Connecticut has announced to spend US$100 million on research in the next 10 years. In the UK, the British government devoted US$73 million of public funds to stem-cell research only in the years between 2004 and 2006, and it has announced that it will match up US$18.5 million per annum over a decade. See also, Gerlin, 2006.

that came out of this review was the Torch Plan (1988) that seeks to push science for technical outcomes rather than resulting in basic research. Projects funded under the Torch Plan are in the later stages of clinical development, and thus demonstrate commercial and marketable prospects. High-technology development and applied science are further facilitated by the setting up of science parks and incubators under this plan. The Torch Plan has also diversified and decentralized R&D funding, by channelling it through state-owned banks and private venture capital as well as the diversification of oversight over research directions.

As a result of this policy, numerous university stem cell labs and centres have founded spin-off companies to commercialize their research (Frew et al. 2008). If companies are spin-offs of university research institutes, the latter owns a share. This has served to strengthen ties between private enterprises and public universities. There are many examples of academic stem cell centres that maintain shell companies in order to commercialize their research and profit from patents (e.g., ibid.; Global Watch Mission 2005). Huizhen Sheng's Centre for Developmental Biology at Xinhua Hospital for instance has formed a shell company between her centre and Shanghai Medical University, as principal shareholders, in order to file several patent applications relating to somatic cell nuclear transfer (SCNT), a technique by which embryos are cloned for therapeutic purposes – in her case by fusing animal egg cells with human cell nuclei. The patent applications cover areas such as cross-species SCNT using rabbit oocytes (Global Watch Mission 2005). Another example is Sino-Cells Biotechnologies Co. Ltd., which is a spin-off from Beijing University's Stem Cell Research Centre. Sino-Cells was founded in 2000 with investment from the Beijing University Health Science Centre, Beijing University Resource Group, scientists investors and Beijing Hezhong Huaxin Science and Technology Development Co. Ltd. Short- and long-term goals comprise drug-screening, genotyping, and cryopreservation (storage by freezing) of human embryonic stem cells (hESCs), as well as using bone marrow stem cells for the treatment of corneal diseases. In the long run, Sino-Cells is planning to raise more capital in order to build a good manufacturing practice facility in order to use hESCs for clinical application.

The most impressive example of a Chinese public-private stem cell enterprise though is Beike Biotechnologies in Shenzhen. In 2001, Beike was founded in order to commercialize stem cell research and clinical work in a collaborative effort between Beijing University, Hong Kong University of Science and Technology, Zhengzhou University and Shenzhen Graduate School of Qinghua University. Capital from Shenzhen city government and the China State National Fund was also invested.[13] Based on a well-organized network, Beike has developed extremely

13 The enterprise is based on a whole supply and exchange network organized on a large scale. It includes satellite hospitals, clinicians, stem cell banks and university research laboratories with main research labs in Shenyang, Shenzhen, Zhenghou and Hainan. On its website, the Beike group states that it conducts and supplies experimental stem cell treatments in 27 hospitals in China and one in Thailand. Blood and stem cell banks in each

rapidly, and the group seeks to expand further inside China and beyond. In terms of clinical services, Beike bets on strategy diversification. While conducting research on a broad range of sources from human embryos, aborted foetuses and various adult tissues, according to their website, clinical work currently mainly uses stem cells from umbilical cord blood and bone marrow, which are delivered by intravenous injections and surgical injection in some cases. Beike has emerged as a world leading provider of such medical services, as thousands of patients from China and internationally have already been treated in Beike clinics on various incurable and terminal conditions, such as spinal cord injury, amytrophic lateral sclerosis, Parkinson's disease, motor-neurone diseases, blindness, Alzheimer's and many others.[14]

Despite the central government's strong push for private sector and applied research, as the heart of China's innovation strategy, private capital funding of academic research, as Murray and Sparr (2006) find, is still immature. In the UK for instance, the Welcome Trust in partnership with the U.S. Juvenile Diabetes Foundation had already donated more than US$35 million into the field before 2006 (ibid.). In China, on the other hand, the unambiguous policy approach to merge private and public research and funding is hampered by the fact that it is enormously difficult for innovative research-driven Chinese biotech companies to raise start-up capital. According to Frew et al. (2008), this is more a reflection of financial policies than a lack of confidence in the science. Chinese small to medium-sized enterprises (SMEs) find it hard to secure venture capital to start up firms. Banks generally turn down their funding applications. Therefore, researchers as well as biotech companies still by and large depend on government funding at all levels, including the state (central), provincial and local, but the central government is by far the most significant supporter of China's national stem cell program (ibid.; Murray and Sparr 2006).

Chinese Policies and Sources of Human Embryonic Stem Cells

In this section, it will be shown how in the interplay of programmatic concepts like 'scientific development' and the regulation of hESCR and human assisted reproduction the population is harnessed as a resource for national development as human capital and as 'experimental' bodies available for stem cell research. The sheer size of China's 1.3 billion population creates an enormous wealth of biological resources and human capital in China (Chen et al. 2007). Lisa Hoffmann (2006) has shown how an important component of the Deng Xiaoping inspired change has been a shift from a reliance on politically 'red' cadres to a preference for

of the many Chinese cities where its labs reside in also belong to Beike's exchange network. Source: Beike's website, on www.beikebiotech.com.

14 In an interview, the chief executive officer Sean Hu stated that 2,500 patients were treated by Beike hospitals between 2001 and early 2008 (Schuster 2008).

those with expertise and talent, thus reshuffling the role of educated and talented personnel. Under the guiding ideology of 'scientific development,' the strategy to employ human resources and talent more effectively is closely intertwined with China's ambition to lead innovation by 2050. As Chen et al. note, 'a talent strategy is a key issue for developing life sciences and biotechnology in China' and, in turn, the key to successful stem cell programs is the procurement of large abundances of human embryos (Heng 2007).

International Society for Stem Cell Research (ISSCR) has recently stated that China's policies towards hESCR are perhaps the most explicitly liberal in the world,[15] and others suggest that presently no other country is pursuing the field more aggressively than China (Liao, Li and Zhao 2007). China's competitive edge is built on strategy diversification. Research on both adult and embryonic stem cells is supported by government funds, and scientists are actively testing also the hypothesis that post-embryonic sub-totipotent stem cells exist in many human adult tissues. In January 2004, the Ministry of Science & Technology together with the Ministry of Health officially implemented the key national policy for the regulation of hESCR in China. In line with the guidelines of the UK Warnock Committee (*British Medical Journal* 1984), the Ethical Guiding Principles for Research on Human Embryonic Stem Cells permit research on human embryos up to the 14th day of embryonic development, when the primitive streak begins to develop. Article 5 of the Guiding Principles defines the sources of hESCs and allows their procurement from 1) spare eggs and leftover embryos from fertility treatments in IVF clinics, 2) aborted foetuses from natural or voluntarily selective abortion, 3) cloned embryos solely for the use of medical research created via the technique called somatic cell nuclear transfer (SCNT), and 4) from germ cells like female eggs and sperm voluntarily donated. Yet, the guidelines strictly prohibit any commercial dealings with and payment for eggs and embryos.

Article 6 of the guidelines also permits the procurement of stem cells from hybrid human-animal embryos. The guidelines strictly prohibit the hybridization of human germ cells with the germ cells of any other species, in terms of creating chimeras, but they permit the fusion of human cell nuclei with enucleated egg cells from animals, such as rabbits, cows or other animals. As the UK Human Fertilisation and Embryology Authority's (HFEA) report on the consultation on hybrids and chimeras points out, studies into the creation of cytoplasmic hybrid embryos have to date only obtained a go ahead in China and the UK.[16]

Another key policy is the Regulation for Human Assisted Reproductive Technology (ART) and Sperm Banks. Implemented by MOH in 2001, the regulations were revised and re-issued with an additional set of Ethical Principles

15 See ISSCR's China profile on its website : www.isscr.org/public/regions/country.cfm?CountryID=52.

16 The report 'Hybrid and Chimeras' is available in electronic version on HFEA's website, on www.hfea.gov.uk/docs/Hybrids_Report.pdf.

for Human ART and Sperm Banks in July 2003. The regulations and ethical principles are also a key policy for the field of stem cell research, as they regulate, among other things, the obtaining of human embryos and gametes like eggs and sperm from fertility clinics, and thus define criteria for the transfer of left-over human embryos and eggs from the IVF clinic to the stem cell lab. According to these guidelines for instance, only couples but not single females are allowed to obtain treatment in a Chinese fertility clinic. In China, these two major policies, which regulate the use of human embryos in stem cell research as well as the use of IVF technology in human assisted reproduction, define the legal framework according to which the sourcing and the use of human embryos is regulated in the People's Republic.

There is general agreement that in China's liberal environment the access to human materials including embryonic and foetal tissues is relatively easy and that this offers an enormous advantage for researchers (Doering 2005, Heng 2009, Yang 2004). In the interplay of one-party state regime peculiarities, policies and medical practice, the PRC offers abundant opportunities for Chinese researchers. Owing to four different reasons, following Boon Chin Heng (2007), it is possible to argue that current legislation creates large abundances of embryonic bodies and makes them available as 'experimental' resources in stem cell research. First, this is because the one-child policy means that couples who have had successful fertility treatment are prohibited from using their leftover embryos for the conception of more children. As a result, in contrast to other countries where reproduction is not limited to one child, Chinese IVF centres produce a steady surplus of leftover human embryos on a systematic basis. Second, under MOH's regulations of assisted reproduction and sperm banks promulgated in 2003 the donation of a couple's leftover embryos to other childless couples is strictly prohibited, even though these may be utilized in scientific research upon the patient's 'informed consent.' Third, China's rapid economic growth means that clinical assisted reproduction is affordable to a rapidly growing proportion of the population. This is due to the fact that rising infertility rates in China pose severe pressures on couples, and in traditional Chinese culture having no offspring is regarded as a most unforgivable and unfilial deed. For many couples, as Heng (ibid.) notes, assisted reproduction is a last resort to avoid stigmatization by society. In essence, this means that the greater the number of couples using assisted reproduction, the greater is the abundance of leftover IVF embryos serving as potential sources for stem cell research. Lastly, as Heng also argues, the use of hormones for ovarian over-stimulation in fertility treatment is widespread as a practice, and this does regularly lead to excess numbers of oocytes and hence fertilized embryos being generated from each individual patient.

In this way, medical practice and Chinese guidelines for hESCR and ART produce unprecedented abundances of leftover IVF embryos on a regular and systematic basis. Under the strict guidelines of the one-child policy and the prohibition of embryo donation to other infertile couples, former IVF patients who attain reproductive success are only given two options to deal with their leftover embryos. They can only discard them as 'waste' or give their consent to their donation to scientific research, e.g. for the derivation of embryonic stem cells. As the traditional Chinese family value system places much emphasis on biological kinship, embryo donation is equated with child adoption, and both symbolize a rupture of ancestral family lineage. Even though it has not officially been put forward as a reason why embryo donation to other infertile couples is prohibited in China while the practice of child adoption is not, the traditional value of family blood relations often serves as an explanation of the ban. According to such traditional beliefs, it is an insult to one's family and ancestors as well as a personal failure to have unknown and unacknowledged biological progeny (Heng 2009; Qiu 2001). This is because traditionally both Confucianism and Taoism have placed much emphasis on the 'spiritual connectedness' between ancestors and members of the family line, a tradition that finds expression in the practice of ancestor worship. Behind this tradition is a decisive patri-linear nature of traditional Chinese society though, according to which male bloodlines and clan ancestry are paramount even to individual identity (Qiu 2001). As ooctye donation 'only' entails a loss of genetic connectedness to the birth mother but not to the blood father, this also means that egg donation for instance is much preferable over child adoption (Heng 2009).

In modern day China, however, the legal practice of child adoption is more common than such culturalist arguments suggest.[17] It can therefore just as well be assumed that the preservation of biological kinship, particularly under the restriction of the one-child policy, is not a value shared by each and every Chinese citizen. As some Chinese citizens are willing to adopt offspring from a different bloodline, this suggests that public attitude varies more than official culturalist viewpoints implicate. It has already been reported since the early 1990's that the state of ancestor worship is declining in modern day China, particularly in areas where the influence of the Communist regime's hostility towards religion was the strongest (Chu and Ju 1993). While in rural areas of China, as well as Taiwan, ancestor worship is still more common, Chu and Ju's finding for instance from

17 Many Chinese couples for instance are now rushing in, willing to adopt the thousands of orphaned children who lost their families in the earthquake disaster in Sichuan Province, driven by the desire to complement their one-child family with another child. See: Eimer 2008. China is also part of an internationally organized enterprise of international child adoption that enables infertile couples to circumvent the shortage and often difficult bureaucratic procedures of child adoption in their home countries. As Chinese citizens become more and more prosperous, more Chinese couples want to adopt children themselves, either because they are infertile, have a girl and are willing to pay the fines to also have a boy, or because they have lost their child in accidents, disease or for other reasons. However, as domestic adoption does not bring in the high fees that orphanages can charge international clients, not so wealthy Chinese citizens often experience tremendous difficulties to adopt a child from a Chinese orphanage. See: Adoption: The Schuster Institute for Investigative Journalism, China – a Report, Brandeis University. Available at: www.brandeis.edu/investigate/gender/adoption/china.html#overview.

Shanghai and adjacent villages is 'that forty years of indoctrination have brought about a sharp decline in religious beliefs among Chinese people along with the virtual disappearance of ancestor worship.' As it may well be the case that more liberal legislation would incite infertile couples to happily accept impregnation with others' leftover embryos, as well as the fact that some couples may also prefer to donate their spare good embryos in order to actualize the potentiality of their leftover embryos (Gomez-Lobo 2005), it seems both unnecessary and unjustified that the law obstructs couples from making such choices. Instead, current legislation only leaves them the option to choose between disposing of their remaining embryos as 'waste' or to donate them to research.

The international and MOH's regulations of artificial reproduction in China is that only one and up to three embryos can be implanted into the female womb, depending on the woman's age. Disregarding the fact that Chinese couples are only allowed to conceive one child, clinicians often fertilize up to 15 or even more mature oocytes as a matter of routine (Doering 2005; Liao et al. 2007). This is possible because the widespread use of follicle-stimulating hormones boosts egg production to an average high number of eggs. With a new set of legislation concerning oocyte donation promulgated in 2006, there is now also some sustentative pressure to obtain large numbers of mature oocytes from individual patients.[18] The Ministry of Health's Decree No. 44 of 2006 (MOH 2006) stipulates that oocytes can only be procured from IVF patients, while obtaining oocytes from non-patients is explicitly forbidden. If 20 or more mature oocytes are retrieved from the patient, at least 15 eggs must be kept for the patient's own use (e.g., Han 2008; MOH 2006), and only the remainder can be donated to other couples.

Donation has to be a voluntary act, which means that donors cannot obtain payment. As Heng (2009) points out, these overly stringent regulations also have led to a severe shortage of donor oocytes in China. As it is common practice that as many eggs are fertilized in China as are of good quality, even though couples can only conceive one child, abundances of spare embryos can be generated from each individual IVF patient.

Mapping the Illiberal Politics of 'Embryonic Life' in China

The last section has shown how in the interplay of current medical and regulatory practices of the illiberal state that restrict the reproductive choices and rights of couples, large abundances of leftover IVF embryos are being generated in

18 While trade with and payment for gametes are strictly prohibited in China, compensated egg-sharing is legal and common as a practice (Heng 2007). Some patients may obtain heavily-discounted fertility treatment. The discount can range from as low as 50 per cent to as high as 100 per cent of total medical fees billed to prospective egg sharing patients.

Chinese infertility clinics. Illiberal biopolitics, as a term, is introduced in order to mark that a regulatory control of life and human embryos has emerged in China too. A number of things can be said about the particularities of 'illiberal biopolitics' and how it distinguishes itself from 'liberal biopolitics' for that matter. The first important thing is that a regulatory control that seizes hold of the biological features of the population, as a species body and as an object of political strategization, has also emerged in the one-party state (see also Greenhalgh and Winckler 2005). As Sigley (2004) notes, 'liberal rationalities of government do not have a monopoly on the biopolitical.' The instance of the governance of China's national stem cell program indicates that state apparatuses may also have a biopolitical imperative, when they are not always concerned with limiting the reach of the state and the governance of the population at a distance. The 'biological' under the control of 'illiberal rule' is the object of the same regulatory mechanisms, such as forecasts, statistical estimates, and overall measures, not to modify but to intervene in life and the population at the level of their generality and their quality. Here, the population has also become a vital political problem that is at once scientific and political, that is at once a biological problem and power's problem.

In stem cell science's need to obtain more embryonic bodies, what is different though is that the *in-vitro* inhabitants of Chinese reproductive centres have become the focal point of illiberal biopolitical strategies to 'improve' the quality of the population, both directly through selection and indirectly as a resource for national development and the development of new therapies and other forms of biological intervention into the diseased and ageing population. A more direct form of illiberal selective intervention into the 'quality' of the population body is stipulated in MOH's Regulations of Artificial Reproductive Technologies and Sperm Banks (MOH 2001, revised in 2003). Article E's 'quality criteria' for medical staff specify that *in-vitro* fertilization and embryo transfer must accord to the principle 'to promote population quality.' The 'contraindications' for IVF treatment in article C further specify the quality of the population according to the overall criteria set out in the Maternal and Infant Health Care Law.[19] Implemented in 1995, the law has been subject to extensive domestic and international critique as a eugenics law.[20] Following much debate, eugenics was officially repudiated at the end of the century and domestic debates in 2002 and 2003 abolished compulsory medical inspection prior to marriage. While revisions of the law have made pre-marital medical check-ups optional since

19 The Maternal and Infant Health Care Law is available at: wwww.unescap.org/esid/psis/population/ database/poplaws/law_china/ch_record006.htm.

20 For instance article 10 calls on physicians to advise couples with inheritable genetic, infectious or mental diseases to use long-term contraceptive measures, for the reason that otherwise they would not be allowed to marry. In addition, article 18 demands physicians to advise termination of pregnancy if the foetus is suffering from genetic disease and any other defects of serious nature, such as mental diseases.

October 2003 (*China Daily* 19/08/03), its prescriptions remain non-optional in the IVF clinic. Here, patients must undergo medical checks and medical staff are required to disapprove IVF treatment and embryo transfer, if a couple and donors are diagnosed for these conditions.

A second important point to make is that about illiberal biopolitics' relationship to sovereign power, in contrast to liberal biopolitics' relation to that older form of power. As noted by Foucault on several occasions (e.g., Foucault 1978, 2003), biopower has not replaced the older form of sovereign power altogether, but it has started to overlay it. What the two forms, liberalism and authoritarianism, share is that they inhere elements of sovereignty and a biopolitical imperative of the optimization of the population. The fundamental difference between liberal and illiberal biopolitics, however, lies in the extent to which both deploy this sovereign power.[21] While new forms of self-governance, choice, liberties and more indirect forms of regulation may be a new trend in some areas of life in late-socialist China, such as professional work life (Hoffman 2006) and reproduction under the provisions of the one-child policy (Greenhalgh and Winckler 2005, Sigley 2004), the regulatory control of life in China, to a greater extent than liberal governmentality, is linked up with a power that is sovereign. This is precisely for the reason that citizen freedom remains an artefact of government intervention (Sigley 2004) which, to borrow from Dillon (2007), creates a radical ambiguity. This ambiguity lies in the claim, on the one side, that only self-governing and responsible citizens can foster social development and ensure national prosperity, whereas vast portions of the population, on the other side, remain under careful surveillance and become objects of administrative measures of the illiberal state. The peculiar relationship of biopower to sovereignty at the general level of state governance also reaches down to the micro-level of China's bioeconomy, the IVF-stem cell interface.

It is a common practice also in China that the legal requirement of informed consent grants individual patients the right to decide over the fate of surplus embryos, fresh or frozen, no longer needed for their own infertility treatment. In the Chinese fertility clinic, the right of life and the right to kill is a radically ambiguous one though. IVF patients can normally decide over the fate of their

---

21 It needs to be mentioned here that the author is aware of but for this purpose cannot engage with a discussion about the relationship between biopolitics and sovereign power, as it is considered by Agamben 1998 and Esposito 2008. Giorgio Agamben has radically questioned Foucault's thesis about the modernity of biopower, by proposing that since antiquity power has always been both sovereign and biopolitical. In Agamben's pessimistic account of politics, the state of exception of 'bare life' is the nomos of the modern. In *Bios*, Esposito analyses the radical transformation of the political into biopolitics. He discusses why none of the categories of modern political thought can completely grasp the essence of biopolitics and reconstructs the negative biopolitical core of Totalitarianism (Nazism). He finally proposes an affirmative response to the current deadly version of biopolitics that is a politics of life capable of being used not on bodies but in favour of bodies.

good but no longer needed embryos, either by granting them the right to live as offspring of other couples or by killing them through disposing them as waste or donating them to research. In China, what is so peculiar is that couples are also called upon as free subjects to decide what to do with their surplus embryos, yet their freedom is radically limited by the choices that they can make. Instead of a right to make life, or to grant life, Chinese couples can only choose between two different possibilities to 'make die,' either by discarding their superfluous leftover embryos as waste or by donating them to scientific research.

The one-party state now also regulates and controls 'life' and the population, but it does so without an internalized principle of limited government. Despotism is the prevailing form of rule in China, but this power now also has a biopolitical imperative, which is also a biopower in excess. As noted in an earlier part, for Foucault an 'excess of biopower' is the ultimate condition, when man must 'not only...manage life, but...make it proliferate, to create living matter, to build the monster' (Foucault 2003, 254). The marriage between the deathly function of sovereignty and the life-investing power of biopolitics, in excess, creates a peculiar form of sovereign biopower which, in analogy to Sigley's notion of 'liberal despotism,'[22] is henceforth termed to be 'biopolitical despotism' as an absolute power of the sovereign over life. In biopolitical despotism, the inter-linkage of sovereignty and biopower in excess creates embryonic life, in excess, whilst at the same time it is able to exercise the death function of sovereignty over the life that was created in excess. Thus, the numbers of harvested eggs and fertilized embryos are in no proportionate relationship to the number of embryos that can possibly be used for reproduction. In this sense, the Chinese IVF-stem cell interface is an instance of 'biopolitical despotism.' Chinese biopolitics does not only make pregnancies 'illegal,' and thus incites high numbers of abortions every year (Hemminki et al. 2005), but it also transforms the human embryo into 'illegal embryonic life,' by preventing it the right to actualize its potency. Prevented from the right to actualize their potency, embryonic bodies can be circulated 'in and through all manner of material in (stem cell science's) martial rage to enhance life at the risk of life' (Dillon 2007).

Conclusions

The preceding sections have shown how China's national stem cell program thrives on the fact that it exemplifies an illiberal politics of 'embryonic life' and the population, for the reasons that have just been mentioned. In the illiberal state, it can be concluded, current state policies and medical practice favour the utilization of leftover embryos in scientific research over their use in reproduction.

22 Gary Sigley's (2004) proposal of the notion of 'liberal despotism' marks that the despotic state in late-socialist China rules by granting Chinese citizens some new rights and liberties.

This is unsatisfactory to the extent that human embryos have become part of our 'imaginary of life' (Dillon and Lobo-Guerrero 2009) and because for some the disposal or termination of human embryos represents a wilful destruction of human life. It is out of this concern for instance that some countries like Germany, Italy and Switzerland restrict the fertilization of oocytes to the number of embryos that can be transferred for fertility treatment into the uterus at a time. As Chinese couples, who already have obtained one child, do not have the right to choose for their 'good' leftover embryos to remain in the 'reproductive trail', an unprecedented stock of good quality IVF embryos is made available as 'experimental' resources in China's national stem cell program.

What this demonstrates is an instance of a co-construction of subjects (in this case human embryos) and technology in illiberal states. Just in the way that there is no polis of man and of ordinary citizens in China, the illiberal politics of embryonic life does not grant the emergent form of life, the human embryo, a place in the polis of man either. In China, human embryos are therefore in a precarious state if compared for instance to their national role in Italy (Metzler 2007), where the law turns 'foetal citizens' (Holc 2004) into citizen subjects. While human embryos are a key resource in China's drive to the top through innovating stem cell research, Chinese human embryos are neither 'nationalized', nor are there penalties or sanctions of a serious nature for those who violate the law. In illiberal biopolitics' relationship to sovereign power, the actualization of the active potency inherent in human embryos is at the will of the sovereign (Foucault 2003), but only where the right to actualize *in-vitro* life's potency is not subject to sovereign juridical power's right to kill and to restrict is this emergent form of life 'secured' (Dillon 2007). In a biopolitical imperative to catch up and to lead, the interplay of Chinese state policies and ethical guidelines turn large parts of embryonic life into resources for medical experimentation, thus serving, in Foucault's own terms, 'to maximise and extract forces' (Foucault 2003).

In-vitro life is created in lavishing riches and large abundances, but as 'life' it is not 'secured' (Dillon, ibid.). In China, this 'life' does not posess a *per se* right to life. Its value neither derives from public discourse about culture and morality nor from ethical guidelines, but the value that the created surplus of 'life' derives is that of its usefulness as an 'experimental' resource.

Bibliography

Agamben, G. (1998) *Homo Sacer: Sovereign Power and Bare Life* (Stanford: Stanford University Press).

Boheler, K.R. et al. (2002) 'Differentiation of Pluripotent Embryonic Stem Cells into Cardiomyocytes', *Circulation Research* 91 (3), 189-201.

British Medical Journal (1984) The Warnock Committee, 289(6439), 238-239.

Chen, Z., Wang, H.-G., Wen, Z.-J. and Wang, Y. (2007) 'Life Sciences and Biotechnology in China', *Philosophical Transactions of the Royal Society* 362, 947-957.

CAS (2006) *China Modernization Report 2006*, edited by Chinese Academy of Science, available at: www.modernization.com.cn/cmr2006%20overview.htm.

China Daily (2003). 'China Simplifies Procedures for Marriage, Divorce', August 19.

Chu, G. and Ju, Y. (1993) *The Great Wall in Ruins: Communication and Cultural Change in China* (Albany: State University of New York Press).

Clifford, J. (1988) *Predicament of Culture: 20th Century Ethnography, Literature, and Art* (Cambridge: Harvard University Press).

Cong, Y. (2008) 'From Chinese Values of Life to Exploring the Ethical Aspects of Stem Cell Research in Mainland China', *Contemporary Chinese Thought* 39(2), 18-31.

Cussins, C. (1996) 'Ontological Choreography: Agency through Objectification in Infertility Clinics', *Social Studies of Science* 26, 575-610.

Deng, X. (1978) 'Speech at the Opening Ceremony of the National Conference on Science', in *Selected Works of Deng Xiaoping (vol. 2)*, edited by *People's Daily Online* (Beijing: People's Daily Online).

Dillon, M. (2007) 'Governing Terror: The State of Emergency of Biopolitical Emergence', *International Political Sociology* 1(1), 7-28.

Dillon, M. and Lobo-Guerrero, L. (2009) 'The Biopolitical Imaginary of Species-being', *Theory, Culture and Society* 26(1), 1-23.

Doering, O. (2005) 'Bioethische und politische Aspekte der Stammzellforschung in China', in Bender, W. et al. (eds) *Crossing Borders. Grenzueberschreitungen* (Münster: Agenda Verlag), 343-368.

Eimer, D. (2008) 'China Earthquake: Chinese One-child Families Rush to Take an Orphan', *Daily Telegraph,* 31 May.

Esposito, R. (2008) *Bios: Biopolitics and Philosophy* (Minneapolis: University of Minnesota Press).

Fewsmith, J. (2004) 'Promoting the Scientific Development Concept', *China Leadership Monitor*, No. 11 (Summer) (Stanford: Hoover Institution).

Foucault, M. (2008) *The Birth of Biopolitics: Lectures at the Collège de France 1978-79*. (London: Palgrave Macmillian).

—— (2003) *Society must be Defended: Lectures at the Collège de France*, 1975-76 (New York: Picador).

—— (1978) *History of Sexuality, Vol. 1: The Will to Knowledge* (London: Penguin).

Franklin, S. (2006) 'Embryonic Economies: The Double Reproductive Value of Stem Cells', *BioSocieties*, 1, 71-90.

Frew, S., Sammut, S., Shore, A. et al. (2008) 'Chinese health biotech and the billion-patient market', *Nature Biotechnology*, 26(1), 37-53.

Gerlin, A. (2006) 'The Hard Cell', *Time Magazine*, 26 September.

Global Watch Mission (2005). *Stem Cell Mission to China, Singapore and South Korea: A Report* (London: Department of Trade & Industry).

Gómez-Lobo, A. (2005) 'On Potentiality and Respect for Embryos: A Reply to Mary Mahowald', *Theoretical Medicine and Bioethics* 26 (2), 105-110.

Greenhalgh, S. and Winckler, E. (2005) *Governing China's Population. From Leninist to Neoliberal Biopolitics* (Palo Alto: Stanford University Press).

Guoqiang, W. (2004) *Statement by Mr. Wang Guoqiang,* at UN General Assembly's 59th Session in Commemoration of 10th Anniversary of International Conference on Population and Development. 14 October, available at: www.mfa.gov.cn/ce/ceun/eng/ chinaandun/socialhr/shfz/t164490.htm.

Han, P. (2008) 'China Bans Commercial Use of Human Eggs', *Press Release of Embassy of PRC in Australia*, 10 April 2006, available at: au.china-embassy.org/eng/xw/t245323.htm.

Hemminki, E., Wu, Z., Cao, G. and Viisainen, K. (2005) 'Illegal Births and Legal Abortions', *Reproductive Health* (2)5.

Heng, B. (2009) 'Stringent Regulation of Oocyte Donation in China', *Human Reproduction* 24(1), 14-16.

—— (2007) 'Growing Opportunities of Frozen Embryos in China offers Opportunities for the Development of Human Embryonic Stem Cell Banks', *Future Medicine* 2(6), 873-874.

Hoffman, L. (2006) 'Autonomous Choices and Patriotic Professionalism: On Governmentality in Late-socialist China', *Economy and Society* 35(4), 550-570.

Holc, J.P. (2004) 'The Purest Democrat: Fetal Citizenship and Subjectivity in the Construction of Democracy in Poland', *Signs* 29(3), 756-782.

Kay, L.E. (1994) *The Molecular Vision of Life: Caltech, the Rockefeller Foundation and the Rise of the New Biology* (New York: Oxford University Press).

Liao, L., Li, L. and Zhao, R. C. (2007) 'Stem Cell Research in China', *Philosophical Transactions of the Royal Society* 362, 1107-1112.

Metzler, I. (2007) 'Nationalizing Embryos: The Politics of Human Embryonic Stem Cell Research in Italy', *BioSocieties* 2(4), 413-427.

MOH (2006) *Decree on the Regulation of Human Clinical Assisted Reproduction Techniques and Accreditation of Human Sperm Banks* (Decree No. 44), issued on 7 February, available in Chinese at: www.jincao.com/fa/10/law10.145.htm.

—— (2001, 2003) *Regulations on Human Assisted Reproductive Technologies*. Enforced on 1 August 2001, revised July 2003.

Murray, F. and Sparr, D. (2006) 'Bit Player or Powerhouse? China and Stem-cell Research', *New England Journal of Medicine* 355(21), 1191-94.

Normile, D. and Mann, C. (2005) 'Asia Jockeys for Stem Cell Lead', *Science* 307(5710): 660-664.

Qiu, R. (2001) 'Sociocultural Dimensions of Infertility and Assisted Reproduction in the Far East', in *Report of a Meeting on Medical, Ethical, and Social Aspects*

of Assisted Reproduction, edited by Vayena, E. et al., 75-80, available at: www.who.int/reproductive-health/infertility/12.pdf.
Qiu, R. (2004) 'Bioethics and Asian Culture', in Qui, R. (ed) *Bioethics: Asian Perspectives – A Quest for Moral Diversity* (Dordrecht; Boston: Kluwer Academic Publishers).
Rabinow, P. (2003) *Anthropos Today: Reflections on Modern Equipment* (Princeton: Princeton University Press).
Rabinow, P. and N. Rose (2006). 'Biopower Today', *BioSocieties* 1(2), 195-218.
Rose, N. (2007) *The Politics of Life Itself: Biomedicine, Power, and Subjectivity in the 21st Century* (Princeton: Princeton University Press).
Salter, B., Cooper, M. and Dickins, A. (2006). 'China and the Global Stem Cell Bioeconomy: An Emerging Political Strategy?', *Regenerative Medicine* 1(5), 671-683.
Schneider, L. (2003) *Biology and Revolution on Twentieth Century China* (Lanham: Rowman & Littlefield).
Schuster, L. (2008) 'Stem Cell Treatments in China: No Regulatory Approvals, but U.S. Patients with ALS or Spinal Cord Injury Line Up', *Neurology Today* 8(7)
Segal, A. (2003) *Digital Dragon: High-technology Enterprises in China* (Ithaca, NY: Cornell University Press).
Sigley, G. (1996) 'Governing Chinese Bodies: The Significance of Studies in the Concept of Governmentality for the Analysis of Government in China', *Economy and Society* 25 (4): 457-82.
Sigley, G. (2004) 'Liberal Despotism: Population Planning, Subjectivity, and Government in Contemporary China', *Alternatives: Global, Local, Political* 29(5), 557-75.
Simon, D. and Cao, C.C. (2009) *China's Emerging Technological Edge: Assessing the Role of High-End Talent* (Cambridge: Cambridge University Press).
Stoler, A.L. (1995) *Race and the Education of Desire: Foucault's History of Sexuality and the Colonial Order of Things* (Durham: Duke University Press).
Svendsen, M. and Koch, L. (2008) 'Unpacking the Spare Embryo', *Social Studies of Science* 38(1), 93-110.
UK Stem Cell Initiative (2005) *Report & Recommendations* (Pattison Report). November. Available at: www.advisorybodies.doh.gov.uk/uksci/uksci-reportnov05.pdf.
U.S. Embassy Beijing (2001) *Beijing Environment, Science and Technology Update*, 21 September 2001. Available at: www.usembassy-china.org.cn/sandt/estnews092101.htm.
Wang, Y. (2003) 'Chinese Ethical Views on Embryo Stem Cell Research. Asian Bioethics in the 21st Century', Eubios Ethics Institute. Available at: www.eubios.info/ABC4/abc4049.htm.
Wang, Y. (2006) 'The Moral Status of Human Embryos', *Asian Biotechnology and Development Review*, 9(1), 45-63.
Yang, X. (2004) 'An Embryonic Nation', *Nature* 428, 210-212.

Index